PEOPLE

CONTRIBUTORS
TO THIS VOLUME INCLUDE

PATRICK ANDERSON

D.S.CARNE-ROSS

PATRICK CARPENTER

RONALD CLARK

J.G.CROWTHER

GLYN DANIEL

CHARLES DIMONT

PROFESSOR BONAMY
 DOBRÉE

DAVID DREW

J.DUMONT

PROFESSOR CYRIL
 FALLS

JAMES FISHER

ORMEROD GREENWOOD

MICHAEL HAMBURGER

ALAN HODGE

GEOFFREY HUDSON

MOLLY IZZARD

ROBERT FURNEAUX
 JORDAN

RONALD LEWIN

DAVID MAGARSHAK

ERIC MOSBACHER

RAFAEL NADAL

PROFESSOR STUART
 PIGGOTT

KATHLEEN RAINE

DAVID STONE

A.J.P.TAYLOR

HUGH THOMAS

ALAN TYSON

BERNARD WALL

FRANCIS WATSON

WILLIAM WATSON

General Editors

GEOFFREY GRIGSON & CHARLES HARVARD GIBBS-SMITH

PEOPLE

A VOLUME OF THE

GOOD, BAD, GREAT & ECCENTRIC

WHO ILLUSTRATE

THE ADMIRABLE DIVERSITY

OF MAN

HAWTHORN BOOKS, INC.
Publishers
NEW YORK

Published in the United States of America by Hawthorn Books,
Inc., 70 Fifth Avenue, New York City 11. All rights reserved
including the right to reproduce this book, or portions thereof, in
any form, except for the inclusion of brief quotations in a review.
Designed and produced by Rainbird, McLean Ltd, London. Printed
in Great Britain by Jarrold & Sons Ltd, Norwich, Norfolk;
color plates printed by Tillotsons (Bolton) Ltd; endpapers printed
by Van Leer of Amsterdam. Library of Congress Catalogue
Number 55-12436.

Second American Edition: October 1957

FROM THOMAS COOK TO VOLTAIRE, Brigham Young to T. S. Eliot, Mao Tse-tung the Chinese dictator to Han Van Meegeren the forger, this volume contains brief accounts of a very wide variety of men and women.

It is not a book of reference or a biographical dictionary. The approach is less neutral. We have intended, rather, to illustrate the delightful diversity of mankind, at a time when we are all of us accused of thinking and feeling in the same way, of becoming an undifferentiated mass, or a series of masses from Moscow to London, London to San Francisco and Tokyo. More than a hundred years ago the concept of the 'Average Man' was invented by the Belgian scientist, Adolphe Quételet, one of the many scientists we have included in People. He is an impossible monster, this Average Man; he may be useful for statistics and sociology, for cartoons and condemnations, but he does not live down any street of any city in the world, in which all of the windows and the front doors may be the same; he does not exist, he never has existed, and never will exist. It is per-haps good to be reminded of that by the example of the saints and the bad men, the saviours and the destroyers, the philosophers and the eccentrics, the inven-tors and the explorers, the poets and the heroes, who fill this book – people of many countries, Europeans and Americans, Chinese and Indians, Persians and Japanese.

Several things we have not done. We have not brashly attempted to pick only those whom we consider to have been the greatest men and women of all time – had we done so, nobody would have agreed with our list. We have not been too attentive, therefore, to the commands of 'ought' and 'must'. Variety has been our aim, and there have been great men, after all, who would make very dull reading. Also we have restricted ourselves in time, more or less, to the modern age; leaving out the ancient world and taking our men and women from that era of conscious personality which begins with St Augustine, and comes down to Freud and Jung.

If the artists – poets, novelists, painters, musicians, etc. – occur through the pages in good measure, it is because they endure more than most by the force of their recorded personality, and have left us a part of their inmost selves it would be unwise to neglect. Often, as the reader will find, poems and extracts from their sayings and writings are offered instead of too dry or too abstract a recital of their lives. Moreover, anecdotes are included when they appear to tell the truth of a man's nature.

A word, also, about the illustrations. These have been chosen so far as possible to be illustrations of character; when it can be safely done, we have aimed to avoid the hackneyed portrait, especially the portrait made of a great man when his work was over and he had become an institution.

GEOFFREY GRIGSON

CHARLES HARVARD GIBBS-SMITH

Color Plates

The endpapers are of Bonaparte Crossing the Alps at Mount St Bernard 1800, by J.-L. David.

Black and White Plates

BLACK AND WHITE PLATES (*continued*)

BLACK AND WHITE PLATES (concluded)

PEOPLE

A

Acton the severe

ACTON, John Emerich Edward Dalberg, first Lord Acton, (1834–1902), English historian and scholar, remembered most frequently for his famous generalization 'All power tends to corrupt and absolute power corrupts absolutely'.

Acton belonged to a Roman Catholic family, partly English, but with wide continental connections. Because of his religion he was refused admission to Trinity College, Cambridge, and as a result he became one of the few Englishmen of his insular time with a knowledge of European culture. Acton's appetite for learning was gigantic, with a bias nevertheless towards the trivial puzzles of history. He acquired a great reputation as a scholar, he built up a vast library to provide materials for a History of Freedom (though freedom has a brief history, compared with oppression) – and yet published practically nothing. At his death all that remained were the lecture notes of his students, from which a few books were compiled.

Acton introduced into English history the standards of German scholarship, which he supposed to be academic and detached. He organized the *Cambridge History of Modern Europe* (prototype of other cooperative ventures), in which each chapter was written by a different contributor, yet the reader was supposed to find a single book with a common spirit. The experiment was a grotesque failure: each chapter remained a separate essay.

Bearing the mark of the lecture-room, Acton's own writings abound in strong generalizations, which no doubt stirred his audience, but are less effective under detached scrutiny. Acton held that the historian must be a moralist. He must first ascertain the facts with strict impartiality; but he must then condemn every historical character who deviates from the highest virtue. As all men in public life often lie and sometimes kill (if only in wartime), there were few who escaped Acton's sentence. His attitude was no doubt more sensible than that of the historian who, by explaining men's motives, manages also to excuse their actions; but there are gradations between black and white which Acton refused to recognise.

The Boston amateur

ADAMS, Henry, (1838–1918), American historian, who spent his life in a fruitless search for power, and, though successful in the eyes of the world, considered himself a failure.

Adams has left us his appraisal of what a successful man should be: writing of William C. Whitney, he says: 'Already in 1893, he had finished with politics after having gratified every ambition and swung the country almost at his will: he had thrown away the usual objects of political ambition like the ashes of smoked cigarettes; had turned to other amusements, satisfied every taste, gorged every appetite, won every object that New York afforded, and, not yet satisfied, had carried his fields of activity abroad, until New York no longer knew what most to envy, his horses or his houses.' This was the Adams dream, in which his social and intellectual leanings ran a three-legged-race. 'All a man's life', wrote his brother to Henry, 'is not meant for books, or for travel in Europe.' For the first thirty-two years there had been little else.

He was a Bostonian: born 'under the shadow of Boston State House' – and from the cold intellectual *ambience* of Boston Brahminism he tried to escape. Against him there was a family tradition of high public service. By the age of ten, he wrote, 'his face was already fixed, and his heart was stone, against State

Street; his education was warped beyond recovery in the direction of Puritan politics'. Harvard he equally disliked: 'It taught little and that little ill.'

After leaving Harvard, he travelled in Europe; read desultorily for the law; and then for seven years acted as private secretary to his father, who was American minister in London. He was his father's *aide* in a difficult – and important – time; 'one began to dream the sensation of wielding unmeasured power,' he said. But where was that power to lie? 'For the law, diplomacy had unfitted him; for diplomacy he already knew too much.' He tried political journalism in Washington – attempting to control power from his study. But that ended half-heartedly; and he went to Harvard as an assistant professor of history and editor of the *North American Review*. They were good years – although he said they were barren, and set him on the task of writing a *History of the United States*. And he married; his wife was a charming woman – before she set off to Europe on her wedding trip she was given such flattering letters of introduction that she never had the courage to use them; but she would read them in front of the fire when she wanted to cheer herself up. A few years later she committed suicide: like Henry, she lacked a real purpose; unlike him, she could not cope with her indecision.

His *History* is still one of the best. Like Macaulay, he had a dramatic flair for character. Thus of a minor figure, Joel Barlow, he wrote: 'His ambition, above the lofty ambition of Jefferson, made him aspire to be a Connecticut Maecenas and Virgil in one; to patronize Fulton and employ Smirke; counsel Jefferson and contend with Napoleon. In his own mind a figure such as the world rarely saw – a compound of Milton, Rousseau and the Duke of Bridgewater – he had in him so large a share of conceit, that tragedy, which would have thrown a solemn shadow over another man's life, seemed to render his only more entertaining.'

Yet Adams now is remembered above all for his brilliant, incisive, ironical memoirs, *The Education of Henry Adams*: they are the splendid testament of a man who never found himself. He was not a dilettante, he worked hard for his ambition. And his goal was clear: power. But he lacked the understanding to find the way to that goal. It was no longer possible, as America boomed in the nineteenth century, and public opinion became important, to control affairs from the study. It was necessary to come out into the market-place; which Adams never did.

' Guardian of mankind '

AKBAR, (1542–1605), grandson of Babar, descendant of Jenghiz Khan and Tamerlane (q.v.), and the third Mogul ruler of Hindustan, who enlarged and consolidated his empire so efficiently that his descendants retained their throne until 1858, when India passed to the British Crown. A man of earnest and inquiring mind, he lived in splendour, described by the Jesuit missionaries who frequented his court.

Here is one of the great individualists of history, a man who defied the prejudices of his time and attempted to create among the warring tribes and unruly states of sixteenth-century India a concept of a political and cultural whole, an India without racial or religious barriers, where all were to be members of one state. He failed, as the British who assimilated his carefully planned and efficiently administered system of government, were to fail 350 years later.

Akbar inherited his kingdom as a boy of fourteen, but he had to fight for it, so weak was his father's grip on Hindustan. Thereafter, campaign by carefully conceived campaign, he extended a kingdom to an empire, till at his death it stretched from the Indian Ocean to the Bay of Bengal, and only the southern part of the sub-continent, the Deccan, kept its independence.

The man himself comes down to us warm, generous, kind and humane, in the pages of his chronicler Abul Fazl and the Jesuit missionaries to his court. Stocky, burly, with a hearty laugh and a healthy air, he has none the less a noble and kingly presence. He radiates energy. Many-sided, he has a boundless appetite for life, a deep intellectual curiosity, and is a Renaissance man, or prince, who has 24,000 books in his library, and yet remains illiterate to the end of his life, delighting to be read to and holding a vast store of memorized poetry and information in his head. A fine rider and huntsman, he delights also in his stables, his 5,000 elephants; he lays out his gardens, and plays with his tumbling pigeons; and there is a weekly inspection of the army of painters and craftsmen in his employ. Twice a day he holds audience, and the fame of his justice is such 'that everyone wronged feels he had the emperor on his side'. He has 300 women in his harem, yet has no sons; and when sons are at last given to him, he hastens to build a new capital, Fatepur Sikri, the City of Victory, on the site of their birthplace. For fourteen years the city grows, walls, palaces, courtyards, gardens, the great metropolis of the Mogul Empire. Then suddenly it is abandoned, and twenty years later a traveller, surveying its deserted streets, remarks 'Fuit Ilium'.

By nature simple and straightforward, the greatest and perhaps the most sympathetic of the Moguls, Akbar had his share of sorrow. Of his three sons, two died of their excesses in early manhood, the third attempted a rebellion. His new religion, the Din-i-Ilahi or 'Divine Faith', which was to provide a unifying spiritual force for his immense empire, came to nothing; and his attempt to weld a corporate whole out of the divergent elements of his subjects was frustrated by their bigotry and conservatism. To the end of his life, despite an increasing hostility to the Moslem faith, he evaded the efforts of Christians, Hindus, Parsees, Jains, to capture him for their own. He died muttering the word God, and was buried quietly and simply beneath a marble slab in the splendid tomb he had built outside Agra.

Fatepur Sikri still stands, desolate, deserted, the home of the bat and the jackal, its great red walls and its noble gateway looking down on the barren plain.

ILLUSTRATION: Plate 1.

Sergey Aksakov

AKSAKOV, Sergey Timofeyevich, (1791–1859), one of the most tender and profound of Russian writers: 'We must understand man as he is and not demand from his nature what it does not possess,' wrote Aksakov to Gogol (q.v.), and this maxim best describes his writings, for he applied it not only to man, but also to bird and beast.

Aksakov was born in Ufa, the capital of the easternmost province of European Russia; he spent much of his childhood on his father's estate, where he grew up to become a passionate fisherman and hunter. It was as a child, he writes in his autobiographical *Family Chronicle* 'that the grandeur and beauty of God's world sank imperceptibly into my soul and lived without my knowledge in my imagination'. But it was not till he was forty-three, after he had retired from the Civil Service, that he gave a literary expression to the grandeur of nature in his first descriptive work *The Blizzard* (1834). The death of his father, a rich landowner, made him independent, and

his house in Moscow, where he settled permanently with his wife and family, as well as his country estate of Abramtsevo, near Moscow, became famous for his patriarchal hospitality and as the meeting-place of the Moscow literary and theatrical world. It was at Abramtsevo that he wrote the books that made him famous.

The first three of these were devoted entirely to his favourite sports: *Notes on Angling* (1847), *The Diary of a Shotgun, Sportsmen of the Orenburg Province* (1852) and *Tales and Reminiscences of a Sportsman* (1855). Turgenev (q.v.), one of his greatest admirers and friends, summarized his genius as a naturalist in one sentence: 'If a black-cock could tell its life story, it would, I am sure, not have added a single word to what Mr Aksakov has told us about it'.

At the age of sixty-four he was beginning to lose his sight, and it was as a distraction from the ailments of old age that he went back to the early years of his life and began his supreme autobiographical trilogy – *A Family Chronicle* (1855) – which he partly dictated and partly wrote, and which has been excellently translated into English. *A Family Chronicle* showed him to be a creative artist of the first rank. It is pervaded by what he himself described as 'a feeling of pity for all suffering humanity'. The unaffected simplicity and directness of his prose made a Russian critic observe that 'Aksakov's works seem to have been written by a man who has never read a book in his life'.

A few months before his death in June 1859 he dictated the last fragment of his memoirs, *A Sketch of a Winter's Day*. Aksakov's *History of My Acquaintance with Gogol* was published after his death.

Destroyer of Rome

ALARIC I, (d. 410), the Gothic King who sacked imperial Rome and massacred its citizens.

The end of an age, the end of over a thousand years of Roman history, perhaps the end of 'ancient times', came when Alaric the Goth sacked the city of Rome in August 410. It was the third time Alaric had besieged Rome. Before he was bought off on the first occasion, he had replied grimly to the half-threats of envoys out of Rome, 'The thicker the hay, the easier mowed'; and after the third siege the hay was mowed with a vengeance. The Western Empire died in frightful destruction, chaos and misery, in one of the most dramatic tragedies in the annals of the world. The destroyer, who was not a complete barbarian and who is believed to have tried to keep his men in hand, died soon afterwards. He was doubtless a great fighting man, but he was still more an instrument of fate, since it was the pressure of the Huns, who crossed the Volga in 375, which set the Goths on the move.

Nor was the sack of Rome more than the climax and final symbol of decay. Rome, the Rome of the west, was spiritually sick; and Italy had already been ravaged up to the gates of the city. The two greatest men who had arrested the landslide, Diocletian and Constantine, had deserted Italy, the first exercising his over-lordship from Nicomedia in Asia Minor, the second building the great new capital which bore his name and was intended to be the capital of the whole empire, though it became that of the eastern branch. Rome had ceased to be a nation of soldiers. The mobile army, rushed from one danger to another, was composed of hardier men, barbarians, while Romans were reduced to garrison duties. The last good soldier who defended Rome, Stilicho, was, significantly, a Vandal. Leaving aside moral decay and its disputed causes, this reliance of a vast and wealthy empire on barbarian hirelings in a world seething with folk movement was fatal. The end might have been less catastrophic and might have come with a transfer of power, but it was inevitable.

Like others who attacked Rome, Alaric had previously served her (he had been a general under the Emperor Theodosius), but her weakness in east and west alike had become too tempting. Before descending upon Italy he had overrun Greece from end to end. The Goths destroyed, but they also preserved. They repeopled Gaul and Spain. Eventually they settled down beside the Romanized inhabitants who were left, learnt their provincial speech and adopted many of their deeply-ingrained customs. They also played the greatest part in defeating the menace of Attila (q.v.) to western Europe. Yet the word 'Goth' survives to recall the sack of Rome, standing for the coarse and the uncivilized. After the sack of Rome, Alaric died in Southern Italy. In the north of the toe of Italy near Cosenza, he is said to have been buried under the river Busento, with his treasures. The river was diverted by captives who were then killed to preserve the secret.

Prince Consort

ALBERT, Prince, (1819–1861), Prince of Saxe-Coburg and consort of Queen Victoria. He conceived the Great Exhibition and much influenced art and architecture and the sciences in the nineteenth century.

Albert was born in the castle of Rosenau, deep in the Thuringian Forest, so that his taste was always tinged with German romanticism – hence his love for the more obvious Scottish scenery and his lamentable additions to Windsor Castle. His taste was also indelibly marked upon his two other royal homes – Balmoral and Osborne. He retained through life a simple Lutheran piety. His parents were unhappy, but the report that he was the son of a Jewish Court Chamberlain is probably untrue. Baron Stockmar, presiding genius of the Coburg family, married several of its obscure princes into great ruling houses; the most brilliant of these marriages was that of Albert to Victoria. 'In less than three hours', wrote the Prince, 'I shall stand before the altar with my bride! God help me!' The next morning the Queen and Prince were about early. 'Strange,' said Greville, 'that a bridal night should be so short.' The explanation was that the newly married couple had, from the first hour, for themselves and others, the one ideal of work. Neither the aristocracy nor the John Bullish public welcomed 'The German Boy', and it was only through work that Albert could succeed. Even the Queen excluded him, to start with, from State affairs. When, however, he dined at the Middle Temple, a member wrote that 'no prince that has ever lived could stand less in need of exhortations to good deeds, or of admonitions against bad ones'. He was thus forced into activities such as the Presidency of the Society for Abolition of Slavery, and of the Royal Society of Arts, into the encouragement of mural painting in the new Houses of Parliament and of the building of model dwellings.

Albert's great achievement – negatively and positively – centred upon the Great Exhibition of 1851 in Hyde Park. He was energetic in its promotion and he was instrumental in choosing the design by Paxton for the pre-fabricated iron and glass Crystal Palace, in which the Exhibition was held, a building of an importance in the development of modern architecture not altogether realized by its designer. The Exhibition and the Crystal Palace are seen now as symbols of the turning of England from a feudal and agricultural state into an industrial and capitalist one. The taste of the 'art' section reached a new nadir – the reaction to it was the Arts and Crafts Movement of William Morris (q.v.) – but the progress, expansion and optimism of the Age had been duly proclaimed.

Upon Albert's death – he had caught a chill at a Sandhurst review – the Queen went into complete seclusion for many years. She retained Albert's rooms untouched, and exhibited all the trappings of mourning to the end of her life. The Albert Memorial (architect: Sir Gilbert Scott) in Hyde Park is a little to the west of the Great Exhibition site. When an inscription was considered, it was thought that one word 'Albert' would be sufficient for purposes of identification. This has proved correct.

Alexander Alekhine

ALEKHINE, Alexander, (1892–1946), Russian chess master, world champion, who left a collection of games of unequalled brilliance.

A lawyer by profession like Morphy (q.v.), Alekhine came from a wealthy Russian family, and showed a great talent for chess from boyhood. He was a recognized master at sixteen. When the first World War broke out he was playing in a tournament at Mannheim, and was interned by the Germans. He escaped to Switzerland, reached home by way of Siberia and joined the Russian army. The Revolution came. Alekhine, as son of a former President of the Duma, had small hope of escaping alive, but his chess saved him, and he made a living by teaching chess in Soviet schools and universities. In 1921 he was allowed to play in a tournament at Tribery, and instead of returning to Russia, made his way to Paris, and started life again with chess as his profession, and one single aim – the World Championship. He triumphed again and again in great tournaments until he earned the right to play Capablanca for the championship. He beat Capablanca at Buenos Aires in 1927. In the meanwhile, Alekhine had qualified as a French lawyer and had become a French citizen – but he lived by chess, taking part, as a world champion should, in great and small tournaments, here, there, and everywhere; and playing and winning sharply realistic games with a brilliant consistency.

In his forties, about 1935, his powers of concentration declined a little, and in the same year he lost the championship to Dr Euwe of Holland, who agreed to an early return match. In 1937 Alekhine summoned all his determination and became champion for the second time, a feat which no other master had achieved. When the second World War began, Alekhine was playing in Buenos Aires; he returned to France to join the army, though he was years over age. In the nineteen-forties, at a low ebb, and cut off from the rest of the world in Portugal, a challenge came to him for a World Championship match in England with the Soviet champion, Mikhail Dofvinnik. A telegram announcing the final arrangements was too much for him, and he died the same night of heart failure. He had played, incidentally, a good deal of blindfold chess (in which the single plays without sight of the boards); and, with the boundless ambition which was his mainstay, he had raised the record to thirty-two simultaneous games. This was a staggering figure, and though it has been passed since Alekhine's day, the opposition faced by later blindfold players has been less formidable, while the quality of play has never been equalled.

'Full-blooded Yankee'

ALLEN, Ethan, (1738–1789), leader of the Green Mountain Boys, whose finely impudent capture of Fort Ticonderoga from the British changed a small rebellion into a great revolution.

He was a rebel long before the first shots were fired on Lexington Green. After a rambling, log-cabin childhood, without much schooling, Allen became a land speculator. His territory was a region north of Massachusetts Bay, between Lake Champlain and the Connecticut river; it was a disputed region, for though the Board of Trade had given it to the Province of New York, the New Hampshire Proprietors continued to make grants for it. With his brothers, Ethan Allen founded the Onion River Company, and obtained the right to some thousands of acres. He was more than a land-hog: he had a deep feeling for the newly developed area as well as that love of liberty which goes with the pioneer. When the New Yorkers began to claim the land, Ethan Allen organized his fellow settlers into that almost legendary band of militiamen, the Green Mountain Boys. They aimed to hold the land and make it into a new state. Allen was outlawed by the Governor of New York; and retaliated by offering a reward for the capture of the Governor.

At the outbreak of war he had an army ready. With his Green Mountain Boys, he entered Ticonderoga Fort while the British were asleep. When the commanding officer appeared – carrying his trousers – Allen told him in famous words (recorded by himself) to surrender the garrison 'In the Name of the Great Jehovah and the Continental Congress'. Shortly after Allen was captured by the British, and then dragged about as a prisoner for three years. General Prescott had told him 'I will not execute you now, but you shall grace a halter at Tyburn, God damn ye'. He was taken handcuffed to England, and brought back to the New World. In his *Narrative of Colonel Ethan Allen's Captivity* (1779), he tells a grim story of the treatment and neglect of prisoners, and manages at the same time to illustrate again and again his own flamboyant character. Soon after his capture he twisted off with his teeth a tenpenny nail which fastened his hand irons, and swaggered over to those who abused him – 'particularly a Doctor Dance, who told me that I was outlawed by New York, and deserved death for several years past; was at last fully ripened for the halter, and in a fair way to obtain it: when I challenged him, he excused himself in consequence, as he said, of my being a criminal; but I flung such a flood of language at him that it shocked him and the spectators, for my anger was very great. I heard one say, damn him, can he eat iron?'

England was roundly whipped and apostrophized before the close of the *Narrative*: 'Vaunt no more old England! consider you are but an island! and that your power has continued longer than the exercise of your humanity! Order your broken and vanquished battalions to retire from America, the scene of your cruelties ... I know you have individuals, who still retain their virtue, and consequently their honour and humanity. These I really pity, as they must more or less suffer in the calamity, in which the nation plunged headlong; but as a nation I hate and despise you. My affections are frenchified ...'

This 'full-blooded Yankee', as he calls himself, deserves his fiery page in American fact and legend with Paul Jones (q.v.), Paul Revere, and the other folk-heroes of America; he lived shrewdly and robustly, maintained individualism in the midst of social change and wore his freedom with a passionate swagger.

First to the South Pole

AMUNDSEN, Roald, (1872–1928), Norwegian discoverer of the South Pole, which he reached in 1911, a month ahead of Scott's ill-fated party.

'To the explorer', Amundsen wrote, 'adventure is merely an unwelcome interruption of his serious labours ... An adventure is merely a bit of bad planning, brought to light by the test of trial.' While preparing an expedition to the North Pole, he heard that Peary had reached it in 1909, and promptly switched from North to South, though Scott's South Polar expedition had already left. For Amundsen, all went smoothly – no bad planning, no adventure. His success was partly due to the use of skis and Eskimo dogs. Scott's failure was partly due to his experiment with Shetland ponies which died and held him up, a delay which contributed to Scott's death in a blizzard thirteen miles from safety.

Amundsen also had the distinction of being the first to sail through the long-sought north-west passage; this was now only a *tour de force*, but he turned the exploit to scientific use. He also sailed through the north-east passage. He was quick to decide that the development of aircraft made previous methods of arctic exploration obsolete, and with the American Ellsworth Vines he was the first to fly over the North Pole in an Italian airship in 1926. Two years later he was killed when flying to the rescue of another Italian airship which crashed in the Arctic.

Architect of Santa Sophia

ANTHEMIUS OF TRALLES, (sixth century A.D.), architect of one of the world's major buildings, Santa Sophia or Hagia Sophia at Istanbul, engineer, mathematician and poet, who brought the sensitive skill of the Greek artist to Roman engineering.

The early basilican church of Hagia Sophia – Divine Wisdom – at Constantinople (Istanbul) having been burnt down early in the reign of Justinian, Anthemius began the new church in February 532. It was finished in December 537. For many centuries this was the largest church in Christendom; its complex of domes still covers the largest uninterrupted floor area in the world (approximately 100 feet by

260 feet). Anthemius, who had the help of Isodorus of Miletus, was the architect, and was said by Procopius to 'have grown frightened at times by the magnitude of his undertaking'. The achievement was indeed remarkable. Anthemius took Roman engineering and adapted it to the covering and enclosure of a vast central space with surrounding aisles, with no aid from that multiplicity of supports which the Gothic architects were to use. He disposed the masses of his building so as to concentrate the thrust of the dome and the arches at a few points, and in this way he left areas where he could introduce windows. These included the ring of windows round the dome, at what is theoretically the point of greatest thrust. So the myth arose that the dome was suspended from Heaven.

The Pantheon – first of the world's great domes – had been a comparatively simple problem to its Roman architects: they placed the circular dome over a circular space with very thick walls. At Santa Sophia Anthemius supported semi-domes upon vaults and arches, leading up in this manner to his central dome. The whole has been compared to a mass of bubbles. He solved the problem of stability, as well as the solid geometry involved in putting a circular dome over a rectangular plan, without which neither St Peter's at Rome (see Brunelleschi), nor St Paul's in London, could have been built.

To this very complicated structure Anthemius gave aesthetic unity. Arch, vault, semi-dome – all have a single springing line; above which is an unbroken area of sombre but glowing mosaic. Below that line everything is covered with thin slabs of marble – the colours of which moved Procopius to poetry.

The angelic doctor

AQUINAS, St Thomas, (c. 1225–1274), i.e. Thomas of Aquino in Italy, the greatest of the scholastic (that is, medieval catholic) philosophers. He is influential even today since in 1879 Pope Leo XIII decreed that in all Catholic colleges teaching philosophy the system of Aquinas must be the basis of all tuition.

Since Saint Augustine (q.v.) philosophy and theology had in the main been dominated by Plato's thought; Aristotle was in disrepute, since some of his doctrines appeared to lead to heresy. Aquinas, whose knowledge of Aristotle was very considerable and who claimed that the heresies were the result of misinterpretation, devoted his life to persuading the church that Aristotle was a better basis for Christian philosophy than Plato, and to demonstrating that a complete theological system could be constructed from Aristotelian concepts.

His great systematizing works were the *Summa contra Gentiles* and the *Summa Theologiae*. In the former he states: 'The purpose I have in view is ... to declare the truth which the catholic faith professes, while weeding out contrary errors.' As pagans do not accept the authority of the Scriptures, 'it is necessary to have recourse to natural reason, to which all are compelled to assent'. Certain truths, such as the existence and the unity of God can, he thinks, be proved by reason without the help of Scriptures: others, such as the doctrine of the Trinity, cannot. These two classes are carefully distinguished.

The meticulous and detailed parade of arguments endorsing catholic theology cannot properly be summarized. Aquinas states the case against any position he is defending very fairly, and often with a realism that suggests the objections were those he had actually heard. In the first three books of the *Summa contra Gentiles* he uses only arguments which are based on reason: not till the fourth does he appeal to revelation, when the doctrine cannot be proved by reason alone or where (we may suspect) reason unaided might lead to the wrong (*i.e.* non-catholic) conclusion. To the Catholic Church Aquinas is the 'Angelic Doctor'; to Dante he was *fiamma benedetta*, a flame of heavenly wisdom, wiser even than Aristotle. Secular philosophers of today tend to think that Aristotle's metaphysics and logic, so far from saying the last word, are largely erroneous, and that Aquinas's system into which they are so closely woven, is therefore inevitably impaired. And they question whether the finding of arguments for predetermined conclusions is to be reckoned among the highest forms of philosophy – however far they are based upon 'natural reason'.

'The courtesies, the daring deeds I sing . . .'

ARIOSTO, Ludovico, (1474–1533), major poet of the Italian Renaissance, author of the huge romance

epic *Orlando Furioso*, which retells the story of Charlemagne's war with the Saracens.

Like other great creators, Ariosto put his energy
into his masterpiece, leaving little for the biographer.
He spent most of his time in and around Ferrara,
which, under the house of Este and Lucrezia Borgia
(q.v.), was one of the most brilliant centres of Renaissance civilization in Italy. He studied law for a
while – 'My father kept me to that rubbish for five
years' – then turned to literature, writing in Latin as
fluently as in Italian. He became an attendant gentleman in the household of the Cardinal Ippolito d'Este,
brother of the Duke of Ferrara. This worldly, not to
say vicious, prelate kept him continuously on the
move, employed in diplomatic missions all over Italy.
It was not a life that suited Ariosto:

> Who wants to gad about, why, let him gad!
> See England, France, see Hungary and Spain:
> For me, I'd sooner stay in my own region.

However, diplomacy took him to Florence in the
summer of 1513, when the city was given over to wild
celebrations in honour of the election of a Florentine
Pope, Leo X, and there he saw and fell deeply in love
with a beautiful married woman called Alessandra
Benucci. Her husband seems to have died soon after,
whereupon she followed Ariosto to Ferrara. There
love gave him happiness and comfort for the rest of
his life, though they were unable to marry for many
years, and then in secret, since Ariosto was nominally
a priest, and held several benefices he could not afford
to give up. The *Orlando Furioso* was published in
1516, and from then on constantly revised. It is the
greatest of pities that this poem is now so little read.
Superficially it is a long tale of knight errants, dam-
sels in distress and magic castles, but an essential
truth to human experience underlies Ariosto's airiest
inventions. Accept the challenge of the opening lines:

> The ladies and the knights, the arms and loves,
> The courtesies, the daring deeds, I sing,

and enter into the timeless world of fable and romance
which Ariosto creates; feel the warm humanity, the
delighted energy which pulses through the plot, the
generous response to whatever is great, beautiful, or
moving in human affairs – and the reader will become
a reader of Ariosto for life. *Orlando Furioso* is the
literary equivalent of the great Renaissance pictures
of Raphael, Titian and Leonardo; it shares the same
belief in the value of the noble works of man and all
the ceremonies of civilized life. The contemporary
triumphs in architecture and painting, rich clothes
and elaborate pageantry, all the colour and vitality
of that extraordinary age are reflected and celebrated
by Ariosto.

Roman of the Dark Age

ARTHUR, (sixth century A.D.), no doubt existed, a
Romano-British general though not a king, behind
all the splendid, and confused weavings of medieval
legend and romance.

In Britain, bearing a Roman name, Artorius, he
was possibly 'the last of the "Romans"; the last to understand Roman ideas and use them for the British
people' (R.G. Collingwood). First to mention him
was the Welsh author Nennius, writing about 796,
and on the whole his account in the Historia Brit-
tonum is quite sober. Arthur was altogether invincible
and dauntless, he 'fought for the kings of Britons,
though he himself was *dux bellorum*', *i.e.* commander
in the field of a special force, or task force, which
engaged Saxon invaders when and where necessary.
Nennius gives the names of the twelve battles in
which Arthur defeated the Saxons; the last of them
was fought about A.D. 500 and checked Anglo-Saxon
aggression for nearly fifty years.

Standing out in the decay of Roman Britain for his
energy and acumen, Arthur may have won his battles by introducing armed cavalry, of which a recol-
lection is possibly preserved in the legendary Knights
of the Round Table. Arthur himself was killed at the
battle of Camlann, Briton fighting against Briton.

Father and schoolmaster of Turkey

ATATURK, (1880–1938), Mustapha Kemal, who
took the title of Ataturk, 'father of the Turks', saved
the core of a reduced Turkish state from extinction
and set Turkey on a new path.

He differed from contemporary dictators by his
sense of the possible, and by moderation in aims,
though not in methods. His other virtues were patriotism, courage and honesty, which he set against

his brutality, his intellectual narrowness, and a taste for debauch. Revolutionary in every fibre, he began on the left by accident because the right was corrupt; his reforms were unrelated to party. He rose rapidly in the army, fighting in the Libyan and Balkan wars before his great achievement of stopping the British on the Gallipoli peninsula; after which he fought in the Caucasus, and finally in Syria. Everywhere he was outstanding, though far from a military genius; his troops lost heavily, he was a rough and headlong tactician, but he was invincibly determined, and had a tremendous grip on the spirits of men. All the while he grumbled, criticized and sneered – with plenty of material for the practice – and was as insubordinate as he could dare to be.

The great days began when Mustapha Kemal raised a ragged unofficial opposition to the Greek invasion of Asiatic Turkey after the First World War. It was no longer the 'When you see me raise my hand, fix bayonets and come out after me!' of Gallipoli. He now commanded from the deep rear, leaving much to subordinates. The Greeks did virtually what they would with his discouraged levies. But when these were at their last gasp and the generals would have destroyed the army and lost the war by fighting on, Mustapha Kemal, though usually an advocate of fighting to the end, intervened and ordered an immediate retreat to the Sakkaria, covering Ankara, the Turkish capital. That was his most successful military act. He commanded in person in the battle of the Sakkaria, which has been deformed by legend. It did not, in fact, lead to the rout of the Greeks, but it wore them out, and so prepared for Mustapha Kemal's ultimate triumph.

The rest was political war, which ended in his dictatorship over a diminished Turkey. He let the Arab lands go without a qualm. He refused to be drawn into proletarian crusades by Russia, or Islamic crusades by anybody. What did he care for Islam? His aims were circumscribed and he did not allow Turkey to play the great power. He became Turkey's schoolmaster: taught it a new script, educated and emancipated its women, reformed its banking and its farming. All was concrete: no mysticism, no tradition. He had broken and destroyed the first opposition with great cruelty; later he decided that modern Turkey could not do without a political opposition. The experiment of creating one failed because the simple people were trained to beat up oppositions. He did not despair: 'Let the people leave politics alone for the present ... For ten or fifteen years more I must rule. Then perhaps I may be able to let them speak.' Strangely, almost incredibly, the experiment has evolved in the way he foresaw.

On the brink

ATTILA, (d. 453), king of the Huns and 'Scourge of God', who ruled unchecked from the Caspian to the Rhine, holding – one day – the fate of the West in his hands – a fate which was decided in one of the most decisive and bloody battles of the world.

There was little of the great captain about Attila: although his origins and much of his personal history are hidden in the mists of an imperfectly chronicled time, we know enough to say he was great by force of circumstance rather than by ability. Nomadic peoples, as the Huns were, have to be conquerors, or they will starve; and for the first eight years of his reign Attila was fighting other barbarian tribes, and making himself supreme in Central Europe. He possessed a rough-and-ready military efficiency of the most brutal kind and some primitive sense of organization, and he was savage in the extreme. Fact and legend about him are intermixed. A Greek sent on a mission from Constantinople to Attila's capital (somewhere near the present site of Budapest) described the scene in his banqueting hall – the gauzy slave-girls dancing around, chanting verses in his honour, the silver tables, the entry at last of the King, still on horseback, who would drink a cup of wine without dismounting. To the rulers of the Roman Empire he was truculent or accommodating, and he seems to have been a master at dissembling, all things to all men; open or wily, just or unjust, ascetic or debauched.

The movement of his huge armies across Europe was devastating. They poured westward like rats. Attila defeated the forces of both the Eastern and Western Roman Empires and placed them under tribute. After these tremendous feats he turned upon Gaul. The continent he scourged was already disrupted by earlier folk movements. In desperate defence against the annihilation which Attila represented, three discordant elements combined to meet him. They were Aetius, the Roman commander in Gaul; Merowig, a Frankish prince; and Theodoric I, King of the Spanish Visigoths. The decisive battle was fought on the Catalaunian Fields near Châlons-sur-Marne, Attila, by tradition, saying to his lieutenants before it began, 'Your natural estate is war, your sweetest passion vengeance. A battle is for you a holiday.' This battle was a defeat. Theodoric, however, fell in the course of it; Aetius was eventually murdered by an Eastern Emperor jealous of his prestige and power; Merowig lived to father a celebrated dynasty. Attila, driven back into the Danube valley, died there two years later during the debauched acquisition of a wife.

Attila stands as a symbol of the impact of barbarism on a divided and in part decadent empire. He is the supreme destroyer (though one famous clemency is attributed to him, the sparing of Lutetia, the ancient Paris, out of respect for St Genevieve). The very name of his people, the Huns, is another symbol which the peoples of the West have never forgotten. Attila boasted – or someone put the boast into his mouth – that the grass did not grow where his horse had passed and he was transformed into the King Etzel of the *Nibelungenlied*, the legendary epic of the Germans.

'We must love one another or die'

AUDEN, Wystan Hugh, (b. 1907), Anglo-American poet, a teacher, preacher, healer and entertainer in verse. As though he were an artesian well in the desert or a geyser in the rock, poetry of most kinds has welled up through this writer of our time, without caution or fear. Son of a medical psychologist, Auden received – and survived – the customary education of the English middle class, going from a 'public school' (one rather more liberal than others) to the university of Oxford. The taste for hanging around words and listening to what they say, which he calls the primal taste or gift of the poet, has blended in him with the English moralist and the generous man concerned for a human society all at sixes and sevens and all homeless at home.

Auden's progress in thought has been from Marxism to a Christian belief, always under the spell of teaching and healing, e.g. of Grimm's *Fairy Tales*, D. H. Lawrence, Groddeck, Homer Lane, Freud, Kierkegaard. In stricter poetry, in manipulating his words, his first master was Thomas Hardy, with his architectural concern for the shape and sharpness of poems and his deep and, in a good sense, 'churchy' tenderness for mankind.

> There is no such thing as the State
> And no one exists alone;
> Hunger allows no choice
> To the citizen or the police;
> We must love one another or die.

These lines are near the centre of his teaching, a belief in the 'open' democratic society where choice is allowed and possibilities are not reduced and controlled, or cancelled:

> ... true democracy begins
> With free confession of our sins;
> In this alone are all the same,
> All are so weak that none dare claim
> 'I have the right to govern', or
> 'Behold in me the Moral Law':
> And all real unity commences
> In consciousness of differences,
> That all have wants to satisfy
> And each a power to supply.
> We need to love all since we are
> Each a unique particular
> That is no giant, god or dwarf
> But one odd human isomorph;*
> We can love each because we know
> All, all of us, that this is so.

Such lines are rather Auden's poetry of instruction; he is a poet also of the heart, of fun, of the self-contained dramatic story – a jester inside one body with the preacher, believing that the different moods in each of us answer to poems of different weight and kind, from the epic to the limerick. Such a sonnet as this might be called a fairy tale for our age:

> He watched with all his organs of concern
> How princes walk, what wives and children say;
> Re-opened old graves in his heart to learn
> What laws the dead had died to disobey.
>
> And came reluctantly to his conclusion:
> 'All the arm-chair philosophers are false;
> To love another adds to the confusion;
> The song of pity is the Devil's waltz.'
>
> And bowed to fate and was successful so
> That soon he was the king of all the creatures:
> Yet, shaking in an autumn nightmare, saw
>
> Approaching down a ruined corridor,
> A figure with his own distorted features
> That wept, and grew enormous, and cried Woe.

* *Isomorphs*: figures of the same shape but different elements.

Auden is much the poet for wading in the human swirl, instead of taking a sentimental refuge in nature; and whereas T. S. Eliot (q.v.) left America for England in search of traditional values, Auden in 1939 left England for Ann Arbour University, Michigan (he is now an American citizen) and immersed himself in that urban society most typical of our age, in a population made up of all the peoples of the earth. It is as though he could feel and know our time only in the three-dimensional din of Seventh Avenue.

ILLUSTRATION: Page 79.

'A son of so many tears'

AUGUSTINE, SAINT, (354–430), bishop of Hippo in North Africa, where he passed most of his life. The greatest of the Latin Fathers of the Church, who by his doctrine, personality and reputation has had a power and influence over Christian thought second only to that of St Paul.

Augustine's father was a pagan, but his mother, Saint Monica, was a Christian of great piety, and the important part that she played in his religious development is described in his remarkable *Confessions*. From this work we learn much about his youth: his early delight in Latin literature and hatred of Greek; his love of tragedies, and the impression made on him by Cicero's *Hortensius*, which first inclined his mind towards philosophy. But the book's real purpose is to record the stages in his moral life (which he paints in the blackest colours); it is addressed to God in a spirit of remorse, contrition and gratitude. The gluttony of the infant was followed by the wantonness of the child, and upon reaching adolescence he was utterly overcome by the lusts of the flesh – especially after he moved to Carthage, 'where debauchery bubbled around me like a frying-pan'. His psychological insight into his heart is acute. He had stolen some pears: 'What I wanted to enjoy was not the thing I stole, but the actual sin of theft.' In Carthage 'I was not yet in love, but I loved the idea of love'. He put away his mistress, but was still unable to wait for his betrothed to come of age, so he prayed: 'Give me chastity and continence, only not yet.'

His concern with the problem of evil attracted him to the dualism of the Manichaeans, who taught that matter was essentially evil. But their intellectual weakness disgusted him, and in Milan he fell under the influence of Ambrose's teaching, to which the prayers of his mother were added: 'A son of so many tears', she had said, 'cannot be lost.' After a passionate inner struggle he was converted, giving up his bride and a second mistress.

As a bishop Augustine wrote much to combat heresies. Against the Donatists he defended the concept of the church as a society of sinners; attacking the Pelagians' optimistic view of human nature, he declared that only God's grace enables man to be virtuous. All are deserving of damnation, and all the unbaptised, even infants, will be damned; but certain of the baptised have been chosen to go to heaven. This doctrine of 'predestination' was stressed by the Reformation. But the reformers largely rejected Augustine's teaching that the State should be subject to the Church in religious matters – a doctrine (expressed in Augustine's *City of God*) which inspired the concept of the Holy Roman Empire and the extremer papal claims.

Miss Austen

AUSTEN, Jane, (1775–1817), English novelist with a shrewd tenderness for the interweaving of life with life which makes up a human society.

As a daughter of a rural rectory, with many relations and connexions among the landed gentry of southern England, Jane Austen had unusual opportunities for observing and enjoying the society around her. All her six novels are set in comfortable but unpretentious manor-houses, generally well populated with young people (she herself had six brothers and a sister); her characters divert themselves with balls, picnics, amateur theatricals, visits to neighbours and country drives and walks, varied occasionally by trips to London and Bath. In every book the business in hand is the making of marriages for the young ladies, a business that is seldom accomplished easily or uneventfully. The vulgarity of a mother and the seduction of a sister may seem to raise an insuperable bar to it; comparative poverty and a position of dependence may make the desired match look unrealizable; the young man's affections may be temporarily running elsewhere, or the girl herself, as Swift said of a statesman of his time, may 'have the misfortune to be perpetually mistaken' about who is falling in love with whom. So a comedy of errors must be played out, always with wit and irony, and often with considerable depth of feeling, before weddings are arranged and happiness reigns.

The first sentence of *Emma* perhaps best suggests the light and teasing tone in which these happenings are described: 'Emma Woodhouse, handsome, clever, and rich, with a comfortable home and a happy disposition, seemed to unite some of the best blessings of existence; and had lived nearly twenty-one years in the world with very little to distress or vex her.' What follows, of course, is the story of how her subsequent vexations were all of her own busy and ingenuous doing. 'I could not sit seriously down', Jane Austen wrote to the Prince Regent's librarian – thus nicely defining her own genius – 'to write a serious romance under any other motive than to save my life; and if it were indispensable for me to keep it up and never relax into laughing at myself or other people, I am sure I should be hanged before I had finished the first chapter.' No doubt in saying this, Miss Austen, as one still calls her almost inevitably, was being over-modest by intention, for admirers of her six completed books can detect in them many differences of mood; *Pride and Prejudice* (1813) is the gayest; *Persuasion* (published in 1818 after her death) the most serene, and *Sense and Sensibility* (1811) the most nearly romantic; *Emma* (1816) is sharpest in satire, *Northanger Abbey* (1818) a polished burlesque; while *Mansfield Park* (1814) is almost a tragedy – saved from becoming so only by its author's resolution to 'Let other pens dwell on guilt and misery. I quit such odious subjects as soon as I can, impatient to restore every body, not greatly in fault themselves, to tolerable comfort and to have done with all the rest.'

Few writers have had a stranger publishing history than Jane Austen. Three of her books were already in draft by 1797–8, yet the first to be published was *Sense and Sensibility* in 1811. *Pride and Prejudice* in its first version was refused by a publisher in 1797; *Northanger Abbey* was accepted, but not issued until after her death. Her three other books were written during the last five or six years of her life. So success was slow to come, nor can anyone now tell how much arduous rewriting of the early books preceded it. When it came she frankly appreciated it; 'I have now, therefore,' she wrote to her brother in 1813, 'written myself into £250, which only makes me long for more'; and we know, besides, that she was much gratified by the favourable notices she received in the formidable quarterly reviews. How all her work was achieved, so neatly and precisely, is hard to imagine, since for the most of her life she had no room of her own, and at Chawton, where she shared a cottage with her mother and sister, would hide her manuscripts at a writing-desk in the drawing-room under the blotter. We must picture a woman remarkably quick and lively in mind, but alarmingly self-contained; tart and sharp, perhaps, in manner, but at heart affectionate and possessed with a deep, though not over-wide, sense of sympathy.

From such gifts came a series of novels that offer the most finished and delightful examples of domestic comedy in the history of English fiction.

B

'It was a rare party'

BABAR, (1483–1530), properly Zahir-ud-din Mohammed, conqueror, founder of the Moghul Empire, first of the dynasty responsible for Islamic rule in Hindustan, with its vast consequence, and for Hindustan's Indo-Persian culture. A man of sensibility and prodigious physical hardihood, who left one of the world's best books of memoirs – from which, while music drifts at the evening prayer-hour through the orange groves of Herat, which he loved so much, his epitaph may be picked: 'It was a rare party.'

Babar ('the lion') has made himself remembered not only as the first of the Great Moghuls but also by the revealing candour of his narrative; the close observation of nature and of character; the love of beauty – flowers, animals, calligraphy; the joy of skill and strength in battle, in the chase, in the swimming of every river between Kabul and Agra (thirty-three strokes for the Ganges); for his courage in exile, comradeship in danger, lordliness in gesture:

'Among these was one famous diamond, the Koh-i-nor which has been acquired by Sultan Alauddin. It is so valuable, that a judge of diamonds valued it at half of the daily expense of the whole world. On my arrival, Humaiun presented it to me, and I gave it back to him as a present.'

In his veins ran the blood of Tamerlane on his father's side and of Jenghiz Khan on his mother's, and there is another facet to his character:

'The expedition against Bajour being thus terminated to my entire satisfaction, I gave orders for the erection of a pillar of skulls on a rising ground.'

The trails of Babar's life and of history begin 'on the extreme boundary of the habitable world' in the hill-girt oasis of Ferghana, where the Stakhanovites of the Uzbek cotton-belt now feed the mills of Moscow, a thousand miles away. In his twelfth year he inherited this tide-pool of the Mongol ebb and flow, a good but circumscribed fief, where tulips and roses filled the gardens, and clover grew in the meadows and game was abundant and the pheasants were fat; and where 'the people have a way of taking the stones out of the apricot and putting almonds in their place, which is very pleasant'.

It was not enough. The trails led on through Samarkand, seat of Alexander, and throne of Tamerlane to failure, peril of the assassin, and exile among the mountain-shepherds; and thence across the Oxus (Amu Darya), and over the passes of the Hindu Kush where the thunder of the small sure-footed horses of Central Asia had echoed before. Herat ('in the whole world there is not such another city') led to Kabul, where Babar laid out a great garden and stayed for several years, pacifying his new kingdom and at times dreaming of another, till at length 'We marched from the garden; I stayed till the first watch, and bestowed the oranges on different persons'. On his fifth invasion into the northern Indian plains the crack of his new artillery shook down the Afghan kingdom of Delhi on the field of Panipat, and then subdued the infidel chivalry of the Rajputs. Four years later, not yet forty-eight, he died in his own new palace at Agra, after praying (it is said) that the sickness of his beloved son and successor, Humaiun, should pass into his own strong body: which was taken home, not to his boyhood's kingdom, long overrun by Uzbeks and Mongols, but to his Kabul garden – 'when the *arghwan* flowers are in bloom, the yellow mingling with the red, I know no place to compare with it'. His successors, in splendour and decline, held the peacock-throne until sea-power took control and closed the land-gates between Central Asia and India. The Koh-i-nor went to the British Crown.

Babar's drinking-habits are a study in themselves. He abstained 'according to the rule of Jenghiz' until Herat brought the new pleasure to his palate, whereafter his drinking-parties took on an epic quality, on boats, in subterranean chambers of delight, in the violet-garden or the garden of fidelity, because of a victory or a good harvest or a haircut, 'or any other reason why'; his companions singing his own compositions until they fell senseless.

'Looking down from my tent on the valley below, the watch-fires were marvellously beautiful; perhaps that is why I drank too much wine at dinner that evening.'

There was vomiting, and worse, and sober repentance lightly cast aside. Yet there was a deliberate artistry in this, as in Babar's whole exercise of living: and as deliberately, on the eve of his final battle with the Rajputs, he shook himself free of drinking with a famous speech:

'Gentlemen and Soldiers, he who sits down to the feast of life must end by drinking the cup of death. ...'

ILLUSTRATION: Plate 7

Johann Sebastian Bach

BACH, Johann Sebastian, (1685–1750), German composer, of whom Beethoven remarked '*Das is nicht ein Bach, das ist ein Meer*' ('That's not a brook, it's an ocean').

To his contemporaries Bach seemed anything but the giant he is today – not because he was out of touch with the spirit of the time, but because his hard-working life was spent far from the more active centres of European life. Bach's family was well known for its musical ability in the neighbourhood of Eisenach, in Thuringia, and this long family tradition of music-making was a magnificent preparation for his career: unlike most musicians, Bach did not need to cut his own path at the beginning. There it was, ready made, leading, either for huge ability or small, to the same thing – the craftsmanlike fulfilment of certain simple but important functions in the life of a small, provincial, God-fearing community.

Bach's education was guided by his elder brother, since both his father and his mother had died while he was young. There is a famous story of how Bach was refused access to some of his brother's scores, and each night stole downstairs and copied out a page at a time, by moonlight. The story stands well enough for his mixture of obstinacy and moral sturdiness. At fifteen, Bach became a chorister at St Michael's, Lüneberg. He had a passion to hear as many of the finest organists as possible, and, having no money, he used to walk the thirty miles to Hamburg. Such austere exercise made him familiar with the German classic composers, including Buxtehude and Schütz (q.v.). To vary his education, Bach used to travel the sixty miles to Celle, where he heard a Court orchestra playing a very different kind of music, more elegant, less serious. These two influences, the religious and the sportive, were the foundation of his own style, though in fact his idiom was so imbued with the Church spirit that he was being wholly himself when he adapted secular music to religious purposes (as in *The Christmas Oratorio*). His music was directed to a greater than earthly power, even in secular cantatas, in which he might be setting a grovelling text dedicated to the dreariest of princelings.

At eighteen, in 1703, Bach became church organist at Arnstadt, where he was overjoyed to discover a fine new organ, but was soon in trouble for embroidering the hymn-tunes and confusing a sober-minded congregation. He was not very happy at Arnstadt. For one thing, he had to look after children, and unlike his great predecessor Heinrich Schütz, he had little success in doing so. He left in 1707, and spent the next sixteen years in a number of respectable but not very remunerative posts, which he changed according to inclination – though not always as easily as he would have wished. On one occasion he was arrested according to the records, 'since he obstinately insisted upon his resignation being accepted at once'.

In 1723 Bach applied to be cantor at St Thomas's Church in Leipzig, and was elected unanimously. Here he stayed for the rest of his life, happily composing and not so happily fulfilling his official duties. He had many undignified quarrels with his superiors – so many, indeed, that Bach sought to equip himself with a Court title to strengthen his position. Accordingly he serenaded the King-Elector of Poland-Saxony, and over a period of months despatched to his Court a series of secular works dedicated to him most ardently. Art, artfulness, and sheer dogged persistence won him the title of *Hof-Compositeur*.

Despite these occasional disturbances, Bach's years at St Thomas's had been a time of superb achievement. Among the works he wrote were *St Matthew Passion* (1728–1729), the *B minor Mass* (1738) and the *Art of Fugue* (1750). His life had been so retiring that when he died of apoplexy in 1750 there was little stir, and his music was overlooked by those who admired the music of his brilliant sons, Carl Philipp Emanuel Bach and Johan Christian Bach. It was to be many years before Samuel Wesley and other musicians were to rediscover for the world what Wesley called 'the immortal and adamantine pillars' of Bach's art.

ILLUSTRATION: Page 26.

'Silent, upon a peak in Darien'

BALBOA, Vasco Nuñez de, (c. 1475–1519?), discoverer of the Pacific.

Keats in his famous sonnet wrote of Cortez as the first man who gazed on the Pacific, from a peak in Darien. He should have written Balboa. It was in 1513 that Balboa first saw the blue Pacific, his thoughts no doubt concentrated on the Peruvian gold to which it might open a way (at that time Balboa needed gold urgently to justify himself to his Spanish masters at home). When he had gazed his full, he hurried down to the Gulf of San Miguel and plunged into the new ocean, waving the Spanish flag.

Balboa was altogether an attractive character, who once had himself exported in a barrel to escape his creditors, fell romantically in love with the beautiful daughter of a native chief, and was notable among the Spanish *conquistadores*, since he did not consider the best way of managing a colony was to enslave and murder the inhabitants. His preparations to discover and conquer Peru were cut short by the arrival from Spain of a brutal governor, who had him arrested and executed on a false charge; the Peruvian adventure was left to Pizarro, who was one of his companions when he discovered the Pacific.

La Comédie humaine

BALZAC, Honoré de, (1799–1850), French novelist. 'What Napoleon could not achieve with his sword,' he announced as a very young man, 'I shall accomplish with my pen.' A generation later, the hundred and more volumes that make up his *Comédie humaine* had been written, and he had indeed staked out an empire in the world of fiction that remains solid, unshakeable and wholly unique.

Born in the town of Tours and educated in Vendôme, Balzac looked upon Paris as the centre of the world which he was to conquer. From the moment when the young provincial moved to the capital, becoming a lawyer's clerk and then a hack-writer, Paris was for him 'the most alluring of monsters'. In 1829 he was successful with *Les Chouans*, an historical novel about the Royalist rebellions in Brittany against the Revolutionary Republic. A Royalist he proclaimed himself to the end of his life, and he was a worshipper, also, of the soldier-heroes of the Napoleonic Empire. So a Romantic element persisted – he came to Paris in the middle of the Romantic movement – in his outlook, though more and more it was overlaid by an ambition to give a portrait in sharp and strong detail of all of French life.

The twenty years in which he wrote his great novels was the time of the citizens' monarchy of King Louis-Philippe. It was an age in which French industry and commerce were rapidly developing, and merchants, manufacturers and money-grubbers were promoted to leading positions in the land. Balzac was fascinated. He had always desired fortune, as well as fame, and he plunged into numerous publishing and printing enterprises in the hope of making money. They failed, leaving him crippled with debt, but nothing could quench his conviction that money was one of the prime springs of human action, and business the most exciting of mankind's ventures. In novel after novel, whether set in a provincial scene, like *Eugénie Grandet* (1833), or in the bustle of Paris, as in *Le Cousin Pons* (1847), and *La Cousine Bette* (1847), the plot is concerned with the effects produced on human desires and emotions by the power of money and the demands of neediness.

All his life Balzac was ingenuously searching for a theory of the passions which would explain how ordinary affections develop into manias and apparently normal people are tragically overwhelmed by lust, avarice and envy – on the part of their neighbours, if not of themselves. Perhaps fortunately, he never discovered for himself a key philosophy, and to the end of his life his remarkable energy was able to pour itself out in uninhibited variety. The study of money and mania stands for only one side of his realistic conception of the novel; the other is illustrated by the use he made of his intense gifts of observation. 'The events of public or private life', he once wrote,

'are intimately linked with architecture.' And so, in most of his novels, minutely detailed and wholly convincing backgrounds are presented: the exact reality of provincial houses and Parisian lodgings. No one, for instance, who has once read *Le Père Goriot* (1835), can forget the intimate daily circumstances of the old man's life. This sense of the significance of physical things Balzac applied also to his descriptions of people: 'I penetrate the soul', he said, 'without neglecting the body.' The passions of the soul he may often have magnified, but the corporal presence of his characters, their features, clothes and habits, are indisputably real.

Not until 1842 did he conceive the grandiose plan of linking all the books he had written, and the still greater number he meant to write, under the general title of *The Human Comedy*. Dressed in his monklike robe, interminably drinking cups of black coffee, altering and re-writing his proofs to the very last moment – sometimes even dictating additions to an impatient printer – for nearly twenty-five years Balzac contrived to work up to eighteen hours a day. A mania for collecting and a talent for unlucky investment only served to drive him on; for the more his debts mounted, the more furiously he wrote. Though he once declared that his ambition was 'to be loved', as well as to be famous, his long liaison with Mme Hanska, a Polish countess, was not allowed to interfere with his writing habits. Work went on, and proofs arrived and were urgently despatched, whether he was at home in Paris or with Mme Hanska in Switzerland, Germany or the Ukraine. It was in the Ukraine on her estate that he died, a few months after their marriage, leaving behind a massive *œuvre*, that may be marred here and there by a tediousness and a lack of grace in style, but which remains one of the mountainous achievements of literature. It is curious to think, yet instructive and understandable, that one great admirer of *The Human Comedy* has been the poet W. B. Yeats (q.v.).

ILLUSTRATION: Page 32.

Arctic adventurer

BARENTS, William, (d. 1597), Dutch navigator and explorer, and leader of the first exploring party to defy the arctic winter. Barents took part in several expeditions that searched for the north-east passage between 1594 and 1597. On his last voyage, instead of finding 'the Coasts of Tartaria, Cathaia, and China' about which he had been instructed by the learned cosmographer Peter Plantius, his ship was frozen into the north-east of Novaya Zemlya, the long, sickle-shaped island in the Russian Arctic. He and his crew spent ten months in a hut built of driftwood, which was found undisturbed and intact in 1871. In June 1597, as their ship was still fast in the ice, they made for safety in two open boats, but after a week Barents died. The survivors were eventually befriended by Russians, who cured their scurvy. They were picked up by a Dutch ship, and caused a stir when they arrived in Amsterdam attired in their arctic dress. Barents has his memorial in the name of the Barents Sea between Novaya Zemlya and the North Cape.

The greatest showman

BARNUM, Phineas Taylor, (1810–1891), the great showman of America, who called himself frankly 'the prince of humbugs'.

Beginning in 1836 with Barnum's Grand Scientific and Musical Circus, he specialized in freaks and oddities. Many of these were faked. Thus a chief exhibit was Joyce Heth, a coloured woman apparently of great age. Barnum claimed she had been George Washington's nurse. On her death, it was proved she could have been no more than seventy years old. A mermaid constructed of a monkey and a large fish, the Siamese Twins, the Missing Link, the Great Living Whale, and General Tom Thumb, who earned Barnum a great fortune, were more of his exhibits.

General Tom Thumb, picked up in 1844, was the midget Charles Stratton, a man in perfect miniature, beautifully proportioned and only twenty-five inches high. In 1845 he was brought to Europe, first to Paris, then to London, where he was presented several times to Queen Victoria.

In 1871 Barnum established The Greatest Show on Earth, a circus and menagerie combined with some of his older exhibits. He was known by this time all over the world, a shrewd master and pioneer of blarney and advertising, of direct and indirect campaigns of publicity. Like others of more repute who are more harmful, Barnum was the ancient showman and cheapjack of the fairs reshaped to play upon the urban masses.

'Completely independent, completely indifferent'

BARTÓK, Bela, (1881–1945), Hungarian composer. Out of keeping as it might seem in a cosmopolitan age, Bartók's nationalism was the force behind music of savage and uncompromising actuality.

In his *Kossuth Symphony* (1904) he had symbolized and satirized Habsburg tyranny by including a distorted version of the Austrian National Anthem which an Austrian trumpeter refused to play during the rehearsal. This was direct flag-waving, whether by composer or trumpeter, and Bartók clearly felt his development was wrong. In the same year as this Kossuth scandal, his Hungarian consciousness was given a different turn: he began his researches into musical ethnology which were to continue till his death and were to reveal a genuine Magyar folk-music – something more virile altogether than the gypsifications which had been used by Liszt and Brahms. Whenever possible he lived with the peasants, learning their customs as well as their music, though sometimes not learning their music at all, since they would often sing only familiar songs of recent origin, and pretend to have forgotten the ones Bartók was searching for.

Slowly Bartók plotted the geography of this vast land of folk-music; more quickly, he absorbed its atmosphere into his own music, imitating its melodic and rhythmic features, and constructing a new harmony to support them. The eighty-five miniature pieces *For Children* (1908) were the foundation of a language that served Bartók well in larger musical forms – in music sometimes 'completely independent, completely indifferent', jagged and angry, and a reflection of the disasters which fell on the Hungary in which Bartók had sunk his artistic self, sometimes tempered and hardened into mastery. Admiral Horthy's Budapest and Hitler's Europe were no place for him, and Bartók crossed to America in 1939, where he had to face illness, poverty and neglect.

'Completely independent, completely indifferent,' were Bartók's own words, admirably fitted to his keen integrity.

Poet of 'Les Fleurs du Mal'

BAUDELAIRE, Charles, (1821–1867), French poet and critic. 'He was profoundly original in this respect: powerfully and essentially, he represents modern man as he has become as the result of the refinements of excessive civilization; modern man with his senses sharpened and vibrant, his mind painfully subtle, his brain saturated with tobacco, his blood boiling with alcohol.' To this description by Verlaine, add Paul Valéry's tribute: 'With Baudelaire, French poetry has at last transcended national frontiers. It has found readers everywhere; it has imposed itself as the very poetry of modern times.'

Baudelaire's poetic fame has been made by a single book, *Les Fleurs du mal* (1857), which is so difficult to classify that it has been suppressed as pornography and given minute attention as a contribution to theology. When he was alive, Baudelaire did his best to baffle the public about his true intentions, even spreading fantastic rumours about his person and his habits. Contradiction and paradox were his element: 'Among the rights which have been discussed in recent times', he noted, 'there is one which has been forgotten, yet which *everyone* is interested in establishing – the right to contradict oneself.'

Even Baudelaire's prose works, his admirable critical essays and the confessions in his private notebooks, do not help to resolve the contradiction between his two main *personae*, the dandy and sensualist on the one hand, the moralist and near-mystic on the other. Dandyism, to Baudelaire, was a complete philosophy based on what he called the 'cult of oneself'; it affirmed everything which is sterile and artificial and a denial of nature and love. It included sensuality, but this sensuality unrelated to religion and art; for the great man (or dandy) 'never takes leave of himself':

In the glowing fire-grate of your hair I inhale the odour of tobacco mingled with opium and sugar; in the night of your hair I see the infinity of tropical azure resplendent; on the downed banks of your hair I inebriate myself with the mingled odours of musk and coco-nut oil.
Long let me bite your heavy black tresses. When I gnaw your elastic and rebellious hair, it seems that I am eating memories.

Like much of his work, this prose poem stems from his long relationship with Jeanne Duval, his mulatto mistress, who served Baudelaire as an embodiment of all that is evilly and viciously beautiful, just as his mother – on whom he depended emotionally and for money – supplied the moral disapproval that was a necessary reminder of the ideal. It was his mother who nursed him through his second childhood, the paralytic stage of the syphilis which killed him. Two other personal relationships were crucial. The first was with Edgar Allan Poe (q.v.), the writer he never met, but translated, glossed and idolized as a master, companion and kindred spirit. The second was with his step-father, General Aupick, who stood for everything Baudelaire loathed and despised; this hatred not only inspired many of his most trenchant aphorisms, but induced him to appear on the barricades during the Revolution of 1848 – for the mere pleasure, he claimed, of shouting 'Down with General Aupick!'

Yet the same poet, who wrote in praise of drugs, drunkenness, squalor and perversity, concluded another of his prose poems with these words:

Souls of those I have loved, souls of those I have sung, strengthen me, support me, rid me of lies and the corrupting vapours of the world; and you, O Lord God, grant me grace to produce a few good verses, which will prove to myself that I am not the lowest of men, that I am not inferior to those whom I despise.

(*The translations are by Michael Hamburger.*)

ILLUSTRATION: Page 33.

Against capital punishment

BECCARIA, Marchese de, (1738–1794), brilliant and persuasive enemy of capital punishment and judicial torture, who was called in his day 'protector and defender of humanity'. It seemed to him absurd, he wrote in his famous book *Of Crimes and Punishment* (1764), 'that laws, which are an expression of the public will, which abhor and punish murder, should themselves commit murder'.

Beccaria was born in Milan of a family of judges, soldiers and clergy. According to himself, eight years of a fanatical education under the Jesuits suffocated all his feelings of humanity. He recovered only by reading Montesquieu and the French encyclopaedists. Friendship with a young enlightened prison governor also gave Beccaria an unusual knowledge of torture, secret accusations, the religious Inquisition and death for the smallest offences.

In his book he argued against legalized revenge. Crime is to be measured by the injury done to society, and punishments are not just unless the law has adopted the best means of preventing the crime it punishes. The abolition of capital punishment in many countries has been due to Beccaria's clear advocacy and arguments.

The giant of music

BEETHOVEN, Ludwig van, (1770–1827), German composer. 'Strength', said Beethoven, like a Bismarck of music, 'is the morality of those who distinguish themselves from the rest, and it is mine too'; and his last gesture before he died was to raise a clenched fist.

Story after story depicts Beethoven as one of the giants of art. When Goethe and Beethoven took their walk together at what is now called Teplice-Sanov in Bohemia, and met the Habsburg Empress and her dukes coming the other way, Goethe stood respectfully to one side, while Beethoven marched straight through the covey, arms folded, head aloft. When the Empress asked him one morning to call upon her, his reply was 'that he was busy all that day, but would attempt to look in the day after'. Men and not titles mattered to Beethoven. His father had worked as a minor musician at Bonn, between bouts of drunkenness, and there as a child Beethoven observed the corruption of aristocrats; and he developed instinctively and unintellectually a desire to establish a new aristocracy of genius, for which anything was to be sacrificed. The meeting with Goethe (q.v.) was a fine opportunity for expounding his beliefs. The rulers of the world, he remembered, 'could make a privy councillor or a minister, but they could not make a Goethe or a Beethoven. Therefore they must be taught to respect that which they cannot make, and which they are far from being themselves; it does them good.'

Beethoven had no doubt that he deserved respect himself. On another occasion he said, 'Music is the wine that incites us to new creation, and I am the Bacchus who presses this glorious wine for mankind and grants them drunkenness of the spirit; when they are sober again they will have fished up much that they may take with them on to dry land'.

Beethoven believed, simply, in the divine inspiration of music, and he championed Genius, not as a glorification of self, but to gain respect for an instrument of Divine Will. Nineteenth-century recognition of the artist's independence was largely due to Beethoven's example.

From the first this giant knew that he must walk alone; and loneliness was increased, though his music was not damaged, by the cruel fortune of going deaf, a gradual process which began in 1802, the year in which he wrote his Heiligenstadt Testament. This was ostensibly a will in favour of his two brothers. In fact, it is a tragic message out of the depths, one of the most terrible things ever set down by a man, in which he declared 'it is so long since real joy echoed in my heart'. Even at this time he could compose music as sunlit and optimistic as the *Spring* sonata, Opus 24, and the *Second Symphony*.

As his deafness grew worse, Beethoven in Vienna turned his porcupine back against all but a very few friends and men of genius. He lived in squalor, dust everywhere, puddles on the floor, ink-pots on the bed, chamber-pots under the table, not a shelf or a corner which did not hide or display some new variety of filth and disorder. Rossini was one of the few to visit the Master in his den. 'When I descended those dilapidated stairs', he wrote, 'I retained of my visit to this great man an impression so painful – thinking of this destitution and shabbiness – that I could not repress my tears.'

Nonetheless, Beethoven's misery was self-inflicted, since he was not altogether a poor man. It was a case of chaos outside, of indifference, absolutely, to circumstances, and of no chaos within. Rossini's visit took place when Beethoven had some five years to live. He had been stone-deaf since 1819, which had no effect on his output, since, like most composers, he made music in his head, in his being, and not on his piano. He worked till the end. The *Ninth Symphony* was composed from 1817 to 1823, the five string quartets, the final revolution of his art, for so long considered obscure and wilfully unconventional, occupied him in 1825 and 1826.

Beethoven was always unconventional. His friend Ferdinand Ries once pointed out what he thought was an elementary musical error in an early quartet. Beethoven growled, 'Who forbids this harmony?' 'Why, Fux, Albrechtsberger, and a dozen other theorists.' 'In that case', Beethoven replied gleefully, 'I allow it.' In all his music, whether in the *Eroica* symphony or the last quartets, Beethoven stalked heedlessly over the academies, going in search of his own and human glory. Lesueur, the French composer, according to Berlioz, after listening to a performance of the *Eroica* in Paris, came out so overcome with emotion, he said, that 'trying to put on my hat, I thought I should never find my head again'. Most appropriately, Beethoven clenched his fist and died in Vienna, in the last days of March 1827, at the height of a spring thunderstorm.

ILLUSTRATION: Page 27.

'Furious Visarion'

BELINSKY, Visarion Grigoryevich, (1810–1848), son of a naval surgeon, fearless and passionate Russian critic, who considered that it was the critic's business to be 'the tutor of society'. 'Ever since I was a child I have considered it to be a most agreeable offering to the God of Truth and Reason to spit in the face of public opinion whenever it was stupid or mean or both' – this saying is characteristic of the whole attitude to life of 'furious Visarion', as Belinsky was known among his friends.

He began his work as literary critic at the age of twenty-three by contributing to Moscow periodicals, after he had been expelled from Moscow University because of his 'poor intellectual attainments', though the real reason was his youthful tragedy *Dmitry Kalinin*, in which he attacked serfdom and the Russian landowning class which lived by it. In Moscow he associated with the group of young Russian Hegelians and for a time shared their ultra-conservative opinions. Then in 1839 he moved to Petersburg, where he became the literary critic of the widely read monthly *Home Annals*. His views changed: he now became the outspoken enemy of Russian absolutism and the most influential writer of his day. 'As a literary critic', wrote Turgenev (q.v.), who became his closest friend, 'Belinsky was what the English call the right man in the right place.' What his friends admired in him and his enemies detested was the boldness, warmth and conviction with which he propagated his literary and political ideas.

'Literature', Belinksy declared, 'is not a drawing-room occupation, but the efflorescence of the civilization of a people and the result of the historical development of its life.' Poetry in its widest sense was 'truth in the form of contemplation'. 'It is', he wrote, 'thinking in images, and hence, if an idea, expressed by an image, is not concrete or fully realized or false, the image itself cannot possibly be artistic.' He demanded that 'a real poet' should possess 'a powerful sympathy with the problems of contemporary life'. 'Let him depict reality as it is,' Belinksy wrote, 'and not look at it through the soot-covered spectacles of a morality that was true in the past.'

Shortly before he died of consumption, he sent a famous letter to Gogol (q.v.), in which he attacked Gogol's reactionary views. 'I can't keep silent when lies and immorality are preached as truth and virtue under the cover of religion and under the protection of the whip. ... The salvation of Russia lies in civilization, education and humanity. ... She needs neither sermons nor prayers (she has had plenty of both!), but the awakening of a feeling of human dignity in the people.'

Defender of Byzantium

BELISARIUS, (c. 494–565), Byzantine general, one of the soldiers who have influenced the fate of the world. By his campaigns he propped up the decaying Empire of the East, under Justinian, and for a while stopped the hands of the clock.

Little is known of him but for the narrative of one partisan, his secretary Procopius, the Byzantine historian. Procopius paints the life and great deeds of his master with a loaded brush. Yet however uncertain the details, nothing is doubtful about the results or the simple tactical methods Belisarius employed. For about a century and a quarter before his birth, warfare had changed. The legion had gone. Cavalry had now that ascendancy on the battlefield which it was to keep, in spite of a check now and then, until after the day of Condé and Cromwell. Belisarius won his victories against Vandals and Ostrogoths by employing a reserve of cavalry in mail, armed with missiles as well as shock weapons: they used bows from the saddle, and could also charge home to decide an issue.

In his day the Barbarians had overthrown the Western Empire. The Eastern, with its capital at Byzantium, was tottering. The simplest proof of the great skill of Belisarius is that he nearly always won against great odds, whereas under other leaders the so-called Romans could no longer withstand the young conquerors from the north or even the Persians. The one exception was the general who replaced Belisarius, the eunuch Narses, but he was equally successful by using the same methods. Like Hannibal, Belisarius lacked the advantage of leading a national and homogeneous army. His troops, of mixed nationality and race, gave their loyalty to him personally, not to Justinian and the Eastern Empire. Unlike Hannibal, he does not appear to have been a first-class disciplinarian. More than once his plans were imperilled or even spoiled by the disobedience or the impetuosity of subordinates. Yet he himself was disciplined. Had he not been loyal to an ungrateful Emperor, he could have hewn a kingdom for himself.

In his most famous campaigns Belisarius followed a path which British soldiers were to tread thirteen centuries later. He reconquered North Africa from the Vandals, crossed again to the European continent, defeated the Ostrogoths and recaptured Rome itself. Byzantium did not manage to keep all that he had won; indeed, when recalled in his old age, he had to face the Bulgars almost at the gates of the city. Nevertheless, he gave the Eastern Empire a chance to breathe and to be active once more. Belisarius and Justinian preserved and prolonged a fragile power and a civilization doomed in any event to progressive decomposition. Without them the legacy of that civilization, which included much that Byzantium had itself inherited from greater ages, would almost certainly have been less rich. Ironically he is best remembered by a legend that in his last years he was disgraced, blinded, and reduced to begging for bread. The legend has no foundation, but it symbolizes the ingratitude of Justinian (q.v.) and of his failure to use the gifts of his great general as he might have done.

Deep, splendid, and serene

BELLINI, Giovanni, (c. 1426–1516), the first of the supreme painters of Venice.

Most of Bellini's paintings are religious, but as a man of his age, helping to create that age, he felt with a new intensity for man and nature. He fed upon colour, he observed and he painted the physical structure of the landscape – the way a river twists, the branching of a tree, the cracks in the brown rock, the grain of clothing, the frisking of a rabbit; as in his *Agony in the Garden* (National Gallery, London).

Yet none of this detail spoils the purpose or dulls the shock of his pictures. The tenderness and strength of his feelings spread from the actors right through the scene in which they are acting. In *The Agony in the Garden*, once more, the head and the beseeching hands of Christ tell their story with all the sharper effect because they are painted against the strongest and whitest light; and Christ's anguish appears the greater because it is echoed in the light, flame and tortuous shape of the sunset cloud and in the angularity and bareness of the rock. (So in an English carol Christ tells his mother that he will die:

> And the stones in the wall,
> Mother, shall mourn for me all.)

Around his Madonnas the landscape becomes itself part of the love of the mother for her child.

Florentine painters gave in their backgrounds miraculously idealized glimpses or scraps of landscape. Bellini, loving the countryside of the Veneto, widened the glimpse: he introduced man to idyllic landscape observed and painted almost for its own sake. So when he was asked for a picture of Paris, he replied that he was unable to paint it because he had never seen Paris.

Bellini was surrounded by greatness. Mantegna was his brother-in-law. Titian and Giorgione were his pupils. Dürer met him in 1506 – old, but as Dürer described him, the King of Painters, kind and courteous. Changing from tempera painting to painting in oil, Bellini was more and more able to spread a glow and intensity of colour over his pictures. In his old age (with Titian's help) he had still to paint the gloriously pagan *Feast of the Gods*, which now hangs in special state in the National Gallery at Washington. Here the colour is Venetian, yet still the vehicle of deep, splendid and serene emotion. The National Gallery in London, the Metropolitan Museum in New York and the Academy in Venice preserve many of Bellini's paintings.

ILLUSTRATION: Page 29.

The great utilitarian

BENTHAM, Jeremy, (1748–1832), English thinker and political theorist, founded the Utilitarian school of morals and politics. He asked of every law, convention or institution: 'What's the use of it?' – a destructive formula which left little of traditional life standing.

Bentham began as an advocate of legal reform with no thought of political change. In fact, he looked hopefully to the enlightened despots, especially to Catherine the Great. He condemned the Rights of Man as even more romantic and absurd than kings and aristocrats. But, when the unreformed parliament failed to follow his advice, he was persuaded by James Mill that only universal suffrage could produce the Utilitarian changes that he desired. Bentham believed that all institutions should promote 'the greatest happiness of the greatest number'; and though this principle does not necessarily imply political democracy, most Benthamites came to accept the view that the greatest number are best capable of deciding how their greatest happiness can be achieved.

Bentham owed his influence entirely to his writings and to his conversation. His only practical act was to invent a model prison, the Panopticon, in which the prisoners could be under constant observation by the chief warder from a central point. For this extraordinary device, which was never used, he received £20,000 from the British Government. The invention was symbolic of his general approach to mankind. Despite his democratic principles, he believed that the life of every citizen should be supervised by Utilitarian philosophers; and his followers acted on this belief in the reformed parliament, when they remade one aspect of life after another. No man has contributed more than Bentham to give modern life its form; his thought and his practical suggestions shaped contemporary European civilization. His writings are crabbed and difficult, enlivened only by the new words that he was constantly inventing.

Though a materialist and an atheist, he has survived after death. His followers founded University College, London (originally known as the godless college in Gower Street); and Bentham's mummy, which is kept in a cupboard there, emerges to preside over the College feasts.

ILLUSTRATION: Page 30.

The horseless carriage

BENZ, Karl, (1844–1929), German inventor of the automobile, who devoted his life to making a horseless carriage, and lived to see it conquer the world.

When Benz's three-wheeled engine-driven machine (the first 'car') appeared on the streets of Mannheim in 1885, people stood aghast to see that it moved without the aid of men or horses. The *Neue Badische Landeszeitung* wrote: 'There is no doubt that this engine-velocipede will make a strong appeal to a large circle, as it should prove itself quite practical and useful to doctors, travellers, and lovers of sport.' It was the beginning of the end of the horse for traction.

To Benz, it was a particular triumph, because he had pleaded for his idea almost alone. There had been horseless carriages before, of course; Murdock and Trevithick (q.v.) had run vehicles on the road which were driven by steam-engines; nor did Benz invent the internal-combustion engine. That was the work of either Étienne Lenoir or Siegfried Markus. It was while Benz was a student at the Karlsruhe Polytechnic that the idea of the horseless carriage driven by a gas-engine fired his mind. One of his professors, Ferdinand Rechtenbacher, had a strong, if advanced following, because of his prophecy of the decline of the steam engine. Benz listened to his words; and in the years ahead, as he worked long hours in factories, he dreamed of putting an engine on a frame with wheels, and making it go along.

He went into the gas-engine business for himself, but his partners were not interested in his crazy scheme, and he had to design his carriage in secret in his spare time. His problem was to build an engine that was both lighter and more powerful than any other; to put it on to a chassis, and to get power from the engine to the wheels. Benz's first car was a great achievement for one man; everything – engine, fuel, transmission, controls – had been developed and designed by him: the wheels were driven by means of a chain, and there were two speeds. Benz cars kept their chain-drive for a long time, for Benz was a conservative man, and hampered his own business expansion by refusing to abandon certain fixed ideas. He also built his cars with three wheels long after all other makes had four.

His early days in Mannheim were made very difficult by the arbitrary speed limits that the police imposed on him: twelve kilometres an hour outside the city limits, six inside. Benz saw that he would never be able to develop his cars if this rule were not altered, and he thought of a scheme to abolish it. He wrote to the Minister of Baden, asking him if he would like a ride in his car. The Minister accepted. Then Benz arranged with a local milkman that he should wait with his horse and van in a certain road. When Benz passed them, at six kilometres an hour, the milkman – it was agreed – would start off, pass the car at a good speed, and jeer at them. The plan worked perfectly: the Minister was so angry at being passed by a milk-van that he urged Benz to go faster. Benz explained the speed limit. 'Never mind', said the Minister: and Benz won the day.

The firm of Benz had little encouragement inside Germany; but their cars sold well in France. And Benz, though he never became a wealthy man, was never in want in his old age. He was always honoured in the motor industry as the maker of the first car; and his name is still current in the famous racing-car marque, Mercédès-Benz.

Bering of the Straits

BERING, Vitus, (1681–1741), Danish navigator in the Russian service and discoverer of the straits that bear his name. 'In the beginning of January, 1725,' writes Nartov, chronicler of the last days of Peter the Great, 'Peter was realizing that he had not long to live ... With his own hands he drew up the instructions relative to the Kamchatka expedition, which should determine the relation between Asia and America' for it was not known whether the north Pacific area was land or water, or whether Asia and America were united. 'Now that the country is in no danger from its enemies we should strive to win for her glory along the lines of the arts and sciences,' said Peter, giving instructions to be carried out after his death. 'In seeking such a passage [to China and India by way of the Arctic Sea] who knows but perhaps we may be more successful than the Dutch and English, who have made many such attempts along the American coast?'

In 1728 Bering succeeded in sailing round the eastern tip of Asia. He supervised a number of expeditions for the discovery of the northern coast of Siberia. In 1740–41 he crossed the Bering Strait to the American coast, explored part of the coast of Alaska and died on the way back. Russian trappers and seal hunters settled in Alaska. The gap in the American coastline between the Russians in Alaska and the Spaniards in southern California was left to be filled in by Captain Cook (q.v.).

God and matter

BERKELEY, George, (1685–1753), Irish cleric and philosopher who is celebrated for his denial of the existence of matter – a thesis which he thought to be the plainest common sense if only rightly understood.

The most subtle work of this charming writer dates from his youth. *The Principles of Human Knowledge* appeared when he was twenty-six and the three *Dialogues of Hylas and Philonous* two years later. His interests were not exclusively philosophical; as Dean of Derry he concerned himself with a plan for establishing a great missionary college in Bermuda, from which America was to be evangelized. In a famous poem he saw America rising out of Europe's decay:

There shall be sung another golden age,
    The rise of empire and of arts,
The good and great inspiring epic rage,
    The wisest heads and noblest hearts.

Not such as Europe breeds in her decay;
    Such as she bred when fresh and young,
When heav'nly flame did animate her clay,
    By future poets shall be sung.

Westward the course of empire takes its way;
    The first four acts already past,
A fifth shall close the drama with the day;
    Time's noblest offspring is the last.

Berkeley spent three years in Rhode Island, but returned home disappointed when the money promised by the Government did not come. His last work, *Siris*, was an enquiry into the virtues of tar-water, to which he attributed wonderful medicinal properties, claiming that it was 'of a nature so mild and benign and proportioned to the human constitution, as to warm without heating, to cheer but not inebriate'. Berkeley's later years were spent as Bishop of Cloyne.

'And whatever the world thinks,' Berkeley wrote, 'he who hath not much meditated upon God, the human mind, and the *summum bonum*, may possibly make a thriving earthworm, but will most indubitably make a sorry patriot and a sorry statesman.' It was religion which prompted his attack on matter, and the title-page of the *Principles* promises to enquire into 'the grounds of Scepticism, Atheism and Irreligion'. Starting from the empiricism of Locke (q.v.), which asserted that all our ideas were derived from experience, Berkeley claimed that what we perceive are (the ideas of) colours, sounds, tastes, smells, etc.

Continued on p. 39

PLATE 1

AKBAR (1542–1605). The Murderer Adham Khan, being thrown from the palace
walls at Agra on Akbar's orders in 1562. In the foreground, the victim, Atgah Khan
(Akbar's foster-father), lying stabbed. *Inscribed:* outline and portraits by Miskin, painting
by Sankar. Mughal (Akbar) period. *c.*1600.

PLATE 2

BENJAMIN FRANKLIN (1706–1790) by J. M. Wright.

WILLIAM BLAKE (1757–1827).
Pencil drawing by John Linnell.

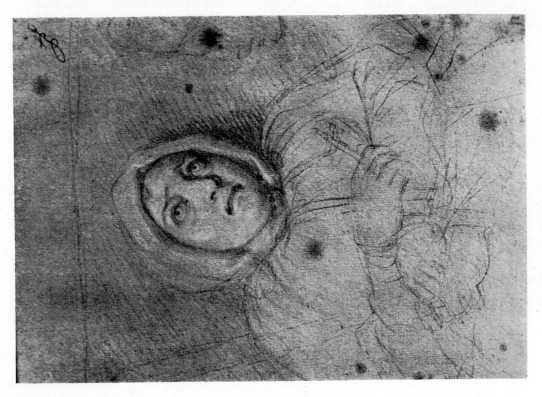

MARQUISE DE BRINVILLIERS (c. 1630–1676)
before execution, by Charles le Brun.

LUCREZIA BORGIA (1480–1519) by Bernardino Pintoricchio. Detail from a fresco in the Vatican.

SANDRO BOTTICELLI (1444–1510) by himself. Detail from *The Adoration of the Magi*.

BACH (1685–1750) by E. G. Haussman.

BEETHOVEN (1770–1827) aged forty-seven, by A. von Kloeber.

HECTOR BERLIOZ (1803–1869) by Gustave Courbet.

GIOVANNI BELLINI (c. 1426–1516). Presumed self-portrait.

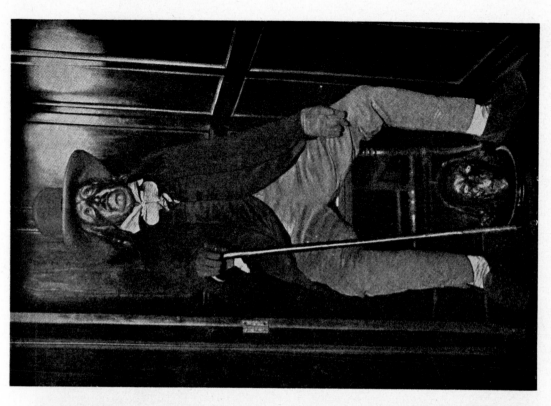

JEREMY BENTHAM (1748–1832).
Effigy (in University College, London) dressed in Bentham's clothes with his embalmed head between his feet.

TYCHO BRAHE (1546–1601) by M. van Mierevelt.

BRILLAT-SAVARIN (1755–1826)
by Angélique Allais from the series of portrait-engravings of Deputies in the
National Assembly at Versailles, 1789.

BISHOP BERKELEY (1685–1753) painted in 1725 by J. Smithers.

BALZAC (1799–1850). Photograph by Nadar.

BAUDELAIRE (1821–1867) about two years before his death.

CARAVAGGIO (1565–1609). Self-portrait, detail from *David and Goliath*.

JOHN BUNYAN (1628–1688) painted in 1684 by J. Sadler.

SIR EDWIN CHADWICK (1800–1890).

CATHERINE THE GREAT (1729–1796) engraved after the oil painting by Michail Schibanoff.

ISAMBARD KINGDOM BRUNEL (1806–1859)
with the hauling chains of *The Great Eastern*, his ship.

PIETER BRUEGEL THE ELDER (c. 1525–1569).
The Painter and the Amateur, by himself.

38

PLATE 3

CHARLES V (1500–1558) at the Battle of Mühlberg 1547. Painted in 1548 by Titian.

PLATE 4

FRANCIS I (1494–1547) by Jean Clouet.

and that the objects in the world are collections of such ideas (as 'sweet', 'rough', 'white', etc. might constitute a lump of sugar). Furthermore, it seemed clear that these ideas could not exist without a mind: 'all the choir of heaven and furniture of the earth, in a word all those bodies which compose the mighty frame of the world, have not any subsistence without a mind ... their *being* (esse) is to be perceived or known ... consequently so long as they are not actually perceived by me, or do not exist in my mind or that of any other *created spirit*, they must either have no existence at all, *or else subsist in the mind of* some eternal spirit'. Berkeley dismissed the view that ideas (or some ideas), though mental, resemble the objects from which they derive: 'an idea can be like nothing but an idea', and if all we are aware of is our ideas how can we compare them with unperceived matter?

Though Berkeley defended his main position with a variety of subtle arguments, it was his fate to be misunderstood and misrepresented. Dr Johnson's treatment of Berkeley's 'ingenious sophistry' is well known, but hardly well informed: striking his foot with mighty force against a large stone, till he rebounded from it, he exclaimed, 'I refute it *thus*!'

ILLUSTRATION: Page 31.

The ultra romantic

BERLIOZ, Louis Hector, (1803–1869), French composer. Berlioz should have started his wild, romantic life on the day of the storming of the Bastille, or else he should have been born earlier still and led the assault with gun in one hand and flag in the other, as in a painting by Delacroix. In fact, his only battles were with obdurate parents, deplorable women, hardheaded academics, poverty, and a temperament that would have swept another man to early suicide.

In his youth he did his best to become a doctor, not a musician, but he saw a performance of Gluck's *Iphigeneia* in Paris. 'Short of fainting', he wrote, 'I could not have been more impressed, than when I saw the performance of *Iphigénie en Tauride*.' Berlioz kept himself alive by teaching and journalism. In 1830 he won the *Prix de Rome* for composition, but the musical authorities disliked his music, remembering perhaps that he had scribbled on the walls of the Paris Conservatoire the words 'C'est défendu de faire la musique contre ces murs'.

C

In 1827 the visit of Kemble's Shakespearean company to Paris had increased the confusion of Berlioz's life. Shakespeare, he said, 'in opening the heavens of art with a sublime crash, illuminated the most profound distances'; and the sublime crash echoed loudly thereafter through Berlioz's own music. Shakespeare had to share his effulgent love with Harriet Smithson, the leading actress in Kemble's company, of whom Berlioz had said, 'She will beautify the last days of my life, which, I hope, will not be long. One could not endure such emotions for long.' Harriet Smithson was not of a like mind; so Berlioz sought 'violent distraction', as he called it, with a pianist named Camille Moke, to whom he became engaged before leaving for Italy. There he received a letter from his prospective mother-in-law reproaching him, and announcing the marriage of Mlle Moke to a M. Pleyel. Berlioz at once set out armed with laudanum, strychnine and a disguise, seriously intending to murder both Camille and her mother. On the way he lost his disguise, and with it his murderous intentions. He still 'harboured a passion for Harriet', and was equipped with a powerful weapon in the shape of his *Symphonie Fantastique* (1830), into which he had emptied the remains of his unrequited love. On his return to Paris some time after the Moke affair, he played this work at a concert of his own music, with the intention of attracting Harriet's regard. This time he succeeded, though he had to attempt suicide by poison in her presence, and save himself with an emetic which he conveniently had with him, before she would agree to marry him, which she did in 1833. The marriage failed, and the two separated in 1840.

The music and the life of Berlioz were alike, from *Sardanapole* (1830) with which he had gained the *Prix de Rome* to *The Damnation of Faust* (1846) and his opera *The Trojans* (1863). At its worst the music recalls in its effect Berlioz's account of his attempted suicide – 'Fearful shrieks from Harriet – sublime despair – mocking laughter from me – desire to live once more on hearing frantic avowals of love – emetic – results which lasted for ten hours'. At its best his music has an heroic and almost godlike strength and tenderness about it. By common standards this music born out of orgies of emotion is illegitimate. It is never orderly, will never be admired by those who are aghast at the composer's claim that 'the idea ranks below the feeling and the passion'. But it has the courage and vitality of great art.

ILLUSTRATION: Page 28.

Giovanni Bernini

BERNINI, Giovanni Lorenzo, (1598–1680) 'Italian architect and sculptor. In the nineteen-twenties an English writer remarked that no sculptor of equal power was so little known in England, 'except perhaps by name'. That is perhaps true of him as an architect, though he designed the Piazza of St Peter's in Rome (1666), which is the high achievement of all European baroque, that style so intricate and incessantly alive, which freed man's spirit from a chilly exact, academic classicism, which at last was all too sane, reasonable and immobile.

His father was Florentine, and he passed his youth in Rome. His first work – a funerary bust of a bishop – brought him work, at the age of fifteen, for Pope Paul V. To the next ten years belong those masterpieces now in the Villa Borghese in Rome: *Aeneas and Anchises*, the *Rape of Proserpine* and *Apollo and Daphne*. More famous was the *Santa Therese* of S. Maria della Vitoria: the art writer, Mrs Jameson, a fair sample of the enlightened Victorian, found this baroque combination of realism and sensuality 'offensive in its materialism', while Taine, the French historian and critic, found it 'adorable'. Bernini never visited England. In 1665 he was in Paris, to be fêted by Louis XIV and to design a façade of the Louvre. Christopher Wren was then studying architecture in Paris, but Wren got only a glimpse, as he said, of 'the old fox's' sketch. Other fine sculpture includes, in Rome, the Fountain in the Piazza Agonale, the Triton in the Piazza Berberini, the famous Fountain of the Galleys in the Piazza di Spagna. In St Peter's Bernini designed the colossal S. Longinus, the *Cathedra Petri*, and the tombs of several popes.

Bernini was a nervous, electrifying, daring sculptor, exacting a crisp obedience from marble, dividing it and reforming it into dynamic shapes. His architecture was grandly conceived. It was Bernini also who designed the whole approach to St Peter's, the piazza, the steps, and the enclosing colonnades, each containing 320 columns nearly four and a half feet in diameter. It is a superb creation, using the least adorned of the classical orders – the Tuscan – and depending for effect upon its majestic sweep, on sunlight and shadow, and on changing vistas of cathedral and fountains. The Piazza itself is cut flat; it is a saucer, subtly designed to hold the crowd which comes there to receive the blessing of the Pope: a stage setting for a drama, and a major victory of Baroque town-planning. The Fascist Government opened up the east side of the Piazza, a monstrous architectural blunder, since much of the sense of enclosure was at once destroyed. There was no excuse, since a sketch by Bernini exists showing how the scheme should have been completed at that point.

Blood and iron

BISMARCK, Otto von (1815–1898), the first chancellor and architect of a United Germany, a Junker squire who once remarked that a man who has not drunk five thousand bottles of champagne and smoked five thousand cigars could not properly be said to have lived. Half of him at first was the grand squire, half the junior administrator. When he was Prussian representative in the Federal Diet he made a reputation as a man of character and power, and he learned to know the weakness of the Austrian leadership of Germany. Later he was ambassador at St Petersburg and at Paris, put 'on ice' until his time should come. A telegram from his friend von Roon, Minister for War, told him laconically 'the pear is ripe. Come immediately.' Von Roon's army reforms, essential to preserve Prussian militarism, had failed to pass a Liberal parliament, and King Wilhelm of Prussia preferred to send for Bismarck the Junker rather than submit to bourgeois democracy.

'Not by revolutions and majority votes ... but by blood and iron, can Prussia be preserved', said Bismarck on 8 October 1862. Bismarck stood firm; the Junkers were saved; and in 1866 the German Liberals finally abdicated (until 1945) and gave Bismarck the power to collect taxes unconditionally. For centuries French policy had been to keep Germany disunited; and for this very reason Napoleon III (q.v.) did not interfere in the Prusso-Austrian War. To French surprise, Prussia beat Austria in a few weeks; and in 1871 France, carefully isolated by Bismarck's superb diplomacy, was herself beaten and Alsace taken from her. After 1871 all the German states joined in the German Empire under Prussian leadership, and Bismarck gave his master Wilhelm the imperial crown of Germany. Ten years earlier, in the war of Italian independence, Prussia had stood as a weak observer hardly daring to give an opinion. Such was Bismarck's achievement.

From now on it was Bismarck's policy to maintain what he had created: which was, in fact, a conservative defence of a revolutionary situation. Here was a new great power in Europe: it rapidly became highly industrialized, for it could plan its development on a vast scale because it had started late. The Reichstag became a show-piece, with universal suffrage and no powers. The Chancellor was responsible only to the Emperor.

The great expansion of German industry was combined with a great expansion of population. Germany, unlike Britain or France or Russia, had no back door: expansion geographically could only mean a Greater Germany in Europe. In 1877, Bismarck had said (during one of his astute diplomatic manœuvres which aimed at avoiding 'the nightmare of coalitions' between France and Russia) that the Balkans were not worth 'the bones of a Pomeranian grenadier'; and by 1890 Germany was so powerful as a politic-economic unit that she *had* to expand to save the unity of the State. Bismarck fell in 1890 over his proposal to drive the Social Democrats out of existence when he admitted that he could not defeat them politically. This was symptomatic of the position of the new Germany which he had created single-handed: there was no room for it in the old scheme of Europe. Germany had either to expand beyond her frontiers or collapse from internal dissension: the captains of industry, for example, had to fight foreigners or each other. The Germans opted to fight foreigners. The 'painted lathe' that was Bismarck's Reich – to employ the phrase he used himself to describe England – really had no other course.

Such was the consequence of the life-work of Bismarck, this Titan who could move – here all the German characteristics are personified – from the utmost firmness to sentimental tears. His work was vast, but like most of the work of trolls and Titans, it was bound to be disastrous.

'Man is all imagination'

BLAKE, William, (1757–1827), English visionary, painter and poet. Blake was condemned in his own day, and has been condemned since, as mad – a journalist called him in 1809 'an unfortunate lunatic whose personal inoffensiveness secures him from confinement'. Study of his writings has slowly revealed, beyond the excellent poet, Blake's powerful thoughts about man and society.

Blake was singularly direct, attractive and winning in his life: one of his younger friends called him a 'man without a mask'; he was always absolutely himself, always rich, as his first biographer wrote, in the midst of his poverty (he made a humble livelihood as an engraver). Sir Thomas Lawrence and other successful painters would visit him in the poor rooms where he and his wife lived, off Fleet Street, in London: 'They pity me,' said Blake, 'but 'tis they are the just objects of pity; I possess my visions and my peace. They have bartered their birthright for a mess of pottage.' Blake was not for sale.

All that he said or wrote explains something of his nature, seriousness and enthusiasm: 'Nothing can withstand the fury of my course among the Stars of God and in the Abysses of the Accuser.'

'Where man is not, nature is barren.'

'"What," it will be questioned, "when the sun rises do you not see a round disk of fire somewhat like a guinea?" O no, no, I see an innumerable company of the Heavenly host crying, Holy, Holy, Holy is the Lord God Almighty.'

'One power alone makes a poet: imagination, the divine vision.'

'Man is all imagination. God is man and exists in us and we in him.'

His poems are exquisitely simple in language, though not always in meaning, as in *A Divine Image*

> Cruelty has a Human Heart,
> And Jealousy a Human Face;
> Terror the Human Form Divine,
> And Secrecy the Human Dress.
>
> The Human Dress is forged Iron,
> The Human Form a fiery Forge,
> The Human Face a Furnace seal'd,
> The Human Heart its hungry Gorge.

– or *The Sick Rose*:

> O Rose, thou art sick!
> The invisible worm
> That flies in the night,
> In the howling storm
>
> Has found out thy bed
> Of crimson joy,
> And his dark secret love
> Does thy life destroy.

Blake as a painter, though his conceptions are often

powerful and his colour is often delicious, has been over-praised. He was too impatient of the outer world to build his designs of strong and valid forms. Perhaps the best eulogy of Blake as a man and poet comes in the course of a severe criticism by a living poet, T. S. Eliot: 'He was not distracted, or frightened, or occupied in anything but exact statement. ... He was naked, and saw man naked, and from the centre of his own crystal.'

ILLUSTRATION: Page 23.

New rights, new clothes

BLOOMER, Mrs Amelia Jenks, (1818–1894), American champion of women's rights, whose harmless, if eccentric, dress, has earned her a memorial she could hardly have expected – or desired.

After a few years as governess to small children in Seneca Falls, N.Y., she married Dexter C. Bloomer, a Quaker who edited the *Seneca City Courier*, and began to write articles on the moral problems of the day. In 1849 she started *The Lily*, the first women's magazine in America. Mrs Bloomer wrote firmly-worded indictments of intemperance, unsuitable marriages, poor education, and the unequal electoral laws. She was an enlightened woman, much respected by the leaders of American women's suffrage.

It was with her concern for dress reform that Mrs Bloomer emerged from the shade of Seneca Falls and burst on to a startled New York. Her favoured costume consisted of an ordinary bodice, a short skirt and voluminous trousers. The trousers were quickly christened Bloomers. Possibly to Mrs Bloomer's surprise, her unusual dress helped her other aims: huge crowds came to hear her speak, as well as to look at the bloomers. She lived to see the more weighty of her ambitions realized in the sensible independence and equality of American women; and perhaps she had enough sense of humour to regard the fate of her rational dress with tolerance.

Author of the 'Decameron'

BOCCACCIO, Giovanni, (1313–1375), Italian writer whose life, like his books, reflects his impulsive character. By nature he was not a man of reason but of passion – passionately amorous and passionately artistic – yet he became in his disordered, slightly inaccurate way one of the most learned men of his age. Like Petrarch he thought his boring and pedantic words in Latin were his masterpieces, and treated his Italian writings as trifles. Whereas the stories of the *Decameron* are triumphs of European literature.

His father was a Florentine merchant in Paris, and there Boccaccio was born. Most of what he knew he taught himself – including Greek. A period spent as a merchant's apprentice in Florence was followed by a stay in Naples, where he studied Canon Law. He soon set aside that rather arid subject when, in 1336, he fell in love with Maria d'Aquino, illegitimate daughter of the Angevin King Robert. This love affair, which was so unlike Petrarch's melancholy devotion to Laura or Dante's apotheosis of Beatrice, was a turning-point in Boccaccio's life, the crown of all his experience at the luxurious Neapolitan Court. It was a tropical passion, and short-lived – Fiammetta (as he called her) soon finding another lover. Boccaccio recovered and wrote plentifully on and around his experience. He never married – indeed, he rabidly denounced the matrimonial tie as a menace and a trap for writers. Most of his remaining years he spent either in Florence, where he was employed in the public service, or at his property at Certaldo. In 1362 he underwent a religious conversion and repented his worldly life. He wanted to destroy his Italian writings, but Petrarch, his great friend, managed to dissuade him. He died at Certaldo in 1375. Generous (he was Dante's greatest admirer), sensual, irrational and yet urbane, in all the works of his genius we seem to feel the warmth of his heart.

The *Decameron*, which Boccaccio wrote between 1348 and 1353, marks his liberation from the weaknesses and conceits of his Italian poetry. Ten young men and women together seek refuge from the plague in Florence and tell each a story a day for a space of ten days – a device for relating a hundred stories of unsurpassed variety and sustained power. The stories are drawn from many sources, classical and medieval, or they are based on the lives of persons well known to his readers; others are plainly suggested by Boccaccio's own experiences in Italian or foreign cities. These are tales of heroism and abnegation, of quickness of wit, of polite manners, of the life of merchants and tradespeople, of friars and nuns. All are infused with poetry. The *Decameron* is concerned with all the manifestations of *amore* or sexual attrac tion; from the love of noble and passionate lovers to the sexual couplings – they are often comic – of the vulgar. On one point Boccaccio is a great snob; he sees passionate love as a patent of nobility (is it not the kind of love he himself has experienced?). The noble passion is rarely experienced by common people; for, as he observes, they lack not only birth but also the food and drink and leisure that nourish love. Hypocritical and cunning friars have these latter advantages, but their love goes to San Giovanni Barbadoro – St John Goldbeard, or filthy lucre. Boccaccio cannot forget the friars – they are as bad as marriage – but he also describes their doings in some of his most brilliant tales. No one can ever forget Fra Cipolla with his miraculous relics at Certaldo, or Ciapelletto, who tells lies even on his death-bed and is afterwards reputed a saint, or Martellino's experience at Trevigi, or the young girl Alibech's stay with the lecherous hermit Rustico. The author moves easily from this mood to one of frank sensuality. He is always on the side of lovers who love truly, but he understands nothing of Dante's or Petrarch's ideas of sublimation – his men and women want to make love, and in the achievement of their aim all is fair; and when they are clever at deceiving their husbands, wives or parents, we see him waiting for the applause.

Thanks to its rich texture of poetry and invention the *Decameron* has been worked like a gold-mine by writers since Boccaccio's time. Here, for instance, are the familiar tales of Romeo and Juliet (a thin piece) used by Shakespeare, and Isabella and the pot of Basil (one of Boccaccio's masterpieces) which was retold by Keats. In the condensed short story Boccaccio has never been surpassed, at his best never equalled.

The divine shoemaker

BÖHME, Jakob, (1575–1624), German shoemaker and mystic.

> Fish in water lives, and plant in earth
> And fowl in air, and sun in firmament,
> Fire is a salamander's rightful home
> And God's own heart is Böhme's element,

wrote the mystical poet Angelus Silesius.

As a little boy this great but unlearned Protestant mystic herded the cattle at Old Seidenburg, where he was born, near Gorlitz. It was perhaps the happiness of his boyhood which led him to compare the life of angels to the life of children in May gathering wild flowers. Once, exploring a cave, he found a wooden vessel full of money, but took none, returning instead to tell the other boys of his find. Neither he nor any other could find the hoard again, which later on he believed to have been shown him by some supernatural tempter. During his apprenticeship to a shoemaker at Gorlitz, a stranger with 'a severe but friendly countenance' told him, after buying some shoes, 'Jakob, thou art little, but shalt be great, and shalt become another Man, such a one as at whom the world shall wonder': he would have to endure misery, poverty and persecution, but God would be gracious to him.

The child now began to think much about God, and once for seven days was 'surrounded with a divine light' – the first of his many spiritual experiences, all of a peculiar joy and radiance, without the 'dark night of the soul' of Roman Catholic ascetics. The vision returned when he was twenty-five. As the young shoemaker sat in a meadow outside Gorlitz 'viewing the Herbs and Grass of the Field, in his inward Light he saw into their Essences, Use and Properties, which were discovered to him by their Lineaments, Figures, and Signatures'. In 1610, after another visionary experience, he wrote his most poetic book, the *Aurora*. Publication led to trouble. The minister of Gorlitz preached against Böhme, by name, from the pulpit and called him a heretic, while the good man sat quietly listening. Taken before the Senate, he was ordered to write no more books. For seven years he obeyed, until he felt a divine and overwhelmingly powerful command. When more writings appeared, Böhme was asked to leave the town for the sake of peace and quiet. Later he was examined before the Elector of Saxony in Dresden, at an assembly of learned doctors of mathematics, divinity and chemistry, and no fault was found in him. On his death-bed he heard 'sweet harmonious music'.

Böhme's writings soon became known in all the Protestant countries, and elsewhere from Russia even to Rome. He expressed himself with great humility and a natural sweetness, though in an obscure symbolic vocabulary which has to be mastered. He wrote of a burning fire which came and went like a sudden shower: so possessed 'I saw and knew the Being of all Beings, the Byss and the Abyss, and the eternal Generation of the Holy Trinity, the descent and the Original of the World, and of all Creatures through the Divine Wisdom. I knew and saw in myself all the Three Worlds, namely the Divine, angelical and paradisical, the dark world, the original of the nature of the fire, and then thirdly, the external and visible world, being a Procreation or external birth from both the internal and spiritual worlds. And I saw and knew the whole working Essence, in the evil and the good, and the original and existence of each of them, and likewise how the fruitful-bearing womb of eternity brought forth.'

Among the Protestant mystics Böhme stood second to none. He was much loved by romantic poets and painters in his own Germany and in England, where his happy nature-mysticism affected Wordsworth – who turns passages out of Böhme into his own verse – Coleridge, Blake, and the artist Samuel Palmer (qq.v.). A romantic delight in nature made sense, if, as Böhme said, it was a procreation of the spiritual, of the divine – an 'outbirth of the eternal'.

The liberator

BOLÍVAR, Simón, (1783–1830), Venezuelan revolutionary and liberator, and one of that small band of patriots who never grow dim, though a legendary light may touch up their portraits.

Sometimes Bolívar is called the Washington of South America. In a sense the title fits him because, like Washington (q.v.), he came of a fine old family of the European kingdom against which he raised a colony in revolt. It fits him less well in the sense that he was a theoretical idealist, whereas Washington, narrower but deeper, was intensely practical, and perhaps for that reason the more successful. The inspiration of Bolívar lay in the writings of Rousseau, Montesquieu, and Voltaire. Their influence was reinforced, curiously enough, by contemplation of the new-born Napoleonic empire during a visit to Europe. On his return to Caracas in 1807 he found a sorry contrast to what he had seen, or what he had imagined, in Europe – stagnation in place of a lively swift-moving world. The rest of his life was largely given to armed revolt against Spain. He was an unbending republican, whose left-wing convictions led to differences between him and the other liberators of his time, San Martín, his chief rival and as great a man as himself, and Miranda.

Bolívar often won quick and brilliant successes, but he also suffered heavy set-backs, notably at the hands of the wild *llaneros* or cowboys enlisted in the service of Spain. His rout by them was followed by the wholesale slaughter of the Spanish creoles he had so much relied upon. He won his surprise victory at Boyacá after a remarkable and grim crossing of the high Andes. In 1821 the battle at Carabobo was decisive, and when the territories which are now Venezuela, Colombia, Ecuador and Panama had been freed, he was able to turn against the Spanish power farther to the south. Victory at Junín in 1822 freed Peru; and Sucre, his chief lieutenant, liberated Upper Peru (which became the state of Bolivia, named after Bolívar) by winning the battle of Ayacucho on 9 December 1824, against the Spanish viceroy. This was the climax of the revolution.

Bolívar was to die in misery while far short of his aims, which still have to be realized. After liberation his goal was federation – a united South America, as he proclaimed in 1826, when the young republics conferred at Panama. Instead, Spanish America has been tormented by many wars since his death. Yet the idea remains. Though it has been submerged again and again by animosities and rivalries, a sense of solidarity is now stronger than ever, and in part at least it can be traced to Bolívar. His spirit, his ideals, his personality have remained alive. His name is still magic, and is revered by men of very different outlook who might have opposed him in his day. Unlike San Martín, he had a vein of fanaticism; but he shared his rival's personal disinterestedness and altruism.

A Renaissance lady

BORGIA, Lucrezia (1480–1519), illegitimate daughter of a Pope, sister of one of the cruellest figures in Renaissance Italy, and herself one of the most notorious – and most maligned – women of history.

Rodrigo Borgia, her father, was renowned as a cardinal for his excessive sensuality: a bacchanalian orgy he arranged at Siena brought a letter from the Pope (Pius II) about his 'wholly worldly manner'. His worldliness extended to several mistresses (the most famous being Giulia Farnese). By one of them, Vannozza Cattanei, he had four children, including Lucrezia and Cesare Borgia. At that time religion had gone from the Papacy: it was the Italian era of great advances in thought, great liberation of feeling, great achievements in art, of self-contained arrogance and pride, and of power politics. When Rodrigo Borgia became Pope Alexander VI and lived in the Vatican with his concubines, the ruling princes were not surprised at his conduct, or dismayed. Power politics were what counted; and in these the Borgias excelled.

Lucrezia was victim of a father's and brother's ambition. Certainly she was aware of the enormous power her position gave her; and the charges of immorality against her (the gravest charge was that she had been incestuous with both Alexander and Cesare) are matters of doubt. She was a charming beauty: 'She is of medium height, and slender figure,' wrote Cagnolo of Parma. 'Her face is long, the nose well defined and beautiful; her hair a bright gold, and her eyes blue; her mouth is somewhat large, the teeth dazzlingly white; her neck white and slender, but at the same time well rounded. She is always cheerful and good humoured.' And another wrote: 'She is very beautiful, but her charm of manner is still more striking.' She was married three times, first to Giovanni Sforza of Pesaro; but when Charles VIII invaded Italy, the Sforzas lost all their power, and Cesare had the marriage annulled. A more profitable liaison was planned. In an attempt to gain a friendship with Naples, Lucrezia was married to Alfonso of Aragon. This also turned out to be against Cesare's best interests; and he had Alfonso strangled. Lucrezia seems to have accepted these trials as part of the vicissitudes of life: she had the Borgia resilience.

With her third marriage she found peace at last; Cesare decided that an alliance with Ferrara would help him, and Lucrezia was married to Alfonso d'Este, heir to the dukedom of Ferrara, in 1501. A cavalcade of fifteen hundred came to fetch Lucrezia from Rome. For six days there was festival in the Holy City; dances, plays, masques, and a bull-fight in the Piazza of St Peter's. And then Lucrezia set off, to spend the remaining years of her life as a dutiful duchess; her Court at Ferrara was brilliant, and there she patronized Ariosto among poets and Titian among painters. No more would she sit between her father, the Pope, and her brother, as they watched 'fifty decent harlots' cavort in one of the rooms of the Vatican. She outlived both of them: and though the world has judged her wicked and immoral, by the standards of the time she was better than most.

ILLUSTRATION: Page 24.

Sandro Botticelli

BOTTICELLI, Sandro, (1444–1510), Italian painter, at once one of the most exalted and delightful artists of the new speculations and new emotions of the civilization of Florence in the fifteenth century.

Exquisite beauty of line and colour, a delicate but strong sweetness, the evocation of a young, fresh and graceful world, untouched by harshness or moral conflict, but tinged with a subtle poignancy or melancholy – these qualities characterize the more familiar masterpieces by Botticelli. His father was a tanner. At fourteen he became a pupil of Fra Lippo Lippi, and he grew to be one of the company of scholars, poets and painters, and sculptors who gathered round Lorenzo de' Medici – Lorenzo the Magnificent, at that time the supreme patron of the arts in Europe. Between 1478 and 1490 Botticelli painted pictures that are among the most famous and familiar in the world – the *Primavera*, or Spring, and the *Birth of Venus*, which hang in the Uffizi in Florence. Yet they are not among the best-understood paintings. It is too little to say that they represent the 'spirit of the Florentine Renaissance', its youthfulness, grace, freshness, etc. The birth of Venus, poised on the wide shell above a gentle, crispy sea, her hair blown by the wind, into which roses are tossed, was in fact the painting of a high mystery, a birth of beauty out of a universal fecundity, or a fertilized soul. Whatever the exact interpretation of Botticelli's mythological or cosmic allegories, they are signed through and through with his own individuality: they 'proclaim the whole of the artist's mind', in the new manner of the age. So do Botticelli's later paintings which he made after his patron's death and after Savonarola, the grim monk and reformer, had preached a burning repentance to the Florentines and a severe cleansing of the spirit.

Lorenzo the Magnificent died in 1492, in 1494 the Medici were expelled, and Savonarola was in the ascendant for another four years. Botticelli was so affected by Savonarola that the whole of himself and the whole spirit of his painting were changed and stiffened, from the time of the execution of Savonarola in 1498 to his own death. The sweet serenity of Madonnas with their little sons, the piercing sweetness of the mythologies, gives way to stern composition and tension, as in the *Calumny* at the Uffizi in Florence or the strong, grandly and starkly constructed *Pietà* in the Old Pinakothek at Munich. The

transformation was the more complete since Botticelli, according to Vasari, was by nature genial and
fond of playing practical jokes on his friends and his
assistants.

ILLUSTRATION: Page 25.

Structure of crystals

BRAGG, Sir William Henry, (1862–1942), with his
son, W. L. Bragg, was joint founder of the analysis of
crystal structure by reflections of beams of X-rays.
This has led to the discovery that nearly all natural
substances are in some degree crystalline – *i.e.* their
constituent atoms are arranged in a systematic order.
The development of the Braggs' method has enormously extended the knowledge of the structure of
minerals, metals and living matter, and has provided
essential data, which could not be discovered in other
ways, for the synthesis of sex hormones, penicillin,
and many substances of fundamental importance.

The Braggs used X-rays to make the constituent
atoms of substances throw their shadows on a suitable screen. From these shadows they could deduce
the exact places of the atoms, and the distances between them. Chemistry, which had described the
combinations between atoms, could now be extended
from a qualitative into a quantitative science, and so
enable mathematics to get at the internal structure of
substances.

At Trinity College, Cambridge, Bragg did well in
mathematics, and then at the age of twenty-three
became professor of mathematics and physics at
Adelaide. From Adelaide he went to Leeds, and from
there to London University. It was an expression of
his consummate gifts and his charm of character that
he made all things seem interesting and easy, as teacher
or lecturer. All of his contribution to the analysis of
crystal structure Bragg made after he was fifty years
old; and in 1915 he and his son were jointly awarded
the Nobel Prize for Physics.

Tycho Brahe

BRAHE, Tycho, (1546–1601), the son of a Swedish
nobleman, studied at Copenhagen and Wittenberg,
and early showed talent in astronomy. The King of
Denmark built a splendid observatory for him on the
island of Hven in the Cattegat, when he was thirty.

Brahe was an observer of unsurpassed skill, who
raised the technique of observation to its highest point
before the invention of the telescope. Besides accumulating a vast mass of observations of a new order of
accuracy, he had a strong critical sense. He observed
the great new star of 1572, and pointed out that it
proved that the stars were not unchangeable. His accurate observation of comets showed that they moved
between the planets, and that the crystalline spheres
which were supposed to carry the planets could not
exist. Though he admitted the simplifications which
the Copernican system introduced into the description of the motion of the planets, he could not accept
it because it seemed to him contrary to the laws of
physics. He could not imagine how a big body such
as the earth, which seemed to be at rest, could really
be in motion. Still more important, in spite of the
most careful observation, Tycho Brahe was unable to
find any parallax of the fixed stars. This is an effect
which must exist if the earth moves in an orbit, for
the direction of motion will be different in different
places in the orbit, which causes the aspect of the star
to be different. Brahe could not observe the effect even
by his careful methods; it was not in fact detected
until nearly three centuries later, by Bessel.

He bequeathed his observations of the planets to
his young assistant Kepler, who deduced from them
his three immortal laws of planetary motion, and
provided Newton with the data for his incomparable
efforts.

ILLUSTRATION: Page 30.

The red deer on the rock

BREUIL, Henri, (b. 1876), French archaeologist,
who has revealed the oldest prehistoric art in the
world.

It is impossible to say when the art of painting began; but when the energetic, vital naturalistic engravings and paintings of Spanish and French caves were
discovered, it seemed incredible that the artists could
have been prehistoric hunters, still more incredible
that they could paint in this way 15,000 to 20,000
years ago. More than any other man it was Henri
Breuil who convinced the world that this was so.

Born in the Soissonais country, he busied himself from his earliest youth with natural history and archaeology, and though he became a priest, he has spent all his life, not in parish cares, but in archaeological research and above all in the problems of this art of the Old Stone Age.

The cave paintings of Altamira in north-east Spain were discovered in 1875. In 1901 Breuil found similar paintings and engravings in the Dordogne valley in Southern France, in the caves of Fonte-de-Gaume, Les Combarelles, and La Mouthe. Breuil not only argued, and argued convincingly, that the paintings were genuine: he proceeded to copy them in as many caves as possible, until (this was before the days of good photography) the world learnt to see Upper Palaeolithic art through Breuil's hands and eyes. Modern photography has confirmed his accuracy as copyist and interpreter (though many of the paintings cannot be well photographed, and many of the engravings cannot be photographed at all). From palaeolithic art (see his *Four Hundred Centuries of Cave Art*) he moved on to the study of palaeolithic tools, from France to South Africa, South Africa to China; and so revolutionized the classification of early man.

Muse of the stomach

BRILLAT-SAVARIN, Anthelme, (1755–1826).

'Animals feed, man eats', Brillat-Savarin wrote in that book, or gospel, of good eating which has made him famous, the *Physiologie du goût*. 'You, first parents of the human race,' he apostrophized Adam and Eve, 'who ruined yourselves for an apple, what would you have done for a turkey cooked with truffles? But in Eden there were neither cooks nor confectioners. – How I pity you!'

Savarin was a lawyer, and eventually a judge of appeal. At the time of the revolutionary terror in France he escaped to Switzerland, and then took refuge for three enjoyable years in the United States. His celebrated book recalls sights and experiences of America, including a word picture of Edward the fat man, who sat upon an enormous armchair in Broadway, with three chins each more than a foot long and fingers 'like those of the Roman emperor who used his wife's bracelets for rings'. Savarin published the *Physiologie du goût* in the last year of a happy life;

and from end to end the book smiles with the quiet, kindly, worldly, plump yet energetic contentment which marked Savarin's nature. He described himself as 'among the number of the *gastrophori*, or paunch-bellied', though he had carefully confined his girth 'to the limit of the imposing'. Gasterea (Greek *gaster*, stomach) he certainly elevated into the tenth Muse, 'fair as the goddess of love', but he had no use for 'those so-called gastronomes who are mere gluttons, whose belly is an abyss, and who eat anywhere, of anything, and to any amount'; nor would he have cared for the modern social game of food snobbery and wine snobbery, since good living and good eating appeared, on the contrary, to this urbane, cultured man as one of the chief links of society, holding the different classes together.

Brillat-Savarin's 'fundamental truths' or aphorisms include 'The fate of nations depends on how they are fed', 'Tell me what you eat and I'll tell you what you are', 'To receive anyone as our guest is to become responsible for his happiness during the whole time he is under our roof'. A fellow judge told the great astronomer Laplace that he considered the discovery of a new dish far more interesting than the discovery of a star – 'for dishes increase the sum of human enjoyment, whereas there are always plenty of stars to be seen'. Savarin agreed.

ILLUSTRATION: Page 31.

Powders of inheritance

BRINVILLIERS, Marquise de, (c. 1630–1676).

This proud, resolute, small, exquisitely pretty and dainty French aristocrat was one of the most celebrated poisoners of all time. The love affairs of this Marie Madeleine d'Aubray began in childhood and continued after her marriage to a French nobleman. It was with her lover Sainte-Croix that she started her use of arsenic, vitriol and 'poison of toads' in 1663, experimenting at first upon hospital inmates (she visited them as an angel of charity) and her own servants. Principal victims of the Marquise were her father and her two brothers. Slightly tipsy upon one occasion, she told a servant that a box she carried contained 'many inheritances' – in other words, many poisons, which became known after her trial as *poudres de succession*.

When her lover Sainte-Croix died, he left papers

and poisons by which she was incriminated. She escaped to England and the Netherlands, but Louis XIV had her arrested at a convent in Liège in 1676. Soon afterwards she was tried and found guilty. While her judges wept at their verdict upon so delicious a woman, the Marquise, without a quiver, fixed them proudly and sharply with her large china-blue eyes. Victor Hugo long afterwards looked with curiosity at the oaken table in the Conciergerie upon which she underwent the water torture; for so much water, she exclaimed, there was no room in her small body. Before she was beheaded, the Marquise did public penance in a chemise outside Notre Dame, barefooted, with a rope round her neck and a lighted torch in her hand. Her husband knew of her proclivities, but at the other end of the dining-table he took precautions always against the fate of his wife's father and brothers.

The Marquise was incontinently and fiercely vicious in expected and unexpected ways from the very beginning; it was the contrast between her character and her station, her frozen cruelty and her exquisite figure and features, her ruthlessness and her altogether feminine charm which captivated the French public, who crowded to see her die, as well as French historians and French writers.

ILLUSTRATION: Page 23.

The soul that felt the flesh

BRONTË, Emily, (1818–1848), poet and novelist – perhaps the one English woman poet whose gift may be described better as genius than as talent.

She was the second daughter of an Anglican curate, and lived for the greater part of her life at Haworth in Yorkshire. Her elder sister Charlotte (born in 1816) survived her by seven years, and her younger sister Anne (born in 1820) by six months. Emily's death followed within two months that of her elder brother Bramwell, for whom she had a deep affection. The Brontës were an Irish, not a Yorkshire family; the Rev. Patrick Brontë was born in an Irish 'cabin', and his father was one of those famous story-tellers who still existed in the youth of W. B. Yeats, and whose influence on his 'Celtic Twilight' school of poetry was more profound than that of any written tradition. Patrick Brontë possessed his father's gift in a lesser degree, and his tales of the supernatural made guests

at the Vicarage afraid to go to bed. The bleak moorland setting, the harsh manners and strength of character of the minor characters in Emily Brontë's one novel, *Wuthering Heights* (1848), are taken from Yorkshire; but the elemental power and beauty of her poetry, and of her conception of the characters of Catherine Earnshaw and Heathcliff are closer to the world of the Irish *sidhe*, and legends of the dead who return, like Catherine's ghost, to the Yorkshire Moors; 'Heaven did not seem to be my home, and I broke my heart with weeping to come back to earth; and the angels were so angry that they flung me out into the middle of the heath on the top of Wuthering Heights, where I woke sobbing for joy.'

The poetic intensity of Emily Brontë's imagination is that of all peasant lore, stories that have long been 'steeped in the heart'. To quote from *Wuthering Heights* again: 'They *do* live more in earnest, more in themselves, and less in surface, change, and frivolous and external things. I could fancy a love for life here almost possible.'

Emily Brontë left Haworth once, in 1836, to teach at a school near Halifax; she returned home after six months. Again in 1842 she accompanied Charlotte to the Pensionnat Héger, in Brussels, to study French, German and music. Her capacity for logical thought impressed M. Héger, who observed that she had the mind of a man, and should have been 'a great navigator' – 'Her powerful reason would have deduced new spheres of discovery from knowledge of the old; and her strong imperious will would never have been daunted by opposition or difficulty; never have given way but with life.' During both these absences she was 'wild for home', and never wished to live anywhere else than in Haworth parsonage. There she kept house for her father, played Mozart on her piano, and could live without any intrusion into her private world. No one knows whom she loved, or if she loved; her passionate poetry, with its Byronically romantic situations, came out of a world of day-dream, in which she and her sister Anne wove a cycle of stories about the lords and ladies of an imaginary island, Gondal, situated in the North Pacific, but having the climate and landscape of Yorkshire. Her latest poems show her in the subjectivity of mysticism. She despised orthodox religion, and in *No coward soul is mine* speaks the pantheistic language of the Upanishads:

With wide-embracing love
Thy spirit animates eternal years
Pervades and broods above,
Changes, sustains, dissolves, creates and rears.

Though Earth and moon were gone,
And suns and universes ceased to be
And thou wert left alone
Every Existence would exist in thee.

There is not room for Death
Nor atom that his might could render void,
Since thou art Being and Breath
And what thou art may never be destroyed.

Her intensity can be thrilling – to use the word deliberately – and complete; as in *Plead for Me*:

And am I wrong to worship where
Faith cannot doubt, nor Hope despair,
Since my own soul can grant my prayer?
Speak, God of Visions, plead for me,
And tell why I have chosen thee!

– or in her description of the messenger of hope in *The Prisoner*:

Still let my tyrants know, I am not doomed to wear
Year after year in gloom, and desolate despair;
A messenger of Hope comes every night to me,
And offers, for short life, eternal liberty.

He comes with western winds, with evening's wandering airs,
With that clear dusk of heaven that brings the thickes stars;
Winds take a pensive tone, and stars a tender fire,
And visions rise and change that kill me with desire ...

Poems by Currer, Ellis and Acton Bell (pseudonym for the three sisters) were published in 1846; and after Emily Brontë's death, Charlotte and her husband, the Rev. Bell Nicholls, edited a posthumous edition of the poems written by this strange, wild woman who died so young.

Imager of man

BRUEGEL, Pieter, (c. 1525–1569), Flemish painter who painted universal images of man and the world, and must be counted among the supreme artists.

Some painters so clearly perceive and render both the shape and nature of things that their pictures never 'date'; their magnetism and their power to convince the magnetized spectator never diminish. This is true of 'Peasant' Bruegel. The facts about him are meagre: he married the daughter of another artist; Pieter and Jan Bruegel, his sons were painters after him; he saw Italy with his own eyes, in the era of Michelangelo; he was a member of the Antwerp Academy; he moved from Antwerp to Brussels; and we know the look of him, from his own hand.

His pictures, some drawings and engravings tell his inner tale. We know his style, his compact, solid, utterly convincing simplifications of form, his clear combinations of colour, his unconventional appetite for the common facts and situations of life, the common people and the common objects, the squat children, the blunt shoes, the flat caps, the brawny, tight limbs, the jugs and pitchers, the coarse stool and bench, the round gaily coloured pies on a flat surface, the corn sheaves, the curling tail of a greyhound, the slide of a hawk across a frosty sky; we know the genre paintings, the proverbs come to life, such as the *Tower of Babel* (Vienna), the *Blind leading the Blind* (Naples), or the *Schlaraffenland* (Munich), in which suet pudding grows around the trees, a boiled egg scampers about; also a roast pig, brown and crisp with a knife in him for carving more slices. We know the landscapes of the Four Seasons, especially the *Winter* (Kunsthistorisches Museum, Vienna), and the broad serene *Corn Harvest* (Metropolitan Museum, New York), which gives the visual sense of Shakespeare's 'sunburnt sicklemen'. In all this work by Bruegel no square inch lacks authenticity and timelessness. Bruegel's effect arises from a tension between the magnetic likeness of things and a fantastic, often disturbing invention. The open pies paraded on a roof or on a baker's tray, a squat child with a Tudor-age cap crushed over its features, men turned into strange beasts because they are wearing bee skips over their heads – fantasy is made out of the straightforwardly unfantastic.

Bruegel's own Flemish time and milieu were topsyturvy. The Middle Ages were meeting and giving way to the Reformation; Spanish tyranny, blood, fire and Inquisition drove through the country, the peasant masses were on the move. Bruegel was open to such spiritual and physical agonies of the time, of which he made timeless employment. In his *Triumph of Death* in the Prado, Madrid, a vast barren landscape lies under a smoky sky; to the north the whole world seems on fire. Gallows mock the leafless trees. An army of skeletons armed with scythes, axes and nets is waging war on mankind, and inexorably it drives the noblemen, peasants, knights and kings toward a great trap-door marked with a cross; some draw their swords and fight back, revellers are surprised at a good meal, and a fool creeps under the table. A bell tolls over the battlefield, above an inquisition of skeletons condemning a wretch to death by drowning; around a chapel by the sea-shore there is a crowd of mourners; and in the calm sea beyond, a ship is slowly sinking.

Bruegel does not depict the individual man, but men, – mankind, in the individual scene or situation. His figures are almost all of them anonymous, all part of the mass involved in mankind's fate or fun. His landscapes, too, may be particularized; yet they stand not for a place, but for the world.

ILLUSTRATION: Page 38.

Railways and liners

BRUNEL, Isambard Kingdom, (1806–1859), English engineer, and one of the major figures, adventurous, individual and self-reliant, of the early age of railways and steamships.

In 1833, a young man of twenty-seven, Brunel was made engineer for the projected Great Western Railway from London to Bristol. It was still a time for the far-sighted pioneer. The Duke of Wellington objected to railways 'because they encourage the lower classes to move about', and people were not entirely convinced that railways would be useful or were desirable, though Stephenson's *Rocket* had made its first journey in 1829 and his Manchester and Liverpool railway had been opened in 1830. In 1835 Brunel was congratulating himself in his journal: 'The Railway is now in progress. I am the engineer to the finest work in England. A handsome salary of £2000 a year, on excellent terms with my directors, and all going smoothly.' He made a brilliant job of his line, which he extended later to Plymouth and into Cornwall, across the great river-bridge which is still in use after nearly a hundred years. Brunel was not only dogmatic in his railway work; he was, aesthetically, very much a man of his time. The railroad to him was a wonder of modernism, to be honoured accordingly by seemly architecture and design. A viaduct might be so contrived as to make an arch of triumphal entry into a town (nowadays it is plastered with advertisements). Some of a crenellated tunnel entry near Bristol was knocked away by a landslide. Was it to be

repaired? 'By no means,' said Brunel, 'leave it, train ivy over it, and it will appear as a beautiful ruin.' Industrialization was still no law to itself.

Brunel's railway from London to Bristol was a fragment of an artery between London and New York. Brunel conceived the completion of that artery by means of a Bristol–New York steamship to be called the *Great Western*. The ship was built, a timber paddle vessel 212 feet long, able to cross the Atlantic without refuelling; she was launched, and reached New York for the first time in 1838, after fifteen days. By 1843 he had completed a new liner, the *Great Britain*, an iron boat 322 feet long, which made the crossing in 1845 in fourteen days and a half-hour. His third ship – five times bigger than any other ship in the world – was the *Great Eastern*, 693 feet long, which took over a year to launch and eleven days to reach New York.

Nor forget I to sing of the wonder, the ship as she swam up my bay
Well-shaped and stately the 'Great Eastern' swam up my bay.
She was six hundred feet long,
Her moving swiftly surrounded by myriads of small craft I forget not to sing

– wrote Walt Whitman, always alive to the new manifestations of power in the nineteenth century.

The *Great Eastern* killed Brunel, this human dynamo who smoked cigars incessantly. Shortly after the boat was launched, he came down with a stroke. Brunel was one of the confident creators of the new Iron Age, utterly forthright, frequently wrong, more frequently right, yet as sure of himself always as any politician, academic painter, or writer of his Victorian times. His expanding world was still one for individuals. He stood up to those who employed him and drove his employees. To one of his assistants he wrote that since 'plain, gentlemanly language' had no effect on him, he must try stronger words, 'You are a cursed, lazy, inattentive, apathetic vagabond' – shortcomings unpardonable to a great Victorian – 'and if you continue to neglect my instructions, and to show such infernal laziness, I shall send you about your business.' Or to a contractor who ran a refreshment room on the new railway, 'I assure you, Mr Player was wrong in supposing that I thought you purchased inferior coffee. I thought I said to him that I was surprised you should buy such bad roasted corn.'

ILLUSTRATION: Page 38.

Building the dome

BRUNELLESCHI, Filippo, (1377–1446). Italian goldsmith, sculptor and one of the great architects of the world. The pure, pristine nature of the Florentine Renaissance, so masculine in its main form and structure, so full of grace in its detail, was, in architecture, largely the creation of this one man, hasty, hot-tempered, violent, small, ugly, self-reliant – staunch friend and staunch enemy.

He was born forty years after the death of Giotto, and some twenty years before Uccello (qq.v.). He and Donatello were students together, his contemporaries include Fra Angelico and Fra Lippo Lippi; his great enemy and rival was the sculptor Ghiberti. This rivalry began with the competition for the sculptured bronze panels of the portals of the Baptistery at Florence; and it continued till Brunelleschi's death. His first important building was the small, exquisite Pazzi Chapel in the cloister of Santa Croce, a perfect blend of solid and void, a perfect handling – virtually for the first time since the fall of the Roman Empire – of classical motifs. The very large church of San Spirito at Florence and the Badia at Fiesole, just outside Florence, are two more of his buildings mixing strength and charm and restraint in the same way.

Brunelleschi had one overriding objective – to crown the cathedral of his native Florence with the first of the great Renaissance domes. He did: and it is still there, still centre of one of the most famous views in the world, dominating the valley of the Arno in unexampled beauty. His problems were how to support the dome on temporary centering without a whole forest of heavy supporting timber from the floor upwards, how to crown the whole with a cupola just at the point where weight is least desirable, how to build a double dome for internal and external effect, and how to perch the whole structure on a high drum, to deprive the dome of lateral support from the main building. All these problems, and more, Brunelleschi solved. He built his centering upon a wooden platform hung by chains from the lower part of the incomplete dome. He tied in the whole dome with a huge chain of timber balks. He made the inner and outer dome into a single structure united by fins at eight points. Yet how cold it would be to think of the dome merely as a problem in architecture: it is a passionate triumph of intellect and aesthetics, of the spirit of man and of mathematical calculation; it is a triumph of engineering, yet also an overwhelming

adventure and exploration without the aid of detailed precedent and text-book; and beside it triumphs of structural engineering in our own day are barbarian – mere essays in bigger-and-bigger-still. Nor would the *duomo* ever have crowned the cathedral, if this angry, impatient little man had not fought for his ideas with authorities who found them too novel and too bold. The *duomo* both states and solves problems inherent in later Baroque domes, St Peter's in Rome, St Paul's in London, Les Invalides and Le Panthéon in Paris, the Capitol in Washington, all derive from it. Yet that is to slip back into architectural history. More than anything else it was this feat of structure and design which makes Brunelleschi the biggest single figure in the first flush of the Italian Renaissance, which flowered in Florence when the Gothic cathedrals of France and England were still in the building.

The Pilgrim

BUNYAN, John, (1628–1688), tinker, and Baptist author, whose one source-book was the Bible, and who with this wrote *The Pilgrim's Progress* and other works famous both as monuments of English prose and testaments of religious experience.

He was a hell-fire Christian, a vigorous believer to whom God was a living reality. And the devil as well. In his autobiography, *Grace Abounding*, Bunyan paints his religious dilemmas with stark allegory: 'I did liken myself in this condition, unto the case of a child that was fallen into a mill-pit, who, though it could make some shift to scrabble and spraul in the water, yet because it could find neither hold for hand nor foot, therefore at last it must die in that condition.' His style is fresh, devoid of any ancestry but the translation of the Bible. While he was playing some gambling game, 'a voice did suddenly dart from heaven', he wrote, into his soul 'which said, wilt thou leave thy sins and go to heaven, or have thy sins and go to hell?'

As a person, Bunyan was undoubtedly a fanatic: an example of the simplicity of complete devotion, who would hardly like to be remembered as a writer, and not a converter. In *The Pilgrim's Progress* narrative and literary skill defeat one's distaste for allegory. Ideas are made the companions of the pilgrim and torments of the mind become the vicissitudes of his uncomfortable journey. Bunyan has a superb sense of idiom, a flair for words: 'So soon as the man overtook me, he was but a word and a blow'; 'his house is as empty of religion, as the white of an egg is of savour'. In *The Life and Death of Mr Badman, The Holy War*, and *Pilgrim's Progress*, part two, Bunyan pursues his theme. It is religion at its most personal, its most appealing: 'When the day that he must go hence was come, many accompanied him to the river side, into which as he went, he said, "Death, where is thy sting?" and as he went down deeper he said, "Grave, where is thy victory?" So he passed over, and all the trumpets sounded for him on the other side.' The words of that great passage have rung in English minds for two and a half centuries.

There was nothing of the theologian in Bunyan: his works are pictures, childlike in their candour, of the common man's religious problems. When those problems were uppermost in men's minds, he was their mirror: today, he is their canvas.

ILLUSTRATION: Page 35.

'Plant inventor'

BURBANK, Luther, (1849–1926), American plant-breeder who might unkindly be called the Trofim Lysenko of the New World, since Burbank also believed with passion (though without a strong-armed method of enforcement) in the same biological heresy.

A singularly lovable, happy, lively, gnome-like man, with uncommon good looks, Burbank was the son of a small farmer in Massachusetts, his father's thirteenth child by a third wife. According to his own account, his *mystique* of plants began in his boyhood when he was kicking the snow about in the timber-piece of the farm, and found suddenly an oasis of green in the cold white desert, a 'microclimate' in which grass, partridge berry and various other plants were braving the New England winter. His uncle introduced him to Agassiz the naturalist, who explained to him the pollination of plants, and remarked that, by breeding, valuable plants could be obtained from weeds. He was passionately interested in the details of life in the fields around his home, gave up employment in a factory to be a market-gardener, came across Darwin's *Variation of Plants and Animals under Domestication*, and bred a new variety of potato, large, smooth and white. He sold the rights in this Burbank Potato for 150 dollars, and in 1875 used the money to go to California.

Burbank believed, as with less excuse the Russian Lysenko has believed in our time, that the environmental characteristics of plants can be inherited – 'Heredity is nothing but stored environment – the sum of all our past environments. I have said that before; I cannot say it too often'. Behind the belief there was only subjective experience – his own remarkable success as a plant-breeder endowed with cleverness, energy, patience, a delight in nature, and the greenest of thumbs and fingers; and his own observation – for example, of the way in which the wild Californian Poppy varies according to habitat. His first big success came in 1881, when he produced 20,000 young prune trees in one summer by grafting upon fast-growing young almond stock. In 1885 he set up as a 'plant inventor'. By the age of sixty-three he had produced 220 new varieties of plants – stoneless plums, white blackberries, blackberries without prickles, cherries that ripen in February, a spineless cactus, dahlias, roses and the famous Shasta Daisy, 'golden-hearted and wax white' developed from English, New English and Japanese ancestry.

Burbank's approach was not unlike that of his friends Edison and Ford. Like Edison, he tried everything, with a Napoleonic attention to detail. He trained all his senses, sniffing and scrutinizing thousands of flowers, tasting thousands of fruits. Like Ford, he worked as a mass producer; and he noticed qualities which other men had missed, breeding new strains which embodied them.

In California, with its middle climate, its warmth and lushness, its enlivening air and sparkling green, and its white rain-clouds off the Pacific, he found the environment of all environments for his plants, the cradle of cradles. Burbank felt himself a servant of mankind – 'When I lapsed, as I did once or twice, and began to find myself a money maker, I was compelled to execute a sharp right-about-face'. His *mystique* (compare the great educational reformer Froebel, q.v.) impelled him to think of the nurture of children in terms of the nurture of plants – men should work 'towards a race of children that will be the Shasta Daisies of the human family'. As inquisitive at seventy-seven as he had been at eight, Burbank was sentimental and shrewd, homely and wise – 'Show me a developed town with no trees, and I will show you a town to avoid for your families': that or 'The planted and tended tree is as sure a sign of civilization as a revered flag or a church spire or a schoolhouse belfry', was advice much needed, if not heeded, by his countrymen in the rapid development of the U.S.A.; and much needed wherever industrialization outstrips a dignity of settlement.

A journalist once wrote an article on 'Burbank versus Nature'. which enraged him, since his principle was 'to go to school with Nature'; to which, or to whom, he gave a capital N and a personality, although in fact he had no religious beliefs at all. 'I believe', he wrote at the end of his autobiography, *An Architect of Nature*, 'in the immortality of influence' – a naive word for a something which does everything; and without which, according to him, we should still be 'cells swimming in warm salt water'. When Burbank died, he was buried under a cedar tree in the yard of his own Californian homestead. Edison described his own genius as 'one per cent inspiration, and ninety-nine per cent perspiration'. Burbank's was of the same kind – a genius helping to put the resources of nature at humanity's disposal.

The great Conservative

BURKE, Edmund, (1729–1797), English political writer, was the greatest exponent of theoretical Conservatism. His contemporaries all testified to his genius. Johnson said: 'If you took shelter from the rain with Burke, you would say afterwards – that was a remarkable man'. Goldsmith in famous lines wrote that he narrowed his mind, giving up to party 'what was meant for mankind'.

Anglo-Irish by birth, Burke came early to England and attached himself to the Marquis of Rockingham. His first political work, *Thoughts on the Present Discontents*, which he wrote in 1770, expressed the view of the great Whig families that they had been excluded from office by a sinister conspiracy to restore the autocratic powers of the Crown. This myth has deluded historians till our own day. During the American Revolution he delivered a series of great speeches advocating conciliation. Though he lacked the arts of delivery, these speeches put him in the front rank of political thinkers.

Burke took office in the Whig governments of 1782 and 1783. He carried through measures to diminish corruption in favour of the Crown; but at the same time executed some gigantic 'jobs' for his cousin and other friends. After 1784 he was associated in opposition with Fox; and took a leading part in the prosecution of Warren Hastings. But his Whiggism was an exaltation of traditional institutions, and he admired the English revolution of 1688 only because it was a long time ago. Fox welcomed the French Revolution when it broke out in 1789. Burke denounced it and separated from his former Whig friends in 1791. He then became, like the ex-Communists of our own day, the foremost advocate of repression and reaction. His campaign culminated in a dramatic scene in the House of Commons, when he produced a dagger – allegedly of Jacobin manufacture – and flung it on the floor of the House. Though now a Tory hero, he complained that Pitt did not carry on the struggle against revolution strenuously enough; and he was a bitter, disappointed man when he died.

His superb literary gifts obscured the weakness of his arguments. Liberty is, no doubt, most secure when it rests on traditional institutions; but there was something absurd in telling people that they could have liberty only if their ancestors won it and that they must do nothing to gain it for themselves. He gave conservatism a romantic gloss, just as his fellow Anglo-Irishman, Bernard Shaw, talked himself into admiring Stalin. Both were remote from reality. But at least Shaw made money from his antics. Burke died a ruined man.

Busoni the innovator

BUSONI, Feruccio Benvenuto, (1866–1924), Italian composer and pianist. 'I seek, I will, I aspire,' he said, 'but I do none of these things to perfection, or with any final result, because I feel myself to be an innovator.'

Busoni the virtuoso pianist is still spoken of with awe and still overshadows the enigmatic figure of Busoni the composer and his aloof, uningratiating music. His father was a Tuscan, his mother, who taught him music, of German descent, and he had somehow to resolve a distaste for much that was Italian with his own Italian loyalties. Italian music was besotted with the glamour of the opera house, and needed revitalizing with the German instrumental tradition, classical and romantic. Busoni, with his German leanings, felt himself predestined for the task, no less so because he could see that German 'too-muchness' was every bit as absurd as Italian excess of ribbons and tinsel. But Italy was not the place for such a missionary, and Busoni did much of his work abroad, scandalizing the Germans by making the central movements of his gigantic Piano Concerto blatantly Italian. The concerto form was the sacred possession of the Germans, and the *Tarantella* in Busoni's concerto seemed an impudent denial of this. Germany had its revenge. When the first World War came, it treated Busoni as an Italian and an enemy alien, whilst to the Italians he was an exile and a pro-German. Busoni withdrew to Switzerland to carry on his search not only for an ideal Italian idiom, but for the 'unattainable Platonic ideal of which all art is only a partial revelation'.

This latter search he expressed in his opera *Doktor Faust*, which occupied Busoni's thoughts and dreams for the last fourteen years of his life. 'Like a subterranean river ... heard but not seen, the music for Faust', he said, 'roars and flows continually in the depth of my aspirations.' This unfinished opera mirrors Busoni's own conflicts, Faust willing his own life and personality into the body of a child who is to rise up and carry out the task which Faust had begun.

There were odd streaks in Busoni's personal life. In a thick London fog he once asked a passer-by the way to a house. The man took him by the hand, and led him there direct, and as he turned back into the fog the light from the doorway fell on his face and Busoni saw that he was blind. Sudden shifts of this kind from the normal to the super-normal occur in Busoni's music, even in such apparently gay works as the *Comedy Overture* and the *Tanzwaltzer*. In the *Second Sonatina* and parts of *Doktor Faust* the normal disappears altogether, leaving a courageous contemplation of 'the infinity which surrounds human life'. Busoni's vision, in fact, is a solitary one, offering no consolation.

ILLUSTRATION: Page 78.

Dear adorable Lord Byron

BYRON, George Gordon, 6th Lord Byron, (1788–1824), English poet, and for all Europe one of the towering representative figures of romanticism. Only Byron could tell the final truth about himself, and Byron is dumb: his friend and biographer, the poet Tom Moore, burned in 1824 the manuscript account of his own life which Byron had written. His own generation thought Byron the apotheosis of the Romantic Hero – except those who thought him an arrant cad. Tennyson is typical. He was a boy when Byron died of fever, at Missolonghi in Western Greece, 'engaged', as the inscription on his ancestral vault puts it, 'in the glorious attempt to restore that country to her ancient freedom and renown'. When the news reached England, Tennyson went out of his father's parsonage to a quarry and on the sandstone he scratched 'Byron is dead'.

Byron was malformed from birth, mentally as well as physically. The nature of the deformity of his foot has never been solved. E. J. Trelawny, lifted the pall over Byron's dead body to solve the mystery, and averred that he had 'the form and features of an Apollo, with the feet and legs of a sylvan satyr'. Later he toned this down by saying that actually Byron had a contraction of the Achilles tendon. Anyway, he was lame – and swam the Hellespont. But the deformity of his mind, which expressed itself as a rebellious flouting of the conventional, he certainly owed to his mother. A woman of caprice and violent temper, she wrecked his upbringing. His life was a Gothic Folly, and she laid the foundations.

He created a new type – the Byronic figure. He looked the part: a musical voice, pale complexion, small white hands, a magnificent smooth forehead and classic nose, and effective chestnut-brown hair (it was alleged that he slept in curl-papers). All his life he used purgatives unstintingly – they may account for the dramatic pallor and the ethereal air his contemporaries found so fetching. Turning his lameness to advantage, he avoided movement in company and struck statuesque poses. His actions supported his appearance in creating a legend. He consumed women. The harem of servants at Newstead Abbey, Caroline Lamb, the Contessa Guiccoli, and the wife of his doomed marriage of whom he wrote

Some women use their tongues – she look'd a lecture,
Each eye a sermon, and her brow a homily.

Stopping at an inn on the way across Europe his lordship, Byron's secretary recorded, 'fell upon the chambermaid like a thunderbolt'.

On the morning of the publication of the first cantos of *Childe Harold's Pilgrimage* Byron awoke to fame. Yet neither *Childe Harold* nor the other Byronic self-portraits (in MSS of the poem Childe Harold is written Childe Burun) are the poems which command attention today. They were a symbol for his generation, as D.H.Lawrence's novels have been the symbol of a modern generation: like *Lady Chatterley's Lover* they gave the order of release; but now the characters seem lay figures and the poetry seems often banal. *Don Juan* persists, that poem his careful publisher and his rakehell friends both thought unfit for print. The courtesan Harriette Wilson, who saw the text, wrote, 'Dear *Adorable* Lord Byron, *don't* make a mere coarse old Libertine of yourself. Ecoutez, mon Ange.' But *Don Juan* has wit, brio, panache; and also the poetry he often missed in other works.

When Byron died at Missolonghi, his faithful valet William Fletcher sent back a heart-broken letter to Byron's publisher: 'I scarcely Now what I say or Do after twenty years service he was More to me than a father and I am much too distressed to know [how to] give a Correct account of every Pertickeler.' He could have given a correct account of every particular of Byron's strange life, which mixed such good and bad, such sense and pose – an account, for instance, of his ambiguous relations with his half-sister Augusta Leigh. But Byron lived and wisely died an enigma, a Napoleonic figure of poetry and defiance who has been intriguing the world ever since.

C

John Cabot and his son

CABOT, John, (c. 1460–1498), Italian navigator, who in 1497 discovered, or re-discovered, the North American coastline. Cabot sailed in an English ship from Bristol, where a tower stands in his memory.

Five hundred years earlier Leif Ericsson (q.v.) had discovered America, sailing from the Icelandic settlements in south-west Greenland. Since the Bristol merchants were in contact with Iceland, they may have had some traditional inkling of land to the west. This may have helped Cabot to gain English support for an enterprise which the Spaniards and Portuguese rejected. Like Columbus five years earlier, Cabot believed he had discovered east Asia, 'the country of the Great Khan', though 'he coasted it for 300 leagues

and landed and did not see any person', in the words of a letter written home by a fellow Venetian – who also reported that 'he is called the Great Admiral, and vast homage is paid to him, and these English run after him like mad'. Henry VII made a grant of £10 'to him that found the new isle', and subsequently gave him a pension.

A year later he sailed again, with ships full of English merchandise, to trade for the wealth of Cathay. His son Sebastian also tried to find a way to Cathay, and in his search for a north-west passage to it may have discovered Hudson Bay, mistaking it for the Pacific. Failure to find the north-west passage led to efforts to find the north-east passage, and so to trade between Elizabethan England and Russia. Apart from the establishment of the Newfoundland fisheries North America remained of little interest to England until later, when colonies were needed for an exportable surplus of population.

The stern Protestant

CALVIN, John, (1509–1564), French theologian, Protestant and Reformer. 'What could be more agreeable to Faith, than to know ourselves stripped of all virtue, to be clothed by God? Empty of all good, to be filled by God? Slaves of sin, to be freed by God? Blind, to be enlightened by Him? Lame, to be made whole by Him? Weak, to be sustained by Him? Deprived of all self-glory, so that in the end He alone may be glorified in and through us?' Calvin wrote in dedicating his great book, *The Institutes of the Christian Religion*, to Francis I of France.

If human things are best understood in pairs, there could be no more perfect contrast than between the two reformers, Calvin and Luther (q.v.), French and German – Luther with his peasant shrewdness, his roughness, his openness, his bluff humour, his constant self-revelation, his perpetual struggles; and Calvin, subtle, fine-drawn, laconic, Latin, a man of wit and distinctions, assured, and never self-revelatory, the first of the great systematic psychologists, before Montaigne, or Richardson, or Rousseau. Their faces show the contrast, Luther's round and jolly, Calvin's fine and hard, with lips set and thin.

In Calvin, as much as in Rabelais (q.v.), is found the passion for the ancient world, and especially the Greek. It is with the language itself, its grammar, its logic, its rhetoric, its capacity for expressing distinctions, that their love, their arguments, their creative impulse began. Calvin found the Stoic philosophy particularly attractive. With the humanists, he was convinced of the fundamental importance of education, which was literally a matter of life and death; and he sharpened his wits on the study of law.

During Calvin's youth, Reform and Humanism still did not seem incompatible; to be a Catholic reformer in the tradition of Erasmus was still honourable. In France, the reformers counted on the support of Francis I, himself a patron of learning. When he appointed Nicolas Cop, son of his court physician, to be Rector of the University of Paris, the reformers were jubilant. Cop lectured at his Inaugural from the text 'Blessed are the poor in spirit', and his ideas were clearly consistent with justification by faith. But instead, it proved to be the dividing of the ways. Cop's hopes of pacific reform went for nothing. Within a month Calvin, who had come out in Cop's support, was in flight and in hiding. In 1535 he was in Bâle; and from there, in 1536, he launched the first – the Latin – text of the *Institutes*. He was not content to appeal to learned men all over Europe in the universal tongue. As a true humanist, he wanted his countrymen to have the opportunity of reading for themselves. He translated this exposition of Protestantism into French; and it is one of the first masterpieces of the French style.

For several years Calvin wandered, from Ferrara returning secretly to France, going from France to Geneva, from which he was expelled, and on to Strasburg, where he married, and then to Geneva again; he remained there until his death, making it the centre of the French reforming movement, and endeavouring to create there a City of God, having always in mind the great book of that name by St Augustine, whom he greatly admired. Without personal ambition, and with absolute sincerity, Calvin exposed himself to the worst of human failings, the conviction of infallibility, and his persecution of Castalion, the scholar and theologian, and his burning of the Spanish theologian Servetus, who went to the stake in 1553, have left a deeper mark on the human mind than other men's crimes, because they were the acts of a good man. 'It suffices that we recognize God's call as being for us our ground and principle, and we shall govern ourselves well in everything,' he says, at the end of the *Institutes*. But who can be sure that he knows his vocation?

Master of light and violence

CARAVAGGIO, (1565–1609) – Michaelangelo Merisi da Caravaggio – may be called the first 'popular' artist, who made the exact imitation of nature one of his aims.

Caravaggio was violent in art and life. In Rome he prowled around after dark, uninvitingly armed. He was quarrelsome and unbalanced, committed murder in a gambling quarrel in 1606, and had to go into hiding. Wounds, wanderings, prison shock tactics and sickness led him to an early death, but not before he had upset the art of painting. The story is told that Caravaggio, taken by friends to look at antique sculptures, so long regarded as the peak of human grandeur and achievement, pointed to the crowd nearby and exclaimed, 'See how many masters nature has provided for me, and for other artists, without your statues.' And he took a gipsy girl off to his lodgings and painted her telling fortunes.

In 1597, in Rome, he finished paintings of St Matthew for the church of San Luigi de' Francesi – his first public commission; and the new manner sent a shock through everyone who saw them. In the first, rejected version of one of these paintings, in which Caravaggio was said to have brought the common people 'on to the altar', St Matthew was presented as a wrinkled old peasant, with 'neither the attitude nor the aspect of a saint, since he sat cross-legged with his feet shamelessly exposed to view'.

Painting things as they are, Caravaggio directed on them the clearest, sharpest and most startling light – a flood-lighting out of his own personality. If Caravaggio paints a bunch of grapes, they can almost be eaten; if he paints a corpse, it can almost be smelt. And the objects are not always so innocent. He liked (and his public liked) the element of electric horror, as in the *Head of Medusa* in the Uffizi at Florence, and in paintings of holy execution and flagellation.

A difficult painter to assess. He was sincere, but he had a mad desire for self-assertion. He loathed the hypocrisy of his times, he had vitality and imagination, but no refinement of spirit to keep them in order. He had the greatest technical accomplishment, but his feelings were flashy. Like a publicity agent, he sensationalized everything he touched; and so – the forerunner by centuries of colour and 3-D in the movies – he appealed to the easy feelings of the common man. His temperature was always above normal.

ILLUSTRATION: Page 34.

Hero-worshipper and historian

CARLYLE, Thomas, (1795–1881), English writer and prophet, was one of the great preachers of the nineteenth century: 'He preached the gospel of silence in forty volumes.'

Son of an artisan in western Scotland, Carlyle tramped for university education to Edinburgh, where he remained five years. He then removed to London; and spent the rest of his life in Chelsea, despite his dislike of England and life in cities. He escaped the conventional education of the time, entered high society only when his mind was formed; and had a knowledge of German rare among his contemporaries. These things produced a style for which English literature had no parallel. 'Carlylese' is German, but very good German, translated literally into English. Sprung from the people, Carlyle was a revolutionary in spirit; but like many Scots, he disliked the people and his revolution therefore took an unusual form. He railed at the age, and preached Woe; but salvation was to come from a Hero, some divine man, who would grasp authority and put everything right. Carlyle never explained how the Hero was to be found: he would somehow announce himself, and others would recognise his claim. Carlyle ransacked history for Heroes, as examples for the future. His first discovery was Oliver Cromwell; his next, and less happy, Frederick the Great. Among his contemporaries he admired Sir Garnet Wolseley.

Carlyle's best work was done before Hero-worship gripped him. *Past and Present* (1843) is the most succesful attempt ever made to recapture the spirit of the Middle Ages; and *The French Revolution* (1837) is certainly the most dramatic work of history ever written – perhaps the best. *Frederick the Great*, on the other hand, in its endless volumes (1858–1865), is probably the dreariest. His private life was unhappy. His wife, Jane Welch Carlyle, had a clever, restless spirit and was slightly above him in class. They never managed to consummate their marriage; and nagged each other as a result. Late in life, Carlyle had a platonic enthusiasm – mostly snobbish – for a titled lady; which did not improve his wife's temper. After her death, Carlyle lamented his bad treatment of her.

Carlyle's message of hero-worship is trivial, where not idiotic. In practice it meant Hitler and Mussolini. But he delivered his message in incomparable language.

ILLUSTRATION: Page 71.

The mighty libertine

CASANOVA, Giacomo, (1725–1798), Italian adventurer and autobiographer, who has passed into history as the typical figure of the elegant libertine.

Most of our information about him is derived from his *Memoirs*, which he wrote to beguile his old age. His father – fittingly enough – was an actor; he was born in Venice, and sent to study law at Padua. Extravagance soon landed him in debt and he was forced to leave the university. It was at Padua that he had the first of his many love affairs. The girl, whom he refers to as 'the pretty Bettina', later married a shoemaker, 'with whom she led such a miserable life that her brother took her back to live with him'. 'The last time I went to Padua', he wrote towards the end of his life, 'I found her old, ill and poor, and she died in my arms.'

There followed a series of amusing and sometimes scandalous adventures. A Venetian Senator, to whom he had attached himself, suggested that Casanova should preach a sermon at the Confraternity Church of which he was patron. Casanova preached successfully, and at the end his alms-bag contained not merely the usual offerings, but also a number of *billets doux*, for he was tall and handsome, if we are to believe his own testimony. Casanova decided to preach again; he arrived in the pulpit dead drunk and endeavoured to preach an extempore sermon on the temperance of St Joseph. We find him, on his travels, rich one day, in the last state of poverty the next, gambling heavily at the tables of the wealthy and playing the fiddle at a theatre; patronized by bishops and cooling his heels in gaol. The one constant factor are the affairs with an endless series of fascinating women.

Perhaps the central incident in Casanova's life occurred during a visit to London, when he met the famous, or infamous, courtesan La Charpillon, at that time seventeen years old. 'It was towards the end of September that I made her acquaintance,' he wrote in his melancholy old age, 'and on that day the period of my physical and moral death set in.' Casanova had loved many women, some out of chivalry he had refrained from loving, all he had made happy and by most his affection had been returned. But in La Charpillon he met his match. Before long the great amorist was himself infatuated; he spent large sums of money on her, but did not succeed in winning her favours. Frustration and a court case finally persuaded

Casanova to leave England for Germany. There he met 'the great Frederick', who, attracted by his personality, offered him the post of tutor to the corps of Pomeranian Cadets. Casanova was amused by the offer, but did not feel that his vocation lay there, and before long he was on his way to Russia and 'the great Catherine' (q.v.), losing the little money his lavish gambling had left him to a charming Polish servant girl. After Russia, Spain – and more splendours and miseries of love. Then Turin, where we find him enjoying the company of the Epicurean English ambassador and recording that during his stay 'a pretty milliner, being at the point of death, swallowed her lover's portrait instead of the Eucharist'. This action, which he found prodigiously fine, inspired him to a couple of sonnets.

His last years were not happy. He returned to Venice and became a state-spy, but before long he was in his beloved Paris again. There he met a friendly nobleman who engaged him as his librarian, and gave him peace for the remaining fourteen years of his life. This is how a contemporary sketched his character: 'He would be a handsome man, if he were not ugly; he is tall and strongly built, but his dark complexion and glittering eyes give him a fierce expression. He is easier to annoy than to amuse; laughs but little, yet makes others laugh by the peculiar turn he gives to his conversation. He knows everything except those matters on the knowledge of which he prides himself, *viz.* dancing, the French language, good taste and knowledge of the world. Everything about him is comic, except his comedies; and all his writings are philosophical, saving those which treat of philosophy.'

A parfit gentil knight

CASTIGLIONE, Baldassare, (1478–1529), an Italian soldier-diplomat, whose life is a rare example of those qualities commonly supposed to have been the stock-in-trade of every Renaissance nobleman. In part, he is responsible for the myth of the courtly *homo universalis,* the soldier, statesman, scholar and paragon, at one with God and his fellow-men.

In *Il Cortegiano* (the Courtier) Castiglione set down, in the form of a discussion among the Duke of Urbino's courtiers, his thoughts and instructions on courtly behaviour. He was well qualified for the job. His teachers at Milan gave him an interest in intellectual pursuits that never left him, even in the fierceness of war. He served Lodovico Sforza, Duke of Milan, who was Leonardo da Vinci's patron. He visited Henry VII of England on behalf of the Duke of Urbino; he went as papal nuncio to the Court of Spain, to solve the dispute between the Emperor Charles V and the Pope. Charles tricked him, and Rome was sacked three years later, in 1527, by Imperial troops from Germany. It was even suggested that Castiglione himself had been guilty of treachery. Sad at the charge, which was almost certainly false, he resigned; and quickly died, it is said, of the shame which would have overcome his own ideal courtier in such circumstances.

'I will not deny that I have attempted all those studies which I state that the courtier should know,' he said. It could have been no easy task. 'The courtier,' Castiglione wrote, 'besides noble birth, should be fortunate not only in a lively mind, but in beauty of face and body as well, and with a definite grace and charm that will make him acceptable immediately by all who look at him.' The perfect courtier should be equally adept, in fact, at the Court and on the battlefield, the twin peaks of the Renaissance. When the courtier had all the necessary accomplishments, Castiglione would not have him rest content, 'but follow bravely the sublime way to the truest joy. He will find this in a beauty which can only be seen by the mind's eye, a beauty that grows more lovely as the corporal eyes lose their power. So his soul, all evil gone, purged by true philosophy and full of holy love, turns to the spiritual life and opens her eyes, as though she has slept, and sees inside her a shining beam of that light that is the image of angelic beauty.'

The Courtier had an enormous success: beautifully written, a best-seller in an age that had a surfeit of treatises, it was one of the milestones of European literature. In England, the English found Castiglione's perfect courtier in Sir Philip Sidney.

Catherine of Russia

CATHERINE THE GREAT, (1729–1796), Empress of Russia, who combined political acumen and love, to the advantage of her country and the scandal of Europe.

Glory and love were the two passions of this obscure German princess, who became Empress of Russia. A marriage was arranged between her and Peter, the feeble-minded heir to the Russian throne. Catherine has left an account of the wedding night: she was put to bed, and 'I remained alone more than two hours and did not know what I should do. Should I get up again? Should I remain in bed? I knew nothing.' The marriage was not a success; and after nine years Catherine had a son by her first lover. When the Empress Elizabeth died, Peter became Czar. He lasted six months, Catherine deposed him with the aid of her lover Orlov, and upon her orders Peter was quietly murdered. Many years later she asked Diderot, the famous French Encyclopaedist (q.v.): 'What do they say in Paris of the death of my husband?' Diderot was overcome with embarrassment, and Catherine quickly changed the subject.

She was a parvenu, and all the legendary favourites of her court were the same. After Orlov, there was Poniatowski, whom she made king of Poland for a little while. When he was deposed, she had his lost throne brought back from Poland and fashioned into a commode. Catherine's less earthy tastes included a diligent study of literature. She corresponded with Voltaire and the Encyclopaedists, toying with their 'dangerous' liberal ideas. She bought back Diderot's library for him when he was forced to sell it, and liked to consider herself the patron of the advanced writers of her time. Her enthusiasm for culture, though, was more superficial than deep. In home affairs she made unavailing attempts to improve life for the serfs; and she issued a new code of laws under the stimulus of Montesquieu's *Spirit of Laws* and the *Essay on Crime and Punishments* by the Marchese di Beccaria (q.v.). Also she had herself vaccinated when most of Europe regarded the operation with horror. Abroad, she divided Poland, and saw her empire firmly entrenched on the Black Sea.

A 'vulture for culture' in eighteenth-century dress, she liked to think of herself in heaven talking to Confucius, Caesar and Alexander the Great: it was more likely that she would talk to Messalina and Theodora, the immoral empresses of Rome and Byzantium. The story of her 300 lovers is a fiction: there were thirteen. 'I was very affectionate,' she wrote, 'and gifted with an appearance which was very attractive. I pleased at the first glance, without employing any arts or pains to that end. I was very sympathetic and possessed rather a masculine than a feminine temperament. As I have already said, I pleased the men. The first half of the temptation was there and the second followed the first according to human nature; for to tempt and be tempted are very close to each other.' She had all her prospective lovers examined by a medical officer, and then tested by her ladies-in-waiting.

After Orlov, the great influence in her life was Potemkin, the one-eyed, bear-like Ukrainian, who was monumentally lazy. He staged huge pageants for her, the greatest being a journey along the Volga to the Crimea. There were twenty boats; Catherine's was furnished with mirrors and Turkish rugs, and a rich green carpet covered the deck. Potemkin lay back in Turkish draperies. Both dreamed of the day when the Russian empire should extend to Constantinople. Her war against the Turks met with setbacks: but she was so undismayed that Voltaire wrote to her: 'I see with joy and surprise that this convulsion has in no way shaken the composure of that great man whose name is Catherine.'

She was not a great empress, but a proud one: liberal ideas or no, the news of the Revolution in France disturbed her. To a French envoy she said: *Je suis une aristocrate, c'est mon métier.* ('I am an aristocrat, it's my profession.') As she grew old, she grew fat, became untidy in her snuff-taking, and took a final lover. When she died she left instructions that on her grave should be carved, '... she was good-natured, easy-going; was of a cheerful temperament, republican sentiments, and a kind heart. She had friends. Work came easily to her; she loved sociability and the arts.' But her tomb was unmarked. She joined the lustiness of Chaucer's Wife of Bath to the manners of a literary *Salon* of seventeenth-century France. She was cruel and immoral but she lived her life to the full with no trace of cant. And though she cannot be regarded with approval, it is hard not to admire her in the end.

ILLUSTRATION: Page 37.

Out of thin air

CAVENDISH, Henry, (1731–1810), 'the richest of the learned, and the most learned of the rich', English chemist, physicist and aristocrat, was the first to identify hydrogen as a gas fundamentally different from air. The Dukes of Devonshire were the heads of his family, and when he died he left £800,000.

Devoted to science and not to company, disliking conversation and careless of fame, Cavendish lived as a recluse in London and received his meals through a hole in the wall of his laboratory. He proved that water is not an elementary substance, but is produced when hydrogen and oxygen are burned together. He then showed that when a mixture of oxygen and nitrogen is exposed to electric sparks, the gases combine, and produce nitric acid; and he even noticed that electric sparks in ordinary air would not produce a complete combination, for there was always a little bubble of gas left, no matter how long the sparking was continued. More than a hundred years passed before this brilliant observation was explained, when, in 1894, Ramsay and Rayleigh showed that it was due to the presence of the inert gases which they had discovered in the atmosphere.

Cavendish made equally important discoveries in electricity and in gravitation. He gave the most elegant experimental proof that electric charges attract or repel each other according to the inverse square of their distance apart, and he measured the force of gravitation between two masses of different size, thus finding the unit by which the mass of the earth, and hence of all the other stellar objects in the universe, could be measured. Cavendish spent many years on this great experiment, carried out with every refinement then possible. It was strange that after such a monument of care, he made a mistake in arithmetic in working out the average from his final results.

The world-famous Cavendish Laboratory at Cambridge University (where Henry Cavendish had studied from 1749 to 1753) was founded in memory of this shy, aloof, shabby, eccentric and brilliant man.

Miguel de Cervantes Saavedra

CERVANTES, (1547–1616), author of *Don Quixote*, the first and still one of the greatest of modern novels.

About the life and personality of Miguel de Cervantes Saavedra, as about his contemporary, Shakespeare (q.v.), we know tantalizingly few details.

In his young days, after a trip to Italy in the service of a future cardinal, he became a professional soldier; his left hand was maimed in the naval battle of Lepanto (1571), which destroyed Turkish naval power in the Mediterranean. Later he served in Corfu and Tunis; when he was returning to Spain with his brother Rodrigo to seek promotion, he was captured by Barbary pirates and held for ransom in Algiers. The ransom money for Rodrigo was paid, but papers found on the future author of *Don Quixote* gave his captors an exaggerated idea of his importance. A high price was put on him, and five years went by (during which he made four attempts to escape) before the money was raised. In 1587 he was employed by Philip II to requisition stores for the Armada, which sailed against England in the following year. He remained a civil servant for ten years, but he cannot have been a good one; his accounts grew more and more muddled, and he ended in prison. Philip II noted against his name that he was not to be re-employed.

After the publication of the first part of *Don Quixote*, Cervantes was in trouble again. A rake who may have had relations with his illegitimate daughter was found stabbed outside his house. Cervantes and his family were imprisoned and he had some trouble in clearing himself. In 1615 a French diplomatic mission to Madrid learned with astonishment that the world-famous author of *Don Quixote* was 'old, a soldier, a gentleman and poor'. Next year he and Shakespeare died within the same fortnight.

Don Quixote continues, like Hamlet, to be analysed, dissected, argued about as if he were a living person. It is true that in the English-speaking world Cervantes has never been carried on the crest of an intellectual fashion, yet the number of English translations down to our own time shows the strength of Don Quixote's fascination. He has been painted (notably by Daumier, q.v.), he has been filmed, and admirably re-created by radio.

No English translation has reproduced all the facets of the original: probably its wit, humour, pathos, sophistication, irony and profound understanding of the human spirit cannot be reproduced in full in another language. *Don Quixote* was composed as a satire on the romances of chivalry. Yet that is irrelevant to enjoying the story of the lean, chivalrous, foolish knight who tilted at windmills and cut at wineskins. Like Galileo the astronomer, who founded a new universe upon observation instead of on theory inherited from the ancients; like Machiavelli, who observed the political world about him instead of writing about it in scholastic abstractions, Cervantes was one of the great 'upsetters' who flourished between the Middle Ages and the modern world. The fabulous heroes, virgins and giants of medieval romance were dead, and Cervantes tumbled the soil on to their coffin. But in doing so, he put his fantastic yet so vivid knight and squire into the midst of the teeming life of contemporary Spain; he brought literature down to earth; and there, ever since, it has largely remained.

Cervantes also wrote poems and stories (of which the *Exemplary Novels* are the most distinguished) and was an unsuccessful playwright; the convention of his time that plays were written in verse acted against him. *Don Quixote* was the work of his later middle age and his first real success. It brought him immediate international fame, but little money.

The cylinder, the sphere and the cone

CÉZANNE, Paul, (1839–1906), French painter, one of the most single-minded and conscientious of artists.

He was born among the strong lights and shadows and emphatic forms of Provence, the son of a prosperous banker, so that, unlike most of the Impressionists, he was independent: after some years in Paris he was able to retire to Aix, unhampered by private patrons or the necessity of sales, and able to devote himself to an art of solidity and composition: 'I want to make impressionism something solid and permanent like the old masters', he wrote.

Cézanne's early associations with Monet and Pissarro led him to pictures in which he used the brilliant, luminous colours of impressionism. However, he became dissatisfied with the lack of volume which their creed demanded and devised a technique whereby he could build colour into solidity and structure. 'When the colour is rich,' he said, 'the form is at its height ... the form and colour of objects are best conveyed to us through the opposition and contrast resulting from their individual colours.' He also remarked, 'I always keep one foot in the Louvre', and from his studies of Courbet, Tintoretto, Rubens, Poussin, etc., he realized the importance of an effect of depth and space in which he could construct and articulate a composition.

As the years went by Cézanne retired farther and farther from his fellow-men, becoming surly, lonely and misanthropic. Forgotten by the world, he was not even very highly thought of by his friends the Impressionists; but ceaselessly he worked on with superb self-confidence, and confidence in the rightness of his aim; he worked to translate into pigment his conception of nature as composed basically of geometric forms. 'Treat nature by the cylinder, the sphere and the cone', he wrote to a friend in 1904. He knew that if he could succeed in painting these simple forms by the use of colour alone, without effects of light and shade, he would be able to impose logic and order upon any scene, or still-life group, without losing brilliance of colour. So he worked out a method of building up his forms by touches of paint, each brush-stroke, by its varying intensity of colour, having a different spatial position. Every stroke had to be considered in relation to every other part of the picture, and sometimes, not knowing what colour was needed to fulfil his purpose, Cézanne would leave patches of bare canvas rather than spoil the harmony already built up.

Slowly, carefully, and with an austere self-dedication, he evolved his method, and at the end of his life he began to be recognized; yet he knew that he had not completely succeeded: 'My age and my health will never allow me to realize the dream of art that I have been pursuing all my life', he wrote in 1905, the year before his death. When the world war came nine years later, the poet Rilke (q.v.) thought of Cézanne as one of the grand old men who might, if he had been alive, have come out and cried to the world of its follies.

Emmanuel Chabrier

CHABRIER, Alexis Emmanuel, (1841–1894). 'I am cultivating the gift of gaiety,' this French composer wrote in one of his letters, and his music happily combined the energy and deliberation and something of the jovial bluntness always ascribed to the people of the Auvergne in Central France, where Chabrier lived until he was sixteen. His father then gave up his practice as a local barrister and moved the family to Paris, where Chabrier spent some years as a minor official in the Ministry of the Interior. He wrote two operettas admirably remote from a civil servant's desk, resigned, and gave himself to music.

Colourful and decorously flamboyant, Chabrier

now included Verlaine and Manet among his friends and moved among the leaders of French art and literature. In his *Pièces pittoresques* the Auvergnat danced with disregard for musical proprieties, and in his operettas the Parisian immortalized the slight and the trivial. But there was a change. Wagner entered into Chabrier: in 1884 *Tristan und Isolde* was presented in Paris and he became wildly intoxicated. The *danses villageoises* and *valses brillantes* ceased, brisk harmonies congealed, and the healthy open-air melodies drooped in the Wagnerian ecstasy. Thus the finale of his opera *Gwendoline* is almost a Wagnerian caricature. Chabrier recovered and began cultivating his gift of gaiety once more, the masterly comic opera *Le Roi malgré lui* (1887) showing that he knew what to accept from Wagner and what to reject in him.

Chabrier can be pronounced one of music's innovators and honourable prophets. But that is too solemn: he made fun of fun, he dressed vulgarity in top hat and tails and slyly left all its buttons undone. He was neither coarse nor genteel, erudite nor amateur. The real Chabrier idiom had originality and subtlety for all its look of nonchalance.

Father of drains

CHADWICK, Sir Edwin, (1800–1890), English reformer, civil servant and eminently curious Victorian whose cleansing of London led to cleansing the cities of the world.

'To investigate the source of a malaria or stench,' wrote *The Times* in 1847, 'Mr Chadwick would swim through the stagnant pools of Avernus and enter the pestiferous jaws of Orcus itself.' He was a civil service reformer, who made an impersonal assessment of human misery, and went straight to its cause – in this case an inadequate sewage system. It is perhaps not surprising that his contemporaries could never take Chadwick quite seriously. There was no grace in him; to a friend he wrote: 'Mrs Chadwick has had a child and I have had a fever and I have recovered first.'

He trained for the Bar, and lived for seven years in a poor part of London, a city at that time of one and a half million people, where three million pounds a year were spent on gin. It abounded with diseased slums, refuse-covered streets and yards, cess-pools that leaked into wells and graveyards which were full to bursting. Chadwick had worked for Jeremy Bentham (q.v.), and was attracted to the Benthamites – those reformers who sought to change everything for the better to the complete disregard of the past. The law was a disappointment to him, and he soon left it. He was given a job as an assistant commissioner of the Poor Law administration; and he appalled the reactionary commissioners both by his industry and his radicalism. Prevention of disease began to claim his energies. In 1842 appeared one of the horrifying books of the age, Chadwick's *Report on the Sanitary Conditions of the Labouring Population*; a supplement, *The Practice of Interment in Towns* came out in the following year. These are model reports, concise, well-written catalogues of horror, which shocked the English. They are Dickens in full detail. One witness quoted said: 'I have seen a child lie in a downstairs room in a corner, dead of small-pox, and another dying, and the house full of lodgers eating their meals.' In footnotes that are worthy of Gibbon, Chadwick's quotations from the poems of Crabbe and from Shakespeare mingle with the account of a bird-fancier whose house was 'exposed to the combined effluvia from a slaughter-house and a tripe factory ... he said, "You may hang the cage out of the garret window ... and if it be a fresh bird, it will be dead in the week."'

Chadwick's solution for disease among the poor was a gigantic sewage system. He brought an evangelistic passion to the disposal of liquid manure; and of dead dogs: 'The Inspector of Nuisances is sent for and he says it is not his place to do it ... the overseer wont allow it and says he would not mind but the Poor Law Commissioners wont allow it. The Inspector of Nuisances says his place is to prosecute the parties who left the animals there, if only he could find them.'

He was contemptuous of public opinion: and his appointment as Commissioner of Public Health was not renewed. The enormous drainage systems of modern urban life are the monuments to his zeal.

ILLUSTRATION: Page 36.

No foolish talk, no laughter

CHAO MENG-FU, (1254–1322), Duke of Wei, is equally famous in China as statesman, calligraphist, poet and painter. He was twenty-five years old when the Mongols occupied China and ended the rule of the house of Sung, to which he was related. He accepted Kublai Khan's invitation to serve his government, and so earned a short-lived stigma as a collaborationist. Chao spoke of economic reform, and found himself a cabinet minister with rough colleagues. The chairman had him flogged for arriving late at a session. He became secretary of the Han-lin Academy and confidential adviser of Kublai Khan's successor. In Chao a passion for law and order had prevailed over that romantic loyalty to a lost cause which kept more fastidious contemporaries away from the Mongol court. He took himself very seriously, 'never indulging in foolish talk or laughing'.

Chao claimed no originality for his art, believing that the most important quality in a painting is its re-creation of the values of antiquity: 'My pictures may be simple and clumsy, but persons of taste esteem them because they know that my work is modelled on the antique.' He reproduced the styles of ancient masters, Kuo Hsi for landscape, Huang Ch'uan for birds and flowers, the T'ang painters for the figure. The black and white calligraphic style and poetic subjects of the academy art fostered by the Sung emperors were alien to him and he despised them.

Ironically, in view of his pretensions, Chao Meng-Fu in recent centuries has gained a popular reputation as a painter of horses, a subject dear to his Mongol patrons but one which was a small part of his total work. The eighteenth-century emperor Ch'ien Lung possessed paintings by him with such titles as *Elegant Rocks among Sparse Trees* or *Water Village*, all in ink, as well as an album of landscapes in light colour. His reputation was established by a virtuoso's technique joined to a backward-looking philosophy, which harmonized with the intellectual atmosphere of his day. In him the Confucian renaissance initiated by Chu Hsi in the preceding century found its ideal painter.

His boots are cracking ...

CHAPLIN, Charles Spencer, (b. 1889), English-born actor, clown, composer, film director, and folk-hero of an age of mass democracy.

> O, the moon shines bright on Charlie Chaplin;
> His boots are cracking
> For want of blacking,
> His little baggy trousers want a-mending
> Before we send him
> To the Dardanelles.

What would anyone want to know about Chaplin that he could not make up for himself, as he watches *The Gold Rush*, *The Great Dictator*, the magnificently funny and ironical *Monsieur Verdoux*, the sad *Limelight*; or as he contemplates some revival of an early film and sees the little man in the little baggy trousers towered by a giant, shrugging his shoulders, and flapping away down the block, cane twirling and boots yawning? Here is the funny clown who is so sad a man (and sometimes the sad clown who is so funny a man); the Lambeth waif who has made a magic pile of money, the London boy of polyglot origin, with one grandfather a cobbler and one a French general, with a father who died of drink while the little boy on the pavement outside watched the lighted window of the hospital ward, and a mother who took in sewing when there were no music-hall dates, and who went one day to the neighbours with a small piece of coal in her hands, saying, 'I have brought you a pretty present.' Here is the boy who came home to the empty room ('An ambulance has took her away'), who at Christmas in the orphanage had no gesture of love beyond an orange and a bag of sweets; the boy whose mother recovered and came back and sat up at night to teach him the script brought home from the Duke of York's Theatre – the part of Billy the office boy in *Sherlock Holmes*; the boy, 'pale, puny, sullen-looking' dubiously accepted by Fred Karno for his pantomine troupe, which performed in America; and at Los Angeles, where Charlie, as the drunk falling out of the box, was seen by Mack Sennett. Months go by; Sennett wires Adam Kessel in New York: 'Try to get hold of a bloke called Chapman, Caplin or something, playing second circuit.' There is a film contract, and fame.

With Chaplin, life becomes art and art life, interchangeably. Which of the two is this? 'A great star at the peak of his fame notices a young girl with shining golden hair and blue eyes who is walking on as an extra. He sends her flowers every day, invites her to dine, waits for her in his car at the studio gates; marries her.' Is it art or life? Life: the story of Chaplin's second marriage in 1917 to Mildred Harris. And which is this, 'A ship is approaching New York harbour. It is full of refugees from the tyrannies of Europe. The longed-for moment has come; they see the Statue of Liberty – and at the same moment a rope falls before them to herd them together; they are immigrants'? – art, from *The Immigrant* of 1917.

But there is something which holds art and life together: the discipline of work, the technical mastery, the iron lung in which art and the artist still breathe, even when everything else fails. Chaplin has that, and he learnt it in the desolate market where nobody comes to buy, where, as William Blake knew, it is bought only at the price of all that a man has.

There are many books about Chaplin, and there will be more. They tell you how he comes out of the *commedia dell'arte* (which they can't prove, any more than they can prove that the *commedia dell'arte* comes from the ancient Greek mimes.) Let us say that he comes out of the theatre which has no literature, and so no history. But it has documents. 'It was punishment to me', wrote one circus performer, 'if I could not practise. ... At thirteen years of age there was not an act that I could not give a good imitation of.' Chaplin could echo that; and in that spirit he made the thirty-five Keystone comedies in one year, 1914 – including his first full-length film, *Tillie's Punctured Romance*. It was in that perfectionist spirit that he approached all his long pictures from *The Kid* to *Limelight*.

No one has made more nonsense of the contrast between realism and fantasy than Chaplin (what is more realistic than a bowler hat?). Even the fairy gold has sometimes seemed a handful of dry leaves. The fairy princesses have sometimes turned into vampires, or have found him as heartless as Harlequin. Other times have demanded a Byron, a Pushkin, a Chateaubriand. Our time for its folk-hero has demanded Chaplin in the role of the individual behind the number, the being in the statistics or inside the card-index; and such folk heroes, whether Byron or Chaplin, have defects to match their qualities – the excessive postures of a Byron, the excessive pathos of Chaplin.

For proof of Charlie's universality, turn to nursery rhyme; there is an old rhyme:

> My young man has gone to France
> To show the ladies how to dance.
> When he comes home he'll marry me,
> Cockalorum gee, gee, gee.

London children and American children have had

their own modern version:

> Charlie Chaplin's gone to France
> To show the ladies how to dance.
> This is the way he taught them,
> Heel, toe over we go,
> Heel, toe over we go,
> Salute to the King
> And bow to the Queen
> And turn your back on the Kaiserene.

ILLUSTRATION: Page 79.

Life in still life

CHARDIN, Jean-Baptiste Simeon, (1699–1779). Onions, bread, peaches, hares, earthenware crocks, shining copper pans, playing cards on a table – all these were depicted by this French painter of the poetry of domestic life with as much love and care as others have given to lovers or landscapes.

French preoccupation with painting, which runs through to Cézanne and from Cézanne to Picasso and painters of the present day, is splendidly strong in the pictures of this humble, devoted and confined Parisian. 'He who has not felt the difficulties of his art does nothing that counts', Chardin remarked in a speech to the jury of the *Salon*. He had felt the difficulties acutely, refusing to allow others to watch him at work, not, a contemporary wrote, because of any mysterious process he wished to conceal, but because he preferred no one to see 'the fumbling, the painful effort, the anguished birth pangs of his work'. Chardin was poor, and remained poor, he hardly ever removed himself from Paris, living there among shopkeepers and small business men, modest, kindly, rather surprised, it seems, when anyone cared to pay him good money for one of his cool, rich and incomparable pictures.

All his pictures appear intimate and friendly and spontaneous, as though the models had stepped into the frame. A kitchen table by Chardin laden with vegetables and jams, or a more frugal dessert table with knobbly crusty bread, seems to have a natural existence on the canvas; if it belongs to Chardin's home, it belongs also to a twentieth century here-and-now. Yet the paintings control, so to say, an unrest:

And even in your Chardin the cursed unrest of the soul
Exudes from the dry fish and the brown jug and the bowl.

ILLUSTRATION: Page 72.

Emperor of the West

CHARLEMAGNE, *i.e.* Charles the Great, (c. 743–813), Emperor of the Franks. 'My duty, with God's help, is to defend the Church of Christ everywhere by armed might from pagans and infidels without; and to strengthen it within by the learning of the Catholic Faith', he wrote to Leo III on his election as Pope.

We know more of Charlemagne in historical detail, as well as legend, than of any European ruler before Louis XIV. That is the measure of his greatness, and of the impression he left on Europe. His was the last Western Court, until the Renaissance, at which Greek was to be heard. His scholars were responsible for the purification of Latin style, and the collection of texts. Their manuscripts are some of the most beautiful things ever made by the hand of man; and no one who has ever looked at them will call their time 'the Dark Ages'.

Charlemagne's counts (and still more his bishops) were chosen without regard to race or origin. He feasted Frank, Saxon, Celt, Lombard and Greek at his table; he moved among them in Frankish dress – a leather jerkin or linen tunic, with a blue cloak; swam with them in the pool at Aix-la-Chapelle (when he was there, for he journeyed perpetually); roared with laughter at them, and led them out to hunt for the venison on which he dined; he listened to poems, music, flattery, ambassadors, and to ecclesiastical documents; he asked riddles, and questions on astronomy, Biblical interpretation and history; he kept his children from improper marriages (sternly, for obvious reasons of state), but allowed even his daughters to have their lovers; and loved a good deal himself. Much of this (and much more) we know from Alcuin of York, one of the greatest men Charlemagne discovered, and one of the greatest Englishmen, who was Master of his Palace School and unofficially his minister of education and Church affairs.

There was a darker side to Charlemagne. His wars against the pagan Saxons were bitter, remorseless, treacherous, on his side as well as theirs; his wars against the Avars, last remnants of the Hunnish hordes, were as bad; his suppression of Lombard and Frankish revolts at home was marked by torture and cruelty. He once put 4,500 captives to the sword. One by one his enemies came to an end. Yet this great king was reasserting Western civilization among the barbarians. Pope Leo III, attacked in the streets of Rome, beaten up and wounded, was reinstated with Charlemagne's help. In 800, Charlemagne visited Rome; where, as he knelt in prayer on Christmas morning, the Pope crowned him Emperor of the West.

The great Habsburg

CHARLES V, (1500–1558), was the Habsburg Emperor who ruled over more territories in Europe and the New World than any other sovereign before or since. His vast dominions were the result of the famous Habsburg policy: 'Let others wage war. You, lucky Austria, marry.'

At the age of fifteen he assumed his Burgundian realm in the Netherlands, inherited from his father, who died in 1506. At sixteen he was also ruling the Spanish possessions which came to him from his mother. Three years later he was elected Holy Roman Emperor in succession to his grandfather Maximilian I, and thus added to himself the Habsburg domains of Austria, Germany and other parts of central and eastern Europe. He extended his influence by further family marriages – his son Philip married the English Queen, Mary Tudor, and was styled 'King of England, France, Jerusalem and Ireland'. Beyond Europe he was overlord of Mexico, the West Indies and Peru.

Charles was deeply religious and had the ambition of uniting Christendom for a crusade against the Turks. But almost all his energies had to be directed to struggles in Europe. Francis I of France (q.v.), who had been his rival for the Imperial Crown at the election of 1519, was a life-long enemy. He formed frequent alliances against the Habsburgs, and Charles had to fight the Turks not so much as infidels but as allies of France. Germany was split by the Reformation. He met Luther at the Diet of Worms, but, unable to come to a solution, embarked on that long war against the Protestants which ended in the compromise of Augsburg: 'Each country to have the religion of its ruler.' He faced continual unrest in the Netherlands, and the extent of his Empire often aroused the jealousy of England and the Italian states, including the Papacy. In 1555 this most powerful of monarchs abdicated of his own will. It was partly to find mental and physical rest. He announced, 'My life has been one long voyage. Nine times have I been to Germany, six times to my Spanish realm, seven times to Italy, and the Netherlands I have visited ten times; four times have I entered France, twice have I crossed to England, and again twice to Africa.'

Charles retired to a palace adjoining the monastery at Yuste in Spain. 'From henceforth', he declared, 'I am nothing', and he lived a simple life, reading and indulging an interest in watches and clocks. Though he kept an eye on the world and issued instructions for the government of the Empire, somewhat eccentrically he ordered a rehearsal for his own Requiem Mass.

He was a man of austere, devout, sober character, with great dignity. He forbade the desecration of Luther's tomb: 'I contest with the living, not the dead.' He showed personal bravery in battle and, if behind the tenor of his times in some respects, he was every inch the great Emperor. Towards the end of his life he said: 'I do not wish to read or hear what has been written of me. Others will read that when I am dead.' He had sent Magellan (q.v.) on his voyage around the world; and he had been an art patron with excellent taste, who appointed Titian (q.v.) to be his Court painter. Charles was not good looking. Of his own appearance in portraits he used to say, 'Artists usually paint me uglier than I am; therefore strangers meeting me are agreeably disappointed.'

ILLUSTRATION: Plate 3.

A cell on the stage

CHATEAUBRIAND, François René, vicomte de, (1768–1848). 'I am content', he wrote in his old age, 'to have been the unrepentant dupe of two or three noble ideas: liberty, fidelity, honour.' Even from this Byron of France, who had Byron's power of self-dramatization and self-deception, this was going a little far. Here was the Royalist who could serve Bonaparte, the Bonapartist who could serve the restored monarchy, the egotistic author for whom liberty and honour were fine words but fluid concepts. As for fidelity, Chateaubriand was a husband with a passion for mistresses. If he was duped by this noble idea, and showed fidelity at all, it was to one of his mistresses, Mme Récamier, whose love for him persisted till his death. This self-dramatizer, indeed, could have devised nothing more dramatic than the scene of the blind old Récamier sitting by the bed of the speechless old Chateaubriand.

An enemy once alleged that Chateaubriand sought 'for all on the stage'; and all his life he had that high romantic capacity, which was pinned to T.E.Lawrence in our day, of 'backing into the limelight'. When he was a child in the romantic land of Brittany, his nurse swore in the Virgin's name that he should wear only blue and white till the age of seven. He made up for this restriction by clothing the rest of his career in all the colours of Joseph's coat. When he was a young man he visited the American forests, letting his hair and beard run wild like a trapper's, and importing to Europe his own version of the myth of the noble savage. When he had fought a little in France on the royal side he starved in an English exile. 'I dipped scraps of linen in water and sucked them. I chewed grass and paper.' Did he? Anyway, he worked as usher in a Suffolk school, where the boys mispronounced his name and called him Shatterbrain. That he never was.

'Since it is our lot to be slaves, let us drag our chains uncomplainingly. Let us learn to beat them into rings for the fingers of kings or tribunes, as the age or custom may dictate.' With this principle, Chateaubriand was generally afloat on the criss-cross currents of Empire and Monarchy which troubled France in the early nineteenth century. Occasionally a dramatic assertion of principle knocked him to the bottom, but he bobbed up. His political career alone, even his affairs of the heart, would not earn Chateaubriand a special claim on immortality. But he has two others. A notable dish of steak was named after him: and he re-vivified French prose. In his writing he was rhetorical, as in his life, but the rhetoric of his books has not faded. *Le Génie du christianisme* and the *Mémoires d'outre-tombe* are classics of the romantic style, broad in sweep and high in colour, powerful, rich and picturesque.

'I was in love with fame as with a woman', Chateaubriand wrote. In literature, at least, his conquest of fame has proved enduring.

The great commoner

CHATHAM, William Pitt, first Earl of Chatham, (1708–1778). English statesman and war minister,

'England has long been in labour and at last she has brought forth a man', said Frederick the Great of his leading English ally. And Pitt himself revealed his imposing self-confidence when he declared, 'I know that I can save this country and that no one else can.'

In this opinion he was to be thoroughly justified. Between 1757 and 1761, during the four and a half years of Pitt's great Ministry, British arms enjoyed an almost unparalleled series of victories. Responsibility for the strategy rested entirely upon Pitt; he exercised a general and detailed direction that has been attempted by few Prime Ministers since, in peace or in war.

A grandson of 'Diamond' Pitt, who had made a huge fortune in India, William Pitt became a Member of Parliament in 1735 for the rotten borough of Old Sarum, acquired by the family out of the proceeds of the famous diamond. He early decided that 'consideration in the House of Commons generally arises from one of two causes – the protection of the Crown ... or from weight in the country, generally from Opposition to public measures'. Opposition was the course he chose, and his gift for impassioned oratory made him the most formidable critic of the Walpole and Pelham administrations. Better than most of his contemporary politicians, Pitt understood how much the prosperity of eighteenth-century Britain depended on trade. 'When trade is at stake', he said, 'you must defend it or perish.' It was not so much the threat of French domination in Europe that moved him to his magnificent exertions in supreme office, as the knowledge that if French rule was extended overseas in North America, the West Indies, Africa and India, opportunities for British trade would be severely restricted, and the whole kingdom plunged into economic depression.

Pitt's most faithful supporters were therefore in the City of London, where, to this day, he is commemorated by a monument in Guildhall, bearing an inscription truer than most of its kind: 'he increased the wealth of his country', it reads, 'by commerce, for the first time united with, and made to flourish by, war'. But if to City merchants he was the admired 'Great Commoner', who spoke for their interests, to the political factions of the House of Commons he was far less acceptable. Among them he never acquired the personal following essential to success in eighteenth-century politics. To silence his dangerous tongue, the Pelhams brought him into the Government as Paymaster of the Forces, and for nine years (1746–1755) he devoted himself to every aspect of military and commercial administration on which he could put his hands. In this period, the foundations were laid of his remarkable grasp of the instruments of government. He has, also, the distinction of being the first holder of the Paymastership to have left the office without having used it to enrich himself.

War made him Prime Minister, and war-weariness drove him from office. Haughty in temperament and lonely in spirit, he would not cultivate the political favour that might have enabled him to stay in power after the war had been largely won. 'Being responsible, I will direct', he declared, 'and will be responsible for nothing I do not direct.' While, to his colleague the Duke of Newcastle, on whose talents as a manager of men and votes he depended for his majority, he once bluntly remarked: 'Fewer words, my lord, for your words have long lost all weight with me.' Not surprisingly, when the crisis was past, he was turned out, and from the political wilderness denounced the Treaty of Paris, concluded by his successors in 1762, by which, he said, 'we retain nothing, though we have conquered everything'.

Always subject to gout, and to fits of melancholy that amounted to mania, Pitt grew worse in health in the years that followed. When, once more, he was appointed Prime Minister in 1768, his was one of the strangest governments this country has seen, for its leader had become a recluse and, for much of the time, was practically insane. In opposition again after 1770, he contrived on occasion to rise to his old noble heights in speeches in the House of Lords (he was now Earl of Chatham). The bungling administration of Lord North found in Chatham its most effective critic, especially on its American policies. 'The American colonies', he proclaimed, 'are the fountain of our wealth, the source of our strength, the nursery and basis of our naval power. ... If you conquer them, you cannot make them respect you' (and, he added characteristically), 'you cannot make them buy your cloth.' His last speech in the House of Lords was a passionate plea for American liberties; and the exertion killed him; he was dead a few hours later.

ILLUSTRATION: Page 73.

In love with man

CHAUCER, Geoffrey, (c. 1340–1400). One of the supreme English and European poets.

Chaucer was a Londoner, his father a wine merchant connected with the Court and himself at first
a young page to a son of Edward III. He spent his life
within the Court atmosphere, early as a valet of the
King's household, later a diplomat who went on
missions to Italy, France, and Flanders. Good posts,
sinecures and pensions and grants of wine came his
way. He was usually in favour; if forgotten or neglected for a while, he was remembered, rewarded
again and raised out of difficulty. Such facts suggest
what the poems – above all *The Canterbury Tales* –
confirm: that Chaucer had a wise, uncarping, generous, shrewd, humorous, sympathetic, tender, happy
and harmonious nature. To read Chaucer is to be
familiar with him as an individual, so much is he im-
manent in his own verse. Coleridge remarked 'How
well we seem to know Chaucer! How absolutely
nothing do we know of Shakespeare!' Half humorously Chaucer described himself as a man with an
'elvish' or rather absent look, remote, shy, rather
stout, and not exactly a doll or a 'poppet' for a girl's
arms.

William Blake admirably called him 'the great
poetical observer of men, who in every age is born to
record and eternize its acts'; which he does 'as a master, as a father, and superior, who looks down on
their little follies from the Emperor to the Miller;
sometimes with severity, oftener with joke and sport'.
He also wrote of the pilgrims to Canterbury that they
are 'the characters which compose all ages and all
nations ... some of the names or titles are altered by
time, but the characters themselves for ever remain
unaltered, and consequently they are the physiognomies or lineaments of universal human life', a proposition to be extended to the characters in every
tale. Or again: 'Every age is a Canterbury Pilgrimage; we all pass on, each sustaining one or other of
these characters.' Each character is 'the image of a
class, and not of an imperfect individual'.

Unfortunately, knowledge of Chaucer now tends
to stick at the opening couplet of *The Canterbury
Tales*,

> Whan that Aprille with his shoures sote
> The droghte of Marche hath perced to the rote,

and to thrust no deeper into the bramble thicket of a
now unfamiliar English. 'Translations' or 'modern
versions' are no substitute, destroying, as they do,
the subtlety, flavour and substance which make
Chaucer into Chaucer. Far better to charge direct at

Chaucer's poems, and use the glossary for second or
third readings:

> The Miller was a stout carl, for the nones,
> Ful big he was of braun, and eek of bones;
> That proved wel, for over-al ther he cam,
> At wrastling he wolde have alwey the ram.
> He was short-sholdred, brood, a thikke knarre
> Ther nas no dore that he nolde heve of harre,
> Or breke it, at a renning, with his heed.
> His berd as any sowe or fox was reed,
> And ther-to brood, as though it were a spade.
> Up-on the cop right of his nose he hade
> A werte, and ther-on stood a tuft of heres,
> Reed as the bristles of a sowes eres;
> His nose-thirles blake were and wyde.
> A swerd and bokeler bar he by his syde;
> His mouth as greet was as a greet forneys.
> He was a Ianglere and a goliardeys,
> And that was most of sinne and harlotryes.
> Wel coude he stelen corn, and tollen thryes;
> And yet he hadde a thombe of gold, pardee.
> A whyte cote and a blew hood wered he.
> A baggepype wel coude he blowe and sowne,
> And ther-with-al he broghte us out of towne.

Ninety-nine per cent of the meaning of that celebrated picture, which itself is a part of universal
human life, can be understood at once, without a glossary. Learn that a *harre* is a hinge, a *knarre* a fellow, a
ianglere and a *goliardeys* a bubbler and a buffoon,
and the portrait is complete. Or the lyric Chaucer is
clear enough, for example, in the Balade in the
Legend of Good Women:

> Hyd, Absolon, thy gilte tresses clere;
> Ester, ley thou thy meknesse al a-doun;
> Hyd, Ionathas, al thy frendly manere;
> Penalopee, and Marcia Catoun,
> Mak of your wyfhood no comparisoun;
> Hyde ye your beautes, Isoude and Eleyne,
> My lady cometh, that al this may disteyne.

> Thy faire body, lat hit nat appere,
> Lavyne; and thou, Lucresse of Rome toun,
> And Polixene, that boghten love so dere,
> And Cleopatre, with al thy passioun,
> Hyde ye your trouthe of love and your renoun;
> And thou, Tisbe, that hast for love swich peyne;
> My lady cometh, that al this may disteyne.

> Herro, Dido, Laudomia, alle y-fere,
> And Phyllis, hanging for thy Demophoun,
> And Canace, espyed by thy chere,
> Ysiphile, betraysed with Jasoun,

Maketh of your trouthe neyther boost ne soun;
Nor Ypermistre or Adriane, ye tweyne;
My lady cometh, that al this may disteyne.

– in which the only puzzling words are *y-fere*, together, and *disteyne*, to dull, to make dim.

To miss Chaucer because of the exaggerated obstacle of his language is to miss one of those poets who have established themselves firmly against all the changes of time and feeling. 'No one can read him', according to one French critic, 'and not be glad to be in the world.'

'The art of abbreviation'

CHEKOV, Anton Pavlovich, (1860–1904), Russian playwright and short-story writer. To a friend he declared, 'The writers we consider immortal or even good all possess one highly important characteristic in common: they get somewhere and they invite us to go with them; the best of them are realists and depict life as it is, but because every line they write is permeated with the consciousness of an aim, we feel, in addition to life as it is, also life as it should be.' Here was the ultimate purpose of Chekov's own mature writings.

He began writing short stories and plays during his last years at the grammar school in Taganrog, where he was born, and first saw his short stories in print as a medical student in Moscow, where he had to keep himself and his family since his father, a bankrupt shopkeeper, could not provide for them. Chekov's first immature contributions to the Moscow and Petersburg humorous magazines were already remarkable for their acute criticism of life and for their deep compassion. He now taught himself that compactness which made him declare later on that 'the art of writing is the art of abbreviation'. Between 1883 and 1890 he fell under the influence of Tolstoy's teachings and, in addition to some of his famous stories, such as *The Steppe* (1888) and *A Boring Story* (1889), he wrote a number of highly didactic and artificial ones with a strong Tolstoyan slant. During this period he also wrote his one-act comedies, his one-act 'dramatic study', *On the Highway* (1885), forbidden by the censor, his drama *Ivanov* (1887–1889), and his 'Tolstoyan' comedy *The Wood Demon* (1889–1890). In 1890 Chekov made his journey to the convict island of Sakhalin, and the experience he gained there made him abandon his Tolstoyan convictions and write the series of anti-Tolstoyan stories, including *The Duel* (1891) and *Ward No. 6* (1892), which are so remarkable for their integration of idea and character.

His wonderful art of fusing subject-matter and form is best shown in his four great plays – *The Seagull* (1896), *Uncle Vanya* (1897), *The Three Sisters* (1900–1901), and *The Cherry Orchard* (1903–1904), which made him famous throughout the world. In them we see a world where great tragedy and comedy are revealed through commonplaces, a world of inaction and apathy that masks a very human interior *malaise*. *The Seagull* was the greatest fiasco of his stage career at its first performance in Petersburg on 17 October 1897. Performed a year later under the direction of Stanislavsky (q.v.) in Moscow, it proved a great success, but by that time Chekov was living in the Crimea where he spent the last years of his life trying to cure himself of consumption. In 1897 Chekov was elected a member of the Russian Academy, but resigned from it as a protest when Maxim Gorky (q.v.) was expelled on political grounds.

Chiang Kai-shek

CHIANG KAI-SHEK, (b. 1887). Successor to Sun Yat-sen (q.v.), as leader of the Kuomintang party in China, generalissimo and head of the Chinese central government during the war against Japan, 1937–1945, and since 1949 head of the refugee government in Formosa.

Chiang Kai-shek's family – he was born in a small town in the province of Chekiang about a hundred miles south of Shanghai – were salt merchants trading under the signboard of Jade Serenity, but his father died when he was eight years old, and he was brought up by his mother, who was a devout Buddhist of austere life. At school he developed revolutionary sentiments and cut off his hair-queue or 'pigtail' which was traditionally worn by the Chinese as a sign of submission to the Manchu dynasty. Nevertheless, in 1906 he was successful in the entrance to the Military Academy and was sent to Japan for training. He spent four years in Japan, and returned to China on the outbreak of the Revolution in 1911; he had already become an adherent of Sun Yat-sen and took part in the uprising in Chekiang. In 1913, Chiang was involved in the defeat of Sun's revolt against President Yuan Shih-kai and went into exile in Japan; he came back to take part in another revolt in 1915, and later helped to organize an army for Sun at Canton. In 1923, Sun sent him to Moscow 'to pay a goodwill call and study the political conditions and party organization of Soviet Russia'. He was four months in Moscow, and gained a knowledge of Russia second only to his knowledge of Japan. It is a curious fact that the two foreign countries of which Chiang had direct experience were the two which became in turn his principal enemies. Unlike Sun Yat-sen, whose foreign background was Anglo-American, Chiang never visited Western Europe or the United States. He married, however, in 1927 (after divorcing his first wife) into the American-educated and Christian Soong family, which made him for a period almost an honorary American.

After Sun Yat-sen's death in 1925 Chiang led the Kuomintang army to victory over the northern 'warlords', and finally set up a 'National Government' with a loose supremacy over China as a whole and *de jure* recognition from foreign Powers. The political alliance with the Chinese Communists which Sun had arranged broke down in the spring of 1927; Chiang crushed the Communists in the principal cities, but they remained locally independent as a guerilla force in certain rural areas. From 1931, the main problem confronting Chiang as leader of the Kuomintang 'tutelage' régime was defence against Japanese aggression; Japan seized Manchuria in 1931 and renewed the invasion of China in 1937. The war lasted eight years, during the second half of which period China had Britain and America as (initially ineffective) allies. Chiang never wavered in his determination to resist Japanese conquests in spite of military disasters and a crippling blockade, but war-time conditions, with galloping currency inflation, had demoralized the Kuomintang administration and left China exhausted and in chaos. Peace had been patched up with the Communists for the purpose of a joint resistance to Japan (with the approval of the Soviet Union), but after the defeat of Japan civil war was renewed and resulted in 1949 in a decisive Communist victory. Chiang with a remnant of his army sailed to the island of Formosa, where he still holds out with support from the United States, separated by a hundred miles of sea from the mainland of China. During his war-time leadership of China against Japan,

Chiang was the object of extravagant and uncritical admiration in Britain and America, but since his defeat by the Communists he has been a target for general abuse. He still, however, has powerful friends in America, and his refusal to become entirely extinct has recently been a cause of embarrassment in Anglo-American relations.

Japan's supreme playwright

CHIKAMATSU MONZAEMON, (1635–1725), Japanese playwright regarded as the Shakespeare of Japan.

Like Shakespeare, Chikamatsu was poet and dramatist in one, and worked in the theatre – as scene-shifter, later as playwright and assistant to the chanter. In the *jōruri* plays of the Japanese puppet theatre the chief element was the chanting of the text, with which music and puppetry were blended. So by themselves, the few out of the many plays by Chikamatsu which have been translated, such as the domestic *Love Suicides at Sonezaki* (1703) or the superb historical play *The Battles of Coxinga* (1715), read somewhat oddly to the westerner. More than with a play by Shakespeare or Synge, the text is decidedly the skeleton and not the whole body; it needs realization in the theatre.

Yet even translation reveals something of Chikamatsu's standing and the dramatic and poetic genius he put into his contests of duty and love. 'I was carried to Japan', says the exiled Ming princess, in Donald Keene's version (1951) of *The Battles of Coxinga*, 'in a boat that drifted over the sad shoals of the world.' Coxinga's mother, roped and rising to her feet, is like 'an old pine tree twisted and bound with wistaria and vines'. Inside the Castle of the Lions, Coxinga's sister promises to announce whether her husband will join him or no in driving out the Tartars and restoring the Ming dynasty, by pouring either white or red colouring into the conduit which feeds the moat. The red she pours out is in fact her own blood: 'The rouge slipped through the moonlit waters of the spring as crimson leaves rush through fords, waterfalls and the shallows of autumn in this passing world, and fell together with the red-tinged bubbles through the conduit down to the Yellow River.' The plays contain ripe horrors of action or

Continued on p. 87

THOMAS CARLYLE (1795–1881).
Detail from *Work* by Ford Maddox Brown.
The hatless figure is F. D. Maurice.

JOHN CLARE (1793–1864)
as a patient in the asylum, 1844. By Thomas Grimshaw.

CHARDIN (1699–1779) by himself.

William Pitt, Earl of Chatham.
Secretary of State, from the Year 1757 to 1761.

This Print is most respectfully addressed to the Patriotic members of both houses of Parliament and to all who preserve a gratefull remembrance of departed worth,

Published as the Act directs Sep.r 1778 by J.B.

by James Barry R.A.

WILLIAM PITT, EARL OF CHATHAM (1708–1778). Etched by James Barry, 1778.

CHOPIN (1810–1849). Painting by Delacroix.

CHRISTINA OF SWEDEN (1626–1689) by Abraham Wuchters.

THOMAS CLARKSON (1760–1846). Watercolour by A. E. Chalon, R.A.

HENRY CHRISTOPHE, KING OF HAITI (1767–1820) by Richard Evans, who was in charge of Christophe's school of drawing and painting.

JEAN COCTEAU (b. 1891).

BUSONI (1866–1924).

78

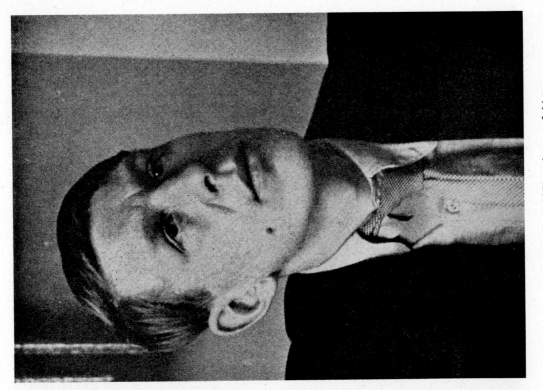

W. H. AUDEN (b. 1907) at the age of thirty-one.

CHARLIE CHAPLIN (b. 1889). A still from *Limelight*, 1952.

CAPTAIN JAMES COOK (1728–1779). By John Webber, R.A.

S. T. COLERIDGE (1772–1834) by Washington Allston, 1814.

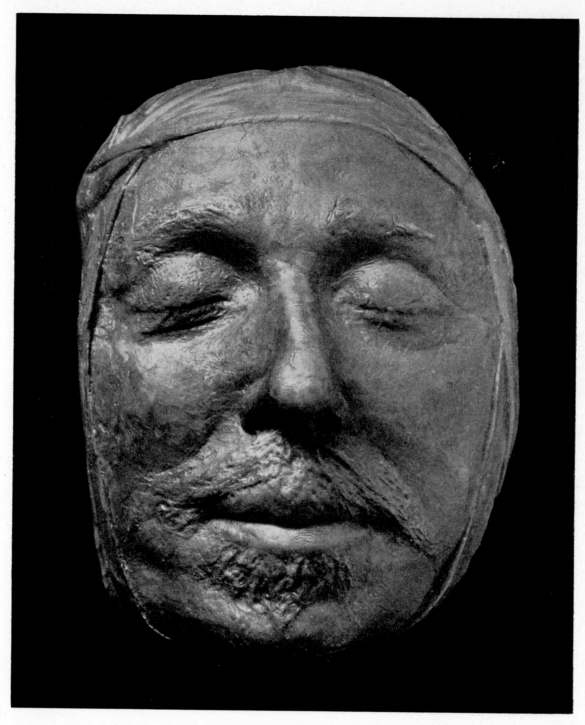

OLIVER CROMWELL (1599–1658). Death-mask in the British Museum.

AARON COPLAND (b. 1900).

SIR FRANCIS DRAKE (c. 1540–1596) by an unknown engraver.

WILLIAM DAMPIER (1652–1715) by T. Murray.

narration which outdo such Elizabethan masters of the horrible as Webster or Tourneur. In *The Battles of Coxinga* these include a caesarean delivery of the dead empress, and a substitution in her womb of a dead baby for the living one, the gouging out of a red eyeball by the owner of the eye, who offers it to the Envoy of the King of Tartary, and the flinging of a soldier against a rock on which he bursts 'like a ripe persimmon'. However, puppetry and chanting removed the action of the plays from a coarse realism. *Jōruri* plays, indeed, are translated, like European operas, from realism into art by their artificiality – a topic on which Chikamatsu himself was eloquent. He defined art as something lifted from the real by stylization: art, he said, is 'something which lies in the slender margin between the real and the unreal'.

The soft-filled centre

CHOPIN, Frédéric François, (1810–1849), Polish composer and pianist, of touching and seductive romanticism.

In Warsaw, where he grew up, one of his teachers declared: 'Leave him alone. His way is uncommon, because his gifts are uncommon.' Schumann in Germany first recognized him with his famous acclamation: 'Hats off, gentlemen! A genius', and before long Chopin had settled into Parisian life with Mendelssohn, Liszt, Berlioz and Meyerbeer, indulging his love for company, pleasure and music; and concentrating entirely on piano works, composing nocturnes, ballades and waltzes, and introducing the polonaise and the mazurka.

In 1837, Chopin and the baronne – George Sand the novelist, that is to say – came together, romantic with romantic. They went to Majorca with her two children, where they lived for some months – described by George Sand in *Un Hiver à Majorque* in 1841 – in acute discomfort in bad weather. The liaison continued for ten years. 'An episode', remarked Chopin, 'without a beginning and with a sad end', for they quarrelled and parted.

Chopin was already consumptive when he met George Sand, and in his later years was at times so ill he had to be carried to the piano. Besides being composer and virtuoso, Chopin was an exceptional piano teacher. Touch, he maintained, was most important,

E

'everything must be made to sing'; and he condemned music which did not obey his own concept: 'Fancy a tree with its branches swayed by the wind – the stem is the steady time, the moving leaves are the melodic inflections.' However, that definition is hardly an absolute for all time. Chopin endures as the irresistible master of celebrity concerts.

ILLUSTRATION: Page 74.

Christina of Sweden

CHRISTINA, (1626–1689), Queen of Sweden, and only child of Gustavus Adolphus (q.v.), who gave up her throne and became a Roman Catholic to amuse herself. In the striking (and very human) tradition of queens who have not let their femininity become obscured by their duty, she surpassed them all by carrying her self-expression to ridiculous lengths.

Gustavus, having expected a boy, gave her an energetic, masculine education: she dressed as a man, and was early accustomed to the sound of gunfire. In later life she often regretted not having taken part in a battle. She was queen at eighteen, and her undoubted brilliance was soon outweighed by immense pride, and by extravagance. Her negotiations to bring about the end of the Thirty Years War revealed a certain talent for diplomacy, and she took some interest in home affairs: but the anxiety of the Senate over an heir ('I can equally well give birth to a Nero as an Augustus,' she once replied to their importuning, and never married) drove her to name her cousin as successor. In 1650 she styled herself king, and the reign of favourites began. Seventeen counts, forty-six barons, and 428 lesser nobles were created by her in ten years, and paid for by public money. One attempt at abdication was prevented by her staunch ministers: and for a while it seemed that she might reform. But the artists, the men of letters from all over Europe whom she attracted to her court (she gave asylum to Descartes the philosopher) filled her with distaste for the simple, often gross, Swedes. Plainly, she was bored with the crown: it pleased her to watch the world gape as she relinquished it voluntarily. She abdicated: it was an action that she never ceased, after the first careless rapture, to regret bitterly.

The *opéra bouffe* actions of the abdicated queen are not without their contemporary parallels: received into the Catholic Church (to Europe's horror), rechristened Alexandra, after her great hero, by the Pope, she settled in Rome at the Farnese palace, and there, surrounded by scholars, cardinals and alchemists, gave herself up to the anodyne of dissipation. She lost her revenue, and she pleaded in vain to have her throne restored. Living on the Pope's charity, Christina died solitary and forgotten.

ILLUSTRATION: Page 75.

Negro majesty

CHRISTOPHE, Henry, (1767–1820), King of Haiti and one of the powerful, enlightened or half-enlightened negroes of the West Indies.

This proud negro, with a solemn carriage and fiery eyes, had helped Toussaint l'Ouverture to liberate Haiti from the French. He had been a slave himself, and in 1806, three years after Toussaint died in a French prison, Christophe, able if uneducated, was elected to a nominal presidency in the island. In 1811, he had himself crowned Henry I of Haiti in a hastily built cathedral; he modelled a Court on the English pattern, and created an aristocracy (not all his leading aristocrats had fortunate names; they included the Duc de Marmelade, and the Comte de Limonade – who was his Foreign Minister). Henry I now began a severe, but improving reign, trying to civilize the freed slaves who were the population of his kingdom. First he was the enlightened despot; then the light began to fade somewhat before his death, and the despotism to increase. In the meantime he had introduced a code of laws, as well as educational, social and agricultural reforms, and he had taken precautions against a possible attempt by the French to recover his territory, building not only a fantastic royal palace, but a vast, massive, improbable fortress or castle on the Pic de Ferrières. To the abolitionists in England – Wilberforce, Zachary Macaulay and Thomas Clarkson (q.v.), Christophe proved, or appeared to prove, how open the slave negro could be to enlightenment. Wilberforce prayed for him every day. Clarkson advised him in letter after letter on government, foreign affairs, education, law and the general conduct of his realm, finding for him the English experts who were required. At Clarkson's instigation he wrote one of his resoundingly royal and dignified letters to the Emperor of Russia, recounting the horrors on the island which had followed the

downfall of Toussaint l'Ouverture, telling him of his labours and improvements and declaring, 'Too long has the African race been unjustly calumniated. Too long has it been represented as deprived of intellectual faculties, as scarcely susceptible of civilization or government by regular and established laws: these false assertions spring from the avarice and injustice of men who have had the impiety to degrade the finest work of the Creator, as if mankind had not one common origin.' For nine years he kept his hold, modelling Court, institutions and reforms after the English. Discipline became too tight, the schoolmastership of a population of ex-slaves became too severe, and the severity too capricious. Soon after Christophe had had a stroke his troops revolted, and he shot himself in the palace of San Souci rather than be captured. His Queen and daughters escaped to England to the kind-heartedness of the Clarksons; his son the Prince Royal was killed and thrown out on a dunghill; and the people took to referring to Christophe as *L'homme*. There was a fine aftermath to *L'homme*'s suicide. They carried his body up the rough, steep path of the Pic des Ferrières. The great citadel was still incomplete. Lime for the masonry was burnt in boilers, and into one incandescent smoking limekiln on the mountain, the dead Christophe was dropped.

ILLUSTRATION: Page 77.

England's war leader

CHURCHILL, Sir Winston Leonard Spencer, (b. 1874), English statesman and war leader.

So thickly do events, experiences, and his own achievements crowd into the portrait of Winston Churchill, in one of the longest public careers of the age, that details of importance are crowded out. It is often said, for example, that his long isolation between the two great wars was entirely due to his unwelcome warnings about Hitler and the threat of National-Socialist Germany. In fact, one cause of that isolation was his stiff antagonism to measures for the political advancement of India. There, as in other things (such as praise of Mussolini and his régime), he has enjoyed good fortune through public forgetfulness. In other ways, misunderstanding has brought upon him undeserved reproaches.

Queen Victoria was still on the throne when he was

first elected to parliament in 1900. The son of a states-man father, he was also already known for other reasons, and much was expected of him. With some aid from Gibbon and Macaulay he had learnt to ex-press himself in speech and on paper. Yet with these and other qualifications, social and inherited, went a defect: he was not a good party man, and it took him a long while to become one. A fair number of men change sides in political life; few do it twice; fewer still then go before the electors as an 'independent anti-socialist'. When first a member of parliament in 1900, Churchill was a Conservative, changing to Liberal before the general election of 1906, and back again to Conservative in the twenties; the truth seem-ing to be that he was all the while a Tory democrat at heart; impatience with his own party and the attrac-tion of some of the Opposition leaders, the enthus-iasm, and ambition, turned him Liberal. In the first World War he was impressed by the looseness of the Government's control – a weakness he took pains to remedy, perhaps too drastically, when his own time came in the second war. The years of 1914–1918 showed in him spirit and brilliant ideas not matched by performance, and triumphs marred by bitter dis-appointments. The twenty-one years between war and war were also chequered, especially after 1929. In the end the gloom of these years was almost un-relieved, and from that gloom Churchill's voice pro-claimed the danger hitherto unexperienced: 'We are for the time being', he said, 'no longer masters of our fate – that fate no longer depends on what we decide here or on what the Cabinet settle in Downing Street. It depends on what may happen in the world, on what other countries may do, for good or ill. It may be hard for our island people, with their long im-munity, to realize this ugly, unpleasant alteration in position.'

Churchill's prophecies fulfilled, and the war a fact, Neville Chamberlain (whom Churchill had called in one of his less public witticisms 'a municipal coun-cillor looking at the world through the small end of a drain-pipe') made him First Lord of the Admiralty, a post he had held nearly thirty years before. It was an interlude. Full power was given to the prophet of dis-aster only when the moment of disaster arrived. Chur-chill became Prime Minister in May 1940, the month in which the Germans invaded the Low Countries and burst into France. No statesman had led an Eng-land in such an evil case, no situation in English his-tory had been so terrible. England was alone, with the Germans in control of the Continental coasts from Scandinavia to the Bay of Biscay. The bombs fell, and Churchill now applied an invincible optim-ism for which there was little foundation in logic; he displayed an inventiveness and imagination which sometimes overran their banks, and a vast capacity for work.

In a few weeks the British Army was evacuated from Dunkirk. In June, Italy joined in the war and France capitulated. He acted with astonishing force, not exhorting too often – that would have been an obvious mistake – nor too seldom, his calls never los-ing their effect. His reputation rose abroad as well as at home to new heights, which was of great value when the untouched reserves of Soviet Russia (June 1941) and the United States (December 1941) were drawn into the war. His defiant oratory in England's phase of isolation had been heard around the whole world, and a language sometimes over-florid and contrived became hard and simple: 'The whole fury and might of the enemy must very soon be turned on us. Hitler knows that he will have to break us in this island or lose the war. If we can stand up to him, all Europe may be free. ... Let us therefore brace our-selves to our duties, and so bear ourselves that, if the British Empire and its Commonwealth last for a thousand years men will say, "This was their finest hour".'

As Great Britain's director of the war, he was the author of notable strategic ideas and remarkable ser-vices, his fervent prolific mind producing enough for half a dozen programmes and sometimes attempting to stuff in items for which there was no room or which were useless or even perilous. His spirit never faltered, but his judgement failed at times, and his best pro-fessional colleagues then found themselves struggling against what appeared to them disastrous Churchil-lian intuitions. Yet all in all for national inspiration, strategic imagination, drive, power to get things done and handling of relations with allies, Churchill must be allowed to be the greatest of war leaders his coun-try has ever known. He contrived to see his own bust on the plinth and read his own biography: he is an institution, without having ceased to be an active politician. Some of Winston Churchill's force as a national leader is to be explained by family history and a strong sense of identification with the fortunes of Great Britain. The first Sir Winston Churchill, knighted in 1663, a small landowner on the borders of Dorset and Devon, bred up among his children a royal mistress, an admiral, two generals, including the great John Churchill, first Duke of Marlborough (q.v.). Lord Randolph Churchill, Winston Churchill's brilliant father, was child of the sixth duke: for more than two centuries the family has been at the heart of power and service.

Soldier of fortune

THE CID, Rodrigo Diaz de Bivar, (c. 1025 or 1045–1099), one of the picaresque figures of medieval legend – in reality a condottiere, in myth the flower of Spanish chivalry, the ideal of heroic virtues. The fable, as always, is the more attractive story: it makes the Cid the apogee of knightly virtue, the selfless patriot, the honourable ideal of his century, although in fact this foremost warrior of the long Christian–Muslim struggle perfectly represented the twelfth-century Castilian, arrogant and exceedingly cruel. He rose to fame in local wars, gaining the nicknames of the Cid (from El Seid, the master) and the Champion. In 1081 he was exiled by Alphonso of Castille, against whom he had formerly fought. 'A man such as the Cid, upright, severe, virtuous, inflexible, of noble sentiments, despised the idle life of the court,' says the romantic historian. Actually, Alphonso and the Cid quarrelled over money. From then, until his death, he was a soldier of fortune, impartially serving Moors and Christians. Eventually he joined forces with the Arab kings of Saragossa, and his greatest achievement was the taking of Valencia in a bloody holocaust. There he ruled until his death, and for some years afterwards Ximena, his wife, held it against the Moors.

In the facts of his life there is adventure, but nothing to touch the heart: there are cruelty, expediency and selfishness, where courtly love demanded honour, sacrifice and chivalry. The Spanish *Poema del Cid* turned its back upon the flaws, and presented a sublime Don Rodrigo, exemplar of an honour which never existed, but which succeeding ages have held as an ideal.

Without these swashbuckling supermen, striding in their seven-league boots through a warring fairyland, we should lack some of our most entertaining tales, many of our finest literary works. But in the end, as with the Cid, the veil tends to become the face, and the age in which he lived, one which was all too golden.

A poet married to nature

CLARE, John, (1793–1864), English poet of the age of Wordsworth, Coleridge, Keats, Turner and Constable, the self-educated son of a farm labourer. Two things chiefly activated Clare's triumph and tragedy – his comfort in nature, or his marriage to nature (after his death, he wrote, nature would be his widow), and his idealized attachment to Mary Joyce, a farmer's daughter who passed out of his life in adolescence. To her many of his most delicious poems were written.

In 1820 the publication of his first book made Clare into a London celebrity. The tide of his fame washed up, and flowed back. Delicate, small, fair-haired and blue-eyed, with the most finely adjusted sensibility, Clare was a misfit in his Northamptonshire village, where after many years he showed symptoms of an increasingly severe psychosis. In 1836, soon after his forty-third birthday, he was sent to a private asylum in Epping Forest, from which he escaped in 1841, walking to Northamptonshire in search of Mary Joyce (who was dead by this time). Later in the year he was taken to the public asylum at Northampton, where he stayed until his death in 1864. Though his mind disintegrated, he contrived for some while to hold a central portion of it intact, writing in the asylum the loveliest and deepest of his poems. These include *I am*, which many subsequent poets have written out for their own comfort, and *A Vision* (1844), the triumphant summary of his life:

> I lost the love of heaven above,
> I spurned the lust of earth below,
> I felt the sweets of fancied love,
> And hell itself my only foe.
>
> I lost earth's joys, but felt the glow
> Of heaven's flame abound in me,
> Till loveliness and I did grow
> The bard of immortality.
>
> I loved but woman fell away,
> I hid me from her faded flame,
> I snatched the sun's eternal ray
> And wrote till earth was but a name.
>
> In every language upon earth,
> On every shore, o'er every sea,
> I gave my name immortal birth
> And kept my spirit with the free.

Much influenced by Wordsworth and Coleridge, Clare defined poetry as hope, love and joy. 'I wrote', he said, 'because it pleased me in sorrow and when happy it makes me happier and so I go on.'

ILLUSTRATION: Page 71.

Champion of the slaves

CLARKSON, Thomas, (1760–1846), English altruistic humanitarian, the inspirer and chief propagandist of the movement to abolish slavery, whom the poet Coleridge called 'the moral Steam-Engine, or the Giant with one idea'.

In his youth it was not looked upon as immoral by the great majority of Englishmen to own slaves in the Colonies and to deal in them. Many drew large profits from the traffic.

As an undergraduate at Cambridge, Clarkson won an essay prize on the subject: 'Is it right to make men slaves against their will?' He published his essay and it put him in touch with evangelical and Quaker groups. Together they formed a Committee for the Abolition of the Slave Trade, since in Clarkson's view the end of the trade would be the first step to total emancipation.

Clarkson was the Committee's propagandist and investigator. He was a tireless letter-writer and pamphleteer and soon had the support of such diverse personalities as Pitt, Fox, Wilberforce, Burke, Johnson and Cowper. He toured the ports to enquire into the conditions of the trade. He was a most conscientious and methodical fact-finder, on one occasion boarding fifty-seven ships in harbour at Plymouth before he found a sailor whom he expected to be a useful witness.

His first success was a bill limiting the number of slaves to be carried in proportion to the tonnage of the ship. When the French Revolution broke out, he had great hopes that Paris might give a lead in abolition, and visited Mirabeau and Necker there. But he was disappointed and returned to the attack at home.

In 1794 his health broke down, and he had not entirely recovered twelve years later when the first part of his plan was achieved with the Act of 1807 which abolished the trade. Wordsworth marked the event with his sonnet: 'Clarkson, it was an obstinate hill to climb.'

After the French wars, he turned to persuading the other European Powers to abolish the trade in their dominions, presenting a long memorandum to Tsar Alexander I in person. In Britain he formed a society for the abolition of slavery. At last, in 1833, the Emancipation Bill was passed, by which all slaves in British possessions were freed. England's lead was not followed by all civilized countries until after Clarkson's death.

Altruists are seldom, alas, the most colourful and fascinating characters; but even if they are colourless they may, like Clarkson, be altogether admirable and as near virtuous as is possible to a human being. As a young man Clarkson gave up his plan to be a clergyman from the moment he learnt of the horrors of the slave trade, and he allowed nothing to divert him, or deflect his cool passion. The colour bar was anathema to him – 'that unhappy distinction between black and white', he called it in a letter to Christophe – the negro King of Haiti, whom he advised – 'which originated in the execrable Slave Trade'. Wilberforce, the politician and philanthropist who led the anti-slavery campaign in Parliament, declared that he appeared to have been 'formed by Providence' for his life's work.

ILLUSTRATION: Page 76.

Sunshine of the heart

CLAUDE LORRAIN, (1600–1682), properly Claude Gelée, French master of landscape, who filled his pictures with air and light and looked the sun full in the eye.

Claude Gelée painted a calm sunshine of the heart. Coming of a poor family, he wandered in France, Italy, Germany and Austria, and then settled in Rome, where with Poussin (q.v.) he developed into one of the great masters of classical landscape painting. His classical and romantic formula was to paint a luminous, infinitely receding sky, a middle distance of half-tones, and a dark mass of trees or buildings in the foreground silhouetted against the sky, with a few tiny figures out of a classical legend. He so much influenced our ways of seeing that thousands of commercial photographs are still based on the typical arrangement of his landscapes. Claude painted numberless variations on the formula, as in his *Enchanted Castle*, which was celebrated by Keats. 'Faery lands forlorn' were never so magically conceived as in this picture. The moon rises above the silent palace by the sea with its empty-eyed windows, its towers and columns, and wild gardens. The luminous sky sends long reflections across the gently rippling sea to the dark masses of the trees, and a shepherdess dreams in the foreground as she watches her sheep.

We know that Claude spent much time sketching in the countryside around Rome, and in the three hundred or so drawings in the British Museum we see that he was able in a few quick strokes of a brush loaded with a wash of brown ink to capture momentary effects of light and space and atmosphere in a way unrivalled until the work of the great nineteenth century landscapists. This air and sunshine he would then transform in his studio into a calm vision of antiquity. With eighteenth-century collectors in England, Claude was a favourite, and in turn his pictures were one of the inspirations of English landscape by Gainsborough, Constable and Turner. His landscapes, suffused with the sun of the Roman Campagna and the Alban Hills, so much affected European painters that for a long while they thought no view was worth while unless it could be made to take on some semblance of the Campagna. Another compliment to Claude is that wealthy landlords altered gardens and landscape to fit with the scheme and sentiment of his pictures. Directly or indirectly, the present look of the English countryside owes much to him.

Politics by other means

CLAUSEWITZ, Karl von, (1780–1831), Prussian general and military thinker whose book *Vom Kriege* (*On War*), prophesies the modern conception of total war.

Clausewitz, the grandson of a Prussian theologian and the son of a disabled Prussian officer, joined the Prussian army as a sub-lieutenant at the age of twelve. At thirty he was one of the circle in Berlin of 'reforming' officers under the leadership of Scharnhorst. They aimed at bringing into being a Prussian national army on the lines of the French People's army created by the Revolution. Because of this, they were dubbed 'Jacobins' by their opponents. However, they soon found themselves fighting against Napo-

leon. Clausewitz was taken prisoner at the battle of Jena in 1806 and spent two years as a captive in France before returning to Prussia. He was appointed assistant to Scharnhorst, who was still planning army reforms, but when in 1811 the Prussian King Frederick William joined Napoleon in his preparations for the invasion of Russia, Clausewitz in disgust fled to the Russian army. In 1812 he negotiated the convention with the Prussians by which they deserted the French on their retreat from Moscow, and the following year he was liaison officer for the Russian army at Marshal Blucher's headquarters. He returned to the Prussian army for the Waterloo campaign. In 1818 he was promoted major-general and appointed Director of the Berlin War Academy, remaining there until 1831, when he was transferred as Chief of Staff to an army corps at Posen. He died of cholera the same year.

Clausewitz was not happy in his career, once writing, 'My life is an existence which leaves no traces.' It was the posthumous publication of his voluminous work *On War* which brought him lasting fame. This book comes from his life-long private studies into the science of war. He surveyed the campaigns in which he had participated and also some 130 previous conflicts, including those of Roman times. He declared that Napoleon, with his mobile warfare and conscription of entire peoples, had brought about a revolution in military thinking. Future wars would not follow the 'chess-board' pattern of the mercenary armies of the eighteenth century fighting for single objectives. They would be 'absolute', 'total' and 'affairs of whole nations', in which peoples would be struggling for their rights to live: 'The more sublime and stronger are the motives of a war, the more it embraces the whole existence of the people.'

The aim of a war was to be the 'complete annihilation' of the opposition. War was part of the coherent life of the State, not an end in itself, but 'the continuation of politics by other means'. It should be the last resort of politics, although military authorities should always be prepared for it.

Once declared, war should be 'violence pushed to its furthest extremes'. Humanitarian rules would be 'scarcely worth mentioning', a stricken foe should 'shed the maximum of blood' before his surrender was accepted, 'moderation' would be 'an absurdity' and terrorism must be employed 'to break the spirit of a civilian population'.

From this brutal approach, which he justified on the grounds that wars should be waged 'as speedily as possible', Clausewitz propounded a political philosophy. With his contemporary Hegel, whom he probably never read, he believed the State should be supreme over individuals. The State's voice should be the Army, and political parties and democratic forms should be suppressed as disruptive influences. Clausewitz allows that there might come a time when war would be unnecessary, but implies that this could be possible only in a world dominated by Prussia and Prussian ideas.

Succeeding generations of Germans have lauded von Clausewitz as 'the High Priest of Strategy', military teachers distorting his views to suit their own purposes. Thus in the twentieth century, General Ludendorff declared himself to be 'completing' Clausewitz by proclaiming a doctrine of Total War in which politics were to play a subordinate part. In fact this is the very contradiction of the Clausewitz theory that war must be a subsidiary to politics. Hitler was often observed with a volume of *On War* open in front of him, but there is little evidence that he understood its content. Perhaps the wisest remark on Clausewitz was made by General von Seeckt in 1930: 'He should be praised less and read more.'

emy on the Left.' But as radical Prime Minister from 1906 to 1909 he proved an indefatigable strikebreaker. In 1914 he set himself up as the virulent critic of each feeble government in turn, heading every number of his paper: 'The Germans are at Noyon.' Called to power in 1917, he established a virtual dictatorship, ignoring the Chambers, and imprisoning the faint-hearted. In the crisis of 1918 it was Clemenceau who proposed that Foch should be put in supreme command of the allied forces. France owed her victory more to him than to any other man. At the Paris peace conference he opposed the idealism of President Wilson and said of his Fourteen Points: 'The Lord God had only ten.' He hoped to annexe the Rhineland; but when England and the United States opposed this, he accepted instead a defensive alliance – which they subsequently repudiated. In 1920 Clemenceau ran for President and was defeated by a candidate who shortly afterwards jumped out of the presidential train stark naked and mad. In old age he visited India and saw New Delhi, the unfinished masterpiece of Lutyens. Pointing to the six former Delhis, he said: 'It will be the most magnificent of all these ruins'—a prophecy soon proved correct.

The Tiger

CLEMENCEAU, Georges, (1841–1929), French politician and leader of France in the first World War. When he took office in 1917 he said: 'You ask, what is my policy? It is to wage war. Home policy? I wage war. Foreign policy? I wage war. Everywhere and always I wage war.' This described his political activities as much as his war leadership. His behaviour and his appearance both earned him the name of 'the Tiger'.

Clemenceau was a radical republican from the Vendée, where the bitter memories of civil war between revolutionaries and royalists still linger. As a young man he voted in the National Assembly of 1871 against the cession of Alsace and Lorraine to Germany. He was relentless against the foreign enemy and against domestic rivals. In the eighteennineties he was involved in the Panama scandal. Accused of taking English gold, the cry of 'Aaoow Yess' lost him the election. He returned to politics with the Dreyfus case, launching the slogan: 'There is no en-

Theatre, film and poetry

COCTEAU, Jean, (b. 1891), French poet who has expressed his poetry in plays, novels, films, ballets, drawings, articles, reminiscences, stunts, lyrics in verse and prose, criticism, and even on gramophone records. What he said of one of his films is more widely true: 'My method is simple: not to meddle with Poetry. She must come of herself, uninvited. Even to name her in a whisper scares her immediately. What I am trying to make is a table, but what you do with it – whether you eat off it, cross-question it, or chop it up for firewood – that is your affair.' (Preface to the journal of *Beauty and the Beast*, 1946.)

If anyone wishes to accuse Cocteau of shocking the bourgeois, he can claim the right to do it; for he is one of them. 'I am born a Parisian,' Cocteau has said, 'my idiom is Parisian; and my accent is Parisian.' Posterity will surely regard his period as one of the great ages of that intellectual capital of the western world.

Cocteau was an infant prodigy, growing up through

the nineties into the time of the Edwardian dandies. He has said of the great people of that time, who launched him at sixteen with a special performance of his early poems at the Théâtre Femina, 'Salute to Mounet-Sully, to Sarah Bernhardt, to de Max; giants who should have for their motto the answer of the Indian Chief who was accused of eating too much at the White House: "A little too much is just enough for me",' – which would often serve Cocteau himself as a good motto.

The Edwardian dandies disappeared; and there came that cosmopolitan age, the age of Diaghilev, of Picasso (q.v.), of Stravinsky (q.v.), in which Cocteau, renouncing the poems and ideas of his youth, was quickly at home. The solvent of it all, according to him, was the arrival of American rhythm, which Cocteau heard first of all in the cake-walk played at the New Circus in 1904; 'The brass and the drums of the band attacked an unknown music, the rhythm of which conjured up the marches Sousa was conducting and punctuating with pistol-shots ...'. For this the highbrow equivalent (the word dates from just this time) was Stravinsky's *Le Sacre du Printemps*, which launched the age in 1913. The war did not submerge the new spirit, but fed it. In 1916, Cocteau and Picasso hatched the ballet *Parade*, to the music of Erik Satie (q.v.), and rehearsed it in Massine's flat; in this ballet appeared those symbols which were to recur here and there throughout the age; the Managers, Italian futurist style, the Chinese, the acrobats, and the young American Miss. After the war came *Les Mariés de la Tour Eiffel* (for the Swedish ballet this time), and Cocteau's connection with the group of musicians called the Six. Remembering his childhood love of the circus and clowns, Cocteau then got the Fratellinis (costumed by Dufy) to mime for him in his *Bœuf sur le toit*, to music by Darius Milhaud. The surrealist title 'Bullock on the Roof' was taken from the name of a famous bar in Paris.

In the late twenties Cocteau began, like other men, to meddle with myth: *Orphée*, in its first theatrical form, dates from 1927. In the thirties he turned to film, with his first surrealist masterpiece, *Le Sang d'un poète*. His later triumphs in film came from bringing myth and film together, in *L'Éternal Retour* (on the theme of Tristan and Iseult), in *La Belle et la Bête* (a magical retelling of *Beauty and the Beast*, made under the impossible conditions he has described in his Journal) and in *Orphée*, which is in some ways a terrible image of our world; Cocteau admits that he has favoured working in the theatre and the cinema – even under the most impossible conditions – because the community they establish holds off that loneliness he has always suffered from, and has sometimes fought with less satisfactory weapons, such as opium.

Cocteau has always lived in an atmosphere of scandal for this and for other reasons – not least for attacking the established masterpieces such as Flaubert's *Madame Bovary*. Cocteau defended himself from these attacks, taking as a simile the game of pelota, in which you need a good strong wall. The wall, says Cocteau, is not a target, you are not shooting at it, you don't want to damage it; no one need be sorry for it; you just want your ball to bounce off, and however hard you throw your ball, it won't leave a mark. Perhaps Cocteau himself may be such a wall. He has, at least, had plenty of things thrown at him. But he has been one of the creators of the modern idiom; and if, being a leader of many fashions, he finds the mob turning at last another way, he may expect that some day they will turn back again. What he said about poetry in the theatre is still current enough: that we need the poetry *of* the theatre, not poetry *in* the theatre. The poetry *of* the theatre has to be seen from a distance. Poetry *in* the theatre is like fine lace held up for our inspection from afar. It is a grave mistake, and it is always recurring.

ILLUSTRATION: Page 78.

A bridler by delight

COLERIDGE, Samuel Taylor, (1772–1834), English poet, critic, metaphysician, political theorist and divine.

'If a man could pass through Paradise in a dream, and have a flower presented to him as a pledge that his soul had really been there, and if he found that flower in his hand when he awoke – Aye! and what then?'

'Bright reflections, in the canal, of the blue and green vitriol bottles in the druggists' shops in London.'

'Idly talk they who speak of poets as mere indulgers of fancy, imagination, superstition, etc. They are the bridlers by delight, the purifiers; they that combine all these with reason and order – the true protoplasts – Gods of Love who tame the chaos.'

To these three notes by Coleridge, add yet another, his description of Shakespeare – 'Our own Shake-

speare, himself a nature humanized, a genial understanding, directing self-consciously a power and implicit wisdom deeper than consciousness' – and they
give between them a notion of the range, gravity, re-
ceptivity and richness of this poet, described by his
friend Wordsworth (q.v.) as 'the most wonderful man
I have ever known' and by Thomas de Quincey as
'the largest and most spacious intellect in my judgement that ever yet existed among men', a view shared
by many who had met and known him. A living critic,
I. A. Richards, speaks of the 'ocean-like' quality of his
mind.

Coleridge's thought, deductive rather than analytic,
included in its sweep the philosophic and the poetic,
the scientific and the moral, political theory and religious musing, together with that minute observation
of his sensations which makes him a remarkable forerunner of psychology. From childhood he read prodigiously ('I have read everything,' he wrote to a
friend, which was essentially, if not literally, true);
and he was perhaps the last man of genius to attempt that universality of knowledge which marked
Renaissance scholarship. He was the son of a Devonshire clergyman – the tenth child of a second marriage. Charles Lamb has described him as he was in
his London schooldays – 'Samuel Taylor Coleridge –
Logician, Metaphysician, Bard! How have I seen the
casual passer through the cloisters stand still, en-
tranced with admiration ... to hear thee unfold, in thy
deep and sweet intonations, the mysteries of Iamblicus,
or Plotinus (for even in those years thou waxedst
not pale at such philosophic draughts), or reciting
Homer in his Greek, or Pindar.' This eloquence, irra-
diating a face white as lard, and this power of holding
his hearers spellbound, lasted through his life, made
him one of the great masters of conversation – or
monologue – and brought him fame in later years,
when all fashionable London, Byron included, came to
his extempory lectures on Shakespeare, Milton, etc.

To some degree Coleridge's life was unfortunate.
He had the supreme good fortune, it is true, to meet
and know Wordsworth, his powers were remarkable,
his achievements considerable; yet from ill-health,
opium taken to alleviate his pains, ill luck in marriage ('Mem:' – he set down in a notebook – 'not to
adulterize my time by absenting myself from my
wife'), and a power and extent of intuition almost too
large to endure, he fell short of his own potentiality.
Yet much remains; not only such fine poems of the
second order as *Dejection, An Ode*, but also *The Rime
of the Ancient Mariner*, and the fragments *Christabel*

and *Kubla Khan*, on which depend his reputation as
one of the major English poets, and which so powerfully evoke a supernatural, visionary world –

> In Xanadu did Kubla Khan
> A stately pleasure-dome decree:
> Where Alph, the sacred river, ran
> Through caverns measureless to man
> Down to a sunless sea ...

The familiar opening lines at once lift the reader into
another orbit. A visit to the peculiar landscape in
which *Kubla Khan* was written explains something of
Coleridge as a poet: the savage wooded cliffs and valley above the quiet, dead, often sunless Severn Sea,
and below the farmhouse at Culbone, where opium,
taken for dysentery, had sent him into a sleep in
which he composed to himself (so he said) a whole
poem. *Kubla Khan* was the opening fragment, and
might not have lived so magnificently by itself but for
the famous interruption by 'A man from Porlock',
who kept Coleridge talking on business until recol-
lection of all the lines was impossible.

Much of his time was embittered by a hopeless and
enduring love for Wordsworth's sister-in-law.

ILLUSTRATION: Page 81.

A fiery particle

COLETTE, Sidonie Gabrielle Claudine, (1873–
1954), French novelist of the charms and miseries of
love, human existence and human environment.

It was Colette's first husband, Henri Gauthier-
Villars – the immortal and unpleasant Willy – who
made her write novels, and pretended that they wrote
them together. These were the Claudine novels, in
which the life of a young girl is seen through eyes un-
clouded by love, but alive to all the delicate shades of
emotion. The first, *Claudine à l'école*, appeared in
1900. 'My name is Claudine, I live in Montigny, I
was born there in 1884, and probably I shall die
there'. Mme Colette's style belongs to the great manner of the brief French novel, concise, without trim-
mings, able to record personal feelings and reactions
with wonderful acuteness, and born of a sharp ear for
the speech of everyday life. In *La Maison de Claudine*
there is this description of her father's death: 'He
died in his seventy-fourth year, holding the hand of
his well-beloved wife and watching her streaming eyes

with an expression that gradually lost its colour, became a curious milky blue, and paled like a sky invaded by mist. He had the most beautiful funeral in a village cemetery, with a coffin of yellow wood, covered only by an old tunic pierced with wound-holes – it was the tunic he wore as a captain in the first regiment of Zouaves, and my mother walked beside it to the edge of the grave without faltering, very tiny and determined under her veils, and murmuring very softly, and for him alone, words of love.'

Willy did not last: if he forced Colette to write (for which he earns our gratitude) he oppressed her: 'I have often imagined', she has said, 'that M. Willy suffered from a form of agoraphobia, that he had a nervous horror of unused paper'.

After her second marriage, Colette's work changed: she was still a brilliant observer, but now she was also a moralist. Claudine has become Renée Nérée: Chéri, the gilded gigolo, is introduced, and Gigi, and an aged Claudine, Julie de Carneilan. In *Chéri* (1920) her world is the world of love – and love that is uncompromisingly illicit and carnal. Yet Colette's ethos is much more than this: love is the *summum bonum* of existence, and she will not allow it to be divided up. A little sadness, a little pleasure – this is love, and life. The activities of the day, the social world, the struggle of the classes, are in Mme Colette's work: but as a frame to the personal relations of her characters. 'There is nothing but passion?' says one of her heroines. 'In the limitless desert of love passion holds a burning – and very small – place; at first one sees nothing else. I am not a callow young girl, to be blinded by his splendour. ... What do I know of the man I love and who wants me? When we shall have found each other in a brief embrace or even in a long night, we must then begin to live together near each other and with each other.' Colette is the timeless observer of dogs beneath the skin. The tones of fulfilled and of aggrieved love clip precisely across her pages: 'Can I forget him, as if I had never known his look nor his mouth's caress ... as if the most important thing in my life was to look for words, words in order to say how yellow the sun is, and how blue the sea, and how the salt shines on the edge of white jet ... yes ... as if there was nothing more urgent in the world than my desire to feast my eyes on the wonders of the earth?'

Colette, in death even as in life, caused a stir. The Church refused a religious ceremony on personal grounds, and open letters – of some warmth – by Graham Greene and the Cardinal Archbishop of Paris appeared in *Le Figaro Littéraire*.

Conquest of the Atlantic

COLUMBUS, Christopher, (c. 1451–1506), Genoese navigator, and in effect the man who discovered America, though he knew nothing of the new continent, and though there can be no doubt it had been visited centuries before by the Vikings, first under Leif Ericsson (q.v.).

The important thing in Columbus's day was to find a short sea route to Asia. Columbus believed that he would find this route by sailing westward, though as he wrote, after he conquered the Atlantic, his proposals had been laughed at and it had taken him eight years to win the necessary support. He had tried first of all to convince the Portuguese, and at last he won over the Spaniards. For half a century the Portuguese had been feeling their way down the endless coast of Africa, in search of an eastern route to the Indies. The Spaniards were jealous of the Portuguese, and eventually this possibility of a short cut via the west must have seemed more tempting. So Columbus sailed from Palos on 3 August 1492, with about ninety men in three little ships estimated to have been about 60 to 75 feet long and to have had a draught of about six feet. He carried with him the King of Spain's commission 'to discover and to gain certain islands and mainland in the Ocean Sea' and a letter of recommendation to the Great Khan. After a call at the Canary Islands, he sailed west on 6 September, and on 12 October made his first transatlantic landfall at what is now Watling Island (San Salvador).

From his first voyage Columbus returned with a great deal of prestige, a few 'Indians' and hardly any gold. He made three more voyages across the Atlantic, but with each his prestige diminished. Instead of the 'Indies' and Cathay, he found only a maze without end of unprofitable islands. Ill-luck prevented him from hitting on the relatively wealthy land of the Aztecs, and once he touched on the South American mainland without recognizing it. He was a practical seaman, not an administrator, and his colonizing efforts were unfortunate. He lost favour; and in May 1498 Vasco da Gama reached India by the eastern route; in other words, the prize of the Indian trade went to the Portuguese after all, and with that disappeared what was left of Columbus's reputation. He died disappointed and more or less forgotten.

In a sense, Columbus enjoys an accidental fame. Born at Genoa of humble origins, he had gone to sea at an early age, and the fact that he never wrote in

Italian, but always in Spanish, suggests that he had picked up his education rather late. He was, of course, a professional. His early voyages were made in the western Mediterranean for Genoese business firms. Later his voyages extended into the Atlantic, and he settled in Portugal and Spain, marrying the daughter of one of Henry the Navigator's captains. Objects thrown up by the tide and seamen's tales must have helped to convince him that land lay farther to the west; but his approach to his great voyage was neither ancient and traditional nor modern and scientific. There was evidence that the distance from Spain to Asia must be far greater than he believed. That did not shift him. In his technique he could skilfully navigate by dead reckoning, by the use of the compass and the estimation of speed and distance; but it seems that he never mastered as much as was known in his day of celestial navigation. He was simply a man with a fixed idea, ready to back it with every or any argument.

A year after the death of Columbus, the German cosmographer Martin Waldseemüller proposed to call the new continent after Amerigo Vespucci (q.v.). This now seems an injustice. But Columbus was unaware that he had discovered America: to his last day he was convinced only that he had found the short western route to Asia.

The perfectionist

CONDORCET, Marie Jean Antoine Nicolas de Caritat, Marquis de, (1743–1794), French aristocrat, perfectionist and mathematician, whose love of independence led him to support the Revolution, and who died for his love.

He was a brilliant youth; at sixteen a golden future was predicted for him by the encyclopaedist D'Alembert. He was a typical cultured man of the eighteenth century, interested in literature and social questions, in natural science and philosophy. Religion and the monarchy were his aversions. D'Alembert's prophecy was never quite fulfilled, for Condorcet dissipated his talents too widely; he published many mathematical works, and wrote for the famous *Encyclopédie*, which did so much to spread the new teachings of liberalism in France.

With the outbreak of the Revolution, he was elected to represent Paris in the Legislative Assembly, and wrote the address to the European powers. He was not always well thought of by his fellows; in particular, an expostulatory letter which he wrote to the king, Louis XV, was thought excessively ill-mannered. Perhaps in power he tended to strut, but this would hardly justify Mme Roland's harsh opinion of him: 'The genius of Condorcet is equal to the comprehension of the greatest truths, but he has no other characteristic besides fear ... such men should be employed to write, but never permitted to act.' He was not to have much longer to act, for his opposition to the king's death had earned him some criticism. When he objected to the execution of the Girondists, he made an enemy of Robespierre: he was proscribed and his goods confiscated. The nine months of his hiding from the Terror revealed an unsuspected depth of spirit. To his poverty-stricken wife he wrote: 'I shall perish like Socrates and Sidney for having served the liberty of my country.' Feeling that the owner of the house where he had been given shelter would be incriminated if he stayed longer, he left, and wandered about the fields. After two days, his hunger drove him to a village inn, where he asked for an omelette. He was carrying a copy of Horace's works, and the innkeeper suspiciously enquired his trade. 'A carpenter.' 'Carpenters don't have hands like yours,' said the innkeeper, and Condorcet was arrested. The next morning he was found dead of poison, administered by his own hand.

While in hiding, he wrote *Esquisse d'un tableau historique des progrès de l'esprit humain*, which is his best memorial. As Boethius in dire straits turned to the consolation of philosophy, so Condorcet wrote this book on the thesis that the evil of life was only the result of bad institutions, from which humanity would free itself in the end. His final section, on the future, revealed Condorcet at his best. He sees the future as a time of equality between nations and between classes: although not absolute equality, but only equal opportunity. Perfectionism is no longer a popular creed, and it may not be wise; but it has stimulated reform and encouraged and comforted mankind.

Jozef Teodor Konrad Nalecz Korzeniowski

CONRAD, Joseph, (1857–1924), Polish–English novelist and master mariner. *A Personal Record* states his creed: 'The world, the temporal world, rests on a few, very simple ideas; so simple that they must be as old as the hills. It rests notably among others on fidelity.'

Until he left the sea for literature, and was naturalized as a British subject, he was a Pole; but born in a Polish province long under Russian rule. As Jozef Teodor Konrad Nalecz Korzeniowski, he had the idea of Honour as a birthright. His patriot father was banished from Poland by the Russians, and Conrad spent his childhood in exile in Russia. His mother died there. He loathed Russia, and gave his verdict later that 'from the very first ghastly dawn of her existence as a state, she had to breathe the atmosphere of despotism'. This land-locked boy read aloud his father's translation of Hugo's *Les Travailleurs de la Mer*, and caught the smell of the sea. At seventeen he became a seaman at Marseilles. He ran contraband into Spain for the Royalists, he left the Mediterranean for the Eastern Seas, Malaya, the Indian Ocean, Australia, and he rose to be a master in the British Merchant Navy. His great stories of the sea are written from the lonely eminence of the captain's cabin, but he writes with full knowledge of the squalor of the forecastle. Once he commanded a river steamer in the Belgian Congo, and that experience was crystallized in one of his most compelling works, *The Heart of Darkness*. His last command was the sailing-ship *Torrens*, on the Australian run, and he had a famous meeting aboard her with John Galsworthy, a passenger, who noted, 'I had never seen before a man so masculinely keen, yet so femininely sensitive'.

Conrad now quitted the sea for letters and came to England. He might have written in French, in which he was equally fluent, but he chose English as his medium. He did not achieve success immediately. *Lord Jim* and *Nostromo* were failures at first. He lived in despair and faith, 'fighting disease and imbecility', he wrote, 'like a cornered rat'. He was profoundly ironical; and it is ironical that one of his worst books gave him wealth and fame in the ten years before he died. Conrad, like Lord Keynes, believed that 'civilization was a thin and precarious crust erected by the personality and will of the very few'. In all his novels, whether they are set in the Eastern Isles, on shipboard or in the underground London of *The Secret Agent*, he is exploring what happens when the crust breaks. His heroes are always fighting for something in this earthquake situation – it may be redemption, like Lord Jim, or an escape from demoralization, like Almayer, in *Almayer's Folly*. He saw mystery in the bat-tle – mystery everywhere. Watching a coast as it slips by, he wrote in *The Heart of Darkness*, is 'like thinking about an enigma. There it is before you – smiling, frowning, inviting, grand, mean, insipid, or savage, and always mute with an air of whispering, come and find out.'

In character a *grand seigneur*, with his pointed beard, his veiled hawk's eyes and his thunderous brow, he made the sheer novel of adventure aristocratic by importing into it the idea of conflict. Man is always against something: the evil in the world, the evil in himself. He wins through by fidelity to a vision. 'There is nothing more futile under the sun than adventure,' Conrad declared, having seen more of adventure than any other novelist. 'Adventure by itself is but a phantom, a dubious shape without a heart.' He gave it a heart: the idea of loyalty.

Light, dew, breeze, freshness

CONSTABLE, John, (1776–1837), English painter of delight in the freshness and sparkle of landscape.

'I shall never be a popular artist – a Gentlemen and Ladies' painter,' Constable wrote, 'but I am spared making a fool of myself. ... I look to what I possess and find ample consolation.' John Constable lived, on the whole, a quiet life without boldly dramatic incidents. His father was a well-to-do miller in Suffolk, from whom he inherited a directness and depth of character and a shrewdness about his own interests. 'Where *real* business is to be done you are the most energetic and punctual of men,' one of his friends wrote to him, 'in smaller matters, such as putting on your breeches, you are apt to lose time in deciding which leg shall go in first.'

Constable's 'real business', above all things, was his own art, about which he was never in doubt. He saw it was his duty to paint in landscape the freshness of nature, to strive to record and combine on canvas those elements of the natural scene which made him happy and calm.

Superior people nagged him (for example, over his marriage to a girl higher in the social scale than the miller's son – her rich grandfather was clergyman of his parish). Superior painters in London, who ruled the realm of painting, could not see the point of his revolutionary art. Constable did not waver: his life, as well as his landscape, is a lesson in honesty, independence, firmness and enlightenment. To his friend, the clergyman John Fisher, who stood by him always, Constable wrote, 'I have no patron but yourself – and you are not the Duke of Devonshire, or any other great ass. You are only a gentleman and a scholar and a real lover of the art whose only wish is to see it advance.'

What was held to be the best painting in his day, he realized, neither sprang from life nor reacted upon life. Constable considered there was 'room for a natural painture'. With him painting was 'another word for feeling'. His duty was to give 'a pure and unaffected representation of the scenes that may employ me'. His art was limited, he wrote, 'it was to be found under every hedge and in every lane, and therefore nobody thinks it is worth picking up'. The light, the dew, the breeze, the bloom and freshness he aimed at were, in his conviction, qualities no painter in the world had managed to perfect. So Constable developed his own vision, instead of seeing and painting in an accepted mode. He had the capacity of living absolutely through his eyes.

To understand the spontaneity and honesty of Constable's art and the degree to which it was new in the world (and therefore helped to change all landscape-painting in the nineteenth century), examine his oil sketches, especially in the Victoria and Albert Museum, London. The works by him which most take us out of ourselves, rather than touching us merely, are the many studies Constable made of the skyscape, of the scenery of clouds, which he examined with the eye at once of painter and scientist.

Pacific explorer

COOK, James, (1728–1779), English explorer, who by his first two voyages of discovery demolished the legend of the *terra australis incognita*, the unknown southern continent (see Tasman).

On his second voyage his instructions from the Admiralty were 'to put an end to all diversity of opinion about a matter so curious and important'. The importance, indeed, was not academic. The French were also after the southern continent. The great French explorer Bougainville had been on the search, but had succeeded only in restricting its supposed

area. If this rich continent had existed, it might have led to war. So Cook conveniently removed a bone of contention.

In proving that the continent did not exist, Captain Cook travelled farther south than any man had done before, and found reason to suspect the existence of Antarctica, which was of no interest to the eighteenth century. 'I will not say it were an impossibility anywhere to get in among this ice,' he wrote, 'but I will assert that the bare attempting of it would be a very dangerous enterprise ... I, who hope ambition leads me not only farther than any other man has been before me, but as far as I think it possible for man to go, was not sorry at meeting with this interruption.'

The ambition of this sober, practical genius, the self-educated son of an agricultural labourer, led him in the course of ten years' exploration to clear up all the major uncertainties about the Pacific. On his first voyage he charted the unknown coasts of New Zealand, which had been seen but not examined, and the east coast of Australia, which many still believed to be a continuation of New Guinea. His second voyage was, in effect, a circumnavigation of the southern ice ring. His third voyage was an attempt to find the north-west passage from the Pacific end and led to much information about the Pacific coast of North America. On the return journey he was killed by the Hawaiians, who long remembered him as a god.

ILLUSTRATION: Page 80.

The first travel agent

COOK, Thomas, (1808–1892), the first travel agent, through whom the tourist with his camera has become a figure inseparable from canyons, mountains, castles, cities and cruise steamers.

The development was bound to come, no doubt, as a consequence of the railways and the new era of swift transport, but it began in a way little to be expected. Cook was a religiously-minded wood-turner, the earnest secretary to a temperance society at Market Harborough in the Midlands of Great Britain. On 5 July 1841, sixteen years after a locomotive had pulled the first passenger train in the world, the Midland Railway, persuaded by Cook, conveyed passengers to and from a temperance meeting, in a special train, at a special price of one shilling per head.

More Temperance 'specials' led Cook to conceive excursions for pleasure and culture. Little by little his labours and those of his son opened first Europe, then all, or most, other countries, to travel – or rather to the 'tourist', a new word of the time which began to mean the traveller of restless, shallow curiosity. Cook, however, had set the world moving. He believed, in his Victorian century, that he had done much to further men's progress, welfare and enlightenment. The American Express, now the world-wide rival of Cook's, did not add travel agency to its vast expressing business until 1912.

Copernicus, earth and sun

COPERNICUS, Nicolaus, (1473–1543), one of the greatest figures in the establishment of the modern scientific outlook.

A Polish son of the Renaissance, he was educated at Cracow, and for ten years in Italy in the time of Leonardo da Vinci. He studied Greek at Bologna and was consulted by the Pope on the reform of the calendar, and received his doctorate of canon law from the Archbishop of Ferrara, one of the Borgias. He returned home at the age of thirty-three, learned in mathematics, astronomy, law, medicine and Greek, and also a competent painter, became secretary to his uncle, the Prince Bishop of Varmia, whose cathedral was at Frauenburg on the Baltic, conducted his uncle's political correspondence, and engaged in the Polish patriotic struggles against the Teutonic Knights, successfully defending the castle of Olstein against them.

The immediate impulse to his revolution in thought was the chaos in contemporary astronomy. This was due, he said, to 'the number of auxiliary means for the study of the heavens ... increasing with the passage of time and with our distance from the founders of this science'. So he looked for a unifying idea which would bring order into the observations collected during 2,000 years, and found it in the notion that the earth went round the sun, which had first been advanced by Aristarchus of Samos. He made systematic astronomical observations to test the point, and at last gave a complete account of his views and arguments in *The Revolutions of the Celestial Spheres* (*De revolutionibus orbium coelestium*), published in 1543, the year in which he died.

In his expressions of opinion, Copernicus was uncompromising, but he was worldly-wise and able to put his ideas in a way which relieved him from attack. He died in high conventional repute, and the wider implications of his theory were not generally appreciated until half a century afterwards, though his first intellectual converts were the English mathematicians, who wrote in his support as early as 1556. By introducing his theory into modern thought, Copernicus initiated a revolution beyond astronomy. He undermined man's egotistic claim to be the centre of creation, and inspired a complete reorientation of human thought in history and social affairs, as well as in natural science. Effectively he raised the modern ideas of motion and relativity against the medieval ideas of fixity and absoluteness, and so made himself the chief scientific spokesman of the Renaissance.

Sidewalk, glass, steel and prairie

COPLAND, Aaron, (b.1900), American composer, whose music is the product of our industrial society. The way he has both accepted that society and reacted against it makes him one of the musical figures of our time.

To a degree Copland is the first of American composers, since he is not merely a composer happening to live in the United States. Also, unlike his elder contemporary, Charles Ives (q.v.), he is by no means a remote figure on the borderland of his country's musical life. His parents were Jews from Russia, and Copland was born in what he has called 'a drab street' among the endless streets of Brooklyn, N.Y. His early music belongs to the America of sidewalks and industrial cities – it is complex, efficient and quite without pity, goaded on by a mechanistic frenzy; its contours are no softer than the skylines of Chicago and New York. Suspiciously one may search the *Dance Symphony* or the *Music for Theatre* (1925) for a betraying sentimentality; but the slow movements are disconcertingly inarticulate, and the fast ones offer a refrigerated impersonal gaiety and a few sinister wisecracks. Beneath this Copland was building a new idiom from the musical equivalents of glass and steel, austere, comfortless, and hardly delightful to the public. In the early thirties he became concerned by the estrangement between the artist and the public, and began to simplify his style; he visited Mexico in 1932. The dancers in *El Salón México* (1936) are creatures of flesh and blood; a humanity closer to soil than to asphalt warms the music of his ballets *Billy the Kid* (1938), *Rodeo* (1942), and *Appalachian Spring* (1944). Copland had now united the influence of Middle Western folk-music with the discoveries he had made in the absolute music of his early years, and so devised a popular art which fulfils its social purpose, in theatre, cinema, or concert hall, without for a moment ceasing to be art. He comments poignantly on prairie and city alike, balancing melancholy and a young American exuberance and exultation.

The fact that both his popular and his graver music have force and individuality shows Copland in control of an artistic situation he has brought about almost single-handed. He has built for himself and his successors a musical idiom that is unmistakably American.

ILLUSTRATION: Page 83.

'Crocodiles would not eat them'

COURBET, Gustave, (1819–1877), French painter of notable vision; and of importance in the development of art in the nineteenth century through his honesty, earnestness and respect for sheer painting.

When the International Exhibition of 1855 rejected most of Courbet's 'realist' paintings, he erected a marquee outside the gates and gave his one-man show. The sign on the marquee announced 'Realism. G. Courbet', and prefacing the catalogue he wrote that it was his aim to be 'not a painter only, but also a man'. Bluff, big, talkative, Courbet might no doubt have talked less and saved the time for painting. The talk was sometimes excessive, sometimes foolish. He knew that he must paint what he saw, he must paint his own vision, and not wander off into that painting of 'ideal' fancies which was choking French art like folds of wet flannel. Delacroix might depict angels. Courbet could not depict angels, he said, since he had never seen one. Renoir was informed by his teacher that there was a difference between the big toe of the classical hero and the big toe of the local coalman: Courbet could not make such distinctions. Coalman and classical hero changed places. Art for him be-

came 'democratic', and democratic art was 'realism'. Democratic sympathies and the revolutions of 1848 were behind his picture *The Stonebreakers*, which he painted from the life: 'I stopped to watch two men breaking stone along the road. It is seldom one comes across a more complete picture of misery.' The men were invited to his studio, and he began the picture – all of which, he said, 'takes place in broad daylight, beside the road. The men stand out against the green slope of a great mountain which fills the canvas; only in the right-hand corner does the slope of the mountain allow a little blue sky to be seen. I invented nothing, dear friend; every day, going out for a drive I saw these men. Well, in this country that is how you and I end up.'

In one sense these admirable feelings are irrelevant altogether. Looking at *The Stonebreakers* to-day, it appears no picture of 'a complete picture of misery', only an honest, selective, carefully constructed, admirable record of two men at their work. Courbet's 'realism' is also questionable, since in his painting things appear not as they were, but as they were to Courbet, arranged and rendered by Courbet's skill and strained through Courbet's own emphatic personality. Flowers, a girl in a hammock, a wave rolling to shore, a green forest, a scene in snow, a dark stream rolling out of the limestone, and under limestone stratifications in his home countryside of Franche-Comté – whatever the subject – Courbet's handling of it is unmistakable and poetic.

Yet Courbet's poetic bluntness seemed, in his day, blasphemy at the high mass of art. He was the 'great stupid painter who put his wooden shoe through the plate-glass window'. When his *Bathers* was exhibited in 1853, Napoleon III put his riding-crop across the huge naked girl whose back and striding thighs fill most of the picture, one critic also saying of the nudes that 'crocodiles would not eat them'. Courbet's art was the broad understructure for impressionism, but his honest poetries endure supremely well on their own account. His democratic sympathies helped him to his object, but the pictures are independent. In front of them one forgets that he talked too much, one forgets what he talked about; and cares nothing for his doings in the Commune in Paris in 1871, and whether or no he had a share in pulling down the Vendôme column. Even the exile in Switzerland, where he died in 1877, seems irrelevant. Convincing pictures are the result.

ILLUSTRATION: Page 167.

English iron

CROMWELL, Oliver, (1599–1658), Lord Protector of England. 'He was a soldier disciplined to perfection in the knowledge of himself', wrote Milton in
the *Second Defence of the People of England*. 'He had
either extinguished, or by habit had learned to subdue,
the whole host of vain hopes, fears, and passions,
which infest the soul. He first acquired the government of himself, and over himself acquired the most
signal victories; so that on the first day he took the
field against the external enemy, he was a veteran in
arms, consummately practised in the toils and exi-
gencies of war.'

Of the formative years of his life, before he put on
the mask of a public personality, we unfortunately
know very little. Cromwell was forty-three (advanced
in middle age, by seventeenth-century standards) before he ceased being an obscure squire from the Fens.
Like most of the best British statesmen, he did not
dabble in ideas ('I can tell you, sir, what I would not
have; though I cannot, what I would', he said when
the Civil War was beginning). Accordingly, and not
without reason in his situation, he distrusted people
with notions, and 'rhetoricians – to whom I do not
pretend, neither to them nor to the things they use
to speak, words. Truly our business is to speak *things*',
as he told the Parliament of 1656.

But a man does not lead a revolution, and become
Lord Protector of England, without a driving force;
and that force Cromwell had found before he exercised it on public events – it was religious faith of a
curious and dogmatic kind. He was born and bred a
countryman, in an England that was still largely
medieval in its ways. His education was at the grammar school of Huntingdon, his native place, and for a
year at Sidney Sussex College, Cambridge, where he
is known to have acted in a morality play (a good one,
too) called *Lingua*. Then his father died suddenly;
and as the only son in a house full of daughters, he
had to take on the management of the estates. He
went to London to acquire the necessary legal knowledge at the Inns of Court; and soon after his twenty-
first birthday brought home as a bride the daughter
of a prosperous merchant, Sir John Bouchier. All
very proper, very regular, very humdrum – 'as if his
highest plot, to plant the bergamot', as Andrew Marvell rightly said.

And then, in the early years of his marriage, he
suffered a nervous breakdown. '*Valde melancholicus*',

wrote the London specialist, Sir Thomas Mayerne, in
his case-book in 1628. He had fancies about the town
cross, nightmares, fearful attacks of rage and midnight terrors of dying. To escape from himself, he
plunged into dissipation: 'You know what my manner of life hath been. Oh, I lived in and loved darkness and hated the light', he wrote to a cousin in 1638.
Even at that time, the best thing he could say to honour his Lord was 'that He giveth springs in a dry and
barren wilderness where no water is'. His Lord still
had trials in store for him: in the following May his
eldest son Robert died, which was a loss he remembered literally to his dying day. For this man of iron
was in private life most tender-hearted, and remained
so. His favourite daughter Betty (Elizabeth Claypole)
begged off all the Royalists she liked most when her
father was in power; and during her illness affairs of
state were suspended while her father haunted the
sickroom.

His interest in public affairs began in 1628, when he
was elected to Parliament for Huntingdon. He continued to sit for Parliament until the Civil War, but
he was no speaker, and no party man; he did not
begin to rise into leadership until the war started, and
he formed his own troop of horse. In a few months
the troop was a regiment; then a double regiment;
from then on, the way to power was open. 'I had
rather have a plain russet-coated captain that knows
what he fights for and loves what he knows, than that
which you call a gentleman and nothing else. I honour a gentleman that is so indeed.' Cromwell had
much in his favour: the character of East Anglia and
his knowledge of it; his skill in choosing men; his
passionate love of horses; his curiously English,
muddled but profound religious sense, which had
been tried in the fire of his own suffering. The furious
energy which had turned in to trouble him, was now
turned outwards into the active life of the campaigns.
And anyone was welcome among the Ironsides who
knew his own mind, and abjured the King, the Pope
and the Devil.

As a ruler, Cromwell had much to recommend
him, yet an impossible position; his measures were
often enlightened, his outlook sensible. But the Tudor
governmental system, which had functioned through
parson and squire, was now wrecked. The succession
problem defeated him, as it has defeated most personal rulers. 'I beseech you in the bowels of Christ,
think it possible you may be mistaken', he shouted at
the Scottish Presbyterians, and in other words, at the
English ones too. But if you think it possible you may

be mistaken, how can you go on? All that is implied in Cromwell's last prayer, which ends: 'Teach those who look too much on Thy instruments to depend more upon Thyself. Pardon such as desire to trample upon the dust of a poor worm, for they are Thy people too. And pardon the folly of this short prayer, even for Jesus Christ's sake, and give me a good night if it be Thy pleasure.'

ILLUSTRATION: Page 82.

Discoverer of radium

CURIE, Marie, (1867–1934), born in Poland as Marie Sklodowska. The daughter of a teacher of physics, she became the most famous of all women scientists. With her husband Pierre Curie she discovered radium.

As a child, Marie Sklodowska was a determined and successful student, who completed her school studies with a gold medal, and became a governess. In country isolation, she dreamed of intellectual freedom in Paris, and gradually focused her attention on the physical sciences, acquiring habits of independent work. With her sister's help she succeeded in entering the Sorbonne in 1891. It was about this time that she wrote that 'life is not easy for any of us. But what of that? we must have perseverance and, above all, confidence in ourselves. We must believe that we are gifted for something, and that this thing, at whatever cost, must be attained.' It was in this spirit that she relentlessly pursued all her aims. She was a passionate, almost a grim, character. In her year she was first in mathematics and second in physics, was awarded a scholarship, and advised to work in the laboratory of a young physicist, Pierre Curie, who, with his brother, had already discovered the important effect by which a vibrating quartz crystal can produce an alternating electric current. Pierre Curie had also made fundamental discoveries in magnetism, and he set Marie Sklodowska to work on this subject. They fell in love, and were married in 1895. In the next year, Becquerel announced his discovery of the radioactivity of uranium. Marie Curie decided to work on the new phenomenon for her doctor's degree. Her first child, Irène, a future Nobel laureate in her own right, was born in 1897, after she had started on her radioactive researches.

Presently she noticed that pitchblende, the mineral from which uranium was obtained, was more radioactive than uranium itself, and deduced that it must contain another more radioactive substance. Pierre Curie now joined Marie in her search. The qualities of both were required in the analysis of the baffling phenomenon. Pierre invented appropriate apparatus, and Marie undertook the work of detection. Within a few weeks, she had discovered two such radioactive substances, polonium and radium; and her problem was now to separate a sensible quantity of radium. Four years of immense and tedious labour were needed to concentrate several tons of uranium residues, and to separate radium salts from them by thousands of crystallizations. This was carried out in an old shed in the Paris School of Physics, and Marie Curie finally obtained about one-tenth of a grain of pure radium chloride, sufficient to cover a threepenny bit. She determined the chemical and physical properties of radium, and proved that it was a new element. All of this she accomplished while rearing her infant daughter.

The Nobel Prize for physics in 1904 was awarded jointly to the Curies and Becquerel. It was in this year that her second daughter, Eve, who became her mother's biographer, was born. Then, in 1906, Pierre Curie was killed in a tragic accident. She was appointed his successor in the Sorbonne, the first woman to be given a post by the university; and in 1911 she was awarded the Nobel Prize for chemistry – the only person to receive more than one Nobel prize. The characteristics of her work were experimental skill, accuracy and caution, and an extraordinary determination. She established a tradition, which has been carried on brilliantly by her daughter Irène and her son-in-law, Frédéric Joliot-Curie.

D

'Don't be a nun in springtime'

DAFYDD AP GWILYM, (c. 1325 – c. 1380), poet of love among the birch leaves and the yellow broom of Wales.

Older by some years, no doubt, than Chaucer (q.v.),

who was born about 1340 and died in 1400, Dafydd came of an aristocratic family in South-west Wales, where Welsh and Anglo-Normans lived side by side. The love-poetry of the Continental troubadours, or wandering singers, must have affected him – with his own Welsh accent, he belongs to their tradition – and he may have been a wandering scholar himself. One can make only broad statements about his life: that it was carefree and sensual, that he liked most of all the freshness of girls, which he extended into the freshness and tenderness of nature, spring, May, etc.

In one poem Dafydd makes a girl at church call him the pale fellow with long hair, who looks affected and in love. In another poem he tells his girl that when he is dead – for love of her – the birch trees will conduct his funeral, himself in a shroud of clover in a coffin of leaves, on a bier of branches carried by a thousand white seagulls; that he will be buried in St Nightingale's church in the woods of song – where the cuckoo (which is the bird of cuckoldry and gallantry) will sing paternosters, hours and psalms for his soul. Or the stars help him to love, he thanks their pure light and calls them clover-flowers on the face of Heaven, and gilded frost, and marigolds of the air.

Gwyn Williams has made this literal translation of a poem by Dafydd:

> For God's sake, no more bread and water.
> Throw aside watercress.
> For Mary's sake, cease your thin prayers,
> The Roman monks' religion.
> Don't be a nun in springtime,
> Worse is the nunnery than the grove.
> Your faith, my pretty paragon,
> Sets its face against love.
> The ring's warrant, a mantle
> And a green garment ordain you better.
> Come to the spreading birch,
> The cuckoo's church in the woods;
> No one will mock at us there
> For winning heaven in a green grove.
> Keep in mind Ovid's book,
> And, please, not too much faith.
> (*An Introduction to Welsh Poetry*, 1953).

Dafydd ap Gwilym has been called the greatest poet of the Celtic races. He is certainly one of the most engaging of the medieval poets of Europe, which would be more recognized if Welsh were better known, or if translations of his poetry were not so few and mostly so feeble.

Self-taught scientist

DALTON, John, (1766–1844), English scientist who elaborated the atomic theory of chemistry. He was born in Kendal, son of a Quaker hand-loom weaver. With his brother Jonathan, he opened a village school when he was thirteen, their prospectus announcing that 'Youth will be carefully instructed in English, Latin, Greek, French; also Writing, Arithmetic, Merchants' Accompts, and the Mathematics'. The school was not a success, 'owing to the uncouth manners of the young masters'.

He moved to Manchester in 1793, and became associated with the Literary and Philosophical Society, though he earned his living throughout his life as a tutor of children. In 1826, when he was world-famous Pelletier, the French chemist, went to Manchester from Paris to see him, and was amazed to find him supervising a child's sums on a slate. 'Have I the honour to address Mr Dalton?' he asked. 'Yes,' said the son of the Quaker weaver. 'Wilt thou sit down whilst I put this lad right about his arithmetic?'

In his Cumberland days, Dalton had begun to study the weather systematically. This led him to 'speculate upon the nature and the constitution of the atmosphere'. It often struck him how a *compound* atmosphere', or a mixture of two or more gases, could behave like a uniform 'simple atmosphere'. He found the clue in Newton's proof that a gas consisting of atoms will obey Boyle's law, *i.e.* its volume will be halved if its pressure is doubled. Dalton gradually explained a large part of the chemical facts then known in terms of his conclusion that '*the ultimate particles of all homogeneous bodies are perfectly alike in weight, figure, etcetera*'. The 'ultimate particle' of a compound body, such as water, which consists of hydrogen and oxygen, consisted, Dalton said, of one atom of each of these elements. Dalton designated the 'ultimate particle' of water as HO (though later it was shown that there are in fact *two* atoms of hydrogen, and one of oxygen, in a molecule of water). He had made a very great advance, and he described his atomic theory in his treatise *A New System of Chemical Philosophy* (1808).

Dalton made other important contributions. He asserted in 1793 that the *aurorae* are electrical in nature, and he independently discovered that when the temperature of a gas is decreased by 1° C., its volume contracts by about 1 part in 273. Joule, who was once his pupil, showed that this implied that there is an absolute zero of temperature. Colour-blind, he also investigated the characteristics of his condition. It is said that when he was given an honorary doctorate at Oxford in 1832, he wore his scarlet doctor's gown in the street, unaware of its conspicuous appearance.

Dalton was one of the last entirely self-taught scientists to make a very great contribution. Like his weaver-father, he belongs to a period of home-industry which has since passed away.

Buccaneer – explorer

DAMPIER, William, (1652–1715), a writer of admirable ability, a second-rate explorer and a third-rate buccaneer, who made England keenly alive to the exploration and exploitation of the South Seas.

Buccaneering was not his primary concern; but it was the only way open to him of seeing strange quarters of the world. 'I came to these seas', he wrote, 'more to indulge my curiosity than to get wealth, though I must confess at that time I did think the trade lawful.' John Evelyn, after dining with Pepys and the man 'who had been a famous buccaneer', remarked that he seemed more modest 'than one would imagine by relation of the crew he had assorted with'; and Dampier made so little out of twelve and a half years of buccaneering and other adventures which took him round the world, that he had to sell his part share in a Malay who was exhibited as a curiosity.

That was after Dampier's return in 1691. Six years later he published *A New Voyage round the World*, which was popular enough to turn him into a literary lion. In 1699 the Admiralty made him commander of the first exploring expedition it had ever organized, but gave him a ship so rotten that on the return journey it 'founder'd thro' perfect Age'. Not unsurprisingly the expedition failed to reach its objective, the east coast of Australia, which no European had yet seen, though Tasman (q.v.) had sailed around it. Dampier discovered New Britain, but the most important outcome of the expedition was another book, his *Voyage to New Holland* (1703). He now sailed in command of two government privateers to harass Spanish shipping – an expedition which was a failure, but is remembered because his subordinate captain marooned Alexander Selkirk (q.v.) on the island of Juan Fernandez.

When he sailed again it was not as a leader – he had no talent for leadership – but as pilot in an expedition of 1708–1711 which picked up Alexander Selkirk and collected £200,000 worth of Spanish booty. Dampier's writing inspired an interest in the Pacific, which had been dormant since the time of Tasman, and stimulated the Admiralty into efforts to find the *terra australis incognita*, the unknown southern continent believed then to exist on the far side of the globe. His accounts of strange men and tropical seas, of beasts, birds and plants fascinated and excited his contemporaries. Thus the Lilliput and Brobdingnag of Swift's *Gulliver's Travels* are South Sea countries, somewhere in the neighbourhood of the still undiscovered and for ever legendary *terra australis*.

ILLUSTRATION: Page 85.

Poet of the Divine Comedy

DANTE ALIGHIERI, (1265–1321), the chief poet of the Italians and one of the major writers of mankind.

In the opening cantos of his most celebrated poem, the *Divine Comedy*, Dante describes how he finds himself lost in a dark wood. He is met by the poet Virgil, who guides him down through Hell, divided into circles according to the type of sin punished, until they reach the centre, where the treacherous are eaten eternally by Satan. From this cold innermost circle of Hell, Virgil leads Dante to the steps of Mount Purgatory, crowded with souls struggling upward to Paradise. In the last book, Virgil and Dante reach the outer spheres of heaven, where Virgil, being a pagan, can see no further and must turn back. Here Dante is met by his youth's love, Beatrice. She leads him upward until for a brief moment by her intercession he is able to look upon God.

The world obstinately continues to read the *Inferno*, if not all of the poem, despite the fact that Dante's theological, metaphysical and political preoccupations become more and more remote from the modern consciousness. He wrote to reprove, to instruct, to edify and to exalt; to show the consequences of error and sin, and the rewards of justice and righteousness. His hell, his purgatory and his heaven are vast edifices described in exact topographical, almost exact architectural, detail; and he populated all three with individuals known to him or to his audience, either personally or by repute. He constructed the poem in harmony with the theology of Aquinas and the philosophy of Aristotle, which gave him such confidence that he did not just castigate his contemporaries in a way which would be normal to a writer in any age: he assumed the divine prerogative of prescribing, item by item, how they would be punished, and how they would be rewarded in eternity. It is this divine insolence in awarding eternal punishment and bliss which measures the gap between our consciousness and his, between modern consciousness and the consciousness of the Middle Ages. It measures, too, the imaginative leap we have to make if we are to come into full contact with this most superb of medieval poets, and if we are to feel more than the brilliant verbal and visual qualities of his art.

Yet the scene is not Hell, Purgatory and Paradise as realities: it is the inside of Dante's own mind, he writes of his own experience, his own descent into Hell and redemption through Love. The poem is a brilliant and terrible statement of the responsibility of man for his own actions. It is full of subtle and moving details such as the fact that Beatrice becomes more beautiful as they move through the spheres and get nearer to God, because Dante's sight is becoming clearer and more filled with love. In the final Cantos Beatrice leads Dante forward in his mind to the very centre of the Universe, which is God – to that final point of meeting which to Dante meant salvation: 'Within its depths I saw ingathered, bound by love in one volume, the scattered leaves of all the Universe ...' (*Paradiso*, XXXIII. 85). Here the book ends, for, as Dante says, his power failed also, but already his 'desire and will moved, even as a wheel moves equally – by the Love that moves the Sun and other stars'.

In one respect Dante broke sharply with medievalism. In his day, not so much had been written in Italian, and to treat of subjects so great and portentous as heaven and hell in anything but Latin was a breach with tradition. For some while Dante hesitated. His decision to use the vernacular caused headshaking, but gained the world a masterpiece. His language is as direct, in fact, as the painting of his friend Giotto (q.v.). To modern Italian it is as close as the language of Chaucer, who was born about twenty years after Dante's death, is remote from modern English.

Dante, whose profile was made familiar to the world by Giotto (Page 119), took part in the political life of Florence, his native city, during the struggles of Guelfs with Ghibellines, Blacks with Whites, which were further complicated by the struggles between the city and the Papacy. He was exiled; and it is ironic that this great poet had almost to beg his way through life. He found protection principally at the Courts of Verona and Ravenna, learning how 'hard is the road going up and down another's stair' (*Paradiso* XVII, 58–60), and feeling for those who, like himself, 'languish in exile, and revisit their country only in their dreams' (*De Vulgari Eloquentia*).

He was also a political thinker, again in the medieval tradition, and wrote many fine poems apart from the *Divine Comedy*. Little is known about his true relations with Beatrice, whom he made his guide to paradise, and whom he celebrated in the *Vita Nuova*. She appears to have been Bice Portinari, a girl whom he first met in Florence when they were both children. She grew up, married somebody else and died young in 1290. Dante, in fact, like other poets, idealized a girl he had met only a few times. His wife does not occur in his writings at all.

ILLUSTRATION: Page 123.

'Tomorrow I shall sleep in glory'

DANTON, Georges Jacques, (1759–1794), French revolutionary, terrorist, patriot and saviour of his country. At the darkest hour of the Revolution, he proclaimed, 'We must dare and dare and dare again – and France will be saved.'

On the scaffold before the guillotine he turned to the executioner and proudly ordered, 'You must show my head to the people. It is worth showing.'

Towards the end of a bold life, Danton said that he 'risked being thought too violent so as never to be thought too weak'. As a young lawyer of poor origins, he had leapt into the Seine in Paris and swam shouting curses at the Bastille – symbol of *l'ancien régime*, which he was convinced had outlived any useful function. He was appointed an advocate and took an oath of allegiance to the Constitution. But on the outbreak of the Revolution, in 1789, he was the first to demand the deposition of the King, voting eventually for his execution. He joined the Jacobin extremists, incited the people to violence against the monarchy, suppressed the moderates, and agitated for war against the countries giving shelter to *émigrés*.

In 1793, as Minister of Justice, he was the power in the Committee of Public Safety. He rallied the nation to defend itself with the cry: 'Everything belongs to the country when the country is in danger.' Well-educated, a linguist, a sound administrator, he felt the need for moderation after the blood bath for which he had been responsible. His open declaration of this change was as bold as his most violent incitements: 'Better to be guillotined than to guillotine.'

Yet Danton was unable to restrain the Terror he had loosed; and he was to be the victim of his own ferocity. After a few months of intriguing and jockeying for power, during which Danton denounced 'false patriots in red bonnets' and openly challenged his detractors 'if they entertained the slightest suspicion to rise and say so', he was arrested on the orders of Robespierre (q.v.) in 1794. He was charged with conspiracy against the Republic and corruption. There may have been some substance in the latter accusation, for he had considerably increased his private fortune during the Revolution. He had no doubt about the outcome of his trial: 'I have lived entirely for my country. I am Danton till my death. Tomorrow I shall sleep in glory.' He concluded: 'One had better be a poor fisherman than meddle with the art of governing men.'

ILLUSTRATION: Page 119.

Theorist of evolution

DARWIN, Charles Robert, (1809–1882), English naturalist. By his concept of evolution, he was the last man, as Julian Huxley has put it, to shake the world with the 'magic force of a single idea'. No subsequent synthesis of thought – not even the theory of relativity – has so humbled man, so purged his self-consciousness, so tempered his purpose and so blessed his wisdom. From *The Origin of Species* (1859), which he wrote in a modest country home with children and the benign ruralities of a peaceful England around him, ignorances, obscurities and superstitions scuttled away like cockroaches from a light.

'It is interesting to contemplate a tangled bank', wrote Darwin in his most famous passage, 'clothed with many plants of many kinds, with birds singing on the bushes, with various insects flitting about, and with worms crawling through the damp earth, and to reflect that these elaborately constructed forms, so different from each other, and dependent upon each other in so complex a manner, have all been produced by laws acting around us.' As Darwin saw these laws,

they were: growth, reproduction, inheritance, variability, competition or struggle for life and natural selection. But it was his synthesis of them, his innocent generalization of the theory of evolution, that at last dissolved the medieval view of man's place in nature.

Since his boyhood, Darwin had 'wasted' his time on doing things which interested him, and those he was told not to do. He was the grandson of an able scientist and thinker, Erasmus Darwin, and of Josiah Wedgwood, the potter, a noble and liberal humanist. He was educated in an atmosphere of tolerance and virtue at Shrewsbury, under Dr Samuel Butler, and at Christ's College, Cambridge. At Cambridge he was supposed to read for the Church; but instead collected plants, insects and geological specimens, went shooting, talked to scientists, and grew passionately obsessed with the investigation of every aspect of the external world, an enthusiasm which led his scientific mentor Henslow and his uncle, another Josiah Wedgwood, to recommend him for the post of naturalist on the voyage of H.M.S. *Beagle*, planned for five years in the Atlantic and Pacific. Captain Fitz-Roy, master of the *Beagle*, at first disliked Darwin, mainly, so it is said, because of the shape of his nose, and was not easily persuaded to take him. Possibly Darwin's nose stood a while between the world and this theory of evolution; for it was on the voyage of the *Beagle*, upon which his opportunities were limited for months at a time to observation and contemplation, that his first ideas on evolutionary theory occurred to him.

The two most important stimuli were the fossils of eastern South America, and the animals of the Galapagos Islands; particularly their finches, now known as Darwin's finches, of which there are many forms, differing greatly from island to island. How these, and other animals such as the island tortoises, became different from each other started a slow but inexorable train of thought. Darwin opened his evolution notebook in 1837, on his return from the voyage of the *Beagle*. 'After five years' work I allowed myself to speculate on the subject', he wrote. Not until 1844 did he make a first sketch of his conclusions. Only in 1858, in a joint communication with Alfred Russel Wallace to the Linnean Society of London, did Darwin's theory reach its full synthesis; this famous communication was followed in 1859 by the publication of the *Origin of Species*.

It is not easy for us to imagine the storm of disapproval that broke on this book, or to revive, at this distance of time, the emotional resistance to the universality of evolution. Never have ideas been subjected to such vigorous and fanatical crticism. Yet the strength of the opposition to Darwinism was so great that its inevitable defeat became a spectacle the world could not overlook. The common ancestry of living matter is so widely accepted now that it has become a creed without an apologia. An edifice of scientific knowledge has been built on Darwinism great enough to test its foundations.

Darwin's occupations in his quiet, busy life admirably show how scientific triumphs depend on the blending of the general and the particular. On the adventurous voyage of the *Beagle* all was grain to his mill. Then came meticulous editing of the results. Then a fanatic concentration on one intricate and difficult animal group, the barnacles, on which he published monographs in 1851 and 1854. Then the great generalizations (*The Origin of Species*, 1859, *Variation of Plants and Animals under Domestication* 1867, *Descent of Man*, 1871). Among these again the *Fertilization of Orchids* in 1862, and towards the end of his life, the *Formation of Vegetable Mould through the Action of Worms*, in 1881. In other words, Darwin was always refreshing general thought by particular investigation; and the reward of particular investigation was the discovery of lessons of general value. Darwin's life was that of the ideal naturalist; he showed his love of nature in the dissection of its parts, and his worship of nature in the putting of them together again.

ILLUSTRATION: Page 86.

Artist of lawyers and Don Quixote

DAUMIER, Honoré, (1808–1879), the French painter and draughtsman, felt to a rare degree the pathos, absurdities, follies, pride, meannesses, weaknesses and eccentricities of mankind. Not to know anything of his lithographs and paintings would be to miss one of the revelations of modern art.

Daumier belonged to that bourgeoisie which stood in his experience for mankind, and so gave him his subjects, suspended often between the respectable and the seedy or between pretentiousness and disaster. His father was a glazier in Marseilles, and for a while the young Daumier was clerk to a process-server

(compare the lower middle-class childhood of Dickens (q.v.)), which plunged him deeper into the human mess. 'One must belong to one's time,' Daumier maintained: he belonged to the time newly interpreted and revealed above all in fiction – by Balzac in his *Human Comedy*, Dickens, Flaubert, etc. Life made a hard bargain with Daumier. He had to keep himself alive in Paris by caricature for comic papers, making in all some 4,000 lithographs. Still he maintained in them a superb standard of design, draughtsmanship and pungency. Lawyers are tearful or wolfish, politicians forget they are men, *les bons bourgeois* contemplate the stars, they come to the art exhibition and fall asleep, or in the exhibition the statue on her pedestal is bored even more than the bourgeois spectators. The players in the orchestra yawn as the pseudo-classical opera grinds on. Or in the garden the pumpkin receives the homage of the gardener and his wife, who are a couple of human pumpkins.

Sometimes Daumier may be savage and ruthless, but he could never forget his humanity for long, in his art or in attitude. Walking through poor streets with a friend of his own calling, he remarked that they had art to comfort them, but what had the poor? His sympathies are clearest of all in the bold, deep, solid, strong simplicity of his oil-paintings, so little regarded in his own day, in his favourite subject of Don Quixote and Sancho Panza, in broad, dark figures of mankind walking over a rockiness of life, as the light dies.

Daumier as well was ultimately victimized by poverty and neglect. The time came in his old age when he could not sell a water-colour for fifty francs, and when – last cruelty and indignity for an artist – he went blind. Offered a decoration at one moment, he refused it quietly and soberly. His friend Courbet (q.v.) exclaimed that dirty decorations ought to be refused with noise and display. 'No, no,' Daumier told him gently; 'No, I did what I thought right, and I'm satisfied. But the whole affair is nothing to do with the public.' Or one may realize his independence of character by the fact that when Corot offered him a house in his distress, he had to pretend he was doing so, not for Daumier's sake, but to annoy a landlord.

Daumier inherits from Rembrandt, Goya, and Rowlandson; and like the two greater of these, who felt all of the human tragedy, he retreated into his own isolation of life and mind. In his day, only a few accorded him his high rank.

ILLUSTRATION: Page 86.

Science and creation

DAVY, Sir Humphry, (1778–1829), physicist, the son of a Cornish wood-carver, who investigated the properties of nitrous oxide, 'laughing gas', which was the first anaesthetic, discovered sodium and potassium, and invented the miner's safety lamp.

Davy had all the conventional attributes of genius. He was a youthful prodigy, and had brilliant eyes and a lightning mind. Though he was of humble origin, his circumstances were not unfortunate. As a boy he learned French from French refugees, and was able to read Lavoisier's great treatise on chemistry. His mother took in James Watt's son as a lodger, so he was in contact with the most progressive scientific minds of the day. He was invited by Thomas Beddoes, the eccentric doctor whose son was the poet Beddoes, to direct his laboratory at Bristol, and there he discovered the anaesthetic properties of 'laughing gas' when he was twenty. He consorted with the poets Coleridge and Wordsworth, who lived in the neighbourhood and had just published *Lyrical Ballads*. The fame of 'laughing gas' brought him an invitation to the newly-founded Royal Institution in London. After a good start, the Institution had slumped. Davy, twenty-three years old when he arrived, delivered an introductory discourse of the utmost brilliance. The Napoleonic wars were preventing the aristocracy from spending their holidays on the Continent, and they flocked to the entertainment which Davy provided. The Institution became a centre of fashionable life, and the young director was launched into society under the wing of the Duchess of Gordon.

Though Davy was snobbish, he did not allow it to interfere with his researches. He worked from ten to four like a whirlwind, rushing from one experiment to another. As soon as he heard of Volta's invention of the electric battery, he exploited it with tremendous power, and succeeded in producing metallic sodium and potassium by electrical decomposition of the alkalis. 'When he saw the minute globules of potassium burst through the crust of potash and take fire as they entered the atmosphere, he could not contain his joy – he actually bounded about the room in ecstatic delight.' In 1812 he received an application from a boy named Faraday for a job. He replied: 'I am far from displeased with the proof you have given me of your confidence, which displays great zeal, power of memory and attention. ... It would gratify me to be of any service to you. I wish it may be in my power.'

This was a magnificent reply from the great man. It has often been said that the greatest of all Davy's discoveries was Faraday (q.v.). To the invitation to investigate coal-mine explosions, Davy replied: 'It will give me great satisfaction if my chemical knowledge can be of any use in an inquiry so interesting to humanity.' As all the world knows, he succeeded. Faraday was his assistant in the experiments.

Great though he was as a scientific discoverer, his conception of the place of science in human life was even more remarkable. In his introductory discourse, delivered in 1802, he said that science had bestowed on man 'powers which may be almost called creative; which have enabled him to modify and change the beings surrounding him, and by his experiments to interrogate nature with power, not simply as a scholar, passive and seeking only to understand her operations, but rather as a master, active with his own instruments'. An extraordinary statement from a twenty-three-year-old boy just arrived in London.

'Only my own pleasure'

DEBUSSY, Claude Achille, (1862–1918), French composer of the time of Aubrey Beardsley, Whistler and Oscar Wilde (q.v.), who was that most unsocial of artistic beings, the professional dreamer. For himself, he remarked, the most sympathetic poet was one who, 'by resorting to discreet suggestion rather than to full statement, will enable me to graft my dream on to his dream'. Debussy, in fact, associated more with Verlaine (q.v.) and Mallarmé and other symbolist poets than with musicians; his first wholly characteristic work was *L'Après-midi d'un faune* (1892), after Mallarmé's poem. Most revealing of all his friendships was one with the skilful, over-heated, earnestly 'decadent' author Pierre Louÿs, which precisely reflected the weaker side of Debussy's music. Debussy, however, had learnt from another friend, Erik Satie (q.v.), the virtues of repose and humility: all his days he had a horror (in music) of the grandiose and self-important – a horror that is instinctive in his Maeterlinck opera *Pélleas et Mélisande* (1892–1902).

To dreams, self-indulgence, the amoral and the sensuous Debussy added a pantheistic love of nature. He was guided, he claimed, rather absurdly, by 'the counsels of the wind that passes and tells us the story of the world'; all the same, nature within the dream was no more close to the real thing than nature in the late Pre-Raphaelite paintings and the Pre-Raphaelite poems (he had composed a setting to D. G. Rossetti's *Blessed Damozel*) which Debussy admired so much, and far from being guided either by nature or the counsels of the breeze, he obeyed nothing but his own sleek and feline self. One of his teachers asked him what rules he observed. 'None', said Debussy, 'only my own pleasure.' He liked to surround himself with oriental bric-à-brac and his company, like his music, was insidiously delightful.

The first World War changed him: he was no longer the Debussy who remarked that 'Liberty, Equality and Fraternity were words which at best are only fit for cab drivers'. Instead the silent, self-enclosed sybarite becomingly a flaming patriot, who proclaimed the greatness of the French tradition, the hatefulness of the enemy and the nobility of the *poilus*, and signed his war-time sonatas 'Claude Debussy musicien français'.

His later music is restrained and a triumph of weakness overcome at last by a carefully nurtured strength. Listening to it reminds one of the title of one of his earliest songs *Il pleure dans mon cœur*. If Debussy had had no heart, his imaginative dreams would not have come to life at all; as it is, the life of them is none too open and pleasant.

Crusoe's begetter

DEFOE, Daniel, (1660–1731), English novelist, journalist, and man of business, wrote his first and greatest novel when he was nearly sixty years of age. This was the *Life and Strange Surprising Adventures of Robinson Crusoe of York, Mariner*, published in 1719, a book that owes its enduring attraction to two chief characteristics, distinct but complementary. It is one of the finest examples of that fantasy, made real, which has for centuries stirred the imagination of men – and of children: the dream of living on a deserted island. And the story is presented with such an extraordinary air of verisimilitude that in reading it all sense of fictitiousness is lost. This is perhaps one of the most acceptable qualities that can be possessed by a work of fiction, as Defoe well understood, for in his Preface to *Crusoe* he adroitly wrote: 'The editor believes the thing to be a just history of fact; neither is there any appearance of fiction in it.'

'The Father of the English Novel' might not relish this title, bestowed on him by later critics, for in all the books that followed *Crusoe* he was at pains to give his narratives of adventure the semblance of authentic journals. So successful was he that it is hardly possible to detect a difference in reality, though there is in breadth of interest, between *The Life of Jack Sheppard* (1724), which is largely a genuine piece of crime-reporting, and his most celebrated 'novel' about thieves and prostitutes, *The Fortunes and Misfortunes of Moll Flanders* (1722). Many a reader, also, has been taken in by the seeming actuality of *A Journal of the Plague Year*, written nearly sixty years after an event that had occurred when Defoe was five. One of his secrets is a plain, straightforward style which, even when it is ungrammatical, has all the appearance of direct speech. Another is his gift for accumulating detail: he had a prudent housekeeper's and shopkeeper's eye for noting what people wore and ate, and especially for how much things cost. What remarkable vivacity he brought to this task may be seen from a single incident in the life of that much-married ruffian and hero in *Colonel Jack* (1722). Observing in an inn an eligible widow, at a time when he is momentarily single, the Colonel decides to tempt her out of her melancholy by treating her 'handsomely, but not extravagantly'. He provides 'what the house afforded, which was a couple of partridges and a very good dish of stewed oysters; they brought us up afterwards, a neat's tongue, and a ham, that was almost quite cut down, but we ate none of it, for the other was fully enough for us both, and the maid made her supper of the oysters we had left, which were enough'.

In his early years a hosier and general merchant – hence his characters' knowledgeableness in matters of trade – Defoe went bankrupt in 1692. His energetic career as a journalist then began; within the next forty years he composed some 250 pamphlets and books, besides for nine years publishing a thrice-weekly newspaper, *The Review*, almost entirely written by himself. If by no means scrupulous in his political attachments, at least he had the courage of his shifting convictions, for he was three times sentenced to stand in the stocks. 'Kitchen reading' the novels of his old age have been called, and except for *Crusoe* perhaps they are; but, after all, there is no reason why the kitchen should not sometimes get the best.

Artist in solitude

DEGAS, Hilaire Germain Edgar, (1834–1917). This Frenchman painted, but not to please: 'They call me', he remarked, 'the painter of dancers, but they do not understand that the dancer has always been for me an excuse for painting lovely materials and rendering movements.' He showed his dancers – and here is all of this painter's disdain, aloofness, and exquisite severity – 'stripped of their coquetry, in the state of animals cleansing themselves'.

Degas was born of a family of bankers, his mother a French creole from New Orleans. Money was not scarce for him. He could work as he pleased, and what pleased him was an ordered grace, a delicious capturing of limbs, body, neck, head and dress, whether of dancer or washer-woman, exactly in the split second of the most thrilling poise and rhythm. Nothing must interrupt: a painter's business was only to paint. A carriage and pair? Not for him. What, Degas asked, did a painter need with a carriage and pair (the outward sign of the success, compromise, vulgarity and indeed imbecility of the bulky academic figures who were contemporaries of Degas in London)? He would make his models take a bath, he would stop them at the right gesture. All he needed for the time being was there, in front of him: 'One must treat the same subject ten times, even a hundred times. Nothing in art should seem accidental, not even movement.' So the women of Degas dance and poise and towel and sponge themselves, lean to their clothes, and make lines of delight as they raise their arms and bend them v-shaped to brush or comb out their hair. A logic of movement and grace demands and receives the embracing tender logic of colour. All coquetry discarded, a human eternity remains.

Two sayings by Degas: 'It is all very well to copy what you see, but it is much better to draw what you will continue to see in your memory.' 'Even in front of nature, one has to compose.' No out-of-door artist (like an aloof cat, he disliked getting wet), but an indoor man, Degas entirely recognized the artificiality of art. If he used models, he assiduously studied and copied existing art. So the story of the lady who called on him for advice about her son:

'My son paints, and is so sincere before nature.'

'How old is your son?'

'Fifteen, Monsieur.'

'So young,' Degas exclaimed, 'and already sincere before nature. Alas, Madame, your son is lost.'

No one is ready for nature, Degas held, till he has copied and re-copied the masters.

His loneliness, his aristocracy of spirit, his dread of losing a sight already impaired by his military duties in the Franco-Prussian War, brought out his peculiarities, which could be undesirable. His tongue was a razor blade. He was violently against the Jews, and his housekeeper had to read him all the anti-semitic journalism in the affair of Dreyfus, the Jewish staff officer tried and convicted of treason. He once dismissed a favourite model on the ground that she was a Protestant and all Protestants supported Dreyfus. If this was one of Degas's less amiable traits, one must respect his loneliness, austerity, and pursuit of perfection: 'It seems to me that today if the artist wishes to be serious, to cut out a little original niche for himself, or at least preserve his own innocence of personality, he must once more sink himself in solitude. There is too much talk and gossip.'

When he was eighty-three he at last freed himself from the world's common lack of grace by committing suicide.

I think, hence I am

DESCARTES, René, (1596–1650), French philosopher, generally regarded as the 'father of modern philosophy', because the impact of the new discoveries in physics and astronomy led him to question some of the traditional medieval teaching, and to attempt the construction of an entirely new philosophical system.

Descartes' life shows the dilemma which faced an enquiring mind of his age – an age in which the astronomical writings of Galileo (q.v.) were burned by the Church for their heresies. To his contemporaries he was primarily a mathematician and a physicist. His philosophy was written to show that his system of physics was the right one and that other (earlier) systems were sinful. Descartes had been brought up in a Jesuit college and always courted ecclesiastics, so it seems that piety rather than timidity moved him to justify his physical theories.

In his book *A Discourse on Method* (1637) he describes his dissatisfaction with the uncertainties in all the sciences taught by the Jesuits, mathematics excepted. 'For these reasons, as soon as my age permitted me to pass from under the control of my instructors, I entirely abandoned the study of letters, and resolved no longer to seek any other science than the knowledge of myself, or of the great book of the world.' He served in various armies, travelled widely, and eventually settled among the tolerant Dutchmen.

The problem that worried Descartes was: Is the 'real world' like our ideas? After meditating all day inside a stove, he tells us, he evolved the philosophical method known as 'Cartesian doubt'. Certainly our senses cannot tell us about the 'real world': we cannot tell that we are not dreaming at the moment, or not subject to hallucinations and optical illusions. Moreover, though we cannot conceive of two and two being anything other than four, a malignant demon might be deceiving us: there might be nothing in the 'real world' to correspond. 'But ... I observed that, whilst I thus wished to think that all was false, it was absolutely necessary that I, who thus thought, should be somewhat; and ... I observed that this truth, *I think, hence I am* (Latin: *Cogito ergo sum*), was so certain ... that no ground of doubt, however extravagant, could be alleged by the sceptics capable of shaking it.' A medieval argument then 'proves' the existence of God, and as God is no deceiver, the principle is established that 'what is very clearly and distinctly conceived is true'. Moreover, the malignant demon is banished. Thus Descartes, after all, satisfies himself that his mathematics – and his physics, which are pure geometry – are like the real world.

ILLUSTRATION: Page 119.

'Galloping through a wild country'

DICKENS, Charles, (1812–1870), English novelist, whose works have been accepted by the whole of mankind.

'I seem to be sending some part of myself into the Shadowy World,' he wrote two days before he completed *David Copperfield*; and no novelist put more of himself into his novels. From childhood life gave Dickens inexhaustible assets – poverty, disgrace and dismay, to begin with. His father was a Clerk in the Navy Pay Office, who lost his position and was imprisoned for debt in London, in the Marshalsea Prison. The boy had to work in a blacking-factory on the Thames. Everything he saw in his father's prison was etched in him for use in the *Pickwick Papers* and

David Copperfield. Everything he experienced in the blacking-factory was stored up, large or small. His father was turned into Mr Micawber. His companion among the rats and rottenness of the blacking-works was Bob Fagin, and the name went into *Oliver Twist*.

All Dickens' life was an upward anguish. His sister was kept at the Royal Academy of Music: Dickens went to see her given a prize, and he could not bear to think of himself 'beyond the reach of all such honourable emulation and success'. So it went on till he died, leaving more than £90,000. Yet with this anguish he combined all the facility of the quick-change actor. In a farce he once played lawyer, waiter, pedestrian, hypochondriac, old woman and deaf sexton. Indeed, he applied at one time for an audition at Covent Garden. A cold kept him away, or he might have become the Great Victorian Actor. He became instead a shorthand reporter, the quickest and most efficient in the House of Commons; and he careered about the country, in the last days of the coaching inn, covering elections, 'writing on the palm of my hand', he remembered, 'by the light of a dark lantern, in a postchaise and four, galloping through a wild country, and through the dead of night.'

After the success of *Sketches by Boz* and then *The Pickwick Papers*, Dickens became as much a national possession as the National Debt. On the surface, his life ran straight and smoothly towards the £90,000. But on *Boz* and *Pickwick* he married a wife, distinguished by 'a sort of bashful sensuality', who could neither help him nor share his thoughts. Carlyle described Dickens at this time as a small man, with 'clear, blue, intelligent eyes that he arches amazingly, large, protrusive, rather loose mouth, a face of extreme mobility which he shuffles about – eyebrows, eyes, mouth and all – in a very singular manner while speaking'. He and his wife had a quantity of children, but the marriage finally collapsed, and he was bedevilled by a liaison, cumbrously unplatonic, with a young actress, Ellen Ternan.

In the magical series of Dickens' novels, the world was given an immortal gallery of minor characters that includes the Artful Dodger, Dick Swiveller, Sarah Gamp, Mr Guppy, the Cheeryble Brothers and Sam Weller. But Dickens' young female characters have a doll-like insipidity, which derives from the unsatisfactory nature of his marriage and his relations with women. His inspiration was always private, inward, personal. Women he did not know; London, as an image of mankind, he did know. He tramped its streets, groped among its sea-coal fogs, felt the sinister damp along its river, breathed the stale air of its law-courts, and was never at fault.

The publication of his novels became an annual rite for the world. When a ship reached New York with a vital number of *The Old Curiosity Shop*, waiting crowds shouted from the quay 'Is Little Nell dead?' His passion for the under-dog and his loathing for conventional society made Macaulay stigmatize *Hard Times* as 'sullen socialism'. However, Dickens was a man of feeling, not ideology. He was never a socialist, but he stood, as one critic has remarked, for 'the native decency of the common man'.

The actor lost to Covent Garden was never suppressed. Throughout his life he ran amateur theatricals. Just before his death he said his daydream was 'a great theatre, in the direction of which I should hold supreme authority'. The obsession killed him. The public readings from his works which he gave in his latter years overstrained his nerves and his physique. He died from a seizure just after writing a letter in which he quoted from Shakespeare 'these violent delights have violent ends.'

Henry James had noted prophetically that the 'force of the Dickens imprint, however applied in the soft clay of our generation' would resist 'serenely the wash of the waves of time.'

ILLUSTRATION: Page 126.

Arguments with God

DICKINSON, Emily, (1830–1886), American poet, who spent her life in Amherst, Massachusetts, looking after her prosperous lawyer-father, regretting a mysterious love-affair, pottering amongst her greenhouse flowers, arguing coyly, brightly, often profoundly with her personal God. This eccentric routine produced 800 poems, startling brevities scribbled on the backs of envelopes, as though a bird had been endlessly engaged in sending telegrams to eternity. Her privacy is to be respected:

> The soul selects her own society,
> Then shuts the door;
> On her divine majority
> Obtrude no more.
>
> Unmoved, she notes the chariot's pausing
> At her low gate;
> Unmoved, an emperor is kneeling
> Upon her mat.

I've known her from an ample nation
Choose one;
Then close the valves of her attention
Like stone.

Emily Dickinson's poems are bound to be uneven, since she was carelessly prolix and never really knew the discipline of publication. At their best, they imply a buried modernity, like that of Gerard Manley Hopkins (q.v.). Often she saw things precisely and tensely and was compact in her thoughts, off-rhymes and unexpected images adding perspective to the quick stanzas. Thus a startled bird

> ... unrolled his feathers
> And rowed him softer home

or a snake, a 'narrow fellow in the grass', 'wrinkled, and was gone'. From immediacies of this kind, granted by her lonely walks, she was not always successful in rising to the comprehensive vision she desired. Sometimes a coy egoism gets in the way, and she is a 'debauchee of dew' or a 'little tippler', who leans against the sun. But it is a mistake to expect consistency of excellence from a poet, and the lapses of Emily Dickinson are fewer than the eccentricity and isolation of her life might have caused.

After the romantic incident in Philadelphia when she was twenty-four, she wore white and glimmered about the house, rarely entering rooms when guests were present, but occasionally pressing a lily into the hands of a visiting clergyman. But then, surmising that the horses' heads 'were towards eternity' or reflecting on the 'heavenly hurt' of loss and difference felt in the mind, she recovers from coyness, and reestablishes herself as amongst the five or so really good women poets who have written in English – perhaps also as a typical American artist in her deviation from the main stream of American optimism.

Light in darkness

DIDEROT, Denis, (1713–1784), one of the great transformers, philosopher, encyclopaedist, writer, the most indefatigable, most prominent and perhaps most effective of that band of liberators of thought, including Voltaire, d'Alembert, Rousseau, Grimm and d'Holbach, who battled against the obscurantism of French eighteenth-century ecclesiasticism, and helped to bring about the French Revolution. Diderot was the father of the great *Encyclopédie*. He had been approached in the first place, as a literary hack, to translate Chambers's *Encyclopaedia*, which he promptly transformed into a compendium of all recent speculative and practical knowledge. Fighting against tremendous obstacles, largely deserted towards the end by his friends, who grew tired of the incessant battle against authority, working furiously, he brought the *Encyclopédie* to almost triumphant conclusion – almost, for at the end the printer, fearing retribution, expunged from the manuscript many enormously valuable passages which he thought too risky; these were lost irretrievably. The *Encyclopédie* was officially banned in 1759.

In the advanced salons of his day Diderot was always to be found, talking and talking, although he was the countryman, rough, gruff, puckish, irreverent, who never acquired the airs and graces of fashionable Paris. He had refused the 'respectable' avocations offered by his father, preferring the dubious career of a writer; and brought up by the Jesuits, he spent his life fighting bitterly against Catholicism. As he talked, fascinating, daring ideas incessantly bubbled up in him, with an energy which made him the most stimulating, even intoxicating, conversationalist of his day. The smallest thing would get him off on a mental adventure astonishing by its originality. Intellectually he had no fear, so much so that many of his writings could not be published in his lifetime, notably the brilliantly ruthless *Neveu de Rameau*, which did not appear till 1823. Early in his career his *Lettre sur les aveugles* (1749), in which he made his first entry into philosophy, earned him three months in the prison of Vincennes; he had foreshadowed survival through adaptation, a commonplace with us now, which was then too much for the delicate consciences of authority. Diderot was amazingly in advance of his time. In his immensely entertaining, and to the prudish, shocking, *Rêve de d'Alembert* he is astonishingly in line with to-day's thought on being and the constitution of matter. In his motives and his feelings he was always completely honest; he was rationalist, materialist even; banishing God as an active agent in living, and urging that the better instincts of man should be cultivated to gentleness and benevolence.

Diderot also wrote a psychologically astute work on acting and the drama, *Paradoxe sur le Comédien*, in which he argued for domestic tragedy, and so influenced the whole development of the drama in the nineteenth century. In the *Salons*, too, he began the modern criticism of art. All his lively writings brought him little money, and when the time came for him to provide for his daughter, he was forced to offer his library for sale. Here the Empress Catherine of Russia stepped in; she bought his books, but left him in possession of them as her salaried librarian. In 1773 he went to St Petersburg to thank her, and spent many argumentative afternoons with that vivacious, philosophic eccentric.

Startling as his doctrine appeared to his contemporaries, outrageously frank in his speech, temperamentally Diderot was a *bon bourgeois*. He was unhappily married and left his wife, yet he spent his days in perfect fidelity to Sophie Voland, who was intelligent enough to appreciate his sallies and follow his acrobatic thought. He was devoted to his ideas, to his work of enlightenment, but he never took himself too seriously, bursting into roars of laughter when he heard that an Amsterdam publisher was going to issue an edition of his collected works. He was the peasant always, tough, unrepentantly realistic, with the spiritual vitality required by those who form or transform the temper of an age.

ILLUSTRATION: Page 120.

Dizzy

DISRAELI, Benjamin, first Earl of Beaconsfield (1804–1881), twice Prime Minister of Britain, Tory democrat and Tory imperialist, was a Jew of Spanish extraction who created the modern British Conservative Party. He was also a prolific author, briskly eyeing his world and writing novels which picture his own ambitions. In everything he followed his maxim 'life is too short to be small'.

In the eighteen-thirties he was notorious for his fantastic clothes, his ringleted locks and his romantic novels. When asked by the Prime Minister of the day what he wished to be, he replied unhesitatingly that he wished to be Prime Minister. He made four unsuccessful attempts to enter Parliament, moving from radicalism to the right, before he was elected as 'both Tory and democrat' in 1837. His maiden speech ended in uproar with Disraeli shouting, 'The day will come when you will hear me'; and in the middle eighteen-forties he made his Parliamentary name by violent attacks on Sir Robert Peel, his Party Chief and the

Prime Minister, because he rejected the traditional Tory policy of protection in favour of the repeal of the Corn Laws.

'The right hon. gentleman', he said in a famous speech, 'caught the Whigs bathing, and walked away with their clothes. He has left them in the full enjoyment of their liberal position, and he is himself a strict conservative of their garments.'

After the death of Peel, Disraeli was accepted as Conservative leader in the Commons, although he offered to give way to Gladstone, who was still a Tory. However, Gladstone (q.v.) moved across to the Liberal benches, and in the brief Conservative administration of 1852, Disraeli was Chancellor of the Exchequer. From this year began the famous titanic rivalry between Disraeli and Gladstone, whom Disraeli once described as: 'that unprincipled maniac ... with one commanding characteristic – whether Prime Minister, or Leader of the Opposition, whether preaching, praying or speechifying – never a gentleman.' However, in his old age he said the trouble was he had 'never been able to understand him'.

Disraeli was Prime Minister for the first time for a few months in 1867, but his famous term came in 1874 and lasted for six years. In 1876 he took a peerage as Earl of Beaconsfield. The outcast had arrived. 'I am dead,' he said after his first sitting in the Lords, 'but in the Elysian Fields.' In his six years as premier, Disraeli showed himself a sturdy imperialist, adding new specks of imperial red to the world atlas. On his own responsibility he bought shares for the country in the Suez Canal Company, with money borrowed from Rothschild; and the greatest of his personal triumphs was to have Queen Victoria proclaimed Empress of India in 1876. His relations with the Queen were a mixture of affection and unbearable flattery (though not unbearable to her): she was 'a sovereign whose large and peculiarly experienced intelligence he acknowledges and appreciates, and whose judgement on many occasions would have more influence with him than that of all his colleagues'. The Queen used to send him gifts of primroses, which she believed to be 'his favourite flower'.

In his long premiership Disraeli had to deal with the trouble caused by Turkish atrocities in the Balkans. Disraeli, who supported Turkey against Russia dismissed them at first as 'coffee-house babble', but Gladstone roused the country with his speeches. A menacing international situation was averted by Disraeli's diplomacy at the Congress of Berlin, from which he returned 'bringing Peace with Honour'. His government fell in 1880 and he died the following year.

Disraeli is rightly held in great honour by modern Conservatives, but in fact his own policy was an individual one: it was an individual romanticism based on the belief that the nation should be a combination of Crown, Church, Empire and the welfare of the people. 'The question now placed before society is this,' he once informed Oxford University: 'is man an ape or an angel? I am on the side of the angels.' His novel *Sybil* had the sub-title 'The Two Nations', the rich and poor, whom he was convinced must work together for the common good.

ILLUSTRATION: Page 126.

The first modern sculptor

DONATELLO – properly Donato di Niccolò di Betto Bardi (c. 1386–1466), Florentine sculptor.

More than most, Donatello shared in that wonderful sense of the discovery of man's life and being which ended the Middle Ages and began the modern world. His father was a Florentine woolcomber; he had training as a goldsmith and was a friend of Brunelleschi (q.v.), one the supreme sculptor, the other the supreme architect of the earlier Italian Renaissance. It is hard to live oneself back into the new wonder and new self-confidence of Donatello's age, when the past was uncovered to launch the future, when the surrounding world was newly grasped, and when a Brunelleschi asked himself how a dome was placed on a building, or a Donatello asked how the problems of a bronze equestrian statue were solved, and both of them triumphantly found the answers.

In the first years of the fifteenth century Brunelleschi and Donatello were in Rome, the 'treasure-seekers' among the ruins, Donatello learning Roman nobility and *gravitas*, from classical sculpture. In 1416 he carved the *St George* for the outside of the church of Or San Michele in Florence, conceiving him as a young man, erect, his hands resting on his shield, his eyes calm, his gaze intense – the carving of a man and a saint rather than a Gothic expression of the idea of a saint. Donatello's individualism and imaginative insight – these are his 'modernism' which puts him at the head of the long succession of sculptors down to a Henry Moore or an Archipenko. These qualities mark figure after figure – the statue of a bald-headed man known as *Lo Zuccone*, with its strong, melancholy countenance, the *David* (1430), the first figure of the Renaissance and the modern world carved entirely in the round, divorced from an architectural setting, or the young *St John the Baptist* (1453), an emaciated figure which burns with prophetic power.

The colossal equestian statue of the professional soldier Gattamelata, which he finished for Padua in 1453, again was the first statue of its kind made since the fall of the ancient world.

Donatello lived austerely, never married and had no care for money. All his money, so the story is told, he hung from the ceiling in a basket, which his friends and workmen could help themselves from at need. When he grew too old for work, his patron Cosimo de' Medici, the ruler of Florence, supported him. Cosimo, on his death-bed, asked his son Piero to settle a property on Donatello, but the old man soon found that property-owning was too much for him, declaring that he would rather starve than have to worry about what was happening on his estate. Piero thereupon took back the property and gave Donatello a pension in its place. The best of Donatello's work is assembled in the Bargello in Florence.

'Death, thou shalt die'

DONNE, John, (1573–1631), poet and divine, who taught English poetry to think and argue and so to deepen its passion.

Donne was a young man of brilliant attainments. He was reared as a Catholic and he made a love match with the niece of his employer – two things which prevented his success at Court. All his bitterness, all his energy, all his passion, all his perplexity at *fin de siècle* uncertainties, Donne superbly hammered into his chosen subject of the contradictions of love. He confessed to an 'hydroptique immoderate desire of humane learning'. This, combined with his dialectical intelligence and his deep feelings, led to a type of so-called 'metaphysical' verse argued over for centuries, accepted, rejected and, in our time, enthusiastically accepted again.

To begin with, Donne was epigrammatic in prose (Why Doth the Pox So Much Affect to Undermine the Nose?), bitter in his adolescent satire –

> Ranke sweaty froth thy mistress's brow defiles,
> Like spermatique issue of ripe menstruous boils

– witty and unconventional in such a poem as *The Flea*, in which he argues for the seduction of a girl since both poet and girl have been bitten by the same insect, yet also profound and moving in poems of love and fidelity. The last verses of *A Valediction: Forbidding Mourning*, written to his wife on his departure abroad, brilliantly illustrate the unity-in-division of their two souls by comparing them to dividers:

> Our two souls therefore, which are one,
>   Though I must go, endure not yet
> A breach, but an expansion
>   Like gold to airy thinness beat.

> If they be two, they are two so
>   As stiff twin compasses are two:
> Thy soul the fixt foot, makes no show
>   To move, but doth, if th'other do.

> And though it in the centre sit,
>   Yet when the other far doth roam,
> It leans, and hearkens after it,
>   And grows erect, as that comes home.

> Such wilt thou's be to me, who must,
>   Like th'other foot, obliquely run;
> Thy firmness draws my circle just,
>   And makes me end where I begun.

In 1615 Donne took Holy Orders in the Anglican Church, becoming a Royal Chaplain and, in 1621, Dean of St Paul's. Renowned alike for his piety and for the eloquence of his sermons, this 'angel speaking out of a cloud' still knew the philosophical *angst* of the new era – 'And new Philosophy calls all in doubt' – but rooted himself firmly and medievally in the Christian faith as in the superb sonnet which begins by ordering death not to be proud, and ends –

> One short sleep past, we wake eternally,
> And death shall be no more; death, thou shalt die.

– a sonnet set in our own day to magnificent, solemn music by Benjamin Britten. During his last troubled illness Donne dressed himself in his winding sheet in the Deanery of St Paul's in London and posed for his monument to Nicholas Stone, the sculptor. This statue survived the fire of London, and stands anguished, fantastic and medievally modern in the crypt of the cathedral.

ILLUSTRATION: Page 121.

Is there a God?

DOSTOYEVSKY, Fyodor Mikhailovich, (1821–1881), major Russian novelist. Discussing the first draft of his last and most famous book, *The Brothers Karamazov*, he wrote to a friend that 'the main question I shall deal with in all parts of my latest novel will be the same; it is one which, consciously or unconsciously, has tormented me all my life – the existence of God'.

That expresses Dostoyevsky well. His father was a retired doctor and managed to get him an entry into the Army Engineering College in Petersburg, but he loathed army life and resigned in 1844. He made up his mind to give himself to writing, and Belinsky (q.v.) at once singled out in his first novel those characteristics of his art which were later to make him one of the giants of world literature – first, the amazing truthfulness of his descriptions of life: secondly, his masterly delineation of character and the social environment of his heroes; thirdly, his profound understanding and wonderful expression of life's tragedy. Belinsky, too, put his finger from the first on the weakest element in his genius: his diffuseness, his tendency to tire the reader by unnecessary repetitions and digressions. Dostoyevsky's vanity, which was boundless, ended his association with Belinsky and Belinsky's friends, who jeered at his wish to be considered, at that early stage of his career, as the greatest literary genius of the age. Instead, he joined a small group of Russian utopian socialists led by Petrashevsky, a disciple of Fourier. It was at one of the meetings of this group that he read Belinsky's forbidden letter to Gogol (q.v.) which formed the chief accusation against him after his arrest with the other members of the group on 23 April 1849. He was sentenced to death, taken to the place of execution and there reprieved and sent to Siberia. It was thus that his first 'unconscious search for God' ended in tragedy.

On his return from Siberia ten years later he started writing once more, and he tried journalism. He failed, and this was followed by a time of aimless wandering abroad to escape from his creditors. His passion for gambling aggravated his straits, and he fell back on obtaining advance payments from Russian periodicals for the serialization of his novels. It was while he was abroad in this way that he wrote three of his masterpieces – *Crime and Punishment* (1866), *The Idiot* (1868) and *The Devils* (1871), in all of which the problem of God's existence is the main pivot of the action. In *The Devils*, indeed, this writer, who had by then turned his back on his liberal past and embraced a philosophy of life based on autocracy and the Church, poses the question directly: Shatov's tragedy is also his own tragedy: both believed in Christ, both were tormented by their disbelief in God.

It was in an earlier work, *The Memoirs from a Dark Cellar* (1864), that Dostoyevsky first met the challenge of the scientific determinism of his day. No one saw more clearly the limitations of the scientific approach to ethical problems. He understood the lure of material prosperity which science was beginning to present to mankind, and the unlimited resources open to exploitation. He saw in this the sign of an advent of a new epoch, which threatened by a new temptation to undermine all the cultural values of European life, and which he expounded so explicitly in the story of the Grand Inquisitor in his last novel, *The Brothers Karamazov*. But even in this greatest of his novels no satisfactory answer is given to the question that tormented him all his life – which is perhaps why he never finished it.

Drake on the Spanish Main

DRAKE, Sir Francis, (c. 1540–1596), English admiral and Queen Elizabeth's principal weapon in the cold and subsequently the hot war against Philip of Spain.

Earlier generations of English adventurers and explorers had searched for a quick route to Cathay, but royal policy had confined them to looking for a north-west or north-east passage, thus prudently avoiding clashes with the Portuguese and Spaniards, who had a long and profitable start. In Elizabeth's time all this changed. English adventurers made money by transporting African slaves – the demand was insatiable – to the colonies on the Spanish Main, and the young Drake took part in this traffic. When Anglo-Spanish tension was intensified by religious antagonism, the Spanish Main offered opportunities for striking at the Spanish power, beside unlimited opportunities for enrichment. Drake, an inspired leader of combined operations who had no objection to being repudiated for diplomatic reasons when necessary, was an admirable instrument for fulfilling both aims ('the gentleman careth not', said Queen Elizabeth, 'if I disavow him').

The Spanish empire depended on the treasure which the Spaniards found in Peru, shipped along the Pacific to the Panama isthmus, transported by mule-train to the Atlantic coast, and then shipped home. By striking at this traffic, both by land and sea, Drake cut at the roots of Spanish power; and by doing so at a time when England and Spain were nominally at peace, he exposed himself to a charge of piracy and the death penalty.

Drake's voyages were not backed by the Treasury, but by private investors, one of whom was the Queen. They were often exceedingly profitable; his voyage of circumnavigation (1577–1580) in the *Golden Hind* is said to have yielded a profit of 1,400 per cent. The voyage so impressed the English that Drake's ship, beached near Greenwich, was a great attraction to the public (until it fell to bits). The Queen never allowed Drake sufficient resources to seize Panama. This was Drake's dream; if Panama could have been taken and held, Spain would have been crippled, and the Armada could not have sailed. His famous raid on Cadiz, when he 'singed the King of Spain's beard', was a spoiling attack, designed to hamper the preparations for the Armada; and when the Armada finally sailed the presence of the formidable *el Draque* among the English commanders had a demoralizing and devitalizing effect on the Spaniards equivalent in value to many warships.

His exploits on the Spanish Main, his circumnavigation of the world, his raid on Cadiz, gave confidence to a young country on the periphery of the civilized world, which was still feeling for its strength. They demonstrated that the Spanish giant was not invulnerable and that English navigators and seamen were the equals of their south European predecessors. Drake's last voyage to the Indies was a failure. The Spaniards had learned their lesson and strengthened their defences, there was little he could do, and he died in his ship, his dream of capturing Panama as distant as ever.

ILLUSTRATION: Page 84.

Naked English

DRYDEN, John, (1631–1700), English poet, also playwright and critic, of majestic energy. No writer has made English a more naked, athletic, pliant, effective means of communication.

His cousin, Honor Dryden, sent him when he was young a gift of sealing-wax, paper and an inkhorn. Dryden replied that they were imperfect emblems of her beauty – 'the white and red of wax and paper are but shadows of that vermilion and snow in your lips and forehead. And the silver of the inkhorn, if it presumes to vie in whiteness with your purer skin, must confess itself blacker than the liquor it contains' – conventional compliments, but a brilliantly sharp foretaste of how Dryden was to live among words. Alexander Pope, the other great English poet of the era, recorded that Dryden was intimate 'with none but poetical men'. The details of his life are unimportant, but the finest of his poems, especially *MacFlecknoe*, *Absalom and Achitophel*, and the fierce translation of Juvenal's Sixth Satire, stand hugely in English literature like the stone pillars of a classical building.

Having a mind which was passionate, balanced and sceptical (Dryden was a member of the Royal Society), he attacked in his satire the sluggish, the dull, the conceited and self-satisfied, the awkward lumps of men who spoilt order, balance and civilization.

Of the quotations which follow, the second ridicules hack writers for the stage, in the third, out of *Absalom and Achitophel*, Dryden transfixed the poet Thomas Shadwell. These are two of his most famous lines. The fourth is from the translation of Juvenal's Sixth Satire. Nos. 5, 6 and 7 indicate the more splendid or the graver elements in his poetry:

1. Fools change in England, and new fools arise,
   For tho' th'immortal species never dies
   Yet ev'ry year new maggots make new flies.

2. Still they write on, and like great authors show;
   But 'tis as rollers in wet gardens grow
   Heavy with dirt, and gath'ring as they go.

3. The Midwife laid her hand on his Thick Skull
   With this Prophetic blessing – *Be thou dull.*

4. Adult'rers next invade the nuptial state
   And marriage-beds creak'd with a foreign weight.

5. In Eastern quarries ripening precious dew.

6. And now time's whiter series is begun.

7. All, all of a piece throughout:
   Thy chace had a beast in view;
   Thy wars brought nothing about,

Continued on p. 135

PLATE 5

EDWARD GIBBON (1737–1794) by H. Walton.

PLATE 6
EL GRECO (*c.* 1541–1614). Presumed self-portrait *c.* 1609.

DANTON (1759–1794) by C. Charpentier.

DESCARTES (1596–1650) from a copy of the portrait by Frans Hals.

DIDEROT (1713–1784) by J. L. Pigalle, 1777.

JOHN DONNE (1573–1631).
Effigy in his winding sheet by Nicholas Stone.

121

ST FRANCIS OF ASSISI (1182–1226) preaching to the birds, by Giotto.

DANTE ALIGHIERI (1265–1321). Detail from Giotto's *Paradise*.

DÜRER (1471–1528) self-portrait.

124

ERASMUS (1466–1536) by Hans Holbein the Younger.

DISRAELI (1804–1881).

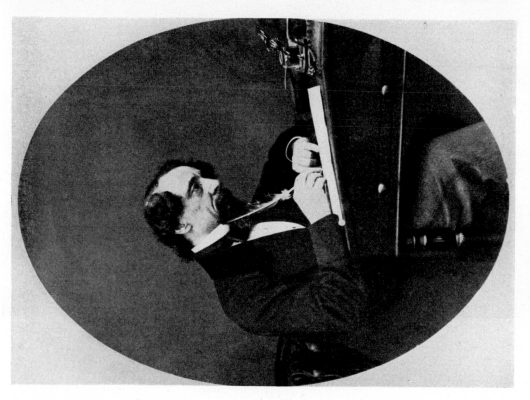

CHARLES DICKENS (1812–1870). Photograph taken in 1859.

EDISON (1847–1931) at thirty-one, with an early model of his phonograph.

MICHAEL FARADAY (1791–1867) with a bar of the heavy glass used in his researches into magnetism.

127

ELIZABETH I (1533–1603). The crowned ermine symbolizes royal virginity. Painter unknown.

GALILEO (1564–1642) by Justus Suttermans.

129

FLAUBERT (1821–1880).

ELIZABETH FRY (1780–1845) before her marriage (she was born Elizabeth Gurney).
Drawing by Amelia Opie.

131

T. S. ELIOT (b. 1888).

132

ANDRÉ GIDE (1869–1951) taken in 1947.

FREUD (1856–1939).

EINSTEIN (b. 1879).

PLATE 7

BABAR (1483–1530) superintending in the Garden of Fidelity 1508. Illustration to
Memoirs of Babar. Inscribed; drawing and colour by Bishan Das, faces by Nanha.
Mughal (Akbar) *c.* 1590.

PLATE 8

OSCAR KOKOSHKA (b.1886). Self-portrait.

Thy lovers were all untrue.
'Tis well an old age is out
And time to begin a new.

In a famous essay (1914) in which he reintroduced Dryden to favour, the poet T. S. Eliot has called him 'one of those who have set standards for English verse which it is desperate to ignore'. An appetite for Dryden he maintained to be 'the test of a catholic appreciation of poetry'.

Pneumatic bliss

DUNLOP, John Boyd, (1840–1921), Scottish inventor of the pneumatic tyre essential to modern transport.

It was bumping round the cobbled streets of Belfast, where Dunlop was a veterinary surgeon, which gave him the idea of inflated instead of solid tyres. In 1887, he conceived that his carriage wheels and his boy's tricycle wheels (his boy had asked him if he couldn't make his tricycle go faster) might be cushioned. Purchasing rubber tubing from a chemist, he filled it with air, and attached it to a wooden wheel with strips of canvas. In order to make a comparison, he took a solid-tyred wheel from his son's tricycle, and sent the two wheels spinning across the yard. The tricycle wheel with the solid tyre fell over half-way. The cushioned wheel flew across to the wall, and rebounded.

Dunlop patented his tyre in 1888.

'Art is hidden in nature'

DÜRER, Albrecht, (1471–1528), German artist, son of a goldsmith at Nuremberg who, on the eve of the Reformation, brought the culture and scientific curiosity of the Renaissance into German art. There are rivers upon which an ebbing tide meets the incoming tide, the two forming a tidal wave which sweeps back inland. The image fits Dürer, who is both medieval and a man of the new age, Gothic and Renaissance, German and Italian.

'Attentively regard Nature', he wrote, 'and take her for your guide. ... Truly, Art is hidden in Nature.'

G

His two visits to Northern Italy encouraged him to teach a 'scientific' art to his less learned colleagues at home. 'It is evident', Dürer remarked, 'that the German painters are not a little skilful with their hand and in the use of colours, though they have as yet been wanting in the art of measurement, also in perspective and other like matters. It is therefore to be hoped that, if they learn these also and thus acquire skill and knowledge together, they will in time allow no other nation to take the prize before them.' To spread his ideas he took advantage of the recently discovered art of printing; he wrote several books, he mastered the technique of the woodcut and of engraving on copper plates, and so produced cheap works of art which would have a wide public. In his large woodcuts illustrating the Revelation of St John he raised the art of pictorial printing to a level which has probably never been surpassed. The same is true of the *Great Passion* and the *Little Passion*, and superb single plates such as *Melancholia* and *St Jerome in his Study*. He was the friend of the Reformers, of Luther and Melancthon, and of Erasmus; and in these and other works he expressed that discontent with the Church which was to develop into the Reformation. His visions of apocalyptic events were topical, for there were many who expected these prophecies to come true within their lifetime. In the print *St Michael's fight against the Dragon* he shows a mighty struggle taking place in heaven: the saint and his angels thrust and hack in their war against fantastic fiendish monsters, whilst below them lies a serene, untroubled landscape.

Yet Dürer knew that he could only make such visions effective, with all the minute detail he loved to put into his paintings, his portraits, his humanistic self-portraits, his engravings and woodcuts, if, in the true spirit of the Renaissance, he studied nature; as he said, 'Never think to do anything better than God has done it, for your power is mere nothingness compared with the creative activity of God.' Thus he studied and drew in watercolour all kinds of plants and animals – plants from grasses to the larger celandine, animals from hare to rhinoceros; and in the later years of his life he devoted far more time to his scientific enthusiasms than to his art.

His fame at his death was widespread, for like the great Italians of the Renaissance, he had shown that an artist is more than a humble workman; he may also be a philosopher.

ILLUSTRATION: Page 124.

E

Scientist and popularizer of science

EDDINGTON, Sir Arthur Stanley, (1882–1944), English physicist and astronomer, the prose-poet of scientific exposition, whose writings have appealed imaginatively to a vast reading public in many lands.

Eddington's scientific reputation is based on his great discoveries about the internal constitution of the stars, and his explanation of why the millions upon millions of stars in the universe are all within a narrow range of mass. This is due to the balance of gravitation against the pressure of radiation, or light, from the centre of the star, which is at a temperature of tens of millions of degrees Centigrade. He succeeded in deducing the luminosity of a star from its mass, and thus discovered a theoretical law which applied to all stars, actual or possible.

Eddington was a Quaker. Like that other famous Quaker in science, John Dalton, he was born in Kendal, and studied in Manchester. He entered Owens College at the age of fifteen, and easily outdistanced all his fellows. Then he studied at Cambridge, where he established a record by becoming Senior Wrangler (first in the mathematical examination) after only two years' work. In 1916 he published his first paper on the Cepheid stars, which vary in brightness in a regular way, a phenomenon he attributed to pulsations in the glowing ball of stellar gas. All of his later discoveries about the internal constitution of the stars grew out of this paper, and in his greatest work, by his magnificent command of mathematics and his physical intuition, he revealed the star as a self-governing engine, driven by atomic energy. As Secretary of the Royal Astronomical Society, Eddington happened to be the first man to receive an account of Einstein's general theory of relativity, which had been published in Germany in the last months of 1915. Through this accident he became the chief expositor of the new theory to the English-speaking world.

Eddington's expository style and philosophical point of view are finely illustrated in the famous concluding paragraph of his *Space, Time and Gravitation*: 'We have found a strange foot-print on the shores of the unknown. We have derived profound theories, one after another, to account for its origin. At last, we have succeeded in reconstructing the creature that made the foot-print. And Lo! it is our own.'

Aesthete and baronet

EDEN, Sir William, (1849–1915), English baronet, amateur and eccentric, though eccentricity may be the wrong word for one who wrote 'Nothing can make me happy, nothing can prevent me from suffering, neither God nor man, or even woman! Art and beauty are the altars of sacrifice in my life, and I wish it so.'

This north-country baronet, wealthy, tall, strikingly handsome, married to a beautiful wife, endeavoured to be the complete aristocrat both of position and taste. He was soldier, master of hounds, first-rate shot, amateur of boxing, talented artist and friend of artists, with a passion for the drawings and paintings of Degas. Only art gave him peace and comfort. Whistler (q.v.) picked a famous quarrel with him on the grounds that he had paid an insulting minimum for a portrait of his wife, but the quarrel was not to the credit of the artist, who painted out Lady Eden's head. Outrages to taste or beauty made Sir William Eden irascible and difficult. He loathed 'vulgar rhododendrons on guard amongst the dirty leaves', declined to stay in a house where the crimson ramblers and calceolarias grew against red brick – 'all of them framed in self-satisfaction'. All the bad architects of Britain he wished to see burned at the foot of the Albert Memorial.

He thought 'the progress of civilization is the decay of taste', and copied out in his notebook, not long before his death 'The worm of the world hath eaten out my heart'. The politician Anthony Eden is his son.

Technological wizard

EDISON, Thomas Alva, (1847–1931), American inventor, of incredible versatility and shrewd business sense, for the rest of the world a symbol of American application, success and plain man's philosophy. He called his own genius 'one per cent inspiration, and ninety-nine per cent perspiration'.

The child Edison, born to a prosperous dealer near Detroit, was marked out by an abnormally large head. At twelve he was in business – on his own account, selling newspapers and candy on the trains between Port Huron and Detroit. To train-men and their wives he sold papers and vegetables at a discount; he carried his goods free by putting them in a U.S. mail van, and he established a small laboratory in a smoking car, making experiments between stops.

Aboard train, the young Edison printed a newspaper, the *Weekly Herald*, containing such items as 'Birth: At Detroit Junction G.T.R. Refreshment Rooms on 29th inst., the wife of A. Little, a daughter'. Lower down, in the same column, as a fill-up he inserted: 'Reason, Justice and Equity never had weight enough on the face of the earth to govern the councils of men.'

He was now fourteen. One day in Detroit he observed the tremendous excitement over the news of the great battle of Shiloh in the Civil War. He telegraphed the news ahead to Port Huron to reduplicate the excitement, and took in the train with him a thousand instead of the usual hundred papers, in which the news was printed. When he arrived, a crowd clamoured for the papers which he sold at 25 cents apiece, making what was for him an enormous sum. 'Then I realized', he stated, 'that the telegraph was a great invention.'

It was in fact the nerve of American industrialism, and, like the telephone, 'a little mother of the big trust'. Edison decided that telegraphy should be his field. A station agent taught him to operate a train telegraph, and he began to make his own instruments. Owing to the call-up of men in the Civil War, he was able to get a telegrapher's job when he was fifteen, and for the next five years he travelled as a 'tramp-operator' through the States. While working for the Western Union in 1864, he invented a repeater for repeating messages at slower speed. This contained the germ of his great invention of the phonograph.

In the wild years after the Civil War, Edison described how, in the Middle West, 'everything was wide open'. He would 'go over to a gorgeously furnished faro-bank' to get his midnight lunch. 'Everything was free. There were over twenty keno-rooms running. One of them I visited was in a Baptist church, the man with the wheel being in the pulpit, and the gamblers in the pews'.

He found work in a factory making telegraph apparatus in Boston. The first invention he patented was a quick means of recording votes in the House of Representatives. He showed it to the politicians, who laughed and told him that they were not interested in quick voting, but in filibustering. Edison said that ever afterwards he never attempted inventions unless there was an obvious market for them. He arrived in New York in 1869, and was a telegrapher in the Stock Exchange. He was present when Gould and Fisk tried to corner all the gold in the United States. 'The mob of brokers and of lookers on surged to and fro, and in and out, some howling, yelling and gesticulating, others silent and confounded and others again, almost crazy, some, indeed, were quite crazy.' The telegraph broke down under the pressure, and Edison was the only man who could quickly put it right.

Edison invented an improved ticker for sending stock-exchange quotations, and received $40,000 for it. At twenty-three he was able to manufacture electrical apparatus on a considerable scale. He soon had fifty men working for him, including Schuckert and Bergmann, who subsequently founded the great German electrical firms of those names. Other employees later on were Kennelly, the discoverer of the Kennelly–Heaviside layer, which makes long-distance radio possible, and Acheson, the inventor of carborundum.

Within a few years he had forty-six patents for stock-tickers, and in 1874 invented quadruplex telegraphy, by which four messages were sent simultaneously on one wire. He worked at the same time on fifty different inventions. He invented the stencil for duplicating papers, and paraffin paper for wrapping sweets. He invented the carbon microphone which made long-distance telephony possible. His telephone inventions were demonstrated by a young assistant in his London office, George Bernard Shaw, whose novel, *The Irrational Knot*, was based on this experience. Then Edison invented the phonograph (or gramophone). This was a brilliant, absolutely clear-cut achievement. And he developed the carbon filament lamp, and the first electricity supply system to keep his lamps going in New York City. By the end of his life he held more than one thousand patents, and he had made one important scientific discovery: he noticed in his experiments with lamps that electricity leaked from hot filaments. Fleming (who was on Edison's English staff) based his invention of the radio valve on this effect.

Edison was known as the *Old Man* before he was

thirty. Up to the age of thirty-nine he led an abnormal life, working twenty hours a day for long periods. On one occasion he worked on the phonograph continuously for five days and nights. When a new man joined his staff and enquired about the regulations, Edison spat on the floor and yelled, 'Hell! there ain't no rules around here! We are tryin' to accomplish somep'n!' He introduced himself as 'Don Quixote' and his chief assistant as 'Santcho Pantcho', and his staff as 'muckers'. When one of his assistants was angry about a rival stealing one of Edison's ideas, Edison asked him why he was so excited. 'Everybody steals in commerce and industry, I've stolen a lot myself. But I knew *how* to steal. They don't know *how* to steal – that's all that's the matter with them.'

Edison aimed at turning invention from a matter of inspiration into a systematic process. He was the most romantic figure in the new science of developmental engineering, the systematic turning of science into practical contrivances, in which America is at the present time supreme.

ILLUSTRATION: Page 127.

Understanding the universe

EINSTEIN, Albert, (1879–1955), German-Jewish theoretical physicist and the most highly endowed of living men of science. He formulated the theory of relativity, from which it follows that mass is a form of energy.

After school at Munich and training in the Federal Institute of Technology at Zurich, Einstein in 1902 became an examiner in the Swiss Patent Office at Bern, reporting upon patent applications. He worked out the theory of relativity in his spare time, making contributions which were almost as important to the quantum theory, which had recently been proposed by Planck. When he was awarded a Nobel Prize in 1921, it was for his work on the photoelectric effect. Relativity, after sixteen years, had not become respectable enough.

Newton had provided a philosophical framework for his theory of gravitation by making the ideas of absolute space and time more precise. He had to overcome the vagueness of his predecessors. Einstein had, perhaps, an even more difficult task. He had to withstand the precision and prestige of a Newton. He arrived at the fundamental role of relativity from a consideration of the electromagnetic field. Ever since Faraday had shown that the relative motion of an electrical conductor, such as a copper wire, and the lines of force in the magnetic field from a magnet, enabled electricity to be obtained from magnetism, or magnetism from electricity, the stage was set for the ultimate discovery that nature has different properties, depending on the point of view from which it is observed. One of the first results of Einstein's theory of relativity in 1905 was his demonstration that the amount of energy in a given mass of matter was equal to the mass multiplied by the square of the velocity of light. (It is not surprising that light should appear in this equation, since it is an electrical phenomenon, similar in nature to radio waves.) As the velocity of light is very large, the amount of energy in a small piece of matter is very great. Thus Einstein, right at the beginning of his career, told scientists exactly how much energy might be obtained from a given piece of matter.

In 1914, Einstein was called to the Prussian Academy of Sciences in Berlin. In the following year, he published his *General Theory of Relativity*, in which relativity was extended to cover gravitation. He showed that space, time and mass were related, and not independent of each other, or absolute, as in Newton's theory. With his general theory, he explained an anomaly in the movement of the planet Mercury, and forecast how much the sun would bend rays of light passing near it. His forecast was confirmed by observation.

Einstein is essentially an original thinker in physics. By an enormous achievement of abstract thought he was able to emancipate scientists from the old ideas established with all of Newton's authority. Once this reorientation of thought was accomplished, the technical calculations were not very difficult. As a mathematician, Einstein is only moderate, having learned just enough mathematics to find the most convenient way of expressing his ideas. He has remained in his outlook more classical than the younger quantum physicists who based science on the laws of chance. He said he could not believe that the Almighty had arranged the universe according to the casting of dice. That would be unfair. The universe is difficult to understand, but not irrational: *Raffiniert ist der Herr Gott, aber boshaft ist er nicht*, or, in the American translation, 'God is slick, but he ain't mean'.

In 1933, after the rise of the Nazis, Einstein announced that he would 'only stay in a country where political liberty, toleration, and equality of all citizens before the law are the rule'; he resigned from the Prussian Academy of Sciences, stood by his persecuted people, and left Germany for the United States, becoming an American citizen in 1940. He has expressed himself as drawn to the simple life, as opposed to class differences, and as having a 'passionate sense of social justice and social responsibility'. But with the latter he has always and increasingly combined 'an obstinate sense of detachment'. Though intensely devoted to liberty he disbelieves in 'human freedom in the philosophical sense'. Since his youth he has been guided by Schopenhauer's saying: 'A man can do as he will, but not will as he will.'

In later years Einstein had repeatedly called for efforts for peace and the control of atomic weapons. In his opinion 'mankind can only gain protection against the danger of unimaginable destruction and wanton annihilation if a supra-national organization has alone the authority to produce or possess these weapons'.

ILLUSTRATION: Page 134.

Poet of 'The Waste Land'

ELIOT, Thomas Stearns, (b. 1888), American-English poet, critic, playwright, whose poem *The Waste Land* (1922) made him the figure of his time in English thought, feeling and literature.

Upon the fringes of the South, in the wide, comfortable residential streets of St Louis, Missouri, where Eliot was born and bred, families of New England origin tend to be more English than the English; at least, more New England than New Englanders. By custom this young man of New England descent went east to Harvard. He then went farther east, back to England and to France, to Oxford and to the Sorbonne, to a London bank, and to the heart of Englishry – classicist in literature, as he has described himself, royalist in politics, Anglo-Catholic in religion. He has never returned to live in America, and he became a naturalized Englishman in 1927.

In 1914 Eliot met the American poet Ezra Pound, then living in England, and a generous, enthusiastic discoverer and promoter of talent. Pound at once knew Eliot's measure and worked to establish him on both sides of the Atlantic. In 1922 a breakdown made it necessary for Eliot to take three months' leave from his bank. 'During that time' (to quote Pound) 'he wrote *Waste Land*, a series of poems, possibly the finest that the modern movement in English has produced, at any rate as good as anything that has been done since 1900, and which certainly loses nothing by comparison with the best work of Keats, Browning or Shelley.' Pound criticized and cut, and to him *The Waste Land* was dedicated; then, like some active creature out of the trees, it dropped among the 'literary world' which was cosily eating its dead dog and resented the interference. One of the *littérateurs* greeted *The Waste Land* with the words, 'A grunt would serve equally well'. Few then foresaw what the influence of the poem or its author would become, although Eliot had already collected a number of his critical essays in *The Sacred Wood*, perhaps the most famous book of literary criticism in this century.

Eliot was exceedingly conscious of the poet in relation to poetry and tradition. He was conscious of the relation of new to old, he saw that English verse needed galvanizing, and in 'free verse' he sought to discover and heighten the essential cadences of modern speech, as in the free verse lines from *The Waste Land* with their characteristic placing of modern (and also town) imagery among historical allusions:

The river's tent is broken: the last fingers of leaf
Clutch and sink into the wet bank. The wind
Crosses the brown land, unheard. The nymphs are departed.
Sweet Thames, run softly, till I end my song.
The river bears no empty bottles, sandwich papers,
Silk handkerchiefs, cardboard boxes, cigarette ends
Or other testimony of summer nights. The nymphs are departed
And their friends, the loitering heirs of city directors;
Departed, have left no addresses.
By the waters of Leman, I sat down and wept. ...
Sweet Thames, run softly till I end my song,
Sweet Thames, run softly, for I speak not loud or long.
But at my back in a cold blast I hear
The rattle of the bones, and chuckle from ear to ear.
A rat crept softly through the vegetation
Dragging its slimy belly on the bank

His poetry has changed and loosened somewhat since *The Waste Land* and *The Hollow Men*. The form of his latest poems, the philosophic *Four Quartets*, is said to be based on the late quartets of Beethoven; they are divided into sections, corresponding to movements, of contrasting verse-form and theme.

Eliot's stern attention to style and morals had, in the twenties, the effect of a salutary frost. Imprecise thought and feeling were killed, literary standards were raised. Attention was drawn by him to Dante, Baudelaire, the Jacobean dramatists and sermon-writers and the Metaphysical poets, as if to make English poetry unprovincial once more. Eliot's withdrawal from Cactus land into an increasing churchiness found its critics and its mockers, *The lips seem bursting with a loud amen*. At last with his plays *The Rock* (1934), *Murder in the Cathedral* (1935), *The Family Reunion* (1939), *The Cocktail Party* (1950) and *The Confidential Clerk* (1953), Eliot has given himself a new public of a different kind from those practising writers chiefly concerned with style who were his first and closest disciples; and the plays have given him wider fame than has been enjoyed by any poet of this century. He has become through Europe and America a great public statue, unrivalled in his influence upon his own and succeeding generations of writers. In the long view Eliot's poetry may seem over-conscious and too deliberate. A younger poet has said of him, 'He is excellent: he is the best we have, but what a pity he is the best', and it is perhaps altogether too easy and too true to repeat of Eliot that he has completed a revolution in the language of poetry, when one should talk, if one could, more of its life-enhancing qualities. With posterity, it may perhaps be his fate to creep backwards into the history of literature, when he will occupy an honourable but seldom-visited niche in the pantheon like the niche of Abraham Cowley.

ILLUSTRATION: Page 132.

The Faery Queen

ELIZABETH I, (1533–1603), Queen of England, gave the most famous description of herself when, as the Spanish Armada was sailing up the Channel, she told her subjects, 'I know I have the body of a weak and feeble woman, but I have the heart and stomach of a king, and a king of England too.'

Elizabeth inherited the charm and imperiousness of her father (Henry VIII), which she exploited to the full with her own femininity. She was too modest about her mental powers when she said: 'My parents took good care that I should be well-educated, and I had great practice in many languages, of which I take to myself some knowledge. ... I had many learned teachers, but they laboured in a barren and unproductive field.' In fact she was a woman of intellect and culture who employed her natural female irresolution with unique success in home and foreign politics. This was marked in the question of her possible marriage. In the first year of her reign she told Parliament: 'As for me, it shall be sufficient that a marble stone shall declare that a Queen, having lived and reigned so many years, died a virgin.' Most of the rulers of Europe sought her hand for themselves or members of their families, but she remained unmarried, although her relations with her Court favourites, especially Essex, sometimes caused scandal. There is a poignancy in one of her own poems:

When I was fair and young, and favour graced me,
Of many was I sought, their mistress for to be;
But I did scorn them all, and answered them therefore,
'Go, go, go, seek some otherwhere,
Importune me no more!'

Elizabeth's strength lay in her ability to interpret the feelings of her subjects. She avoided war with Spain until it was absolutely necessary. Then she proclaimed on behalf of all Englishmen: 'Let tyrants fear. I have always so behaved myself that, under God, I have placed my chiefest strength and safeguard in the loyal hearts and goodwill of my subjects ... and think foul scorn that Parma or Spain, or any prince of Europe, should dare to invade the borders of my realm.' On occasions she would speak her mind to fellow rulers, as, for instance, when the French king Henry IV changed his religion from Protestant to Catholic on the ground that it might help to unite France. She wrote to him: 'It is a perilous thing to do ill that good may come.' She was often high-handed with her Parliaments: 'And therefore henceforth, whether I live to see the like assembly or no, or whoever it be, yet beware how you prove your Prince's patience as you have now done mine.'

Life in Elizabethan England was by no means comfortable, abounding in intriguers, conspirators, spies and informers and chances of sudden death, including the plague –

Wit with his wantonness
Tasteth death's bitterness;
Hell's executioner
Hath no ears for to hear
What vain art can reply.
I am sick, I must die.
Lord, have mercy on us!

Or as another of her poets, Sir Walter Ralegh (q.v.) wrote in a bitter poem:

> Tell men of high condition
> That manage the estate,
> Their purpose is ambition,
> Their practice only hate:
> And if they once reply
> Then give them all the lie.

However, in her last speech to Parliament she undoubtedly spoke the sentiments of all the nation: 'This I count the glory of my crown, that I have reigned with your loves' – which helps also to explain the flattering cult of the 'Faery Queen', the love-magnet of all hearts, which poets of the reign took to such extremes. Imperious she was and an imperious queen she remained in her final illness, characteristically rebuking her minister, Cecil, when he told her she must go to bed: 'The word *must* is not used to Princes. Little man, little man, if your father had lived you durst not have said so much, but you know I must die, and that makes you presumptuous.'

As for her appearance, Elizabeth, hardly fairy or nymph, was described in her youth as 'pleasing rather than beautiful ... a good complexion ... beautiful eyes, and above all a beautiful hand, which she likes to shew'; and a German who saw her at the end of her reign reported that she was very majestic, 'her face oblong, fair but wrinkled; her eyes small, yet black and pleasant; her nose a little hooked, her lips narrow and her teeth black ... her hair was of auburn colour, but false ... her hands were slender'.

ILLUSTRATION: Page 128.

Skeletons in carnival

ENSOR, James, (1860–1949), Belgian painter and fantastic satirist of mankind.

'All rules, all canons of art, vomit death' – a saying typical of this strange man and marked individualist among modern painters. His life was outwardly uneventful. Ensor's father was an Englishman who had taken to drink, his mother kept a curio or junk shop, at Ostend, where he was born. Nearly all his life he lived above this shop, which, with its masks and shells, was endlessly fascinating to him, endlessly symbolic of mankind.

Scandalized Masks, an eerie picture of 1883, may be taken as a key to his vision. A skinny masked man sits at a table by candlelight, a door opens, a woman, also hideously masked, stands there in a moment of appalled and horrible recognition: in carnival is the truth of our society, and the truth is beyond tragedy, only to be understood through irony and fantasy. So, too, Ensor painted a portrait of himself peering out with keen amused eyes from among the jostling masks of mankind, he painted a bonneted skeleton which looks in surprise at a disintegration of human bones upon the floor, or skeletons fighting for the body of a hanged man, or the bizarre reception of Christ come back to earth, in the huge fantasia of *Christ's Entry into Brussels*, which is one of his master works (1888). Christ is a tiny figure on a donkey hardly noticed among the bigotry, the blare and the banners, 'Up with the Socialist State', 'Long Live Jesus, King of Brussels', etc., which the self-interested people wave instead of palms.

When Belgian critics discovered the kind of painter they had and reacted against him bitterly, Ensor, in 1896, painted his *Dangerous Cooks* (p. 180). Diners are visible through a kitchen door, and a cook is about to enter with a dish; on this dish Ensor's own head reposes with a look of content. Another cook fries the head of another artist, beneath a row of heads. In the corner hangs a slaughtered chicken with the features of a woman painter. Beyond, in the restaurant, napkins around their necks, the foul diners smugly await their cannibals' meal.

'The world without morality or order reaches beyond the logic of tragedy to its own wild grotesque comedy,' one of Ensor's interpreters has written of his art. The description is incomplete, because the design and superb shimmering colour which Ensor could manipulate, often carried him beyond irony or fantasy or the macabre into the deliciousness of the kingdom of light. The full range, quality, power, and beauty of his pictures have not yet been sufficiently appreciated, perhaps, as Ensor himself wrote, because his art tends towards the literary. 'My pictures tend towards the outskirts of painting.'

ILLUSTRATION: Page 168.

The humanist

ERASMUS, Desiderius, (1466–1536), Dutch humanist and one of the lights of the new learning in

...rope; though like his friend Sir Thomas ...v.) he remained firm in his faith when Pro-...tism was abroad.

He was illegitimate (though he denied it), and was put into a monastery; but while he found that he could get drunk in the cloisters as often as he wished, study – for which he had a passion – was frowned on. It was no easy matter to leave, but he managed to, and for many years had to lead the life of a poor scholar: 'All I ask for is leisure to live wholly to God,' he wrote, 'to repent of the sins of my foolish youth, to study Scripture, and to read or write something of real value.' Little of Erasmus's work is read today, except his incisive, ironical letters. Of a pupil he disliked, he wrote: 'Imagine a pair of sullen eyes under shaggy eyebrows, a forehead of stone, a cheek which never knew a blush, a nose thick with bristles and swollen with a polypus, hanging jaws, livid lips, a voice like the barking of a dog, his whole face branded like a felon's, with the stamp of deformity to warn off approach as we tie hay to the horns of a shrewd cow. To think that I should have taught classics to such a creature as this.'

In England he found many friends, and one delightful custom. 'When you go anywhere on a visit the girls all kiss you. They kiss you when you arrive. They kiss you when you go away; and they kiss you again when you return. Go where you will, it is all kisses; and ... if you had once tasted how soft and fragrant those lips are, you would wish to spend your life here.' Oxford he liked, but Cambridge earned nothing but his scorn: 'The wine is horrible', he wrote. His reputation as a teacher spread; and as a writer. His *Moriae encomium – The Praise of Folly* (1509), in which worldly ecclesiastics are damned with faint praise, riled and amused Europe. There was nothing he enjoyed so much as the urbane chit-chat of donnish wit: he was malicious – 'I will say no harm of the Bishop of London except that he was a superstitious and malignant Scotist'. And he was ready with advice to those who asked: 'Never work at night; it dulls the brain and hurts the health. Remember above all things that nothing passes so rapidly as youth.'

Europe at the beginning of the fifteenth century was a testing-ground for the Catholic Church. Religion was indistinguishable from superstition; the sale of pardons was big business (see Jakob Fugger). Erasmus saw the evils. So did Luther; but Erasmus was more content to enjoy the good things – rich living, and fine learning – that went hand in hand with ecclesiastical abuse. And it was Luther (q.v.) who detonated the explosions of reform; while Erasmus settled into obscurity, faithful to Rome. 'Christ I know,' he wrote, 'Luther I know not. The Roman Church I know, and death will not part me from it till the Church departs from Christ.' The world has never forgotten his face through the portraits of him by Holbein.

ILLUSTRATION: Page 125.

Eric the Red

ERIC THE RED, (c. 950–c. 1003), Norse settler in Iceland who explored and colonized Greenland; his son Leif Ericsson (q.v.) appears to have touched on the continent of America.

Another Icelander, Gunnbjorn Ulfsson, had sighted Greenland when driven westward from his course and when Eric was banished for three years because of two deaths in a feud, he set out to explore this land instead of returning to Norway. His exile over, Eric went back to Iceland, collected settlers and in A.D. 985 established two farm colonies in south-west Greenland. He named a formidable country the Green Land possibly to attract European merchants. Eric's colonies were eventually weakened by a deterioration in climate, which also brought the Eskimos down from the north. Contact with Europe dwindled and ceased, and the exact fate of the colonies is unknown. One came to an end by 1325, the other soon after 1450. Eric was typical of the roving resourceful Viking navigators, forced overseas by land hunger and pressure of population. His story is told in the Icelandic *Saga of Eric the Red*.

'The discoverer of Wineland'

ERICSSON, Leif, discoverer of America and son of Eric the Red (q.v.). He sailed westward from Greenland in the year 1002 to explore land previously sighted by one Bjarni Herjulfsson, who had earned some contempt among the Norsemen for not investigating it. He found the land seen by Bjarni, called it Helluland ('land of the flat stones'), went on to another land, which he called Markland, and finally came to a third land, which he ordered to be explored in shifts.

They had with them, according to the Icelandic saga, a small, flat-faced, freckled (or pockmarked) German named Tyrker, insignificant in appearance but very clever at all kinds of handicraft, who against orders one day became separated from his party and caused anxiety by failing to return with it. When he did return, and Leif started asking him questions, he saw that he was greatly excited.

'Tyrker began to reply in German,' the saga continues, 'rolling his eyes in all directions and writhing his lips; and none understood what he said. After a time he recovered himself, and spoke in Norse in these words: "I did not go much farther than the others. But I have important news for you. I found grapes and grape-vines." "Is that the truth, foster-father mine?" Leif asked. "Surely it is true," he answered. "I was born where there are plenty of vines and grapes." ... Leif gave the land a name in terms of its products and called it *Vinland* (wineland). Then they sailed away, and had fair wind and weather until they sighted Greenland, with its glacier-clad mountains.'

The sagas have been dissected and redissected to establish which were the lands explored by Leif Ericsson, and there is no absolute agreement, but it is tempting to believe that the land where the excitable German found the vine was Massachusetts. Species of vine still grow there wild, including the Summer Grape or Pigeon Grape (*Vitis aestivalis*) and the Fox Grape (*Vitis labrusca*).

Discoverer of a civilization

EVANS, Sir Arthur John, (1851–1941), English archaeologist, excavator of the palace of Knossos, on the northern coast of Crete, and discover of the Minoan civilization.

His father was another distinguished archaeologist and pioneer of the study of prehistoric man, and from his youngest days he was brought up to understand antiquities. Schliemann (q.v.) had guessed that an earlier civilization must lie behind his own discoveries in Mycenae and Troy and he had thought of excavations in Crete. Evans, Keeper of the Ashmolean Museum at Oxford (which he made into one of the finest archaeological museums in Western Europe) was led to Crete by his study of ancient seals; and in 1900 he began his work at Knossos, and at once revealed a metal-using prehistoric civilization preceded by a stone-using village economy. He named this civilization 'Minoan' after the legendary Minos, king of Crete and son of Zeus and Europa.

It is given to few people to discover an entirely new civilization in this way. Evans showed that his Minoans were the earliest city-dwellers and navigators of the Mediterranean, whose city states and thalassocracies, which flourished from well before 2000 B.C. to 1400 B.C., foreran the Greeks and the Phoenicians. His long years of excavation were described and evaluated by him in the *Palace of Minôs* (1922–1935); and in *Scripta Minoa* he began to study the still undeciphered writing of the Minoans.

Forerunner of mass production

EVANS, Oliver, (1755–1819), American inventor, was one of the ingenious, adaptable, conscious and foreseeing artificers of the machine age, and a notable pioneer of mass production for mass appetite.

Engaged in 1782 to build a water-mill on Red Clay Creek, near Wilmington, in his own state of Delaware, Evans began by analysing the whole complex of small jobs which millers had to perform by hand. It seemed to him that the power which moved the millstone could be made to do all the other work, thus saving time, labour, dirt and waste. Within three years his famous automatic mill was in existence; it combined unloading and elevation, descent by gravity, and horizontal transport inside the mill house.

Evans wrote what has so often been true: 'He that studies and writes on the improvement of the arts and sciences labours to benefit generations yet unborn, for it is not probable that his contemporaries will pay any attention to him ... therefore improvements progress so slowly.' Yet necessity compelled a fairly quick acceptance of his revolutionary concept, which was ready for the extended wheatlands of America. This clear-headed man was one of those who responded to the special circumstances of American livelihood, in which old tradition was not so much an interference as a drag, and to the need of special adaptations to fit the scale of American production. Other things he devised include a means of making ice; steam engines, and a steam dredger.

The analysis of space

F

FARADAY, Michael, (1791–1867), English scientist, son of a blacksmith, who proposed the electromagnetic theory of light. His discovery of electromagnetic induction revealed the principle of the electric motor and dynamo, the transformer and the telephone. He set out the laws of electrolysis, the decomposition of solutions by electricity, invented the terms *cathode, anode, ion,* etc., discovered benzene, the basis of the synthetic dyestuffs industry; and invented the instrument which contained the principle of the cinematograph.

This strange man, who had no collaborator or scientific assistant, belonged to the very small and severe Protestant sect of Sandemanians. They believed in the literal inspiration of the Bible, and washed each other's feet. Faraday became an elder. He was very strict in his Sunday observances, and used always to return to London at the week-end to attend the service. However, when he had become famous, Queen Victoria commanded him to dine with her on a Sunday evening. Faraday pondered deeply on his duties to God and to Caesar, and decided that he must render unto Caesar the things that were Caesar's. He obeyed the Queen's command. The sect condemned his decision, and suspended him from membership. For long he was allowed only to sit in the gallery during service, and many years passed before he was restored to eldership. The Sandemanian sect has since died out. The chapel where Faraday used to pray and preach has recently – and ironically – been turned into a telephone exchange.

When he was a boy, Faraday was apprenticed to a bookbinder. He sometimes read the pages that he was to bind, and in this way became interested in electricity. One of the bookbinder's clients, who was a member of the Royal Institution, noticed his concern for science, and gave him tickets to hear lectures by Sir Humphry Davy (q.v.). He wrote careful and well-illustrated notes, and sent them to Davy, and asked for a job. To his eternal credit, Davy complimented him on them, and presently engaged him as assistant.

Immediately afterwards he left on a grand tour of Europe, with special passports from Napoleon to enter France, though England and France were at war. He took Faraday with him. The boy had never been more than twelve miles from London before in his life. With Davy he now met most of the great scientists and personalities of Europe. Faraday saw Napoleon in a procession, and noted with scientific precision how 'he was sitting in one corner of his carriage, covered and almost hidden by an enormous robe of ermine, and his face overshadowed by a tremendous plume of feathers that descended from a velvet hat', and how 'his carriage was very rich and had fourteen servants stood upon it in various parts'.

After returning to England, Faraday helped Davy with the research on the miner's lamp. He did not publish any research of his own until he was twenty-five, and none of importance until he was twenty-nine. Ørsted of Copenhagen discovered in 1820 that an electric current could deflect a magnet. All the scientific world was excited, and tried to secure a continuous rotation of a magnet round a current. Faraday succeeded first. Davy was vexed and jealous, and thought he had stolen the idea from Wollaston and himself. He was president of the Royal Society, and tried to black-ball Faraday's election.

Ten years later, after innumerable attempts, Faraday discovered that if a coil of wire is moved across the lines of force from a magnet, an electric current is produced in the wire. He conceived the idea of the electromagnetic field to explain the phenomenon. Light he thought of as waves in this field. One evening, at the Royal Institution, Daniell, the inventor of the zinc and copper electric battery, was due to lecture. He was a very shy man, and at the last moment before the lecture was due to begin, he lost his nerve, and ran out of the building into Albemarle Street. The lecture theatre was full, and to meet the situation, Faraday gave an extempore lecture, which he described as *Thoughts on Ray-Vibrations.* In it he propounded the idea of electromagnetic waves, and suggested that light was a species of them. Clerk Maxwell worked this idea out, and forecast the existence of electromagnetic waves other than light – that is, radio waves, which were demonstrated experimentally by Hertz. Faraday conceived the physical idea from which radio and the theory of relativity have been deduced – not to mention electrical engineering.

Newton had imagined space as rigid absolute emptiness. Faraday introduced the idea of space as the seat of mobile, flexible, ever-fluctuating electromagnetic forces. For him space was, as it were, alive with physical happenings. By establishing this mode of thought, he created the conditions in which scientists could gradually arrive at the notion of the combination of space and movement and time, and the theory of relativity. Yet in all his works Faraday never used mathematics more complicated than simple arithmetic.

ILLUSTRATION: Page 127.

Fielding the novelist

FIELDING, Henry, (1707–1754). Sometimes called the Father of the English Novel, he proclaimed his originality in his greatest work, *Tom Jones*: 'As I am, in reality, the founder of a new province in writing, so I am at liberty to make what laws I please therein. And these laws my readers, whom I consider as my subjects, are bound to believe in and obey.'

Coleridge once said that there are three perfect plots in the world, those of *Oedipus Tyrannus* (by Sophocles), *The Alchemist* (by Ben Jonson), and *Tom Jones*. A full-blooded harum-scarum general was Fielding's father; when his mother died, the General married the keeper of a London eating-house. The son perpetuated his father's robust *joie de vivre*, in his own life and in his novels. 'His happy constitution', it was said, 'made him forget everything when he was before a venison pasty or over a flask of champagne.' He was burnt out, in his forties, by a mixture of dropsy, asthma, jaundice and gout. By then he had enjoyed a perfect marriage and immortalized his wife in his heroines. He had launched the English novel on its career, he had written more than twenty plays and imposed his personality on the Augustan theatre. The actor Murphy, who edited his works, said: 'He would go home rather late from a tavern, and would, the next morning, deliver a scene to the players, written upon the papers which had wrapped the tobacco in which he so much delighted.' He ended as a London magistrate who vastly improved the rude justice of the eighteenth century.

Before Fielding the English novel hardly existed. *Joseph Andrews, Amelia* and *Tom Jones* gave it a pullulating life. As a barrister on circuit, Fielding mastered the world of chambermaids and coaching inns and criminals, and Thackeray rightly said 'he had an eye that brightened up a rogue like a constable's lantern'.

He projected in his novels the bustling what-happens-next of eighteenth-century travel, and he did so with both honesty and the balance of a cultured man, who read Cicero's *De Consolatione* in his many moments of poverty and depression. He once wrote a poem, *On True Greatness,* in which he called himself 'a great, tattered bard'. True enough. He was the bard of eighteenth-century England. All in all, Dr Johnson was wildly out when he called Fielding a blockhead, and then emended his judgement to 'what I mean by his being a blockhead is that he was a barren rascal'.

Poetry of the Shāh Nāmah

FIRDAUSĪ, (c. 940–1020), Abū'l-Qāsim Mansūr, known as Firdausī, Persia's epic poet, wrote the *Shāh-Nāmah,* or Book of Kings, as often quoted in Persia as Shakespeare in England.

About the age of forty Firdausī began his immense poem of some 60,000 couplets, which was to collect and preserve the tales of the ancient kings of Persia, from Gayūmarth, the first king of the world, and Hūshang who discovered fire, to the Sasanian kings. It took him some twenty years, after which the Sultan Mahmūd became his patron. For Mahmūd he worked at a fuller version, on the promise, it is said, of a thousand gold dinars for every thousand couplets. Delighted with the complete epic, the Sultan proposed to send Firdausī an elephant-load of gold coins, but he was persuaded to send no more than a load of silver. Chagrined and proud, Firdausī gave the money to a sherbert seller and a bath attendant, and escaped from Ghazna, Mahmūd having ordered that he should be trampled to death by elephants. He paid the Sultan back in satirical verses. Eventually he came home and the Sultan repented and sent him 60,000 dinars' worth of indigo. It arrived through one gate of Tūs, as the corpse of Firdausī was carried out through another.

Until twenty years ago, Firdausī's tomb was lost, a patch of rubble in the remains of a garden among the mounds and ruins of the old city of Tūs. In 1934 Shah Riza Pahlevi opened a memorial garden, pavilioned, with a long pool, flanked by rows of trees, and a white stone cenotaph raised up on a broad flight of steps. In Teheran, the Persian capital, the main street is named after Firdausī, as well as the best hotel.

The realist

FLAUBERT, Gustave, (1821–1880), French novelist. 'I should like', Flaubert grumbled in his later life, 'to find some way of making a lot of money, so that I could buy up every copy of *Madame Bovary* in existence, throw them all into the fire, and never hear of the book again.'

In part he was expressing the natural distaste of an author for being thought of as a 'one-book man' (which he was not); but in part, also, he was revolting against the current conception of him in his days of fame as 'father of the realistic school of novelists' (which he was). In Flaubert's highly sensitive nature, two elements, from the start, conflicted. Born at a time when the Romantic movement was in triumph throughout Europe, he shared as a young man in the large hopes and exotic longings of the generation immediately preceding his own; yet, at the same time, a mercilessly sardonic turn of mind led him to question, mock and, in the end, scarify the conventions of his age, as accepted both in literature and in ordinary life. In one of his letters to his mistress, Louise Colet, he put it this way. 'There exist within me, speaking from a literary point of view, two distinct persons: one in love with eloquence, with lyricism, with the soaring of eagles, with all the sonorities of phrase and mountain-peaks of idea; another seeking and probing the truth as much as he can, liking to state the small fact as forcefully as the large, wanting to make you feel almost tactilely the things he describes; the latter loves to laugh and take pleasure in man's animalities.' From these contrasting sources of inspiration sprang, on the one hand, the oriental 'sonorities' of his Carthaginian novel, *Salammbô* (1862) and, on the other, the ironic realism of *Madame Bovary* (1857).

Who was Emma Bovary? Flaubert was frequently asked, and his reply was always 'myself'. Nor was this answer merely a paradox. As an ambitious young man of uncommon gifts, he had been profoundly bored by the banalities of life at home in Rouen. One of his earliest projects had been a Dictionary of *idées reçues*, in which the shop-worn phrases and almost meaningless clichés of everyday conversation were listed and satirically anatomized. 'Hatred of the bourgeois is the beginning of virtue' became a kind of password between himself and his school friends. Looking for escape, he must often have experienced the feelings he ascribes to Emma Bovary, when she is first becoming disillusioned with wedded life in Yonville: 'Like sailors in distress, she gazed around with despairing eyes upon the loneliness of her life, seeking a white sail on the immensities of the misty horizon. She did not know what chance, what wind would bring it to her, to what shore it would carry her. ... But each morning when she awoke she was agog for what the day might bring forth. She listened for the sounds of the world, jumped from her bed, and never ceased to be surprised that nothing happened.'

What, in fact, befell Emma Bovary was a slowly consummated tragedy. Married to a doting, boorish country doctor, and encompassed by what she and her creator regarded as the depressing materialism of small-town life, she found an outlet for her dreams in successive adultery with two young men, each, from Flaubert's point of view, as vulgar in his pretentiousness as were the local shopkeepers so despised by Emma. There follows the pathetic downhill course of lies and borrowing that leads to bankruptcy, suicide, the break-up of the household and the orphaning of the Bovarys' charmless daughter, left with a total capital of 12 francs, 75 centimes. To this theme Flaubert devoted, over a space of four years, all his gifts for finely accurate description, and for the most conscientious use of language – he would spend laboured days re-writing, searching for exactly the right form of words, and hours eliminating from his pages unnecessary 'buts' and 'ands'. He was, in fact, lacerating himself; transferring to Emma Bovary a caricature of his own romantic youthful aspirations; and in depicting the self-important inanities of her acquaintance, ironically avenging himself on the provincial bourgeois, whose deadly *idées reçues* had once tormented him.

The facts of Flaubert's life may be quickly told. He was a Norman doctor's son. Illness cut short his studies for the law, and his father's death left him with a decent competence on which he was able to dedicate himself to writing. For the most of his working life he lived at Croisset, on the Seine in Normandy, looked after by his mother and his niece. Having long promised himself that he would begin 'with a thunderclap', he did, indeed. When *Madame Bovary* appeared serially in the pages of a Paris review, he and the publisher were prosecuted for obscenity. All discriminating critics came to his defence. During the next two decades the rest of his works gradually appeared, some of them having been planned and first drafted years ago – *Salammbô* (1862), *A Sentimental Education* (1869), *The Temptation of St Antony* (1874), and, eventually, the posthumous and unfinished final epitome of *idées reçues*, his *Bouvard and Pécuchet* (1881). In his later years, Flaubert was the *cher maître* of the best among rising young writers, and he died the paragon of professional men of letters, having been, as sometimes happens, more genial and agreeable in his private life than in his books.

ILLUSTRATION: Page 130.

Assembly line

FORD, Henry, (1883–1947), American automobile engineer and manufacturer, who introduced mass-production into his factories and so revolutionized large-scale industry.

Though a farmer's son (of Irish descent), Ford showed a strong mechanical bent from childhood. He had a passion for mending clocks: 'Every clock in the Ford home shuddered when it saw him coming.' Clocks and watches entertained him more than his schooling, which was of the simplest kind, based on the McGuffey Readers, which consisted of extracts from famous authors, recommending love of dumb animals, fair play, truth and honour. Henry used to spend his time mending watches underneath the desk. He received no secondary education or technical training.

Though he could easily have followed his father as a farmer, he went into the city at the age of sixteen to find work as a mechanic. He became a service man for portable steam engines. In his spare time he built a steam farm locomotive. The substitution of engines for horses was one of his driving notions from the beginning of his career. His aim was to make a mechanical horse which could be used by all farmers and any man who had a horse and cart. This helped him finally to escape from the set of ideas which enclosed all the other founders of the motor industry: their aim was only to produce a luxury for well-to-do people, a hand-made mechanical work of art.

His rise was not at all rapid. He became steam engineer in the Detroit Edison Company in 1891, and remained with the firm until 1899; spending the spare time of seven years on building his first motor-car, which he ran in 1896. In 1901 his own Henry Ford Company was founded.

During the next ten years Ford developed his firm, like half-a-dozen other able men in Detroit. His cars were assembled from parts made by sub-contractors.

By 1907 the annual production had risen to 8,759 Ford now announced that he would make a light four-cylinder touring car of at least 20 horse-power, at a low price. This was the famous Model T. It was an immediate success. 10,607 were sold in 1909, 34,528 in 1911. These results were remarkable, but not revolutionary. Ford obtained them by applying the usual methods of production with exceptional force and drive. The motor-car was still built in essentially the same manner as a house. In 1913 there were a hundred spots in the factory hall at which the cars were assembled. Five hundred men put the parts together, while another hundred handed parts to them from piles beside the assembly spots. This system was beginning to break down; there were dozens of streams of parts coming to the piles, and it became very difficult to arrange that the supplies moved at an even pace down all the separate streams. The supply and assembly system had grown to a stage where a radical rationalization of procedure had become necessary, or chaos would intervene.

Ford first introduced a moving assembly line for the assembly of magneto parts. He started it at five feet a minute, and the time of assembly of a magneto was reduced in the first experiment from twenty to thirteen minutes. But the line was moving far too fast. It was reduced to three feet eight inches a minute – as much as the workers could keep up with.

The assembly line for chassis was introduced in the autumn of 1913, after experiments had been made by towing a car slowly with a rope. Six men walked beside it and picked up parts for incorporating in the assembly from piles made beforehand along the track. The time of assembly went down from fourteen hours on the old system to six hours on the new. The annual output of cars leapt up to 168,220. The design of the Model T remained unchanged for nineteen years, and ultimately 15,000,000 were made. This was Ford's mass-production revolution.

The comprehensive introduction of these methods created new problems. There was a tremendous labour turnover. Workers were utterly exhausted, especially by the first crude systems. They collapsed after getting out of the factory, and fell asleep in droves in the tram-cars. Ford met this situation by suddenly doubling the rate of pay from $2·50 to $5 a day, and creating the most efficient and ruthless private police to force the workers to keep to their tasks. Thousands of men stormed the factory for jobs at the amazing wage rates. They were engaged on probation, and their habits carefully investigated. If they did not spend their wages in the approved manner, they were warned, and then fired. Ford's director of this scheme, a clergyman named Marquis, said that some men – as well they might – resented this supervision as 'humiliating'. The labour turnover went down, and Ford acquired a highly-paid long-service staff, permeated by informers backed by a formidable organization of ex-boxers, wrestlers, footballers and other strong-arm men.

The new system required a steady flow and unchanging product for its maximum performance. Big fluctuations in kind of demand upset it. Consequently Ford preferred peace to war; and in 1915 he joined a group of American pacifists in favour of trying to secure peace by negotiation, and he financed the famous voyage of the *Peace Ship*. He faced a flood of hatred and ridicule for his peace activities with almost as much indifference as he had ignored the complaints of exploited workers, dismissed collaborators and beaten competitors. When the United States entered the war, he turned over to armament manufacture, but without the genius that he believed was best deployed under conditions of peace, agreed or enforced.

Though nominally a Republican, Ford supported Woodrow Wilson, and stood as a Democratic candidate, on Wilson's platform, to keep the United States out of the war. The Republican *Chicago Tribune* subsequently announced that *Ford is an anarchist*. He prosecuted the paper for libel. He spent a week in the witness-box, while lawyers asked him whether he could 'read or write'. He confused Benedict Arnold with the English novelist, Arnold Bennett, who had recently been staying with him. When he was asked what the United States was originally, he replied: 'Land, I guess.' In 1916 he had said that 'records of old wars mean nothing to me. History is more or less bunk. It's tradition.' He now shortened this to 'History is bunk'.

After the first World War, Ford built his firm into the biggest one-man business ever known.

The first Quaker

FOX, George, (1624–1691), son of a Leicestershire weaver, Christopher Fox ('Righteous Christer'), of Drayton-in-the-Clay; and founder of the Religious Society of Friends. 'I saw', he said, 'that there was an Ocean of Darkness and Death; but an infinite Ocean of Light and Love, which flowed over the ocean of Darkness: and in that also I saw the Infinite Love of God; and I had great Openings.'

He was a priggish child ('I was taught how to walk to be kept pure'), and at nineteen went to a fair where he saw his Puritan friends drink healths and make a night of it: 'I was grieved that any, that made Profession of Religion, should offer to do so.' He therefore abandoned his job and his relations, and travelled the country questioning and reasoning with any who had a local reputation for wisdom in those first Commonwealth days of ferment. Amongst the advice he received was to get married, to join the army, to take physic, to be bled, to take tobacco and sing psalms; but 'tobacco was a thing I did not love, and psalms I was not in an Estate to sing'. Despairing of human help, he turned within himself: 'The Lord God opened to me by his invisible Power, how that *Every Man was enlightened by the Divine of Christ*; and I saw it shine through all.'

Henceforward Fox taught the doctrine of unity with the creation, not of detachment from it. 'Now was I come up in Spirit through the *flaming Sword* into the *Paradise of God*. All things were New, and all the *Creation* gave another smell unto me than before, beyond what Words can utter.' He was received, however, as a Blasphemer. Persecution grew when he gathered adherents in the Midlands and North-Western counties among the groups of Seekers there. He organized them in Silent Meetings without pre-arranged form, outward Sacraments, or consecrated buildings. All were Ministers, for 'to be bred at Oxford or Cambridge, was not sufficient to fit a man to be a Minister of Christ'. Holding that women have souls (he quoted the Magnificat) Fox gave them equality with men in his organization. Quakers practised a fierce equality both among themselves and with others; 'hat-honour' was refused to social superiors, and all were addressed indifferently as 'thou', and by their plain names.

Fox was imprisoned in 1650 at Derby, the first of eight major imprisonments. Closely questioned, he declared himself without sin, but denied that he was Christ ('Nay, we are nothing; Christ is all.') For bidding the magistrates tremble at the Name of the Lord he received the nickname Quaker, which stuck. He was offered release if he would take a commission in the Commonwealth army, mustering for Worcester fight: 'I told them I lived in the Vertue of the Life and Power, that took away the Occasion of all Wars.'

Fox lived to see Quaker Meetings set up from Danzig to Carolina, and visited most of them, surviving 'dangers and perils by sea and land'. He died in London, 'in great contentment and peace', treating death, said William Penn (q.v.) as if it were 'hardly worth notice or a mention'. Penn declared that 'his authority was inward and not outward; and that he got it and kept it by the love of God, and power of an endless life'.

The Renaissance monarch

FRANCIS I, (1494–1547), King of France, in the great era of the Renaissance, who led a life of outward magnificence, but was a vacillating ruler.

In 1519 Francis failed to obtain election as Holy Roman Emperor; he borrowed vast sums to bribe the Electors, but Charles V, his rival, with the aid of Jakob Fugger (q.v.), out-bribed him. He turned against Charles (q.v.) in angry disappointment, though at the battle of Paria, in 1525, his forces were routed, and he was taken prisoner. After the battle he sent a message to his mother saying, 'Of all things nothing is left to me but honour and life, which are safe'. His policies against Charles and the Empire were vacillating: combining against him with German and other Protestants, he veered between Catholics and Reformers, and coming down on the Catholic side lost goodwill among his allies by allowing the massacre of the Protestants in Vaudois.

His grandeur was exemplified in the famous meeting with Henry VIII of England in 1520 on the Field of the Cloth of Gold, staged – the most gorgeous of all diplomatic conferences – among emblazoned pavilions and fountains running with wine. Splendour, favourites, mistresses, occasioned expense and taxes which made him unpopular. He had no scruples; but none the less encouraged learning and patronized all manner of artists, foreign as well as French. He was patron to Rabelais and to Leonardo da Vinci.

ILLUSTRATION: Plate 4.

Embracing my Lady Poverty

FRANCIS OF ASSISI, (1182–1226), Italian saint and founder of the Franciscan Order. These words of William Blake are the best clue to him: 'How wide is the Gulf & Unpassable between Simplicity and Insipidity.'

Simplicity may be simple, but it is not easy. Francis, whose father was a rich cloth merchant (and therefore one of the freest and most travelled men of his time) and whose mother was probably French (like Boccaccio's) and whose language in youth was certainly Provençal, was brought up in the subtlest civilization of his time – the civilization which produced the poets of courtly love and the heresies of the Albigenses, the Manichaean dualists of good and evil.

Insipidity may be comforting to the world; but simplicity is disturbing – it is the little boy who stands at the Emperor's levee and remarks calmly that he has no clothes. When Francis embraced my Lady Poverty (exactly in the spirit of *l'amour courtois*) he knew what an ugly look she had; and, like many of the best saints, he was a rake reformed. A beggar asked alms in the name of God, and Francis sent him off with a curse. Then, thinking he might have come to ask for something in the name of a count or a baron, Francis left his friends and ran after him. Later, to give money seemed to him too little. On a pilgrimage to Rome, he exchanged his clothes with a beggar in the cathedral, and grovelled among the beggars for a day, hungry, with his hand stretched out. Nor was that enough: he was hungry, but he was fit, and most of the beggars ill. Later still, he was riding out of Assisi when he found himself face to face with a leper. This was the horror he most feared; he turned the bridle and galloped off, then stopped, returned, gave the man money – and dismounted, and kissed the leper's hand as though he were a priest.

Late in his career, in 1218, a General Chapter of the Franciscans was attended by Cardinal Ugolino as well as St Dominic and some of his followers. Ugolino pressed Francis to accept a more elaborate organization, and especially to profit by the example of the older rules. Francis, the layman, gave what a later age would have called a Protestant reply: 'Brothers, the Lord has called me to the way of simplicity and humility. Through them, He has shown me the truth which is for me and for those who wish to believe in me and to follow me. So don't come talking to me of the Rule of Saint Benedict, or Saint Augustine, or Saint Bernard, or any other Order, but only of that Rule which God in His mercy has been pleased to show me; and He has told me that it is His will, by this means, to make a new pact with mankind; and

He does not wish us to have any other means but this.'

He had to give in, however, and elaborate his rule; he had to agree to the omission of the clause which bade his friars to take nothing with them, and he had to watch the old simplicity give way to learning. Stories of St Francis – such as the story of his sermon to the birds (painted by Giotto) – were collected and preserved in the *Fioretti di San Francesco* – the 'Little Flowers of St Francis'.

ILLUSTRATION: Page 122.

'The wisest American'

FRANKLIN, Benjamin, (1706–1790), the archetype of the successful American and a leading figure of the American Revolution. He was almost everything: by profession a printer, by inclination inventor and scientist, he was statesman, publisher, philosopher, diplomat and man of letters. Sober, but so little overcome with solemnity, he was not allowed to write the Declaration of Independence in case he hid a joke in the middle of it.

From his beginnings in Philadelphia with one Dutch dollar and a copper shilling, Franklin quickly became a man of substance, and his success may be explained by a passion for self-improvement, in mind and in character, that is unequalled. He ruled his life. In his search for moral perfection, he made a list of the useful virtues, of which he found thirteen. 'In order to secure my credit and character as a tradesman', he wrote in his famous autobiography, 'I took care not only to be in *reality* industrious and frugal, but to avoid all appearances to the contrary.' A book of rustic apothegms carried his name to a wide circle. Two examples are: 'A countryman between two lawyers is like a fish between two cats,' 'It is hard work for an empty sack to stand upright.' All was thus raised in Franklin on a broad basis of common sense. In community life he became incessantly active: his reputation won him a place as a Pennsylvania delegate at the Albany Congress in 1754, where he presented a Plan of Union for the colonies; and he was sent to London as the colonies' unofficial representative. The repeal of the hated Stamp Act was due to the force of Franklin's testimony before the Commons.

His early love of Britain, where he had thought of settling, did not last. To Lord Howe, who commanded the British troops against the colonists in the revolutionary war, he wrote in 1776, 'Directing Pardons to be offered the Colonies, who are the very Parties injur'd, expresses indeed that opinion of our Ignorance, Baseness and Insensibility, which your uninform'd and proud Nation has long been pleased to entertain of us.' At the signing of the Declaration of Independence, his suppressed wit reasserted itself: 'Yes, we must, indeed, all hang together, or, most assuredly, we shall all hang separately,' he said. After the war, he spent most of his remaining years on an ambassadorial mission to France, revered, in the land of Rousseau and Voltaire, as the natural man incarnate.

He was indeed a perfect exemplar of the Age of Reason; humane, practical, liberty-loving, combining the optimism of a Pangloss with the industry of a Gibbon (q.v.).

ILLUSTRATION: Plate 2.

Enlightened despot

FREDERICK THE GREAT, (1712–1786) – Frederick II, King of Prussia – was the most famous and most boastful of the enlightened despots. He was accustomed to say: 'I am the first servant of my people', but like other servants refused to take orders from his master.

In youth Frederick was artistic and tender. He attempted to escape from his father's severity: he was captured, and forced to see his companion's head cut off; and was nearly executed himself. Coming to the throne in 1740, he claimed Silesia and attacked Austria: 'Ambition and a desire to make myself talked about, these were my motives'. He waged war on and off until 1763, sometimes against a coalition of Powers; and ended up with Silesia in his possession. He was reputed the finest general of his age, manoeuvring his troops with unparalleled rapidity. But others learnt the trick; and in his last war – the Potato War of 1778 – not a life was lost on either side. Napoleon said of Frederick's campaigns, in which no more than a few farms changed hands: 'Only a small ambition could be satisfied with such victories.' Frederick thought this himself and, in later life, preferred diplomatic methods. These brought a fine slice of Poland in 1772.

He ruled Prussia on the most advanced principles. He abolished torture; he also revised commercial policy and improved roads and harbours – the stage-tricks of despots in every age. He impoverished his peoples by his wars and did nothing for their political advancement. Though he deprived the nobility of the last scraps of political power, he did not emancipate or even much alleviate the condition of their serfs. He is supposed once to have allowed a decision in the royal courts of law to go against him; but this is a legend. He aspired to write French verse and invited French writers to his palace. Voltaire, the greatest of them, came, argued and quarrelled. Carlyle wrote a long-winded book, in which he presented Frederick the Great as a hero. The book is unreadable. Frederick was not a hero, but he had some distinction. Like most men with power, he was wicked; but unlike most men with power he was not ashamed to say so.

'*A whole climate of opinion*'

FREUD, Sigmund, (1856–1939), Austrian scientist and originator of psycho-analysis. Psycho-analysis is the name of a technique by which mental processes may be examined and certain mental illnesses (the neuroses) cured. It is also the name of the theory of the mind upon which such treatment is based.

Born at Freiberg in Moravia of Jewish parents, Freud was educated in Vienna. After some years of physiological research he qualified in medicine and became a clinical neurologist. In 1884 a colleague, Dr Breuer, told him of a hysterical patient who had been relieved by the process of recollecting painful memories while in a state of hypnosis; this treatment Breuer called the 'cathartic' method. A visit to the eminent Charcot in Paris deepened Freud's interest in hysteria, and a period of collaboration between Breuer and himself produced a joint book; but after the partnership was dissolved Freud abandoned hypnosis and went on to evolve the psycho-analytic technique of 'free association' – a process in which the patient relaxes his conscious attention and relates the thoughts that occur spontaneously to his mind.

Freud's chief discoveries were made between 1890 and 1900: the existence of the unconscious, and its dynamic effect on the conscious mind; the operation of repression – of a process, that is, whereby a variety of thoughts and wishes are kept from consciousness; and the existence and importance (which he only fully understood a few years later) of infantile sexuality together with the part played by it in the formation of character and neuroses. Freud was also able to explain dreams as the disguised representation of repressed wishes and regarded this as his most valuable discovery: 'insight such as this', he wrote in his *Interpretation of Dreams* (1900), 'falls to one's lot but once in a lifetime'. But it was his emphasis on the importance of sexuality in early childhood which aroused most opposition, calling forth from many of his contemporaries first incredulity and then hostility.

For some years Freud worked alone, but from about 1906 he was joined by an increasing band of collaborators; a few of these, notably Adler and Jung (q.v.), later followed independent paths after theoretical differences. In his old age Freud received world recognition. In 1938 he left Nazi-occupied Vienna, where he had lived for close on eighty years, to find a haven in London. There he died a year later.

Freud's is one of the great fertilizing minds of our time. There are few branches of human endeavour which his discoveries and speculations do not illuminate. Though mainly a psychiatrist, he made surprising discoveries in anthropology and mythology, and as a critic of civilization and art. But perhaps his greatest influence will be found to have been in morality, religion and the bringing up of children; for, in the words of W. H. Auden, the poet, 'he is no more a person now but a whole climate of opinion'.

ILLUSTRATION: Page 134.

The Movies

FRIESE-GREENE, William, (1855–1921), English pioneer of motion pictures whose talent was ill-rewarded in his life-time and whose work is still not fully appreciated.

He was the son of a Bristol iron-worker: and from his early days was interested in photography, learning much from the inventor of photography, William Henry Fox Talbot (q.v.), who lived not far away at Lacock Abbey in Wiltshire; and for a time he earned his living as a journeyman photographer. Friese-Greene wanted the pictures to move – he wanted to see the world moving, unlike the American Eadweard Muybridge, who at the same time was producing his famous still shots of animal movement. With J.A.R.Rudge, the inventor of the 'bio-phantascope' – a machine that worked on the principle of a rapid series of lantern-slides – he worked on the project for some years; and then came to London and opened a photographer's shop in Piccadilly.

His chief difficulty was to contrive a satisfactory film. In 1888 he used a strip of sensitized paper made transparent with castor oil. This saved the required negatives, but not the positives. It occurred to him to try celluloid; in June 1889, with the engineer who made his taking and projecting machines, he applied for a patent for this new sensitized film.

In October of that year, he took his first picture on this material. He asked a cousin to meet him at the Apsley Gate entrance to Hyde Park. Friese-Greene arrived early and set up his machine. When he saw the cousin coming with his dragging three-year-old son, he began to turn the camera. The next day was Sunday; while the family was asleep after luncheon, Friese-Greene went into his laboratory and started the projector. There, jerky and blurred, were his cousin and the little boy. The story is told that Friese-Greene rushed into the street crying 'I've got it', and dragged a startled policeman into the house to see the film again.

He had neglected his business and was now a poor man. His remaining years were spent in impotent struggles against the new interests in the growing film industry. He went on experimenting, especially with colour film. In a law suit Friese-Greene's patent for a motion picture camera was recognized as the first, but it was cold comfort. He died at a protest meeting organized by the Cinematograph Exhibitors Association on a trade problem. He stood up to speak and was heckled callously because he could not be heard; quite suddenly he collapsed. On his tomb in Highgate Cemetery in London there is the misleading inscription 'His genius bestowed upon humanity the boon of commercial photography'. But on him, alas, it bestowed nothing but a tardy fame.

Garden of children

FROEBEL, Friedrich Wilhelm August, (1782–1852), German educational reformer, inventor of the kindergarten.

His childhood taught him, in his own words, that 'where for trust we find distrust, where for union we find disunion, where for belief we find doubt, there but sad fruit will come to the harvest, and a burdensome and narrow life alone can follow'. Froebel's father was an earnest, severe, orthodox and narrow Lutheran pastor in the Thuringian Forest, much moved (as Froebel himself was to be) 'by the conviction of the rectitude of his actions'. His mother died when he was nine months old; his stepmother treated him, after a child of her own had been born, 'with worse than indifference' – 'by word and deed, I was made to feel an utter stranger'. Hence Froebel was a creature both of his time and his circumstances. Like many poets and painters of the era, he turned to nature, in which he found meaning, refuge, and the warm motherhood he had lacked.

For a while he was apprenticed to a forester, and after an interval at Jena University was clerk to the Office of Woods and Forests. 'My religious church life now changed', he wrote of his first forest spell, 'to a religious communion with nature, and in the last half-year I lived entirely amongst and with my plants, which drew me towards them with fascination, notwithstanding that as yet I had no sense of the inner life of the plant world.' Dreamy, excitable and receptive, in 1805 he put down that 'the more intimately we attach ourselves to Nature, the more she glows with beauty and returns us all our affection'. He found his vocation through teaching in the Model School at Frankfurt, under a headmaster who had been one of the pupils of the Swiss educational reformer, Pestalozzi. He now desired 'to educate men whose feet shall stand on God's earth, rooted fast in Nature'. The ideas and methods of Pestalozzi, whom Froebel visited and admired, seemed to him insufficient: they were not comprehensive enough, and were not enough based on the unity of man and nature. This poet of education, who wandered out to catch the sunset after his day's work, and walked under the glitter of the stars till midnight (one of his nightly walks around Göttingen was suddenly illuminated by the superb comet of 1811, on which he focused his meditations), felt that 'Joyful and unfettered work springs from the conception of all things as one whole, and forms a life and a life work in harmony with the constitution of the universe and resting firmly upon it'.

Froebel emphasized play and creativity in children and 'employment in keeping with their whole nature'. In the eighteen-thirties he worked out his notion of the right beginnings, the right educational institution for the small child. Walking with two of his disciples over the Steiger Pass on the way to the village of Blankenburg, he cudgelled his head for the right name to give the institution, suddenly shouting out to the mountains, 'Eureka! I have it! It shall be called *Kindergarten*!', and the first of the world's kindergartens was opened at Blankenburg in 1837. Kindergarten in English is a word without overtones: translate it back into 'Garden of Children', and at once Froebel's ideas are clear and his relationship to the world of Blake, Wordsworth, Coleridge, Constable, Hölderlin, etc. becomes obvious. Like plants, children are to be helped to grow according to their nature.

'A mere philanthropic din'

FRY, Elizabeth, (1780–1845), Quaker and prison reformer. The American Ambassador once said: 'I have seen the two greatest sights in London; St Paul's Cathedral and Mrs Fry reading the Bible to the prisoners of Newgate.' And Lord Byron had a verse on her:

Oh Mrs Fry! Why go to Newgate, Why
Preach to *poor* rogues? And wherefore not begin
With Carlton, or with other houses? Try
Your hand at harden'd and imperial sin.
To mend the people's an absurdity,
A jargon, a mere philanthropic din,
Unless you make their betters better: – – – FY!
I thought you had more religion, Mrs Fry.

Elizabeth Fry was born a Gurney of Earlham Hall. The Gurneys were 'wide' Quakers; the women did not wear the grey dress and bonnet, nor the men the broad-brimmed hat. Elizabeth or Betsy Gurney, the fourth of twelve children, grew up in a house of red cloaks, purple boots, ponies, hide-and-seek in the eighty cupboards, music, dancing to the 'dear, elating fiddle', play acting, republican sentiments, deism and free-thinking. To some degree Betsy was the odd one out, a neurotic child, afraid of the dark even in her teens ('I sometimes think it right to go into the garrets that are said to be haunted'), afraid of death and the sea – subject to a recurrent dream of drowning. Her periods of depression were known to the

family as 'valleys'. Of herself she wrote in 1797, 'I am a bubble, without beauty of mind or person. I am now seventeen, and if some kind and great circumstance does not happen to me, I shall have my talents devoured by moth and rust.'

The great and kind circumstance occurred in February 1798, when William Savery, a Quaker tanner from Philadelphia, arrived in Norwich on a religious visit. He found Goat's Lane Meeting so unsympathetic that he 'expected to pass the meeting in silent suffering', but at last he was enabled to speak. After spending the day with him, Elizabeth went home and wrote in her diary: 'Today I have felt that there is a God.' Soon afterwards she dreamed again of the rushing sea; but she was in a safe place and it could no longer reach her.

No immediate and drastic change was made in her life. She went to London, called on Mrs Siddons, went to the Opera. 'Mrs Twiss gave me some paint for the evening. I painted a little, I had my hair dressed, and did look pretty for me.' Soon afterwards she became a 'plain' Friend, wearing the grey costume and taking to 'thee and thou'. But it was long before she found the work of her life. She had married a London merchant, Joseph Fry, and borne him eight children, before she entered Newgate Prison for the first time in 1813.

The commission was brought to her by another visiting Quaker from America, the French *emigré* nobleman, Stephen Grellet. On a religious impulse he had gone to Newgate, and 'was astonished beyond description at the mass of woe and misery' which he saw. He begged Elizabeth Fry to do something for the women. This account of what she found there is given by a companion:

'The railing was crowded with half-naked women, struggling together for the front situations with the most boisterous violence and begging with the utmost vociferation. I felt as if I were going into a den of wild beasts. I recollect quite shuddering when the door closed upon us and we were locked in with such a herd of novel and desperate companions.'

But in 1817 the Rev. C. B. Taylor had a different story to tell:

'I was present when she read a portion of the word of God to the women. ... There they sat in respectful silence; every eye fixed upon the grave, sweet countenance of the gentle lady who was about to address them ... never till then, and never since then have I heard any one read as Elizabeth Fry read that chapter.'

An enquirer asked her method. 'I never refer to their past. We have all sinned and come short.'

Elizabeth Fry's aims in prison-reform included separating men and women, classifying prisoners, and giving them employment and instruction; and with energy she furthered this programme in England, Scotland, Ireland, in France, Germany, Switzerland, Belgium, Holland, Denmark, until her influence spread throughout the world. One of the energetic sociological saints of the nineteenth century, Elizabeth Fry said before her death, 'Since my heart was touched at seventeen years old, I believe I never have awakened from sleep, without my first waking thought being how best I might serve my Lord.'

ILLUSTRATION: Page 131.

Money, money and more money

FUGGER, Jakob, (1459–1526), German banker, the most powerful financier of his day, whose influence in European politics showed for the first time the absolute power of hard cash. The old feudal system of waging war had declined, it was the age of the freelance generals, the Condottieri, and their mercenaries, who fought for money and had to be paid. Money therefore was power, and Fugger belonged to the Renaissance, as the age of power.

Jakob Fugger was fourteen years old when he began in his family business at Augsburg, but spices, silks and woollens attracted him less than 'various undertakings of greater profit, such as bills of exchange and mines'. In 1487 he made a loan to Archduke Sigmund of Tyrol; in security, he received some highly profitable silver and copper mines. When Sigmund handed over the Tyrol to the Emperor Maximilian I, it was the beginning of the famous partnership between Jakob Fugger and the Habsburgs. Maximilian, careless of his empire, mortgaged many profitable revenues to gain the ready money he needed. Fugger was always there to act for him. He played a part, too, in the evils that led to the Reformation. Money he had lent to the Archbishop of Mainz could only be repaid by the sale of pardons. It is said that the Archbishop's pardoner was accompanied everywhere by an agent of Fugger's, who impounded all the takings.

By 1517 the house of Fugger was so powerful that its wealth could decide who should succeed to the Roman crown. The negotiations show exactly what is meant by the phrase 'The Age of Fugger'. When the Habsburg king of Spain, Charles V, decided that he wished to become king of the Romans, Francis I, the French king, let it be known that he was prepared to spend vast sums to compete for the honour. The bargaining with the electors went on for years. In the end, Fugger supported Charles; the total cost was 850,000 florins, of which Fugger provided 543,000.

Little is known of his personality. He was said to be a merry man, modest, but ready to speak his mind. None of the worries that the twentieth century associates with big business oppressed him: he told his nephews that he always slept soundly every night. Louis XII of France asked the condottiere Gian Giacomo de Trivulzio what was needed to get the dukedom of Milan. 'Money, money, and money', was the reply – and one which Jakob Fugger would have approved, as the perfect agent of the new diplomacy.

G

'No end to your nose'

GAINSBOROUGH, Thomas, (1727–1788), English portrait-painter and landscape-painter, master of grace and shimmer and evanescence. In his formative years as a journeyman painter, he loved to draw and paint the countryside around Sudbury and Ipswich as the background of portraits. The landscape of these early pictures is always fresh, young and open-aired. It makes one understand how in 1768 he came to write, 'I'm sick of portraits and wish very much to take my viol-da-gamba and walk off to some sweet village where I can paint landskips in quietness and ease.'

In 1759 Gainsborough arrived in Bath, the fashionable spa of eighteenth-century England. The lightness and elegance of his painting fitted the fashion, he exhibited in the Pump Room, and soon received commissions for portraits of aristocrat and *nouveau-riche*. He was independent, nevertheless, and did not identify himself with his sitters.

From Bath he moved to London, where in a few years he challenged the position of Sir Joshua

Reynolds. The temperaments, as well as the styles, of the two men were very different; Reynolds, the scholarly eclectic, constantly laboured to rival the old masters; Gainsborough, the spontaneous, natural-born painter, was concerned only to use his technique to the best advantage. Both artists painted Mrs Siddons the actress, and it is typical of them, that whilst Reynolds depicted her as 'The Tragic Muse', Gainsborough painted her as a fashionable lady (National Gallery, London). Reynolds signed his name with a flourish at the bottom of the picture, saying, 'Madam, my name shall go down to posterity on the hem of your garment.' Gainsborough's only recorded remark about his sitter was, 'Madam, there is no end to your nose!'

At the height of his career, showered with commissions, he longed to get away from the drudgery of his London studio. 'Damn it!' he wrote, 'I hate a dust, and kicking up a dust, and being confined in harness while others ride in the waggon, under cover, stretching their legs in the straw at ease, and gazing at green trees and blue skies without half my Taste.' In one sense Gainsborough's longing was real; but he also subscribed to a view that the landscape proper to art was an improved and imaginary one; and this he realized in what he called his 'fancy pictures'. At his death, his house in London was full of these unsold dreams. Gainsborough wrote of his portrait-painting that he was 'encouraged out of his way'; but we need not regret a departure which gave us so much exquisite elegance, grace and poignancy – the *Lady Innes* and the *View in the Mall*, in the Frick Collection in New York, the *Blue Boy* in the Huntington Collection at San Marino, or the *Perdita Robinson* in the Wallace Collection in London.

ILLUSTRATION: Page 167.

Prototype of the scientist

GALILEO GALILEI, (1564–1642), son of a Florentine merchant, founder of modern physics and the first completely modern scientist. He was born in the same year as Shakespeare, and he died in the year in which Newton was born, having a genius of similar magnitude. He discovered the laws of motion, which are the basis of physical science, reaching his conclusions by experimental analysis of the way balls drop (this is the origin of the story that he dropped balls from the top of the Leaning Tower of Pisa) and roll down inclines. By comparison with his pulse, he observed that the great lamps in the Cathedral of Pisa swung with a constant period. From this he invented the pendulum, and explained why, from his laws of motion, it has a constant period, though the size of its swing may vary. Galileo also founded the science of the strength of materials, deducing from the strength of their construction material the maximum size of animals, trees, houses and bridges. He was led to study the vacuum, and his pupil Toricelli invented the barometer.

In 1609 Galileo heard of the Dutch invention of the telescope, and made one for himself. He turned it on the heavens and found he had opened a new window on the universe. He saw the mountains on the moon, the phases of Venus, the moons of Jupiter, and the myriad stars of the Milky Way. 'All which facts were discovered and observed a few days ago by the help of a telescope devised by me, through God's grace first enlightening my mind ... I am filled with infinite gratitude to God that it has pleased Him to make me alone the first observer of such wonderful things, which have been hidden in all past centuries.' Galileo's mind was equal to the unparalleled facts he had discovered. He instantly perceived their full significance, and expounded it in the simplest, liveliest style. The phases of Venus, which had crescents like the moon, were a proof that it went round the sun. The revolution of the moons round Jupiter showed that such revolutions of small bodies round big was a celestial commonplace. Therefore there was nothing surprising in the assertion of Copernicus (q.v.) that the earth went round the sun.

At first, his magnificent celestial discoveries were well received by the Church, but as their undermining effect on old ideas became clearer, opposition grew. In 1615 the Inquisition took official notice of his work, and in 1616 banned it. He was required to surrender his erroneous opinions, and officially he did so. In private, he composed splendid accounts of his scientific discoveries, cast in the form of fascinating dialogues. The first of these, *Dialogues About the Two Great Systems of the World*, was published in 1632, and the latter, *Conversations on two New Sciences*, in 1638.

A few months after the publication of the *Dialogues*, he was again summoned by the Inquisition. He arrived in Rome, a frail man of sixty-nine. He seems always to have regarded the question of the earth's motion as purely scientific, and never understood its wider implications. He was surprised at being 'vehemently suspected of heresy', and was menaced with torture. 'Do as you please with me,' he said, according to the minutes of his last examination. He was commanded to abjure his heresies, which he did. The story that he murmured under his breath *'E pur si muove'* – 'it does move, all the same' – appears to be apocryphal.

Galileo was quite typical of the scientists of the last four centuries, who have tried to draw a sharp line between science and social affairs. He thought that he was engaged merely in a struggle with ignorance, and he had recorded his belief that 'there is no greater hatred in the whole world, than the hatred of ignorance for knowledge'.

ILLUSTRATION: Page 129.

The great soul

GANDHI, Mohandas Karamchand, (1869–1948), Indian leader known as the Mahatma or 'great-souled one'. The most remarkable man to come out of India in many generations – who was more than half saint and (it is tempting to say, defying logic as Gandhi did so often) more than half politician.

No world figure was more familiar than Gandhi in the last years of his life, the dark, gentle spider in his loin-cloth, half humorously surveying the scene or the people around him. All his life he had been a vegetarian and a total abstainer from alcohol, and he won respect as the politician who was more than a politician, and more than an artist in expediency; a man devoted to his own people, but also devoted to all of mankind. At the age of thirteen he was married to a child of the same age, but from 1906 was a Brahmacharya, a celibate within the married state for the purpose of realizing that God, who on the lips of Western politicians, tended to be only a pious word or sentiment. In early life he had admired Western ways, he had been called to the Bar in the Inner Temple in London, and had worn the top hat and frock coat of the period. In 1893 a legal case took him to South Africa, where he spent twenty-one years opposing discriminatory legislation against Indians and where he devised the methods of fighting for Indian independence by 'non-violent non-co-operation'. Among writers, he much admired Thoreau (q.v.) for his essay on Civil Disobedience.

When he returned to India, Gandhi became prominent in the Congress Party, its spokesman, and thus, he believed, the spokesman of the Indian masses. His 'non-violent' campaign against British rule led occasionally to violence and bloodshed, and when this occurred it was his custom to call off the campaign and express his contrition in public: the more 'Himalayan' the mistakes to which he confessed, the greater became his reputation for saintliness and the greater his hold on the Congress Party. He often courted arrest and imprisonment, and his well-advertised fasts were often effective in securing his release or causing the authorities to do his will in other ways. British viceroys who dealt with him could never be sure whether they were confronted with the saint or with the politician, and negotiations with Gandhi therefore tended to be extremely unsatisfactory. In 1915 he had backed 'with all his heart' a resolution of support for Great Britain in the war, but by the time of the 1939 war, though he detested the German doctrines, he had decided that only a free India could give moral support to Britain, and he advised the British to oppose Hitler by his own methods of non-violence. In 1942 he concurred in the decision of the Congress Party to use the weapon of mass obstruction of the war effort, which led to his detention, for the last time. In the final period before Indian independence was granted, his methods had their greatest triumph. A fast of his ended riots between Hindu and Muslim in Bengal, which armed force had failed to check. He exercised immense influence over the first Indian Cabinet but, perhaps to its private relief, remained outside it. His successes in moderating Hindu–Muslim antagonism earned him the hatred of extreme orthodox Hindu sects, and in 1948 this practice of non-violence came to a violent end: a Hindu bullet killed him at New Delhi; and his passing was mourned by good men throughout the world.

Death, life and gypsies

GARCIA LORCA, Federico, (1899–1936), Spanish poet and dramatist, whose poetry and personality were so powerful that long before the publication of his main works the word *lorquismo* was coined to describe them.

This son of an Andalusian farmer, who delighted

in music and folk-lore, wrote his poems and lived with a sensuality at once bold and delicate, and with a powerful spontaneity which was always under control. He preserved the freshness of what is felt rather than thought; and he could reveal the drama of the universal in the minute or the second, his imagination pouring out startling images and similes, not as ends in themselves, but to convey the idea and tone of his verse.

In the ballads of Lorca's *Romancero gitano* (1928), the most widely read book of verse in all Spanish-speaking countries, Lorca attained perfection in the type of poetry based on popular and *culto* tradition. Their external theme is the Andalusian gypsy, their form the centuries-old Spanish *romance*. Their humour and delight in life combine with fundamental topics – sex, passion, jealousy, envy, blood and death; and their plots, settings, action, even dialogue (foretaste of the coming dramatist) account for the popular success of these in fact difficult poems, where dream and reality often fade in and out of each other and where daring metaphors flow with astonishing ease. A faithless wife and her lover, lying in a field, hear 'a horizon of dogs barking far away from the river'. The cut hands of St Olalla roll on the ground 'still crossed in a tender, decapitated prayer' while the outpouring blood 'moans its mute serpent song'. The hooves of galloping horses can 'beat the plain's drum', or be 'four resonances', or 'light a fever of diamonds', or 'put four moons on the stone'. Although their superb musicality is inevitably lost in translation, we can easily appreciate such plastic metaphors as:

> White-washed façades made
> The night white and square

or this one depicting how a gypsy lad, 'bronze flesh and dreaming soul',

> Cut off the round lemons
> And kept throwing them into the water
> Till he turned it into gold.

Lorca's *Canciones*, unlike this glittering type of exuberant poetry, are short, intimate poems, of poetic essence and delicate beauty:

> Above the high pine grove
> four pigeons sweep through the air.
> Four pigeons
> fly and turn over.
> They carry
> their four wounded shadows.

> Below the pine trees
> four pigeons lie on the ground.

The so-called surrealism of Lorca's work is fully expressed in *Poeta en Nueva York* (1940) – 'A Poet in New York'. This book was the outcome of a year's stay in America and of the impact on this Spaniard of a technological civilization, 'the crude challenge of a rootless science'. There Lorca saw the king of the negroes 'imprisoned in a porter's uniform'. He denounced the crime against man and nature and saw every dawn 'moaning through endless stairs looking for fresh buds', though 'nobody is there to welcome it in his mouth'.

Lorca's masterpiece is probably the long *Llanto por Ignacio Sánchez Mejías* (1935), his lament for a bull-fighter gored and killed by a bull. One of the most impressive poems in modern literature, it opens with a sad tolling refrain like a litany:

> At five o'clock in the afternoon.
> A little boy brought the white sheet
> at five o'clock in the afternoon.
> A coffin with wheels is the bed
> at five o'clock in the afternoon.
> Already dove and leopard fight
> at five o'clock in the afternoon.
> Death laid eggs in the wound
> at five o'clock in the afternoon.

Lorca also renovated the Spanish theatre. His tragedies, farces and other plays are nothing but 'dramatic poetry', though not necessarily written in verse. He resurrected the old chorus, he bound music and poetry to action, and the reality of human passions and characters to eerie motifs. Yet the dramatist in Lorca did not live long enough to reach the maturity of the poet.

Drunk always with life, and haunted also with the idea of his own death, Lorca often seems to have glimpsed the future. In 1930 he wrote:

> Then I realized they had murdered me.
> They looked for me in tunnels, in cemeteries, in churches but they did not find me.
> Could they not find me?
> No. They could never find me.

In 1936 he was indeed murdered by the followers of Franco in the Civil War, on the outskirts of his native Granada. Many of his poems and some of his plays have been translated into English.

ILLUSTRATION: Page 169.

From Tin-Pan Alley

GERSHWIN, George, (1898–1937), American composer, the child of Russian parents in Brooklyn, N.Y. In a memorial programme a few days after his death, Arnold Schönberg (q.v.) broadcast his opinion that Gershwin shared with Johann Strauss and Offenbach a certain rare quality of genius. From a Viennese composer no praise could have been more telling. Yet in one thing Gershwin was quite unlike his European predecessors: he was the untrained professional out of tin-pan alley, who sought to increase, not his prosperity – that was considerable enough – but his musical skill.

Gershwin's talent was hedged with limitations. His early songs and musicals were excellent in their way, but when Paul Whiteman invited him to write a work for the concert hall, he needed more than a natural inventiveness. The result, likeable and muddle-headed, was the *Rhapsody in Blue* (1924), the first of a succession of symphonic works, of which each one bore the grotesque scars of Gershwin's battle for technical mastery. This slightly inept genius composed with the text-book in one hand, knowing that somehow, against the rules, his music was improving. All the while, he was turning out witty musicals, culminating in the political satire *Of Thee I sing* (1931). Friends and admirers made a joke of Gershwin's efforts to improve his technique. 'It cannot be necessary', they said, thinking of his income. Among his works are *An American in Paris* (1928) and *Porgy and Bess* (1935). There was an engaging egotism about Gershwin. 'George,' he was asked by Oscar Levant, 'if you had to do it again, would you fall in love with yourself again?' But Gershwin was a humble artist in a section of the musical world which encourages technical incompetence and banal invention.

History in the balance

GIBBON, Edward, (1737–1794), English historian, whose *Decline and Fall of the Roman Empire*, though it may have been superseded academically, will stand for ever as the noble monument of a man and an age. The age was the eighteenth century, the time of civilized scepticism. It was the temper of the time to doubt, and to prefer Reason; and to the study of the Roman Empire in its dog-days, Gibbon brought scholarship, urbanity, wit.

From his childhood he read incessantly; perhaps far too well for the University of Oxford, which was a great disappointment to him. He was converted for a while to Roman Catholicism, and was sent by an angry father to Switzerland. It was there that he fell in love with Mlle Suzanne Curchod; so intense was his passion that he would hold up travellers on the roads near Lausanne, and only let them go after they had admitted Mlle Curchod's superiority. His father forbade their marriage, a blow commemorated by Gibbon in one of the falsest notes of English letters: 'I sighed as a lover, I obeyed as a son.' He never married.

He was a long time in deciding what would be his life's work: a visit to Rome crystallized the yearnings of a latent historical sense, a passion for antiquity, and his extensive, often curious learning. The *Decline and Fall* was not a popular success: but his genius was immediately recognized – although never, alas, by the Duke of Gloucester, who received the third volume with the genial words: 'Another damn'd thick, square book! Always scribble, scribble, scribble! Eh, Mr Gibbon?'

Gibbon's view of history is as balanced as his prose: each is at times excessive. His tendency was to detract from any person or event that might possibly support revealed religion: 'at the sound of his trumpets the walls of this city [Angoulême] imitated the example of Jericho, and instantly fell to the ground: a splendid miracle which may be reduced to the supposition that some clerical engineers had secretly undermined the foundations of the rampart'. There is also a certain salacity in his narrative: 'Nor does his humanity ever slumber,' said Porson of Gibbon, 'unless when women are ravished or the Christians persecuted.'

He led a severe, often lonely life: and he has left an affecting memoir of it, an incomplete work that is, in its way, as brilliant as the history. To the study of history he brought the colour of personality and the fire of prejudice. In the present swiftness of newspaper-headline history, a time of terse prose and capsuled ideas, it is a tonic to delve into Gibbon's stately periods, to find in his dispassionate ethos a needed tranquillity, and to observe, through the quizzical glance of the eighteenth century, how another empire behaved in decline.

ILLUSTRATION: Plate 5.

The little boy and the clergyman

GIDE, André, (1869–1951). This French writer describes in his very frank autobiography, *Si le grain ne meurt,* how as a child he was walking in the street when suddenly, out of the blue, a bright canary flew towards him and perched on his shoulder. When this happened on another occasion it seemed prophetic, not only of his nature as an artist – 'I am not like the others' – but of a *constante fugacité* which was to dominate his ideas. Gide described himself as 'a little boy who amuses himself, combined with a protestant clergyman who bores him'. Brought up in strict and wealthy surroundings, sunk in torpor, gnawed by guilt, physically delicate, he suddenly discovered the joy of a sensuous paganism. The little boy amused himself, the protestant clergyman protested. 'Everything I find pleasant is also antagonistic to me', he wrote: he had 'a passion for teaching', yet nothing in his life was constant, so in his curriculum there could be no fixed laws.

No sooner did Gide discover his true nature in the North Africa he was to love and celebrate so long – and here is the famous Gidean irony and paradox, amounting to perversity – than he immediately entered a platonic marriage with his extremely religious cousin. A chaste ideal love, a preoccupation with God (to be seen in the figure of Alissa in *La Porte Etroite*), always runs parallel with the adolescent rebelliousness and sensuality of *Les Nourritures Terrestres* (in which he so wonderfully enjoys the sensuous delights of North Africa) or *l'Immoraliste.* We know now that his wife suffered much from his habits of confessing – or rather teaching – his emotional attitudes, as in the defence of homosexuality contained in *Corydon.*

Gide is protean: he turns to the moment rather than duration, to the future, not the past. He believes in reaching beyond, in hedonistic detachment, sincerity and curiosity. He himself claims not to have written a real novel until in late middle age he produced *Les Faux-Monnayeurs* (The Coiners) – a masterpiece so self-conscious that it is about a novelist trying to write a novel, further supported by Gide's journal of how he wrote it. Although Gide was bitterly disappointed in his later association with communism, his work grew mellower, more rationalist, from this point to the end of his long life.

ILLUSTRATION: Page 133.

A French Bluebeard

GILLES DE RAIS, (1404–1440), nobleman, Marshal of France, and companion of Joan of Arc, a Bluebeard, remembered as one of the most monstrous characters of mankind.

He inherited estates of great wealth in his native Brittany and added to these in 1420 by marrying the heiress, Katharine of Thouars, who left him in due time. In his early twenties he raised his own companies of soldiers for the war against the English and fought by the side of Joan of Arc. With Joan he entered Orleans in triumph, and for his part in the victories over England he was created Marshal of France by Charles VII. Gilles recognized that Joan was moved by 'an incomprehensible force', and there is no doubt her trial and execution had a profound effect upon him.

After the war, he lived extravagantly, moving in kingly state between his many castles. 'I was born', he declared, 'under such a star that no one in the world has ever done, or ever can do again, the things which I have done.' He entertained, he patronized the arts, and was himself a skilled illuminator and binder of books.

Vastly rich as he was, he found himself in difficulties over money, and tried to mend matters by alchemy and necromancy, surrounding himself with astrologers, unfrocked priests, magicians and sinister charlatans of every kind. He turned from Black Mass and blasphemy to far viler obliquities. His servants bought or kidnapped children, usually boys, on whom he practised the grossest abominations before and after killing them. The number of his victims was at least 140. For several years he was unsuspected in his own society, although the murkiest rumours floated among the peasants. At last in 1440 he was brought before the Ecclesiastical Court at Nantes on charges of sacrilege. To these were soon added charges of heresy and murder. There may have been certain legal irregularities in the trial, as well as political machinations behind it, but there is no question that Gilles de Rais was guilty. He confessed to his crimes as an act of expiation, which absolved him from heresy; and as he recited his foul misdeeds, the judges are said to have turned pale and sick, and ordered the crucifix behind them to be veiled for the sake of decency. Gilles told them: 'Nothing and no one suggested these crimes. It was my imagination alone that led me to them. I conceived them, from my thoughts, for my daily pleasures. I had no other purpose than to gratify my desires.'

He was hanged and his body burnt in Nantes. Where the pyre had been, an expiatory monument of the Virgin was erected.

Artist with brush and lute

GIORGIONE, (c. 1478–1510), Venetian painter, who gave his pictures a vibrant ecstasy unknown in art before or since.

Giorgione de Castelfranco's life was short and lyrical. Brought up in Venice, 'he displayed very amorous leanings', according to Vasari, the historian of Italian painting, 'and was exceedingly fond of the lute, playing and singing so divinely that he was frequently invited to musical gatherings and meetings of noble persons.'

His greatest pictures (out of the few which survive) are *The Fête Champêtre*, the *Sleeping Venus* and *The Tempest*; each of which entices one into a timeless poetic world, where paint, colour, light at their perfect, momentary climax, flood into one's being, and round one's being, like music. Giorgione's 'music' is that kind which belongs to youth, fountains, gardens, love, and the fulfilment of love. His master was Giovanni Bellini (q.v.), who had felt a tender link between man and his natural environment. But Bellini's religious concern held him back, whereas Giorgione painted man and nature as though they were of a piece, harmonizing with each other in a felicity of paganism. In *The Tempest*, the two unrelated, mysterious figures of the soldier and the naked gypsy exist in serenity and stillness, although sky and landscape are pregnant with storm. Everything is hushed. Is *The Tempest* a picture of two figures in a landscape? Or of a landscape containing two figures – just as it contains trees, earth, air, colour, light?

Giorgione's summer-softness without tiredness or weakness, and his absorption in nature, made him a puzzle to his contemporaries, but they never doubted his brilliance. They called him Giorgione (great George) for his powers of mind. Humbly born, gentle and good-mannered, Giorgione loved the effect of brightness held in the air.

He died young, like Raphael and Keats. This is how his death came, according to Vasari: 'He fell in love with a lady, so that they became greatly enamoured of each other. However ... she caught the plague, and Giorgione, being unaware of this, associated with her as usual, and died soon after.'

When he died, Titian, who was of about the same age, finished a number of his pictures, including the *Sleeping Venus*.

ILLUSTRATION: Page 176.

The artist of love

GIOTTO DI BONDONE, (c. 1267–1337). Italian artist recognized as the founder of painting in Italy, as if by himself he had made an immense visual leap – as if, in fact, he achieved in a single life what is usually accomplished step by step by generation upon generation of artists.

Whether this view is strictly tenable or not, there is no doubting Giotto's revolutionary influence. On his tomb in the cathedral at Florence is a fifteenth-century epitaph by Poliziano: 'I am he by whose undertaking the dead art of painting was restored to life ... Nature lacked what was lacking in my art. To no other was it given to paint better or more ... But what need is there for words? I am Giotto: my name alone tells more than a long poem.'

Lorenzo Ghiberti, the Florentine sculptor, maintained that Giotto put the 'crudity' of the Byzantines behind him, and that in art he had created (in those words which are now a familiar bugbear of the arts) 'truth to nature'. Byzantine art upon wooden panels or in mosaic was stiff, grave, immobile, hieratic, superhuman in its grandeur. In the frescoes in the Arena Chapel at Padua Giotto painted the story of the Virgin and her son in coloured movement altogether of an earthier and more human kind. The gestures are those of something which happens, of a convincing story within the experience of men. So, too, in the earlier scenes of the life of St Francis (q.v.) which he painted in the Upper Church at Assisi. Giotto's landscape, his buildings, his accessories to action are all simple, but there Giotto's figures are – poised upon the floor of this ordinary world, beings in that terrestrial setting which all of us are surrounded by. He constructs his scenes from our environment as the poet Dante, his coeval in Florence, puts that environment into his similes.

Stories are told of Giotto's youth – for example

that the painter Cimabue saw him as a little Tuscan shepherd boy drawing sheep on a stone, and so took him as a pupil. He grew to be a favourite with everyone, partly for his wit and humour, yet the essence of his painting is love. Tender and tough, Giotto is the artist of love as his favourite St Francis is the saint, and Dante, the poet, of love.

The Grand Old Man

GLADSTONE, William Ewart, (1809–1898), four times Prime Minister of England and 'Grand Old Man' of the Liberal party. 'Gladstone will soon have it all his own way,' wrote Palmerston of his then Chancellor of the Exchequer, 'and, whenever he gets my place, we shall have strange doings.' In fact, what the country got in the years of Gladstone's first and most successful Ministry (1868–1874) was one of the two or three greatest reforming administrations in British history.

'At last, my friends,' Gladstone declared to the electors when he became Liberal leader, 'I am come among you, and I am come unmuzzled.' Largely by the votes of the newly enfranchised town labourers, he was returned to office with an ambitious programme for extending and liberalizing the semi-democratic institutions of the age. A system of national primary education was started, intended to make Parliament's new masters worthy of their votes. The Ballot Act was passed. The Civil Service was opened by competitive examination to all talents. Entry to the universities was made possible for men of all creeds (Nonconformists and Catholics had hitherto been banned). The Army was reformed, and the purchase of commissions abolished. Ireland, as Gladstone had already forecast, it was his mission to pacify; and his first administration took two steps towards doing so: they disestablished the Irish Church, and carried out a measure of Land Reform, directed against absentee and rack-renting landowners. Altogether, theirs was an impressive record of radical legislation; it is no wonder that in aristocratic drawing-rooms Gladstone was denounced as 'the people's William'.

A singular feature of Gladstone's career is that the older he grew the more radical he became. When he first entered the House of Commons in the Reformed Parliament of 1832, he was a Tory and a follower of Peel. As the son of a rich Liverpool merchant, with wide interests in the West Indies, he was a natural free-trader, and in sympathy with the Anti-Corn Law League. On the splitting of the Tory party, after Peel had decided that the protection enjoyed by English landowners must go, and the Corn Laws be abolished, Gladstone willingly went with his leader into opposition. For him there followed a long period of earnest soul-searching before he elected to join the Whigs in 1859. It was then that he was appointed Chancellor of the Exchequer, a post he held for six years, and in which his great gifts as an administrator, and as an imaginative master of facts and figures, made him an unqualified success. In these years, too, he established beyond doubt his position as the country's next Liberal Prime Minister.

The end of his first Ministry in 1874 probably marks the apogee of Gladstone's political achievement. His second Government (1880–1885), which followed on Disraeli's, was much less happy. To its credit is the passage of the Third Reform Bill, enfranchising agricultural labourers, but it came to some grief in colonial and imperial matters.

In 1886, during his brief third Ministry, he concluded that all must be staked on a drastic proposal for Home Rule. Had he achieved his purpose, Anglo-Irish relations might have been saved much misery, but his decision split his party. Joseph Chamberlain and the Liberal Unionists deserted him; his administration fell, and though he became Prime Minister for the fourth time in 1892 at the age of eighty-three, his government was weak and divided, wholly dependent on the Irish vote. Unable to make headway, he retired in 1894, disgusted with his colleagues, whom he described as the 'blubbering Cabinet'. He died in 1898 at the age of eighty-nine.

He was a remarkable combination of qualities. He was a man of the highest principle, who was notoriously devious and inscrutable in his political dealings with colleagues. He was both zealot and practical man, Oxonian High Churchman, classical scholar (he wrote *On translating Homer*), and popular demagogue. To his genius it fell to unite the interests of the commercial middle classes with those of the industrial working man, and to guide with skill the destinies of Victorian Britain at a time when the rule of benevolent oligarchs was giving way to the promptings of mass democracy.

ILLUSTRATION: Page 171.

Sage of Weimar

GOETHE, Johann Wolfgang von, (1749–1832), was the most gifted of all German writers and the most varied, and in his long and fertile life he completely transformed art and letters in his country.

Goethe is too vast a subject to be described easily. Apart from his poetry, plays, essays and novels, which in themselves have an unusually large auto-biographical content and were often inspired by love affairs, he wrote an account of his youth, *Dichtung und Wahrheit* (Poetry and Truth – it is one of the best pictures of a young man's life ever made), and observations on travel such as the *Italienische Reise*. He also left a voluminous correspondence. And in later years his protégé, Eckermann, served as a Boswell and noted down impressions of his table-talk, his habits and even the clothes he wore from day to day. Goethe's life was so favoured by circumstance that it is hard to think how he could have been more fortunate. As a young man he had superb health and was as handsome as Apollo. The versatility of his character astonished all who met him. He was capable of writing magnificently in a whole range of different styles, he would act in amateur theatricals, travel in disguise, drink long and deep (taking care to avoid coffee, however, which he thought a danger to health) and he was always in love. He was the poet of a fortunate age for Germany, that of the great musicians and of the Emperor Joseph II, when every little baroque court modelled itself on Versailles and the Germans reached the apex of humanism and toleration.

Goethe was born to comfort. His parents were prosperous and cultivated burghers in Frankfurt-am-Main. He pursued his education at Leipzig and subsequently at Strasbourg, but though he took a degree he was never bound down to the hack-work which was later so to cripple Schiller, and had leisure to cultivate the humanist temper of his age. Apart from poetry and drama, he was enthusiastic about the new developments of science, and his scientific studies were considerable, though amateur. In literature this was known as the 'Storm and Stress' (*Sturm und Drang*) period. Goethe was soon in full reaction against the French classical drama and its laws about the unities; Racine was long dead and the greatest star was Voltaire. Goethe's best 'Storm and Stress' drama was *Götz von Berlichingen* (1773). But what brought him immediate fame was his melancholy novel of a young man who commits suicide in the frustrations of love and ambition – *Werthers Leiden* (The Sorrows of Werther), 1774. *Werther* was read throughout Germany (and the rest of Europe), and suicides were attributed to its influence – to Goethe's great sorrow and irritation.

The turning-point in Goethe's life came the following year when he accepted the invitation of the young Duke of Saxe-Weimar to visit the Duke's tiny principality. Eighteenth-century Weimar had only a handful of inhabitants, but Goethe, supported in all things by the liberality of his patron, who hero-worshipped him, and with the assistance of the distinguished men that he brought there, such as Herder and Schiller, was able to turn it into 'the German Athens'. His arrival was the excuse for a riot of carnivals, operas, plays and masques in which the whole Court joined – a spectacle not seen in Europe since the Italian Renaissance. Goethe gives us an idyllic picture of this eighteenth-century world of courtiers, actresses and *fêtes champêtres*, in his novel *Wilhelm Meister*, the first seven books of which appeared in his early years at Weimar. In 1782 the poet was ennobled and made President of the Ducal Kammer. But in 1786 he took leave of absence for two years and visited Italy. He described some of his experiences there in the *Italienische Reise*. Italy confirmed Goethe in a radical change of outlook – he had already finished with the romantic 'Storm and Stress' period, outstripping his admirers, and was now looking to the harmonies of the classical world. The change was made apparent in his dramas of the time: the poetical version of *Iphigenie auf Tauris* (1876), *Egmont* (1786) and *Tasso* (1789). *Iphigenie* has a poetic sensibility that was entirely new in Europe. Racine had tackled the same subject; but whereas Racine saw Greece through Roman eyes, Goethe's Greece, though harmonious and Apollonian on the surface, had strange undertones that were thoroughly German yet echoed the sense of mystery to be found in early Athenian dramatists. A well-known instance is the *Parzenlied* (Song of the Fates); the Gods remain –

> But they, they remain
> In eternal feast
> At golden tables.
> They stride from crest
> To crest of mountains:
> From the deepest abysses
> Steams up the breath
> Of the stifled Titans,
> Like the smoke of a sacrifice,
> In a light cloud.

Goethe's new development coincided with the French Revolution, but no poet ever was less impressed by political events. He was irked by the unreasonable clamour of the mob, which threatened that true progress which he thought of as essentially personal; for Goethe the Revolutionaries, like the Lutherans long before them, were disturbers of peaceful development. All Goethe's sympathies were on the side of the established authority; in these troubled years he wrote *The Metamorphoses of Plants* and the *Essays on Optics*. In 1792 he dutifully followed his Duke to the French war, but found soldiering unbearably tedious. During the bombardment of Verdun he could not endure the roar of the cannon – he had always been sensitive to loud and unpleasant noises – and as he noted: 'We [*i.e.* Goethe and Prince Reuss] walked up and down behind some vineyard walls, protected by them from the cannon balls. After talking about sundry matters ... the prince asked me what I was occupied with at present and was much surprised when, instead of speaking of tragedies and novels excited by the phenomenon of today, I began to speak with great admiration of the doctrine of colours.' During the Napoleonic years he was also busy – in his characteristically 'desultory' way – with *Faust*. He completed the first part in 1801 and published it in 1806. He planned the second part in 1798, after the completion of *Hermann und Dorothea* (1797), but he put the finishing touches to it only in the year before he died. Meanwhile Goethe proved his gifts as a theatrical manager and, especially through his close collaboration with Schiller, founded the modern German theatre.

Goethe's domestic life was eccentric. He was a man of many loves, some of which developed into passionate affairs. Women outstanding in his life and poetry were Frederika of Drusenheim, whom he had known in his Strasbourg days, and Anna Elizabeth Schönemann (the 'Lili' of the Autobiography), Frau von Stein, Corona Schröter the actress, and Minna von Herzlieb, who inspired the *Wahlverwandtschaften* (Elective Affinities). But in 1788 Goethe began living with Christiane Vulpius, a poor girl who was considered much beneath him, though to his love for her we owe among other things his *Roman Elegies*. She bore him a son in 1789 to whom the Duke stood godfather, and Goethe's mother accepted her as a daughter, yet Goethe could not make up his mind to marry her until eighteen years afterwards, in 1806. Indecision, such as he ascribed to Wilhelm Meister, was one of his notable characteristics. Christiane died in 1816,

but she lost her looks well before then, and her enemies said she drank.

ILLUSTRATION: Page 174.

'My subject was life'

GOGOL, Nicolai Vassilyevich, (1809–1852), Russian novelist, short-story writer and playwright: 'My subject has always been the same: my subject was life and nothing else,' he wrote in *An Author's Confession* (1847).

Born in the Ukrainian township of Sorochintsy, he spent his childhood on his father's small estate. His father was the author of some Ukrainian comedies, performed at the rich mansion of a distant relative, and there Gogol had his first introduction into the world of art: there he found a large library, a picture-gallery and a theatre. But his father's position as one of the numerous hangers-on of his wealthy relative both impressed and depressed him so much that he never felt comfortable in the presence of highly placed dignitaries. Coupled with the influence his mother's deep religious feelings had on him, this accounts for a great many of his fanatically held beliefs which drove him into mysticism and the defence of autocracy and which finally found expression in his *Selected Passages from Correspondence with my Friends* (1846), the book which provoked Belinsky (q.v.) to write him his famous open letter.

Gogol's first publication was *Hans Kuechelgarten*, a romantic poem he had written at school, which appeared in 1828, soon after he had arrived in Petersburg (1828). It failed; and the failure sent him scuttling out of Russia to Lübeck. He returned almost immediately to Petersburg, where he obtained a miserably paid job in the Civil Service, gave private lessons in rich houses, attended a course of painting at the Academy of Fine Arts, tried unsuccessfully to become an actor, and in between managed to write two volumes of Ukrainian tales of unsurpassed imaginative power, published under the title of *Evenings in the Hamlet of Dikanka* (1831–1832). These established him as a writer of considerable talent. Unsatisfied with his success, Gogol began writing a history of his native Ukraine and obtained a post as lecturer in medieval history at Petersburg University, a career which came to an ignominious end after a year. He went back to literature, he wrote two more volumes of short stories, *Arabesques* and *Mirgorod* (the latter including his short historical novel *Taras Bulba*), and his three plays, *The Government Inspector, Marriage* and *The Gamblers*. 'In *The Government Inspector*', he said in *An Author's Confession*, 'I decided to collect everything that was evil in Russia, all the injustices committed in places where justice is most of all expected of man – and laugh it all off.' The comedy was first performed in Petersburg on 19 April 1836, arousing not only laughter but also the anger of many influential people. Gogol was only twenty-six, he was recognized as the greatest living author in Russia; but the attacks which followed that most delicious of comedies made him leave Russia; and it was in Rome that he wrote the first volume of his famous novel *Dead Souls* and his most moving short story *The Overcoat* (1842).

The last ten years of his life were years of bitter frustration. He went on a pilgrimage to Palestine in the hope that it might restore his lost powers as a creative artist. On his return to Russia, he settled in Moscow, attempted to finish *Dead Souls*, and failed; he burnt the second volume of *Dead Souls* shortly before his death in 1852.

aristocracy and the newly emerging class of the Russian bourgeoisie. It was naturally the bourgeoisie that Goncharov defended. Next he spent more than ten years writing his second, most profound and most celebrated novel *Oblomov*, in which he again drew a highly idealistic portrait of a business man in the character of Stolz, the friend who comes to the rescue of the gentlemanly Oblomov, but never succeeds in reforming him. His novel lacks Dostoyevsky's violence, Turgenev's brilliance and compactness and Tolstoy's monumental force, but in it he achieved something none of these great writers was able to do: he transformed the humdrum life of his totally insignificant hero into a great human tragedy. He made his lazy, supine, will-less Oblomov a universal human type only to be compared with the great human types created by Gogol (q.v.) in *Dead Souls*, and such gigantic figures of world literature as Don Quixote and Falstaff.

He was a self-centred and lonely man. When *Oblomov* was published, he was already showing a tendency to paranoia which led him into a violent quarrel with Turgenev (q.v.), whom he accused of stealing his plots.

ILLUSTRATION: Page 182.

Oblomov's creator

GONCHAROV, Ivan Alexandrovich, (1812–1891). 'Depict a thief, a prostitute, a defrauded fool, but don't forget that they, too, are human beings,' declared this Russian in his novel, *Oblomov*, which he published in 1859.

Goncharov's father was a well-to-do grain merchant of the small town of Simbirsk. After his father's death, he was sent to Moscow to be trained for business at the Moscow School of Commerce, but he left, became a student of the philological faculty of Moscow university, and entered the Russian Civil Service in the Ministry of Finance. Then for three years – the happiest years of his life – he served as secretary to a Russian vice-admiral in command of an expedition around the world, a description of which he published in *Frigate Pallas* (1858). Finally, he was appointed censor and later editor of the official journal of the Ministry of the Interior.

His first novel, *An Ordinary Story* (1847), dealt with the conflict between the decaying class of landed

Poet of Gongorism

GÓNGORA Y ARGOTE, Luis de, (1561–1627), Spanish poet whose poems (suppressed in the year he died by the Inquisition) were celebrated for a fantastic, extravagant, baroque use of language.

Though he took orders, Góngora was more poet than cleric, with a youthful zeal for cards and the demi-monde at variance with that grave, aloof, mature face so splendidly recorded by Velasquez. When he was a young prebendary of Cordova Cathedral, he was reprimanded for attending church too seldom and bull-fights too often, for gossiping, keeping company with actors, talking in service and writing profane poetry – all a counterpart to paying 'a thousand pensions to melancholy'. Góngora continued to write, reprimand or no, and his poetry went around in manuscript – love poetry, court poetry, satire, culminating in the *Fable of Polyphemus and Galatea* and the unfinished *Solitudes*, both of which are crusted and packed with his verbal magnificence, wit and daring, his brilliance of metaphor, his topsy-turvying of normal verbal and syntactical usage. A sonnet on a rose, cleverly translated by Sir Richard Fanshawe, will give a notion of his rich, sensuous artificiality, still short of the extreme:

Blown in the morning, thou shalt fade ere noon;
What boots a life which in such haste forsakes thee?
Thou'rt wondrous frolic, being to die so soon,
And passing proud a little colour makes thee.
If thee thy brittle beauty so deceives,
Know then the thing that swells thee is thy bane;
For the same beauty doth, in bloody leaves,
The sentence of thy early death contain.
Some clown's coarse lungs will poison thy sweet flower,
If by the careless plough thou shalt be torn;
And many Herods lie in wait each hour
To murder thee as soon as thou art born –
Nay, force thy bud to blow – their tyrant breath
Anticipating life, to hasten death.

The *Solitudes* maintain such virtuosity with more strength and surprise, as when Góngora writes of the ships of Covetousness reaching the Indies

To penetrate the aromatic lawn,
That builds both pyre and nest
For the Arabian bird, whose outstretched wing
Uncurves a flying rainbow in the sky,

or of Magellan's ship discovering 'the elusive hinge of silver fine' – the straits which unite the Pacific and the Atlantic. Góngora was in some ways akin to his English contemporary John Donne (q.v.), but he is a more indulgent poet in his verbal play, more extravagant, in the manner of Crashaw, his nearest equivalent in English. Gongorism was long a word of reproach, but Góngora's poems, like Donne's, were rediscovered and newly admired in our century.

Bitter and tender

GORKY, Maxim, (1868–1936), pseudonym of Alexey Maximovich Peshkov, Russian novelist. 'The aim of literature', wrote Gorky in his story *The Reader* (1898), 'is to help man to understand himself, to strengthen his faith in himself and develop his striving for truth, to fight vulgarity in people, to learn to find goodness in them, arouse their feelings of shame, anger and courage, and do everything possible to make them noble and strong so that their lives should be inspired by the holy spirit of beauty.'

His pseudonym of 'Gorky', *i.e.* 'bitter', with which he signed his first published story *Makar Chudra* (1892), epitomizes his own attitude towards the appalling conditions of his early life which he described so magnificently in *Childhood* (1913), *Apprenticeship* (1916), and *My Universities* (1923). After seeing his mother kicked in the breast and after attacking his stepfather with a bread knife, Gorky wrote in *My Childhood* that 'Often, recording such atrocious memories of our bestial Russian life, I wonder whether there is any point in recalling them. And, with revived assurance, I tell myself, "The point is that this continues to be the actual, loathsome fact to this very day, that this fact must be traced back to its source and uprooted from our memories, from the souls of our people, from our confined and squalid lives."'

He was born in Nizhny-Novgorod (now renamed Gorky in his honour). His father, a cabinet-maker, died when he was four and his mother three years later. It was his grandmother who awakened in him his love for literary expression by her rich store of folk tales and who was most of all responsible for his remarkable prose style. Unlike Chekhov (q.v.), he took an active part in the Russian revolutionary movement, was arrested and imprisoned several times and spent much of his life abroad, mostly for health reasons (he suffered from tuberculosis) at Capri.

One of the most important themes in all his writings is man's conflict with his environment. His fight against social injustice is first conducted in his stories and novels by highly idealized characters who are symbols personified rather than creatures of flesh and blood. In *Mother* (1906) his protest against economic enslavement became more concrete in the portraits of the revolutionary leaders, most of which were taken from life. In his last novels, for instance, in *The Artomonovs* (1906), he still argues emotionally against capitalism. His sense of social injustice and the dignity of man is so acute that he presents the life the workers were compelled to live under private enterprise in Russia with brutal realism; but then he reacts so overwhelmingly against that kind of existence that he is often blind to his characters as true men and women: 'I always regarded as real heroes only those men who loved work and who knew how to work, men whose only aim in life was to release the creative forces of humanity for the adornment of the earth and to make life worthy of man.'

Gorky's plays mainly have to do with social and political problems and the exposure of 'middle-class vulgarity'. He knew his own shortcomings as a dramatist. 'I wrote about twenty plays,' he declared in his essay *On the Drama* (1933), 'and all of them are more or less weakly connected scenes, in which the continuity of the plot is never sustained and the characters are colourless, unsuccessful and not properly worked out.' His plays, though, have always been popular in Russia, and one of them at least, *The Lower Depths* (1904), has been popular abroad.

ILLUSTRATION: Page 170.

Light out of darkness

GOYA Y LUCIENTES, Francisco José de, (1746–1828), painter to the Spanish king, compassionate and satirical engraver of the sorrows, follies, cruelties and superstitions of his age, and one of the most powerful and possessed image-makers of European art.

'I have had three masters,' wrote Goya, 'Velasquez, Rembrandt, and Nature.' Rembrandt taught him to feel in pigment and to compose, Velasquez and nature taught him to see; but Goya saw with his inward as well as his outward eye, looking into a twisted and tortured canyon underneath man's superficial normality. We know only the broad facts of his life. Goya, vigorous, robust, passionate, walking on a line between health and psychosis, was the child of a poor home. He studied in Madrid, then in Rome, lived wildly, and returned to Madrid in his late twenties, showing for a time a delightful, fresh, gay-coloured lyricism in designs for tapestry.

We poets in our youth begin in gladness
But thereof comes in the end despondency and madness.

These early paintings recall the best and airiest of Gainsborough's work; but there soon spills into Goya's art a gall of personality and experience. From 1790 Goya worked on the *Caprichos*, his first collection of satirical etchings, in which he pilloried dandyism and wantonness, superstition, ignorance, servile courtiers, corrupt women, hypocritical priests. These were at first withdrawn at the Inquisition's understandable displeasure, but the king had accepted a set and Goya was protected. Goya wrote that he had chosen the follies of civilized society which were 'most apt to provide an occasion for ridicule and at the same time to exercise his imagination'. He knew both his business and his danger, writing that

'the sleep of reason begets monsters', whereas 'Imagination united with reason is the Mother of the arts and the source of their wonders'. In 1800 Goya painted his frank and brutal *Family of Charles IV* (in the Prado, in Madrid), which Gautier described as the representation of 'a grocer's family who have won the big lottery prize'. Goya appears to have been one of the lovers of the Duchess of Alba whom he painted several times. Unfaithful to him, she died in 1802; and seems to have increased Goya's bitterness and his sense of the follies of man. The French invasion of Spain in 1808, instead of sweeping away corruption, instructed Goya in all the shades, degrees and depths of man's cruelty to man; and the terrifying and compassionate result was that set of etchings, *The Disasters of War*, which are perhaps the most powerful protest ever made against war's cruelty, unreason and futility. Goya's titles emphasize the horror of his designs by their brevity and irony – the brutality and torture, '*What bravery, on the dead*', '*What more can they do to him?*'; the ruthless executions – '*Hard Journey*', '*Nothing to be done*'; the stripping of dead bodies, '*So much profit.*' In literature something of a parallel for *The Disasters of War* may be found in Ambrose Bierce's stories of the American Civil War.

Self-portraits painted at one date and another through his life are a comment on Goya's pilgrimage. Cut off all the more by deafness, he lived from 1819 to 1823 at the Quinta del Sordo, the 'house of the deaf man', painting round the walls the terrible quintessence and climax of his nightmare, though it would be too simple and too evasive to pretend that these murky pictures, such as the *Saturn Devouring His Children* (in the Prado), are simply monsters begotten at last by Goya's sleep of reason. Goya's savage indignation also begat them. The Prado, which houses the fullest collection of Goya's work, contains other paintings from the Quinta del Sordo, including *The Pilgrimage of San Isidoro*, in which it seems that all the beggars from all of Goya's pictures have gathered into one foul-smelling heap, and *The Witches' Sabbath*, a crouching huddle of witches intent upon one black crone, every gesture, every turn of the head, the yellow faces, the brown and black rags, expressing degradation and disgust. In his extreme old age, still drawing and painting, Goya moved outside Spain, to Bordeaux, where he died. One of his last engravings, for all the extreme thrust of his art, he called *Lux ex tenebris*, 'Light out of Darkness': owls, ravens and priests hurry in fear from a dazzling stream of light.

GUSTAVE COURBET (1819–1877).

GAINSBOROUGH (1727–1788) self-portrait with his wife and child.

JAMES ENSOR (1860–1949). Self-portrait (on the plate), detail from *Les Cuisiniers Dangereux*, 1891.

GARCIA LORCA (1899–1936) by Gregorio Prieto.

MAXIM GORKY (1868–1936).

GLADSTONE (1809–1898) taken about 1859.

171

GUSTAVUS ADOLPHUS (1594–1632) by an unknown painter.

HENRY VIII (1491–1547). Attributed to Hans Holbein the Younger.

173

GIORGIONE (c. 1478–1510) self-portrait.

VICTOR HUGO (1802–1885) about the age of thirty-five, by an unknown painter.

177

THOMAS HOBBES (1588–1679) by J. M. Wright.

DAVID HUME (1711–1776) by Allan Ramsay.

ALEXANDER VON HUMBOLDT (1769–1859) by F. G. Weitsch, painted in 1806.

T. H. HUXLEY (1825–1895) as a young man.

Russian Writers: A group of *Sovremennik* staff contributors in 1856.
Behind: Tolstoy (in uniform) and Grigorovich. *Seated:* Goncharov, Turgenev, Druzhinin and Ostrovsky.

The Greek of Toledo

GRECO, EL, (1541–1614), properly called Domenicos Theotocopoulos, Greek-born artist of the Spanish School, an enigma of swirl, flame, flash and lividly expressive colour.

Crete, in El Greco's day, was in the Venetian Empire. There he was born of a Cretan family, and may have had experience in painting ikons in the Byzantine manner. He came to Venice, as a young artist from Jamaica or Nigeria might come to London, and found his own manner there under the revealing influence of Tintoretto. Eventually he reached Spain, settled in the decaying city of Toledo, and painted 'orgasms of the soul', as they have been named. An expressive painter, but precisely of what? Though his strange pictures include saints and martyrs, Virgins and Crucifixions, the *Agony in the Garden* (National Gallery, London) and the *Resurrection* (the Prado, Madrid), he is rather too easily called a painter of religious ecstasy and mystical fervour; whereas he may be more the painter of a personal fermentation in terms of his age, painting subjects which passed well enough in the fanatically religious atmosphere of Spain. 'A worthy man,' El Greco said of Michelangelo, 'but he never knew how to paint' (he was ready if required, to repaint Michelangelo's *Last Judgement* in the Sistine Chapel without offensive nudity); and, asked whether drawing or colouring was the more difficult, he replied 'colouring'. He was the friend of the intellectuals of Spain, including Gongóra the poet (q.v.), and he lived in the house of a Marquis de Villena who dabbled in sorcery. The painter Clovio, who knew him in his young days in Rome, found him, on one delicious day when everyone was out and about, alone in a darkened room: 'He refused to come out with me, explaining that the light of day impaired his inner light.' But it might be rash, in spite of the literal subject of his paintings, to conclude that the inner light was religious. Gongóra's light as a poet was superbly and extravagantly verbal; the light of El Greco seems to be an ultimate light or fire of pigment, an intelligent, extravagant, daring and personal manipulation of the means of painting – by means of which he has appealed so much to our own century of cubism and abstraction.

In El Greco's *Agony in the Garden*, clouds and hills – or shapes – billow and swirl in suddenly frozen whirlwind forms: a moon illuminates this cut and divided landscape, through which soldiers led by Judas advance towards Gethsemane. In the foreground, revealed in a sudden shaft of light, Christ kneels in blue and red. Above him an angel in yellow bears the cup of sorrow; 'he prayed saying, "Our Father, if this cup may not pass away from me, except I drink it, thy will be done"', while the disciples lie asleep, enclosed in a cave of unconsciousness. Whether El Greco paints and feels Christ's agony and sweat, or whether he brilliantly paints a concept of agony, the spectator has to judge, and may judge wrong.

ILLUSTRATION: Plate 6.

Lion of the North

GUSTAVUS ADOLPHUS, (1594–1632), Swedish king, bulwark of Protestantism and Lion of the North, whose intervention in the Thirty Years War was a compromise between religious duty and territorial anxiety.

This iron man, so brave and so pious, was brought up to be the champion of Lutheranism. He was a reforming, just king at home, and a clever, innovating general abroad; and all his affairs he conducted with humanity: 'In order to render oneself master of a place,' he said, 'clemency counts as much as force.' His humanity, all the same, was tempered by his religious bigotry.

His father left him with wars against Denmark, Russia and Poland: Gustavus concluded the first two, and carried on the war against the Poles until they defeated him in Prussia. He then intervened in the Thirty Years War. His motives were divided. Gustavus, all on the side of the Protestants, sympathized when Protestants were persecuted by the Roman Emperor, Ferdinand II. He believed himself their God-appointed deliverer. Also the Emperor in time might occupy the Baltic sea-ports and menace Scandinavia. Watched by Europe, and scorned by Ferdinand, who wrote, 'This snow king will melt as he comes South', Gustavus left Sweden in 1630, convinced he would die in battle. Early advantage gave him the alternative of invading Austria or pursuing Tilly, who commanded the forces of the Catholic League, to the west. Unwisely, it now seems, he chose the latter, and wintered at Mainz; there, surrounded by princes and foreign ministers, he was regarded as the arbiter of Northern Europe. There were more victories, the result of Gustavus's new, mobile tactics; Ulm, Augsburg,

I

Munich fell. Richelieu tells us that 'After Munich, all Europe trembled'. And then, engaging the condottiere Wallenstein suddenly at Lutzen, Gustavus, armourless because of old wounds, was butchered in the mist.

The spectacle of religious wars is rarely satisfactory to modern eyes: the protagonists appear as muscular Christians whose emotions have overcome their reason. Gustavus, who added to his religious beliefs a statesmanlike mind and sound common sense (he forswore his early love, to marry elsewhere for the good of Sweden!) rises higher than that, and deserves respect.

ILLUSTRATION: Page 172.

H

Hāfiz of Shiraz

HĀFIZ, (1320–1389, or 1390), often accounted one of the two most remarkable poets of Persian literature, the other being Rūmī (q.v.).

Shams al-Dīn Hāfiz (Hāfiz means 'he who remembers' *i.e.* who knows the Koran by heart) was born, lived and died at the city of Shiraz, a contemporary of Chaucer and more or less of Petrarch and Boccaccio. His lifetime was one of bloodshed and insecurity, culminating in the cruel invasions of Tamerlane. One of the legends told of him, which may or may not be true, is that Tamerlane charged Hāfiz with diminishing the importance of his conquests: he would give Samarkand and Bukhara, he had written in one poem, for the mole on his beloved's cheek. Hāfiz replied, 'Alas, O prince, it is this prodigality which is the cause of the misery in which you see me.' The reply pleased Tamerlane so much that he treated the poet kindly and well. There are stories, too, of Hāfiz's love of wine and dissipation; but he was far from being the fifth-rate hedonist, the Cavalier lyricist or the Victorian cousin of Meredith and Rossetti which so many English translations suggest.

There indeed is the trouble. Hāfiz is a poet uncommonly hard for us to appreciate through translation, partly because his translators, old and new, scholarly and amateur, have been 'forsooth poets',

inept manipulators of English to the verge of illiteracy, and partly because translation has been so difficult. Hāfiz writes simultaneously in different planes, erotic and mystical, worldly and sacred; he plays upon words, he is allusive, uses many figures of speech, is compact in his meaning and close in the design of his poems, as well as exquisite in his cadences. Gertrude Bell is thought of as the best of his translators. Here is her version of *The Joyous Return*, Hāfiz on reunion with God, as amended, or reordered, by a modern Persian:

I

Where are the tidings of union? that I may arise –
Forth from the dust I will rise up to welcome thee!
My soul, like a homing bird, yearning for Paradise,
Shall rise and soar, from the snares of the world set free.

When the voice of thy love shall call me to be thy slave,
I shall rise to a greater far than the mastery
Of life and the living, time and the mortal span.

Pour down, oh Lord! from the clouds of thy guiding grace
The rain of a mercy that quickeneth on my grave,
Before, like dust that the wind bears from place to place,
I arise and flee beyond the knowledge of man.

II

Rise up! let mine eyes delight in thy stately grace!
Thou art the goal, to which all men's endeavour has pressed,
And thou the idol of Hāfiz' worship; thy face   [arise
From the world and life shall bid him come forth and

Though I be old, clasp me one night to thy breast,
And I, when the dawn shall come to awaken me,   [rise.
With the flush of youth on my cheek from thy bosom will

When to my grave thou turnest thy blessed feet,
Wine and the lute thou shalt bring in thine hand to me,
Thy voice shall ring through the folds of my winding-sheet,
And I will arise and dance to thy minstrelsy.

This is one of the poems inscribed on his white alabaster tomb surrounded by roses, orange trees and cypresses on the edge of the river Ruknabad outside Shiraz. Another story is told of the poet's death. His loose-living caused such anger that there was talk of refusing him a Moslem burial. The matter was decided by putting some of his couplets into a vase and bidding a child draw one out. The couplet was

> Fear not to approach Hāfiz's body.
> Though he is sinful, he will enter heaven.

The federalist

HAMILTON, Alexander, (1757–1804), American statesman and powerful advocate of representative government, one of the chief figures in the making of the new country after the turbulences of the Revolution.

He was the illegitimate son of a Leeward Island merchant; and an orphan at eleven. To go to college was his ambition, and his relations sent him to New York. There revolt was kindling; and Hamilton spoke brilliantly and persuasively against the English parliament at mass meetings: 'a collegian, a collegian', shouted the crowds as the seventeen-year-old fought his way to the platform; but they cheered his words and agreed with the pamphlets he wrote.

In the war he became Washington's private secretary, and had to work hard. It was a good opportunity to find out what happened behind the curtain of affairs, and Hamilton's quick mind saw which political system would suit the new America: 'A representative democracy, where the right of election is well secured and regulated, and the exercise of the legislative, executive and judiciary authorities is vested in select persons, chosen really and not nominally by the people, will, in my opinion, be most likely to be happy, regular and durable.'

But he wanted to leave Washington and acquire honours in battle. One day Washington reprimanded his talented young assistant for being late; Hamilton resented this, and took the occasion to leave. He commanded an infantry regiment, and was prominent in the attack on Yorktown. After the war he was called to the Bar, and went into Congress. He believed in a Constitution, a federation of the states, as opposed to Jefferson (q.v.), who was more concerned with states' rights; and wrote his famous series of 'Federalist' articles. He became the Secretary of the Treasury. 'In that office I met with many intrinsic difficulties,' he wrote, 'and many artificial ones proceeding from passion, not very worthy, common to human nature, and which act with particular force in republics. The object, however, was effected of establishing public credit, and introducing order into the finances.' This was true: his report on America's financial problem, and his solution, were brilliant. It was the peak of his career. His proposals were carried through Congress by a splendid deal: in return for Jefferson's support, Hamilton agreed that the national capital should be north of the Potomac.

Out of office until his death, Hamilton worked hard at building up a law practice. Talleyrand, the French statesman (q.v.), who passed Hamilton's window late one night, and saw him working, said afterwards: 'I have seen a man who made the fortune of a nation, labouring all night to support his family.' He was often a petty man; but never dishonest, as his enemies alleged. When Aaron Burr stood for the governorship of New York, Hamilton worked successfully to prevent his election; an action that was good for America (Burr was a secessionist who wished to form a Northern confederacy) but bad for himself. Burr said that Hamilton had insulted him, and challenged him to a duel. On a summer morning, on the banks of the Hudson, they met, and Hamilton was mortally wounded.

He had charm and a taste for intrigue: but he was always a strong patriot. The idea of the 'common man' did not please him at all. His version of democracy was a strong, central representative government, and the years have shown how right it was.

Mynheer Handel

HANDEL, George Frederic, (1685–1759), German-English composer – English inasmuch as he became a naturalized Englishman in 1726 and worked in London most of his life – who was born at Halle in Germany in the same year as J. S. Bach.

After three inevitable years in Italy, Handel was made Kapellmeister to the elector of Hanover. But he had cast his eye upon London, its wealth and liveliness, in the era of such men as Swift, Pope, Prior, Gay and Congreve – a London moreover which was thin in musical genius. He visited London in 1710 and again soon afterwards. Queen Anne commissioned him to write a Te Deum for the peace of Utrecht (1713), which ended Marlborough's war against the French and allowed for England's rise to a European or world supremacy. She bestowed a pension on him, Handel quietly deserting his German master and transferring himself to London for good and all. Anne died the year after. Awkwardly for Handel the new king was his old employer. However, George I forgave him and confirmed him in the royal patronage.

Chamber music, orchestral music, operas poured out from Handel; from the Italianate operas he turned to oratorios, which were in key with the ordered grandeurs of his century. *The Messiah*, today no doubt the most popular choral work in the English-speaking world, was first performed in Dublin in 1742. It took some time to conquer, but long before the century came to an end Haydn wept when he heard the 'Hallelujah Chorus', declaring, 'Handel is the master of us all'. One may reflect that *The Messiah* is the one great monument of early eighteenth-century art to hold its own, without first aid or special pleading. Yet with justice Donald Tovey has written about 'the burial of Handel's art beneath mammoth performances'; and he is thought of too much by one extreme or another – either he is the composer of *The Messiah* interpreted in every provincial town by keen amateurs (true fame, after all), or the composer of the occasional pieces, the repertory pieces, the airs which conveniently fill up intervals. Handel was a composer of genius whose ideas were no less of the eighteenth century than the ideas of Alexander Pope (q.v.). Art was then inspired common sense. It was meant to be understood, grand, if need be, but not singular or eccentric. If Handel was a 'musical opportunist', then so were all great artists, in all arts, of that time. It is typical that Handel should have remarked of *The Messiah*, 'I should be sorry if it only entertained people. I wish to make them better'; typical that he should be a good judge of popular taste. When someone objected that a chorus in *Judas Maccabeus* (1747) would never catch on, Handel replied, 'It will be more popular with the people than my other fine things' – and the chorus in question was 'See, the Conquering Hero Comes'.

Sometimes choleric, always generous, Handel was no recluse, but a travelled man of the world who enjoyed the best London society had to give in one of the best of its intellectual periods. He worked with amazing speed – *The Messiah* was composed in twenty-three days – and left a prodigious quantity of music. He remained, it is true, mynheer Handel to the last, with a strong German accent ('He is ein damn scoundrel and good for nothing' someone heard the old Handel muttering to himself as he walked in Hyde Park), but how much the great occasional pieces are part of English life! Handel was buried in the English pantheon of Westminster Abbey, where at every coronation his anthem *Zadok the Priest* rises grandly; and the pomps of English death have their dignified climax still in Handel's 'Funeral March' from *Saul*. Beethoven declared, 'Go and learn of Handel how to achieve great effects with simple means'.

ILLUSTRATION: Page 175.

Inventor of the new journalism

HARMSWORTH, Alfred, (1865–1922), afterwards Lord Northcliffe, London 'Press Lord' who revolutionized the English newspaper.

Harmsworth became his own proprietor at twenty-two, when he founded the London weekly named *Answers*. This was in 1888. In 1900 he founded *Comic Cuts*, in 1894 the *Sunday Companion*, in 1895 *Home Chat*. These papers show how skilfully he could satisfy the new mass public created by universal elementary education. In 1896 he took the greater plunge into daily journalism, and the first number of the *Daily Mail* appeared.

A *Daily Mail* of 1896 now appears very sedate; but Harmsworth had broken with the old practice of column upon column of closely-printed leading articles and interminable reporting of political speeches; he concentrated on brevity and readability. Though he used the *Daily Mail* to support his political views and promote causes of his own, it was bought simply because it was easy to read; and it became the first newspaper in the world selling a million copies.

Clearly news was a commodity. For the popular newspaper the important thing now was to collect news with skill and present it attractively. By way of the advertising revenues, this new journalism was so immensely rewarding that it attracted other men for profit alone. Harmsworth, it is true, made wealth and was ennobled, but fundamentally he was indifferent to money; from first to last he was devoted to his craft of journalism.

In 1903 he also launched the first illustrated newspaper, the *Daily Mirror*. In 1908 this inventor of the new journalism in the age of the masses acquired a controlling interest in *The Times*, gravest, most sedate and most monumental of the world's newspapers. *The Times* was in difficulties; and Northcliffe, in fact, was its saviour. Obsessed with power, he died mad in 1922. By then the finances of *The Times* were in good order.

The heart and the blood

HARVEY, William, (1578–1657), English physiologist, physician and discoverer of the circulation of the blood.

He was an undergraduate at Caius College, Cambridge, founded by John Caius (1510–1573), who had studied anatomy under Vesalius at Padua.

Harvey himself went to Padua from 1597 to 1602 to continue his anatomical studies, at the period when Galileo (q.v.) was in his prime; and it was his greatest achievement to introduce Galileo's principles of dynamics, the science of motion, into the explanation of biological processes. The first fruit of this was Harvey's proof of the circulation of the blood.

All the elements of the problem had been more or less well known for some while: but they needed linking by the appropriate conceptions and modes of thought. Harvey, as a first-rate anatomist, knew the facts: he knew the blood proceeded through the arteries in one direction and was prevented from flowing backwards by the valves. The student in Galileo's Padua had learnt about pumps and valves: it was natural to him to conceive of the heart as a pump, propelling blood through the artery pipes. The difficulty was to find the precise place where the blood passed from the arteries to the veins. It seemed evident that it must occur in the lungs, but microscopes were still not invented and the capillary tubes which the blood passes through could not be seen.

Harvey used an indirect proof for the circulation. He employed Galileo's methods of quantitative calculation of moving objects and calculated the amount of blood pumped steadily by the heart in one direction. He measured the capacity of the heart: it held two ounces of blood. But the heart beat seventy-two times in every minute, so that it pumped $2 \times 72 \times 60$ oz., or 540 lb. of blood in an hour. That was about three times the body-weight of a man; and on an average, a man's body contains only about 9 lb. of blood. Where, then, could all the blood pumped by the heart come from? Obviously, it pumped the same blood over and over again, in 'a motion, as it were, in a circle'. In this master work, published in his *Exercitatio anatomica de motu cordis et sanguinis* (1628), Harvey incidentally founded comparative anatomy, since he had to compare the function of the heart in a wide range of mammals; and he was the first since Aristotle to advance embryology.

In politics Harvey was a cavalier, and physician to the Stuarts. His discoveries about the embryology of mammals he had to explain to Charles I in the deer park at Hampton Court.

Novelist of the half-darkness

HAWTHORNE, Nathaniel, (1804–1864), American novelist and writer of short stories, who explored some of the closed rooms of human personality – the half-light of evil, sin, guilt, conscience and repentance.

Of the room he worked in, Hawthorne wrote: 'This deserves to be called a haunted chamber, for thousands and thousands of visions have appeared to me in it.' Author and room were haunted; and he continued haunted and withdrawn all his life. He was withdrawn in his New England childhood at Salem. He was lame; his father died when he was a small boy, his mother was all too black-weeded and thorough as a widow. Well trained in the consciousness of sin, Hawthorne did not switch on the full light in its shuttered rooms, so much as feel his exact way through the half-darkness; out of which came his short stories – such inner glimpses as *The Minister's Black Veil* or *The Birthmark*, in which the cost of removing a single blemish from the wife's beauty is the wife's death, or *Wakefield*, a parable of the man whose weakness of will makes him an outcast of the universe – and his novels, particularly his great New England tale of sin, *The Scarlet Letter* (1850).

Fascinating brief entries in his notebooks show his caste of mind and his way of conception.

'A man to swallow a small snake – and it to be a symbol of a cherished sin.'

'A person with an ice-cold hand – his right hand; which people ever afterwards remember when they have once grasped it.'

'To inherit a great fortune. To inherit a great misfortune.'

'To symbolize moral or spiritual disease by disease of the body; – thus, when a person committed any sin, it might cause a sore to appear on the body; – this to be wrought out.'

A late marriage when Hawthorne was 38 revealed to him the nature and excellence of love, making him say that we are shadows till the heart is touched – 'then we begin to be'. Herman Melville, who greatly admired him for his honesty and insight, saw that Hawthorne found good by exhibiting evil: he wrote that Hawthorne was one of those who said No, in thunder – 'for all men who say *yes*, lie'.

Music for the careworn

HAYDN, Franz Joseph, (1732–1809), Austrian composer. To some amateurs who had banded together in a small town in Northern Europe to perform his Oratorio *The Creation*, Haydn sent a grateful letter: whenever he became discouraged in a composition, he told them, one thought made him persevere – his music might 'become a spring from which the careworn may draw a moment's rest and refreshment'. This was typical of Haydn as man and as musician, the Haydn of the *Trumpet Concerto* and the Haydn who comforted his servants, when the French were bombarding Vienna in 1809, by saying, 'Don't be frightened, my children. Where Haydn is, no harm can come to you.' The French, indeed, courteously posted sentries at Haydn's door, though death came in by the back entrance and caught the aged composer soon afterwards.

Haydn's early childhood had been in different circumstances. There were no servants. He was the son of a wheelwright in Lower Austria; but from the thatched house he went to Vienna and had his musical training as one of the choir-boys in St Stephen's cathedral. Service as a court musician to Prince Nicholas Esterházy did not greatly raise his social status. Until Beethoven challenged convention, a composer was still looked upon as a servant; and Haydn only rose to a social eminence when he came to England in 1791, at the invitation of the impresario Salomon. Simple, direct, dignified, optimistic and uncomplicated as ever, he would not desert Salomon for a rival and a higher reward, feeling himself dedicated, not to banknotes, but to the service of his public.

Haydn was a craftsman in his treatment of the conventions and an artist in his ability to fuse the necessarily orthodox with the justifiably eccentric. When he begins the *allegro* of his *Surprise* symphony in a blithely irrelevant key, he allows this indiscretion to electrify the whole movement, so that the external gaiety of the music is strengthened by that inward tension which is so characteristic of Haydn. His music has none of Mozart's disquieting ambivalence, yet it can be deep and serious, as in the *Seven Last Words* or the *Nelson Mass*, or it can be droll, as in the variations of the *Surprise* symphony. Haydn can make comedy out of what was noble, or contrive nobility out of comedy. It is a fair criticism to say that there is no undercurrent of tears in Haydn's music, to suggest that he is too urbane.

Henry the Eighth

HENRY VIII, (1491–1547), King of England, a Renaissance monarch, minor poet and musician, the central figure in the start of the English Reformation, and an absolute ruler who showed political insight and acumen in a difficult era of change.

Two things give Henry VIII a lop-sided reputation – the tale of wives, which will raise a laugh always in a variety show, and the portraits which emphasize a certain grossness and cruelty. As for the six queens, it was perhaps better to marry than to have had six or sixteen mistresses. As to looks, a foreigner described him in his younger days as 'the most handsome potentate I ever set eyes on'; which to us may appear exaggeration. Erasmus declared him a 'happy genius'. He was a good scholar, kept minstrels in his retinue, and played expertly himself on lute, harpsichord and organ. His treatise against Luther in 1521 was praised by Pope Leo X, who conferred on him the title *Defender of the Faith*, which is still one of the styles of English sovereigns in their Protestant world. His anthem *O Lord, the creator of all things* is not forgotten, his poems still find a place in anthologies. One or two of them read ironically in view of the wives:

> As holly groweth green,
>   And never changeth hue,
> So I am, ever hath been
>   Unto my lady true;
>
> As the holly groweth green
>   With ivy all alone,
> When flowers cannot be seen
>   And green wood leaves be gone,
>
> Now unto my lady
>   Promise to her I make.
> From all other only
>   To her I me betake.
>
> Adieu, mine own lady,
>   Adieu, my special,
> Who hath my heart truly,
>   Be sure, and ever shall!

He was fond, too, of hunting, entertainment and gambling, playing tennis, shovelboard and Pope July –

> Pastime with good company
> I love and shall, until I die

Grudge who list, but none deny!
So God be pleased, thus live will I

– he began another of his poems. To all his qualities he added a great belief in himself – 'Nor do I see any faith in the world save in me, and therefore God Almighty who knows this prospers my affairs'.

As a ruler he progressed in three stages towards complete autocracy. The first was to rid himself of the influence of his early adviser, Cardinal Wolsey. The second was the Reformation. In the third stage he consolidated his control over the whole country. Henry wanted a male heir, which his first Queen, Catherine of Aragon, was unable to bear him. When for political reasons the Pope refused to grant a divorce, Henry took action on his own. But in throwing off Rome, he was only expressing the feelings against external influence in their affairs which his insular subjects had held for a long time. Theologically and religiously, however, he had no great sympathy for the Reformers.

The boisterous temper of his early life quietened, and if he was at times brutal and callous, he was doing little more than reflect his age. Personally he was a moral character in comparison with many of his contemporary rulers. To the end of his life he never lost the look of what were termed by Sir Thomas More (q.v.) 'his quick and penetrable eyes'. To his credit also he was father to Queen Elizabeth (q.v.).

ILLUSTRATION: Page 173.

The way to Good Hope

HENRY THE NAVIGATOR, (1394–1460). This Portuguese prince, who navigated no ships and the limit of whose sailing was across the Straits of Gibraltar, initiated the great age of exploration. The known confines of the world were doubled within a century by the discoveries which Henry promoted.

Henry convinced himself that Africa did not end, as everyone believed, roughly opposite the Canaries at Cape Nam (*i.e.* in Portuguese 'Cape Not'). This once impassable barrier became a convenient landmark for his navigators; and it was succeeded in terror by Cape Bojador ('the outstretcher'). No man could pass Cape Bojador and live. For twelve years Henry sent out men who failed to pass it. 'You cannot meet there a peril so great', Henry said to Gil Eannes, who was one of them, 'that the hope of re-

ward shall not be even greater. In truth I marvel at these misgivings that have possessed you all ... I am astonished to think you have them from the opinion of some few mariners who know only the navigation of Flanders ... and do not know how to handle a compass or make use of a chart of the seas.' Gil Eannes thereupon doubled Cape Bojador and dispelled the bogey. By the time of Henry's death his mariners had pushed on nearly to Sierra Leone, and the way was open to rounding the Cape of Good Hope and reaching the fabulous 'Indies' of Marco Polo, which were the goal of all early exploration.

Henry's seamen were authorized to take possession of suitable territories in the name of the King of Portugal. Thus Henry was a precursor of European expansion overseas, though the voyages he sponsored were unprofitable. His mariners were ordered not to capture the natives they met, but to trade with them peacefully. However, since princes and rich men desired exotic human ornaments in their households, a trade developed in slaves; to be increased enormously when America was discovered and slave labour was required. Henry's activities thus led unwittingly to a disaster for Africa and a moral disaster for Europeans.

Modern cosmogony

HERSCHEL, Sir William, (1738–1822). Born in Hanover as Friedrich Wilhelm Herschel, this astronomer was the founder of modern cosmogony and first suggested that our own Galaxy, or Milky Way, formed an 'island universe' of stars, like a nebula.

Herschel was a skilled musician, and came to England in 1757, playing the organ and conducting a small orchestra before high society at Bath. Passionately interested in the stars, he used to go to bed with a basin of milk and text-books of astronomy, waking up in the morning with thoughts about acquiring telescopes. There was nothing for it but to make his own instruments and grind his own lenses in his spare time. Finally, after music had been abandoned for science, he made and set up his great telescope with a focal length of forty feet, and a mirror four feet in diameter.

His grand aim was to survey the whole of the heavens and to discover their general structure. In 1781 he discovered the planet Uranus. In 1782 George III invited him to become his private astronomer. Herschel introduced the method of 'star-gaging' – of counting the number of stars in a certain region and deducing the way in which they are distributed. He showed that all the visible stars lie in a disc-shaped assemblage, and that the sun was not far from the centre of it. On his method of star-gaging depend the recent extensions in our observational knowledge of the structure of the universe which have been made with the giant telescopes at Mt Wilson and Mt Palomar. Herschel's telescopes gave an image of new magnitude and definition, the stars appeared without rays. The great and eccentric Henry Cavendish (q.v.) asked him at a dinner, 'Is it true, Dr Herschel, that you see the stars round?' 'Round as a button,' he replied. After silence between the two men till the end of the meal Cavendish turned to him again, 'Round as a button?' 'Round as a button,' Herschel said again.

Pictures of the passing world

HIROSHIGE, Ichiryusai, (1797–1859), Japanese landscape painter, held in special affection in the West, where his work (with that of Hokusai (q.v.)) influenced Whistler, Van Gogh and other artists.

Except for journeys after landscape, Hiroshige spent all his life in Yedo (the present-day Tokyo), where he was born. His father was a fire-brigade officer, who sent him to be trained by an artist of the aristocratic Kano School. But it was the tradition of Ukiyoye – 'Pictures of the Passing World' for the common people – which attracted Hiroshige. For more than two generations it had already produced an art both refined and popular in the form of coloured wood-cut prints. The constant theme of Ukiyoye had been scenes and personalities of the theatre and the gay quarters of the city. Hiroshige and Hokusai preferred landscape, scenes of the city and its country surroundings.

Like many other wood-cut artists, Hiroshige began as a book-illustrator. He rose to fame in 1826, when he published his *Views of the Eastern Capital*. His landscape was something never seen before either in Japanese or Chinese art. He draws with a gift for directness, local atmosphere, balance and simplification, hardly equalled by the supreme Hokusai. It has

been well said that 'with Hokusai the accidents of nature are an occasion for entertaining novelty of composition; to Hiroshige they are dear for their own sake', though Hiroshige is the coarser draughtsman.

In the spring of 1834 appeared the first set of views illustrating the posting-stations along the Tōkaidō, the road joining Yedo to Kyoto. To make the sketches Hiroshige had attached himself to the retinue of the annual mission which brought the Shōgun's gift of a horse to the Emperor. He made further Tōkaidō sets and views of Yedo under various titles, as well as a series of thirty-six views of Mount Fuji and sixty views of the provinces. *Passenger Boat on the Yodo River, Kameido Shrine in the Snow, White Rain on the Nihonbashi, Full Moon at Takanawa*, are the titles of some of his best-known prints, which indicate his feeling and his choice of subject. If the prints are tinged with sentimentality, it is a sentimentality redeemed by the naturalness of his human figures, and the drama of his composition. Towards the end of his life Hiroshige was more and more fond of Kakemono-ye, *i.e.* narrow vertical prints in the style of a painting to be hung on the wall – as in his celebrated *Monkey Bridge* and *Kiso Gorge in the Snow*.

The Nazi leader

HITLER, Adolf, (1889–1945), German leader responsible for some 25,000,000 deaths, who left behind him a devastated Germany and a devastated continent. Suffering from delusions of persecution and grandeur, he was well fitted to Germany's historical, geographical and psychological sickness in the period from 1918.

Hitler's father was a minor customs official in Austria at Braunau-on-the-Inn, where he was born. He went to Vienna in hopes of becoming an artist and in revolt against his father's humdrum situation. But he had no gift and the academy would not take him as a student. For a while he lived by drawing picture postcards and advertisements for tailors and furniture dealers. During these years, spent mostly in the dosshouse, Hitler formed his political beliefs. Theories about 'race' he imbibed from reading Houston Chamberlain and Gobineau. The doctrine of the will came to him from Schopenhauer. The rest of his political education he acquired from newspapers.

The noisy claims of the other nationalities which made up the ramshackle Austro-Hungarian Empire exaggerated Hitler's German nationalism. The ineffective Parliament in which these claims were aired taught him to hate democracy. The ineffective Habsburgs – in Hitler's view they should have been the champions of Germanic supremacy instead of yielding to the Czechs and other 'subject' races – taught him to hate traditionalism. He despised the working class (to which he felt an inborn superiority as an official's son), and so could not join the Social Democrats – particularly when he discovered that a number of the founders and leaders of Social Democracy were Jews. He admired Karl Lueger, the leader of the anti-semitic Christian Social Party (who organized a youth movement which marched through the streets in uniform), but Lueger's anti-semitism was not enough for him; it was religious, not racial; *i.e.* it did not apply to baptised Jews. Communism and capitalism were hateful to him 'because' they were Jewish. Anti-semitism, in fact, was the driving force in Hitler's mind. Belief in its counterpart, the Aryan master-race, was secondary.

In 1912 Hitler went to Munich. A chance photograph of a crowd on the day war was declared in 1914 shows him with an expression of bliss. Though an Austrian, he immediately volunteered for the German army, and served on the western front until 1918, becoming a lance-corporal and battalion and regimental runner. His comrades regarded him as a crank, and he bored them with political harangues. The armistice found him in hospital with temporary blindness, which may have been caused by mustard-gas or hysteria or both (the hospital records disappeared after his accession to power).

War and the inflation in Germany created a new class of cranks, misfits and down-and-outs, which now kept Hitler afloat. When he returned to Munich, he was at first employed by the German army to report on political activities. At a discussion during the preliminary training course he replied to a speaker, who defended the Jews, with a passionate harangue, which taught him that he could sweep an audience off its feet. He intervened in the same way at a public meeting of the infant National Socialist Workers' Party attended by twenty-five people, and was thereupon invited to join. He did so half-heartedly, became party-member No. 7, and found the party an instrument he could use. He ousted its founder and leader and took his place.

The party grew and became noisy in Bavaria, though it was still thought to belong to the lunatic side of politics, particularly when Hitler in 1923 attempted a *putsch* or insurrection against the Bavarian Government. It was a fiasco. The party was banned. Hitler was confined in the fortress of Landsberg, where he wrote his unreadable political handbook *Mein Kampf* (my 'struggle'). He also had time to reflect that power could be gained, not by insurrection, but by exploiting the legal opportunities in the insecurely based republic. Released after eleven months instead of four years, Hitler rebuilt the party. So far he had been the political agitator looking for an Aryan Messiah who would lead his people to the promised land. His own ambition was to be this Messiah's propaganda minister, but in answer to his followers' enthusiasm he found the Messiah in himself, and now developed into the *Führer* or leader.

His intense activity, the newspapers he acquired or founded, the speeches he made, the demonstrations he led, the civil disturbances he provoked, were not enough to turn the Nazi movement into a major political force until the slump of 1930, which increased its representatives in the Reichstag from twelve to 104. In July 1932, with 230 members, it became the strongest single party. In November 1932 it lost 2,000,000 votes and thirty-four seats; but in January 1933 Hitler was made Chancellor in a coalition Government.

The Reichstag fire enabled him to get rid of the Communists; the other political parties, including right-wing elements who helped him to power, were also disposed of, and the Nazis became the only party in the state. In June 1934 he murdered many of his own supporters whom he believed to be a threat. Within a few years he turned the disarmed, democratic Germany of the Weimar Republic into a heavily armed, totalitarian war machine. One daring international *coup* after another made it appear for a while that he might succeed without a war. Austria and Czechoslovakia were absorbed; and in 1939 Hitler astonished the world and his own followers by concluding a non-aggression pact with Russia. When his invasion of Poland in 1939 made Britain and France declare war, it seemed for the first time that he had overreached himself. Yet he went from triumph to triumph. Poland was overrun, then Denmark and Norway, followed by Belgium and Holland. France collapsed, the British were driven from the Continent. In 1941 a plan to invade Britain was abandoned, but the Germans took Yugoslavia, Greece and Crete. So far Hitler had dealt with one enemy at a time: he now invaded Russia with Britain undefeated in his rear.

Failure to win decisively in the first advance left the German army unprepared for the Russian winter. Next, against the advice of his generals (discredited in his eyes because they had refused to sanction the armoured thrust through the Ardennes which had put France out of the war), Hitler ordered an advance towards the Caspian instead of pressing forward to Moscow. He thus exposed his extended right flank to the defeat of Stalingrad. Failure to understand the importance of Malta meant that Rommel's army in North Africa was always short of supplies, and Rommel was defeated at Alamein. A ban on the development of the German Air Force after the fall of France and failure to concentrate on the necessary fighters, left Germany open to devastating bombardment from the air. The initiative, particularly after America entered the war and the weight of American supplies became effective, passed irresistibly away from Hitler.

His order that the Germans must give no ground and must fight where they stood was lunacy. It deprived his generals of mobility and the weapon of strategic withdrawal; and it did not prevent the Germans from being driven back by the Russians and expelled from Africa; Italy and France, finally Germany itself were invaded. 'The greatest military genius of all time', as he had appeared to some a few years earlier, survived an attempt at assassination, but now influenced the war only by prolonging it to no purpose. In April 1945, in scenes of maniacal horror, nemesis caught up with Hitler. The Russians drove remorselessly into the centre of a bomb-shattered Berlin. From his bunker the Führer dictated instructions to armies which did not exist. He sentenced Himmler and Göring to death (they were out of his reach, but had dared to think of overtures to the enemy); and at last he admitted defeat. National Socialism was a failure, he was a failure, the Germans were unworthy of him, let them perish with him.

Then came suicide by poison and the burning of Hitler's body.

Man and Leviathan

HOBBES, Thomas, (1588–1679), English moral and political philosopher, who taught in his *Leviathan* (1651), his most famous book, that if men are to pursue their happiness they must guard against human greed and fear by surrendering their rights to an all-powerful authority, the 'sovereign' – which may be a single man or an assembly.

The condition of men 'living without a common Power to keep them all in awe' Hobbes calls 'Warre': war need not consist in actual fighting, but only in 'the known disposition thereto'. His interest is in the circumstances that arise when law (with the power to enforce the law) is removed. For it *is* sometimes non-existent! Hobbes instances 'the savage people in many places of *America*', though he does not want to say that this was the original condition of mankind. In such a situation the greed, suspicion and ambition of some men – not necessarily a majority – reduce social relations to chaos: 'there is no place for Industry ... and consequently no Culture of the Earth; no Navigation ... no commodious Building ... no Arts; no Letters; no Society; and which is worst of all, continuall feare, and danger of violent death; And the life of man, solitary, poore, nasty, brutish, and short.'

Hobbes' solution is the creation of the Leviathan (which is the name of the whale in the Psalms), a sovereign to which each man will surrender all his rights – save that of self-preservation. 'Covenants, without the Sword, are but Words': but the sovereign will have power – and swords – enough to enforce the law. Under this absolutism each man places voluntary limits on his own self-seeking, in return for a similar surrender made by his neighbours.

More comfortable centuries than Hobbes's – or than our own – dismissed his account as too cynical. Certainly there is a positive desire to live in society: man is a social animal. 'Do the bees rebel against their queen?' Hobbes asked: 'do the ants lock up their houses when they take the air?' But men do not regard each other merely as competitors.

Hobbes confessed to being naturally timorous and afraid of death; he was solitary by taste, and his extreme Royalist sympathies made him flee to France in 1640 on the fall of Laud and Strafford. Personal danger, and England divided by civil war, thus lay within his experience and shaped his views. But between nation and nation we are all as cynical as Hobbes: we believe that most states will observe their treaties, but not that all will all the time. Greed and ambition are too strong. And we now recognize an atmosphere of suspicion with a 'known disposition' towards fighting as 'cold war'.

ILLUSTRATION: Page 178.

Guerilla leader

HOFER, Andreas, (1767–1810), Austrian and Tyrolese folk-hero.

After being defeated by Napoleon, Austria was compelled in 1805 to cede the Tyrol and Vorarlberg to Bavaria. Three times the inabitants rose in revolt under the leadership of Andreas Hofer, who had been a sharpshooter and captain of militia in the war, and three times the Bavarians were defeated. Known as the *Sandwirth*, from the name of his father's inn, *am Sand*, Hofer, though little more than a peasant against the centralized authority of the Napoleonic system, maintained successful guerilla attacks on the French and Bavarian troops. He administered the Tyrol in the name of the Emperor, Francis II, who gave a lukewarm support. When Austria was defeated at Wagram in 1809, Hofer's successes were nullified, there was no hope of evading Napoleon's dictate, and the Tyrol and Vorarlberg were confirmed in Bavarian ownership. Hofer and some of his companions now surrendered to the French under an amnesty, though he refused to acknowledge the Bavarians. Later in the year, misled by rumours of an Austrian rising, he escaped with a price on his head and attempted a new rebellion, only to be betrayed, taken to Mantua and shot – on the direct orders, so it is said, of Napoleon.

Poet of a doomed Austria

HOFMANNSTHAL, Hugo von, (1874–1929), Austrian poet, dramatist and man of letters. While the Austrian Empire was disintegrating, Hofmannsthal did his best to re-create it in his works.

'It is hard to struggle against a ruling society, but harder still to have to represent one that doesn't exist.' This aphorism from his *Book of Friends* (1922) is a modest summary of all he achieved; for he did succeed in representing a whole culture already doomed to extinction. His best lyrical poems were written before he was twenty; but they were an end, not a beginning; a true product of the *fin de siècle*:

And children slowly grow with their deep eyes
That know of nothing, slowly grow and die,
And every one of us goes his own way.

The harsh fruits gather sweetness gradually
And like dead birds come hurtling down at night
And for a few days fester where they lie ...

And roads run through the grass and strewn around
Are cities full of torches, ponds and trees,
And threatening cities, withered ones are found ...

From having seen such things what profit comes?
Yet he says much who whispers 'evening',
A word from which grave thought and sadness flow

Like rich dark honey from the hollow combs.

(Translated by Michael Hamburger.)

To progress from such lines in his early poem, *Ballad of the Outer Life*, Hofmannsthal had to make a new beginning; he did so, and no one can blame him for turning, less subjectively, to the drama, the short story and the essay. None of his later works – except the unfinished novel *Andreas* and the tragedy *The Tower* – was wholly and strikingly original, but they must be judged in the light of Hofmannsthal's special function: to preserve, rather than to revolutionize, the highest standards of literature. Even his libretti for the operas of Richard Strauss, such as *Der Rosenkavalier* (1911) and *Ariadne auf Naxos* (1912), and three plays, *Das Grosse Salzburger Welttheater* (1919, written for the Salzburg Festival), *DerSchwierige* (1921) and *Der Turm* (1927), have great merit.

'The man mad about painting'

HOKUSAI, (1760–1849), Japanese artist. In his biography published in 1892 Edmond de Goncourt called Hokusai 'one of the most original artists in the world'. His wood-cut prints had only recently become known in Europe. Artists were fascinated by his spontaneous draughtsmanship, endless invention, the humanity and pungency of the popular life he depicts, and hailed him as the greatest oriental artist – though they hardly knew of another.

In his own country, admiration of Hokusai has not been universal. He belonged to the school of Ukiyo-ye, artists of the Passing World, celebrated by the humble and unsophisticated, but despised by the educated. He drew from the age of six, but, he tells us, to the age of seventy he had no skill – 'at eighty I shall have considerable talent ... at a hundred I shall be sublime, at a hundred and ten I shall render life to a single line, to a single point'. He died at eighty-nine, saying 'If I had had but five years longer I could have become a great painter.'

Hokusai was the son of a poor mirror-maker. He lost his first job in a book-shop through inattentiveness. For seven years he was apprenticed to a wood engraver and in 1790 was received into the studio of the artist Shunshō. He chafed at the narrow studio tradition, angered Shunshō by studying the style of the aristocratic Kano school and was expelled. Thereafter he was self-made. In 1796 he founded a studio and school of his own. He was slow in finding his own style. His first prints – of actors, signed with the name Shunrō bestowed on him by Shunshō – show little originality; and he supported life by illustrating cheap books as well as by hawking red pepper and calendars in the streets. He first achieved fame by the production of 'surimono', elegant little prints used as invitations and greeting cards. In the first years of the new century he began to take the interest in landscape on which his reputation came to be firmly established. His volumes of Tokyo views, depicting broad landscape in delicate colour, appeared between 1800 and 1806. The scenes nearly all contain figures whose attitudes and occupations interpret the humanity, sympathy and humour which informs all his later work. He sometimes signed his work 'gwakyōjin', 'the man mad about painting', or added 'humorously drawn by Hokusai'. Hokusai's five greatest serial works began in 1810 with the publication of the *Six Poets*. These are marvels of rapid brush painting in which the figures are each composed of the characters forming their names. The *Ippitsu Gwafu* (Album of Brush Drawings) of 1823 has an equal vitality. Meanwhile he had begun the publication of the volumes of Mangwa, random sketches in black with light colour, depicting an endless variety of figure subjects full of humour and sly observation. The two series of views of Mount Fuji, the best known of all his works, appeared in 1823–9 and 1834–5. For the sense of design, the colouring, and the quiet comment on the place of man in the natural world, these prints are unsurpassed.

Hokusai earned little by his art and was seldom out of debt. He dressed like a peasant in a straw coat and sandals. Among the artists of the East he is unique in having influenced the art of the West and being known in the West almost as well as he is in Japan.

ILLUSTRATION: Page 175.

A major poet of Germany

HÖLDERLIN, Johann Christian Friedrich, (1770 –1843), one of the most limpid and deep of German poets. Like William Blake in England, he was not content with lyrical, narrative or didactic poetry. In middle life he wrote a series of great prophetic 'hymns' in an unrhymed, irregular form adapted from the odes of the Greek poet, Pindar.

Hölderlin's early enthusiasm for the French Revolution, together with his burning love of Nature and the Greek gods, told him he would be a poet, and nothing but a poet. For nine years after he graduated at a theological college in Tübingen, he made a wretched living as a private tutor, with brief intervals of leisure at the cost of dependence on his mother or on his friends; meanwhile he wrote poems, a novel, *Hyperion*, a tragedy, *Empedocles*. The one woman he loved and who loved him – the Diotima of his poems – was the wife of his wealthy employer, J.F.Gontard; so it was a love doubly and insuperably barred by society and morality. Susette Gontard died at Frankfort in 1802; about a fortnight later Hölderlin, who cannot have known of her death, returned insane from the South of France, where his last tutorial post had taken him. By 1806 his madness (schizophrenia) was complete and incurable. The second half of his life was spent in a small tower at Tübingen, where a carpenter's family looked after him till his death.

His poetic mission was an ascent to unpermitted heights which had to be expiated by a fall no less extreme. Throughout his mature work Hölderlin foretold the course of his life, but never more poignantly than in a brief poem written shortly before his final breakdown, *The Middle of Life*:

> With yellow pears the land
> And full of wild roses
> Hangs down into the lake,
> O graceful swans,
> And drunk with kisses
> You dip your heads
> Into the hallowed-sober water.
>
> Alas, where shall I find, when
> Winter comes, the flowers, and where
> The sunshine
> And shadows of earth?
> The walls stand
> Speechless and cold, in the wind
> Weathercocks clatter.

(*Translated by Michael Hamburger.*)

The first strophe, with its images of fertility and the harmonious balance of land and water (which symbolize the conscious and unconscious parts of the human mind), corresponds to his creative years; the second strophe, with its images of blank desolation, to his presentiment of the long years of expiation, the death-in-life of his madness.

'I fear', he wrote in 1801, 'that in the end it will be with me as with old Tantalus, who got more of the gods than he could digest.' Yet he went on to write those prophetic hymns, of which *Patmos* (1803) is the most magnificent. In it he establishes a link between the Greek gods and Christianity, but leads up to our present age, a period of Night in which there is no divine revelation, but only preparation for a greater and happier age to come.

Hölderlin's later poetry – not including the naive products of his madness – seems to have been uttered through him, rather than by him; it has the primitive power, and the ambiguity, of an oracle.

ILLUSTRATION: Page 174.

An English Republican

HOLLIS, Thomas, (1720–1774), English eccentric, champion of liberty, and benefactor of Harvard. He lies ten feet down on his estates, in a grave which by his own orders is unmarked.

Hollis devoted his life and wealth, in his words, to 'upholding liberty and preserving the memory of its champions, so as to render tyranny and its abettors odious'. He collected writings about freedom, republished them in new editions, in leather bindings ornamented with the cap and dagger of liberty, and then despatched them to the universities and libraries he approved of – including Harvard, Zurich and Berne. He himself took no butter, milk, sugar, spices or salt, never married, never went to church, never became a member of Parliament since election was then impossible without bribery. Succeeding to estates in Dorset, this Fellow of the Royal Society devised an odd way of commemorating the champions of freedom. He renamed in their honour all his farms and fields. The farms (still bearing the names he bestowed) include Locke Farm, after the philosopher, Harvard Farm, after John Harvard of New England, Sidney Farm, after the republican Algernon Sidney, executed in 1683, and Milton and Marvell Farms,

after the two poets who were against the King in the Civil War. Philosophers, New England puritans, regicides, tyrannicides, law-givers, reformers, etc., are spread across the fields like fertilizer. A farmer today drives his tractor from Cromwell to John Knox, Luther to Wycliff. He may sow mangolds in Machiavelli or turnips in Toleration, set his potatoes in Plutarch, or Plato, or Peters (after Hugh Peters, chaplain of the court which condemned Charles I to death), or turn his cows out into Confucius.

Eccentrics upset others by existing at all. Hollis was disliked and called 'democratical' in the time when the adjective had today's savour of 'communist' or yesterday's of 'fascist'. Dr Johnson and Mrs Carter spoke of Hollis one day:

Mrs Carter: He was a bad man. He used to talk uncharitably.
Johnson: Poh! Poh! Madam; who is the worse for being talked of uncharitably? Besides he was a dull poor creature as ever lived.

Dull, poor creatures can have worse manias than one for liberty. Hollis, at any rate, was self-effacing. He gave orders, not only that his grave should be unmarked, but that the field in which he lies should be ploughed immediately after the burial.

The Green Man

ROBIN HOOD, an English outlaw and folk-hero of the Middle Ages. Did Robin Hood ever exist? Can he be ascribed dates and a life-history? Rhymes about Robin Hood are mentioned in the fourteenth-century poem of *Piers Plowman*, and thereafter ballads have long described him, with Little John, Scathlok and Much the miller's son, as the ideal outlaw of the green forest.

The ballads make him of yeoman stock, living off the King's deer, preferring virtue to vice and befriending the virtuous and the downtrodden. Little John asks Robin Hood in *A Gest of Robyn Hode*:

Where we shall rob, where we shall reeve,
Where we shall beat and bind?

And Robin warns him not to harm the husbandman 'that tilleth with his plough', or the farmer who walks by the greenwood thicket, or the knight or the squire that 'would be a good fellow'; but he is against the greedy sheriff, against the King's servants, though not the King; against greedy bishops, or abbots or monks, though not against the Virgin. So far Robin Hood is that type of 'virtuous criminal' who crops up again and again in literature (*e.g.* Raffles the Gentleman Crook). Attempts are made to fit him with an historical suit of clothes as a fourteenth-century outlaw. These are not convincing. By origin Robin Hood seems more likely to have been a wood goblin –Robin of the Wood, the goblin known as 'the Man in the Oak', the magical figure associated with fertility and May Day and the May Cycle, who survives in the stories of Charles II in the oak, the Jack-in-the-Green, the Green Man after whom inns are named, and who is so frequently carved on corbels, bosses, etc., in medieval churches as a head among oak leaves or hawthorn leaves, often with the oak or hawthorn growing from his mouth. There are fifteenth-century churchwardens' accounts which include payments for 'gathering of the Robin Hood' on May Day.

The ballads which make Robin Hood an outlaw border upon magic, as in Robin's attachment to his Trystell tree, or when Robin and his associates are in danger and he has only to blow upon his horn for immediate rescue. Thus in the ballad of *Robin Hood and the Three Squires*. Robin, disguised as an old man, offers his services to the Sheriff of Nottingham as hangman, and asks leave to wind his horn:

> The first blast that he did blow,
>   He blew both loud and shrill;
> A hundred and fifty of Robin Hood's men
>   Came riding over the hill.
>
> The next loud blast that he did give,
>   He blew both loud and amain,
> And quickly sixty of Robin Hood's men
>   Came shining over the plain.
>
> 'O who are you,' the sheriff he said,
>   'Come tripping over the lee?'
> 'They're my attendants,' brave Robin did say,
>   'They'll pay a visit to thee'.
>
> They took the gallows from the stack,
>   They set it in the glen,
> They hanged the proud sheriff on that,
>   Released their own three men.

Robin Hood fits well into the large English family of supernatural beings, including Robin Goodfellow, Tom Thumb, and Kit with the Canstick.

Discoverer of vitamins

HOPKINS, Sir Frederick Gowland, (1861–1947), English scientist, the discoverer of vitamins, and pioneer of biochemistry. He was the son of a London bookseller, and a cousin of the poet Gerard Manley Hopkins (q.v.).

His father died when he was a baby, and he had a lonely childhood. He was sent to the City of London School, where at the age of fourteen although he had already shown chemical talent, he played truant for six weeks, and had to be taken away. He attributed his action in later life to 'sheer boredom'. Now a frail outcast, he was sent to a school where they moulded 'character', and at seventeen he was put into an insurance office in the City, but after six months was articled to an analytical chemist. He learned no theory, but mastered practical analysis in a remarkable degree, becoming analyst for Sir Thomas Stevenson, the great medical jurist. Hopkins prepared the analytical evidence for him in many famous poisoning trials. Through Stevenson he gained the opportunity to graduate in medicine, at last, when he was thirty-three.

While walking the wards at Guy's Hospital, Hopkins noticed the nutritional disorders of girls brought into the City by the recently-invented typewriter. The old male clerks had lunched in the public-house on a cut from the joint and two vegetables, but the girls went to the new tea-shops and lunched off a bun and a cup of tea. They suffered from vague malaise, which was not understood.

Meanwhile, Hopkins produced the standard method of analysing urine, and was invited to teach chemical physiology at Cambridge. He discovered an improved method of crystallizing the protein in the whites of eggs and next began to investigate the role of protein in the diet of rats. He found that rats fed on chemically pure protein, pure fat and pure sugar, languished, but recovered when very small doses of milk were added to the diet. He announced in 1906 that milk must contain 'an accessory food factor' (later called a vitamin), present in very small quantity, but necessary for life. This was his most spectacular discovery, but scientists esteem him even more as a leader and thinker. In 1913 he said that the life of a living cell 'is the expression of a particular dynamic equilibrium'. He visualized living processes like a fountain, which has a permanent shape, and yet is in incessant motion. He struggled against the idea that the chemistry of living things is different from the rest of chemistry, and was never tired of telling how, when he was young, a very distinguished chemist had said to him: 'The chemistry of the living? That is chemistry of protoplasm; that is super-chemistry; seek, my young friend, other ambitions.'

Because he refused to take this advice, he became the main leader of modern biochemistry.

'I took him for a natural'

HOPKINS, Gerard Manley, (1844–1889), one of the most intense, flaming and forcible poets of modern English.

Sensitive, scrupulous, with a first-rate brain and a passionate response to the world around him, Hopkins belonged to a well-to-do family of the middle classes. At twenty-two he was received into the Catholic Church while still an undergraduate at Oxford; and soon afterwards he became a Jesuit. In his journal on one occasion Hopkins recorded the sight of a dead sheep under a stone hedge: 'There ran slowly from his nostril a thick flesh-coloured ooze, scarlet in places, coiling and roping its way down, so thick that it looked like fat.' Such observations are part of the key to his peculiar poems. Like a Darwin or a Preraphaelite painter, he observed with precision, or with a passionate science. But then he believed also that the world is 'charged with the grandeur of God'. Lacking consciousness, everything in the world gives out what Hopkins called a 'dull glory'; but man is different: man is created to praise, and could make in his life or poems a conscious bright glory out of the dull glory. So Hopkins as a poet transformed the dull glory of sunset, or stars, leaves, plums, metals, swirls of water, anemones in a rock pool, or a kestrel hovering on the wind:

> The world is charged with the grandeur of God.
> It will flame out, like shining from shook foil.

Honest, precise, passionate observation had to be matched by a precise, passionate, re-burnished, poetically unpoetical or unstaled language, also in God's honour. Hopkins could begin a poem on seeing a kestrel against the dappled sky of early morning in a way syntactically and verbally unfamiliar, yet brilliantly apt and not difficult to construe:

> I caught this morning morning's minion, kingdom of
>   daylight's dauphin, dapple-dawn-drawn Falcon, in
>   his riding
> Of the rolling level underneath him steady air ...

He was always perfecting his knowledge. There are stories of him tucking up his robes and ploughing a furrow to 'know' ploughing, and of the gardener at the Jesuit seminary, who could not believe that Hopkins was a great scholar because he had seen him staring at a piece of glass in the drive – 'I took him for a natural,' said the gardener. At times the sense of God and the ability to praise deserted Hopkins: out of such spiritual desolation he wrote, in his 'terrible sonnets', some of the most remarkable religious poems since those of Donne (q.v.) and George Herbert:

> I am gall, I am heartburn: God's most deep decree
> Bitter would have me taste: my taste was me.

In 1889 he died of typhoid in Dublin, where he was professor of Greek at the Royal University, leaving the bulk of his poems still unpublished (publication was delayed till 1918), and leaving also a series of letters filled with some of the most piercing criticism of literature in the English language. Hopkins – a little uncomfortably – saw a kinship between his poetic nature and that of Walt Whitman (q.v.).

Hudson of Hudson Bay

HUDSON, Henry, English navigator of the seventeenth century, who gave his name to Hudson Bay and the Hudson River, and whose attempts to find a north-east and north-west passage greatly extended the knowledge of the Arctic.

His first voyage, in 1607, was intended to find a quick way to China by way of the North Pole, but resulted instead in the establishment of the Spitzbergen whale fisheries. In 1608, in the service of the Dutch East India Company, he sailed 150 miles past the site of New York up what is now the Hudson River, before satisfying himself that that was not the way to the East. In 1610, sailing in the *Discovery*, he explored what is now Hudson Bay (which others had visited before) and was frozen in. Dissension broke out among his crew, and in the spring came hunger. The men went into the 'Woods, Hilles & Valleys, for all things that had any shew of substance in them, how vile soever: the mosse of the ground, then the which I take the powder of a poste to bee much better, & the Frogge (in his ingendring time as loathsome as a Toade) was not spared'.

His crew mutinied. On the way home Hudson and his young son were set adrift in an open boat and perished. The evidence provided by the survivors made the authorities more than ever convinced of the existence of a north-west passage. but the practical result was the establishment of the Hudson Bay fur trade.

Harken to the sacred dreamer

HUGO, Victor Marie, (1802–1885), a leader of the French Romantic Movement, poet, novelist and dramatist. He bade the French

> Listen to the poet's voice,
> Harken to the sacred dreamer.

The French and the world have obeyed, for a while, though Hugo's reputation has declined no less than the reputation of Scott (q.v.).

Owing to disagreements between his parents, his childhood was unhappy. In old age he recalled 'the dwarfing of childhood by physical and spiritual night' and considered 'the supreme happiness of life is the conviction we are loved'. His father had been one of Napoleon's generals, and Hugo declared his ambition as a writer by saying histrionically that he wished to be Chateaubriand (q.v.) or nothing. In 1827 he lifted the banners of a romantic crusade (romanticism coming belatedly to France after climbing to its peaks in England and Germany), to show that 'the object of modern art is not beauty but life'. In this period came the novel *Notre Dame de Paris* (1831) and the tragedy *Hernani* (1830). Swinburne rashly said that *Hernani* made it 'evident for ever to all but the meanest and most perverse of dunces and malignants' that Hugo 'was the greatest tragic and dramatic poet born since the age of Shakespeare'. The malignants included the classicists: there were riots between classicists and romanticists when *Hernani* was first acted in Paris.

Victor Hugo plunged also into politics, a flamboyant orator. He opposed Napoleon III (q.v.), and incited troops against him in Paris at the time of the *coup* of 1851. In 1852 he went into exile in the Channel Islands, where he wrote the novel *Les Misérables* with its theme of redemption through suffering and love. In 1870 he returned in triumph to France. For the rest of his life he was regarded as a national institution and was the idol of literature, given a grave in the Pantheon when he died.

Hugo was a strange mixture of meanness and extravagance, caution and daring, imagination and lack of feeling. He is now perhaps under-estimated. In verse or in prose he unites at his best the open eye and a romantic intuition:

'The sea never tells what it means to do. There is everything in this abyss, even chicanery. One might say that the sea had designs; it advances and retreats, it proposes and retracts, it prepares a squall and then gives up its plan, it promises destruction and does not keep its word. It threatens the North, and strikes the South.'

Swinburne, ending a brief account of Hugo (which may stand for his effect in, and for a while after, Hugo's own lifetime) said of him, he was 'unsurpassed in sublimity of spirit, in spontaneity of utterance, in variety of power, and in perfection of workmanship; infinite and profound beyond all reach of praise at once in thought and in sympathy, in perception and in passion; master of all the simplest as of all the subtlest melodies or symphonies of song that ever found expression in a Border ballad or a Pythian ode'.

Impact, if not always merit, is to be measured by the reading of prime ministers. Gladstone ruled England on Homer, Stanley Baldwin on Mary Webb, and Lloyd George always carried *Les Misérables* with him wherever he went.

ILLUSTRATION: Page 177.

Tackling the world

HUMBOLDT, Alexander von (1769–1859), German explorer and scientist, author of *The Cosmos*. In his day this son of a Prussian officer became, after Napoleon, the most famous man in Europe. He owed this great reputation to his universal knowledge and diplomatic gifts. He was trained as a mining engineer, was interested in botany by one of the companions of Captain Cook (q.v.) and entered the Weimar Circle of Goethe and Schiller; Goethe (q.v.) wrote that he was 'always struck with fresh amazement in his company', and regarded him as without a rival in extent and versatility of knowledge.

Humboldt set out to join Napoleon in Egypt, but unexpectedly found himself in Madrid, where, even more unexpectedly, the Spanish minister d'Urquijo proposed that he should explore Spanish America. He sailed in 1799, and returned to Europe five years later, with a tremendous mass of notes, which he was to publish in thirty volumes. He now settled in Paris. Here, a German living in France, he conceived of science as a supra-national activity; and he became the founder of the international organization of science by persuading the Czar to establish a chain of magnetic and meteorological stations throughout Russia, and the Duke of Sussex, then President of the Royal Society, to set up a similar chain throughout the British Empire. His world-view of science was expressed in his *Cosmos*. 'I have been seized with the mad idea', he wrote, 'of representing in a single work the whole material world.' He assembled material for this throughout his life and published the first volume at the age of seventy-six, and the last when he was eighty-nine.

In one aspect he was the H. G. Wells of his time: he succeeded in giving a readable and comprehensive outline of contemporary science, approaching nature in the spirit of the German Romantics; he was, in fact, the outstanding figure on the scientific side of their movement. His famous description of the effects of an earthquake is typical. 'A single instant annihilates the illusion of our whole previous life; we feel the imagined repose of nature vanish, and that we are ourselves transported into the realm of unknown destructive forces. Every sound affects us – our attention is strained to catch even the faintest movement of the air – we no longer trust the ground beneath our feet. Even in animals similar inquietude and distress are produced; dogs and swine are particularly affected, and the crocodiles of the Orinoco, which at all other times are as dumb as our little lizards, leave the agitated bed of the river and run with loud cries into the forest.'

Humboldt's synoptic view of all nature gave a strong impetus to scientific exploration. It helped to inspire the voyage of the *Beagle*, which carried Charles Darwin over regions where Humboldt had blazed the scientific path; and without making any major discovery himself, he laid the foundations of physical geography and meteorology.

The fame of Humboldt declined almost as quickly as it had risen. His description of the universe, enormously valuable and widely read in its day, was scientific journalism of the highest class, which was quickly outdated with the advance of science. His function as an organizer of international science was taken over by societies and governments, and his personal investigations in a score of different sciences were taken over by specialists. But his 'mad idea' of representing in a single work the whole material world strengthened the conception of the unity of science, of nature, and of mankind. It was never more valuable than it is today, in the split society and the split world of the twentieth century.

ILLUSTRATION: Page 180.

The sceptic

HUME, David, (1711–1776), Scottish philosopher and historian, developed the empirical philosophy of Locke (q.v.) and Berkeley (q.v.) to what seemed to be its logical conclusion, a complete scepticism concerning the rationality of the beliefs we hold: 'If we believe that fire warms, or water refreshes, 'tis only because it costs us too much pains to think otherwise.'

Hume's serene disposition made him proof against the hostile reception of many of his works. Of the publication of his most important book, the *Treatise on Human Nature: being an Attempt to introduce the experimental Method of learning into Moral Subjects* (1738) he wrote: 'Never literary attempt was more unfortunate. ... It fell dead-born from the press. ... But being naturally of a cheerful and sanguine temper, I very soon recovered the blow.' His *History of England*, written from a Tory standpoint, also met with disapproval from all parties, and it was fortunate that Hume was 'ever more disposed to see the favourable than the unfavourable side of things'. Shortly before his last painful illness, which he bore with his customary resignation, he wrote a short paper *My Own Life*, containing a 'formal oration' of himself: 'A man of mild disposition, of command of temper, of an open, social and cheerful humour, capable of attachment, but little susceptible of enmity and of great moderation in all my passions. Even my love of literary fame, my ruling passion, never soured my temper, notwithstanding my frequent disappointments.'

In the *Treatise* Hume's empiricism led him to accept the view that every idea has an antecedent impression: 'All our simple ideas in their first appearance are derived from simple impressions, which are correspondent to them and which they exactly represent'. When later he came to consider the idea of causation he therefore asked from what impression it was derived. Presumably it was from some relation between objects; but his analysis of the possible relations between cause and effect (contiguity, priority of cause to effect in time, constant conjunction) led to nothing but the sceptical conclusion that 'objects have no discoverable connexion together; nor is it from any other principle but custom operating upon the imagination, that we can draw any inference from the appearance of one to the experience of another'. This demonstration by a rational eighteenth-century man that there is no such thing as a rational belief was unlikely to disturb Hume himself: 'I dine, I play a game of back-gammon, I converse, and am merry with my friends; and when after three or four hours' amusement, I wou'd return to these speculations, they appear so cold, and strain'd, and ridiculous, that I cannot find in my heart to enter into them any further'.

ILLUSTRATION: Page 179.

'Darwin's bull-dog'

HUXLEY, Thomas Henry, (1825–1895), English biologist. In 1860, one year after the publication of Charles Darwin's *Origin of Species*, the British Association for the Advancement of Science met at Oxford. Bishop Wilberforce (a mathematician) announced his intention to 'smash Darwin' (who was not present). After speaking 'for full half an hour with inimitable spirit, emptiness and unfairness', he turned to the young Huxley, already known as an avowed Darwinist, and 'begged to know, was it through his grandfather or his grandmother that he claimed his descent from a monkey?'

'If then', said Huxley 'the question is put to me, would I rather have a miserable ape for a grandfather, or a man highly endowed by nature and possessing great means and influence, and yet who employs those faculties and that influence for the mere purpose of introducing ridicule into a grave scientific discussion – I unhesitatingly affirm my preference for the ape.'

It was this moment in his life – this unsought controversy with a pompous ignoramus – that established this great anatomist as a powerful figure in Victorian science; a fearless and ingenious debater. Huxley's first scientific paper was published when he was twenty. Like Darwin, he had formative years of travel (on H.M.S. *Rattlesnake*, from 1846 to 1850), and like him specialized on particular groups of sea-animals. Most of his early papers were on invertebrates. But it was his acceptance of, and keen development of, Darwinism (which can be dated to his review of the *Origin of Species* in *The Times* for 26 December 1859) that made him into the greatest comparative anatomist of his day, the great classifier, the consolidator of Darwin's principle, the agent of order.

It is impossible to give an idea of Huxley's extraordinary output of work, or of the remarkable variety of the subjects in his knowledge – knowledge as profound as it was catholic. Endowed with a restless energy, which may be hereditary, his talk (as his son Leonard describes it) 'was at once copious and crisp'. So was his writing: he wrote nearly 100 essays, nearly 200 scientific papers, and over twenty books, some of which went through over a dozen editions in his lifetime. Physiology, the cell, evolution, comparative anatomy, geographical distribution, physiography, geology: to all these subjects he contributed major papers of analysis and major works of synthesis. Yet (and in this he was unlike Darwin) he found time for art, music, literature, even fiction.

Notwithstanding his vast and fundamental contribution to the modern arrangement of animals, Huxley is valued as a zoologist by – zoologists. To humanity his greatest contribution was perhaps another, which can be best expressed in the words of Lord Hobhouse: 'His strongest claim to reverence and gratitude ... is the steadfast courage and consummate ability with which he fought the battle of intellectual freedom, and insisted that people should be allowed to speak their honest convictions without being oppressed or slandered by the orthodox.'

ILLUSTRATION: Page 181.

I

Peer Gynt among the trolls

IBSEN, Henrik, (1828–1906). 'Enjoyment of Ibsen', wrote Bernard Shaw of the plays of this Norwegian dramatist and poet, 'is a question of strength of mind. The quantity of truth the average man can bear is still very small; and every increase of the dose is met by piteous protests and cries of "Pessimist", "Cynic", "Morbid" and the like.' Ibsen's dramas of social realism were certainly so greeted. 'Dramatic impotence, ludicrous amateurishness, nastiness, vulgarity, egotism, coarseness, absurdity, uninteresting verbosity, suburbanity' was the reaction of the London *Daily Telegraph*. Shaw, his defender, replied: 'Ibsen supplies the want left by Shakespeare. He gives us not only ourselves but our situations. ... One consequence is that his plays are much more important to us than Shakespeare's.'

Perhaps. It was certainly a portent or a menace in 1879 when the 'new woman' slammed the door in Ibsen's *Doll's House*; but Ibsen would now be in that mist which so neatly enwraps, for example, John Galsworthy, had he depended solely upon a dramatic reflection of social problems. From that point of view *Ghosts* (1881) is altogether *vieux jeu* in our world of Kinsey Reports. Ibsen, in fact, survives since he was a poet. Even in apparent realism he made use of the poet's weapons and creations of symbol and myth.

In his creative life Ibsen never allowed himself to grow stiff and dead. 'There are actually moments', he wrote in despair about his own country, 'when the whole history of the world appears to me like one great shipwreck, and then the only important thing seems to be to save oneself' – which Ibsen did by withdrawing fom Norwegian stuffiness to the larger air of Germany and Italy, fleeing from 'all those cold and uncomprehending Norwegian eyes in the windows and streets'; and by changing (as it appeared) from poet to realist, and back again to poet in his old age.

The poet, it is true, seemed to modify into a man with top hat and frock coat, avid for decorations, who was even reconciled with a Norway, and an 'average-ness', he had rejected; but underneath was always the seer who in 1867, before the first of his social dramas, had fashioned the magnificent dramatic poem of *Peer Gynt*. The essential Ibsen is in Peer, one of the universal beings of world literature, the man who lived with the trolls but in the end rejected their teaching of 'to thyself be enough'.

'Worthy of respect'

IVAN THE TERRIBLE, (1530–1584). Czar of Russia, a monstrous tyrant at a time when cruelty was quite common, the first despot of modern Russia, but not the last.

'A goodlie man of person and presence,' wrote an English observer of Ivan, 'well favoured, high forehead, shrill voice, a right Sithian.' Queen Elizabeth regarded him favourably – from a distance, and even agreed to a proposed marriage between the Czar and Lady Mary Hastings (though it was never effected). To foreign visitors, Ivan was full of bearish charm; and he was never called 'terrible' – the Russian adjective, which usage has translated as 'terrible', really means 'respected' or 'worthy of respect'. Ivan was certainly that.

It was an age of violence: Henry VIII, Philip II, the Inquisition, the St Bartholomew's Day massacre – Ivan was no lone tyrant; it was just that he was crueller (and to less purpose) than anyone else. His youth, under a regency, was callous: torture and sudden death were commonplace, and Ivan learnt an early lesson: that ruthlessness was the only way to ensure complete control. Yet the first years of his reign were very equable: he called a general assembly of nobles and clergy, and proposed certain Church reforms. He disliked the nobles very much – they were too independent; and when they refused to swear an oath of allegiance to his son when Ivan was dangerously ill, he began to destroy them.

He was alternately depressed and elated. He would pour burning brandy over those who irritated him; and then be contrite. One of his palaces he turned into a complete parody of a monastery, with himself as Abbot. Bears would be let loose in the courtyard on visitors; and the 'Abbot' would shake with laughter, before hurrying off to perform some Holy office; that done, he would spend an evening in the torture cells, often assisting with the torment. His professed aim was the destruction of the nobles: but he was undoubtedly a pathological sadist as well. He had absolute power: and he used it. When some English women laughed at his odd behaviour he had them stripped in front of everyone, and four or five bushels of peas emptied on the floor. Then the women were made to pick up all the peas; when this was done, Ivan gave them some wine, and said that he hoped they would think twice before they laughed at an Emperor again.

Sometimes his revenges were more severe. Hearing that the people of Novgorod had been in touch with the King of Poland, and had sworn allegiance to him, he resolved to punish the town, and set off with his *Oprichniki*, his personal troop, each one of whom had on his saddle-bow the insignia of a dog's head (to devour enemies) and a broom-handle (to sweep away treason). First, all the monks were flogged to death, then the townspeople were roasted over slow fires, and some drowned in the icy river. Ivan always carried his sadism to the ultimate: he would visit widows of his tortured victims and then torture them. Something like 60,000 died in Novgorod. His wrath satisfied, Ivan summoned the remaining townspeople to the market square; 'Inhabitants of Novgorod,' he said, 'you whose lives have been spared, pray God to grant us a happy reign. ... Now let lamentation and groaning cease! Let all regrets be hushed! Live and prosper in Novgorod. .... Depart in peace to your dwellings.' In Moscow he built a giant frying pan for the light grilling of his victims. Madness could not go much further.

He would get so angry over trifles that he would foam like a horse. The man who had been hailed as a 'very Christian prince' had become a Slav Nero. So powerful an autocrat was he that for hours after he died no one dared approach his body – they could not believe he was dead. He was the first despot of modern Russia; but not, unfortunately, the last.

Charles Ives

IVES, Charles, (1874–1954), American composer. As a young graduate of Yale, Charles E. Ives founded a successful insurance firm of Ives and Meyrick; and there he worked until 1930, when illness made him retire. Business man or no, Ives had been composing since childhood, when he wrote a dirge on the death of one of the family pets – much performed in the family and in his Connecticut village. Ives became a business man for perhaps two reasons – it freed him from any need to compromise, and he believed it to be his duty. He disliked art for art's sake or for the artist's sake, and he believed that a man whose intellectual and moral muscles had not been toughened in everyday life could never be a full artist, and would lack what he called 'spiritual sturdiness'. Not surprisingly, Ives attacked the effete Debussy (q.v.), and he suggested that the content of Debussy's music would have been worthier of his manner 'if he had hoed corn or sold newspapers for a living'.

The spiritual home of Charles Ives was Concord, Mass., and his spiritual atmosphere has been New England transcendentalism, which has helped him to be a courageous individual, equipped him with a social conscience, set him on a search for the infinite, and has also made him too content with the simple and the commonplace. He has worked by a kind of ecstacy and logic of inspiration to compose music which is large in scope, virtues and vices. His work varies from the uproarious vulgarity of such a song as *The Circus Band* to the classical counterpoint of the first movement of his Second Symphony and the anarchic aspirations of his great *Concord Sonata*. Those who have recently discovered the music of this astonishing man have made too much of its 'modernity'. In his New England isolation, Ives was certainly making technical discoveries many years before the great European innovators Schönberg (q.v.) and Stravinsky (q.v.). But to call Ives modern, as Ives himself said of Emerson, is 'as futile as calling today's sunset modern.'

J

'A world called Henry James'

JAMES, Henry, (1843–1916), American novelist. His father, a Swedenborgian with means, believed that the Divine Guidance would lead to the Divine

Truth. This meant *laissez-faire* in his children's education. They were shuttled between schools and tutors in America, France, Germany, Switzerland, England. So Henry, born an American, was bred a cosmopolitan. Though he once said, 'The mixture of Europe and America which you see in me has proved disastrous', it made him. He declared he would have loved to be popular. Today he is universally accepted as the supreme interpreter of 'the international situation', in terms of the American-in-Europe. He had to find a base. First, a young man, he tried Rome, saying, 'It beats everything'. Then he tried Paris. But though Flaubert read his stories and said they were *proprement écrit*, Paris wouldn't do. 'I must be a born Londoner', he decided, and took permanent root there. And in London the unique style developed. First straightforward, as in *Roderick Hudson*; then alembicated; then what Hardy described as 'a ponderously warm manner of saying nothing in infinite sentences'. In London he succumbed to what he called 'the great dining-out business', and the famous conversation flowered. He spoke, it was said, in 'a Chinese nest of parentheses'. These proliferated more and more in his prose, particularly when he began to dictate his novels. Steadily he settled down to what a wit called the 'simple dynastic arrangement. James the First, James the Second and the Old Pretender.'

His appearance ripened with his style. At last his secretary saw him as 'an eminent cardinal in mufti, or even a Roman senator amusing himself by playing the part of a Sussex squire'. But the magisterial air and the taste for duchesses – 'I can stand', he said, looking round a gilded Mayfair drawing-room, 'a great deal of gold' – never ossified his incredibly delicate and sensitive perception of the nuances of human behaviour. In his essay on *The Art of Fiction*, he speaks of 'an immense sensibility, a kind of huge spider-web, of the finest silken threads, suspended in the chamber of consciousness and catching every air-borne particle in its tissue'. Such a sensibility he retained to his death. He enjoyed hugely the process of *being* Henry James, of watching the great oiled cylinders of his mind throbbing smoothly like a liner's engines. In such a mood he would send a telegram, 'Will alight precipitately at 5.38 from the deliberate 1.50', or call a dog 'something dark, something canine'. All that was a veneer for the dedication to his art – a remorseless, lifelong dedication.

He wrote of his own 'wasteful habit or trick of a greater feeling for people's potential propriety or felicity or full expression than they seemed able to have themselves'. The sequence of novels, the interpretation of which has now become a major industry of the major critics, made a triumph out of the wasteful habit. 'Never cease to watch whatever happens to you', was his bequest to younger writers. His whole life consisted in a steadfast observation of himself and a conversion of what he saw into fiction. 'As there is a world called "Dickens", another called "Balzac", so', it has been said, 'there is a world called "Henry James".'

ILLUSTRATION: Page 215.

Countryman-composer

JANÁČEK, Leoš, (1854–1928), Czechoslovakia's most original composer, whose masterpieces are too seldom performed in the West.

The culture from which Janáček emerged is foreign to Western Europe; its artists are unnamed, its painting and craftsmanship are exhibited only in the half-light of churches, and its music is made not in the concert-hall, but in the houses and the fields. He was born in a Moravian village, one of the fourteen children of a schoolmaster, who began Janáček's musical education. At ten the child received a bursary which enabled him to go to a monastic school for several years. There Janáček and other boys formed a small band which played at banquets and marriages. In later life his own music, even at its most abstract, retained this nexus with common life. Inflections and rhythms of Moravian speech and a delight in Slav folk-music influenced him in a style which expressed national sentiments in a highly individual way; and since he was a Slav, much of his work was suggested by Russian literature – Tolstoy, Gogol, Ostrovsky, Dostoyevsky (qq.v.). Janáček's operas may deal with tragic, introspective or neurotic subjects – *Katia Kabanova* is based on Ostrovsky's great tragedy *The Storm*, the nightmarish *Aus einem Totenhaus* on Dostoyevsky's *House of the Dead* – but musically they are free from sophistication, though every bar reflects the austerity of the composer's upbringing.

Janáček was a countryman-composer in an urban, cosmopolitan age. He had a peasant roughness and shrewdness, and intolerance of authority. At the Prague Conservatory as a young man he wrote too honest a review of a concert given by one of the professors, and was expelled for a while. Yet typically he combined his dislike of the academic with an academy of his own which he set up at Brno in 1881. There he spent the greater part of his life in obscurity, teaching and composing.

Jenufa, Janáček's most famous opera, reached fame in the least probable way. It had been given a production in the country and had then been quickly and quietly put aside. A countrywoman was overheard singing airs at her work, the airs proved to come from *Jenufa*, which thus found its way to Prague, and from Prague to the opera houses of the world. To the old man's surprise *Jenufa* made him famous. When he died in 1928, he left behind him in manuscript his *Festival Mass*, a hymn of joy at once sacred and profane.

'Life, liberty and the pursuit of happiness'

JEFFERSON, Thomas, (1743–1826), American statesman, whose finest memorial is in the words of the Declaration of Independence.

'Within a few days I return to my family, my books and farms,' he wrote on leaving Washington for the last time as an old man, 'and having gained the harbour myself, shall look on my friends still buffeting the storm, with anxiety indeed, but not with envy.' Nearly all of Jefferson's honours were thrust upon him. He was often misguided, and lacked far-sightedness in politics, but he provided a good balance to Hamilton (q.v.) in the Congress. Of a good Virginian family, he always regarded Virginia as his real native land: his youth was gay, and charmingly blighted by a forlorn love-affair. Of the girl in question, he wrote, on the flyleaf of a book: 'Rebecca Barwell is the devil; if not the devil, she's one of his imps.'

He entered Congress, and from the beginning was anti-British. He denied that the English parliament had any rights over the colonists: but he was no political philosopher. 'State a moral case to a ploughman and a professor,' he said, 'the former will decide it as well, and often better than the latter, because he has not been led astray by artificial rules.' He was one of those chosen to draw up the Declaration of Independence, and wrote most of it himself: its sentiments are an accurate reflection of Jefferson's own. He sincerely believed in an aristocracy based on talent, and not on wealth or birth. 'We hold these truths to be self evident' says the Declaration, 'that all men are created equal, that they are endowed by their Creator with certain and inalienable rights, that among these are life, liberty and the pursuit of happiness.'

He did not like public office: and returned to Virginia as often as he could. But his ability caused him to be sent to France as ambassador; and then, in 1789, he was offered the Secretaryship of State. He tried to co-operate with Hamilton, but they were too opposed to get on well together. In the end Jefferson resigned in protest at Hamilton's financial policy. In 1800 he was urged to be President. Though he had little personal ambition, he felt it was his duty to agree. His credo was that of the staunch republican: he believed that a government's job was to stop men hurting each other, but otherwise to leave them to their own affairs. He was an unassuming leader, and would infuriate foreign diplomats by receiving them in carpet slippers. His greatest achievement as President was the Louisiana Purchase, (1803) by which France sold the United States the vast territories now comprised in Louisiana, Missouri, Arkansas, Iowa, Minnesota, Kansas, Nebraska, Colorado, North Dakota and South Dakota, Montana, Wyoming and Oklahoma. His greatest error, which turned his supporters from him, was the embargo on British ships, an action that harmed America much more than it did Britain. He was not a handsome man; 'it must be owned', someone once said, 'that his greatest personal attraction was a countenance beaming with benevolence and intelligence.' He was proud that no blood was shed while he was President. To America he left a legacy of the kindly liberal, who through good works and good faith could inspire a nation. 'Enlighten the people generally,' he wrote, 'and tyranny and oppression of both mind and body will vanish like evil spirits at the dawn of the day.'

In his own words, all his life he was as 'busy as a bee in a molasses barrel'. And he was busy till the day he died; he fell ill on the third of July, and kept himself alive until the fourth, exactly fifty years after the signing of the Declaration of Independence.

ILLUSTRATION: Page 218.

'The perfect warrior'

JENGHIZ KHAN, (1162–1227), the savage, barbarous and brilliant founder of the Mongol empire.

To the credulous Europeans of the thirteenth century, the Mongols were the inhuman off-spring of Hell. Their sudden unpredictable appearances, and their ferocity, enhanced the legend.

Jenghiz Khan unloosed the first horde of invaders upon the West. His father had been chief of a Mongol confederacy in the steppes of Central Asia, who died when he was young. By 1206, after suffering and persecution, Jenghiz Khan was master of the nomad world and acknowledged as such by a council of tribal notables. He now abandoned his old name of Temuchin for Jenghiz Khan, 'the perfect warrior'; and launched upon that tide of conquest that caused his people to be called 'the scourge of God'. First to fall were the Kin Tartars of northern China, who had displaced the Sung dynasty. Pouring through the Great Wall, his disciplined armies, led by himself, his sons and his brothers, were so completely successful that by 1214 he was ready to turn his attention to the West. Here his already enormous empire bordered the territories of Korezm. This was a powerful and prosperous empire which stretched from the Persian Gulf to the Indus, and northwards to the Caspian and Aral Seas, but a foolhardy gesture on the part of its Turkish shah was to loose an unprecedented torrent of destruction, and it was from the ruins of the Korezm empire that the Mongols made their appearance in Europe. The Russian princes of Kiev were the first to challenge the then unknown invaders, and from their rout Christendom learnt for the first time the horrors of a Mongol sack. Jenghiz once more turned his attention to China, and was preparing to annihilate the Sung dynasty of southern China, when he was made uneasy by a certain conjunction of the planets. He turned back towards his tented capital in Karakorum, and died on the way by the Sale river in Mongolia. His funeral escort slaughtered everyone they met on the road, so that news of his death should not cause trouble before the great tribal assembly had endorsed his division of the Empire among his sons. His burial-place is secret to this day.

Jenghiz Khan was tall, robust, scantily bearded, cat's-eyed, just, resolute and cruel, a genius in warfare and a ruler wise in his selection of counsellors. His personal attitude is best summarized in his own words: 'The pleasure and joy of man lies in treading down the rebel and conquering the enemy, in tearing him up by the root, in taking from him all that he has, in making his servants wail so that tears flow from the eyes and nose, in riding pleasantly upon his well-fed geldings, in making one's bed a litter upon the belly and navel of his wives.'

The tide of Mongol conquest ultimately receded, but left behind it more than the pyramids of skulls and the depopulated provinces that so appalled the Islamic and Christian worlds. Two brilliant courts, the Timurid court of Oxiana, and the Mogul court of Hindustan, were created by the descendants of Jenghiz Khan, and the Renaissance of Europe itself was fostered by the open trade-routes of the Mongol empire.

Fire in the deep cave

JOHN OF THE CROSS, Saint, (1543–1591), Spanish Carmelite friar, mystic and poet.

He was from Castile, the most severe province of Spain. After taking orders, he followed the calling of St Teresa of Avila (q.v.) for stricter discipline in religious houses. 'Though small in stature, I know he is great in God's eyes', St Teresa wrote of him; he was her ideal apostle in the work of reform. He lived in cramped caves, he prayed all night, he starved himself. In 1577 he was kidnapped by friars of an unreformed and less austere section of his order. For nine months they tortured him. His mind was dazed by a barrage of questions. But he survived, escaped from the monastery by twisting a rope of blankets and took refuge in St Teresa's convent. His pursuers could not suggest that the holy nuns would be likely to shelter a recalcitrant friar.

There was nothing of the man of action in St John, apart from this escapade. He was no religious leader. He was too rapt in the mystic union of the believer with God, and his poems are the proof of his utter devotion – especially the *Living Flame of Love* and the *Dark Night*. The latter starkly and superbly begins

En una noche oscura –

Upon a gloomy night
With all my cares to loving ardours flushed
(Overture of delight!)
With nobody in sight
I went abroad when all my house was hushed.

The lover through the dark night reaches his beloved, and the poem ends with the superb image of St John of the Cross discarding his cares among the lilies. In the *Living Flame of Love*, St John writes of the lamps of fire in his deepest caverns, of the living flame of love piercing to his soul's most profound centre.

His life consisted in the pleasure of shedding the possibilities of pleasure. 'To have pleasure in all things, have pleasure in nothing', he said; or 'Live in this world as if it contained only God and your soul, so that your heart may be held up by nothing which is human'. On his death-bed he announced, 'I shall sing Matins in Heaven'; and he lived till midnight, saying, 'It is time for Matins' as the bell began to sound. St Teresa's comment on him was 'So *good* a man'.

The Grand Cham

JOHNSON, Samuel, (1709–1784), English poet, critic, moralist and everlasting presence, 'that strange figure', wrote Macaulay, 'which is as familiar to us as the figures of those among whom we have been brought up, the gigantic body, the huge massy face, the black worsted stockings, the grey wig with the scorched foretop, the dirty hands, the nails bitten and pared to the quick. We see the eyes and the mouth moving with convulsive twitches; we see the heavy form rolling; we hear it puffing; and then comes the "Why, Sir!", and the "What then, Sir!" and the "No, Sir!" and the "You don't see your way through the question, Sir!"'

Macaulay sketches only the façade – the outwardness of the man who booms through Boswell and looms in portraits by Barry or Reynolds, the Grand Cham with the big bow-wow manner, the man who claimed, 'every man has a right to utter what he thinks truth, and every other man has a right to knock him down for it'. But his friend Goldsmith said, 'he had nothing of the bear but his skin'. Inside lurked compassion and a melancholia reaching the fringe of madness.

Johnson's line, 'Slow rises worth by poverty depressed', describes the source of his idiosyncrasies. The Lichfield bookseller's son had to leave Oxford without a degree for lack of funds. He was nearly fifty before his *English Dictionary* brought him fame, a pension and relative ease. Between lay failure as a schoolmaster; hack-work as a Grub Street translator; the bitterness of using great talents to little ends. But after the 'Dictionary', as George Saintsbury

wrote, 'eighteenth-century literature is centripetal and centrifugal to and from Johnson, as if he were a sort of maelstrom'. This is Boswell's period. It is easy to forget that most of the biography covers only the last third of Johnson's life. His writing was mainly over; the solemn and splendid poems, now too little read or regarded, the *Rambler* and *Idler* essays, and *Rasselas* (composed to meet his mother's funeral expenses). There was still the edition of Shakespeare to come, and his finest work in prose, the *Lives of the Poets*. But these were his years as a mighty talking-machine; the Great Bear relaxed at the Club among the intelligentsia or at the table of the brewer's wife, Mrs Thrale. 'A tavern chair', he said 'is the throne of human felicity.' Enthroned, he talked to kill. Boswell has preserved for ever the cannonade of his conversation: 'Were it not for imagination, Sir, a man would be as happy in the arms of a chambermaid as of a Duchess,' 'Patriotism is the last refuge of a scoundrel.'

Behind the self-assured common sense he wielded like a club in his conversation lay darker matters. He had a horror of being alone. A few days before he died he thanked God for preserving his understanding, particularly as he had had a great disposition to insanity. The great business of his life, he said, was to escape from himself. Religious obsession, a scrofulous disorder, this constitutional melancholia are the thunder-cloud behind his lightning epigrams. They condone his quirks: the wolfish gluttony, the odd tricks of saving up bits of orange-peel and touching posts as he walked the streets, the convulsive twitching and muttering. They make his humanity the brighter – the tenderness of his care, in his later years, for the strange crew he housed, the negro Frank, the blind Mrs Williams, the cat Hodge. His Dictionary is superseded; there are other critics and better essayists. But 'the shadow of his great rock', as Saintsbury put it, will long stand as 'so welcome a refuge in a waste and sweltering land of paradox and mirage, of crankery and quackery'.

ILLUSTRATION: Page 219.

Hero of the sea

JONES, John Paul, (1747–1792), sailor, fighter and adventurer, celebrated in American naval tradition as fervently as Nelson or Sir Richard Grenville in the naval tradition of the English.

This son of a Scottish gardener went to sea at the age of twelve. Disliking the slave-trade in which he found himself, he left his ship and had to make his way back from the West Indies to Scotland. On the voyage two of the officers died, and as the only man capable of navigating, he brought the vessel safe to port. The owners were so pleased that they gave him a command, whereupon he made one or two voyages to the West Indies. Here scandal and an ugly note came into his life when a sailor died after Jones had flogged him for disobedience. He was not an easy captain, for on another voyage some of his crew mutinied.

For reasons never explained, though it was probably to avoid rumours about himself in Scotland, he now changed his name, adding Jones to the original John Paul, and he settled on the estates of a dead brother in Virginia, intending to stay there. But when in 1775 Congress decided to form a navy 'for the defence of American liberty', Jones was the senior first lieutenant. He was an arrogant, proud man, and his relations with the American naval authorities were never very good: he always demanded higher rank and paid little attention to those above him. Coming from Virginia, he was regarded as a 'foreigner' by the New England sailors, and this irked him; 'America has been the country of my fond affection since the age of thirteen,' he said. He was given a commission to 'distress the enemies of the United States by sea or land'. His crews were motley and his ships small and ill-armed, but he sailed for Europe and began to harry the English ships that came his way.

In 1779, near Leith, on a raid to seize British shipping, he saw forty merchantmen, defended by a few men-of-war, among which was the *Serapis*, of forty-four guns, commanded by Captain Pearson. Jones, with his old Indiaman, *Bon Homme Richard*, gave battle to *Serapis*. When the ships were accidentally fouled, he lashed them together, and began one of the bloodiest sea-conflicts in history, comparable in some ways to the fight of the *Revenge* under Sir Richard Grenville. Jones, tough, cool and determined, saw his main battery of guns go, half his crew lying dead. But to Pearson's question, 'Have you struck?' when it seemed that the *Bon Homme Richard* was lost, he replied, 'I have just begun to fight,' and won the day. 'The scene was dreadful beyond the reach of language,' wrote Jones.

He was lionized in Paris, and drifted from the American service (where he felt he never got his due preferment) to the Russian navy. But there were some unpleasant allegations over his behaviour to a young girl, and he returned to Paris. He died there in obscurity. His remains were eventually recovered from France and interred in state at the U.S. Naval Academy at Annapolis.

His secretary has left a description of him. 'A man of about five foot six inches high, well shaped below his head and shoulders, rather round shouldered, with a visage fierce and war-like.' He 'wore the appearance of great application to study, which he was fond of'. Although he was vain, and more than deserved the label of adventurer – and perhaps of pirate – Paul Jones was first and foremost a patriot, and revealed, in his tough resilient nature, those qualities that have been so marked in the American character in the days since the Revolution.

ILLUSTRATION: Page 222.

Concept of energy

JOULE, James Prescott, (1818–1889), English physicist, the chief establisher of the principle that energy is neither created nor destroyed, but only passes through various forms. It is the fundamental principle of modern physics; according to which electricity, heat, and mechanical motion are different forms of energy. Latterly Einstein has shown that mass itself is a kind of congealed form of energy.

Born at Salford, the son of a brewer, Joule was educated at home and tutored by John Dalton (q.v.). He owed his achievement to his keen mind and exceptional experimental skill, his industrial surroundings in Manchester, and his freedom from academic education and conventional scientific ideas. Unconsciously Joule adopted the engineer's method of measuring the amount of work done by a steam-engine (introduced by James Watt as a unit by which he could fix the price of his engines) and introduced it into physics. In this way he showed that the amount of work done by electricity in driving an electric motor was equivalent to the amount of heat it could produce in an electrical resistance. Thus electricity, heat and mechanical work were merely different manifestations of the same thing – energy, the capacity for doing work.

As he was an obscure young man in the provinces,

his first papers were rejected by the Royal Society. 'I was not surprised, I could imagine those gentlemen in London sitting round a table and saying to each other: What good can come out of a town where they dine in the middle of the day?' However, the Royal Society elected him a Fellow at the age of thirty-one. Joule was the first to point out that an absolute zero of temperature must exist, at −480° F. or −273° C.

The first public support for Joule came at the British Association meeting at Oxford in 1847. A youth of twenty-two in the audience got up and supported him. This was William Thomson, later Lord Kelvin. They became friends, and together discovered the effect used in liquefying air, which became the basis of the modern liquid air industry.

Ulysses and Finnegan's Wake

JOYCE, James, (1882–1941), Irish novelist and the most original of the pioneers who have influenced contemporary European writing. A Dubliner, he spent most of his life in exile from his own country, in Trieste, Paris and Zurich (where he died). Even as a young man teaching elementary English for a living to Trieste businessmen, Joyce never seems to have doubted his literary destiny; he suffered singular hardships and poverty for his vocation, and even in his latter years in Paris, when he had become famous, he did not escape misfortune – he began going blind.

Joyce's importance depends on the three books which occupied the greater part of his adult life: *Portrait of the Artist as a Young Man* (1916), *Ulysses* (1922) and *Finnegan's Wake* (1939). There is a continuity between them; each begins in the literary *genre* of the former, but pushes the experiment further. Unlike in form (the first is more or less conventional, the last two break completely new ground), they have in common Joyce's musical lyricism and Celtic traditions, his inherent sense of sin, his obsession with Catholicism, and his feeling for Dublin (many years after he had left his native city for ever it is said that he could recall the exact order of shops in a side street and would dwell for hours on local personalities).

One of Joyce's constant themes is revealed in the extract from Stephen Daedalus's diary on the last page of the *Portrait*. Stephen, *i.e.* Joyce, is writing of his forthcoming exile:

'April 16. Away! Away!

'The spell of arms and voices: the white arms of roads, their promise of close embraces and the black arms of tall ships that stand against the moon, their talk of distant nations. They are held out to say: We are alone, come. And the voices say with them: we are your kinsmen. And the air is thick with their company as they call to me, their kinsman, making ready to go, shaking the wings of their exultant and terrible youth.

'April 26. Mother is putting my new secondhand clothes in order. She prays now, she says, that I may learn in my own life and away from home and friends what the heart is and what it feels. Amen. So be it. Welcome O life. I go to encounter for the millionth time the reality of experience and to forge in the smithy of my soul the uncreated conscience of my race.

'April 27. Old father, old artificer, stand by me now and ever in good stead.'

'To forge ... the uncreated conscience of my race' is no bad description of the task he attempted in *Ulysses* and *Finnegan's Wake*. Joyce's books always exceeded their immediate predecessors in scope and ambition. The plot of *Ulysses* is carefully formal in every detail: a day in the life of Stephen and his Jewish companion Bloom, divided up according to corresponding books of Homer's *Odyssey*, is both an unrivalled picture of Dublin in 1904 and a symbol of man's pilgrimage through life. To convey what he has to say, Joyce had recourse to every variety of style in English literature. In *Ulysses* he begins probing the subconscious as a theme for literature – which is exemplified in the disconnected *tour de force* of Molly Bloom's soliloquy.

It is from the disconnected flow of such dreams that *Finnegan's Wake* comes. But Joyce pushes the experiment further, and language itself is broken up and words are re-formed. We have now left the conscious world of reason and logic. Joyce's new language attempts to express the hidden consciousness by an elaborate pattern of associations. So that though the heart of the book is man and the cosmos expressed in terms, primarily, of Celtic myth, the symbols used are charged with different currents of images as in our dreams, and the characters themselves are shadowy and changing:

'riverrun, past Eve and Adam's, from swerve of shore to

bend of bay, brings us by a commodious vicus of recir-
culation back to Howth Castle and environs.

'Sir Tristram, violer d'amores, fr'over the short sea, had
passencore rearrived from North Armorica on this side
the scraggy isthmus of Europe Minor to wiederfight his
peninsolate war: nor had topsawyers rocks by the stream
Oconee exaggerated themselves to Laurens County's gor-
gios while they went doublin their mumper all the
time. ...'

Finnegan's Wake was constructed over years of
labour, and Joyce weighed every word. It demands
time and application from the reader that few are
ready to give. Commentaries are helpful, but many
of Joyce's image-associations are 'private', and it
seems doubtful whether anyone can ever grasp them
in their fullness. Gramophone records of readings by
Joyce himself have survived the author, and these
help to bring out some of the musical and oratorical
qualities of his strange masterpiece.

Extrovert and introvert

JUNG, Carl Gustav, (born 1875), Swiss psychiatrist, and the most widely known of living psychologists. Opinions at the present day are sharply divided
on the value to be placed on his work, which can only
be understood as a modification of, and to some extent a reaction against, the doctrines of Freud (q.v.).
Jung's early experience as a psychiatrist in Zurich
led him to champion the new discoveries being made
in Vienna by Freud, who at the time was working
almost alone. The two men met personally for the
first time in 1907; and there followed several years of
friendship and the fruitful exchange of ideas, during
which Jung did much to help the new science of psycho-analysis. He became editor of the first psycho-
analytical journal and later (1911) President of the
newly-formed 'International Psycho-Analytical Association'. These appointments were fostered by Freud,
who was impressed by 'his exceptional talents, the
contributions he had already made to psycho-analysis,
his independent position' – *i.e.* the more liberal atmosphere of Zurich and the advantages he derived from
not being Jewish – 'and the impression of energy and
assurance which his personality conveyed'. But Jung
had already begun to follow a line of thought which

he has pursued ever since, giving the facts of analysis
a fresh interpretation of an abstract, impersonal and
non-historical character, and placing less emphasis on
the sexual aetiology of the neuroses. In 1913 theoretical differences came to a head, and after much bitterness (Freud later described Jung as 'one who was incapable of tolerating the authority of another ... and
whose energies were ruthlessly devoted to the further-
ance of his own interests') Jung left to found his own
characteristic school, which he calls 'Analytical
Psychology'.

Jung turned to the delimitation of types of personality, and classified men as 'introverts' and 'extro-
verts', these representing two fundamental attitudes
towards reality. He placed increasing emphasis on
transcendental aspects of unconscious mental activity,
and especially on the 'collective unconscious', which
contains primordial images or 'archetypes'. These
Jung derives from the common past experience of the
race; some, such as the *persona*, the *shadow*, the *animus* and *anima* and the *earth mother* have been isolated, and typically occur in dreams, phantasy, myths
and mystical experience. In his psychotherapy Jung
considers favourably the possibility of co-operation
between the conscious and the unconscious, regarding the latter as undeveloped rather than repressed.
In general Jung's psychology has proved more con-
genial than Freud's to many persons of a speculative,
mystical or religious caste of mind.

Codifier of Roman Law

JUSTINIAN I, (483–565), Flavius Anicius Iustin-
ianus, the greatest of the Emperors of the Roman
Empire in the East, whose reign was a tongue of fire
from the ashes of a decline which continued after his
death. It has been claimed that modern history begins
with this Emperor.

Justinian did so much, and yet his fame appears so
diffuse, that it has to be asked whether he was, after
all, a great man, and not just, as his many detractors
suggest, a very clever one. From humble origins, he
was adopted by his uncle Justin (Emperor, 518—527)
and went to Constantinople. There he made sure of
his own fortune by governing for his illiterate uncle,
whose successor he was. His ascension to the throne
was marked by one of the largest festivals Constanti-

nople had ever seen: and with him, equal receiver of the people's tribute, was Theodora, his empress, the daughter of a bear-master. She had been a byword throughout the Empire for licentiousness and depravity, and Justinian had married her against all advice. Yet for the rest of her life she was a model of rectitude, always at hand to strengthen her husband's indecision.

In an age of theological controversy, Justinian excelled by devoting himself to problems of the nature of God that no one could ever settle. After diligent persecution of both pagans and heretics, he himself became guilty of heresy at the end of his life. If his passion was theology, his talent was for imperial peculation, or extravagance. Wars against Persia, Italy and Spain sapped his exchequer. Enormous public works, a taste for splendid festivals, and superb buildings (the greatest which remains is the church of Santa Sophia in Constantinople) had to be paid for. The money was extracted from a burdened people in taxes: if they rose up in protest, the risings were crushed bloodily and savagely (30,000 people were killed in the rising of A.D. 532). Justinian was no tyrant himself, but he was willing to employ despotic ministers, and he closed his eyes to their methods, provided that they served him well. Above all, he is remembered for one thing – for consolidating the vast, haphazard mass of law. This codification of Roman Law, carried out under his command by the jurist Tribonian gave the Middle Ages a chance to know the meaning of civilized order. It has been a tap-root of our civilization.

K

'A quite impossible bird'

KAFKA, Franz, (1883–1924), Czech novelist and short story writer. The name, in Czech, means jackdaw. He said one day to Gustav Janouch: 'I am a quite impossible bird, I am a *kavka*. The coal merchant in the close of the Tein Cathedral has one. Have you seen it?' 'Yes, it flies about outside his shop.' 'Yes, my relative is better off than I am. It is

true, of course, that its wings have been clipped. As for me, this was not in any case necessary, as my wings are atrophied. For this reason there are no heights and distances for me. I hop about bewildered among my fellow men ... a jackdaw who longs to disappear among the stones.'

Kafka was Jewish, but not a Jew. He was Czech, yet not a Czech, for his language was German, and he only learnt to speak Czech in his adult life. He was a novelist, yet not a novelist: for his novels were unfinished, and if his instructions had been obeyed, they would have been destroyed at his death. He had a love affair, yet it was not a love affair, with Milena, the Czech translator of his early stories. 'Few things are certain, but this is one of them: we shall never live together, in the same apartment, body to body, at the same table, never, not even in the same town.' And while he was involved with Milena, he was engaged – three times, twice to the same girl. But he never married. He was religious, yet he was not religious, for he never had any revelation of God. Has the reader lost patience with this impossible person? But exactly – he was a jackdaw, as he said himself, hopping about bewildered among his fellow men. Life is not really as sad as all that? Then consider the end of Kafka, dying unable to speak with tuberculosis of the throat (and the end of Milena, after four years in Ravensbruck concentration camp, only three weeks before the allied invasion). And what God rules over a world like that? Kafka lived and wrote to find the answer; impatience, he said, was the only sin. Like Luther (q.v.) he had to find 'the deep hidden yes under the no'.

There is more to his life; more even to the end of it. In the summer before his death he was staying on the Baltic at Muritz, near the Berlin Jewish People's Home. In the kitchen he noticed a girl in her late teens scaling fish. 'Such gentle hands, and such bloody work', said Kafka, disapprovingly. At the end of the holidays Kafka decided to go to Berlin and set up house with her. This time he carried through his decision, and so did she, though she came from a respected orthodox home. Before he died, Kafka wrote to her father asking to be accepted, not as a practising Jew, but as 'a repentant one, seeking conversion'. He was not accepted; but Kafka was happy with his 'little family' – Dora Diamant, and his friend Robert Klopstock, who gave up his studies in Berlin to nurse him.

Above all his books, including *America* (1927) and *The Trial* (1925) and his stories, and a handful of profound epigrams and gnomic sayings, it is *The Castle* (1926), which stands out, a marvellous book (for once the word may be used literally) in which the world of folk-lore is reborn among us. The effect of it might be described by a note in the *Journal* of Kierkegaard (q.v.) that Danish magician whom Kafka loved and hated and resembled:

'One evening at dusk out at Peblingesøen there were two little girls and one of them said: "then a long way off she saw an old castle". I do not believe that even the greatest poet could produce such an effect as those thrilling memories of fairy stories, with the old castle "a long way off", and the "then" or "they went on a long way until ...".'

It was just so with Kafka:

'It was late in the evening when K. arrived. The village was deep in snow. The Castle hill was hidden, veiled in mist and darkness, nor was there even a glimmer of light to show that a castle was there ...'

Timepiece of Königsberg

KANT, Immanuel, (1724–1804), German philosopher. His influence, if now on the wane, has reached further than that of any other philosopher of modern times.

The contrast between Kant's teaching, which dominated philosophical thought for a century and a half, and the narrowness of his life is striking. Many philosophers have lived uneventfully, but Kant swam in a particularly small pond. At no time in his life did he venture more than forty miles from Königsberg: born and educated there, he refused all appointments elsewhere and eventually, at the age of forty-six, obtained the chair of logic and metaphysics in the university. Kant remained a bachelor, and his daily round was one of meticulous regularity: he was called by his man-servant at 5 a.m., studied for two hours, lectured for a further two, and then returned to his desk till it was time for his mid-day meal – the only regular meal of the day. From four to five he walked in all weathers, and spent the evening in lighter reading till he retired at 10 p.m. This routine Kant followed with such regularity and punctuality that the citizens of Königsberg used to set their watches by him. He appears to have been somewhat deficient in feeling; but against the austerity of his private life, and of his published writings, must be set his popularity as a lucid and likeable teacher, and his enjoyment of the evenings he spent in society during his earlier years, where because of his brilliant conversation, he was much in demand. Just over five feet tall, round-shouldered and feeble in voice, he owed his long life to the few demands he placed on a frail constitution.

As a philosopher Kant accepted the empiricism of Hume (q.v.) who had, he claimed, aroused him from his dogmatic slumbers. Now some 'sciences', *e.g.* mathematics, physics (in part) and metaphysics, appeared to give us knowledge in advance of experience, *e.g.* the knowledge that $7+5=12$, or that every event has a cause. Such propositions appeared to be not empirical but *a priori*: at the same time, according to another philosophical distinction, they did not seem to be true in virtue of the meanings of the words they contained, *i.e.* they were not analytic but synthetic. Accepting that we *do* have such knowledge, and realizing the need to account for it, Kant was led to ask in his *Critique of Pure Reason* (1781): 'how are synthetic *a priori* judgements (or propositions) possible?' and to deduce the nature of the 'categories' which are the necessary pre-conditions of all our thinking. At the same time he undertook to demonstrate the plausibility but essential meaninglessness of metaphysics. Philosophers today, while at one with him in his attack on metaphysics, do not share his initial assumptions concerning mathematics and the 'pure' parts of physics: they accept that these are analytic, and that their synthetic applications are empirical.

When the *Critique of Pure Reason* first appeared (besides his immensely influential *Metaphysic of Morals*, 1785, it is his most important work) it was almost ignored. Goethe once said that to read it was like stepping into a brightly lighted room; but its obscurity and the novelty of its terminology made it a formidable work to study. Nevertheless recognition was not long in coming to Kant: soon Königsberg became a shrine of philosophy, and he was consulted on a wide variety of problems – whether, for example, inoculation for the small-pox was lawful.

At the full height of his reputation Kant became involved in a clash with the Government over his religious doctrines. After some defiance he was forced by King Frederick William II to pledge that he would not lecture or write on religious subjects any more. This collision with the outside world is said to have depressed Kant so profoundly that he withdrew from society; soon after (in 1797) he ceased all academic lecturing. But as Kant was now seventy-three, this may not have been a major tragedy.

'The roaring of the wind is my wife'

KEATS, John, (1795–1821), English poet. 'I feel the flowers growing over me,' Keats said before dying of consumption.

No English poet was more compact of sensation. His friend Haydon the painter declared that he 'once covered his tongue and throat as far as he could reach with cayenne pepper in order to appreciate 'the delicious coldness of claret in all its glory' which was his own expression. Keats himself wrote, 'If a Sparrow come before my Window I take part in its existence and pick about the Gravel.' 'The roaring of the wind is my wife and the Stars through the window pane are my Children.' 'I feel more and more every day, as my imagination strengthens, that I do not live in this world alone but in a thousand worlds.' 'No sooner am I alone than shapes of epic greatness are stationed around me and serve my spirit the office which is equivalent to a King's own bodyguard – then "tragedy with scepter'd pall comes sweeping by''. According to my state of mind I am with Achilles shouting in the Trenches, or with Theocritus in the Vales of Sicily Or I throw my whole being into Troilus, and repeating those lines, "I wander, like a lost soul upon the Stygian Banks staying for waftage", I melt into the air with a voluptuousness so delicate that I am content to be alone.'

This 'voluptuousness so delicate' has brought a critical lash on to Keats – by persons as various as Byron, Gerard Manley Hopkins, and Carlyle, who accused him of wanting 'a world of treacle'. Keats was in no more than his twenty-sixth year when he died in Rome; and now that all his letters have been collected and published, we know more of the intensity of his feelings and judgements – 'I am certain of nothing but of the holiness of the heart's affections and the truth of imagination' – and of his exalted and balanced view of the poetical character; he may have exclaimed, 'O for a life of sensations rather than of thoughts!' but the thoughts crowded in. The poetical character 'does no harm from its relish of the dark side of things any more than from its taste for the bright one; because they both end in speculation'. A poet, he went on, 'is the most unpoetical of any thing in existence; because he has no identity – he is continually infor[ming] and filling some other Body – the Sun, the Moon, the Sea and Men and Women who are creatures of impulse, are poetical and have about them an unchangeable attribute – the poet has none;

no identity – he is certainly the most unpoetical of all God's Creatures'. To a poetical sensibility, this son of the keeper of a livery-stable joined a poetic gravity and intelligence. 'I find that I cannot exist without poetry' – but he added 'without eternal poetry'. 'My imagination', he wrote to Shelley, 'is a Monastery and I am its Monk.' In his brief life as medical student, poet and dying consumptive, a monk in the strict monastery of imagination, Keats was finely gifted in raising the mind to the pitch of expectation:

> Who are these coming to the sacrifice?
> To what green altar, O mysterious priest,
> Leadest thou that heifer lowing at the skies
> And all her silken flanks with garlands drest?

Again and again there is about to be a revelation –

> And as I sat, over the light blue hills
> There came a noise of revellers: the rills
> Into the wide steam came of purple hue –

And the revelation is revealed:

> 'Twas Bacchus and his crew!
> The earnest trumpet spake, and silver thrills
> From kissing cymbals made a merry din –
> 'Twas Bacchus and his kin!

So, too, in the *Ode to a Nightingale*. Four stanzas go by: the fifth begins

> I cannot see what flowers are at my feet
> Nor what soft incense hangs upon the boughs
> But in embalmed darkness, guess each sweet
> Wherewith the seasonable month endows
> The grass, the thicket, and the fruit-tree wild.

But that stanza has to be finished, and most of the next stanza has to pass, before the nightingale is revealed in full song, and before the poem continues in Keats's most familiar and singular lines, which are above label or change:

> Thou wast not born for death, immortal Bird!
> No hungry generations tread thee down;
> The voice I hear this passing night was heard
> In ancient days by emperor and clown:
> Perhaps the self-same song that found a path
> Through the sad heart of Ruth, when, sick for home,
> She stood in tears amid the alien corn;
> The same that oft-times hath
> Charmed magic casements, opening on the foam
> Of perilous seas, in faery lands forlorn.

He could contrive also the most life-enhancing images and lines –

Aye, on the shores of darkness there is light
And precipices show untrodden green.

His friend Leigh Hunt described Keats as under middle height – 'his lower limbs were small in comparison with the upper, but neat and well turned. His shoulders were very broad for his size; he had a face in which energy and sensibility were remarkably mixed up, an eager power checked and made patient by ill-health. Every feature was at once strongly cut, and delicately alive. If there was any faulty expression it was in the mouth, which was not without something of a character of pugnacity. His face was rather long than otherwise; the upper lip projected a little over the under; the chin was bold, the cheeks sunken; the eyes mellow and glowing, large, dark, and sensitive.'

ILLUSTRATION: Page 221.

Founder of the Labour party

KEIR HARDIE, James, (1856–1915), English politician, was the founder of the English Labour party in its present form. Without him the alliance of Trades Unions and Socialists might never have taken place.

Keir Hardie was by origin a Scottish miner and, at first, a miners' official. Early on he became a Socialist, whose Socialism was based on ethical principles, not on Marxism. It represented, in fact, the last flowering of British nonconformity. He rejected an alliance of Labour and Liberalism, and in 1893 took the lead in founding the Independent Labour Party at Bradford. The programme of the I.L.P. mixed Marxist phrases and religious phrases in a way calculated to appeal to British working-men; though Bernard Shaw claimed to have put into the programme the little sense that it possessed.

In 1892 Keir Hardie was elected to parliament, the first representative of labour. It was the day of top-hat and frock-coat. Hardie caused a sensation by going to the House of Commons in a cloth cap, attended by his supporters in a brake. This gesture of class consciousness has not been imitated by Labour M.P.s of a later generation. Keir Hardie took the lead in winning the Trades Unions for a federal association with the Socialist parties; and this, in

time, became the Labour party. In the House of Commons he led the party from 1906 until the outbreak of war in 1914; but as a parliamentary leader he was not a success. He was too simple. His simple nature and his way of appealing to the emotions cut him off from the practical issues. In foreign affairs he was a pacifist. When the war broke out he resigned his leadership, and soon afterwards died broken-hearted. The I.L.P. did not survive him so very long as a separate organization; but the Labour party has always retained something of his spirit. The rebels of the party can still protect themselves from Trades Union disapproval by arguing that Keir Hardie would have agreed with them. They are quite right. He was the greatest saint that the Labour movement produced, though saintliness is not a qualification for workable, everyday politics.

Planetary laws

KEPLER, Johannes, (1571–1630), German astronomer who discovered that the planets move round the sun in ellipses.

Kepler became a professor at twenty-three, but obtained most of his income from astrology, which he called 'the foolish and disreputable daughter of astronomy, without which the wise old mother would starve'. He was Tycho Brahe's assistant in Prague, and inherited his careful observations, from which he deduced the laws of planetary motion by a tremendous exertion of scientific genius and labour.

Besides his immortal discovery of the planetary laws, Kepler founded the modern theory of optics, under the impulse of the recent development of the telescope by Galileo and himself. The two great men corresponded, Kepler fully realizing Galileo's magnitude, though Galileo did not perceive in Kepler a genius as great as his own. Kepler, in fact, stood between the medieval past and modern present. He was deeply influenced by Pythagorean number-mysticism, and regarded the numerical coincidences that he found between the sizes of the planetary orbits as his greatest discovery. But Kepler knew his own importance. In the preface to his most comprehensive book he exclaimed: 'Let it await its readers for a century – God Himself has waited for six thousand years.' The book did not have to wait so long, for within a generation it was read by Isaac Newton (q.v.). By his theory of gravitation, Newton explained Kepler's laws, and the motion of all objects in the universe.

Student of God

KIERKEGAARD, Soren, (1813–1855), Danish student of God and man and the crisis of the modern age, whose thought now affects literature and theology in many countries of the world.

Severely brought up by an elderly father, a self-made Copenhagen merchant over-conscious of his sins, the young Kierkegaard went through familiar levels of experience – rebellion, dissipation, reconciliation (with his father) and conversion. While he was still an undergraduate reading theology, Kierkegaard fell in love with a young Copenhagen beauty, Regina Olsen, and she with him. But he then considered himself religiously bound to break the engagement and release the girl; which he did, and so plunged into a deeper suffering; this made him, he declared, a 'poet', someone as yet incompletely inside existence, though on the way to the divine.

Kierkegaard had before him now a brief fourteen years of thought, experience, thorough sense of mission, and authorship. 'A man must get out of the poetical and into the existential, and ethical.' He felt himself 'hardly more than a poet', and not be to what he indeed was, 'a strong ethico-religious character'. As men we *exist*: what can resolve those puzzling situations which are common to all of us? Not reason: and we must not refuse participation in the anguish of life – to do so is to lapse from individuality into the crowd which is 'untruth' – we must be individuals and dissolve our tensity and anguish in the only possible way – in faith, in God. Kierkegaard saw sharply the choice of individual or crowd – crowd which 'renders the individual completely impenitent and irresponsible'.

'The crowd is untruth. Therefore was Christ crucified, because, although he addressed himself to all, he would have no dealings with the crowd, because he would not permit the crowd to aid him in any way, because in this regard he repelled people absolutely, would not found a party, did not permit balloting, but would be what he is, the Truth, which relates it-self to the individual.' Loving the crowd denies loving your neighbour. Loving the crowd, 'making it the authority in matters of taste, is the way to material power, the way to temporal and earthly advantages of all sorts'. It was his concern not to presume to call himself a Christian, but (humbly) to know what Christianity is, and to attempt to re-introduce it into Christendom; he must unpick the crowd into its constituent individuals, since with the category of individuals, each 'alone in the whole world, alone before God', Kierkegaard said, 'the cause of Christianity stands or falls'. He remarked that the only inscription he could desire for his tombstone was *That Individual*.

For all the subtlety, vigour and wisdom of his writing, and the tactics and strategy of his books, Kierkegaard suffered from being the genius of a small provincial town. He suffered bitterly from attacks in the press. He was ridiculed for spindly legs and trousers too short to meet the socks, he was mocked at as a simpleton, though he has proved to be Denmark's greatest and most provocative writer.

ILLUSTRATION: Page 220.

Royal chaplain

KIRK, Robert, (c. 1641–1692), Chaplain to the Queen of the Fairies.

Then a spirit passed before my face, the hair of my flesh stood up; it stood still, but I could not discern the form thereof; an image was before mine eyes. – The spirits before Robert Kirk, who so aptly made this quotation from Job on the title page of his *Secret Commonwealth*, were the fairies – 'of a middle nature betwixt man and angel, as were demons thought to be of old'. Kirk was a Highland minister and scholar labouring at Aberfoyle in Perthshire. He translated the Psalms into Gaelic, but has a small and delightful immortality because of his knowledge of the Good People, which he imported in the pamphlet usually known as the *Secret Commonwealth of Elves, Fauns and Fairies*, written by him in 1691, and at last printed in 1815.

In Scotland the fairies had not dwindled under literary influence to elegant, airy-fairy, leaf-tripping miniatures of men and women. The Good People, so

Continued on p. 231

PLATE 9

LOUIS XIV (1638–1715) by Hyacinthe Rigaud.

PLATE 10

FLORENCE NIGHTINGALE (1820–1910), seated, and her sister. Water colour by W. White.

NEHRU (b. 1889).

HENRY JAMES (1843–1916).

LEONARDO DA VINCI (1452–1519). Presumed self-portrait.

LE CORBUSIER (b. 1887).

THOMAS JEFFERSON (1743–1826). Detail from *Declaration of Independence* by John Trumbull.

DR JOHNSON (1709–1784) by James Barry.

KIERKEGAARD (1813–1855) by N. C. Kierkegaard.

JOHN KEATS (1795–1821). Painted in Rome by Joseph Severn.

PAUL JONES (1747–1792). Mezzotint by an unknown engraver.

LERMONTOV (1814–1841) by P. E. Zabolotsky in 1837.

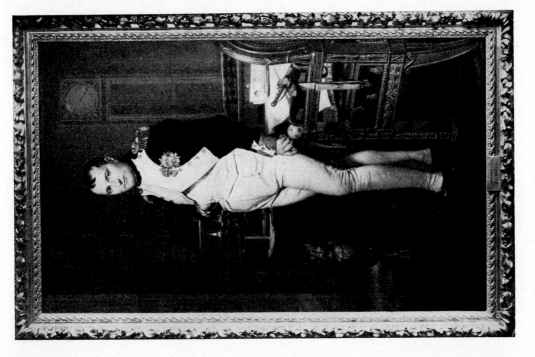

NAPOLEON (1769–1821) by David.

NELSON (1758–1805)
as a young captain, painted in 1781 after his return from the West Indies, by
J. F. Rigaud.

ANTONY VAN LEEUWENHOEK (1632–1723) by J. Verkolje.

JOHN LOCKE (1632–1704) by Godfrey Kneller.

LUTHER (1483–1546) by Lucas Cranach.

226

FRANZ LISZT (1811–1886) about the age of twenty-eight. By Ary Scheffer.

NICCOLO MACHIAVELLI (1469–1527) by an unknown Florentine sculptor.

MANTEGNA (1431–1506) self-portrait.

MARAT (1743–1793) murdered in his bath. By David.

MARIE ANTOINETTE (1755–1793) by Elisabeth Vigée-Lebrun.

PLATE 11

THE POMPADOUR (1721–1764) by François Boucher.

PLATE 12

RUBENS (1577–1640) and his first wife, Isabella Brant, in 1609. Self-portrait.

called 'to prevent the dint of their ill attempts', were a society behind society: they haunted small hills, struck hammers, baked bread, stole both nurses and children, shot stone arrow-heads at men and cattle, were inclined to partake of funeral feasts uninvited, made trysts with men and also women, as in the border ballads, and dressed (though their bodies were 'somewhat of the nature of a condensed cloud, and best seen in twilight') in 'plaids and variegated garments'. On quarter days these Good-bad People were apt to change their lodgings, when there was special danger of 'terrifying encounters with them even on high ways'.

Robert Kirk was a seventh son, and as such was no doubted credited with special powers. The story of his death or disappearance was told – and retold by Sir Walter Scott – that he swooned when walking on a fairy-hill, was taken to be dead, and was then buried in Aberfoyle graveyard, appearing afterwards to one of his relatives and saying that in fact he was a prisoner of Faery. In his role as anthropologist, Andrew Lang considered the *Secret Commonwealth* (which he edited and had reprinted) the best description of the fairies; in his role as poet, he wrote charmingly on the Fairy Minister:

> ... No more shall any shepherd meet
> The ladies of the fairy clan,
> Nor are their deathly kisses sweet
> On lips of any earthly man.
> And half I envy him who now,
> Clothed in her Court's enchanted green,
> By moonlit loch or mountain's brow
> Is Chaplain to the Fairy Queen.

Going for a walk with a line

KLEE, Paul, (1879–1940), Swiss painter and master of fairy-tales within the frame.

It was typical of Klee to paint what he called a 'Twittering Machine', a delicately drawn, linear, wiry, fantastic bird, equipped with a handle. Turn the handle – if you can catch hold of it, which you cannot – and a strange twittering will emerge from the beak and from the silent, plane surface of the picture. Klee, in his own words, wished art to 'sound like a fairy-tale and be at home everywhere'. He thought art should be 'a holiday, a change of atmosphere, and a point of

L

view, a transfer to another world, which presents a diverting spectacle', so that we come back to everyday life with our vitality renewed.

He was born at Münchenbuchsee, near Bern, and at first could not decide whether to be a musician (like his father) or to paint. His eyes made the choice, opening more and more to a world filled by items of enchanted animation. Going to Naples at twenty-two, he was delighted by the forms and oddities seen in the aquarium. Things became lively with the magic of their own personality (such a thing might be a firework, an eye, a crescent moon or a scarlet exclamation mark) – much as the toys come to life in the music of Bizet's *Jeux d'Enfants*. In 1914 Klee crossed the Mediterranean to Kairuan, where he discovered the perfect intermingling of fantasy and realism. Inner and outer worlds overlapped, paintings could be contrived like the carpets of Kairuan, the pattern coming to life; and Tunisian colour flooded into this quiet, gentle, hallucinated artist, who was able to boast before long 'Colour and I are one: I am a painter.'

'Nothing can replace intuition' was one of Klee's remarks. 'I want to be as if new-born' was another. He talked of going for a walk with a line, but he was always master of his own art: his fairy-tales were controlled and disciplined. When Hitler came to power, Klee was teaching at Dessau; and his art was well liked in Germany. His best pupil now turned informer, he hated the Nazis and was hated by them, he was ill and unhappy, and in 1933 he left Germany for Switzerland. There years before his death, the Nazis, thick and humourless, confiscated 102 of Klee's works. Some of his most intriguing masterpieces – including the *Twittering Machine* and *Around the Fish*, now in the Museum of Modern Art, in New York – were ridiculed in Hitler's Exhibition of Degenerate Art, which travelled around the Third Reich, every picture lopsided in its frame or mount. The action of the Nazis was like firing a fifteen-inch gun at a humming-bird, except that jewelled, whizzing, twittering, hovering art of this kind is indestructible.

The heart laid bare

KLEIST, Heinrich von, (1777–1811), German dramatist and story-teller. 'Oh,' he wrote of himself in a letter, 'there is a sad sort of clarity which nature has spared all those lucky ones who see only the surface of things. As for me, it shows me the thought behind every look, the meaning behind every word, the motive behind every action – it shows me everything around me, and even myself, in all their miserable bareness, and in the end my heart recoils in disgust from that nudity.'

Like his military forebears, Kleist spent his early life in the service of the King of Prussia; he joined the Army at the age of fourteen, saw active service at fifteen and was commissioned at twenty. Soon after, he resigned his commission to satisfy his longing for enlightenment; but his philosophical studies led to a shattering disillusionment: far from revealing absolute truth, they convinced him that it was not to be found on this earth. From 1802, when this crisis occurred, to his early death, he lived through a nightmare of vain projects, half-hearted resolutions and violent, but fruitless passions. His early cosmopolitanism changed to a fanatical hatred of the French and of Napoleon, whom he planned to assassinate; but his real enemy was himself. At the age of thirty-four he could stand it no longer, but formed a suicide pact with a married woman suffering from cancer and died after shooting her not far from Berlin.

As for his writings, their great strength is that 'he only wrote because he couldn't help it', as he himself remarked. Ambitious as he was, literature was only one of the many possible outlets for his restless energy and extraordinary gifts; and even his literary works were not safe from the self-destructive frenzy that thwarted all his other ambitions. He managed to destroy all but a fragment of his tragedy, *Robert Guiskard*, as well as his only full-length novel and an autobiographical work written shortly before his death. Yet his extant works – seven plays, eight long stories and two ingenious essays – have rightly won him a place among the five or six greatest German writers. One reason is the clarity of which he speaks, a clarity combined with the most intense emotional pressure.

The nature of disease

KOCH, Robert, (1843–1910), German bacteriologist and a major benefactor of mankind. Pasteur (q.v.) founded modern bacteriology, Koch converted it into a great instrument of medicine.

Pasteur's discoveries had opened up brilliant possibilities, but the means of exploring them had not been worked out. Koch possessed the peculiar combination of exactitude and thoroughness which this required. In his spare time as a country doctor, armed only with a good microscope, he made a detailed investigation of anthrax, in which he gave the first complete proof that a particular disease was due to a particular bacillus. He worked out the modern methods of investigating, preserving and staining bacteria and he produced photomicrographs of bacteria which have rarely been equalled. Koch persevered with all this technical work, he explained, because research on infective disease had led to such conflicting results.

His genius was immediately recognized by the German Health Office, and he was given an appointment and a room for research. Here he solved the problem of cultivating bacteria outside the body, by adding gelatine to the nutrient medium. He worked out the technique of disinfection and sterilization, introducing steam sterilization in place of dry heat. Within ten years Koch and his pupils elucidated the nature of eleven important human diseases, including tuberculosis, cholera, typhoid, diphtheria, pneumonia, meningitis, influenza and plague, besides that of many animal diseases.

At the Institute of Hygiene, founded for him in Berlin, in 1885, Koch not only directed research, but taught the new branch of medical science to students from his own country, and from all the world. His genius for consolidation and development was the perfect complement to Pasteur's originality.

Interpretation by pigment

KOKOSCHKA, Oskar, (b. 1886), Austrian painter, and one of the most energetic, flaming and productive masters of our age.

Kokoschka has lived in many places, Vienna, Berlin, Dresden, Paris, London. His father was Czech, his mother Austrian, and he himself belonged to Vienna, where he broke into strange flower under the special guardianship of the functional architect and pioneer of modernism, Adolf Loos. Coming to be known as 'the mad Kokoschka', he was writer and painter in one; and his energies and his attitudes broke provocatively with that faded, empty and easy charm which is the Austrian delusion and the Austrian bait for tourists. He has explained the wild tactics of his early life, his early painting, and writing, 'not as adventures of a bravado, but rather as a student's way to put his own nature to the test ... I was following up primarily two motives, which I saw reappearing like threads in the weft of modern society: to what limits will the individual nature flexibly accommodate itself and how rigid is the framework of modern society.'

Painting to Kokoschka has been a language with its own valid way of conveying ideas, and interpreting life. In one sense Kokoschka is the baroque artist (Viennese version) who threw an eye up to the restlessness and fecundity displayed upon painted ceilings in Vienna; but this baroque restlessness and extravagance unite with expressionism (see Edvard Munch), with expressive sacrifice of the literalness of things – or persons – in the search, even by paint, for what appears to be their message or their significance. After life, not after appearances, he has stated that for the most part 'we avoid human life, with the alternative of committing suicide or becoming a robot'. This painter of portraits, including portrait after portrait of himself, has declared that his problem is the man he meets in life ... 'he is the central figure in my thoughts because there are no egotistic interests to blur my vision. I myself am only interested in myself' (and the truth of this is in the self-portraits) 'when I am human as the others are'.

Neither the expressionist nor the baroque elements in Kokoschka are as much appreciated as they should be in England or America, as Kokoschka found when he came to London as an exile from Hitler's Central Europe. One of the leading English painters of a younger generation had the jocular habit of dismissing everything Kokoschka has ever painted, and talking of him as 'Oskar Kokoschka the beautiful spy', as though he were a character of Ruritanian romance. The reason, though, is less subservience to French painting, than the deliberate way in which the English have used French and Southern influences to counteract their own more or less Teutonic tendencies to excess.

From the early nineteen-twenties Kokoschka took to landscape, a good deal under French influence, especially the landscape of mountains and cities, so observing the subjects and so arranging the pictures that each painting of mountainous country seems an image of the universe, each painting of a modern city an image of a humanity without boundaries. They have the extent and sweep of a landscape by Rubens, though a Rubens of Austrian baroque, soaked in the German and Scandinavian desire to *express* and explain. Kokoschka has always chosen the high point for these orgiastic views, as when he painted the sweep of the Thames from a top window in the Savoy Hotel. The *Self-portrait of a Degenerate Artist* reproduced here (Plate 8) he painted in 1937, when the Nazis cleared his work out of public galleries and included several of his pictures in their travelling exhibition of Degenerate Art.

ILLUSTRATION: Plate 8.

The great Khan

KUBLAI KHAN, (d. 1294), the great Mongol, founder of the XXth dynasty of China, the first of his race to rise above the barbarism of the Mongols.

More than any other Eastern conqueror, he has become a talisman, a Nietzschean figure, the evocation of whose name conjures up all that is fabulous, all that is mysterious in history. When, in 1279, the Sung dynasty (the XIXth) fell before his lieutenants, it was the end of a 4,000-year monarchy, as well as the culmination of fifty years of Mongol effort to drag all China into their Empire. He was a man who destroyed history as he made it, soaring like a tower over the limitless fields covered with his mighty armies.

As the grandson of Jenghiz Khan, Kublai Khan fought his way to be Mongol leader; at his death, his rule was acknowledged by princes of his house on the Volga, by those whose dominions stretched from Oxus to Arabia, and by the far distant provinces of China, from the Arctic to Malacca; and he was the first emperor of China whose name and character were known in the West. The Venetian Marco Polo (q.v.), carried back tales of his splendid palaces, his luxurious Court and huge hunting expeditions, which delighted a disbelieving Europe. Kublai, in his turn, delighted in tales of the West and welcomed Europeans to his Court with possessive civility.

Although not a particularly cruel man, Kublai's way of living demanded an amount of money that could only be produced by cruel means, to which he was deliberately blind. He was excessively superstitious, he is said to have been over-fond of gold and his concubines. However, he endeared himself to the Chinese by the esteem in which he held men of letters. He became a discerning patron of Chinese culture. He had astronomical instruments designed, and made a not inconsiderable effort to procure European priests for the education of his people, although this was primarily a political move. When it failed, he used Tibetan Buddhism as a means of civilization.

Although an able administrator and a good general, Kublai made a number of disastrous military expeditions: one to Japan cost him 1,000,000 men. He always endeavoured to repopulate areas emptied by war, however. A man large on a scale that puts the titans of today into baby clothes, he was a tyrant, but not a despot, who built, even though he had to destroy first of all.

'Beautiful paintings are things bewitched'

KU K'AI-CHIH, (344–406), is the first Chinese painter whose authentic personality has come down to us and the first of whose work we have an example – or at least an early and faithful copy. This, the most famous Chinese painting in the world, illustrates a treatise called *The Admonitions of the Instructress to the Court Ladies*, and is now in the British Museum in London.

At Nanking, under the petty Chin dynasty, Ku K'ai-chih was famous alike for art, wit and buffoonery. At the age of twenty he scandalized nobles and ministers by offering ten times as much as they did on a temple subscription list. Challenged to make good his promise, he asked for a wall to paint on. His picture of the Buddhist saint Vimalakirti (the patron of exquisiteness) aroused such enthusiasm that his liability on the subscription list was quickly met by the money paid for admission to see the work. He is credited with the simplicity which the Chinese often discern in the artistic genius. Told that a certain magic leaf would render him invisible, he would wear it on his head. To tease him, some of his paintings were removed from a closed box without damaging the seals. He never enquired after them, saying, 'Beautiful paintings are things bewitched; it is not strange that they should change their shape and fly away like holy men who are transformed into fairies.' He ate sugar cane

always from the wrong end, because he preferred 'to enter gently into Paradise'.

A landscape pleased K'ai-chih by its imposing multiplicity: 'A thousand peaks vie in tapering grace, ten thousand valleys contend with rival streams. Trees and grasses, like misty clouds that rise and gather, film them with a cloak of green.' In portraiture, for which he was specially celebrated, the eyes fascinated him: 'The delineation of character depends entirely upon them.' In descending order of difficulty he placed human figures first, and then, landscapes, gods, horses and buildings.

The scenes in the scroll painting in the British Museum are in thin black line with light colour, each illustrating a scene described in the accompanying text. The most engaging quality of the design is the ease and clarity of the grouping of the figures in space. One scene shows a lady in a curtained bed in conversation with her husband, who remains seated on a bench outside. It illustrates the maxim 'If the words you utter are good, all men for a thousand leagues will respond to you. But if you depart from this principle, even your bed-fellow will distrust you.'

L

The art of apophthegm

LA ROCHEFOUCAULD, François, duc de, (1613–1680), French author who is remembered by posterity for his *Réflexions ou Maximes morales*, a collection of over six hundred epigrams that glitter concisely, and a little coldly, on the mannered surface of French classicism.

The maxims are liqueurs to be sipped and savoured. They present, not a view of life, but a commentary upon a section of it; that section is the turbulent, intriguing French Court in the middle of the seventeenth century. The French nobility was divided between Mazarin, who influenced the Queen, Anne of Austria, and the duc d'Enghien, 'Le grand Condé'. La Rochefoucauld was a supporter of Condé, and played a prominent, but unimportant, part in the events of the *Fronde*, that strange half-revolution which disturbed France. 'One is never quite sure about M. de La Rochefoucauld,' said the powerful Cardinal de Retz, one of the Queen's supporters; though this was perhaps because La Rochefoucauld had once shut his head in some folding doors.

He was an average soldier, an undistinguished courtier, a half-hearted lover. It was not until 1660, when he left the political stage, that he found his *métier* in the world of letters. His epigrams, encouraged in the literary *Salons* of Paris, ensured him a greatness he had looked for in vain at the Court.

'What corruption of spirit and of heart it must have taken to imagine all that,' was the comment on the epigrams by Mme de la Fayette, whose *Salon* he favoured. But La Rochefoucauld was not corrupt, he was disillusioned. He had reduced his considered account of humanity to its essence – self-love. 'The most violent passions allow us a breathing space, but vanity works on us all the time', he wrote. His epigrams have been called cynical. But cynicism can be more than flippancy or sophistry, it can be a whole morality. La Rochefoucauld was an early master of the mannered band of French moralists. In a self-portrait, he writes that 'I am scarcely ever angry and I have never hated anyone'. Like Dr Johnson, he wished to clear our minds of cant.

'Few people understand death,' he wrote. 'For the most part one doesn't suffer it with resolution, but stupidly and by custom; the mass of men die because no one can prevent himself dying.' Yet he died equably enough, in the arms of his good friend Bossuet. He could look back on life as a banquet at which he had arrived late; but the guests had waited, and he had been a success after all.

Towards modern chemistry

LAVOISIER, Antoine Laurent, (1743–1794), son of a well-to-do French lawyer; a founder of modern chemistry, tax-gatherer, state-manufacturer of gunpowder, inventor, experimental farmer, organizer of the Academy of Sciences, reformer of weights and measures, and scientific standards, first man to propose a National Health Service and an educational system for a modern industrial state; a liberal bourgeois born a century before his time, who died by the guillotine.

Lavoisier showed his high abilities early in life, and an adoring father had him educated in the Mazarin School, the best in France, so advanced that even science was taught. He graduated in law at the age of twenty-one, but was drawn to geology. He next appeared as an inventor, competing for the Academy's prize for the design of an efficient street-lamp. He was awarded a gold medal for his design, and in 1768 he was elected a member of the Academy at the unusually early age of twenty-five. During the next twenty-five years he was virtually the director of the institution, preparing two hundred reports for it on a vast range of subjects from steam pumps to Mesmerism.

In 1768 he bought a position in the *Ferme générale*, the organization which collected taxes for the French Crown. With the utmost brutality it dragged out of the wretched peasants the money which paid for the luxury and extravagance of the court. Lavoisier conducted his office efficiently and honestly, but he accepted the system, and this helped him to the guillotine.

Lavoisier's scientific achievement was essentially theoretical. Since the Renaissance and the Industrial Revolution there had been an immense increase in knowledge of chemical facts, but this accumulation had run far in advance of theoretical assimilation. A synthetic mind of the first order was required to embrace the vast accumulation in a rational system. The chemists of the eighteenth century tried to relate their facts with the aid of a hypothetical entity called phlogiston. As nearly all of them were far more interested in discovering astonishing new facts and performing fine experiments than in giving consistent accounts of their results, they were happy to jog along with this vague notion. Lavoisier's capacious, efficient and critical intellect could not brook this. He wrote that phlogiston 'is the *deus ex machina* of the metaphysician, a theory that explains everything and explains nothing, to which, in turn, contrary qualities are ascribed'.

He sought for experiments the results of which could be explained without invoking phlogiston, and finally found them in oxidation. All the parts of this process were discovered by others, but Lavoisier put them together and brought out their scientific significance. But he could not bear to admit superior experimental skill of other men, conscious as he was of his philosophical superiority. He tried to appropriate their discoveries, and pretended that he had found them independently. He had a slight megalomania, which made him want to feel that he had achieved everything.

In his nature there was a tough, insensitive element, which was probably the chief cause of his unfortunate end. Marat had had scientific interests, and Lavoisier had treated a communication of his on combustion somewhat brusquely. Years later, Lavoisier found himself attacked by a leader of the Revolution who was acquainted not only with the activities of the *Ferme*, but also with his chemical appropriations. If he had not been executed, he would probably have become the perfect technical instrument of Napoleon's designs.

His treatise on chemistry, published in 1789, was completely modern in method and tone, and is the foundation upon which modern chemistry is built.

'Simply talking about ROOMS'

LE CORBUSIER, (b. 1887), properly Charles Édouard Jeanneret, architect, painter, writer, high priest, *enfant terrible* and publicist of the Modern Movement. 'Throughout my career I have devoted myself to one thing above all else, the housing of human beings.' Le Corbusier has not been content to think of the architect as the man who takes orders from society. On the contrary, 'a great architecture must not only express a manner of living, it must inaugurate and impose one ... in an ailing society it is the duty of the artist to build'. Not surprisingly, this romantic radical and man of the Left, energetic in rebuffing rebuffs, was long proscribed by French academic caution; while in Great Britain he was a symbol of Bloomsbury and the *avant-garde*. At last in 1953 he was given the *Legion d'Honneur* and the Gold Medal of the Royal Institute of British Architects.

Jeanneret changed his name forty years ago, when he became architect rather than painter, setting himself up in Paris. His book, *Vers une architecture* (1927), proclaimed liners and aircraft as our equivalent of the Parthenon, and Le Corbusier owes much both to machine forms and to Greek purities and proportions. In *La Ville radieuse* (1930), a book which blew a gale of fresh air through French and English studios in the thirties, Corbusier proclaimed his idea of the city – his concept of 'vertical living', as the antithesis of the American skyscraper. The American has

built high partly because land is money – on Manhattan or along the boulevard in Chicago. Le Corbusier would build high to preserve a 'carpet of verdure' between the well-spaced towers. Part of his aim in housing is *back to nature*: 'Nature has been stamped out of town life, and paradoxical though it may sound, it is well on the way to being stamped out of country life too. Those who have given thought to this subject speak of the ESSENTIAL JOYS. A happy term. The essential joys are Sun, Space and Verdure', which should be 'the foundation of machine-age town planning in every continent of the world'.

As for his buildings, the Pavilion Suisse, a hostel in Paris's Cité Universitaire, was a landmark: his first real expression of the clean surfaces, the simple mass and the well-lit rooms of a modern building. It employs the famous *piloti* – the motif which restored the *piano nobile*, the grand first floor, to its classic position above ground, while allowing space to pass under the building. To stay or live for the first time in a Corbusier flat – in the block which he built in Geneva – is a strange exhilarating experience, one feels oneself a part of the environment of light and air, and also secure from its inclemencies and vagaries. Sun enters the living-room, rain beats against the glass, snow falls noiselessly against it. At night the moon shines through the wall, now low at one's feet, now high over one's head.

'We have built', begins one of Le Corbusier's books, 'a block of 360 flats in Marseilles – a box of homes'. This is the *Unité d'Habitation de Marseille*, now complete and inhabited – Le Corbusier's first 'vertical city' of 1600 dwellers, with shops, restaurant, school, gymnasium, hotel, etc., within the long, tall, rectangular tower. 'First of all one must lay down the four essentials of urbanism: they are dwelling, working, cultivating mind and body, and circulating'; so all the flats of L'Unité – or maisonettes, as they are more exactly – have sun, light, air, and view. Yet the 'city' remains incomplete until other towers are ranged at wide intervals on the same park-like site. Each dwelling of L'Unité 'is regarded as a thing in itself. It is a container. It contains a family. A thing in itself, with its own reality, its own criteria, its own requirements. It's a bottle'; and as wine-bottles are ranged in the bin, so the flats or dwellings are thrust like bottles each into its space. Designed in accordance with Le Corbusier's 'modulor system' of units of measurement related to the proportions of the human body and suitable for building, L'Unité has only fifteen dimensions, all harmonically related. Of this 'modulor', the symbol of which decorates the concrete surface of L'Unité here and there, Einstein has said 'it makes it easier to design well, harder to design badly'.

Le Corbusier, in short, is one of the major advocates of using the machine creatively and without fear for human benefit. He rejects the sentimental reaction of 'artisanry and folk-lore', maintains that in the machine age architecture has been left behind, that our habit of building in streets, straggling this way and that, is a relic of military necessities, whereas modern building should be 'a product of its environment and true to type', like a native hut or a nomad's tent – which 'like the aeroplane, are not arbitrary in form', but 'dwellings of men bowing to a rule of law'. Le Corbusier writes that he proposes no journey to Utopia: he is 'simply talking about ROOMS'.

ILLUSTRATION: Page 217.

Robert E. Lee

LEE, Robert E., (1807–1870), American general who led the Confederate armies in the Civil War. He is bedecked in the romantic light of private virtue and unmerited doom, yet was beyond doubt the greatest soldier since Napoleon.

Lee was a professional soldier who graduated from the Military Academy at West Point as an engineer, and fought in the Mexican War; he was a loyal Virginian, but it was only with reluctance that he entered the conflict between North and South. He did not become Confederate General-in-Chief until the last months of the war in 1865, after the great victories of the Seven Days Battle, Bull Run, Fredericksburg and Chancellorsville. Some modern observers in iconoclastic mood find Lee irritating. He is almost impossible to fault: his armour is not gaudy, but it is virtually impenetrable. One of the critics, who is no iconoclast, the late Lord Wavell, has perhaps found a weak point: 'His chief defect may have been a lack of hardness; he was possibly too much a gentleman for the ungentle business of war.' This verdict, though, only heightens the romantic light and gives it brighter colours. Perhaps in the Antietam Campaign (September 1862), when he invaded Maryland and Pennsylvania, only to be blocked in one of the grimmer battles of the war Lee was imprudent; at Gettysburg the following summer he

certainly was indecisive – and not ruthless enough with his subordinate, General James Longstreet. But hardly another criticism can be sustained. Moreover, the way in which he was handicapped in resources must always be remembered. One of his handicaps was more subtle, and is less appreciated. Lee had what he considered to be a good cause, but it was a defensive, negative, cause: the sanctity of states' rights. There was no aim but that of recognition of the Confederacy; complete victory was out of the question. Again, his genius for doing much with little was hampered, because the President of the Confederate States, Jefferson Davis, kept the conduct of the war tightly in his hands, and Lee was appointed supreme commander too late.

What was Lee's secret? Endow an engineer with strategic and tactical genius, and he becomes theoretically the ideal commander; but most engineers tend to be narrow. Lee was broad. So he was almost the ideal commander. In him, grafted on to the highest strategic and tactical genius, were all the special virtues of the engineer: a sure eye for a defensive position, an unerring appreciation of where fortification would tell most. This quality was displayed above all in the last desperate battles in the Wilderness Campaign of 1864. He was not generally a defensive fighter. In fact, his strategy was daring and his manoeuvres were often founded upon dividing his army in what seemed a perilous way before reuniting it to deliver one of his terrific surprise strokes. He defended this method as the only one by which he could hope to compensate for the enemy's vast superiority in strength. It never failed him while he had Stonewall Jackson to command the detached force, striking out of the blue. After Jackson's death in 1863, he could not find another instrument of such power.

The Civil War is still to the people of the United States the most important event in their history, a part of themselves. It was the one great set-back to their progress, a terrible tragedy, but in retrospect it was possessed of the loftier elements which distinguish the noblest of tragedies. It is still constantly studied and debated: and Lee, unquestionably noble, stands as the symbol of whatever nobility can justly be discerned in a bitter and bloody conflict. In this sense he has become a figure which belongs to the nation. In the South the romantic light is naturally stronger. There Lee, on his horse Traveller, commonly hangs above the rocking-chair in the parlour. Our age is shy of unqualified praise and unfriendly to the paragon; but it cannot deny Lee was both great and good.

Death on Everest

LEIGH-MALLORY, George Herbert, (1886–1924), English climber, master-technician of mountains. Climbers, he wrote, 'claim that something sublime is the essence of mountaineering. They can compare the call of the hills to the melody of wonderful music, and the comparison is not ridiculous.'

Mallory, in fact, saw in mountain-climbing a spiritual as well as a physical adventure, and as a member of the Everest expeditions in 1921 and 1922 he was able to stress this spirituality in a way given to few other men. He scaled buildings as a boy at Winchester and then graduated through the hard school of British rock-climbing. His Slab route on Leiwedd in North Wales, first made by him in 1908 as a casual vertical 'stroll', so it is said, to recover a lost pipe, is still rated as a 'good very difficult' even by modern standards. Indeed, his ability on difficult rocks was such that legends sprouted around him.

'Have we vanquished an enemy?' he wrote after one great climb in the Alps – 'None but ourselves. Have we gained success? That word means nothing here. Have we won a kingdom? No ... and yes. We have achieved an ultimate satisfaction ... fulfilled a destiny ... To struggle and to understand – never this last without the other; such is the law.' It was by explaining mountains in this way, as much as by the perfection of his profile or his grace on difficult rocks, that Mallory became the 'Galahad of mountaineering'. Asked while lecturing in the United States why one should climb Everest, he replied, 'Because it is there'.   And it was as a speck upon this greatest of the world's mountains that he was last seen, with A.C.Irvine, during the expedition of 1924. Whether the two of them reached the summit none can say. No trace of them was discovered when Everest was at last climbed by Hillary and Tensing in 1953; but to that satisfaction and that feat, Mallory made an immense contribution. (*See also Whymper, Mummery*).

The master revolutionary

LENIN, (1870–1924), creator of the Bolshevik Party and leader of the Russian revolution, who lies embalmed in the Red Square in Moscow.

Vladimir Ilyich Ulyanov, known as Lenin, was an organism as completely devoted to a single end as certain marine creatures which have been described as killing machines. The end, however, was not massacre, but revolution. 'There is no other man', it was said of him, 'who is absorbed by the revolution for twenty-four hours a day, who has no thoughts but the thought of the revolution, and who, even when he is asleep, dreams of nothing but the revolution.' Karl Marx, his master, was a revolutionary, but also a scholar with a taste for literature. Marx knew much of Shakespeare by heart. For Lenin, Shakespeare would have been a diversion and a waste of time.

He was one of six children, all of whom grew up to be revolutionaries. The execution of his eldest brother when Lenin was a boy, must have reinforced his revolutionary single-mindedness; and in the Social Democratic Party in St Petersburg in 1893, he met a revolutionary comrade whom he married. Before this, Lenin had had his share of exile in Siberia.

He quickly became a leader of the party, and in its Marxian dialectics he found that all-embracing faith which he required. From 1893 until the Russian revolution, Lenin was a professional agitator, at home or in exile. At the famous conference in London, in 1903, the party divided into a minority group (Mensheviks), and a majority group (Bolsheviks). According to the Menshevik idea of Marxism, so backward a country as Russia first needed to pass through a capitalist phase, before Socialism could be introduced. Lenin, who led the Bolsheviks, took a different view: he believed that in Russia the capitalist phase could be jumped – with the aid of the revolutionary proletariat of the other countries.

He was in Russia during the abortive revolution of 1905, though Trotsky at that time was more prominent. However, during the next few years it was Lenin who made the party efficient and ready for the October Revolution; and among these ruthless and brilliant agitators and conspirators party democracy was coupled with a rigid party discipline, until there was more discipline than democracy.

In October 1917 came the military *coup*, eight months after the Tsarist régime had collapsed. The Bolsheviks seized power in the name of the workers, soldiers and peasants. Lenin, now on top, had Trotsky as an exceedingly capable lieutenant. He looked continually to the West, waiting for the proletarian revolution to come and rescue the Russian Communists from a situation he knew was untenable in the long run. The peasants were starving, industry was ruined, Russia was in chaos after the war. To keep control Lenin had to act ruthlessly. War-weary Russia accepted the humiliating peace treaty he made with the Germans; and the party he dominated accepted the New Economic Policy, which was a deliberate return to free enterprise as a temporary expedient. There was no other way. Agriculture and industry had to be re-started.

In these conditions democracy in the party followed democracy in the country – into the dustbin. The problems of Russia were superhuman, and the text-books of Marxism gave no solution. More and more, Lenin became the arbiter who settled all questions of importance. His immense efforts told on his health. When he died in 1924 – a death hastened by an attempted assassination – the situation was ripe for a dictator of another kind (*see Stalin*).

'Climbing after knowledge infinite'

LEONARDO DA VINCI, (1452–1519), Italian painter, sculptor, engineer, architect, scientist, perhaps the most diverse and towering genius the human race has yet produced.

In a letter to Ludovico il Moro of Milan, Leonardo recommended at great length his services and qualifications as an engineer and military adviser. In a few words at the end he mentioned that he was also a painter. That famous letter is a warning not to call Leonardo one thing more than another. His notebooks in modern editions are classified, in a long list – philosophy, aphorisms, anatomy, physiology, natural history, human proportions, medicine, optics, acoustics, astronomy, botany, geology, geography, atmosphere, flight, flying-machines, movement and weight, mathematics. The list goes on and on – the nature of water, hydraulics, canalization, warfare, colour, landscape, light and shade, perspective, artist's materials, sculpture, casting, architecture, music.

His father had noticed his 'soaring spirit' and apprenticed him to Verrocchio, the Florentine sculptor, painter and engineer. Florentine culture gave him all the stimulus he needed, and he is both its synthesis and its climax – man being more important than any single one of his possibilities or functions. Like Shakespeare he cannot be known as a man, as a personality, since he is a type to himself. Examine Leonardo's achievements, his interests, his remarks, and you cannot select some central being and say, 'This is Leonardo.' He conceives the *Mona Lisa* and puts upon the portrait the enigma of the veiled smile. He paints *The Last Supper* and leaves the head of Christ unfinished, 'feeling that he could not give it that celestial divinity which it demanded'. He is accused of homosexuality, he delights in curious heads 'bearded or hairy', follows such heads about for a whole day, and goes home and draws them, he sings to a silver lute shaped like a horse's head to make it more sonorous. He entertains his friends with tricks, making animals of soft dough and blowing them to roundness, keeping a pair of smith's bellows and blowing up sheep's guts till they filled the room and pushed everyone back and out. He speculates on flight, on submarines, on prehistory, fossils, gravity; he invents a life-belt, an alarm clock, a camp bed or a machine for excavating earth. He anticipates invention after invention, machine after machine. His eyes are always open, analysing light, shade, colour; watching, learning: 'You should often amuse yourself when you take a walk for recreation, in watching and taking note of the attitudes and actions of men as they talk and dispute, or laugh or come to blows one with another, both their actions and those of the bystanders who either intervene or stand looking on at these things.' He is an anatomist – 'Would it might please our Creator that I were able to reveal the nature of man and his customs even as I describe his figure.' He says that 'the natural desire of good men is knowledge'.

In all his roles, not painting alone, he leaves much unfinished – 'He brought few works to completion,' said Paolo Giovio, 'for his masterly facility and his fastidious disposition caused him to discard many works he had already begun.'

In his old age he said he had 'offended God and Man, since he had not worked in his art as he should have done'. And he wrote – so inevitable was his loneliness – 'If you are alone you are completely yourself, but if you are accompanied by a single companion, you are only half yourself.' Yet neither saying, painting, drawing, speculation, invention can pin down Leonardo's nature for a satisfactory analysis. His nature was Faustian and elusive,

Still climbing after knowledge infinite,
And always moving as the restless spheres.

ILLUSTRATION: Page 216.

A poet alone

LEOPARDI, Giacomo, (1798–1837), Italian poet and prose-writer, who during a brief life of illness and desperate unhappiness wrote some of the most exquisite lyrics in Italian; and some of the saddest utterances on human affairs in any language.

Leopardi came of an ancient but impoverished family. At the age of ten he took to his father's library as though it were a tomb, and emerged after seven years or so one of the finest classical scholars in Italy – and also a melancholy diseased hunchback. Long before he grew up he felt what he called *noia*, boredom, a sense of despair springing from his reasoned belief in the inevitable futility and misery of man's condition. 'I was terrified to find myself in the midst of nothingness,' he wrote at twenty-one, 'myself a nothing. I felt as if I was suffocating, considering and feeling the nothingness of everything – solid nothing.' He felt – like so many writers of his time – the sense of a lost enormous paradise which he had known as a child. But around him he felt also the arid desolation of a circumscribed reality. So he is a poet of sorrow; but not of sorrow alone. Because he was cut off by his sickly body and his philosophy of despair from the common good of life, he could look out on the everyday world of man and nature and see it lit by unearthly radiance:

> Dear to me always was this lonely hill,
> This hedge which from so great a part
> Of the horizon's ultimate shuts out my view;
> And as I sit and look, endless
> Spaces far beyond it, and unearthly
> Silences, profoundest quiet,
> Are fashioned in my thought; my heart's
> Dismayed almost; and as I hear
> The wind storm through these leaves,
> To its voice I now compare that infinite
> Silence; and I call to mind eternity,
> Dead ages, and this present, living
> Age, and how that sounds. So in the immensity
> My thought is drowned; and sweet
> To me is wreck in such a sea.

The young girl returning from the fields in the evening and thinking of the *festa* next day; the sounds of village life starting again after a sudden storm; a servant singing as she goes about her job; the noise of a carpenter working late in his shop – such things in Leopardi's poems are charged with all his longing for a happiness he believed to be unattainable by men.

Again and again he writes of a young girl who dies on the verge of her youth and beauty, as in his poem *To Sylvia*, a girl he had known as she sat and sang over her spinning wheel 'in sweet-scented May' –

> Before winter dried the grass, attacked
> And conquered by a hidden malady,
> You died, young tender one; and did not see
> The flower of your years.
> Nor did sweet praise of your black hair
> Or of your loving timid glances
> Melt your heart,
> Nor did girls with you on the feast-days
> Talk of love.
>
> Now shall you rest for ever,
> Wearied heart. Perished is the last illusion
> I believed eternal. Perished. I know:
> In us the hope of dear illusions
> Not alone is dead, but the desire.
> Rest for ever. You have
> Pulsed enough. Nothing is worth
> Your throb, the earth deserves
> No sighs: Bitter and tedious
> Life is, and there's no more to it; the world
> Is dirt. Calm now: For the last time
> Despair. To our race fate's
> Only present is to die. Now disdain
> Yourself, and nature, and that filthy
> Power ruling in secret to our common hurt,
> And all things' endless emptiness.

With a devoted friend, Antonio Ranieri, he moved to Naples, a doomed if not yet a dying man. There he wrote his last great poem, *The Broom, or The Flower of the Desert*, the poem of a supreme master of the resources of language. The technical power remained, but the spirit was failing, and on 14 June 1837, Leopardi died, a man who had wanted love and never kissed a woman in his life.

A hero of his time

LERMONTOV, Mikhail Yuryevich, (1814–1841), Russian poet and novelist, much influenced by Byron, and one of the great romantic realists.

At the age of twenty-seven, Lermontov was killed in a duel in the Caucasus. He was there as a soldier. Turgenev (q.v.), recalling the two occasions on which he met him in 1840, wrote that he 'was choked in the close social atmosphere into which fate had pushed him'. In his appearance he found 'something ominous and tragic'. 'His swarthy countenance and his large, dark, motionless eyes conveyed the impression of dreamy contempt and passion; their heavy stare was in strange contrast with the expression of his almost childishly tender, pouting lips. His whole figure, stocky, bow-legged, with a large head on broad, stooping shoulders made one aware at once of its inherent strength ... As I watched him, I thought that I caught a beautiful expression of poetic inspiration in his face.' Belinsky (q.v.), who saw him almost at the same time, but in prison after his arrest for fighting a duel with the French ambassador's son, wrote: 'I visited him in prison a few days ago and I spoke to him for the first time as man to man. What a profound and mighty spirit! How true his views on art! Oh, this will be a Russian poet as great as Ivan the Great's tower! He reveals his greatness in every word he utters – his whole nature in all its profundity and integrity!'

Born in Moscow, Lermontov lost his parents in early childhood and was brought up by his aristocratic grandmother on her estate in the Penza province. He began writing poetry at the age of thirteen, and he finished his first cycle of love poems, after an unhappy love affair, when he was sixteen and a Moscow student. He was expelled from Moscow University for his revolutionary sentiments and for writing a poem which hailed the Polish insurrection. For the same reason Lermontov was refused admission to Petersburg University, so he joined the army, entered the Cavalry College in 1832 and was commissioned two years later – the strangest of professional soldiers – in the Guards regiment of Hussars. During the next eight years, spent mostly on active service in the Caucasus, he wrote over a hundred lyrics, among the finest in the Russian language, eleven long narrative poems in which he condemned tyranny and war and praised freedom, and his famous novel *A Hero of our Time* (1840), making his 'hero' Pechorin, as he wrote in his introduction, 'a composite portrait of all the vices of our generation'.

Lermontov's lyrical poems do not easily translate, depending as they do so much upon hidden undertones, combinations of sound and suggestiveness. One of the most magic of them goes literally

In the wild north a pine on a bare summit
    Stands alone, and sways
And as it sways, it dozes, and with a chasuble
    Of powdery snow it's clothed;

And all the while it dreams – that in the far
    Off desert, in that land where
The sun uprises, sad upon the burning rock,
    Alone, a lovely palm tree grows.

Lermontov first clashed seriously with the authorities after he had written his poem *On the Death of a Poet* (1837). In this he openly accused the court of plotting the death of Pushkin (q.v.) and he threatened the retribution of the people. The last lines of the poem ran

You'll not wash off with every drop
Of your black blood the poet's righteous blood.

The duel in which he was killed, and also the duel with the French Ambassador's son, seem to have been carefully arranged by the Russian Secret Police. Prince Vyazemsky, a contemporary minor poet, commenting on an attempt on the life of Louis-Philippe, which occurred at the same time as Lermontov's death, drily remarked: 'They are much more successful in shooting at our poets. It is the second time that they have not missed.'

ILLUSTRATION: Page 222.

All men must be loved

LESKOV, Nicolai Semyonovich, (1831–1895), Russian novelist and writer of short stories. As a child, in his own phrase, he 'learnt to love the common people', and he owed much to his nurse, who gave him his regard for the illiterate, often inarticulate peasant. His own father was a poor civil servant, and he was born in a village in Oryol province. He left Oryol grammar school without finishing his studies, became a civil servant himself, and served for a while in Kiev. The 'stigma' of having no university education stuck to him all his life, the question 'Aren't you a graduate of Kiev university?' always infuriating him.

Leskov had a wide range, loving mankind, seeing the good in the evil, holding that all men must be forgiven, yet always reporting, or making, his characters and presenting his vision of life with an inflexible honesty. 'I love literature', he remarked, 'because it enables me to express what I regard as the truth and what I esteem to be good for mankind at large.' He began as a journalist, writing his first articles about

Russian social and economic life in 1860, and his first stories in 1862. It was in the spring of 1862 that an article by him on a mysterious outbreak of fires in Petersburg, for which the radical students were blamed, was misinterpreted, releasing floods of abuse against him in the left-wing press. In reply Leskov furiously indicted the 'nihilists' in *Nowhere*, his novel of 1863, in which they were accused of wanting to break from their past, though they had nowhere to go. *Nowhere* made matters worse. Angrier still, Leskov wrote a second novel *At Daggers Drawn* (1870–1871), in which, declared Maxim Gorky (q.v.), he 'seemed anxious to prove that malice is sometimes more pitiful and poorer in spirit than stupidity'. His third and most famous novel, *The Cathedral Folk* (1872), was not so inflammatory and was soon appreciated. After this Leskov gave himself to writing short stories, or long short stories, fresh-aired, tender, strong, racy, humorous, ironic, terrible, profound and fantastic, most of them told by himself as a character in the story, and all of them remarkable for style. Gorky, no mean stylist himself, called Leskov a 'magician of the word', who obtained his chief effect by 'the skilful weaving of the nervous tracery of colloquial speech'.

Stories by him vary from the early terror of the *Lady Macbeth of Mzensk* to the wonderful comedy of *The Iron Will* (the tale of a German in Russia who ruins and kills himself by never changing his mind), or the sharp surprising study of *The Procuress*, or the longer tale of *The Enchanted Wanderer*, picaresque but an image of life; they easily make themselves part of the unforgettable furniture and instruments of the mind. Commenting on the tales which deal with 'righteous people', Gorky pointed out that Leskov, unlike Dostoyevsky, did not treat them 'with hysterical tears, but with the good-natured irony of a thoughtful man'. 'By its force and beauty,' Gorky said, 'Leskov's talent yields little to the talents of Turgenev, Gogol, Goncharov, and Tolstoy, and by the scope and breadth of his understanding of life and the depth of his insight into its riddles, he often excels them ... Read him, and you get a better idea of Russia, with all her good and bad qualities, and the muddleheaded Russian, who even when he sincerely believes in beauty and freedom, manages to become the slave of his beliefs and the oppressor of his neighbour.'

Towards the end of his life this deep and lovable writer became, as one might expect, a devout Tolstoyan. Chekov, who first met him in 1883, said that he looked 'like an elegant Frenchman and also like an unfrocked priest' – a duality which went into his nature and can be detected easily enough in all his stories, several volumes of which have been translated into English.

'I sing of nature'

LI KUNG-LIN, (c. 1040–1106), oftener called Li Lung-mien, excelled as a figure painter in China during the Northern Sung period (960–1126). 'When I paint', he said, 'I do it as the poet composes his poems: I sing of nature and of my heart's desire.'

Lung-mien studied the painters of the T'ang Dynasty (618–905), copying hundreds of their paintings in the powerful black outline established in that period. His friend, the Master of the Emperor's Stables, allowed him to study the marvellous tribute horses brought to the capital from Khotan, and horse-painting absorbed him altogether for a while. The poet Su Tung-po, another of his friends, remarked, 'In Lung-mien's mind are a thousand horses; he paints their bones as well as their flesh.' Then either because he was converted to Buddhism, or because a monk told him he risked metempsychosis as a horse, or merely because the Master of the Stables was moved elsewhere, Lung-mien abandoned horses and turned to Buddhist subjects.

It was he who probably created the type of the elegant long-robed Kwan-yin (the Buddhist Goddess of Mercy) seated among rocks, and according to tradition he also invented a new 'spiritual' type for portraying Lohans or Buddhist patriarchs. Of his Buddhist paintings none survives.

Hundreds of other paintings are supposed to be his, but only a few are regarded as genuine. These include a scroll of dancing figures in the National Museum of Peking, and a beautiful fantastic landscape and a delicate picture of a palace, both in the Freer Gallery in Washington.

Lung-mien's life showed a sobriety of greatness, a typical mixture of spontaneity and severe training. He had great charm, a lively cultivated mind, and a scorn of mere social patronage. He lived quietly as an official for thirty years.

'Lincoln was the green pine'

LINCOLN, Abraham, (1809–1865), sixteenth President of the United States, is one of the very few political leaders in whom the glamour of a man of destiny has been lastingly allied with deep humanity and incorruptible moral purpose. Here was the horseback lawyer from the forties, full of quirks and clumsiness, melancholy abstraction and coarse cracker-barrel jests, at once politically ambitious and slow to set and to mature, who deepened in character and changed to the magnetic bearded figure immortalized in the photographs.

> Shawl around his shoulders,
> Letters in his hat.
> 'That's Abe Lincoln.'
> They thought no more than that.
>
> That is how they met and talked,
> Knowing and unknowing.
> Lincoln was the green pine.
> Lincoln kept on growing.
>   (Stephen Vincent Benét.)

Ignorant of much that goes to make political society, living always in an untidy office and lapped by administrative muddle, Lincoln belongs to a brief series of great facts: he saved the Union; he abominated slavery without deserting his essentially conservative attitude to the treatment of the problem, for he was never an Abolitionist; he became associated, as a Whig, with the birth of the Republican party, and he was the first Republican to enter the White House; even his assassin turned out to be an artist and a moralist, translating Lincoln's career into a legend by the gift of martyrdom, and pouring some sombre extra drops into the vast bloodbath of the Civil War.

> O powerful western fallen star!
> O shades of night – O moody, tearful night!
> O great star disappear'd ...
>   (Whitman.)

Lincoln was born in the slave-owning state of Kentucky, but soon moved to the frontier state of Illinois (New Salem and then Springfield), where he grew up, became a shopkeeper, faced bankruptcy, briefly joined the Indian Wars, won for himself the minor position of postmaster, and was self-taught in the law. He served in the state legislature as a Whig and was sent to Congress in 1846, having pledged himself not to stand at the subsequent election. Thus he reached middle-age without having made any particular mark. 'In 1854', he said of himself, 'his profession had almost superseded the thought of politics in his mind, when the repeal of the Missouri Compromise aroused him as he had never been before.' The Compromise had regulated the slave problem. The Kansas–Nebraska Act by which it was repealed in 1854, with its doctrine of popular sovereignty in the new territories (a doctrine promulgated by Lincoln's old associate, Stephen A. Douglas), meant the extension of slavery beyond the previous line of division; and besides, it caused much disharmony in Kansas, with both North and South packing in their supporters. Lincoln was stirred to action. Yet even here he was determined to put the saving of the Union before everything else; and it was the futility of the Kansas–Nebraska Act from this point of view which made him oppose it: 'Much as I hate slavery, I would consent to the extension of it rather than see the Union dissolved, just as I would consent to any great evil to avoid a greater one.'

It was against the growing inevitability of conflict on the slavery question that Lincoln reappeared, to gain fame by his debates with Douglas in 1858, to profit by the split in the Democratic party and finally to secure, on the third ballot, the nomination for the Presidency. (Five new states had been admitted to the Union since 1845, and all of them had come in as 'free' states; the South were in a minority of fifteen to eighteen and the situation was unlikely to improve.) Lincoln's attempts at conciliation failed to avert the outbreak of war. It was a long, desperately-fought and often muddled contest, with Lincoln as a civilian having to cope with an ambitious Cabinet, a series of not very competent generals and no very clear indication of what his Presidential powers were expected to be. His job was to support, to encourage, to hope and, in the early days, to dismiss reluctantly, for it was only with Grant and with Sherman that he found his finest instruments. Certainly he strengthened the Presidency, perhaps beyond the limits of the constitution. Certainly he grew to be the expression of the sorrow and striving of those days, as when, at Gettysburg, his squeaky voice and ungainly manner framed the resolution 'that government of the people, by the people, for the people, shall not perish from the earth'. When the war was won he wished to treat the South with decency and moderation. He was murdered before this difficult plan, so soon repudiated by his own party, could be put to the test.

Lincoln's belief in the Union was described by the

Vice-President of the Confederacy as 'mystical'. 'Plainly the central idea of secession is the essence of anarchy', Lincoln stated in the First Inaugural, to continue, in a later speech, that 'it is now for [us] to demonstrate to the world that those who can fairly carry on an election can also suppress a rebellion; that ballots are the rightful and peaceful successors to bullets ... Such will be a great lesson of peace; teaching men that what they cannot take by an election, neither can they take by a war, teaching all the folly of being the beginners of a war.' This 'mysticism' is inevitably connected with the mystery of being a great man, and the kind of backwoods saint combined with powerful intellect that Lincoln was. Close associates described him as having a 'cold, intellectual glare ... not impulsive, fanciful, or imaginative, but cold, calm and precise', not to speak of an 'intellectual arrogance and unconscious assumption of superiority', while others regarded him as an artist. And it is to him that artists continually turn. Such as Whitman:

> But O heart! heart! heart!
> O the bleeding drops of red,
> Where on the deck my Captain lies,
> Fallen cold and dead.

All in order

LINNAEUS, (1707–1778), Karl von Linne, Swedish naturalist and taxonomist, who enjoyed before his death a fame comparable to that of Isaac Newton (q.v.), though his powers and achievements were of a lower order. Of Newton it had been written by Alexander Pope:

> Nature and Nature's laws lay hid in night:
> God said, Let Newton be! and all was light.

Of Linnaeus it was customary to say 'God created, Linnaeus set in order'. Newton set the universe in order, Linnaeus had a world fame for setting in order, not only plants, but all living things known in his time. Thus it was natural for William Blake to write in 1809, 'As Newton numbered the stars, and as Linnaeus numbered the plants, so Chaucer numbered the classics of men.'

Linnaeus was an enthusiastic, shrewd, earthy, independent man, at once self-satisfied and humble, at once capable of saying blandly that no other man had been a greater botanist or zoologist, or 'Became so all over the world', and of describing the small plant *Linnaea borealis* as 'lowly, insignificant, disregarded, flowering only for a short while, named after Linnaeus, who resembles it'. In his twenties he explored Lapland, travelling nearly 4,000 miles in four months, reaching the Arctic Ocean on foot. In 1737 he proposed his new system of naming plants. 'The difficulty which has been caused to botanists from the revival of the sciences down to the present day by the invention of new names is known to everyone who has handled the subject', he wrote. He showed that the kind or species of plant – and of all other living things – could be known by two words describing it and indicating its relationship. He described each organism by a regular rule, and placed it in its appropriate class, order, genus and species. A species has thus a binary name of two elements; the first element distinguishes the genus to which the organism belongs, the second element (the 'trivial' name) describes the organism; the first is a noun, the second an adjective, both either Latin or in Latin form. Thus a Wood Anemone is *Anemone nemorosa* – *anemone* distinguishing it from other families, *nemorosa*, 'growing in woods', distinguishing it from other anemones. It was Linnaeus, in the same way, who classified man as *Homo sapiens*.

Scientists of all countries were thus given a standardized set of names, an orderly conspectus of all living things, a clear, complete, cut-and-dried view of living nature. The system Linnaeus devised was artificial, since groupings were not always made by a criterion of true relationship; but it was a tremendous advance, a new starting point for biology.

Linnaeus applied his powers of description to himself, recording that he was 'moderately big, rather short than tall, lean than fat, with fairly muscular limbs and prominent veins since childhood ... large head, pale face, eyes brown, very sharp, lively, gladsome, sight excellent, descrying the smallest object'. He had two warts and weighed 178 lb., his walk was 'very easy, quick and lively', he 'lived moderately and was no toper', in winter slept from nine to seven, in summer from ten to three. He was well equipped and self-trained for a life of immense and incessant labour. As for his self-satisfaction, in a family prayer he said that 'God provided him with the greatest herbarium in the world', and had 'bestowed on him the greatest insight into the knowledge of Nature, more than anyone had hitherto enjoyed'. When arranging the

Queen's museum, Linnaeus was invited to play blind man's buff with the Court. It was against etiquette to catch the Queen, but when Linnaeus was blindfolded, he caught her, clapped her on the head, and said according to the rules 'Clap, woman, sit on the bench'. The Queen protested 'It is I', to which Linnaeus replied 'Those who play, must put up with the rules'.

Far more than the mere if mighty indexer of living things, Linnaeus had force of character, was a keen, ruthless observer of the oddity of his neighbours, and wrote with a descriptive power comparable to that of his English contemporary Gilbert White (q.v.).

Being somebody

LISZT, Franz, (1811–1886), Hungarian composer and pianist, distinguished in life and music for a theatricality of self-indulgence.

Success came to Lizst while he was still a child, and to the end of his days it remained his favourite toy. The dangerous appeal of an infant prodigy was replaced by the dangerous appeal of a colourful, too-handsome adult, who was mobbed wherever he went. Maddened women plucked hair from his head. Those who were not fortunate enough to get within reach of the master contented themselves with applauding his art with a fervour that was scarcely artistic, and Liszt very soon became a virtuoso of the bed-chamber as well as of the concert-hall, his distinguished career in the one room undoubtedly influencing his fortunes in the other.

To the stimulants of women, wine, coffee and tobacco, all of which he took immoderately, Liszt added the friendship of the young French Romantics, including Hugo and Lamartine, a last indulgence which was fatal. His life was transformed into a romantic masquerade, the true meaning of which is hard to discover. Religion blossomed into heroic ideas of sainthood and martyrdom, states which Liszt aspired to in one of the wilder dreams of his youth. Love was one moment an idyll (which he shared, after a fashion, with the two chief women in his life) and the next a burlesque.

In the 'programme' of such a work as *Les Préludes* (1856), founded on a poem by Lamartine, Liszt might vaguely pose the supreme question of existence; but in his own life he constantly evaded the issue, and

plunged with a sickening lurch into an abyss of vulgarity. Liszt's snobbery was a matter for laughter and disgust throughout Europe. His plebeian origins – his father was a clerk employed on the Esterhazy estates – gave him an exaggerated respect for titles, and his letters are full of delighted references to his meetings with aristocracy. Saint-Saëns describes how at one concert Liszt arrived very late, and instead of going at once to the platform, strolled ostentatiously around the auditorium, pausing to gossip with the fashionable ladies in boxes. Still, that was conventional enough behaviour for the nineteenth-century virtuoso, and may be forgiven for the merit of Liszt's piano-playing. Not everyone was so impressed as the man who during one performance saw Liszt's countenance 'assume that agony of expression, mingled with radiant smiles of joy, which I have never seen in any other face, except in the paintings of Our Saviour by some of the early masters'. Heine's reaction to Liszt was very different: 'He often rages all too madly upon the ivory keys, and lets loose a deluge of heaven-storming ideas. One feels both blessedness and anxiety, but rather more anxiety.'

His music at its finest – in the *Piano Sonata*, for instance – is equal to anything written towards the end of the last century. In his smaller piano works he had even begun to investigate, a little timorously, those twilit regions that were to be fully explored by his successor Busoni (q.v.).

ILLUSTRATION: Page 227.

Frost, delicacy, dew and transience

LI T'AI-PO, (701–762), Chinese poet of the T'ang dynasty, who wrote during the break-up of the peace of China.

> White dew forms on her stairs of jade:
> Night now, it wets her silken shoes.
> She goes indoors, lets down her crystal screen,
> Stares through it to the autumn moon.

Li Po wonderfully presented such eternal moments, or situations, of feeling. Two tales show how the Chinese reacted to this great poet of theirs. Before his birth, his mother dreamt that the Star of Love, the Evening Star, the *t'ai-po* or 'great bright (star)', had tumbled into her lap – so Li T'ai-po's name. Drunk, it was said, he fell from a boat and was drowned, having leant over to kiss the exquisiteness of the moon's image on the river – which may be legend, but is true in spirit.

Between the two events, this poet of appetite, tenderness, toughness, and the finest antennae, indulged in drink, women, extravagance, perhaps murder, certainly alchemy, magic, ravines, cataracts and mountains. He belonged to two groups – the Six Idlers of the Bamboo Brook, then the Eight Immortals of the Wine Cup. Unlike other poets, he had no official post and never sat for the customary examinations. At Court for a while, the Emperor then allowed him to depart with the privilege of free wine wherever he might travel.

> Girls on the Yueh river have jade faces,
> And dark-skinned foreheads. They wear
> Red skirts, and sandals spiked
> With gold. And, O, as white
> As frost their feet!

Li Po wrote of youthfulness, sheen, colour, flowers with the gaiety and sensuality of a Herrick – but a Herrick built over the graver substratum of a Wordsworth. Indeed, Li Po was not for nothing a friend of the great Tu Fu (q.v.), living through the same times of distress, blood and civil war. Poems were so much Li Po's inevitable blossom, and came to him so abundantly, that he could set down the characters, then fling poems into a brook which floated them away forever. Li Po's eyes – since he was the bright one in all senses – stared out of him, so it is recorded, with an extraordinary glitter.

The Welsh Wizard

LLOYD GEORGE, David, (1863–1945), Prime Minister of Great Britain from 1916 to 1922. He began a social revolution and energetically inspired his countrymen to victory in the first World War.

He was a Welshman, who once declared rhetorically that 'God has chosen little nations as the vessels by which he carries his choicest wines to the lips of humanity'; and he started from small beginnings. His father died when he was an infant, he was educated at a Welsh village school, and by his own efforts established himself as a solicitor. He took to politics, was elected to parliament when he was twenty-seven,

and stayed there for fifty-five years, a radical with the nonconformist conscience, a Welsh fervour and a power of magnificent oratory.

From 1899 to 1902 he violently opposed the Boer War, and made himself a hated bogey or hobgoblin for the staid, admirable for frightening the children. Rising step by step, he became Chancellor of the Exchequer in 1908, and the real leader of his Government's programme of social reform. His budget of 1909 made provision for social insurance – a turning point in the history of our times; and when it was rejected by the House of Lords, the Welsh Wizard roused the country with his tongue – notably in the speech at Limehouse, in which he contrasted the opulence of the wealthy with 'the old workman having to find his way to the gates of the tomb, bleeding and footsore, through the brambles and thorns of poverty'. Triumphing over the Lords and the Tories, Lloyd George and his colleagues made National Insurance a fact; and began to point the way to the future establishment of the Welfare State, whose citizens, contained by the instrument of taxation and death duties, would be neither vastly rich nor poor.

Before 1914, Lloyd George had taken little interest in foreign affairs, but all his dynamism was roused in the war against Germany, and he saw 'the great pinnacle of sacrifice pointing like a rugged finger to heaven'. After reorganizing the flow of munitions to the war, he became Premier in 1916 at the head of a coalition government, proving a magnificent war leader, quick and determined and aggressive. The war over, he led the coalition, with his famous slogan of making Great Britain 'a land fit for heroes to live in', but in the settlement of peace and unsettlement of foreign affairs lost his hold of domestic politics. The Conservatives could not stomach his policy towards Ireland by which the Irish Free State was established in 1921, and in 1922 he was forced to resign. The public had turned against him, though not all at once, as in his own and other countries it has turned, with a new, peacetime mood, against those who have been leaders in war. Also the fires of Liberalism were dying away, as the fires of Socialism and the Labour Party, for which Lloyd George had supplied the matches if not the fuel, began to flare up; and to the end of his days Lloyd George was the Great Man, and then the Grand Old Man, in the wilderness.

It is hard to think that there have been many more successful orators than this skilled, emotional Welshman, whose style grew out of that oratory which filled the grey Bethesdas of Wales with warmth and all the rockets and catherine wheels of enthusiasm. The short man on the platform, impish or grave, commanded perfectly a voice which climbed Snowdons and Plynlimmons and leapt off into the clouds, and then pushed itself down to musical whispers. A hand raised up, a finger shaken, a tiny hesitation, could mean volumes. Images, audacious and always well enough founded in fact or emotion, came with irresistible effect at the exact moment. Thus, on a lack of houses, Lloyd George, after describing the long journey that a particular working man had to make to and from his work, mornings and nights, ejaculated unanswerably, 'If that man was a horse, you would build him a stable.'

Alpine guide

LOCHMATTER, Franz, (1878–1933), Swiss guide from St Niklaus in the Pennine Alps, whose name to modern climbers is nearly legendary.

The Lochmatter family lived by, and for, the mountains. The father, Joseph-Marie, was killed with his eldest son Alexander, on the Dente Blanche in 1882. All the remaining sons became great guides, Franz developing into a superb mountain artist, shaping each facet of a peak's physical character to his own ends as a musician uses notes. 'He had long, beautifully-modelled hands, each sensitive joint a potential steel hook,' wrote Winthrop Young in *The Alpine Journal*. 'And upon exceptionally severe rock his bodily substance and shape would look to have actually changed, and to be distributed between four telescopic limbs, each shifting or attaching itself of its own volition, and yet all accordant in a single smooth upward or downward movement. This movement was grace itself: not even upon the most hazardous passages did it ever give one the anxious sense of a personal conflict.'

Tall, thin, of an aristocratic countenance such as distinguished Rey, Maquignaz, and others among the Italian guides, Lochmatter carried about himself the air of having a personal, confidential, relationship with every mountain which he climbed. He had just that 'feeling' for mountains, just that understanding of them that is hardly explicable in physical terms.

Though he climbed on the great Chamonix Aiguil-les and made extensive explorations in the Karakorams and Himalaya, it is for his great ascent of the south face of the Taschhorn that he will always be remembered. There, with Winthrop Young, he reached out and tickled the limit of human possibility on a mountain. On the Aiguilles his climbs set a new standard. His record raised him so far above the ordinary run of guides that the word 'guide' itself hardly seemed applicable.

Common sense mind

LOCKE, John, (1632–1704), English philosopher. Though not especially distinguished for acuteness or originality, Locke has had a very extensive influence as the founder of the British empirical tradition in philosophy, and as the advocate of toleration in political and religious matters.

As an undergraduate at Oxford, Locke suffered from the Aristotelian tradition, which struck him as 'perplexed with obscure terms and useless questions'. His own philosophy was stimulated by the writings of Descartes (q.v.), and it was to bear the marks of a 'common-sense' approach; though his cheerful confession that he was 'not nice about phrases' led him into the confusions which result from imprecise language. He rejected the doctrine, in part Cartesian, that there are innate (inborn) ideas and principles. All the ideas that we possess must therefore be derived 'empirically', *i.e.* from our experience. Locke set himself 'to enquire into the original, certainty, and extent of human knowledge, together with the grounds and degrees of belief, opinion and assent'. The result of this enquiry was his massive *Essay Concerning Human Understanding*, which was over seventeen years in the writing and published in 1690. 'Let us ... suppose the mind to be, as we say, white paper, void of all characters, without any ideas; how comes it to be furnished? Whence comes it by that vast store, which the busy and boundless fancy of man has painted on it with an almost endless variety? ... To this I answer, in one word, from EXPERIENCE; in that all our knowledge is founded, and from that it ultimately derives itself'. This thoroughgoing empiricism, together with the refutation of the doctrine of innate principles which fills the first of the *Essays*' four books, constitutes the most original part of Locke's contribution to philosophy. It had a marked influence on Berkeley, Hume and Kant.

Locke's weakness lies in the naivety of his model of the mind, which is crudely physical. Thinking is something that goes on in the mind: ideas are the things it goes on with. These ideas were not innate, so how did they get there? They were fished in through the sense organs, and 'furnish' the mind. Locke never realized that knowing what something is ('having an idea of something') does not involve *literally* having anything.

Locke's personality, cautious, ever timid, patient and tolerant, is clearly shown in his two *Treatises on Civil Government*, which were a theoretical justification of the English revolution of 1688. They defend natural rights and a mixed constitution with balanced powers, and not only helped formulate the principle 'no taxation without representation', but largely shaped the constitution of the United States of America. In his political thinking Locke was more optimistic and naive than Hobbes (q.v.); he well expresses the somewhat muddled views of the man of common sense, and a reasoning contempt for bigotry and authoritarianism rare in any age.

ILLUSTRATION: Page 225.

Le Roi Soleil

LOUIS XIV, (1638–1715), reigned longest and was the most magnificent of French kings. Voltaire attributed to him the saying: 'I am the state' – apocryphal but appropriate.

Louis invented a new formula for monarchy when it had ceased to be divine: he was the Sun King, his rays illuminating society at any rate in its higher ranks. As a man he was undistinguished. Though a pious Catholic, he had a series of flighty mistresses, until one of them, Mme de Maintenon, caught him for respectability. She was first governess to his children; then mistress; finally his morganatic wife. To please her, Louis revoked the Edict of Nantes, issued by Henri IV, his grandfather, in 1598, and persecuted the Protestants. This deprived France of the most industrious and skilled part of her population – a high price to pay for Louis's respectability.

He had succeeded to the throne as an infant, and at first left everything to Cardinal Mazarin. In 1661 he became his own chief minister, a post he filled for

more than sixty years with bureaucratic plodding. He failed to appreciate Colbert, his greatest minister; and ran into a series of wars from incompetence and folly as much as from ambition. At one moment he almost succeeded in overrunning Holland; but his plans for conquering Europe (if they ever existed) were thwarted by William III, Prince of Orange and King of England. Louis allowed James II to be expelled from England, and then provoked new wars with England from mistaken loyalty to him. For Louis, war was more a matter of glory than of policy or of practical achievement; and he always insisted on arriving to receive in person the surrender of a besieged town. The greatest monument to his glory is the palace of Versailles, which he built on a swamp. This grandiose and uncomfortable building put monarchy on show. The nobles were encouraged to squander their wealth at Versailles instead of living on their estates. Literary life flourished. Molière and Racine were its greatest figures, though Louis did not appreciate them. Louis exhausted France by his extravagance. On his deathbed he said to his great-grandson, who succeeded him: 'Do not imitate my wars and my love of building.' The French people overthrew the Monarchy seventy-seven years after his death, but they inherited his craze for glory, much to their cost.

Acton calls Louis XIV 'the ablest man ever born on the steps of a throne'. This, if true, does not say much for the others.

ILLUSTRATION: Plate 9.

Soldier – musician

LOUIS FERDINAND, (1772–1806), properly Frederick Christian Ludwig, was Prince of Prussia, general, composer, and friend and inspirer of Beethoven. This outstanding soldier-musician combined, in his romantic life, genius, chivalry, love and a heroic death on the battlefield at an early age. An army career was inevitable for a Prussian prince, and this nephew of Frederick the Great sprang from military as well as musical stock. He spent fourteen of his thirty-four years of life in military duties, but he was also among the foremost musicians of his time. Beethoven, hearing him at the piano in 1796, declared him superior to the best contemporary performers, adding he played 'not like a king or a prince but like a thorough, solid pianist'. So began a friendship of mutual respect and admiration. The Prince invariably treated the older composer as his social equal – a fact which Beethoven never forgot.

Louis Ferdinand was promoted general at an early age. He was a conscientious and dashing commander, but appears to have kept musicians with him whenever possible. The composer Ludwig Spohr (1784–1859) has left a description of a visit to the Prince's headquarters at Magdeburg in 1805, when L. F. Dussek, another of his musical mentors, was also present:

'We were often dragged from our youthful beds at six o'clock in the morning and called in our dressing gowns and slippers to the Prince's reception room where he, often in shirt and drawers (owing to the extreme heat), was already at the pianoforte. The study and rehearsal of the music continued for so long that the hall was filled with officers in stars and orders, with which the costumes of the musicians contrasted strangely enough. The Prince however never left off until everything had been studied to his satisfaction.'

He never married. His greatest passion was for Pauline Wiesel, a married woman of 'bewitching beauty'. Their letters have been published in Germany. He was killed at the battle of Saalfeld against the French, where he was cut off leading a charge. His last action was to shout to those coming to his help that they should let him fall and ride to another part of the fighting where their services were really needed. In so short and active a life, his musical output was necessarily limited. He wrote no large-scale symphonic work, but his chamber music has been praised by successive generations of composers. Schumann rated him with Schubert as a 'Romantic of the Classical Period'. However, he has remained something of a musician's musician. His work is performed on the Continent, but rarely heard in English-speaking countries.

'Here I stand'

LUTHER, Martin, (1483–1546), Protestant reformer and evangelist and one of those men who have changed man and his mind. Watching his baby son Martin at the breast one day, he said, 'Child, your enemies are the Pope, the Bishops, Duke George,

Ferdinand, and the Devil. And there you suck and take no heed.'

Yet even when you have the courage of a Luther (no man ever had more), it is dangerous to be concerned first, foremost and always with your enemies. Luther upset an old world in founding a new one: he remoulded the faith and conscience of the Germans – or a great part of them; and in a life of conflict and determination there were many critical acts and moments and periods for this man who had been trained in the Church of Rome as an Augustinian friar – to name a few, his protest against the sale of indulgences (*see Jakob Fugger*) in 1517, his excommunication in 1521, his marriage in 1525. By temperament and circumstances Luther was forced always to be on his guard, but he knew this was not enough; because he was also a man, and there were those terrible times – the *Anfechtungen*, as he called them, frequent with him even to the end – in which he lost his faith in divine goodness. 'I was shaken by desperation and blasphemy of God,' he wrote after one awful week in 1527. 'David must have been plagued by a very fearful devil. He could not have had such profound insights, if he had not experienced great assaults.'

Luther had worked out all manner of techniques for dealing with these depressions. Harnessing the horse and going out to spread muck on a field was one. Music was specially good; but anything social would help; the fellowship of the Church, feminine society, dancing, jokes. Eating and drinking were essential, fasting the worst expedient; and solitude was to be avoided: 'Eve got into trouble when she walked in the garden alone. I have my worst temptations when I am by myself.' But then at night one is forced to be alone, or almost alone: 'When I go to bed, the devil is always waiting for me.' Sometimes he would wake up his wife Katherina, lying beside him; 'Don't let me be vexed; forbid me to be tempted.' Sometimes he would tackle the devil directly – scoffing, flighting, teasing, sneering: 'St Satan, pray for me. Of course you have never done anything wrong in your life.' The devil would present a list of his sins, and he would answer: 'Yes, old fellow, and here are a few more you have overlooked.' At other times this seemed to him futile: 'Don't argue with the devil, he has had five thousand years of experience.' Dare he, on the other hand, argue with God, as the Samaritan woman had done? 'All Christ's answers sounded like no, but he did not mean no. Yet all his answers were more like no than yes. This shows how our heart feels in despondency. It sees nothing but a plain no. Therefore it must turn to the deep hidden yes under the no, and hold with a firm faith to God's word.'

God's word is the Scriptures, and to these Luther clung; and through them he saw and interpreted his world. As Coleridge said, no one but Luther is fit to translate and comment on the writings of Paul. Luther's affirmations indeed are in his devotion to the Bible, and in his exaltation of the state of marriage. To marriage he came hesitantly, after many doubts about the vow of celibacy which he had taken as an Augustinian monk. But this at least was a positive step; the old exaltation of virginity was broken. So many of his other acts were negative – renunciations of indulgences, of the cloister, of the Mass of the Pope. In the destruction of the images, there is a vast symbolism of the destruction of a world; the images were not mere stones that perished, beautiful or idolatrous. A whole way of thinking, the whole medieval world of allegory, of pictured ideas, went with them.

We do not yet know the end of that most daring and terrible decision that mankind took at the Reformation to strip and wrestle alone with God. Perhaps it has won the blessing that will go with us into the unknown country. But in Luther we see the nakedness of it, and we are afraid as he was afraid. Nevertheless we have to say, as he said: 'Here I stand, I can no other. So help me God. Amen.' The Reformation was kind to portraiture, giving it a new starkness and honesty; and we know the heavy build and features of this man – who said that God as creator was present in the intestines of a louse – from the portraits of his friend and fellow Protestant, Lucas Cranach.

ILLUSTRATION: Page 226.

M

'*A book in breeches*'

MACAULAY, Thomas Babington, first baron, (1800–1859), English historian who wrote only in black and white, never in those objective greys which so-called scientific historians now employ.

This squat figure with an inexhaustible supply of anecdotes and vast learning (whom Sydney Smith once called 'a book in breeches') burst upon London in the late eighteen-twenties by writing trenchant, formidable essays in the *Edinburgh Review*. His father was the great evangelical anti-slaver Zachary Macaulay; he had had an austere childhood soaked in the classics, which he read and re-read throughout his life; and from the moment his first article appeared in the *Edinburgh Review*, his opinions never changed or developed: he remained a Whig, an imperialist, always confident, always successful. Member of Parliament, orator, champion of the Reform Bill, in 1834 he took a seat on the Supreme Council of Bengal, amassed wealth enough during four years in India to be comfortable for life, and then turned home to politics for a while, and to the composition of a great history. One of his rash and pregnant achievements in Bengal, in keeping with all he read and practised and with his re-reading of the Greek and Latin classics, had been to write the famous *Minute of Education*, in which he advised that Western education should be adopted in India and that native culture should altogether be neglected.

Sydney Smith had noted 'flashes of silence' in Macaulay when he came home. At last in 1849 there appeared the first two volumes of *The History of England from the Accession of James II*. Nothing since Byron's *Childe Harold* had had a success so immense and so sustained. Macaulay had wished, so he remarked, to write a history which would combine the informatory with the imaginatory and for a while replace the latest novel on the fashionable lady's bedside. He meant the history to run to 1830: in fact, he reached only 1702, in a colossal fragment of five volumes, a great epic of the making of the English Constitution, which in Macaulay's thought was only concluded by himself and his contemporaries in the passage of the Reform Bill in 1832. England of the seventeenth century is blackened to emphasize the splendid achievement of his own century, but he contrived a series of superb historical tableaux of statesmen, heroes and villains. Melbourne once said, 'I wish I could be as sure of anything as Tom Macaulay is of everything.' Macaulay was apt to be incredulous that everybody else was not as well-informed as himself: 'every schoolboy knows' is his favourite way of introducing an abstruse fact. This utter self-confidence and his tremendous popular success have made later critics emphasize too much the obvious defects of Macaulay's mind: his insensitivity to art and the spiritual or speculative side of human life.

Macaulay never married. It is uncertain that he was ever in love. He was devoted to his sisters, loved children and was most generous to honest paupers and charlatans alike. He died at fifty-nine: before any suspicion of doubt about the values for which it stood had seriously affected the complacency of the Victorian conscience.

With a devil's reputation

MACHIAVELLI, Niccolo, (1469–1527), observer, analyser and scientist of politics. His book, *The Prince* (1513), was long the primer behind the politics and statecraft of Europe.

Machiavelli was a Florentine civil servant, whose career was wrecked by a change of government – in fact, by the triumph of the Medici family, who became the Lords of Florence in 1512. Ruined, unoccupied by affairs of state, lucky to be free, Machiavelli turned none too willingly to literature, writing poetry, comedies, history, etc. – and *The Prince*. As the Florentine artists of his century observed the world of objects with fresh and honest eyes (cf. Leonardo da Vinci), so Machiavelli was the first man to observe the State. He did so as a naturalist might observe and describe the way of life in a nest of ants.

Himself, he preferred a democratic form of government, similar to the government of Republican Rome; but the conditions of Rome could not be reproduced in Italy of the sixteenth century. In the age of Italian despots, therefore, Machiavelli accurately described Italian despotism. The Prince obtained power (unless he had the good fortune to inherit it, which made disagreeable means less inevitable) by the judicious employment of force and fraud. Machiavelli gave the facts; it was for others to apply them, if they wished.

The Prince earned this great political scientist a devil's reputation, which four centuries have not destroyed, and which gave to English the word 'machiavellian' – for the ruthless, unscrupulous and subtle. Theologians and moralists discovered *The Prince* to be atheistic and corrupting.

In 1557 Machiavelli's name was put on the papal index (with Erasmus, Boccaccio and Savonarola): so his books were not to be sold, kept, copied, printed, published or accepted as a gift. Protestants also attacked *The Prince* for immorality, impiety, etc. Its defenders were few and apologetic, but the more *The Prince* was condemned the more popular it became. A cynic observed that posterity had condemned Machiavelli while continuing to practise his doctrines.

One of the things that might have been achieved by a suitably equipped prince, in Machiavelli's opinion, was the unification of Italy. When the statesman Cavour achieved this 300 years later, he admitted that if he had done for himself some of the things he did for Italy he would have been a scoundrel.

ILLUSTRATION: Page 228.

Wednesday into Thursday

MAGELLAN, Ferdinand, (c. 1480–1521), Portuguese navigator in the service of the King of Spain, known as the first circumnavigator of the globe, though he did not complete the journey; but he is entitled to the credit, for he had reached familiar waters, in which he had previously sailed, when he was killed in a fight with natives in the Philippines.

The purpose of his voyage was to find a western route to the Spice Islands (the Moluccas), which he had previously visited after sailing east; he had convinced himself that the American continent, like the African, must have a southern extremity round which he could sail. After calling the people of the area Patagonians ('Big Feet') because of their enormous size, he discovered and penetrated the strait which bears his name; and he called the ocean that he met Pacific – 'peaceful', because of the fair winds and weather that helped him to cross it. But his expedition was entirely unprepared for crossing an expanse of water, the vastness of which was unsuspected.

'We remained three months and twenty days without taking in provisions or other refreshments,' writes Pigafetta, who sailed with him, 'and we ate only biscuit reduced to powder and full of grubs and stinking from the dirt which the rats had made on it when eating the good biscuit, and we drank water that was yellow and stinking. We ate also the ox hides which were under the mainyard' – which they first softened by leaving them for four or five days in the sea.

When the survivors neared Spain, after nearly three years' absence, they were greatly astonished to discover that 'it was Thursday ... since with us it was only Wednesday ... I was more surprised than the others, since, having always been in good health, I had every day, without intermission, written down the day that was current. But we were afterwards advised that there was no error on our part, since, as we had always sailed towards the west, following the course of the sun, and had returned to the same place, we must have gained twenty-four hours, as is clear to anyone who reflects upon it.'

Vice, misery and population

MALTHUS, Thomas Robert, (1766–1834), English clergyman of gentle, placid and cheerful character, often maligned for advancing a theory of population in a famous book which those who have maligned him and misrepresented the theory have not always troubled to read.

Malthus – pronounced *Malt-hus* – was born to a cultured father who was intimate with the philosophers David Hume and Jean-Jacques Rousseau. Living in the years preceding the French Revolution, filled with hope for mankind, his father took the view that society was perfectible (he admired Godwin and Condorcet (q.v.)), that Utopia was not a dream, that man, having advanced from savagery, would advance still further to a golden age of happiness and equality. From denying this in arguments with his father, Malthus is said to have conceived his *Essay on the Principle of Population*, first published in 1798, when he was a young Fellow of Jesus College, Cambridge.

Malthus concluded that man's 'power of population' is greater than the power 'to produce subsistence for man': the disproportion between these two powers always has led, and always will lead, to vice and misery. Therefore a golden age of happiness and equality is never possible. Vice and misery, however, are checks on the increase of population.

That did not make Malthus into a champion of vice, misery, famine, epidemic, war, etc., as 'benevolent remedies' for a redundant population. But he had to meet that accusation. He answered that nothing, in fact, 'could be more desirable than the most rapid increase of population, unaccompanied by vice and misery' – if that were possible – and that all he wished to do was to diminish vice and misery. Malthus has also been attacked for favouring contraception as a check upon increase, though in his belief contraception was vicious and deplorable. The check he did

favour was moral restraint. Malthus used the now familiar and cheapened phrase 'struggle for existence'; and Darwin in 1838 read his book, which certainly helped him to his hypothesis of natural selection. However, the *Essay on the Principle of Population* will always be important in its own right, in the vital study of its own subject.

The very name of this man, when pronounced in the wrong way with a *th*, does sound appropriate to immoral theorizing; it seems rather foreign and queer. As a later Cambridge economist, Lord Keynes, remarked, Baachus, as an English surname, comes from 'bakehouse', and Malthus is only 'malt-house' in a slight disguise – Thomas Robert's surname being as English, after all, as he was himself. For years Malthus lived on amiably and quietly as England's first professor of political economy.

Light and dark, good and evil

MANI, (c. 216–c. 276), Persian founder of Manichaeism, long extinct, but for centuries one of the powerful religions of the world.

Tradition makes Mani a lame Persian boy, well-born, from the Persian city known today as Hamadan, anciently as Ecbatana; he received visions and revelations and then on Sunday, 20 March 242, preached his first sermon before King Shāpūr I, when he was crowned at Ctesiphon, which was the capital of the Sasanian kings. He announced himself as the final prophet, and the loftiest of all prophets, who was superior to Zoroaster and the Buddha in divine revelation, and acknowledged Jesus, the last prophet before himself, whose apostle he claimed to be. Mani wrote his gospels, he preached his doctrines of good and evil, light and darkness – the world is a creation of light, Adam a creature of darkness embodying a sparkle of light, when the world ends in fire the realms of God's light and the devil's darkness are made disparate – throughout the East, until Manichaeism was firmly rooted and a rival force to Christianity. King Bahrām eventually sacrificed him to appease the followers of Zoroaster. Mani was first crucified, and then flayed. His skin was stuffed with grass and was swung above a gate at Ctesiphon (in what is now Iraq) known for centuries as the Mani Gate.

Babylon and Samarkand became the great controlling centres of Mani's religion, which travelled to the West (St Augustine, for example, was a Manichean for nine years) as well as flourishing in the East. Mani attempted to solve the problem of evil in a God-made world; his teaching stressed asceticism and continence, and avoided the knotty problem of Divine Incarnation – all points of magnetism to the convert.

To Christianity Mani's dual concept of good and evil was anathema, since it denied the omnipotence of God. Moreover, he held Christ only to have been human in appearance, so that the Christian idea of resurrection was neither necessary nor valid. Not surprisingly Manichaeism in the West was bitterly attacked and cruelly suppressed; though it survived for the best part of a thousand years.

Statues into paint

MANTEGNA, Andrea, (1431–1506), Italian painter, one of the pioneers who introduced into Northern Italian art the stern ideals of classical antiquity. 'He was of the opinion that good antique statues were more perfect and displayed more beauty in the different parts than is exhibited by nature', Vasari wrote; and he mixed an inborn taste for the Gothic and its sharp naturalism and tortured bodies with an austere grandeur of stone.

Working at first in the university town of Padua, a centre of the revival of classical culture, he became a passionate antiquarian, collecting Greek and Roman statues and studying ancient monuments. This painfully accumulated erudition he used in painting classical subjects and incidents in the New Testament. In Padua he painted on the walls of the Eremitani chapel frescoes illustrating the legend of St James. This subject of the period of the Roman Emperors allowed him to use his knowledge of Roman architecture, dress and armour, and to indulge his conception of sculpture in paint. The church was badly damaged by bombing in the second World War and little is now left of one of Mantegna's major works. In 1459 he entered the service of the Gonzaga family, rulers of Mantua, and for them he worked many years, becoming famous and honoured so that 'the greatest princes in Italy begged for work from his brush'. In Mantua he painted the great decoration in

nine sections representing the *Triumph of Julius Caesar*, which may now be seen at Hampton Court. Here again he found a subject for his antiquarian knowledge. In the rich triumphal car the hero is carried in procession, surrounded by incense-bearers and figures carrying the spoils of war; here are works of art, vases and vessels of all kinds, trophies borne aloft on spears, models of conquered cities and fortresses, elephants and chariots. In the well-ordered phalanx of soldiers we see a great variety of helmets, armour and weapons: amongst the spectators all kinds of incidents are depicted, giving the whole scene an authenticity and authority which at that time were new to art.

Or compare for grandeur of conception, nobility of sentiment and severe beauty Mantegna's amazing *Dead Christ* in the Brera Palace at Milan – where the body is seen as by a kneeler at the feet of Christ. What could have been a dry solution of a problem is made powerful and mysterious by the greenish-white grave clothes, the brownish-grey and white of the dead body, and the warmer colours of the stone and the cushion on which Christ lies. The stillness of the body is emphasized by the contorted faces of the two mourners crouching near the head. Mantegna, it is refreshing to know, was 'touchy, self-opinionated, and above all, arrogant', which are not uncommon qualities of the classicist; his features confirm this statement.

ILLUSTRATION: Page 229.

I Promessi Sposi

MANZONI, Alessandro, (1785–1873), Italian novelist whose reputation is based upon one book only – *I Promessi Sposi* (The Betrothed).

As a man, he was anything but exciting or remarkable. Born into the lesser nobility of Milan, he spent a desolate childhood in Lombard schools, his brilliant mother having fled to Paris and settled there with a Milanese banker. As a young man in Italy and Paris, Manzoni was affected by the revolutionary ideals of his time. But his life completely changed after his first marriage in 1808 when a Jansenist priest brought him back to Catholicism. He wrote poems and two lyrical dramas, and his one and only novel, *I Promessi Sposi*, appeared in 1827.

Manzoni spent most of his long lifetime either in

Milan or managing his estate and looking after his family. He was famous for the rigidity of his morals; and some Italians called him a saint, others a hypocrite. He always supported Italian unity, yet was too timid and neurotic to act in public life. He was terrified of crowds and suffered so much from cold that he used to weigh his clothes several times a day and put them on more or less according to the temperature. But in his old age he became a national hero of the Italians, and received visits from many distinguished pilgrims, who included Cavour, Verdi, Gladstone, Newman, Balzac and Garibaldi.

All Manzoni's other works are overshadowed by *I Promessi Sposi*, still probably the most widely read book in the Italian language. His compatriots feel that it reflects character as the Spanish character is reflected by *Don Quixote*.

The plot is extremely simple, and it may appear to be just another romantic and melodramatic historical novel, typical of Manzoni's age. The time is the early seventeenth century; the place near Como. A simple, hard-working youth is in love with a blushing, virtuous maiden, and the two of them, Renzo and Lucia, are prevented from marrying by a tyrannous local potentate, Don Rodrigo. Renzo flees to Milan, is involved accidentally in a riot and escapes to the Veneto. Lucia takes refuge in a convent, but is kidnapped by a super brigand. The super brigand undergoes a religious conversion. Finally Renzo and Lucia converge on Milan, which is ravaged by the plague. The plague kills Don Rodrigo, Lucia recovers. Renzo and Lucia are married at last.

Goethe and Edgar Allan Poe admired *I Promessi Sposi*, but the immense enthusiasm of the Italians was not widely shared. Manzoni was said to be an imitator of Sir Walter Scott, and translations were so few – and so bad – that the mistake in this judgement was never properly corrected. In fact, the romantic paraphernalia only covers a deep poetic realism, Manzoni owing less to Scott than to Shakespeare. Like Shakespeare, he gives his least important characters – tailor, sheriff, innkeeper, carnal friar – a throbbing individuality and actuality. He is wonderfully alert to natural scenery, and his major characters, Don Rodrigo the tyrant, the timid priest Don Abbondio, Lucia's mother Agnese, Perpetua, Don Abbondio's housekeeper, to name a few, have become proverbial in Italy.

Manzoni spent years revising and improving his book until it became one of the most condensed of novels.

The Chinese leader

MAO TSE-TUNG, (b.1893), Chinese Communist leader (since 1949 Chairman of the Central People's Government of the People's Republic of China), and poet.

Mao Tse-tung's father was a well-to-do peasant of the 'kulak' class, and he was born in a small village in Hunan province in the interior of China, south of the Yangtse. During his early years he witnessed a local famine and a peasant insurrection which was severely repressed. He was sent to school in Changsha, the provincial capital, and afterwards went to Peking, where he worked as a library assistant in the Peking National University, which at the beginning of the twenties was the principal centre of radical political thought in China; in 1918 Marxist study groups had been formed in the university, and in 1921 a Chinese Communist party was formed at a conference in Shanghai with Mao as one of the delegates from Peking. In the same year Mao became secretary of the Hunan branch of the party and began to organize propaganda among the peasants. His special interest in the agrarian problem soon brought him into disagreement with the party leadership, which with the approval of the Comintern was following a policy of co-operation with the middle-class Kuomintang party against the reactionary 'war-lords' and was opposed to extremes. Mao considered that the Chinese Communist party must incite and support an agrarian *jacquerie* even if it meant breaking with the Kuomintang. In February 1927 he drew up a report on the peasant movement in Hunan in which he vigorously criticized the compromises made by the party leaders.

'Within a short time [he wrote] hundreds of millions of peasants will rise in south, central and north China, with the fury of a hurricane; no power, however strong, can restrain them. They will break all the shackles that bind them and rush towards the road of liberation. All imperialists, war-lords, corrupt officials and bad gentry will meet their doom at the hands of the peasants ... To give credits where they are due, if we allot ten points to the accomplishment of the democratic revolution, then the townsmen and urban units rate only three points, while the remaining seven should go to the peasants.'

This emphasis on the peasants was a deviation from Communist orthodoxy, even though Lenin had laid down that the (basically individualist) land hunger of peasants should be utilized by a Communist party for the ends of the proletarian socialist revolution. Events were in Mao's favour. When the break with the Kuomintang came in the spring of 1927, the Communists were quickly crushed in Shanghai, Canton and other large cities, and the only Communist armed forces left in the field were peasant guerilla units which Mao organized in Hunan and the neighbouring province of Kiangsi. At the same time, in order to divert reproach from Stalin, who had laid down the Comintern directives to the Chinese Communists, the blame for the disastrous outcome of the alliance with the Kuomintang was put on the chairman of the Chinese party, Ch'en Tu-hsiu. He was deposed from the leadership and was succeeded by a certain Li Li-san, who made a fresh attempt to overturn the Kuomintang power in the cities, but failed and was discredited in his turn. Mao now became the acknowledged leader of the movement, and his control of the party has never since been seriously challenged.

From 1927 to 1937 the Chinese Communists remained at war with the Kuomintang, holding certain rural areas under their administration in the interior of China, but not controlling any large town. Driven from South China by superior forces of the central government, they made the famous 'Long March' to the north-western province of Shensi, where they established their power locally with their capital at Yenan. In 1935 the Comintern proclaimed a new phase of 'united front' tactics for Communist parties throughout the world, and after the kidnapping of Chiang Kai-shek (q.v.) by one of his own generals, a new alliance was arranged with the Kuomintang for the purpose of a Chinese national resistance to the aggressive expansion of Japan. This turn of policy was unpopular with the rank and file of the Chinese Communists, who wished to go on fighting the hated Kuomintang, and Mao had to explain to them that it did not mean any abandonment of Communist objectives:

'Why has the Communist party announced the abolition of the Soviet (the separate Chinese Communist state) and the cessation of land confiscation ... It is not that these things are undesirable, but that armed invasion by Japanese imperialists has brought about changes in class relations in China, thus making imperative and making possible the alliance of all classes in the fight against Japanese imperialism. ... On these grounds we proposed the slogan of a democratic republic to replace the slogan of the Soviet.'

He implied, that is to say, that the revolutionary struggle would be renewed as soon as the Japanese menace had passed. In the meantime the nationa united front tactics greatly increased the power of the Communist party. It retained its own separate armed forces, and though these were supposed to operate under the supreme command of Chiang Kai-shek as Generalissimo, their strategy was largely determined by the political objectives of the party. Their skill in guerilla warfare enabled them to penetrate behind the Japanese lines and set up local administrations within Japanese-occupied territory. When the war ended they were astride the main railways of North China; they also made their way into Manchuria, and with the connivance of the Russian forces of occupation took over the munition stocks of the surrendered Japanese army. With this great accession of strength, Mao now bargained with Chiang Kai-shek for the formation of a coalition government – a solution at that time strongly favoured by the American Government, which applied economic pressure to induce Chiang Kai-shek to agree to it. General Marshall was sent to China as President Truman's special representative to mediate between the two parties, but negotiations over the terms of the coalition eventually broke down and civil war was resumed. During this period Mao continued to use united front slogans in order to win over sections of the middle classes from the Kuomintang. In a manifesto in 1945 he declared:

'Some people suspect that the Chinese Communists are opposed to the development of individuality, the development of private property. These fears are unfounded. Imperialistic and feudal oppression has cruelly fettered the development of individualism and private capital ... The task of our New Democratic system is ... to promote the free development of a private capitalist economy that benefits instead of controlling the people's livelihood and to protect all honestly acquired private property.'

These assurances went far to neutralize the hostility of the Chinese bourgeoisie, which was suffering from Kuomintang maladministration and was inclined to believe that any change would be better. In 1948 the Nationalist forces suffered military defeat in Manchuria and their retreat soon turned into a rout. In the following year a 'People's Government', nominally a coalition of parties, but with all real power in Communist hands, was set up in Peking (now again declared the capital of China as against Nanking, which the Kuomintang had made the seat of government). Mao became 'Chairman' of the new body in a position equivalent to that of President, and shortly after his appointment he went to Moscow and concluded a military alliance with the Soviet Union. This was the first time in his life that he had been outside China.

Writing after the conquest of power, Mao defined the factors of his success as –

'a disciplined party, armed with the theories of Marx, Engels, Lenin and Stalin, employing the method of self-criticism and linked up closely with the masses; an army led by such a party; a united front of various revolutionary strata and groups led by such a party ...'

Internationally he declared his policy to be –

'To ally ourselves with the Soviet Union, to ally ourselves with all the New Democratic countries, and to ally ourselves with the proletariat and broad masses of the people in other countries, to form an international united front.'

In his private life Mao Tse-tung has always been frugal and even ascetic; by origin a man of the people, he has preserved that indifference to material enrichment which is highly esteemed in China as an ideal, but is extremely rare in practice. In addition to his theoretical writings in prose, Mao has been a poet, whose verse is much admired by his followers, and with reason, if one may judge by translations – for instance, of his poem *The Snow*:

All the scenery of the North
Is enclosed by a thousand *li* of ice
And ten thousand *li* of whirling snow.
Behold both sides of the Great Wall!
There is only a vast confusion left.
On the upper and lower reaches of the Yellow River
You can no longer see the flowing water.
The mountains are dancing silver serpents,
The hills on the plains are shining elephants.
I desire to compare my height with the skies.

In clear weather
The earth is so charming,
Like a red-faced girl in white.
Such is the charm of these mountains and rivers,
Calling innumerable heroes to vie with each other in pursuing her.
The emperors Shih Huang and Wu Ti were barely cultured,
The emperors Tai Tsung and Tai Tsu were lacking in feeling,
Jenghiz Khan knew only how to bend his bow at the eagles.

These all belong to the past – only today are there men of feeling.

He has twice married; his first wife, who was a student of Peking University when they married, was captured and shot by Kuomintang troops in Hunan in 1930, and his second was an actress who became a convert to Communism and left the Shanghai stage in order to work for the Communist cause. Mao appears to have been very successful in maintaining good personal relations with colleagues in the inner circle of the party leadership, and – so far – he has not had to resort to killing to suppress rival factions within the party. Mass executions and forced-labour camps have up to now been confined to real or suspected foes outside the party. Apart from these inevitable concomitants of Communist dictatorship, Mao's only known weakness is excessive smoking; he formerly consumed sixty cigarettes a day, but his doctors are said to have succeeded in reducing the figure, and at the age of sixty he should still have many years of active life ahead of him.

A taste for blood

MARAT, Jean Paul, (1743–1793), French revolutionary, journalist, and agitator, has little to recommend him. He was the first in modern times to discover the simple remedy for all political ills: 'Blood must flow.'

Perhaps this political principle derived from Marat's original profession. He was a doctor, with a large and fashionable clientèle. He practised in Paris and, for some time, in London, where he is thought to have acted as a police spy. With the outbreak of the revolution in France, Marat came forward as an advocate of extremism. He exploited the nervous anxiety inseparable from revolution, and stirred up suspicion: 'treachery' was his explanation for every failure. His newssheet, *L'Ami du Peuple*, discovered arts of demagogy which even Joseph Goebbels was not to improve upon a century and a half later. Marat was also shrewd enough to see that a dictator would follow on the terror which he himself did so much to create.

His greatest influence came after the fall of the monarchy in the autumn of 1792. Early in 1793 the Girondins organized his prosecution for extremism, but he was acquitted and soon had the pleasure of seeing the Girondins condemned and guillotined. Charlotte Corday, an idealistic girl who admired them, called on Marat and assassinated him in his bath. She supposed that this would end the Terror; in fact, Marat's death accentuated it. Marat became the symbol of Jacobinism, and David's picture, painted after his death, turned him into a revolutionary saint. His body was buried in the Pantheon, only to be flung out again, when the tide ran away from terror and towards moderation. His writings were vile – hysteria and abuse without any attempt at thought; but they would make little stir nowadays if they appeared in the columns of the popular press.

ILLUSTRATION: Page 230.

Servant of Kubla Khan

MARCO POLO, (c. 1254–c. 1324), Venetian traveller, author of the earliest first-hand account of Asia; he set foot in certain parts of it that were visited by no other European for 600 years.

'... and I doe beleeue that there was neuer man, Christian, nor Iew, nor Paynim, that hath seene so much of the Leuaunt Parties as I *Marcus Paulus* haue seene, for I haue seene *India* both the greate and the lesse, and *Tartaria*, wyth other prouinces and Ilands, which are so many, that the age of one man, yea peraduenture of ij men, would not suffice to trauel them all.' (From the translation of the *Book of Marco Polo* by John Frampton.)

Marco's father and uncle were dealers in precious stones, who traded with Constantinople and the East. They were persuaded to undertake the journey to the court of the great khan Kublai, which they reached either at Cambaluc (Peking) or at Kublai's summer residence at Shangu (the 'Xanadu' of Coleridge's famous poem *Kubla Khan*) north of the Great Wall of China; thanks to the Mongol domination, Central Asia in the thirteenth century was open to travellers as it had never been before and soon ceased to be again. Kublai had an inexhaustible thirst for knowledge, kept them at his court for several years, cross-examined them about Christianity, and asked them to be his ambassadors to the Pope. They returned to Venice in 1269, and two years later set out again, this time taking with them young Marco, aged fifteen.

Marco learned the Mongol language, entered Kublai's service, and went on missions for him to various parts of his dominions, making copious notes for his master's information. For three years he was the governor of Yangchow. More than twenty years went by before Marco Polo came back to Venice, where his relations did not recognise him. Marco soon went to sea again, became the commander of a galley in a war with the Genoese, and was captured by them in a naval battle in the Adriatic. They allowed him to send home to Venice for his notes, and he set about compiling a record of what he had seen and heard. But he was a man of action, and no writer, and a lifetime of travel in Asia had shaken his command of his native tongue, to say nothing of his Latin: so a fellow prisoner of war, a professional composer of French Arthurian romances, was called in to act as 'ghost'.

Marco Polo's famous *Travels* are not really an account of his travels at all; they refer little to the man himself, and it would be more sensible to call them a *Description of the World* based on the journeys of himself, his uncle and his father. The book is stuffed with marvels, odds and ends about fantastic animals, strange customs, etc., based upon hearsay and travellers' tales. But there is no doubt that Marco Polo permanently altered men's idea of world geography. Columbus, for example, covered his copy of the book with notes, and he discovered America while searching for a western route to Marco's Indies and Cathay. Marco gave Europe its first reliable information about the climate and geography of Russia, Siberia, Persia and India, about the deserts of Central Asia and the unknown waters of the Pacific and the monsoons of the Indian Ocean; about the combustible oil of the Caucasus (which seemed a tall story) and the incombustible asbestos of Mongolia, not to mention innumerable exotic plants and animals.

The martyred queen

MARIE ANTOINETTE, (1755–1793), Queen of France, has become a symbol of romantic reaction. Her most famous remark was made on hearing that the people were short of bread: 'Let them eat cake.' The French people later took her advice and grabbed some of the cake reserved previously for the richer classes.

Marie Antoinette was born a Habsburg, as daughter of the Empress Maria Theresa. She was married early to the successor to the French throne in order to strengthen the Austro-French Alliance. Her husband, who became Louis XVI in 1774, was clumsy, dull-witted and, for some years, unable to consummate the marriage, until advice from his brother-in-law, Joseph II, put matters right. At Court, Marie Antoinette tried to introduce some gaiety and led the fashion of returning to the life of a shepherdess, with a model farm at the Trianon. A less innocent venture was the affair of the Diamond Necklace, in which the brainless Cardinal de Rohan came to suppose that he could enjoy the Queen's favours for the high price of the diamonds. Marie Antoinette was involved unwittingly, but her reputation suffered much harm.

At first without political ideas, she gradually shouldered some responsibility and encouraged Louis XVI against his natural weakness. Once the French Revolution had started, she became increasingly unpopular and increasingly active in trying to preserve the monarchy. She had no confidence in the moderate politicians, who wanted a compromise; and, though she subsidized Mirabeau in this matter, she also distrusted him. Her real hope lay in foreign intervention; and she urged this strongly on her brothers Joseph II and Leopold II. When they proved reluctant, she organized the flight of the royal family in order to force their hands. But Louis and she were caught at Varennes and sent back to Paris, hopelessly discredited.

When the monarchy fell in August 1792 she was imprisoned with Louis in the Temple; and followed him to the guillotine in October 1793. David's grim sketch of her, on the way to the scaffold, shows a woman prematurely aged. Edmund Burke (q.v.) made her the central figure of his conservative rhapsodizing. Her own family was not so loyal to her memory. Her niece, Marie Louise, was married off to Napoleon, who was thus in a roundabout way nephew to the martyred Queen.

ILLUSTRATION: Page 230.

Begetter of Communist revolution

MARX, Karl, (1818–1883), philosopher, and the father, or better (since he would have had difficulty in recognizing his offspring) the grandfather, of Communist revolution.

Marx was born at Trier, the son of a Jewish lawyer, who was baptised with the whole of his family. His radical views made it impossible for him to become a university lecturer, and he worked for a radical newspaper, the *Rheinische Zeitung*, until it was suppressed in 1843. In Paris, where he went to study Socialism, he met Engels, who became his life-long friend and collaborator. During the revolutionary upheavals of 1848 he edited the *Neue Rheinische Zeitung* in Cologne, and went to Paris as a refugee before settling in London. He remained in London for the rest of his life, working in the British Museum Reading Room, and living, for the most part, in great poverty, until Engels was able to make him an allowance. In 1864, when the International Working Men's Association (the 'First International') was founded, he became in effect its leader, though dissensions caused it to be dissolved by Marx a few years later. He published the first volume of his great work, *Das Kapital*, in 1867.

Like all nineteenth-century revolutionaries, Marx was fascinated by the French Revolution, the central feature of which he saw in the forcible displacement of a feudal régime by a revolutionary bourgeoisie, releasing the productive forces of capitalism and putting in the saddle a new class which controlled these forces. Capitalism, however, created another new class, the factory-employed proletariat destined to make its own revolution to displace the exploiting bourgeoisie. As there were no more classes behind the proletariat, the proletarian revolution would be the last.

Though anti-Marxist literature is copious enough to fill libraries, the fallacy in this doctrine is commonly ignored. With Marx's starting-point, his analysis of the nature of the French Revolution, there is no quarrel; it is generally accepted by historians. But Marx goes on to argue by analogy: just as the revolutionary bourgeoisie overthrew feudalism, so will the revolutionary proletariat overthrow the bourgeoisie; which is not logic but guess-work. There is no inherent reason why the guess should be either right or wrong, but the conclusion does not follow from the premise. Marx professed to be the founder of scientific socialism: scientists do not draw conclusions from unproved assumptions.

Yet the guess was not foolish; when it was made in the first half of the nineteenth century, the Chartist movement in what was then the most advanced capitalist country, England, and the movements culminating in the revolutionary outbreaks of 1848 on the Continent, provided evidence enough to colour his belief that the new class of factory workers was indeed revolutionary. The history of the next hundred years failed to bear this out. In spite of the recurrent crises of capitalism which Marx foresaw, the working class became progressively less revolutionary in the more 'advanced' countries as the development of trade unionism and social insurance increasingly entrenched its position: in the most advanced country of all, the United States, the industrial worker, so far from having nothing to lose but his chains, has a house, a car, a refrigerator and a television set to lose. Communist revolutions where they have not been imposed by force from without (which to Marx, who happened to be a democrat, would have been abominable) have taken place only in predominantly agricultural countries; and in the non-Communist world the strength of a country's Communist party tends to be in inverse proportion to that country's industrial progress.

The failure of history to adapt itself to the Marxist scheme does not, however, weaken its adherents' faith in it, so the faith must have an irrational explanation. It is an irony of history that Marx, who called himself a scientist and a rationalist, became the founder of a secular religion now dominant over much of the earth's surface and the central, critical feature of twentieth-century world politics.

Apart from producing a doctrine which succeeded within a century in dividing the world into two hostile camps, Marx was the first to draw attention to the great importance of the productive processes in history, which is now generally taken for granted. Marx on his death was buried in Highgate Cemetery in the north of London, where his grave, grown over with red roses, is a place of Communist pilgrimage.

Painter of man's dignity

MASACCIO, (1401–c. 1428), major, short-lived genius among the artists of Florence, who painted a new vision of humanity, a race of statuesque heroic men raised almost to the power and dignity of gods.

His works are rare, and little is known of his life or character. He died at the age of twenty-seven or twenty-eight. Masaccio was his nickname (his real name was Tommaso Cassaio), meaning the helpless one or the dolt, since he was regardless of himself, always forgetting to collect what people owed him. To feel Masaccio's uniqueness means a journey to Florence, since the frescoes there in the Brancacci Chapel at the church of Santa Maria del Carmine are his most weighty efforts of grandeur. His influence on the world's art and on the concept of man is due to these scenes of the Tribute Money, St Peter, and the Expulsion of Adam and Eve. Here the figures are not delicate or graceful or finicky, or touched with the old jeweller's colouring of Gothic art: they are massive, they are three-dimensional, and firm, as if limitless power were embodied in them – power, although centuries have gone by, which is always upon the verge of release. Adam and Eve are expelled from Paradise: they are human greatness in misfortune, they are not worm-like creatures or vehicles of sin. Here, in fact, is Michelangelo's man or Hamlet's man at the beginning of his career, noble in reason, infinite in faculty, angelic, and like a god, the beauty of the world and the paragon of animals; but not yet, in Shakespeare's words, a quintessence of dust.

Masaccio's figures have been studied by generation after generation of painters and sculptors – from his day to ours, from Fra Angelico, Raphael, Michelangelo to Picasso and the English sculptor Henry Moore, who paid a daily visit to the chapel in his student days in Florence. After the lapse of centuries it is fascinating to observe the effect of Masaccio's vision upon Moore's famous drawings of mankind sheltering from bombs. Fascinating, as well, to mark the difference between a renaissance and a modern concept of man, in the age of the masses.

ILLUSTRATION: Page 265.

A major physicist

MAXWELL, James Clerk, (1831–1879). Scotsmen have not yet awoken to the fact that the greatest of their countrymen is not Hume, Napier, Burns or Scott, but Clerk Maxwell, the leading theoretical physicist of the nineteenth century. As Max Planck, the deviser of the quantum theory, has said, 'It was his task to build and complete the classical theory, and in doing so he achieved greatness unequalled ... His name stands magnificently over the portal of classical physics, and we can say this of him: by his birth, James Clerk Maxwell belongs to Edinburgh, by his personality he belongs to Cambridge, by his work he belongs to the whole world.'

Clerk Maxwell's scoreboard is full. He deduced that radio waves existed, twenty-two years before their existence was proved experimentally, he worked out the complete electromagnetic theory of light from the ideas of Faraday, suggested the experiment of Michelson and Morley, which was the starting-point of Einstein's discoveries, and introduced the theory of statistics into the explanation of the properties of gases. This led to Planck's discovery that energy exists only in quanta or packets of finite size, and to the explanation of the properties of matter in terms of the theory of probability. Indeed, trace every line of modern physical research back to its starting-point, and you come to Clerk Maxwell, who founded, for instance, the now fashionable science of cybernetics, the theory of self-governing machines, as used in 'electronic brains', automatic pilots, range-finders, etc. In addition to all this, he was the first professor of experimental physics at Cambridge, and so launched upon its way the tremendous tradition of the Cavendish Laboratory.

From the age of six, there are records of Maxwell pondering on the way things worked. He used to ask his elders for 'the go of things', and if their explanations were inadequate, persisted: 'But what is the *particular* go of it?' His father was an independent gentleman of modest means. He took his boy to hear scientific lectures, and one of these was by Hay, who had worked out a mathematical theory of aesthetics, based on the shapes of the curves in Greek friezes. When the boy returned home, he experimented with pencil, string and pins, in order to find out how the Greeks had drawn their curves. He discovered several new kinds of curves of his own. His father sent them to the noted Professor Forbes at Edinburgh, who looked up the literature, and found that the previous contributors in the field were Descartes, Kepler and Newton. He sent the child's paper to the Royal Society of Edinburgh, but had it read for him, since it was not considered seemly that a boy of fourteen in short trousers should address that august society.

Maxwell was not always appreciated in his own time. At Peterhouse at Cambridge, he was told he had no prospect of a fellowship, since their standards were so high. When he was professor at Aberdeen, and Aberdeen's two universities were amalgamated, it was Maxwell who was passed over and without a job: and when the Cavendish professorship was founded in the eighteen-seventies, it was offered first to Kelvin, then to Helmholtz, and finally to Maxwell, no one realizing that in fact they had elected the greatest of those three great men.

Cliff, pine, haze, and man

MA YÜAN, (flourished about 1190–1224), Chinese Court painter and master of extreme romantic landscape. With his contemporary Hsia Kuei he created in black ink the vision of tranquil, mysterious, soulful nature which first in Japan, then in Europe (where Chinese art was originally seen through Japanese eyes) appeared to be the quintessence of Chinese landscape painting.

Ma Yüan painted 'the single boat with a lonely man rowing on the moon-lit sea'. Yet among artists of the Sung period his manner was peculiar to himself, or at least to a small group of painters associated with him. These included other members of his family, since the style in some measure was a family invention. Conventional Chinese landscape had dramatized nature: mountain peaks were like clouds, rocks like coiling dragons. Kuo Hsi, the eleventh-century theorist of landscape, had said that landscapes are so much loved by good men 'because amid orchards and hills a man has ever room to cultivate his natural bent ... noise and dust, bridles and chains – these are what man's nature is ever weary of. Haze and mists, saints and fairies – for these man's nature pines eternally, and pines in vain'. This unquenchable longing is absent from Ma Yüan's pictures. He resolves the duality of man and nature into a deep harmony. His figures are not the stooping pygmies of the convention: they gaze boldly from a cliff at the moon, or across mists at shadowed mountains, or they fish from little boats and stare raptly at their lines. Man shares with the trees, rocks, and water, a timeless moment in which reality blends with the infinite. Ma Yüan studied his effects, and the economy of his means, with academic deliberation. Usually the space in the picture preponderates over the solid forms, but exquisitely balances them, the solids being set at one side in the manner called 'side-horn' by Chinese critics. Trees, rocks and objects projecting against mist and vacuity in the immediate foreground are drawn in bold brush-strokes for which Ma Yüan is famous.

The rocks have 'wrinkles like the scars of a big axe'. His pine-trees are 'strong like iron', they have an 'old spirit'; sometimes he painted them with a stump-brush.

Ma Yüan's best known picture, now in a private collection in Japan, is *The Moonlight Night*. On the eft, on a beetling cliff, a gnarled pine projects across the haze, and an old man, turned towards the back of the picture, lies gazing at the moon. The British Museum has a painting of a fisherman, alone in his boat on the grey moonlit water, which is attributed to the master, and in the Boston Museum there is a picture by Ma Yüan of the Buddhist female mystic Ling-chao shivering in the snow beneath a willow-tree.

Il Magnifico

MEDICI, Lorenzo de', (1449–1492), known as Lorenzo the Magnificent, *de facto* ruler of Florence, statesman, poet, scholar, and perhaps the most discerning patron of art and letters the world has ever known.

Patrons are usually inferior to those they patronize – except in wealth and position. Lorenzo the Magnificent, of the great banking family which controlled Florence, was indeed the most civilized ruler of the modern world's most civilized city. He came to power when his father died in 1469, a boy of twenty, talented and well educated; and he managed the affairs of Florence with uncommon shrewdness and ability for more than twenty years, contradicting the rule that those who are skilled in the arts cannot be skilled in government. It is curious to examine Lorenzo's death-mask, which belongs to the Società Colombaria in Florence, to look at the squashed nose, the low forehead, the features, which suggest strength and brutality, and then to think that it was the owner of this head who discerned the genius in Michelangelo, and was the early patron of Leonardo da Vinci. Lorenzo gave the young Michelangelo a place in his household, in which his friends (who included Ficino, Poliziano, Alberti and the humanist Pico della Mirandola) gathered for philosophical discussions and in which a lamp was kept burning before a bust of Plato.

Lorenzo was ugly, with an ugly voice, and ugly movements, but in contradiction to his death-mask

though how it would change if the large eyes could come again to life and if the generous, though firm, lips could open) he had the gifts of enjoyment: enjoyment of nature and ideas, country life and speculation, sensuality and works of art, women and poetry, the present and the ideal past which the Renaissance recovered. He was determined, decisive; also sensitive and magnetic, a man of action, and a man in love with the opposite of action, with retreat into the spirit and retreat into country life. Quant' è bella giovinezza – Lorenzo wrote in his most famous lines –

> How beautiful youth is,
> Yet how it flies away!
> Let who will be happy now,
> Tomorrow is unsure.

He had an acute poignant sense of the limits of delight. Signorelli painted melancholy pictures for him; against his wealth and power, he wrote of death in his poems:

> Death has become so noble and so beautiful
> I think the Gods themselves might wish to die.

And he died himself, with pain and difficulty, at 43, in the year in which Colombus discovered America, opening up horizons vastly beyond the city states of Italy and the once altogether blessed Mediterranean.

Hunting and hawking, talking with philosophers and poets, examining pictures and sculpture, listening to music and making music, buying Greek and Latin manuscripts, arranging tournaments – and also governing, Lorenzo was one of those rare men, such as Sir Walter Ralegh (q.v.) a century later in England, who enjoyed a universality of experience. See also Simonetta Vespucci.

ILLUSTRATION: Page 263.

Author of 'Moby Dick'

MELVILLE, Herman, (1819–1891), American author of *Moby Dick, or the Whale*, first published in 1851 and among the inexhaustible and more wonderful monuments of nineteenth-century literature.

'All Fame is patronage. Let me be infamous', Melville wrote in a letter to Nathaniel Hawthorne (q.v.), and neither he nor *Moby Dick* was famous during his lifetime. Genius has been described as going counter to the wind, like a thunderstorm, which is apt for Melville. He was born in New York of Dutch and Scottish descent, and he was at sea, first as a cabin-boy to Liverpool, then on the whaler *Acushnet* to the Pacific, when other young men of his origins might have been at Yale or Harvard. Tossed about on seas of doubt, insecurity, danger, contradiction, Melville was for ever asking questions of life and looking for answers; and he was indifferent, like Whitman (who also was born in 1819), to the small talk and ordinary successes of a career.

He recognized the grandeur of the seas of life, and for all doubt and unbelief, he saw a divinity in man, in himself and in Hawthorne, the only friend he had approaching his own stature. To Hawthorne he wrote 'I feel that the Godhead is broken up like the bread at the Supper, and that we are the pieces'. Hawthorne, himself, and a few others, in his view, formed 'a chain of God's posts round the world'.

No single sentence can condense or explain the huge personal or cosmological myth and mythical adventure of *Moby Dick* – and the contest it describes between Captain Ahab, the captain of the whale-ship, and the White Whale. It expresses the pride and tragedy of individualism. The first words, memorable as the opening of any of the world's major epics, are 'Call me Ishmael' (who was the outcast). The last tranquil words, or words, at any rate, of resignation, after the death of Captain Ahab, are 'the great shroud of the sea rolled on as it rolled five thousand years ago'.

For a sense of Melville's magnificent prose and some hint of his intentions, try two intervening passages. Captain Ahab, just described as 'like a blighted fruit tree', who shook, 'and cast his last cindered apple to the soil', talks to his first mate, Starbuck, about the force by which man is driven:

By heaven, man, we are turned round and round in this world, like yonder windlass, and Fate is the handspike. And all the time, lo! that smiling sky, and this unsounded sea! Look! see yon Albicore! who put it into him to chase and fang that flying-fish? Where do murderers go, man! Who's to doom, when the judge himself is dragged to the bar? But it is a mild, mild wind, and a mild looking sky; and the air smells now, as if it blew from a far-away meadow; they have been making hay somewhere under the slopes of the Andes, Starbuck, and the mowers are sleeping among the new-mown hay. Sleeping? Aye, toil we how we may, we all sleep at last on the field. Sleep? Aye, and rust amid greenness; as last year's scythes flung down, and left in the half-cut swathes.

Early in the book comes the stupendous sermon preached in the Whaleman's Chapel in New Bedford:

Delight is to him', the sermon ends, 'a far, far upward, and inward delight – who against the proud gods and commodores of this earth, ever stands forth his own inexorable self. Delight is to him whose strong arms yet support him, when the ship of this base treacherous world has gone down beneath him. Delight is to him, who gives no quarter in the truth, and kills, burns, and destroys all sin though he pluck it out from under the robes of Senators and Judges. Delight – top-gallant delight is to him, who acknowledges no law or lord, but the Lord his God, and is only a patriot to heaven. Delight is to him, whom all the waves of the billows of the seas of the boisterous mob can never shake from this sure Keel of Ages. And eternal delight and deliciousness will be his, who coming to lay him down, can say with his final breath – O Father! – chiefly known to me by Thy rod – mortal or immortal, here I die. I have striven to be Thine, more than to be this world's or mine own. Yet this is nothing; I leave eternity to Thee; for what is man that he should live out the lifetime of his God?

Melville's greatest book was the triumph and his life was the travail of a questioning man who could not believe or enjoy peace without belief. He neither approached the magnificence of *Moby Dick* nor plunged so deep in his other tales or in his poems. In 1866 he became a customs inspector on the piers of New York, living in a house on East Twenty-third Street. Almost unknown and forgotten, he died in the black iron bedstead in his study in 1891. A few months earlier he had finished *Billy Budd*, his tale of the hanged foretopman, which has been described as a Nunc Dimittis, or a blessing and a reconciliation between Melville and God.

Chancellor of Europe

METTERNICH, Clemens Wenzel Nepomuk Lothar, Fürst von, (1773–1859), the powerful Chancellor of the Austro-Hungarian Empire, first under the sleepy old emperor Franz, and after, under his mad nephew Ferdinand.

'Pull one stone out of the structure and the whole will crash': this was Metternich's view of the empire

Continued on p. 279

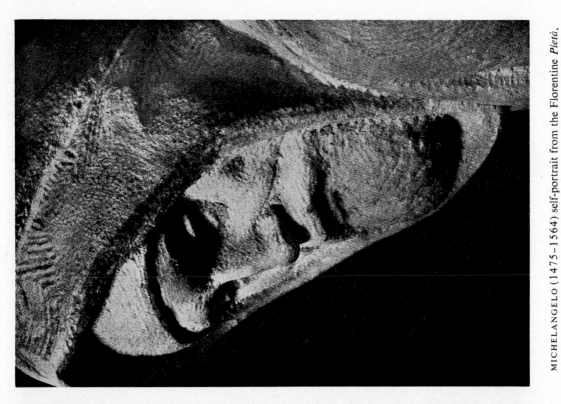

MICHELANGELO (1475–1564) self-portrait from the Florentine *Pietà*.

LORENZO DE' MEDICI (1449–1492).

Tho: Moor L'Chancelour

SIR THOMAS MORE (1478–1535) by Hans Holbein the Younger.

MASACCIO (1401–c. 1428). Presumed self-portrait.

CLAUDIO MONTEVERDI (1567–1643). Painter unknown.

MOZART (1756–1791) about his twenty-sixth year. By Josef Lange.

JOHN PIERPONT MORGAN (1837–1913).

NAPOLEON III (1808–1873).

JOHN STUART MILL (1806–1873).

WILLIAM MORRIS (1834–1896).

ROBERT OWEN (1771–1858). Attributed to Sam Bough.

OSTROVSKY (1823–1886).

271

WILLIAM PENN (1644–1718) by an unknown artist painted in Ireland in 1666.

PITT (1759–1806) by James Gillray.

A. W. N. PUGIN (1812–1852) by an unknown painter.

PUSHKIN (1799–1837) by W. A. Tropinin.

ROCKEFELLER (1839–1937) taken about 1900.

276

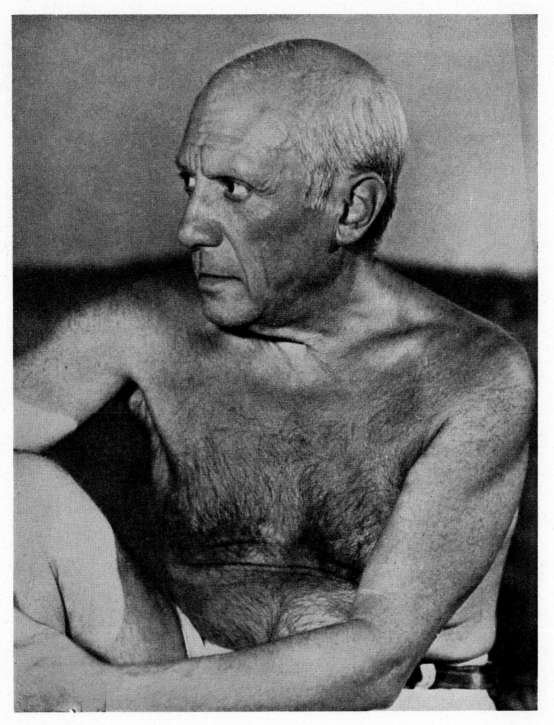

PICASSO (b. 1881).

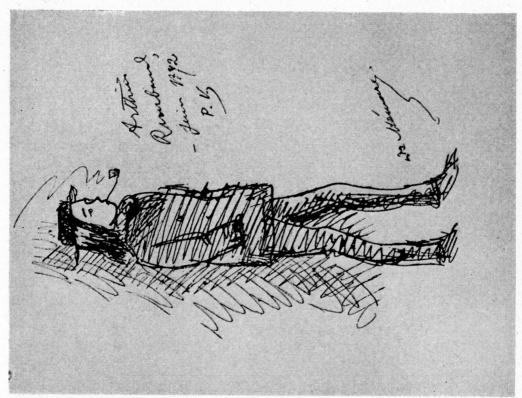

ARTHUR RIMBAUD (1854–1891)
by Paul Verlaine, enlarged from the cover of *La Revue Blanche*, 1895.

SAMUEL PALMER (1805–1881). Drawn by George Richmond in 1825.

he served. His function was to preserve the structure for as long as possible; which he did chiefly by asserting Austria's influence in Europe: he claimed to have ruled Europe for forty years, but Austria never, and he denied any validity in the empire to the theory of nationality, which he considered to have been the worst outcome of the French Revolution.

In the early part of his life he was ambassador at Paris, where he lived – he was a great amorist – with Napoleon's sister Caroline and manœuvred against the Revolution and the French empire: the rest of his life was dedicated to conserving both the victory which the Powers won over France in 1815, and the anti-revolutionary settlement he made at the Congress of Vienna.

Metternich was always willing to negotiate with Napoleon: it was he who made possible Napoleon's marriage to Marie Louise: it was he who offered peace to Napoleon in 1813, at the famous nine-hour interview at the Marcolini Palace during which Napoleon threw down his glove thirteen times and concluded with the remark: 'A man such as I am does not concern himself about the lives of millions of men.' By the Congress of Vienna he ensured effective collaboration between the Great Powers – a system which endured, without a major war, for a hundred years. Before 1815 the very idea of powers meeting to discuss common problems round a table was unheard of.

After 1815 there was a rise of liberal and national feeling in Europe. In Greece, Italy, France, Poland and Spain there was constant intriguing against the *status quo* established by the Congress. After the main outbreaks of unrest in 1829, the empire was ruled by Metternich with an iron hand: the so-called Carlsbad decrees of that year imposed censorship throughout Germany. In 1835 Metternich's old master Francis I died: to be succeeded by a nonentity. The rulers of Austria, besides Metternich, were Kolovrat and Archduke John. These two intrigued against him, and he was left only with foreign affairs to deal with.

It was indeed Metternich's personal enemies at the palace who eventually brought about his fall and the collapse of his system in 1848, after the news of revolt in Paris had turned Europe into an uproar. Metternich and his wife fled abroad to London, where they lived at 44 Eaton Square, and where the old statesman encountered the leaders of the old and the new conservatism in England – Wellington and Disraeli. After the Revolution, Metternich returned to die in Austria in 1859.

N

Sculptor of the mountain rock

MICHELANGELO BUONARROTTI,

(1475–1564), painter, architect, poet, sculptor, and complete embodiment of the Renaissance concept of universal genius. His terrifying mastery won him unique honour in his own life, and has never been called in question.

Michelangelo was born in the rocky land between the Tiber and the Arno. 'If I have anything good in me,' he declared to Vasari, 'it comes from my birth in the pure air of Arezzo, and perhaps also from the fact that with my nurse's milk I sucked in the chisels and hammers with which I make my figures' – since the nurse came of a family of stonemasons. Lorenzo de' Medici took him into his household, and there he studied antique sculpture, and drank in the new learning, and began to give his life to releasing his conceptions in 'the living, mountainous stone' (his own words). The revival of Platonism affected him; so did the strict zeal and the fierce spirituality of Savonarola – visible in Michelangelo's religious sonnets and the greatest of his sculptures, which are no anatomical exercises, but habitations of a soul, 'images of God in earthly clay'.

Vasari called his first masterpiece, the *Bacchus*, in the Bargello at Florence (1497), 'a marvellous blend of both sexes, uniting the slenderness of a youth with the fleshy roundness of a woman'. The *Pietà* of 1498, in St Peter's, at Rome, struck many people at the time as heretical. Here is the Virgin as a young woman, and Christ as a man in middle age – explained by Michelangelo as imaging the immaculate virginity of the one and the bitter suffering of the other. It perfectly expressed Dante's line '*Vergine Madre, figlia del suo figlio*' – 'Virgin Mother, daughter of thy son'. The long lassitude of Christ's body lying in his mother's lap, as he might have lain when a baby, still has that gracefulness he discarded in his figures for a more masculine and severe strength. Vasari talked of the *David* of 1501–1503 as a resuscitation of the dead. The adolescent body, large hands and feet, have a new uncouth interpretative strength, an age away from the Greek sculptural ideal. The sculpture develops to the figures for the mausoleum of Pope Julius II, the great carvings for the sepulchral chapel of the Medici, the Rondanini *Pietà* which he did not live to finish and the *Pietà* for his own monument, which is in the Duomo in Florence, and in which he included his own likeness. In the sculpted figures of his old age, conceptions of the spirit find their own form, with less respect for the common shapes of experience. Yet before Michelangelo came so far, he had conceived and painted the frescoes in the Sistine Chapel – the great ceiling first of all, which took him years of incessant and entirely personal labour from 1508 to 1512; then, more in keeping with his final sculpture, *The Last Judgement* (1534–1541). Here are Christ's ancestors, the prophets, the sibyls; and here are the Creation and the Fall, the grand proclamation of final beauty and strength in the human form, the making of figures more than human if less than divine. 'No one', said Goethe, 'who has not seen the Sistine Chapel can have a clear idea of what a human being can achieve'. There can almost be seen in *The Last Judgement*, damaged and draped for decency's sake, a powerful, fantastic twilight of the Christian God, as well as of man.

Among his achievements in architecture, the silver dome of St Peter's rides the Roman skyline, as a constant witness to his æsthetic dominance of Rome. The dome was completed after his death. No single artist has left behind work of such completeness, such apparent totality of fulfilment. But it is no surprise to find Condivi, his friend and his pupil, saying in the life of Michelangelo which he published before Michelangelo's death in his eighty-ninth year, that he was 'little contented with his works ... his hand not appearing to carry out the ideas he has conceived in his mind'.

ILLUSTRATION: Page 263.

A 'modern' artist

MI FEI, (1051–1107), eccentric Chinese painter whose name is associated with a peculiar, revolutionary technique, a kind of pointillisme constructed of brush-dabs slightly elongated horizontally. A fascinating figure in Chinese art, since he uniquely defied the most tyrannical academic tradition of painting that the world has ever known.

Mi Fei's mother had attended on an empress, so he was given a military commission in the provinces. Later he was summoned to court as an official painter, and made a secretary in the Board of Rites. A fanatic for cleanliness, he was for ever washing and he refused to use plates or towels which had been used

by anyone else. He called a certain large and strangely shaped stone his brother. On a boat trip he threatened to drown himself to secure the gift of a famous piece of calligraphy by Wang Hsi-chih of the fourth century – and was given it. Mi Fei painted both in colour and in monochrome black. He began to draw 'when Li Lung-mien (see *Li Kung-lin*) lost the use of his right hand', deplored the linear element in Lungmien's style derived from the eighth-century master of linear figure-drawing, Wu Tao-tzŭ, and would never 'admit a single brush-stroke from Wu'. The paintings traditionally assigned to Mi Fei, all in the 'pointilliste' manner, bear out that recorded prejudice. Certainly nothing could be farther from the calligraphic brush style of tradition, or more startlingly at variance with the maxim, preached in East and West alike, that brush writing and painting are a single art. But probably only a minority of his pictures were in his iconoclastic style, which shocked his contemporaries and assured his immortality. Mi's reverence for the old masters (he even dressed in the T'ang fashion) must have inspired the usual imitative work. Yet he was sensibly sceptical of attributions to famous old names, ridiculing rich collectors who boasted of possessing large numbers of pictures by his *bête noire*, Wu Tao-tzŭ.

Perhaps paintings actually from Mi Fei's hand no longer survive. One of the landscapes with the best claims to authenticity is in the Freer Gallery in Washington.

'I never was a boy'

MILL, John Stuart, (1806–1873), English philosopher and political economist (and godfather of Bertrand Russell). The son of James Mill, the disciple of Jeremy Bentham (q.v.), he was in his childhood the subject – today we would think the victim – of an extraordinary educational experiment which was to colour his whole life.

'I have no remembrance of the time when I began to learn Greek,' Mill wrote in his *Autobiography* (1873): 'I have been told that it was when I was three years old.' His first studies were in Greek, English and arithmetic; in his seventh year we find him reading the first six dialogues of Plato from the *Euthyphro* to the *Theaetetus*: 'which last dialogue, I venture to

think, would have been better omitted as it was totally impossible I should understand it'. To this rigor-
ous curriculum were added Latin at eight years, and
logic and political economy – two pursuits he was to
make especially his own – at twelve and thirteen. His
father was his sole teacher; there were no holidays,
and little relaxation in the country walks of father
and son, which usually took the form of peripatetic
examinations.

'Through the early training bestowed on me by my
father I started, I may fairly say, with an advantage
of a quarter of a century over my contemporaries.'
Yet this advantage was bought at a price: starved of
affection, always secluded from other children and
from youthful diversions ('I never was a boy'), at
twenty he found himself in the midst of a 'mental
crisis', disillusioned with that happiness that was the
mainspring of the Benthamite system and with a
psychology which weakened sympathies as it analysed them. 'The whole foundation on which my life
was constructed fell down.' Later he found that his
feelings were not, after all, dead; and consolation
came from a study of philosophy and Romantic
literature – Wordsworth, in particular, and Shelley –
and from a broader estimate of the needs of the human mind, in which the crude hedonism of his father
and of Bentham was replaced by a more complex
idea of man's nature.

The books by Mill now most often read are the
Autobiography and the *Essay on Liberty* (1859). Less
confident than his predecessors in the power of argument and reason to influence men's behaviour, he was
equally sure of the duty to find *some* scientific criterion of right and wrong and to apply it ruthlessly to
every belief, tradition or institution. Mill never escaped the effect of his upbringing in emphasizing the
critical spirit at the expense of the feelings and sympathies, though emotion gathered in him around
ideas. One evening in 1870, Mill dined with Lord and
Lady Amberley, the parents of Bertrand Russell –
'After dinner Mr Mill read us Shelley's *Ode to Liberty*
and he got quite excited and moved over it, rocking
backwards and forwards and nearly choking with
emotion; he said himself: "it is almost too much
for me".' By his ceaseless examination of practical
problems, social and political (*e.g.* female suffrage, the dangers of deferring to the standards of
the crowd), he helped to form and invigorate public
opinion.

ILLUSTRATION: Page 270.

Truly eminent and noble?

MILTON, John, (1608–1674), English epic, lyric,
and dramatic poet, and one of the major writers in
English, and a propagandist of the Commonwealth.

> Mortals that would follow me,
> Love virtue, she alone is free,
> She can teach you how to climb
> Higher than the sphery chime;
> Or, if virtue feeble were,
> Heaven itself would stoop to her.

Milton is the hardest of poets to know – if not to
follow – as Handel is the hardest of musicians. The
reason lies partly in circumstance. He belonged to the
first generation in which biographical curiosity had
been aroused, the generation of Pepys and John
Aubrey and Anthony à Wood. The last two wrote
about him; so did the nephews he brought up; and
there are four other *Lives* drawing on first-hand information. But the double reputation of regicide and
poet made them take attitudes of attack or defence,
from Wood's 'John Milton, a rogue' to Toland's
'truly and eminently noble'. The division persists, as
Mr T.S.Eliot (chief prosecutor in our time) has admitted: 'The Civil War is not ended: I question
whether any serious civil war ever does end.' Yet
perhaps more damaging than political prejudice is
Milton's self-consciousness; he sees himself at the
bar of history: 'Do you ask what I am meditating?
By the help of Heaven, an immortality of fame', he
wrote in 1637 to Charles Diodati. The thread runs
through his verse from the high tone of the *Vacation
Exercise* of 1626 ('Hail, Native Language ... here I
salute thee') to the coarsely jocular *Tetrachordon* sonnet ('Cries the stall-reader, Bless us! what a word on
A title-page is this').

To see him afresh, then, let us set him against the
stenotype of a puritan. Was Milton *Of a narrow and
rigid orthodoxy*? On the contrary, he sampled every
heresy from Arianism to Mortalism. Was he *Regular
in attendance at public worship*? 'In the latter part of
his life, he was not a profest Member of any particular
sect among Christians, he frequented none of their
Assemblies, nor made use of their peculiar Rites in
his Family' (Toland). Was he *An enemy of the arts*?
'He made his Nephews Songsters, and sing from the
time they were with him' (Aubrey). He shipped home
from Italy 'a Chest or two of choice Musick-books of
the best Masters flourishing about that time' – *i.e.*

1640 (Edward Phillips). Was he *Strait-laced*? 'He would so far make bold with his Body, as now and then to keep a Gawdy-day.' (Edward Phillips); he was 'extreme pleasant in his conversation, and at dinner, supper etc: but Satyricall' (Aubrey). Was he *Monogamous*? On the contrary, he could not find that polygamy was contrary to Scripture; and after his first wife, Mary Powell, had returned to her mother, he not only wrote in favour of divorce, but had 'a design of Marrying one of Dr Davis's daughters, a very Handsome and Witty Gentlewoman, but averse, as it is said, to this Motion' (Edward Phillips).

There is another stenotype that fits him better: the Renaissance humanist. He had all the traits: the fervent belief in education, the intense delight in physical beauty, the power to take the classic past into his system, the faith in the written word to inspire virtue and nobility, the passionate individualism. But what singles him out from other humanists is the life he breathes into the classic myths. In this passage of *Areopagitica* (1644):

Good and evil we know in the field of this world grow up together almost inseparably; and the knowledge of good is so involved and interwoven with the knowledge of evil, and in so many cunning resemblances hardly to be discerned that those confused seeds which were imposed upon Psyche as an incessant labour to cull out, and sort asunder, were not more intermixed. It was from out the rind of one apple tasted, that the knowledge of good and evil, as two twins cleaving together, leaped forth into the world. And perhaps this is that doom which Adam fell into of knowing good and evil; that is to say of knowing good by evil.

The parable of wheat and tares, the myth of Psyche, the myth of Genesis, are of equal weight; one cannot say that he believes one more than the other. Or, in *Paradise Lost*:

> Not that fair field
> Of Enna, where Proserpin gath'ring flow'rs
> Herself a fairer flow'r by gloomy Dis
> Was gather'd, which cost Ceres all that pain
> To seek her through the world.

The fair field of Enna out of Greek mythology is not less real than Eden; and it is his power of believing in both, rather than disbelieving in either, that makes Milton a truly epic poet.

'There is no God but God'

MOHAMMED, (c. 570–632), Prophet and Founder of Islam.

'According to the tradition of his companions [wrote Edward Gibbon in *The Decline and Fall of the Roman Empire*] Mahomet was distinguished by the beauty of his person, an outward gift which is seldom despised, except by those to whom it has been refused. He possessed the courage both of thought and action; and although his designs might gradually expand with his success, the first idea which he entertained of his divine mission bears the stamp of an original and superior genius ... At the distance of twelve centuries, I darkly contemplate his shade through a cloud of religious incense; and could I truly delineate the portrait of an hour, the fleeting resemblance would not equally apply to the solitary of Mount Hera, to the preacher of Mecca, and to the conqueror of Arabia.'

As we look through the 'cloud of incense' for Mohammed the man, we are as uncertain as Gibbon whether the shade we perceive is substantial; and we have to remember that with Mohammed, as with other great teachers, understanding does not begin with detached observation. He came of good family, but was left an orphan and grew up in a poor home. 'Did He not find thee an orphan and give thee a home, And find thee erring and guide thee, and find thee needy and enrich thee?' says the Koran. At twenty-five (some say earlier) Mohammed's uncle suggested that he should offer his services to the rich widow Khadija, whose caravan was about to leave for Syria.

The caravan made good profits; Mohammed showed his capacity for leadership, and ended by receiving a proposal of marriage from his forty-year-old employer, which he accepted.

According to a tradition which may well be true, he made on this journey his first active contact with Christianity: a long conversation with a monk, in a cell which was a regular stopping place for the caravans, gave him a sense of mission. But it was long before his prophetic call developed. Until he was forty he lived rich and respected (his surname was Al-Amin: 'The Reliable'). He married Khadija; his marriage was happy, and while she lived he took no other wives.

In middle age he began to withdraw himself from active life and to spend long periods in silence and solitude on Mount Hera, perhaps remembering the Christian anchorite he had known long before. At last, one night in Ramadhan, the archangel Gabriel came to him (as to Caedmon in far away England, who was almost his exact contemporary) and bade him recite.

'I cannot recite,' said the Arab on the mountain; like the Englishman in his stable.

'Recite!' said Gabriel, choking Mohammed until he believed that he would die.

'What shall I recite?' asked both the man of the east and the man of the west; and to each the answer was the same:

'Sing the Lord, the creator, who hath made man and taught him what he knoweth not.'

Only Khadija accepted the reality of Mohammed's call. ('She believed in me when all others were unbelieving; she took my words to be true when all others treated me as a liar.') Mohammed's tribe, the Khoreish, lived like other Arabs in a world of taboo and fetish, haunted by the *jinn*. They already believed in Allah, but only as a God behind the Gods – a remote and inaccessible first cause. To Him was dedicated the most important shrine and sanctuary of Central Arabia – the Vadba, the house of the Black Stone. Mohammed kept this shrine as the centre of his worship, but the 'Lord of the House' drove out all the lesser gods and goddesses, in the sternest and most uncompromising monotheism known to the world. To Mohammed neither Jews nor Christians, though they worship the same god, were single-hearted enough about it. Nor were the Khoreish. The great struggle came over their three fertility goddesses. Persecution threatened Mohammed, and he hesitated. Satan suggested to him, as he recited, the interpolation of a couplet in praise of the goddesses: 'These are the exalted females, and truly their intercession may be expected.' The tribesmen, mollified, were ready to accept his revelation and to honour him. But at night, going over his lines, Gabriel stopped Mohammed: 'Did I teach you those two lines?' Ashamed, Mohammed withdrew them. The result was uncompromising hostility. 'A prophet is not without honour, save in his own country.'

Islam dates its beginning from the Hegira, the flight of Mohammed to Yathrib, later called Medina ('The City'). This was in 622, the Year One of the Mohammedan era.

Soon Mohammed was Lord of the City and at war with Mecca. It was at first a matter of skirmishes, and he was not particularly successful as a commander. But he withstood a siege; and during a truce conversions began to come thick and fast. It was not until 630 that he took possession of his native city and then he had only two years of life remaining. They were years of incredible expansion; when he died, Islam was already threatening Byzantium. Six years later, Jerusalem had fallen. Within a hundred years Mohammed's creed was threatening France in the West and India in the East. But it was more than a military success. Arts and sciences flourished; and in Islam, as in other great religions, wonderful sanctity, devotion and purity of life, and the liberating power of a new revelation, lived alongside old surviving superstition and narrow intolerance (see, for example, Rūmī, Hafiz, Rab'ia). But it was a great day for mankind when Mohammed returned to Mecca, and having entered the Kaaba and destroyed the idols, stood at the door with the key in his hand and faced the people. 'Now Allah is finished with pride of position. You are all descended from Adam, and the best man among you is the most pious.'

There is no God but God; and Mohammed is the Prophet of God.

The very Frenchman

MOLIÈRE, stage name of Jean-Baptiste Poquelin, (1622–1673), French actor, showman and playwright. 'Certainly there are places better worth frequenting than the theatre,' he said in the preface to *Tartuffe*, 'and if all those things not directly connected with God and our salvation are to be blamed, it is quite clear that comedy is one of them, and I shall be happy to see it condemned with the rest. But grant (as you must) that pious exercises must sometimes submit to interruption and that mankind needs some diversion; and I maintain that a more innocent diversion than a play would be hard to find.'

Was there ever anything more French than Molière's style? In the passage above, how can one really translate '*les exercices de la piété souffrent des intervalles*'? The rapier has drawn blood, but the fencer looks calm, gracious and elegant. He puzzles Anglo-Saxondom; but let us take comfort – he puzzled his own age just as much. 'C'est une étrange entreprise que de faire rire les honnêtes gens,' says Dorante in *La Critique de l'École des Femmes*; and a strange enterprise Molière found it, this business of making worthy people laugh.

We always want to place him – is he a French Shakespeare or a Ben Jonson? Certainly in his most serious moods his voice is Jonson's:

'La tragédie, sans doute, est quelque chose de beau quand elle est bien touchée; mais la comédie a ses charmes, et je tiens que l'une n'est pas moins difficile à faire que l'autre'

is almost translated by Jonson's

'The parts of a Comedy are the same with a Tragedie, and the end is partly the same. For they both delight and teach,'

but he would not have agreed with Jonson's next words:

'Nor is the moving of laughter alwaies the end of Comedy, that is rather a fowling for the peoples delight.'

But in temperament he was a Shakespeare: a quiet man in company, a disappointment to meet if you expected a pyrotechnic display of wit, but a good mixer, a good listener, a good business man – as he should have been, being the son of Jean Poquelin, *valet-tapissier du roi*, the royal upholsterer. He suffered fools gladly, but he hated knaves.

There is someone, however, whom in his life Molière resembles more than either of our great playwrights, and that is Charlie Chaplin (q.v.). It is Chaplin who comes to mind when one remembers Molière accused of neglecting his aged father (with Chaplin it was his mother), accused of marrying a woman young enough to be his daughter (some went further and said that Armande Béjart *was* Molière's daughter) accused of a destructive attack on society ('A man, or rather a demon in flesh and habited as a man, the most notably impious creature and libertine who ever lived throughout the centuries ...'). As Chaplin is denied the soil of America, so Molière was denied burial with religious rites, and no one knows to this day the facts about his burial or the place where his bones lie. One has to remember Chaplin as the author of *A Woman of Paris* and *Monsieur Verdoux* as well as *The Rink*; one has to remember Molière as the author of *Gorgibus dans le Sac* and *La Jalousie du Barbouillé* and the ballet-entertainments of Versailles on a Cecil B. de Mille scale, as well as *Le Misanthrope*.

The differences are those of his period and upbringing. Molière had the best education possible in his time under the Jesuits at Clermont: his plays show his learning in their plunderings of Plautus and Terence, of Molina and Lope de Vega, of Lorenzino de Medicis and Beltrame and Luigi Groto. But before all he was a man of the theatre, at a moment exactly comparable to that of the Shakespearean theatre in England. He played in his youth in provincial innyards, in companies which were rising out of vagabondage by taking service with the noble houses. He came to Paris when the battle against the privileges of the Hôtel de Bourgogne had been won; the Hôtel de Bourgogne representing the medieval theatre, which in France had survived longer than in England, by being professional and well organized, instead of amateur and dispersed. He won royal favour, as Shakespeare's company did in Elizabethan London. With royal favour went the classical rules and philosophy which were *de rigueur* at Louis XIV's Court. He set loose to the rules; his staging has only fictitious unity of place and time; his comedies mix comedy with farce, and often contain latent tragedy as well. The philosophy he accepted; he wanted his portraits to be universal, not studies of individuals. And he held deeply the doctrine of the golden mean, which is an excellent philosophy for man capable of going to extremes, as most men of his age and certainly Molière might do:

La parfaite raison fuit toute extremité
Et veut que l'on soit sage avec sobriété.

'Perfect reason flees all extremes, and realizes that even in wisdom we need to be sober' – which has a sting in the tail.

Painter's eye

MONET, Claude, (1840–1926), French painter, the purist of the impressionist movement, of whom Cézanne exclaimed, 'He is only an eye, but my God, what an eye.'

In 1874 Monet unwittingly suggested a name for the famous movement to which he belongs. At the first exhibition which he and his friends organized he showed a picture called 'Impression, Sunrise'. A journalist derisively coined from this the name 'Impressionism'. Provincial, stubborn, tough and determined, it was the strong-willed Monet who put into practice most completely the theories of his more intellectual fellow impressionists. Knowing that the appearance of nature was constantly changing as the sun moved through the sky, and that a landscape took on different aspects as the weather changed, he would paint the same subject under varying effects of light and atmosphere. He sometimes set out at sunrise with fifteen or more canvases, working on them one after the other at different times of the day, endeavouring to catch the fleeting, subtle changes of the scene, which he recorded with different schemes of tone and colour. To him the association and nature of the object he was painting mattered not at all; a hay-stack, poplar trees, a lily-pond, the façade of Rouen Cathedral, it was all the same – he fixed his eye upon the light it reflected: 'I wish I had been born blind and then suddenly gained my sight so that I could begin to paint without knowing what the objects were that I could see before me.'

Putting his paint on in broken touches without first mixing the colour on his palette, he left it to the eye of the spectator to unite these touches into colours, in a sparkling, vibrating effect of shimmering light which would envelop the scene completely, obscuring rather than revealing the details of the landscape. Concerned only with light, his work makes no attempt to express any spiritual experience. 'Monet's art', said Degas, 'is that of a skilful but not profound decorator.' However, the impressionism of Monet has affected much of the painting of the last eighty years. He has made life a little gayer, a little more joyous by introducing sunlight and fresh air into pictures and art galleries.

'Pictures aren't made out of doctrines,' Monet wrote. 'Since the appearance of impressionism, the official salons, which used to be brown, have become blue, green and red ... But peppermint or chocolate, they are still confections.'

'Nothing in excess'

MONTAIGNE, Michel Eyquem, sieur de Montaigne, (1533–1592).

Most of what we know about him comes from his *Essaies* or 'attempts' – from him we derive our word 'essay'. He was a country gentleman, comfortably off but not rich. His life was not particularly striking. He was employed on occasion in the King's service and was mayor of Bordeaux. 'Nothing in excess' would have been his ideal motto. At a time when

France was torn by civil war between Catholics and Protestants he managed to keep up the friendship of both sides. What he hated above all was exaggeration or fanaticism. For, as he pointed out, 248 sects arose in antiquity to dispute the nature of the common good. He himself was a Catholic because his parents' family was Catholic; he went to Mass and saw no reason to change, though, as he added: 'A different latitude, different parents, similar praises and threats, could have produced in the same way a quite contrary belief. We are Christian in the same way as we are German or Périgordian ... And since I am in no position to choose, I follow the choice of others and remain in the groove where God has put me. For otherwise I would roll and roll without end.' Though he rejected the Reformation, he was of those who would 'light one candle to Saint Michael and the other to the Dragon' and thought that 'the truest opinion of the supernatural is to have no opinion'.

Montaigne began writing his *Essaies* in the year of the Massacre of St Bartholomew. In his foreword he said:

'I wish to be seen ... without art or affectation: for it is myself that I portray. My faults will be found here as they are; also my plain nature as far as decorum will allow. Had I lived among the peoples of whom it is said that they dwell still under the sweet freedom of nature's first laws, I assure you I would have willingly pictured myself entirely naked ...'

He wrote in a desultory way as pleased him best, taking refuge in his little book when he came in from his ordinary outdoor duties. His system was to have no system, he wrote ideas down higgledy piggledy as they came into his head. He would begin a chapter 'Of the Inconstancy of our Actions' or 'Of Drunkenness' or 'Of Cruelty' or 'Of the Parthians' Arms' with some stray thought about the ancients or with an observation that had struck him when he was riding over his estate, or with a comment on the politics of the age. But he would rapidly stray from this first thought, one idea leading on to another, with only a casual connection – like that between the different sights one sees when going a journey. And he would never end up anywhere near where he began. He had a vast Latin learning, though he was no fanatic about that, unlike some of the Italians, and we can see him pottering about among his books, looking up the half-remembered quotation and putting it down – he could never resist bringing in a few appropriate lines from the classics, indeed his pages are littered with them.

His *Essaies* portray him as the foreword would

lead us to expect, benign, sceptical, no cynic, with the touch of pedantry that becomes the perfect dilettante; he portrays himself with gentle humour as he proceeds through life and grapples with minor ills. He had children, but apparently did not love even them too much or too little. Interminable books have been written about what exactly Montaigne thought. But Montaigne's thinking cannot be divorced from the manner of his thinking, from our picture of the country gentleman, the man Montaigne, and the circumstances in which he thinks or writes.

The first English translation of the *Essaies* by Sir John Florio was published in 1603, eleven years after Montaigne's death in Périgord; it had a wide influence on Englishmen, including Shakespeare.

Innovator and traditionalist

MONTEVERDI, Claudio Zuan Antonio, (1567–1643), Italian composer.

One of the few portraits of this contemporary of Shakespeare, Rubens and Caravaggio shows him as a middle-aged man, leaning forward with an expression at once alert and composed. In his eyes there is no Renaissance cruelty, and no weakness either; no gaiety, no disillusionment; yet perhaps the melancholy of a man of aristocratic intellect, wise and humane, who has suffered and understood. There are lines from Shakespeare which would go well beneath the portrait; or from a less-known contemporary, Sir John Davies:

> I know my soul hath power to know all things,
>   Yet is she blind and ignorant in all;
> I know I am one of nature's little kings,
>   Yet to the least and vilest things am thrall.
>
> I know my life's a pain and but a span,
>   I know my sense is mocked with everything;
> And to conclude I know myself a man,
>   Which is a proud, and yet a wretched thing.

Monteverdi was innovator and traditionalist, and his own life witnessed the secularization of the musician. From 1590 to 1612 his patrons were the Dukes of Mantua, and their treatment of him was not always as noble as their rank. His faithful service was not rewarded with regular or sufficient wages, nor did he at first obtain the promotion he deserved. In 1607 his wife died, and in 1608 his financial and official posi-

tion was at its worst, a miserable time for the father of two children (whom he cared for with a self-sacrificing devotion). The sorrow and hardship of these years stimulated and deepened Monteverdi's art, and to this period belong his opera *Orfeo* (1607), the first opera composed by a professional musician, and the towering achievement of the *Vespers* of 1610.

Unlike Heinrich Schütz (q.v.), whom he resembles in so many and such startling respects, Monteverdi obtained his release from the irritations of an uncongenial post. After a brief interlude he took up the position of *maestro di capella* at St Mark's in Venice, having at last security and an office in keeping with his dignity and eminence. The grandeur of black and green in the mosaics of San Marco fit Monteverdi, yet at Venice the paradox of his life was most evident. His duty at St Mark's was to revive the half-forgotten traditions of the polyphonic church music of the time of Palestrina, who had died in 1594; and he carried out this conservative-reactionary task while continuing to compose music of his own which was revolutionary and forward-looking.

At Venice in 1637 the first public opera-house in the world was opened; and Monteverdi devoted himself to the composition of operas. As with Schütz, his old age was a time of great creative industry. His last work, *L'Incoronazione di Poppea* (1642), was as revolutionary as anything he had written.

The *Vespers* of 1610 show us one aspect of Monteverdi's adventurous genius. He had introduced to the world of church music the splendours of opera, uniting the rich sonority of an orchestra of brass and strings with the dignity of the organ, and bringing passionate arias and expressive recitative into the frame of a sacred service. Monteverdi's deeply humanistic outlook is responsible for his technical and formal daring. His search for the expressive and dramatic led him to discover new tonal combinations prophetic of the work of the nineteenth century Romantics. He scrutinized his libretti for every absurdity and extravagance, and established a precedent for dramatic honesty which has all too often been ignored. The essence of his humanism is contained in one of his letters about opera: 'Ariadne shudders because she is a woman, and Orpheus was stirred because he was a human being and not a wind; whereas these mythological personifications, these Tritons, these Sirens, are not capable of interesting and moving the spectator.'

ILLUSTRATION: Page 266.

Montezuma of Mexico

MONTEZUMA, (c. 1480–1520), ruler of the Aztec Indian tribes of central Mexico at the time of the Spanish Conquest.

The years before the conquest of Mexico had been full of evil portent for the Aztecs. Montezuma had played a ritualistic game of basket-ball with his chief ally, the war-chief of Texcoco, on the issue of strangers ruling in the land of the Aztecs. The wager was the kingdom of Texcoco against three turkey-cocks, and Montezuma lost. Other phenomena were observed: columns of fire, comets, voices crying in the night. By tradition and legend the first chiefs of the dynasty of the errant Quetzalcoatl, god of civilization, were to come from the east; and when rumours drifted up from the coast of four-legged monsters with white-faced men growing out of their backs, legend clearly was fulfilled.

As Cortés and his four hundred men came up from the coast, Montezuma, tied by practical and psychological considerations, waited apprehensively, and barring a few attempts at magic, apathetically. The invaders, with their Indian allies, approached Tenochtitlan, the Aztec capital, which is the modern Mexico City, and were astonished at the beauty and splendour of the town, which they likened to a scene from the romance of Amadis of Gaul. Montezuma came out to meet them with his nobles, and at first all went smoothly, but a feeling of resentment grew among the Indians, fostered by Spanish interference in religious matters. There was trouble, and the legend of the Spaniards' immortality was disproved when an ally despatched to Montezuma a Spanish head. Cortés's position was critical, but going with his officers to the palace, he seized Montezuma, chained him, and forced him to acknowledge the Spanish King. Although he ransomed himself for a large treasure, Montezuma remained a virtual prisoner of the Spaniards for the remainder of his days.

He is often portrayed as weak and vacillating, but he was the victim of the social organization in the valley of Mexico, with its divisions, its tribal units, its loose confederation, in which the needs of the vassal states had priority over the needs of the empire. The Spaniards started their ascent from the coast at harvest time, when every available inhabitant was busy in the fields, bringing in the grain on which survival depended. Montezuma's authority over his vassals and allies was not enough to direct them away from this task, even if the whole of the Indian approach to the Spaniards had not been psychologically exploitable.

Meanwhile difficulties among the Spaniards themselves necessitated the absence of Cortés, and the Aztecs of Tenochtitlan revolted, driving the Spanish garrison to take refuge in the palace of Axayacatla, in the main square. But again the structural weakness of the Aztec organization allowed Cortés to bring up troops to the rescue of the garrison. Montezuma himself, attempting to calm the rage of his people, came out on his palace roof, but was stoned and died three days later, though Indian tradition says that he was poisoned by the Spaniards. His brother succeeded him, and then his nephew, but neither had the power to weld the Stone Age weapons and the tribal jealousies of the Indians into an efficient counter to the steel and precision of the Spaniards. The splendid airy palaces, the reeking temples, where Montezuma himself once delivered 12,000 captives to the sacrifice, the featherwork, the gold and the precious jade of the Aztecs were all destroyed.

The brothers Montgolfier

MONTGOLFIER, Joseph Michel, (1740–1810) and Jacques Etienne, (1745–1799), French papermakers and inventors of the balloon.

There is always a sense of historical exasperation if one contemplates a simple invention which could easily have been thought out a thousand years sooner. The man-carrying hot-air balloon could have provided Alexander or Caesar with aerial reconnaissance, had someone only drawn the simple conclusions from watching a camp-fire and seeing the fragments which rise above the flames and drift off into the night. All that is necessary for such a balloon is a light fabric such as silk, and a fire; but the world had to wait until 1783 for the first aerial voyagers, and the inventors of the vehicle which carried them. The brothers Montgolfier, paper manufacturers at Annonay, near Lyons, watched a fire in 1782, and drew the right conclusions. They made small bags which rose to the ceiling, and then larger bags which rose even higher. At last they staged a dramatic demonstration at Annonay on 5 June 1783, before official witnesses and a gaping crowd.

The balloon they sent aloft on this occasion did not carry either cargo or passengers. But after they had been invited to Paris to continue their experiments, the two brothers set to work in September 1783 and built full-size balloons, at the same time inspiring Professor J.A.C.Charles to build in 1784 the first hydrogen balloon – as it turned out, a much more practical affair.

The Montgolfiers themselves seldom ascended in their linen and paper creations. Aeronauts were sent up, first of all, in large tethered balloons. A miniature zoo then made a free flight, and man's first aerial voyage took place at last in Paris on 21 November 1783, when Pilâtre de Rozier and the Marquis d'Arlandes piloted a gaily decorated Montgolfier balloon. It was inflated by a fire built under the launching platform, and bore aloft a straw-burning brazier to keep up the temperature of the air. The voyage lasted twenty-five minutes and covered four and a half miles.

Montgolfières, as the hot air balloons were called, made other spectacular ascents in 1783 and 1784, but were soon ousted by hydrogen balloons. However, they survived through the nineteenth century as a cheap method of taking up parachutists.

Sculptor of our day

MOORE, Henry, (b. 1898), English sculptor and draughtsman, a leading sculptor of the modern world.

This quiet, steadfast man was born and reared in the small coal-mining town of Castleford, near Leeds, in the West Riding of Yorkshire. As a child Moore was impressed by early carvings in a local church and by the great waste heaps of this mining district which burned and glowed powerfully and mysteriously through the night. The story of Michelangelo, also, was read to him in his childhood, out of Vasari's lives. As an art student in Leeds, he had his first chance of seeing pictures by Van Gogh and Gauguin, and through books he discovered the new appreciation of negro sculpture. As a student transferred to London, Moore was absorbed by the pent life and formal strictness of African, Pacific and Mexican carvings in the British Museum. As a student in Italy, he delighted and has delighted ever since in the grave sculptural figures painted by Masaccio

(q.v.) in the Carmine chapel at Florence. In the famous drawings in which Moore depicted mankind sheltering from bombs, it is curious to see elements from Masaccio woven into the *mise-en-scène* of the London tunnels. Among modern artists Picasso has affected him most; and in a sense Moore is the Picasso of modern sculpture.

Artists work within a dual environment of art and nature, finding in both of them aid to the realization of their ideas and a stimulus to new ideas. So Moore has always been widely alert to 'natural sculpture', not only to man or woman and child, but, for example, to ranges of hills, the structure and mass of trees, boulders, pebbles; to shells, bones, and the wave-ground, beach-ground objects of wood or stone along the foreshore. It is typical of his wide delight that Moore has visited Altamira for the cave-paintings of the Old Stone Age and turns as well to his television set (especially to boxing matches) as a nightly gallery of form and movement.

Himself a shortish, stocky, small-fingered, straightforward man, calm, happy and determined, he has never acted the Master's dubious part of oracle or dogmatic law giver, in spite of his celebrity through the world. 'By trying to express his aims with a rounded-off, logical exactness,' he has affirmed of the artist, 'he can easily become a theorist whose actual work is only a caged-in exposition of conceptions evolved in terms of logic and words' – so the essentials of Moore's art, including his at times exquisite and mysterious drawings, are not to be pinned down in his own few utterances. He is an addict of the shapes of life and tensity. His sculptures are a series of controlled adventures in the 'meaning' or effect of three-dimensional shapes, in endless combination, neither wholly natural nor altogether removed from nature. A definition of art quoted in this volume under *Chikamatsu Monzaemon* admirably applies.

St Thomas More

MORE, Sir Thomas, (1478–1535), author of *Utopia*, humanist, Lord Chancellor of England, Catholic martyr and Saint. The publication of *Utopia* in 1516 added a word to the language and a recurrent theme to literature and speculation. In this political essay in Latin, Utopia – meaning 'No place' – is the land or ideal state reported upon by a traveller, in which there is freedom of worship, education for all, no poverty and none of the evils of society.

More's character we know in rare detail. 'Whenever did Nature mould a character more gentle, endearing and happy, than Thomas More's?' his friend Erasmus asked Robert Fisher in a letter on 5 December 1499. His wit, which went with him to the scaffold, was one trait, and a family one inherited from his father, Sir John More, Justice of the King's Bench. He tells us himself how Sir John defined marriage as a blind man's choice out of a bag full of snakes and eels – seven snakes to one eel. Thomas More, after having hesitated about entering the cloister, made two dips into the bag. His first wife was Jane Colt, who was the eldest of three daughters; and he married her in spite of preferring the second sister, because 'it would be both great grief and some shame to see her younger sister preferred before her'. She died young after about six years, having brought her husband a child every year – Margaret, Cicely, Elizabeth, and John. Margaret, as she grew, became her father's dear and loving favourite.

For his second wife, More chose the widow Alice Middleton, *nec bella nec puella*, or as Erasmus described her, 'aged, blunt and rude'. He seems to have delighted in her as Shakespeare did in Juliet's Nurse, or Desdemona's Emilia – both of whom she resembled; 'cherishing her no less lovingly and tenderly than if she had been his first young wife'. We should think her legendary, devised as perfect counterpoint to his own subtlety, if it were not for the evidence of his own works.

It was a happy house at Chelsea, where the children learnt the Greek alphabet by shooting with bows and arrows at the letters, and the rod was barred. Away on an embassy, Thomas whiled away the hours in the saddle writing them letters in Latin verse:

'Kisses enough I have given you forsooth, but stripes hardly ever,
If I have flogged you at all it has been with the tail of a peacock!'

Erasmus from Rotterdam came to stay, and tells how he was taken into the garden to see the monkey, the rabbits, the fox, the ferret, and the weasel (the monkey you may see in Holbein's *Household of Sir Thomas More*, nestling in the folds of Dame Alice's robes).

But someone else felt the charm of the Chelsea household – King Henry VIII. More's son-in-law William Roper (who had married Margaret) was overcome to see the King walking in More's garden 'holding his arm about his neck'. More's comment was sober and prophetic: 'I may tell thee, son Roper, I have no cause to be proud thereof, for if my head could win him a castle in France it should not fail to go.'

Henry VIII repeated the miscalculation of Henry II with that other Thomas – St Thomas à Becket (More's biographer, Nicholas Harpsfield, noted the parallel): the clever young lawyer, idol of the Londoners, adored for his probity and swift despatch of cases, never without a wisecrack, showing his courage equally among the mob and as Speaker of the House of Commons, was taken up first as good companion and then as Lord Chancellor (1529) in the game of power politics. But that was a game More did not choose to play: he resigned in 1532 to the private life of Chelsea, and since he had not approved of the King's divorce, and would take no oath which would contradict his obedience to the Pope, the end was the Tower of London and the scaffold. Dame Alice went to the Tower to see him:

What the good yer, Master More, I marvel that you, that have always hitherto been taken for so wise a man, will now so play the fool as to lie here in this close, filthy prison, and be content to be shut up amongst mice and rats, when you might be abroad at your liberty, and with the good will both of the King and his Council, if you would but do as all the Bishops and best learned of this realm have done. And seeing that you have at Chelsey a right fair house, your library, your books, your gallery, your garden, your orchard, and all other necessaries so handsome about you, where you might in the company of me, your wife, your children and household, be merry, I marvel what a God's name you mean here thus fondly to tarry.

– I pray thee, good mistress Alice, tell me one thing.
– What is that, quoth she.
– Is not this house as nigh Heaven as my own?
To whom she, after her accustomed homely fashion, not liking such talk, answered: Tilly vally, Tilly vally.
– How say you, mistress Alice, is it not so?
– Bone deus, bone deus, man, will this gear never be left?
– Well then, mistress Alice, if it be so, it is very well. For I see no great cause why I should much joy either of my gay house or of anything belonging thereunto; when, if I should but seven years lie buried under the ground, and then arise and come thither again, I should not fail to find some one therein that would bid me get out of doors, and tell me it were none of mine. What cause have I then to like such a house as would so soon forget his master?

The scaffold they had built on St Thomas's Eve, 6 July 1535, was very wobbly, 'I pray you, master Lieutenant, see me safe up,' said More, 'and for my coming down, let me shift for myself.'

ILLUSTRATION: Page 264.

Khan of Wall Street

MORGAN, John Pierpont, (1837–1913), American financier, the titan of big business at the turn of the century and in his day one of the most powerful men in the western world.

To a man who was enquiring the price of a steam yacht, Morgan said, 'Anybody who even has to think about the cost had better not get one.' Everything about this Great Khan of industry was in keeping. As a child, he is said to have played finance in his well-to-do business family when other children played trains. As a young man he bought a shipload of coffee on his own initiative, plunging his employers into panic – till they found that he had arranged to sell all the coffee, at a profit, even before the purchase. His real career began in the turbulence after the Civil War, when rugged individualism and devil take the hindmost were the order of the day; and his achievement is best seen in the evidence before the House Committee on Banking and Currency, which sat in 1912. A handful of New York bankers, it was maintained, led by Morgan, controlled money, credit, the big industries and the railways, indeed most of the U.S. economy. Morgan's banks, allied companies and subsidiary holdings added up into a large business certainly: it was estimated that 'Morgan men' held 341 directorships in 112 companies, involving a capital of 22 billion dollars; but though he was Morgan the wicked capitalist to thousands, there is no indication that he was ever cruel or avaricious in an ordinary sense. There seemed nothing wrong to Morgan in what was going on in America: the idea of big business was new, there were opportunities to grasp of selling nationally and internationally. Morgan saw no reason why combinations should not be combined to make money into more money.

Before the Senate Committee, the Government attorney tried to make Morgan admit, or betray himself with admitting, some nefarious purpose behind his huge business:

'Is not commercial credit based primarily upon money or property?'

'No, sir, the first thing is character,' replied Morgan.

'Before money or property?'

'Before money or anything else. Money cannot buy it ... Because a man I do not trust could not get money from me on all the bonds in Christendom.' It was a testament that amazed Wall Street.

Morgan himself lived like a Renaissance prince: town house, country house, a huge steam yacht; he entertained royalty and travelled through Europe from one luxury hotel to another. His art collecting activities, to which he applied business principles, have been acutely described by the English critic and painter Roger Fry, who acted as Morgan's art adviser for some time. Fry talks about his 'triumphant progress through Italy ... at Siena the whole of the wooden floor of the Cathedral was taken up that *il Morgan* might see the mosaics. The Queen of Italy had visited Siena a little before and had asked in vain for this.' 'A crude historical imagination was the only flaw in his otherwise perfect insensibility,' added Fry.

He could do a year's work in nine months, he once said, but not in a year. He was not a time-waster: when a new medical centre was planned for Harvard, Morgan jabbed the plan, saying, 'I will build that – and that – and that. Good morning, gentlemen,' and left. He was a gourmet, with a nose hideously bulbed by *acne rosacea* – and eyes that blazed with almost unbelievable fire. And, from his youth until his death, he was a staunch Episcopalian: 'I commit my soul into the hands of my Saviour', wrote Morgan in his will, 'in full confidence that having redeemed it and washed it in His most precious blood He will present it faultless before my Heavenly Father.'

ILLUSTRATION: Page 268.

Pride and sorrow of chess

MORPHY, Paul Charles, (1837–1884), American chess-player, and the outstanding genius of chess in the nineteenth century.

Morphy was born in New Orleans of a well-to-do family which, in spite of its Irish-sounding name, was partly of French, partly of Spanish descent. He was given a first-class education and learnt chess by watching a member of his family at play. In that respect he can fairly be called a child prodigy, and soon he could find no one to match him in his home town. When J. Lowenthal, a famous Continental master, passed through New Orleans, he played two games against Morphy, then aged twelve, and lost both.

Chess was not allowed to interfere with the boy's Law studies, and it was not until 1857, after he had been called to the Bar, that he played in an important tournament, the American Chess Congress, in which this twenty-year-old player was first, ahead by four points of Louis Paulsen, a leading Continental player. Americans were delighted, since their players till then had not been outstanding; and Morphy was encouraged to make the trip to Europe, challenging all and sundry, especially Howard Staunton of England. He crossed the Atlantic in the summer of 1858, and though the match with Staunton never took place, in set matches he beat all the masters of rank who played with him, especially Adolf Anderssen, the victor of the great London Tournament of 1851.

Morphy returned home in 1859; it had been a case of 'I came, I saw, I conquered', but the triumph went sour on him. He began to dislike a game in which he had played more than once against players less chivalrous than himself, and he gave up chess altogether.

Two baffling questions arise from Morphy's chess career. How is it that even now, after a hundred years, his name among all chess players has still an almost legendary ring, and why did he give up the game after these two years of unsurpassed success? His superiority was overwhelming, his style of play was a remarkable step forward in the technique of the game, both tactically and strategically. America was proud to have the greatest chess player of the time, and his prowess was acclaimed no less in Europe than in America. Yet that does not answer the first question. The answer may possibly be that Morphy's style was all his own, and that he combined the sound positional play which prevails today, with the brilliance so much admired in players of his generation. Even today some particularly brilliant coup is frequently described as 'a bit of Morphy'.

As for the second mystery, Morphy, as the years went by, became more and more depressed and morose and at the end suffered from acute melancholia. The Civil War may have affected him, and also his failure as an attorney, for which, rightly or wrongly, he blamed his celebrity as a chess player; people would not entrust their legal business to a man best known for his prowess at chess, a state of affairs not improbable in his times. Towards the end, his doc-

tors urged him to take up chess again, but he refused, interesting himself only in music, especially the opera. He died of congestion of the brain at the early age of forty-seven, the 'pride and sorrow of chess'.

Medievalist and revolutionary

MORRIS, William, (1834–1896), English designer, craftsman, cabinet-maker, smith, weaver, typographer, printer, shopkeeper, poet, essayist, writer of romances, reformer and revolutionary. Morris wrote of himself in *The Wanderer*: 'Dreamer of dreams born out of my due time, Why should I strive to set the crooked straight?'; in fact, he passed his days trying to straighten the crooked to accord with the dreams.

His father was a rich City bill-broker, he grew up in Essex and saw the lovely country of his childhood devoured by suburbia. As a boy he visited the 'Art' section of the Crystal Palace (see *Prince Albert*), and was instantly sick. At Oxford – which still preserved the enchantment of the Middle Ages – he allied himself to the painter Burne-Jones and others; they revelled in Keats, Shelley and Tennyson, but soon turned to older literature – Chaucer, Mallory and the sagas of Iceland, to which Morris made an excited journey. The Middle Ages they found 'jolly' as well as poetic, and a robustious enthusiasm pervaded all their activities.

Morris himself founded Morris & Co. to make and sell furniture fashioned to his ideas. Even when simple, it was expensive; it involved the employment of good designers and much research into lost arts: dyeing, weaving, block printing, etc. Tapestry and stained-glass were mostly designed by Burne-Jones, wallpapers and textiles by Morris. The Red House, Bexley Heath, built for Morris by Philip Webb, and filled with these products of the Morris group, is now regarded as a turning point in the history of domestic architecture. 'Have nothing in your home', Morris said, 'that you do not know to be useful and believe to be beautiful.' This may not be functionalism, but it comes very near to it.

The socialism of this prophet and missionary with a red beard had the medieval guilds as its inspiration. He was not afraid to preach it in Trafalgar Square, a proceeding which landed him in court, and in some of his romances, *e.g. News from Nowhere* and *The*

Dream of John Ball, with its picture of the white chips of stone below the window of the newly made medieval church, he depicts in the same spirit a lost medieval Utopia. His socialism also made him write some of his less inspired verses:

> Come, comrades, come, your glasses clink;
> Up with your hands a health to drink,
> The health of all that workers be,
> In every land, in every sea.
>
> And he that will this health deny,
> Down among the dead men, down among the
>   dead men,
> Down, down, down, down
> Down among the dead men let him lie!

but, though he thought a man should make and sing his verses while working at the bench, Morris is a finer poet than is commonly allowed, at extreme length in *Sigurd the Volsung* or *The Earthly Paradise*, or briefly in such tales as the unforgettable *Blue Closet*, or *Riding Together*, or *Shameful Death*, which plunges brutally into a past which Morris made more than ornamental and merely 'romantic':

> There were four of us about that bed;
>   The mass-priest knelt at the side,
> I and his mother stood at the head,
>   Over his feet lay the bride;
> We were quite sure that he was dead,
>   Though his eyes were open wide.
>
> He did not die in the night,
>   He did not die in the day,
> But in the morning twilight
>   His spirit pass'd away,
> When neither sun nor moon was bright,
>   And the trees were merely grey ...

Such poems (and other aspects of this latter-day medievalism) laid themselves open to parody

> Her pale feet glimmered, in and out,
> Like tombstones as she went about.
>   ℗ miserie !
>
> From right to left and left to right;
> And blue veins strekt her instep white;
>   ℗ miserie !
>
> And folks did ask her in the street
> 'How fared it with her long pale feet?'
>   ℗ miserie !

Morris, however, eschewed that dead 'poetic' language which was the disease of so much Victorian writ-

ing. In architecture and design (if not in poetry as well) Morris is the link between a romantic medievalism in the middle years of the nineteenth century and the functionalism of our own day. His ideal craftsman has never been realized; his clarity in design is now universally accepted. His socialism – minimized by his official biographer, Mackail – came from his conviction that beauty rose from joy in work, which the medieval workman experienced and which is impossible under the factory system. Only at the end of his life did Morris make one important admission – that we must design for the machine, instead of destroying the machine.

ILLUSTRATION: Page 270.

Wolfgang Amadeus Mozart

MOZART, Wolfgang Amadeus, (1756–1791), Austrian composer; by common consent one of the world's supreme masters.

When Mozart was a child the world treated him well. He was the son of Leopold Mozart, a musician of some ability who worked at the Court of the Archbishop of Salzburg. Leopold was a man of the highest moral principles, and can be excused for wishing to show off his prodigious son, who had begun to compose at the age of five. Leopold obtained permission from the Archbishop to tour Europe with his son and daughter, and was rewarded with success (though little else) wherever he went. In London Mozart was subjected to 'scientific tests' to prove that his powers were genuine, somewhat as if the boy had been the bearded lady of a circus or one half of Siamese twins. Instead of being sentimental over these rather degrading years, it might be better to examine the delightful little opera *Bastien and Bastienne* which Mozart wrote when he was twelve.

Good fortune departed from Mozart with his childhood; he could no longer count on startling and delighting the unmusical. In 1776 he set out for Paris, alone, his father having decided that the success of his son in earlier years would recommend him for an official post. But the impresario who had greeted the infant prodigy so eagerly fifteen years before was not interested in a mature artist; indeed, wherever Mozart turned, he found nothing but polite disinterest. He consoled himself in a characteristic way – by playing the fool. Leopold ordered his son back to Salzburg. After a while Mozart returned, and busied himself with a new opera, *Idomeneo* (1781), a serious and dignified work; though the composer was still treated at Court like a common servant.

Salzburg now had a new Archbishop, who behaved towards Mozart with ungodly meanness and arrogance. Despite the efforts of Leopold (who was contented enough) there was a violent upset, and Mozart was expelled, forcibly, from the Archbishop's household. At twenty-five he was now left to his own devices. Unwisely, he found himself a wife; and in the year of his marriage wrote six string quartets which he dedicated so humbly and so affectionately to Joseph Haydn. He also had the happiness of meeting his librettist, Lorenzo da Ponte, and writing with him two operas, *The Marriage of Figaro* (1785), and *Don Giovanni* (1781).

Mozart was now appointed Court composer to the Austrian emperor at a salary that barely paid his rent. He had an ill wife to keep, and he was anything but well himself. He took pupils, he wrote dance music, he played the piano concertos he had written for himself; he was forced to ask a fellow Freemason for a loan, not once or even twice, but time after time, in a series of letters the pathos of which is not visible on the surface; as in his music, the feeling is so controlled that it bears little relation to the torments through which the sensitive and generous nature had to pass.

In his last year, Mozart wrote two string quartets, a piano concerto, and *The Magic Flute*. He also began work on his Requiem, which had been mysteriously commissioned by a stranger 'dressed from head to foot in grey'. Mozart's state of mind was far from healthy at this time, and he became convinced that his visitor was a messenger from Death. 'But', he wrote in a letter, 'since death ... is the goal of our lives, I have made myself so well acquainted during the last two years with this true and best friend of mankind that the idea of it no longer holds any terror for me, but rather, much that is tranquil and comforting. ... I never lie down in bed without considering that, young as I am, perhaps I may on the morrow be no more. Yet not one of those who know me could say that I am morose or melancholy ...'

Mozart died at the age of thirty-five. There were a few friends at the funeral service, but it was cold and raining outside, and two undertakers were the only ones to see his body into a pauper's grave.

The world has Mozart on its conscience, and has been anxious to make amends and smother him with belated love. Musicians, too, have been stricken at the thought of him, rebuked into self-denunciation by the purity and composure of his music. Thus Brahms wrote 'that people in general do not understand and do not respect the greatest things, such as Mozart's concertos, helps our kind to live and acquire renown. If they would only know that they are getting from us by drops what they could drink there to their hearts' content!' Mozart stands back from life, observing, without seeking to resolve, its tragedies and comedies. The grace of his music is a worldly grace; its delicate and sensuous ornament is still a part of the eighteenth century. But from the form, from the ordering of materials in a manner that can make the innocent and the child-like into a thing of tragedy, there arises a power which is more than worldly. The pattern becomes divine.

Mozart was the last great musician to preserve a flawless equilibrium. He neither sins nor sits in judgement, but remains poised in a paradisiacal calm which we can taste through him, but never wholly attain. 'All the emotions play in his music,' wrote André Gide, 'but as if they were transposed celestially.'

ILLUSTRATION: Page 267.

Mountain life and death

MUMMERY, Albert Frederick, (1855–1895), English mountaineer and rock-climber. 'The gaunt bare slabs, the square, precipitous steps in the ridge, and the black, bulging ice of the gully' were life to him, he wrote in *My Climbs in the Alps and Caucasus* (1895).

As partner in a tannery at Dover, Mummery could indulge himself in mountaineering, and he is the textbook example of the climber who went to the mountains for excitement and compensation. He was born with a defect of the spine which made him unable to carry heavy weights: in one sphere of physical action at least he had to prove himself supreme. Epitomizing that age of mountain-climbing during which old peaks were being conquered by ever more difficult routes, he started young, making the first of his seven ascents of the Matterhorn (see *Whymper*) when he was eighteen. After a series of spectacular rock-climbs on the Chamonix Aiguilles, he visited the Caucasus, and then returned to the Alps to make more exceptionally difficult, and many guideless, ascents on the Aiguilles. To the Alps, Mummery brought the newer, higher standards of rock-climbing then being developed in the English Lake District and North Wales, even though his own British experience was almost entirely limited to climbing the chalk cliffs of Kent and Sussex. Mummery emphasized that mountaineering was a sport, dangerous, stimulating, and not necessarily tied to science. 'I fear no contributions to science, or topography, or learning of any sort are to be found sandwiched in between the story of crags and seracs, of driving storm and perfect weather,' he wrote of his book. 'To tell the truth, I have only the vaguest ideas about theodolites, and as for plane tables, their name is abomination.'

Sure of his powers – 'He knew mountains', wrote Lord Conway, 'as some men know horses' – Mummery hated artificial aids to climbing such as pitons. When he could climb no farther up the Dent du Géant he left behind him a famous card, found by another climber: 'Absolutely inaccessible', he had written on it, 'by fair means'. When he took risks, he did so knowingly and with enjoyment; and as he lived by mountains, so he died by them. It was hardly a surprise that Mummery came to an unknown end in 1895 on the slopes of Nanga Parbat in the Himalayas. Possibly he was overwhelmed by an avalanche. (*See also Leigh-Mallory*).

The Strindberg of painting

MUNCH, Edvard, (1883–1944). The outstanding genius of Norwegian art, who belonged to the northern, tortured world of Strindberg and Ibsen.

Born at Löyten, in Norway, the son of a slum doctor, Munch grew up against unmitigated squalor, harshness and poverty; and lived always in dread of sickness and of death. Virile and with handsome strong features, he played no games for fear of wetting his feet, he kept his rooms always at an even temperature, and would retire to bed if someone said that he looked unwell. He represented woman as the destroyer of man's life and the instrument of malignant fate. Munch, in fact, was the friend of Strindberg (q.v.) – the difficult friendship of two difficult men; and in 1896 he designed sets for Ibsen's *Peer Gynt* and in 1906 for Ibsen's *Ghosts*.

'No more painting of interiors with women knit-

ting and men reading,' Munch wrote in 1886, 'I want to show men who breathe, feel, love and suffer. I want to bring home to the spectator the sacred elements in these things so that he takes off his hat just as he would in church' – and the climax of his art was the *Frieze of Life*, which he exhibited in parts, and for which he painted picture after picture of people dancing, suffering, dying, etc.

Munch, in brief, has been the great protagonist of Expressionism; and Germany, rather than Paris, London or his own country, was where he triumphed. Compare with Munch's statement of his aims, Matisse's cheerful wish that his gay pictures should be like a comfortable armchair to a tired businessman. However, aesthetic preferences for the picture as an object-in-itself should not blind us to the Expressionist picture as a dive into human perplexity and tragedy; though one may detect in Munch and some of his German followers that 'too-muchness' of which the English critic S. T. Coleridge accused the Germans. In Munch's Expressionism, nature, form, paint, colour may all shriek around the poor battered individual at the centre, as in his famous *Puberty*, in which a terrified girl sits on the edge of her bed while her strange new feelings are expressed in a dark blue shadow shaped like a fungus, or in the later and more emphatic picture, *The Scream*, in which the man's head appears softened and distorted by the scream which tears from his mouth, and the landscape closes around him without form.

Condemning them as 'degenerate', the Nazis removed many of Munch's pictures from public galleries in Germany. At home, after the invasion of Norway, Munch refused to join the Quisling 'Council of Art', and he fixed the suffering of his last years in a harrowing series of self-portraits. Munch once wrote of his fellow Norwegians, 'I was sold by my brothers, but unlike Joseph, I became a soldier in the country of the Pharaohs', yet he bequeathed all his unsold paintings to the city of Oslo.

The Lady Murasaki

MURASAKI SHIKIBU, (born about 978), Japanese court-lady and novelist. Her long novel *The Tale of Genji* she finished in 1004, so it may claim to be one of the oldest prose fictions in the world.

The Lady Murasaki came of a noble family of the middle rank; her father was a governor of two provinces, who after his retirement took vows as a Buddhist priest. In her childhood Murasaki was quick to learn. She was often present at her brother's Chinese lessons and picked up the language. When she was about eighteen she married an officer in the Imperial Guard, who gave her two daughters and left her a widow. At the age of about twenty-six she entered the service of the pious, serious-minded young Empress Akiko as Lady-in-waiting. By 1031 she appears to have been dead.

The Tale of Genji, her masterpiece (which Arthur Waley has translated for English readers), depicts with fascinating exactitude the multitudinous duties, conventions and ceremonies of the ancient Japanese court. The five parts easily encompass the adventures of four generations, and the whole is interwoven with great skill and acute observation of men. Yet the story is enchanting most of all by the constant evocation of atmosphere and setting: It is night, the rain never stops, and Prince Genji sits by his lamp reading old love-letters. There is a storm, sighing dismally as it sweeps the pine-trees clustering around the house. Dew glitters on the bamboo clumps, and the morning light floods in through the opened lattice. A message comes on a sprig of plum blossom still white with the hoar frost. The people who move so deftly through the long action of the book are human in the extreme, their motivation is complex, their actions in their impact upon each other are tragic. That the book was written nearly a thousand years ago, by a court-lady, to amuse herself and her circle, detracts not at all from its charm and readability.

Most of our direct knowledge of the Lady Murasaki comes from a diary which she kept till 1010. With rather a wan frankness, she notes 'that I am very vain, reserved, unsociable, wanting always to keep people at a distance – that I am wrapped up in the study of ancient stories, conceited, living all the time in a poetical world of my own and scarcely realizing the existence of other people, save occasionally to make spiteful and depreciatory comments upon them – such is the opinion of me that most strangers hold, and they are prepared to dislike me accordingly'. Her writings show her to us as quick, sensitive, intelligent, often lonely, a little bitter, chafing within a narrow conventional employment, yet shrinking from the looseness and boisterousness of the worldly elements around her.

Duce, Duce

MUSSOLINI, Benito, (1883–1945), blacksmith's son, teacher, stonemason, socialist and newspaper editor, then founder of Fascism, and Italian dictator, who enlivened the twentieth century with ideas as novel as 'non-belligerent non-neutrality' and a political 'anti-party'.

Mussolini's 'anti-party' was born in what appeared the most inauspicious circumstances after the resounding defeat of the Italian army at Caporetto in the first World War. The Communists looked forward to a revolution in Western Europe which never came. Instead came this baby of a different type, this illegitimate baby of Marxism, a revolution based, not on Communism, but on fear of Communism. It was a vigorous child, fostered by its midwife, Mussolini, to the uttermost. The situation was more promising than Mussolini can have been aware. Years later, when his Fascists had long ceased to be an 'anti-party' (if that term ever meant anything), Mussolini wrote in his famous article on Fascism in the *Italian Encyclopaedia* that when he called together the few followers he had acquired in March 1919, 'there was no specific doctrinal plan in my mind'. Indeed there was not. His watchword was 'action', and his flair caused him to launch himself on an incipient political wave without knowing where it was going to take him – and certainly without guessing that he would end heels up and head down in a street in Milan.

The irresistibility of 'action' had previously led him to throw overboard his Socialist past and advocate Italian intervention in the war, and now it led him to emulate in his own way the ruthlessness of the Bolsheviks. In 'action' he had to be the leader and not the led, and that saved him from committing himself except in words to D'Annunzio's unfortunate expedition to Fiume in 1919, at the head of the first Blackshirts. A consummate actor, he created the part of the Duce, and took in the world (Hitler never acted; he *was* the Führer). Mussolini's best single performance was the famous march on Rome, in spats, in 1922; it was a fake, because he had already 'squared' the army and the King. He took longer to consolidate himself in power than Hitler did; but he was an innovator, and the impunity with which civilized conventions could be defied had not yet been convincingly demonstrated. However, the classic Fascist methods of castor oil and the club did their work; even the Fascist murder of Matteotti, the Socialist deputy, which shook the dictator so much for a few days in 1924 that he thought that the end had come for him, too, was seen in retrospect to have produced hardly more than a ripple.

Inside opposition eliminated, Mussolini turned to international affairs. But the rise of Hitler roused both his jealousy and his cupidity, and before long he started imitating his pupil – he invaded Abyssinia in 1935, intervened in the Spanish civil war in 1936, over-ran Albania in 1939. But in 1940 the flair that had saved him a generation earlier from committing himself to D'Annunzio's adventure in Fiume, the flair that now saved General Franco from committing a blunder of the same stripe, deserted him. He committed himself to Hitler's war just before the French collapse, a mis-calculation this time from which there was no recovery. The Germans had to come to the rescue of his battered and obsolete armies in Greece and Africa, and in the long run could not save Italy itself from invasion. The Italian people had long since had enough of him, and at this point his own Fascist Grand Council revolted, and he was arrested on 25 July 1943. Once more the Germans rescued him, and for a little while longer he survived as a German puppet, the nominal leader of the nominal Fascist republic in north Italy, until the final collapse, when he and his mistress, Clara Petacci, were captured and shot by Communist partisans.

N

Founder of the Sikhs

NANAK, (1469–1539), Luther's contemporary, religious teacher and revered founder of the Sikhs.

On his preaching itineraries through his native Punjab (and by all accounts more widely afield through India), Nanak's companions were a Hindu peasant and a Muslim musician. Behind him were the centuries-old reforming movements of the Sufis, the mystics of Islam, and the Bhaktis, the mystical and direct devotees of Krishna, in Hinduism. Like other Hindu reformers, Nanak attacked the rigidity of caste and the extremes of asceticism, though he had passed through his own probation as mendicant and

recluse. His dissent, monotheistic, devout and toler-ant, was enlivened by humour, which helped to gain disciples (*shish* or *sikh*) among a peasantry which has always listened to the God-inspired. Reproved by a Muslim for sleeping with his feet towards Mecca (the kind of accident which has started riots in our own day), he answered, 'If you think I show disrespect by having my feet towards the house of God, turn them in some direction where God does not dwell.'

Within a century of Guru Nanak's peaceful death his Punjabi disciples had developed, under successive but not hereditary Gurus (Guru is 'teacher'), their own script, their own sacred writings and literature and their own adaptation of the temple as a meeting-place, as well as an independence of spirit which could proclaim

I will not pray to idols nor say the Muslim prayer,
I shall put my heart at the feet of the one Supreme Being,
For we are neither Hindus nor Mussulmans.

This was an invitation to be persecuted, and it was accepted by the Moghul Empire (*see Babar*). Between the hammer and the anvil, the followers of the gentle Nanak saved themselves from extinction by becom-ing a nation – a militant brotherhood with symbols (such as the long hair and beard) almost suggestive of racial distinction, and a third force with its brief taste of power in the Punjab, under the mighty Ranjit Singh, between the crumbling of the Moghul Empire and the expansion of the *Pax Britannica*.

Through that great cloud of dust which hung over the Sikh exodus from the Pakistan side of the Pun-jab in the post-partition fury of 1947, one sees the bearded, benevolent figure of Guru Nanak patiently proclaiming: 'There is no Hindu, there is no Mussul-man.' Hindu and Mussulman have persisted; but now caught between two fires and inevitably choosing the secular state of India, the more thoughtful of Nanak's followers look back on a history of glory and treach-ery, power and chaos, martyrdom and cruelty, all lit by an obstinately simple faith, and they are begin-ning to murmur at last: 'There is no Sikh.'

But they are the world's best field hockey players.

Inventor of logarithms

NAPIER, John, (1550–1617), Scottish mathema-tician, laird of Merchiston near Edinburgh, inventor of logarithms, and, in the opinion of David Hume, the greatest of Scotsmen, was born before his father was sixteen years old. His ancestors had long been prominent at Court and in affairs. He entered St Andrews University at the age of thirteen, and acquired the intense Calvinistic zeal of the period. Napier wrote of being so moved at this time in his tender years 'in admiration against the blindnesse of Papists' and so possessed by the *Revelations* of St John the Divine that he determined to employ his 'studie and diligence to search out the remanent mysteries of that holy book'. He published his treatise on the Apocalypse in 1593. It was far more famous in his day than the invention of logarithms, and went through more than twenty editions in various languages. In it he deduced that 'the day of God's judgement appears to fall betwixt the years of Christ 1688 and 1700'.

Napier was regarded as a magician, and as his family were the hereditary Poulterers to the King, he was supposed to possess a familiar jet-black cock, which revealed to him the most secret thoughts of his domestics. He entered into a covenant with the notorious desperado Robert Logan to discover secret treasure 'by the grace of God'. Also 'by the grace of God and worke of expert craftsmen' he designed burning mirrors, 'devises of sayling under water' and other 'Secret Inventions, profitable and necessary in these days for Defence of this Island, and withstanding of Strangers, enemies of God's Truth and Religion'. Nor did he neglect the ideological front. In his letter to King James accompanying his *Apocalypse*, he wrote, 'Let it be your Majesty's continuall study (as called and charged thereunto by God) to reform the universall enormities of your country, and ... purge the same of all suspicion of Papists and Atheists and Newtrals ... For shall any Prince be able to be one of the destroyers of that great seate, and a purger of the world from Antichristianisme, who purgeth not his owne countrie? Shall he purge his whole countrie who purgeth not his owne house? Or shall he purge his house who is not purged himself by private meditations with his God?'

Besides dealing with religion and politics he also improved the technique of industry. He introduced the use of salt as a fertilizer, and designed a hydraulic screw for pumping water out of coal-pits.

It is not known exactly how Napier's mathematical interests developed. But from an early age he was familiar with many aspects of practical life. Though isolated from mathematicians, he was by no means isolated from those activities which require calcula-

tion for their better performance. He was the first to propose the invention of a calculating machine. He discussed the imaginary roots of equations, and developed the decimal system into its modern form. His invention of logarithms was a natural product of his age. The advance of astronomy and navigation made improved methods of calculation essential. Various partial efforts were made by mathematicians in many lands. But Napier succeeded in thinking out the whole system clearly, by twenty years of intellectual labour. His work was at once appreciated by the great computors, such as Kepler and Henry Briggs.

The Emperor

NAPOLEON I, (1769–1821), soldier and Emperor of the French, one of the inexhaustibly fascinating characters of mankind, dowered with a variety of genius which has seldom been equalled.

Napoleon was first a soldier, secondly a ruler, thirdly a law-giver. He might have been a great explorer, an industrialist, a banker, a mathematician, a physicist or a chemist; and he was a man of rare charm of personality which worked upon all who knew him, even aboard the ship which took him into exile, and on the gloomy heights of St Helena. Adventurous dictators seldom leave behind them a long enduring bequest. Napoleon's ideas and institutions, on the contrary, have lived: and in France some of his institutions which were admirable in their time, have thrust roots deep – and too deep – into the social and political humus.

To begin with, he transformed the art of war. Nothing comparable to his tactics of 1796 in the first Italian campaign against the Austrians had been witnessed, and perhaps they were never excelled even by himself. All was founded on the simple notion of local superiority in strength and defeating the enemy piecemeal. His plans were often elaborate, but plans for him were secondary. He declared that the art of war was 'all in the execution'. By his *coup d'état* Napoleon became emperor in 1804, and soon showed his versatility by measures of genius, establishing the Civil Code, founding the Bank of France, radically reforming French finance, and concluding with Pope Pius VII the Concordat of 1801. However, French historians split into two schools about his record after the founding of the Empire. For one school the record is stained by an ambition which grew with every success, and finally by a megalomania which made him incapable of moderation. The other school, headed by Sorel, sees Napoleon drawn into wars he would have been glad to avoid, and caught by the teeth of events he was unable to control. Both schools protest too much. But it is fair to say that his war with Prussia in 1806 was one he had not sought and had not brought about by his own conduct; in the Rhineland, Italy, and above all Poland, Napoleon was never regarded as a hateful conqueror. A tradition favouring Napoleon lingered in the Rhineland even after the Franco-Prussian war of 1870.

Three streams of ideas have proceeded from this giant. The most malign is the tradition of dictatorship, of which he was the founder in the modern world and which was carried on and transformed by his nephew, Napoleon III (q.v.), in the middle of the last century. Napoleon as dictator was not absent from the minds of Hitler, Mussolini and others. The ideas of the second stream are entirely different, and they have never reached England, which was always united as a whole unalterably against Napoleon. These are the ideas of liberation, the breaking of bonds, the sweeping away of cobwebs, by force of arms, which have been so powerful in various parts of continental Europe and in Latin America. Men such as Bolívar (q.v.) owe much of their inspiration to Napoleon. Third and last come Napoleon's ideas on the conduct of war. No other soldier is so deeply studied or has so influenced the way in which states since his time have gone to war and in which generals have conducted the operations. With Napoleon are associated the exploitation of interior lines and central positions; economy in force by massing superior strength at the vital point; pinning down the enemy with a strategic advanced guard while manœuvring with the rest of the army; preparing the attack by heavy artillery bombardments; and making decisive use of a powerful reserve kept intact during the earlier phase of a battle of attrition.

All of these notions are part of the paraphernalia of strong-minded and enterprising commanders (including some who scarcely recognized their origin). Above all the search for maximum mobility is an acknowledgement of Napoleon's military thought.

Possibly he was fatal to France in more than the obvious sense of defeat. He keyed France up to his own conception of greatness, he maintained the pressure so fiercely that he seems to have exhausted her

fibre; so much indeed that the French spirit has seldom and only for brief intervals reached the same height. He determined that France should be, and should recognize herself to be, a great nation. Even his ideas upon education, so high-minded in themselves, were applied to this end. 'Temper the young spirits in the Greeks and the Romans,' he ordered his Minister of Education. The spiritual strain of striving for greatness may have been more lasting and more severe and harmful than the immense, and more obvious, physical strain.

Indisputably he encouraged the sciences. The Empire was a great age of French physicists, and he patronized science in other branches as well. Also there is more to be said for his encouragement of the painter David and classicism in French painting than it has been the fashion to allow. Napoleon, it should not be forgotten, had his intelligent admirers in every country, including Goethe and Beethoven, who composed the *Eroica Symphony* in his honour, and Hazlitt in England, who wrote a life of Napoleon and was so upset by Waterloo that 'he walked about unwashed, unshaved, hardly sober by day, and always intoxicated by night ... for weeks: until at length wakening as it were from his stupor, he at once left off all stimulating liquors and never touched them again'. Like Byron in literature, he was a supreme figure of romantic individualism, of its volcanic release and sense of flame and power.

When Napoleon died, the painter Wilkie brought the news to his fellow artist Benjamin Robert Haydon, who recalled in his diary how the two of them in 1806 had walked to the Academy, just after the battle of Jena, 'both groaning at the slowness of our means of acquiring fame in comparison with his'. 'Ah, Napoleon,' Haydon went on, 'what an opportunity you lost! His death affects me to deep musing. I remember his rise in 1796, his glory, and his fall. Posterity can never estimate the sensations of those living at the time.' But posterity has never forgotten him.

ILLUSTRATION: Page 223.

Mountebank dictator

NAPOLEON III, (1808–1873), Emperor of France, 'the first mountebank dictator of modern Europe', was the nephew and eventually heir of

Napoleon I, and had never been allowed to forget this, even as a child. He was brought up abroad, and passed his young manhood in insurrections against the monarchy in France and the status quo everywhere. Lord Malmesbury met him when he was twenty-one, in 1829, and found him convinced that one day he would be ruler of France: he asked Lord Malmesbury to trust in his Napoleonic 'star', which led him to be captured in 1840 and imprisoned in the fortress of Ham. In his six years of confinement he made a careful study of political theory, and he then made a sensational escape to England. Back in London, Napoleon frequented Whig drawing-rooms, and stole the mistress of A.W. Kinglake, the historian.

After the revolution in Paris in 1848, Napoleon returned to France and became candidate for the presidency. The name of Napoleon worked wonders. He was supported by all those who dreaded the violent changes which the urban socialists were supposed to want. Napoleon set himself up as a friend of the people, and was elected by a huge majority. Both Napoleon I and Napoleon III established themselves by a *coup d'état*. But whereas Brumaire was bloodless, the massacre of 1 December 1851, was long remembered. Louis Napoleon turned his presidency into a ten-years' rule by means of the loyalty of the army and by capturing the printing-presses in a daring night-conspiracy. Yet he was popular: he alone, it was felt, stood between the State and anarchy. After the *coup d'état* Napoleon toured France and was fêted everywhere. The phrase *L'empire c'est la paix*, was on everyone's lips: the troops at a military review cried *Vive l'empereur*, and were not reproved. 'The name Napoleon', said its bearer, 'is a programme in itself: it stands for order, authority, religion, the welfare of the people, within: without, for national dignity.' The French people chose to elect Napoleon emperor by plebiscite; and, again, there was a vast majority in his favour.

The Second Empire, the great *opéra bouffe* of modern Europe, has left its stamp on France. Baron Haussmann built Paris anew – huge new buildings and avenues are the peculiar signature of dictators of Napoleon's kind. Eugénie, the beautiful Spaniard whom Napoleon took as his empress in 1855, gave the court a brilliance and popularity Paris had lacked for generations. The Emperor himself, the melancholy visionary with drooping moustachios, remained obsessed with the memory of his uncle. After the Crimean war – into which France was plunged primarily to gratify Napoleon's need for Napoleonic glory – the emperor could justly consider himself arbiter of Europe; but it was soon clear that a conservative policy at home and a revolutionary policy abroad would clash. In supporting the Piedmontese bid for a united Italy, Napoleon offended the Pope and consequently the Catholics at home, and by supporting Poland in the abortive rising of 1863, he lost the friendship of both Russia and Prussia. After the Risorgimento in 1859, France was the world's enemy, with her army much weakened; even Italy was offended because France had made a separate peace with Austria.

Meantime Eugénie became fired by the idea of establishing a Catholic monarchy in Mexico. Though Napoleon was now far less under his wife's influence than in the earlier days of their marriage, the idea seemed to him to be likely to help the fading prestige of his empire. The Austrian Archduke Ferdinand Maximilian was made Emperor of Mexico, but after Napoleon withdrew the French troops, Maximilian was defeated, captured and shot by a firing squad – a disaster which deeply impressed Europe. Napoleon made a worse mistake: he supported Prussia in her bid to lead Germany. Bismarck had decided to fight Austria: this he confided to Napoleon in a meeting at Biarritz, promising him Belgium if he would remain neutral. Napoleon agreed, imagining that the war would last a long time and that he would be called in to arbitrate a peace. Prussia won in seven weeks, and from then on a war between France and Prussia was inevitable. In the crisis that led to the Franco-Prussian war in 1870, Bismarck disclosed the Belgian agreement of 1866, and so alienated England from France. Other potential allies were also manœuvred out of position by Bismarck. When Napoleon was tricked into war, the weaknesses of the army soon showed themselves and Napoleon himself was taken prisoner at Sedan. France declared itself a republic, and the emperor whose star had failed slunk across the channel to die at Chislehurst.

ILLUSTRATION: Page 269.

India's first Prime Minister

NEHRU, Jawaharlal, (b. 1889), first Prime Minister of independent India, and one of the most paradoxical figures of the twentieth century.

Nehru belongs to a family of Kashmiri Brahmins,

a caste famous in India for its culture. Yet he grew up almost entirely ignorant of Indian languages, religions and philosophy. As a boy, he was sent to England to be educated at the public school of Harrow and the university of Cambridge; and to India he returned more of a western liberal than an Indian nationalist. He practised at the Bar at Allahabad, his native city, became president of the municipality, and was soon under the spell of Gandhi (q.v.), though the two of them had life-long differences – thus Nehru accepted, and Gandhi rejected, industrialism.

He now began his life as an agitator against English rule. He travelled into country districts, listened to poverty-stricken peasants, took part in demonstrations, and became a leading member of the Indian National Congress. Under Nehru's guidance, Congress declared the goal of the Indian people to be complete national independence; and for the illiterate peasants of India, this liberal-minded product of western education, this believer in democracy and socialism, crystallized into the classic type of Indian hero – the wealthy young man who (like the Buddha) renounces the pleasures of the world to devote himself to poverty and asceticism for the public good. He was not an ascetic, he commonly travelled by air, or in not inexpensive motor-cars, but that did not upset the legend. The hold he obtained on the Indian masses was second only to the hold of Gandhi himself. Indeed, an article once appeared about Nehru saying: 'Men like Jawaharlal ... are unsafe in a democracy. He calls himself a democrat and a socialist ... but the mind is ultimately a slave to the head ... A little twist, and Jawaharlal might turn into a dictator, sweeping aside the paraphernalia of slow-moving democracy. He might still use the language of democracy and socialism, but we all know how fascism has fattened on this language and then cast it away as useless lumber.' The remarkable thing about this anonymous attack was that the author was – Nehru.

Perhaps no national hero was ever so strikingly self-effacing, or so candid about himself in his own writings. Nehru is a product, if ever there was one, of East and West, and he has admitted he sometimes feels a stranger to them both. His agitation against English rule entailed thirteen years in prison, but he has never been bitter towards England; and he has admitted that the Indian Nationalists drew upon the weapons of English liberalism. Out of her own experience Asia had produced only the ideal of wise and benevolent autocracy – and in practice that autocracy was seldom either wise or benevolent.

If Nehru's democracy endures, then Europe will have paid some of the enormous cultural debt that she owes to Asia.

ILLUSTRATION: Page 215.

Admiral of admirals

NELSON, Horatio, Viscount, (1758–1805), the supreme genius of naval warfare.

Differences of opinion are possible, and disputes occur, about the relative eminence of soldiers: even against a Napoleon a Hannibal may be set up. There has never been any serious doubt that this son of a Norfolk clergyman, this slight, frail-looking man, was the greatest genius in the records of war at sea. His influence on the course of history and the fate of the wars in which he took part was immense. Before the Treaty of Amiens his intervention in the Battle of Cape St Vincent (1797) was decisive and his action at the Battle of the Nile (1798) ended the phase of French predominance in Mediterranean waters. When the war was renewed after the Treaty of Amiens, his victory at Trafalgar (1805) effectively made an end of Franco-Spanish naval power and allowed Britain to exercise hers in conquest, in transportation of armies where she would, in commanding every trade route, and in support of her allies, without opposition.

His great qualities have been obscured by occasional sayings, some of which have nothing to support them except gossip. Impetuous by nature, he was in fact careful and methodical in tactics – and this has the proof of his written instructions. It is true his ideas were simple, but all naval tactics are or should be that. He was also a great leader in the moral sense. He got the best out of his subordinates and made them new men. Such a constellation of talented and brave men as surrounded him has had no equal. With his good qualities Nelson had weaknesses. High among them was childish vanity. Thus he could say, 'It was during this period that perhaps my personal courage was more conspicuous than at any other period.' On one occasion he was grossly insubordinate. His infatuation for Lady Hamilton even led him to forsake his duty in the Naples period, though without evil results, since he had Troubridge to take his place.

Admirals are inarticulate, commonly more so than generals. Nelson is one of the few whose letters and despatches belong to literature, though the form and the content are very uneven. At his best Nelson is a splendid writer. Here is a passage on the Battle of the Nile in a letter to Lord Howe:

' I had the happiness to command a band of brothers; therefore, night was to my advantage. Each knew his duty, and I was sure each would feel for a French ship. By attacking the enemy's van and centre, the wind blowing directly along their line, I was enabled to throw what force I pleased on a few ships ... At twenty-eight minutes past six, the sun in the horizon, the firing commenced. At five minutes past ten, when *l'Orient* blew up, having burnt seventy minutes, the six van ships had surrendered. I then pressed further towards the rear; and had it pleased God that I had not been wounded and stone blind, there cannot be a doubt but that every ship would have been in our possession.'

It should be noted that when several captains of this band of brothers were serving under Lord Keith in 1801, they showed themselves disrespectful and undisciplined. It was Nelson who made them brothers: they relied on him absolutely and at the same time loved him.

Nelson's professional skill, his impetuosity and courage, his loss of an arm in the attempt on Santa Cruz de Tenerife, the empty sleeve, the loss of an eye at Calvi, the story of the telescope, the famous signal before Trafalgar and the death in action in the *Victory* – each are elements in the total legend of greatness, the strange process of the making or the growth of a hero; of which the seed is neither success nor failure nor genius in the conduct of war, but rather the personality of the man; and Nelson in his talk and his animation exercised an uncommon radioactivity. Thus in naval war, adding all of the man together, he founded a tradition which has been transposed from the age of sail to the age of steam.

ILLUSTRATION: Page 223.

Russian hero

NEVSKY, Aleksander, (1220–1263), Russian prince, general saint and national hero. By his victory at the historic 'Battle on the Ice' in 1242, he saved the Russian people from Teutonic domination.

In the thirteenth century Novgorod, in north-west Russia, was the most important of the principalities into which the Russian tribes were then divided and it was to become known later as 'the Cradle of the Russian nation'. Here Aleksander grew up, the second son of Prince Yaroslav. From the east at this time Russian territories were being invaded by the Mongol hordes of Jenghiz Khan, which encouraged the Baltic nations to attempt their expansion into Russia from the west.

In 1240 the twenty-year-old Aleksander led an army against the Swedish knights at the river Neva, which flows through modern Leningrad. Birgev, the Swedish leader, sent him a personal challenge, and during the battle they met in single combat, Aleksander seriously wounding the Swede. The Russians were victorious, and for his leadership Aleksander was accorded the title of 'Nevsky', from the river. However, within a few months domestic Court intrigues and jealousy from the nobles of Novgorod had sent him into exile.

Soon a larger alliance of the Teutonic Knights (Germans, Balts, Swedes and Danes) combined for another invasion. According to modern Soviet sources, this enterprise was blessed by the Pope as a crusade, although Novgorod had adopted Christianity for two centuries. The Teutons overran the Principality with that exceptional brutality for which they were noted in an age used to brutality. Even the local language was forbidden; and in despair Novgorod called on the exile. Aleksander Nevsky collected an enthusiastic but poorly equipped army and met the Teutons on 5 April 1242, at Lake Peipus, which had not yet thawed from the winter frosts: which is why the engagement is known in history as 'the Battle on the Ice'. The Teutons followed their usual tactic of concentrating their heavily armed mounted knights in the centre for a break-through. Aleksander could oppose them only with foot-soldiers and showed originality and daring in out-manœuvring them. He deliberately placed very weak forces in his centre and at the crucial moment threw almost his entire forces against the enemy flanks. The Teutons fled over the dark ice, Aleksander sending after them his famous message:

'Go and say to all: "Whosoever comes against us with the sword, shall perish by the sword. Such is the law of the Russian land, and such it will always be."'

In 1260, Aleksander Nevsky succeeded his brother as Prince of Novgorod. He never attempted to oppose the domination of the Mongols on his eastern border, but paid tribute to them and ruled with their permission.

Tsar Peter the Great created the order of St Aleksander in his honour, he was canonized by the Russian Church, and is a national hero of the Soviet Union.

Father of ornithology

NEWTON, Alfred, (1829–1907), English zoologist, the father of the modern study of birds, who helped to make bird-watching the scientific hobby of thousands in England, in the other European countries and in America.

His career, like that of many Victorian scientific naturalists was inspired by Gilbert White (q.v.) and his *Natural History of Selborne*, and shaped by travel, and by the views of Darwin (q.v.) on organic evolution. Newton visited Lapland, the eastern U.S.A., Iceland, Spitzbergen and most European countries. A cripple in his old age, he made adventurous yachting excursions among the remoter Scottish islands. Those who knew his unchanging and unchangeable rooms in Magdalene College, Cambridge (where Newton was Professor of Zoology from 1866 till his death) would never have guessed that he was in constant communion with a world outside quadrangles and the senior common room, and Newton's eccentricities must have reinforced the impression. Outwardly he was an ultra-traditionalist. He had accepted Darwin's *Origin of Species* when it appeared in 1859; at Cambridge no fundamentalist could have looked more early or mid-Victorian: he always wore a top hat, his clothes always belonged to a style out of date for thirty years and he made a point of referring to matches by their old name of 'Vesuvians'. Yet long before it was customary for dons to acknowledge the existence of undergraduates outside the lecture room, Newton believed in friendship and personal discussion with his students.

He was instrumental in founding the British Ornithologists' Union in 1858, in launching the movement for the protection of birds in the seventies, and in planning co-operative studies in bird migration in the eighties. He hated obscurantism and inaccuracy, was ruthless, resolute, yet scrupulously fair in argument, and he fostered and inspired generation after generation of young naturalists.

And all was light

NEWTON, Sir Isaac, (1642–1727), the greatest scientist so far of mankind, who compassed in his mind a diversity of enquiries, scientific, alchemical, theological, and still managed to steer a course through them to revolutionary triumphs of intellect.

His childhood, which began in a Lincolnshire farm-house, was not particularly distinguished: he was neither outstanding nor dull, although it is said that after he had thrashed a boy who bullied him, he made much better progress in his studies. He contrived a number of mechanical models as a boy, one of them a small windmill worked by a mouse. On the advice of relations, he was sent to Cambridge. One of the first books he read there was Kepler's *Optics*, which impressed him greatly. It did not take him long to create an interest among his masters: especially Isaac Barrow, the mathematician, who was struck by his mental powers and put him in the way of both academic and financial encouragement. By 1665 he was doing brilliant and original work in pure mathematics and physics. It was the year of the Great Plague: and fear shut down his college. Back home for nearly two years, Newton (at the age of twenty-three) worked out, almost in its entirety, his Universal Law of Gravitation.

Secretive about his researches in gravitation, he shelved them for nearly eighteen years. In 1684 he was urged by the astronomer Halley to prepare for publication a proof (which Halley had seen) that a body, attracted to a centre with a force inversely proportional to the square of its distance from that centre, would describe an ellipse about this centre; this was the heart of the Law of Gravitation. It was a monumental achievement, not least in its simplicity. Newton's problem had been this: that since the planets move round the sun, and the moon round the earth, there must be a force acting upon them and stopping them from flying off at various angles. It seemed to Newton that the force that keeps the planets in their orbits might be the same as the force we know on the earth as gravitation. It was Newton's genius to have propounded a set of principles that applied to all forms of motion, by whatever kind of force they were caused. He certainly could not have achieved the results he did if it had not been for the earlier work of Galileo and Kepler; but it was Newton who had the capacity to generalize, to conceive a pattern in the universe, and to open to men's minds an enormity that few of them can understand. And Newton's achievement had an added glory in that he constructed the necessary tools for it: the Method of Fluxions, which we know as the Differential Calculus. It was in 1687 that his major conclusions were published as the *Philosophiae naturalis principia mathematica*, incomparably the greatest scientific book yet written, in which the vague ideas of the material universe, which had spasmodically developed during the previous two thousand years, were now ordered, and in which all in the heavens above and the earth beneath was represented in one blow as a unity, operating according to precise and known laws, and subject to mathematical calculation. It was an astounding example of what was in the power of the human mind, giving a great impetus to the spirit of progress. Two hundred years of labour by mankind were required before an important departure from Newtonian principles was made, when Michelson and Morley found that the speed of a ray of light is independent of the speed of its source, a fact which required the theory of relativity for its explanation. In 1704 he published the *Opticks*, on his discovery of the resolution of white light into the spectrum of colours, each colour having its own degree of refrangibility, which also deeply impressed the eighteenth century:

> Even *Light itself*, which everything displays,
> Shone undiscover'd, till his brighter mind
> Untwisted all the shining robe of day;
> And, from the whitening undistinguish'd blaze
> Collecting every ray into his kind,
> To the charm'd eye educ'd the gorgeous train
> Of *Parent-Colours* ...

– though perhaps one should not quote from the poets about one who borrowed a bad opinion of poetry from his teacher Isaac Barrow – that poetry 'was a kind of ingenious nonsense'.

Newton had been a staunch, if silent, Whig member of parliament, and his devotion was rewarded. In 1696 he was made Warden of the Mint at a time when the Government had debased the coinage – it was the contemporary equivalent of deflation – and a strong, incorruptible man was needed to control the monetary situation. Newton was ideal in the job, and showed that capacity in public administration which occasionally distinguishes a brilliant scientist. He was an efficient and not very merciful tracker down of coiners, and he now shunned scientific research for fear he would be accused of pursuing it when he 'ought to be about the King's business'.

Newton's amanuensis, after his death, sketched the habits of the great man in his daily life at Cambridge, alone in his rooms. His 'chief design', he wrote, was the alchemical one of the transmutation of metals. He was absent-minded – minded, that is, upon his own thoughts. 'At some seldom times when he designed to dine in the hall [he] would turn to the left hand and go out into the street, when making a stop when he found his mistake, [he] would hastily turn back, and then sometimes instead of going into the hall, would return to his chamber again.' He walked about incessantly in his room, and left much of his food untouched, though he liked apples, and in winter would sometimes eat a baked quince at night. 'As to his private prayers I can say nothing of them; I am apt to believe his intense studies deprived him of the better part. His behaviour was mild and meek, without anger, peevishness, or passion, so free from that, that you might take him for a stoic.' His amanuensis never saw him wear a night-gown: he put off his clothes, slept a few hours each night, and put the same clothes on again in the morning. Only cold weather could draw him unwillingly to sit by the fire. All through his life he showed signs of persecution mania; on the Continent, they were quite convinced that he was mad, and at about the age of fifty, he had a mental breakdown, during which he accused the philosopher John Locke of trying to 'embroil him with women' (he never married). Religion, as the secretary suggested, was probably no comfort to him; and J. M. Keynes, who collected Newton's writings, was of the opinion that his secretiveness about his discoveries was due in part to heretical opinions and doubt of the divinity of Christ.

It cannot be said that Newton led a happy life, or that he was at all free from the infirmities and quirks of genius; but happiness and the silences of space, which were his mental home for so long, are not perhaps easy companions. 'I do not know what I may appear to the world,' he wrote towards the end of his life in a famous statement never too often reprinted, 'but to myself, I seem to have been only like a boy playing on the seashore, and diverting myself in now and then finding a smoother pebble or a prettier shell than ordinary, while the great ocean of truth lay all undiscovered before me.' His pebbles and shells were mountains to the grains of sand held by others; and we can only admire him from a distance, for an intellect which surpasses most human understanding.

Glorifying life

NIETZSCHE, Friedrich Wilhelm, (1844–1900), German philosopher. One of the most powerful and striking of all German writers, whose ideas still cause violent revulsion in some readers and have been twisted and misrepresented by his admirers.

He was born the son of a small-town clergyman in Saxony, and after distinguishing himself as a classical scholar at Leipzig, he was appointed to teach at the University of Basle. As a young professor he made the acquaintance of Richard Wagner and Cosima, and in his first book, *The Birth of Tragedy*, we see Wagner's influence when he links the cult of Dionysus in ancient Greece with Wagner's work which, so Nietzsche then thought, heralded a new age. Later, when Wagner reverted to Christian themes, Nietzsche broke from him and denounced him with tortured and ineffectual fanaticism. After the Franco-Prussian War, in which Nietzsche served as a medical orderly and contracted the malady that destroyed his health, he returned to Basle, but was obliged to retire on a small pension in 1879.

Nietzsche's great creative period lasted only nine years – from 1879 to 1888 – and if we remember that he was a martyr to pain and aggravated neuroses, his achievement must seem one of the most remarkable in literature. During this time he wrote *Human All-Too-Human, The Joyful Wisdom, Beyond Good and Evil, The Genealogy of Morals, The Anti-Christ, Ecce Homo, The Will to Power* and *Thus Spake Zarathustra*. Apart from *Zarathustra*, which is deliberately written in a Biblical and prophetical manner, most of his works took the form of loosely connected apophthegms on philosophy, sociology, literature, morals and religion. He also wrote some exquisite short verses. Nietzsche eked out these nine years as a solitary wanderer in second-class *pensions* in Rome, Turin, Genoa, Nice, and Sils Maria in the Engadine; secretly drugging and dieting and taking lonely walks for his health. Though his correspondence was often acrimonious and quarrelsome (he prided himself on his revolutionary views on morals and religion), he seems to have been personally timid and retiring, and made a good impression on fellow-guests such as old ladies. But one day in Turin in 1888 his mind gave way. He was found weeping and embracing a horse, and was taken home to Germany incurably insane. He survived another twelve years – serene and remembering nothing.

It is quite unfair to use Nietzsche's eventual madness to dismiss his works – though this has been done. Still more unfortunate for Nietzsche's reputation was the fact that among his admirers were many of the racial megalomaniacs who prepared the way for National-Socialism in Germany. True, like the Nazis – but also like his master, Schopenhauer – Nietzsche despised women, though to what extent this was because he was frightened of them would be difficult to say; certainly in his sexual relationships he was the caricature of the inhibited professor. But Nietzsche loathed the new German nationalism. Of the Germans he said: 'Every great crime against culture for the last four centuries lies on their conscience.' He viewed the Reformation as a backdoor attempt to undo the splendid achievements of the Renaissance Neo-Pagans and to re-establish Christian morality; he preferred French civilization to German, pretended that his ancestors were Poles, and quarrelled with his sister when she married a man who hatched the absurd project of founding an anti-Semitic colony in South America. And if he advocated a civilization for 'aristocrats' and 'warriors' against the 'decadence' of commercialism, social equality and democracy upheld by 'that blockhead' John Stuart Mill, there can be no doubting how he would have reacted against the Nazis. 'Plebeian', 'servile', 'rootless', 'herd-minded' were his favourite expressions.

If Marx turned Hegel's philosophy inside out, Nietzsche did the same for Schopenhauer's. Schopenhauer took the concept of will as the primary explanation of the universe; but whereas Schopenhauer taught that we should overcome the Will-to-Live by asceticism, Nietzsche maintained that we should assert the will and glorify life with the object, ultimately, of bringing 'the Superman' into being. Nietzsche conceived of the Superman as the deadly enemy of the Christian 'slave ideal' and its pale modern echoes such as democracy or socialism; the Superman would be 'Beyond good and evil', a-moral, ruthless and pagan like the men of the Renaissance.

We are not to suppose, of course, that Nietzsche's ideal of 'blond and beautiful beasts of prey' was merely physical; it was a poetic expression of an excellence that would be first and foremost a thing of the mind. Nietzsche, remember, despite his physical handicaps, considered himself to be extremely 'healthy'. And in his view the Universe was only justifiable as 'an aesthetic phenomenon'. Yet his general ideas are far from clear and coherent. He was more of a poet or a creative writer than a systematic philosopher, and his fragmentary intuitions are as important as an attack on the vices of society – for all his 'amorality' he was a born moralist and preacher – as for their content in themselves.

The Lady with the Lamp

NIGHTINGALE, Florence, (1820–1910). Her revolutionary success in the reform of hospitals in England (and all over the world) is summed up in Queen Victoria's comment: 'Such a *head*! I wish we had her at the War Office.'

Replacing the blood and filth of the British hospitals in the Crimean War with order and decency, Florence Nightingale belonged to the stern century of English social ameliorators; and, like Joan of Arc, she believed that four times in her life she had been spoken to by God. The first time came early, but for years she convinced neither herself nor her parents of her vocation. Ultimately the truth broke through: she must surrender herself to improving the lot of the broken and lost. Her comfortable, upper-middle-class parents were scandalized. 'My people', she wrote of them, 'were like children, playing on the shore of the eighteenth century. I was their hobby horse, their plaything.' But she got up at dawn to annotate sanitary reports, she forced her family to let her train as a nurse; and then came the war in the Crimea, the determining event of Florence Nightingale's life. The Army hospital service collapsed: prepared by years of study, Miss Nightingale stepped in. The result was a revelation. She knew everything. She would not accept the noble-minded ladies who refused to empty bed-pans: she would not kow-tow to doctors who preferred catastrophe to an interruption of their routine. The image of Miss Nightingale walking lamp in hand through the wards among the sick and dying became part of the mythology of Victorian England. The war ended, and Florence Nightingale was a heroine; but she had half a century to live, and she spent the years in unremitting work on behalf of nursing, the British Army's health services, and the improvement of India's millions. She was prisoned on a sickbed in London, but no one in the nineteenth century knew more of what could be done for the health of nations.

Early in her life, touring Egypt, she noted in her journals: 'God spoke to me again, sitting on the steps of the portico at Karnak.' And again: 'Today I am 30, the age Christ began his mission.' In a century when nurses in Great Britain tended to be prostitutes and nearly half of the soldiery died in hospitals when they went to war, the genius of the Lady with the Lamp forced up the standard of public health throughout the world. At one time, in the Cave of the Furies in Greece, she had asked God to deliver her from the body of this death. That was before the Crimean War. The human race may well be thankful that the Furies were not listening.

ILLUSTRATION: Plate 10.

'Poets are the princes of words'

NĪZAMĪ of Ganja, (1145–1207), Persian religious and romantic poet, who wrote the *Five Treasures*. Persians have considered Nīzamī at once among the gravest, wisest and most delicious masters of Persian literature – a poet, one of his countrymen wrote, who was 'the unique pearl of the Ocean of God's benevolence, the royal jewel of the sea of life'.

A strict and devout Sunni or orthodox Moslem, austere and wise, tender, given to meditation and gazing at the stars, preferring poverty to the betrayal of his mission as a poet, indifferent to courts and kings, Nīzamī was certain of his own genius: he maintained that he had delivered poetry from the tavern and established the 'temple of poetry'. Though stories out of the *Five Treasures* are still some of the most popular entertainments of the Middle East, delightfully told with a multiplication of imagery and allusion, Nīzamī is, like Hāfiz (q.v.) and other great Persians, a poet not always to be estimated by the outward mask of his poetry. In the famous love-story of Leila and Majnūn, or in the seven tales called the *Seven Beauties*, said to have been told by the seven favourite wives of Bahrām Gūr, the Great Hunter of Fitzgerald's *Rubaiyat*, Nīzamī creates the Persian miniature in skilful sweetness of words: he gives us the world within a golden border of lilac-coloured hills, azure skies and noble horses, plants in blossom, and determinate dream-clear figures, the sharp oriental feeling for romance and the marvellous. Bahrām Gūr listens to the owls talking in the ruined palace, poor mad Majnūn wanders lovelorn in the desert.

But in the *Five Treasures* romance is not only justified by romance, God is seldom out of sight and the
world is not the best of all things:

> Curse this world which burns the heart:
> Throw a stone at this glass of blood.

Poets, according to Nīzamī, are 'the princes of words',
but he himself turned the 'diamond of his tongue into
a sword'; and before God there stands two ranks,
'in front the prophets, and behind the poets', since
poetry is 'the curtain of mystery' and 'a shadow of the
prophetic veil'.

Few details of Nīzamī's life have been recorded.
He lived and died at Ganja, which is now Kirovabad,
a factory town and the second city of the Azerbaijan
Soviet Socialist Republic. At the moment of his death
he is said to have remarked cheerfully and with a
laugh that the Forgiver had made him hope to be
Forgiven.

Peace and nitro-glycerine

NOBEL, Alfred, (1833–1896), Swedish chemist and
inventor; his development of high explosives made
modern warfare possible, and he founded the Peace
Prize which bears his name, awarded to the 'person
who shall have most or best promoted the Fraternity
of Nations and the Abolishment or Diminution of
Standing Armies and the Formation and Increase of
Peace Congresses'.

He was a self-made man, with a restless spirit and
literary aspirations; a poem that he wrote in English
at the age of eighteen shows the influence of Shelley,
whom he admired very much and imitated very
badly:

> 'I have not shared the pleasures of the crowd
> Nor moved in Beauty's eye compassion's tear,
> But I have learned to study Nature's book
> And comprehend its pages and extract
> From their deep lore solace for my grief.'

All his life he had the ideas of a perplexed and in-
active radical. His scientific education had been very
limited: but his father, a scientist also, sent him travelling to learn engineering. He went to America
(where he is said to have worked for John Ericsson,

who built the *Monitor*, the first armour-plated war-
ship). Back in Sweden, he began to develop the newly-
invented nitro-glycerine. The chief problem was how
to explode it safely. After many experiments, Nobel
used fulminate of mercury in a lead cap – the same
detonator that is in use today. Nobel's small factories began to expand as men realized the value of
nitro-glycerine in all blasting operations; but 'Nobel's
Patent Exploding Oil', as it was called commercially,
had one drawback: the liquid would escape from its
containers; and it caused some unfortunate explosions.

The containers of the liquid nitro-glycerine were
packed in *kieselguhr*, a kind of clay which was absor-
bent, light, and constant in quality. Some nitro-
glycerine trickled out into the clay: and there was the
solid they had been looking for – dynamite – or
'Nobel's safety powder', the sales of which jumped
from eleven tons in 1867 to 3,120 tons in 1874. Nobel's
other major achievement in explosives was to devise
blasting gelatine.

Although there were patent troubles, and fierce
competition for the right to make the new explosives,
Nobel never suffered very much from other armament manufacturers. His factories waxed and increased. In England, for example, the Nobel Dynamite Trust Co. was merged into Explosive Trades,
Ltd.; then reformed into Nobel Industries (with
assets of £24,000,000) and then, in 1927, merged with
other firms into Imperial Chemical Industries, with a
share capital of £95,000,000.

It is not true, as is often said, that Nobel's great en-
dowments were a form of expiation for the evils his
invention had brought; at first, his new high explosives did much more good than harm. But nor was he
a myopic scientist who was content to give the control of deadly weapons to others, and take pride in
his invention. He was merely a puzzled man; and a
very kind and selfless one. 'If only you could understand', he wrote, 'that one can help a human being,
without any ulterior motive: amongst the Israelites
this suggested itself to only one person, Christ, and so
strange was the idea that he was awarded the diploma
of divinity.' The idea of a Peace Prize came to him,
not because he was sorry for what he had done, but
because he genuinely hated war. And he left, as well,
the famous prizes for Chemistry, Medicine, Physics;
and for Literature – for the most distinguished work
– the influence of Shelley again – of an idealistic tendency. Apart from his early poem, there is one other
original work of Nobel's in existence: *Nemesis*, a

play about Beatrice Cenci. 'The incest motive', said Nobel, 'is rendered so inoffensive that the most censorious public would scarcely be shocked.'

'I drift about without rudder or compass,' he wrote to his sister-in-law, 'a wreck on the sea of life.' His brother once asked him for a brief biography. 'Principal virtues: keeping his nails clean and never being a burden to anyone,' he wrote. 'Principal faults: that he has no family, is bad tempered and has a poor digestion. One and only wish: not to be buried alive. Greatest sin: that he does not worship Mammon. Important events in his life: none.'

Horoscopes and prophecies

NOSTRADAMUS, (1503–1566), Michel de Notredame, French astrologer and soothsayer, who rocketed to fame when some of the rhymed predictions in his book *Centuries* (1555) appeared to come true. In one of them he had written 'The young lion will overcome the old one in cruel battle by strange duel'. When Henry II was accidentally killed in a tournament in 1559, it seemed that the prophecy had referred to him, whereupon Nostradamus gained an enormous following. Another of his predictions ran:

> The great shouter, shameless and audacious
> Will be elected chief of the army;
> His attempts will be impudent,
> The bridge broken, the city faint with fear.

After the event again, this was taken to refer to Cromwell – the broken bridge being Parliament.

Nostradamus began life as a doctor. He studied at Montpellier, and settled near Aix-en-Provence, at Salon, where he was supposed to have invented that specific so much desired in the sixteenth century – a remedy for the plague. Astrology and magic were more profitable than medicine, and Nostradamus shrewdly understood how to flatter men's credulity and bring himself wealth and honour. Catherine de' Medici and later Charles IX were among his devotees and patrons; and Catherine sent him to Blois to read the horoscope of the young princes. He was of Jewish origin, and his fame may be connected with the great reputation of the *cabbala*, the Jewish occult system of interpreting the Scriptures.

A people's writer

OSTROVSKY, Aleksandr Nikolayevich, (1823–1886), Russian playwright. Like other literary masters of nineteenth-century Russia, he felt that literature was a social and not merely a polite avocation. 'Poetry as expressed in drama', he maintained in a paper *On the Establishment of a National Theatre in Moscow*, written towards the end of his career, 'is closer to the common people than any other branch of literature, and this closeness does not debase it. On the contrary, it redoubles its strength and prevents it from becoming vulgar and small-minded.'

Ostrovsky's grandfather was a priest, and his father was trained for the priesthood, but became a lawyer with a practice among the Moscow merchants. He himself studied law and then worked in the Moscow Juvenile Court and the Moscow Commercial Court, where he became more thoroughly acquainted with the merchants who were the main subject of his first cycle of plays. But there is not a class of the Russia of his day and not a type of mankind which cannot be found in his plays, grave and gay. These include *The Storm* (1859), the greatest tragedy in the Russian language, *The Snow Maiden* (1873), an exquisite poetic drama, and all the brilliant comedies about Russia's idle rich, the landed gentry, and backstage life in the provinces. In the merchant comedies Ostrovksy shows the havoc which power-seeking, self-assertive types of humanity can cause on family life and social life in general; and he did this without sacrificing what Stanislavsky (q.v.) called his 'grand epic serenity'. Goncharov, Chekhov and Tolstoy all testified to the power of his drama. 'You brought a whole library of works of art as a gift to literature,' Goncharov wrote to him, 'and created your own special world for the stage.' Writing to a fellow-dramatist, Chekhov declared: 'You must either become an Ostrovsky or give up the stage', and referring to one of Ostrovsky's plays, *The Gulf*, in a letter to another correspondent, he wrote: 'It is quite a remarkable play. The last act is something that I could not have written if I had been offered a million. This act is a whole play and if I ever have a theatre of my own, I shall put on this act alone.' Tolstoy wrote to him shortly before his death: 'Your aim and mine has been to publish everything that is accessible, needful and intelligible to every Tom, Dick and Harry and not only to a small coterie. There is not one Russian writer who satisfies these demands more than you. I know from my own experience how widely your works are read and how greedily they are listened to and memorised by the common people. And for this reason alone, if for no other, I consider you to be a writer who in the fullest sense of the word is a people's writer.'

ILLUSTRATION: Page 271.

No Utopia

OWEN, Robert, (1771–1858), Socialist, reformer, and dreamer of Utopian dreams who did not see that a prophet should pretend to walk in step with his age.

Everyone who met him agreed that Owen, who belonged to the generation of Wordsworth, Coleridge and Turner, was tedious though amiable; he would repeat his guiding principles again and again, until it was seen that they rested less upon reason than unshakeable conviction. Owen grew up with the new Industrial Age; he was one of the first to see the evils of the system, and almost the only man of his time to do something about them.

'All the world is queer save thee and me, and even thou art a little queer,' he said to an early business partner; it is not difficult to imagine the world's opinion of him. Yet he was much admired. When, as textile manufacturer, he took over the New Lanark mills in 1800, he had a clear notion of what he must do. Working conditions in industry at that time were very bad: the men drank and stole, and pauper children were casually exploited. Owen had long maintained his conviction that character is made by circumstances; that men are therefore not responsible for their actions, and should be led into good ways, not punished. He introduced the 'silent monitor' system into his works: a label, coloured to indicate the quality of each man's daily behaviour, was placed near each workplace; he opened stores that sold good quality things at fair prices. But by far the most striking of his innovations was his 'Institution for the formation of character' – the first infant school. With Mazarin, he believed in training the children early. His efforts in this direction were universally admired;

from far and wide potentates came to inspect his model factories. Owen did not see that their interest was less humanitarian than prompted by interest in keeping workers happily subservient. Nor did he realize that his own success was the fruit of his business acumen and single-minded benevolence. He became, to himself at least, a prophet.

'He looks to nothing less than to renovate the world, to extirpate all evil, to banish all punishments, to create like views, and like wants, and to guard against all conflicts and hostilities,' wrote one of his admirers, Duke Bernard of Saxe-Weimar. With misguided zeal, he publicly announced his hostility to all current forms of religion. It was an ill-received announcement, and his support waned. His later years saw his American community venture on the lines of New Lanark which he called New Harmony; but by now Owen appeared only an enthusiast, a crank, and a harmless butt.

ILLUSTRATION: Page 271.

P

Defender of the rights of man

PAINE, Tom, (1737–1809), radical thinker and writer, was the greatest English advocate of democratic principles. He answered Burke's lamentations for Marie Antoinette with the devastating phrase: 'He pities the plumage and forgets the dying bird.'

Paine was of Quaker origin, a stay-maker by trade, and the first great writer since Bunyan to rise from the people. He went to America just before the Revolution; and his pamphlet, Common Sense, which he published in 1776, gave the Americans the decisive push into declaring their independence. Paine remained as a radical journalist in America during the revolutionary war. Afterwards, he ran into economic difficulties and returned to England, where – among other speculative projects – he raised money to build an iron bridge. The French Revolution brought him back to pamphleteering. His Rights of Man was written as an answer to Reflections on the French Revolution by Edmund Burke (q.v.), and far transcends the occasion which provoked it. No finer defence of democratic principles has ever been written; and Paine's *Rights of Man* will remain valid long after Burke is forgotten. Paine also wrote at this time *The Age of Reason*, a statement of moderate deism or, as it came to be called in the nineteenth century, agnosticism. That as well is a classic of humanist thought.

Paine was elected an honorary citizen of the French republic and a member of the French Convention. He went over to Paris and associated himself with the high-minded Girondists, who combined extreme principles and feeble practice. When the Girondists were overthrown by the Terror, Paine was involved in their disgrace and spent nearly two years in prison. He was ultimately released at the request of the United States, in gratitude for his literary activity there at the time of the Declaration of Independence. Thomas Jefferson was Paine's warmest patron and, when he became President, invited Paine to the United States. Paine remained there for the rest of his life, broken in health and somewhat of a drunkard.

Reactionaries then, and even now, have used these trivial failings to cloak the fact that Paine was a man of noble character who ranks among the greatest political writers in the English tongue. If he had used his gifts to defend privilege as Burke did, he could have been drunk and (as Burke was) corrupt into the bargain. Instead he preached democracy and rationalism – two causes that will never be forgiven him.

'My pinions never loved the middle air'

PALMER, Samuel, (1805–1881), English artist and religious, or visionary, landscape painter.

Something of a prodigy, this child of a London bookseller was exhibiting pictures by the time he was fourteen. He had a childhood passion for antiquity, churches and ruins, a yearning for an ideal primitivism much strengthened by his acquaintanceship with Blake (q.v.), and his delight in Dürer. If the deeper properties of nature were brought out, Palmer wrote, pictures would be 'what would have pleased men in early ages, when poetry was at its acme, and yet men lived in a simple, pastoral way'. He had 'delicious visions' of Christ at Emmaus, the thief on the cross, etc. When he first met Blake, who was lying in bed

'like one of the Antique patriarchs, or a dying Michael Angelo', Blake said he began the designs he was working on with fear and trembling. 'O,' said Palmer, 'I have enough of fear and trembling.' 'Then you'll do,' said Blake.

For some ten years of his life Palmer created a visionary world of growth and landscape, often in small sepia and Indian ink drawings of hill and valley and harvest and moonlight. An inheritance enabled him to live for a while in a rich Kentish valley at Shoreham, outside London, where he read, prayed, looked, meditated and painted, as the leader of a small group of like-minded young artists, who watched for moonrises and sunrises, and acted Macbeth in deserted chalk pits. He wrote that 'bits of nature' were 'improved by being received into the soul'; and there were times when his excessive art was raised to a high and timeless intensity of imagination. His pinions, as he wrote, 'never loved the middle air': he could at times 'bound upwards; pierce the clouds; and look over the doors of bliss'. To himself his huge full moons and moonlit valleys were on the edge of heaven and they reflected heavenly radiance. The green mountains of the evening, and the moon 'opening her golden eye, or walking in brightness among innumerable islands of light, not only thrill the optic nerve,' he wrote, 'but shed a mild, a grateful, an unearthly lustre into the inmost spirits, and seem the interchanging twilight of that peaceful country, where there is no sorrow and no night.'

After an unfortunate marriage and the cooling of his visionary heat, Palmer lived on as an able but unenthralling Victorian landscape painter. His early drawings and paintings were buried. Coming to light again in our own times, like the poems of Gerard Manley Hopkins or of Hölderlin, or the paintings of the German romantics Runge and Friedrich (which are hard and dry by comparison), they have influenced English painting and have been much admired in other countries, though Palmer's full stature still waits acknowledgement.

ILLUSTRATION: Page 278.

Votes for women

PANKHURST, Emmeline, (1857–1928), inspirer of the Suffragette Movement in Great Britain.

VOTES FOR WOMEN
Men & Women
HELP THE SUFFRAGETTES
To Rush
THE HOUSE OF COMMONS
ON
TUESDAY EVENING, 13th OCTOBER,
AT 7.30

Now, when women have the vote, and use it as carelessly as most men, and when the spirit of Mrs Pankhurst and her fiery daughter Christabel has long departed, it is difficult to imagine the passion and the earnestness of the suffragettes. Yet England in the late nineteenth century was not kind to women's ambitions; upper- and middle-class women were expected to be no more than good wives; working-class girls provided cheap labour, and were thought only to respond to the firm hand. It was natural that Women's Suffrage should be mixed up with the rise of Socialism. About each of these movements there was an air of revolt; and at first Mrs Pankhurst (who had lived in an atmosphere of reform from her earliest days and delighted to discover that she was born on the anniversary of the Fall of the Bastille) supported the Independent Labour Party; but she was impatient of their lack of enthusiasm for women's rights, and formed the Women's Social and Political Union, the spearhead of the suffragette movement. The general question of women's rights occupied her at first; but gradually, her campaign narrowed itself down to votes for women. It was still a novelty for women to be seen agitating in public, and there was much opposition. 'This is what I call life,' said Mrs Pankhurst to Christabel.

The political leaders of the day were pleasantly scornful: 'Votes for women would do more harm than good,' said Asquith, 'Parliament is not elected on the basis of universal suffrage, for children are not represented there.' And even Lloyd George, hearing some suffragette hecklers, said: 'Some rats have got in; let them squeal.'

Though Mrs Pankhurst held the Union together, it was Christabel who inspired the mystic devotion of the girlhood of England. When she was ejected from the House of Commons lobby and screamed at a policeman, 'I shall assault you, I shall spit at you,' crowds of adoring young women followed her example as though she was a new Joan of Arc. For almost ten years before the war the fight went on; there were demonstrations, window-smashings, and prison sentences for the leading suffragettes. One of them, Lady Constance Lytton, tried to cut 'Votes for women' on her chest while in a cell. On Christabel's release from Holloway a huge crowd gathered outside, saying, 'Maiden warrior, we give you rapturous welcome.'

'The old cry was, "You will never rouse women",' said Mrs Pankhurst, 'but we have done what they thought, and what they hoped, to be impossible. We are roused.' With the war, and the forced equality of the sexes, there came first a limited suffrage, in 1916; and then, in 1928, women had the vote. Taking it as a matter of course, perhaps they are no longer grateful. The world does not take kindly to Amazons, and the Women's Social and Political Union will perhaps never get quite the respect it deserves.

ILLUSTRATION: Page 311.

Monarch of physicians

PARACELSUS, (c. 1493–1541) – Philippus Aureolus Theophrastus Bombastus von Hohenheim, known as Paracelsus – Swiss alchemist, chemist, and doctor.

He was the only son of a Swabian nobleman and physician and a bondwoman of the Benedictine abbey of Einsiedelm in Switzerland, his birthplace. The home of his parents was 'quiet and peaceful', and he revered his father as his first model of the good physician. On the death of his mother when Aureolus was nine years old, father and son removed to Villach, in Carinthia. Following his father's calling, he studied at Vienna, then travelled from one university to another, winning his 'doctor's hat' in Ferrara in 1515, at the same time adopting the surname of Paracelsus. He continued to travel the length and breadth of Europe – from England to Moscow, from Spain and Poland to Constantinople and Alexandria. He insisted that medical knowledge should be based upon experience and experiment, not upon tradition: 'The physician does not learn everything he must know and master at high colleges alone; from time to time he must consult old women, gypsies, magicians, wayfarers, and all manner of peasant folk and random people, and learn from them.' He regarded the physician as the servant of God: 'No one requires greater love of the heart than the physician. For him the

Continued on p. 327

PLATE 13

JOHN RUSKIN (1819–1900). *Vanity Fair Cartoon.*

PLATE 14

VOLTAIRE (1694–1778) by Jean Huber.

MRS PANKHURST (1857–1928) with her daughter.

Ætatis suæ 21. A°. 1616.

POCAHONTAS (c. 1595–1617) by an unknown artist.

311

JOHANN STRAUSS (1825–1899) by L. S. Horovitz.

312

STENDHAL (1783–1842) by G. Stryienska.

313

JONATHAN SWIFT (1667–1745) by Charles Jervas.

SPINOZA (1632–1677) by an unknown artist.

TOLSTOY (1828–1910).

J. M. W. TURNER (1775–1851) by Cornelius Varley.

TURGENEV (1818–1883).

W. H. FOX TALBOT (1800–1877).

323

VELASQUEZ (1599–1660). Self-portrait, detail from *Las Meninas*.

TENNYSON (1809–1892) reading *Maud*. By D. G. Rossetti.

326

PLATE 15

DUKE OF WELLINGTON (1769–1852) by Sir Thomas Lawrence.

PLATE 16

J. A. MCN. WHISTLER (1834–1903) by Spy. *Vanity Fair Cartoon.*

ultimate instance is man's distress. Privilege and lineage pale into nothingness, only distress has meaning.'

In 1515 he had to leave Salzburg on suspicion of supporting the Peasant War. In the following year he was appointed city physician at Basel, where his contempt for tradition, his insistence on lecturing in German and his outspoken contempt for his colleagues and their methods, involved him in such violent opposition that he had to leave the city. A sample of his controversial style may seem to justify the use of his name, 'Bombast', for such extravagant claims, until we reflect that in his own case these claims were abundantly justified:

'I am Theophrastus, and in addition I am *monarcha medicorum*, monarch of physicians, and I can prove to you what you cannot prove. I will let Luther defend his cause, and I will defend my cause, and I will defeat those of my colleagues who turn against me; this I shall do with the help of the arcana ... It was not the constellations that made me a physician: God made me ... Let me tell you this: every little hair on my neck knows more than you and all your scribes, and my shoebuckles are more learned than your Galen and Avicenna, and my beard has more experience than all your high colleges.'

From 1526 until the end of his life, Paracelsus continued a poor wandering scholar; yet he wrote countless treatises on medical and kindred subjects, and more than a hundred on religion and metaphysics. At the age of forty-five he was broken in health and fortune, and three years later died at Salzburg, leaving his few possessions to 'the poor, the wretched, and the needy'.

Luther had hoped that so revolutionary a mind would embrace the cause of the Reformation, but Paracelsus died in the old faith. The truths he sought lay deeper than the level of the controversy that engaged the Reformers, being the ultimate mysteries of the nature of man, matter, soul and spirit. He taught that man is a microcosm, comprising in his body all the elements of nature, and in his soul those of the astral world. In order to study man, we must study nature. He followed the teaching of the Cabbala and of Hermes Trismegistus: 'that which is beneath is like that which is above, and the things beneath are so related to the things above as man and wife'. Thus, the senses 'have their proper insensible and impalpable body, even as on the contrary the other part of the body is tangible, for every man is composed of two, *viz.* of a material and of a spiritual body. The materiality gives body, blood and flesh; but the spirituality

P

gives hearing, feeling, smelling, touching and tasting. So then, if one be born deaf, it proceeds from the defect of that mansion place in which the hearing is to abide. For the spiritual body doth not perfect its operation in an ill disposed place'.

ILLUSTRATION: Page 318.

Inventor of the turbine

PARSONS, Sir Charles Algernon, (1854–1931), English engineer and inventor of the steam turbine, which has been described as 'one of the greatest inventions ever made in the history of engineering'.

His professional career began in 1877 when he entered the Armstrong works at Elswick; the turbine was invented seven years later in 1884. Involving the action of steam jets on curved vanes, it applied steam to a revolving, rather than a reciprocating engine; and many experts looked askance at this disturbing innovation. Seldom has any inventor had so delightful a chance of scoring off pompous officialdom as came Parsons' way in 1897. In 1894 he had built the *Turbinia*, the first turbine-powered ship. This wonderful little craft was taken secretly to Cowes in the Isle of Wight at the time of the naval review which helped to mark Queen Victoria's Diamond Jubilee. Suddenly irate and powerless admirals were confronted by the *Turbinia* dashing in and out among their beloved ships at the then astounding speed of thirty-four-and-a-half knots. When tempers had cooled, and when stubborn stupidity had been overcome the Parsons steam turbine was widely adopted for the world's fast steam shipping.

Explorer of infinities

PASCAL, Blaise, (1623–1662), French mathematician and man of religion. His most famous sentence, '*le silence éternel de ces espaces infinis m'effraie*', is in a sense his fitting memorial. For as scientist, mathematician and student of God, Pascal spent most of his brief but incredibly intense life perambulating infinity.

His father, a distinguished lawyer, found him, before his twelfth year, and before he had been taught mathematics, proving for himself a proposition of Euclid. On conic sections, on the theory of probability, on hydrostatics, he did pioneer work while hardly out of his teens; and he invented the first calculating machine. His view of man and of God lifts Pascal out of the record of the history of science (though he was one of the greatest of mathematicians) into a more general, and absolute, distinction. And in the religious and polemical *Lettres Provinciales* (1656), he created modern French prose. Pascal was connected with the Jansenists, an ascetic and puritanical order within the Catholic Church, both by predilection and because his sister had taken vows at Port-Royal. On 23 November 1654 he had a mystical experience, a record of which he always kept about him: after his death it was found sewn into his coat.

'From about half past ten at night, to about half after midnight, Fire. God of Abraham, God of Isaac, God of Jacob, not of the philosophers and the wise. Security, security. Feeling, joy, peace ... Righteous Father, the world has not known you, but I have known you. Joy, joy, joy, tears of joy ...' – In such ecstatic terms, half fumbling, half articulate, Pascal registered his experience and his vision. But there is nothing fumbling about the *Provincial Letters* which he wrote shortly afterwards. They are a counterblast against the Jesuits, with whom the Jansenists were fighting for survival. They have the lucidity and point of a mathematical demonstration and the controlled passionate invective of a great controversialist. Pascal's last and uncompleted work was also intended to be controversy, of a different type: his famous *Pensées* are notes for an elaborate Defence of Christianity. Sainte-Beuve called them a tower of which the stones have been laid on each other, but not cemented. But the stones are diamonds. In the *Pensées* he makes 'The Everlasting Nay' to mankind and 'The Everlasting Yea' to God. Pascal's version of the Shakespearean *What a piece of work is a man!* runs 'What a chimera is man! how odd, how monstrous, how much a chaos, how much a contradiction, how much a prodigy! Judge of all things, and a poor earthworm; depository of truth, cesspit of error and uncertainty, glory and reject of the universe!' Man cannot be understood by man. As an exit from this horror he could only recommend listening to God. Not surprisingly, this explorer of infinities dismissed the moment of death in an epigram of terrible pathos: 'The last act is tragic, however pleasant all the comedy of the other acts. A little earth on our heads, and all is done with for ever.'

Bacteriology

PASTEUR, Louis, (1822–1895), founder of modern bacteriology, was born at Dole, in France, where his father was a tanner. A slow school-boy whose performance in chemistry, when he took his science degree in 1842, was described as 'mediocre', Pasteur soon came to a maturity of mind. In his twenties he wrote that 'three things, will, work, and success, between them fill human existence'.

Right at the beginning of his researches, Pasteur found himself confronted by the chemical secrets of life, and he pursued them ever afterwards, with supreme genius. He proved by clarity of mind, and finality of experiment, that there is no mystery in the chemistry of life, only unsolved problems, which would gradually yield to 'will' and 'work'. He was fond of saying that discoveries were not accidental, they came only to the mind prepared to receive them. Pasteur was appointed professor at Lille in 1854. This was a centre of the brewing and distilling industries. His passionate attachment to his home and his father's interests had left him with a permanent sympathy for the chemical problems of industry. The brewers and distillers of Lille found that he did not disdain their problems, but was prepared to investigate the occasional souring of their beer. As a result of these investigations, he discovered that fermentation was due to germs. He showed that in the absence of these germs, milk and beer did not turn sour; 'the chemical act of fermentation is essentially a correlative of a vital act beginning and ending with it'.

Pasteur now pursued these germs. Where did they come from? Were they spontaneously generated, or were they the offspring of similar germs? He proved conclusively that they were not spontaneously generated. They did not spring into existence from nowhere. These results, published in 1864, were almost as disturbing to conventional ideas as Darwin's *Origin of Species*, published five years earlier. Though he was a devout Catholic, Pasteur had delivered a severe blow to the current beliefs in creationism. Following on Pasteur's demonstration that fermentation depended on germs, Lister set out to try to reduce the incidence of blood-poisoning, which seemed to be a kind of fermentation, by killing the germs which caused it. He thereby introduced antiseptic surgery.

In 1865 Pasteur was asked to investigate the disease which was overwhelming the cultivation of silkworms in France. He discovered the bacilli which caused it, and a method of dealing with them, thus saving the silk industry. Next he investigated anthrax and chicken cholera. He isolated the bacilli, and produced a mild form of them by chemical treatment When animals were inoculated with these, they had a slight attack of the disease, and then became immune, for a period, to the virulent strains.

Pasteur extended this method to the treatment of human disease through his investigations of hydrophobia, caused in man by bites from dogs made mad through infection. He found that preparations could be made from the tissues of the infected animals, in which the infective agent was reduced by suitable treatment to a milder form. Persons inoculated with these preparations were protected from the effects of the virulent forms conveyed into the bite with the mad dog's saliva. The success of this experiment in 1885 led to the founding of the Pasteur Institute, for the extension of this and allied methods of combating disease.

Pasteur was a scientist of prodigious ability, who kept his science and his religion in two separate departments. He had an inspired common sense which sprang from the tanners and craftsmen among whom he was born, and whom he loved. When he was ill, he ached for the smell of the tannery of his childhood. He never became a member of the intelligentsia. Consequently, his ideas and discoveries cut across traditional boundaries, and he became one of the greatest and most original scientists of all time.

The Free Trader

PEEL, Sir Robert, (1788–1850), British Prime Minister, who founded the first civil police force in the modern world, and gave us Free Trade. About his conversion on this latter subject Disraeli remarked, 'He found the Whigs bathing and went off with their clothes.'

Peel was the son of a wealthy Lancashire mill-owner (himself the product of the industrial revolution). Though educated into the upper classes at Eton and Christ Church (Oxford), he retained all his life a broad Lancashire accent. He entered politics early as a government Tory and distinguished himself by his severe administration when Chief Secretary for Ireland. In 1819 he was converted to the gold standard,

and this – the first of many intellectual awakenings – began his estrangement from the Tory squires. He was Home Secretary from 1822 to 1827, when he invented the Metropolitan police force, called at first Peelers and later Bobbies – both in his honour. He opposed Catholic Emancipation strongly, but carried it in 1829, rather than risk further discontent in Ireland.

In the reformed parliament Peel led the Tory remnant and transformed it into the Conservative party, which Disraeli defined as 'Tory men and Whig measures'. Peel's party was supposed to attract propertied men of all sorts and to accept moderate reform. William IV made Peel Prime Minister in 1834, but he failed to secure a majority even after a general election. He was within sight of office again in 1839, but when Victoria refused to dismiss her Whig ladies-of-the-bedchamber, Peel declined the call to form a government. The general election of 1841 brought at last a strong Conservative majority; and Peel had five years as Prime Minister. His main concern was in the reform of finance, where he lowered duties and acted on Free Trade principles. By 1846 only the Corn Laws remained; but these were dear to the Tories both as a social symbol and an economic advantage. Peel tried to shift the burden of repealing them on to the Whigs; when this failed, he did it himself, exploiting the alarm of a famine in Ireland. Though he repealed the Corn Laws and founded Free Trade, he broke the Conservative party. He and a few followers became Peelites; the Conservatives were not in sight of a majority for a generation. He died in 1850 after a fall from a horse.

Peel is always quoted, perhaps correctly, as the greatest symbol of British compromise. He taught the governing classes to yield rather than fight, and so, it is said, preserved them. Perhaps this is true.

Onas and the Indians

PENN, William, (1644–1718), Quaker, Fellow of the Royal Society, and founder of the State of Pennsylvania (1681). 'I eyed the Lord in the obtaining of it, that an example may be set up to the Nations; there may be room there, though not here, for such an Holy Experiment.' The Holy Experiment was made possible by the fact that Charles II owed Penn's father,

Admiral Sir William Penn, £16,000. The Charter paid the debt; as for Pennsylvania, 'the name', said Charles 'is in honour of your father'.

'Rather a mythical than an historical person,' wrote Macaulay of him, preparing to turn on the heat ('Not a man of strong sense. He had no skill in reading the characters of others ... bribes may be offered to vanity as well as to cupidity,' etc.). But what a myth; and what a blessing that there are men who will grow into myths, and myths that will feed men! Think of Penn travelling the canals of his ancestral Holland with George Fox; standing in the bail-dock of the Old Bailey and shouting: 'I appeal to the Jury, who are my judges, and this great assembly, whether the proceedings of the Court are not most arbitrary, and void of all law?'; talking religion at Herwerden with the fabulous Elizabeth of the Palatinate ('You meaner beauties of the night, what are you when the moon shall rise?'); courting Gulielma Maria Posthuma Springett; hobnobbing with the ladies of the Restoration Court; reading the *Maxims* of La Rochefoucauld in the Tower of London; riding to Haverford Meeting in the American wilderness, and taking up before him little Rebecca Wood, her bare feet dangling down on either side; outjumping the Indian braves. Think of the pathos of the last years, 'His memory almost quite lost, and the use of his understanding suspended; and yet as near the Truth, in the love of it, as before.' Above all in Penn's life, think of the scene at Shackamaxon, under the elm tree, where the Indians pledged themselves to live in love with Onas, as they called him, and his children, as long as grass shall grow, and rivers run, and the sun and moon endure. 'William Penn appeared in his usual clothes. He had no crown, sceptre, mace, sword halberd, or any insignia of eminence. He was distinguished only by wearing a sky-blue sash round his waist, which was made of silk net-work.' The few Quakers were surrounded by the tribes, 'who were seen in the woods as far as the eye could carry, and looked frightful both on account of their numbers and their arms'. When the chief of the Sachems put on 'a kind of chaplet in which appeared a small horn', the Indians threw down their bows and arrows, and squatted in a half moon on the ground. Thus was made with them 'the only treaty that was never sworn to, and never broken' (Voltaire).

Penn 'rowed against wind and tide all his life', as he said himself; sometimes compromising, often muddled, often cheated, more than once bankrupt, misunderstood by his own time and by posterity – but hear the man himself: 'Seek and ye shall find, I testify for God. But then you must seek aright, with your whole heart, as men that seek for their lives, yea, for their eternal lives, diligently, humbly, patiently, as those that can taste no pleasure, comfort, or satisfaction in anything else unless you find him whom your souls want and desire to know and love above all. O, it is a travail, a spiritual travail, let the carnal, profane world think and say as it will. And through this path you must walk to the City of God that has eternal foundations, if ever you will come there.'

ILLUSTRATION: Page 272.

Emperor of all Russia

PETER THE GREAT, (1672–1725), Tsar and Emperor of Russia, who brought Russia into the Western orbit. After the Peace of Nystad, concluded with Charles XII of Sweden in 1721, he was proclaimed 'Father of the Fatherland, Peter the Great and Emperor of all Russia', and in the U.S.S.R. today he is greatly revered as the founder of the modern state.

He was never intended to be Tsar, since he was the youngest son of the Tsar Alexis and his wife Natalya Naryshkin. His stepbrother, Feodor IV, died in 1682, and Peter and his half-brother Ivan were raised to a double throne. Peter was too young to rule and his sister Sophia Alekseyevna was regent for six years. It was not a wasted time for Peter. He stayed in the country, enjoying himself with a mock army, and gathered round himself the nucleus of his famous band of 'amusers'. Dwarfs, cripples, adventurers, anyone who could entertain the young prince was welcome. He was not the easiest of companions: since seeing a friend butchered by a mob in the risings that preceded his accession to the throne he had suffered from convulsions, which would begin with a twisting of the neck to the left, while his facial muscles would contract violently. Sometimes a sedative was given to him made from the stomach and wings of a magpie pounded together.

By the time he was seventeen, Peter was tired of his sister ruling Russia; he made Ivan abdicate, and put his sister into a convent. Some of the faction that supported Sophia were executed in Moscow, Peter taking a hand in the business. There is no doubt that he was a complete sadist. He enjoyed seeing people tortured and touching them in their agonies. When Frederick of Prussia showed him the wheel, Peter – to whom it was new – demanded to see an experimental victim; and was unhappy when no victim was forthcoming.

His famous visit through Europe was to have a lasting effect on Peter. There was something of Heathcliffe (the hero of Emily Brontë's *Wuthering Heights*) in the way in which the huge gawky monarch (he was six feet seven) gazed at the fine ladies, and secretly despised them. He was an avid picker-up of new trades, and took a particular interest in carpentry. Charles II of England visited his house in London: and asked for the windows to be opened, so powerful was the stench of the coarse Russian and his *entourage*. By the time the Russian party embarked at Amsterdam for Archangel, it was 640 strong. At a ball given by the Princess Sophia Charlotte, wife of the Elector of Brandenburg, in his honour, he amused the company by making his troupe of dwarfs cavort; but when he saw that the smutty jokes of his jester, Turgenev, were ill-received, he picked up a broom and beat him in the middle of the dance-floor.

His first action on his return to Russia was to cut off the beards of the nobility; it was a symbol that the West had arrived. From then until his death, he worked passionately to change the state. He saw that the only hope for Russian expansion was to obtain better seaports, and his ambition stretched to the shores of the Baltic and the Black Sea. He conquered Azov (from the Turks) and in 1699 made a peace with Turkey. The following year, in alliance with Denmark, Poland and Saxony he began the Northern War, defeating Charles XII of Sweden at Poltava in 1709. At Nystad, Peter was confirmed in his conquest of Karelia, Ingermanland and Livonia.

Inside Russia, his prime task always was to substitute new for old forms. The capital shifted from Moscow to a site on his newly-conquered Baltic territory – St Petersburg. The use of stone instead of wood in building was encouraged, to stop the risk of fire; he founded Academies of arts and sciences, brought in a system of universal taxation, built hospitals and schools. The great flaw in all this progress was his imperviousness to the plight of the serfs: in his whole reign he did nothing to alleviate their miserable condition. For the sake of the new régime, he had his son put to death: the son did not agree with the father's ideas, and Peter did not propose to allow any falling-down after his death.

The greatest love poet

PETRARCH, (1304–1374), Francesco Petrarca, Italian poet and greatest of all poets of love. He has been called the herald of the Renaissance, and the first writer of the romantic mood.

As a young man Petrarch was obliged to take holy orders, but this by no means meant shunning the world. Rather the reverse, for in Avignon 'on the sixth day of April', 1327, on Good Friday, in the church of St Clare, his eyes fell on Laura de Sade, and from that day onwards he was overwhelmingly in love. Petrarch could do no less for Laura than Dante had done for Beatrice. His love sonnets made her as famous as Dante's beloved, but clad her with more flesh and blood. Laura never yielded to Petrarch's passion:

> In wintry midnight, o'er a stormy main
>   A ship I, laden with oblivion, go
> By whirlpool and by rock, while love my foe,
>   And Sovereign ruler, at the helm must reign
> And ardent thoughts and vain intentions strain
>   Each oar, and scorn the storm and waves below
> And winds of sighs and hopes, and wishes, blow
>   With endless rage and rending sails in twain,
> And storms of tears and clouds of scorn, make slack
>   And spoil my feeble cordage, which is found
> Of nought but ignorance and error twined,
>   And those two lovely eyes that lit my track
> Are gone, and reason in the wars is drowned,
>   And I cannot the destined haven find.
>   *(Translated by William Barnes.)*

If she shared – as she may well have done – some of his feelings, that did not prevent her living a normal married life with her husband and begetting a large family. Though he had illegitimate children of his own, Petrarch loved her always, his love becoming more ethereal with the years. At the same time, he was incurably restless and a prodigious traveller. In 1330 he was in Flanders and Germany in the service of Giacomo Colonna. In 1336 we find him on an expedition climbing Mont Ventoux (with the *Confessions of St Augustine* in his hand). In 1337 he paid his first visit to Rome, and the contrast between the ruins of past greatness and the contemporary degradation made a lifelong impression. He may have visited England that same year. Yet his longing for solitude was as great as his restlessness, and for the next fifteen years he returned whenever he could to his famous hermitage in the Vaucluse. In 1340 he was crowned poet laureate in Rome on the Campidoglio.

The tension between his longings for solitude and study – *Le città son nemiche, amici i boschi* (cities are enemies, woods are friends) – and his duties as a public figure had by now become permanent. For a while he was fired with enthusiasm for the Roman adventurer Cola di Rienzo, who established a short-lived and rhetorical 'republic', and then wrote the most famous patriotic *canzone* in the language – *Italia mia*. He visited nearly all the cities of Italy, was revered by great potentates, ecclesiastical and lay, corresponded with the learned, and on one occasion attempted to make peace between Genoa and Venice. When his life was drawing to a close he found another hermitage, this time at Arquà in the Euganean hills near Padua. The house still exists and in the upstairs room where he died they preserve some of his furniture and his cat (embalmed). There he died in 1374.

Like scholars of his age, Petrarch had two languages, Latin and 'the vulgar tongue'; his 'vulgar' writings are incomparably superior to his 'learned' ones. The *Canzoniere*, the love poems, are his masterpiece, from the early passionate expressions of love to the later poems which are more resigned to melancholy. Petrarch's melancholy, his search for solitude in nature scenery and his devoted sad love are really different aspects of a continuously developing life. There is a natural transition from the sight of Laura's angelic form, 'with the golden hair scattered in the wind in a thousand sweet knots', to his flight from mankind:

> And I keep my eyes intent to avoid
> Any human footprint in the sand.

Or again

> No sparrow on any roof was ever lonely
> As I am, nor any animal untamed.

As he considered the illusions and fleetingness of life – 'What the world enjoys is a passing dream' – Petrarch made something of a cult of melancholy. For centuries his sonnets were read far more than the austere theology of Dante.

Chess player and musician

PHILIDOR, François André Danican, (1726–1795), French master of chess and the world's greatest player of the game. There is a strong affinity between chess and music, which was exemplified in Philidor, who was one of the foremost musicians of his day, coming from a famous musical family, in which talent went from father to son, as with the Bachs.

At the age of six Philidor was attached to the Chapelle du Roy, the King's Band. He composed church music – the first piece was written and performed when he was eleven years old – and no less than twenty-three operas. Up to modern times, his scores were used at the Paris Conservatoire as models of style and orchestration. Chess was a favourite pastime with the players in the King's Band, and at ten Philidor had few equals in the game. In 1745, when he was nineteen he played a match against Stamma, a famous Arab from Aleppo, gave his opponent odds and scored an overwhelming victory. From that time his supremacy was never challenged and chess was a support to him when his musical fortunes were low. His travels took him to England, which became a second home: Philidor returning year after year to London during the last thirty years of his life. An English translation of his *Analyse du jeu des échecs* (1749) was immediately successful, and his modesty and friendliness, a personality which must have been dynamic as well as endearing, had such an effect that membership of the British Chess Club, of which Philidor was a member, soon rose to 300, greater than the membership of any chess club in England today. Among its members were illustrious men from the Church, the Bar and society, statesmen and writers.

He was the first to teach the great importance of pawn playing in scientific chess; and one of his most admired accomplishments was playing blindfold, taking on several games simultaneously against leading players. It was not known at the time that blindfold chess had been practised centuries ago by Arab experts, and since Philidor's day other masters have played blindfold against a greater number of opponents. None the less, Philidor's blindfold games, which have been preserved, show a steadiness and certainty of touch which could be admired in a single player, playing over the board.

The French Revolution was a great blow for Philidor, who spent the last three years of his life in England, waiting for the passport which was to enable him to return to his homeland. It never came; and he died in London, among the people who loved him so well and was buried in the fine church of St James, Piccadilly.

'What Nature is not'

PICASSO, Pablo, (b. 1881), Spanish-born artist working in France, the colossus of modern art who has uncovered images of our period, not all of which are the most pleasant, or the prettiest objects. 'When I paint, my object is to show what I have found and not what I am looking for,' he has said.

No painter of the twentieth century, perhaps of any period, has been more prolific; he has originated many and participated in all of the modern movements in art – running through impressionism, post-impressionism, cubism, abstraction and surrealism, vastly digesting the forms of Toulouse-Lautrec, Van Gogh, El Greco, negro sculptors, Cézanne, Ingres, Raphael, the Greeks, primitive art, Moorish art, Byzantine art. With his insatiable desire to create, he has exploited all media – painting, drawing, etching, lithography, sculpture and pottery. Yet his interest in these movements, forms and techniques has never been merely one of research in art: 'I have never made trials or experiments. Whenever I had something to say, I have said it in the manner in which I felt it ought to be said.'

Picasso has never theorized. 'Everyone wants to understand art. Why not try to understand the song of a bird?' Supremely gifted himself as a designer and a draughtsman, Picasso has been a dozen artists inhabiting a single body. At fifteen he made his first naturalistic paintings. At twenty he was painting his pictures of poor people by the edge of the sea; and a few years later his sad jugglers and acrobats, somewhat sentimental symbols of misery. In the years leading up to the first World War, and during the war, he began a fragmentation of reality which led to the formulae of cubism; at the end of the war his abstract paintings became gay decorations, and he made something of a return to realism.

Yet sorting out the Picassos within Picasso is none too easy. He suffers from extremes of condemnation and praise; it is certain that posterity will have to sieve through his work, will reject a great deal of triviality and perversity and failure, and will continue to wonder at the achievements which remain. Whatever he may have said or painted, Picasso is in some ways the supreme playboy inhabiting his own margin; or if you look at him in another way, the first outstanding exponent of an art delivered from the need to imitate or represent. If one statement by him covers his art, it is the reasonable one to which most artists would agree, that 'through art we express our conception of what nature is not' (though Picasso was speaking of Velasquez). Art and nature are different worlds, of which no one has made us more aware than Picasso. When he had attempted to paint the universal masterpiece-with-a-message, the result, though acclaimed, has been patchy and, if the truth be told, ineffectual. Between the wars Picasso the Spaniard began the series of bull-fighting canvases in which the bull symbolizes brutality, the bull-fighter the fighter for liberty, the horse the innocent non-combatant, and the spectators those who watch but will not intervene. The huge grey-and-black *Guernica*, painted after the German bombing of the village of Guernica during the Spanish Civil War, has the best of intentions. By the harsh light of an electric bulb we see the bull, the screaming horse, the broken bull-fighter, the mother with a dead child, the frightened spectator and the serene figure of truth. During the occupation of Paris a German showed Picasso a reproduction of *Guernica*. 'Did you do this?' 'No,' said Picasso, 'you did.' Yet the whole long picture remains a series of ill co-ordinated fragments, varying from the sublime to the silly. If this strikes the reader as an unorthodox and perverse judgement, he should remember the intentions of Picasso and those of his fellow countryman Goya (q.v.), and should then compare the odds and ends of *Guernica* with the intense impact of any one of Goya's etchings in *The Disasters of War*. However, an artist has a right to his failures, and giants and heroes have their weak places. Since the second World War, Picasso has shown his political sympathies: 'What do you think an artist is? an imbecile who has only his eyes if he is a painter, or ears if he is a musician? On the contrary, he is at the same time a political being, constantly alive to heartrending, fiery or happy events, to which he responds in every way. How would it be possible to feel no interest in other people ... to detach yourself from the life they so copiously bring you? No, painting is not done to decorate apartments. It is an instrument ... for attack and defence against the enemy' – which is a dogma not always applied in the way Picasso may have intended.

For good or ill Picasso is so little to be brushed away that his influence is everywhere. There are oddments of Picasso's vision wherever you look; his vision has seeped into the homes, into the streets, and into the people of the great cities of the world.

ILLUSTRATION: Page 277.

God and mathematics

PIERO DELLA FRANCESCA, (c. 1420–1492), one of the mathematician-artists of Italy, and in the complete realization of his power among the most profound painters the world has known.

Piero's vision of mathematics is used to develop and fix the essence of how things look, and the grandeur of Christian story – of Christ, the Madonna, the saints: he forms a world of men and women visibly bold and full and tense, who are yet withdrawn into religious grandeur and solemnity.

His native town was Borgo San Sepulchro. As a boy and a young man he was in Florence, then the cultural centre of mankind, where he developed his passion for mathematics, and learnt to build up his pictures geometrically, to make them self-contained, clear, inevitable, and so compellingly sublime. Caught in the spell of the event, bodies are smooth and unbroken. Colours are quiet and cool, yet they add up to a celestial happiness. Christ is baptized – and he stands, as it were, in the midst of a geometrical theorem (*The Baptism,* National Gallery, London): he carries his solemnity on firm legs, and in the pale sky above him the clouds stretch like the dove, and the dove repeats the shape and stretches like a cloud. Or Christ is born (*The Nativity,* National Gallery, London), and the eye is taken direct to the singing mouths in the smooth young heads of the angels. Each mouth in this band of heads and mouths is differently open: together they make a bar of music, if not audible, at least visible.

Between 1452 and 1466 Piero painted his major work, the frescoes in the church of San Francesco, in Arezzo, which portray the Legend of the True Cross in a splendour of simplified complexity. In his old age Piero della Francesca gave up painting to compose treatises on mathematics and art. Eventually, as if he had lived too much by his eyes, he went blind.

British leader against Napoleon

PITT, William, the younger, (1759–1806), was the second son of the great Earl of Chatham. Canning called him 'the pilot who weathered the storm', though the storm of Napoleon had by no means blown itself out at Pitt's death.

Pitt entered politics when barely twenty-one, invoking from the first the prestige of his father's great name. In 1784 he rescued George III from the coalition of the politicians, Fox and North; and became Prime Minister at the age of twenty-three. He had few followers and never acquired a party. He was strictly a King's man, dependent on the King's support, though the King also needed him. In his first years as Prime Minister he made some slight effort to reform parliament, though without success. His financial reforms were more successful. Pitt's talents were those of a peace minister; but much against his will he was drawn into the struggle with revolutionary France. In 1793, when war broke out, he abandoned such liberal principles as he possessed, announced a Jacobin peril, and harried the English radicals. He claimed to possess his father's genius, but his conduct of the war was muddled and unsuccessful.

In 1799 he advocated Union with Ireland in order to resist Jacobinism there; but he coupled this with emancipation for the Irish Catholics, in order to win over the propertied classes. When George III rejected this, Pitt resigned, not in protest, but rather in apology; and he promised not to renew the idea in George's lifetime. Pitt was too proud to oppose the government of Addington, his incompetent successor; besides, he had no followers with which to make an opposition. He did not criticize the Peace of Amiens (1802); but when Napoleon renewed the war in 1804, public opinion insisted on his return to power. Pitt attempted to organize a European coalition against France. It was shattered at the battle of Austerlitz (1805), after which Pitt said: 'Roll up the map of Europe; it will not be wanted these ten years.' The shock is supposed to have killed him. A more practical cause was his excessive consumption of portwine, prescribed by his doctors from youth. He is alleged to have said on his death-bed: 'My country! How I love my country.' But a more reliable authority reports as his last words: 'I think I could eat one of Bellamy's meat pies.'

ILLUSTRATION: Page 273.

The autocratic excavator

PITT-RIVERS, Augustus Henry Lane-Fox,(1827–1900), English archaeologist, general, landowner and *grand seigneur,* the one man who made the study of prehistory possible. By inventing with inspired common sense the modern theory of excavation and putting it into practice with autocratic vigour, Pitt-Rivers changed antiquarianism into scientific archaeology within a decade.

When Pitt-Rivers was a young officer at Hythe the typology of muskets (he himself invented the use of this word 'typology') led him to study the ethnography of weapons; and when at last he was invalided out of the army as Lieutenant-General after a staff appointment in the Crimea, he turned first to anthropology, then to archaeology. In 1880 he inherited the vast Pitt-Rivers estates in Dorset, a field laboratory in which his ideas could be carried out, for here on Cranborne Chase (a hunting ground of the medieval kings) were Romano-British village sites, barrows, linear earthworks. Excavations were conducted with military precision and with a due sense of rank: the General in his carriage bowling along the roads of Cranborne Chase in the mists of a fine summer morning, followed by the staff of draughtsmen, photographers, recorders, pedalling their penny-farthings, wearing their boaters with the blue-and-yellow ribbon of Pitt-Rivers and the Rushmore estates. In blue and gold also he bound the great volumes of excavation reports, privately, lavishly produced, almost unapproachable models of perfection in their kind.

In the park a band played in uniforms designed by the General. Llamas grazed there, and yaks. Herbert Spencer the philosopher or W. H. Mallock, influential author of *The New Republic*, would come to stay. 'The masses', stated the General, 'are ignorant, and knowledge is swamped by ignorance ... The knowledge they lack is the knowledge of history' and since 'for good or evil ... we have thought proper to place power in the hands of the masses', as well, thought the General, to teach them evolution and the gradualness of change by a new museum which might counteract 'scatter-brained revolutionary suggestions'. That great ethnological museum is now housed in Oxford. And another museum, flanked by a statue of Caesar Augustus, stands in isolation at Farnham, Dorset, on his estates, containing Benin bronzes, Easter Island statuettes, and the great demonstrations by model and potsherd which drove this irascible old rationalist through campaign after campaign in summer and winter alike, seeking to lay a firm basis of ascertained fact about the knowledge of ancient man; and providing the original 'documents' to which the prehistorian will turn again and again.

Pitt-Rivers, in himself an extraordinary character,

set new standards in the recovery and recording of archaeological data. He was determined to present the total evidence recoverable by excavation – 'Tedious as it may appear to some', he wrote, 'to dwell on the discovery of odds and ends.' Without such methods our historical horizons could never have been extended into prehistory. (*See Schliemann.*)

Population and poverty

PLACE, Francis, (1771–1854), English reformer and political economist, who endeavoured to check over-population, poverty and vice by birth-control.

Place knew poverty at first hand and developed an indefatigable passion for social justice. He was born in a London 'sponging house', or private debtor's prison, kept by his father. Educating himself, first he was a leather-breeches maker, then a tailor, and then a successful business man. In 1798 Malthus (q.v.) had published his world-famous *Essay on the Principle of Population*, in which he laid down that over-population was attended with vice and misery and that the check upon it that lay within man's power was moral restraint – or postponement of marriage. To Place this remedy seemed wrong, dangerous and unnatural. Over-population was then thought to be round the corner, and a solution was required without delay. So Place argued for mechanical contraception, publishing in 1822 his *Illustrations and Proofs of the Principle of Population*. In 1823 he circulated handbills of instruction in London and the industrial areas, explaining that it was his aim 'to destroy vice, and put an end to debauchery'.

Late marriage, he maintained, only led to vice and prostitution. Early marriage, feasible if child did not crowd upon child, led to virtue. 'By limiting the number of children', he stated in a handbill addressed to 'the Married of Both Sexes of the Working People', 'the wages both of children and of grown-up persons will rise; the hours of working will be no more than they ought to be; you will have some time for recreation, some means of enjoying yourselves rationally, as well as some time for your own and your children's moral and religious instruction.'

Place and his wife, an ironist may observe, themselves brought into the world no fewer than fifteen children. This remarkable man was active also in the cause of trade unionism.

Nonpareil of Virginia

POCAHONTAS, (c. 1595–1617), the nickname of Matoaka, a Red Indian princess, later Rebecca Rolfe.

Legend and fact in the story of Pocahontas are mixed, and for the legend Captain John Smith is largely responsible, though other contemporary accounts help to put the story in perspective. She was one of the daughters of Powhatan, chief of the Potomac confederacy in Virginia. In his *True Relation of Virginia*, published in Pocahontas's lifetime, Smith writes of her as a 'child of tenne years old' when the English arrived (1606), 'which in feature, countenance and proportions much exceedeth any of the rest of her people'. She was 'the only nonpareil of the country'.

In 1613, Captain Samuel Argall, of the *Treasurer*, came down the Rappahannock River, and took Pocahontas as hostage for some English prisoners held by the Indians. She was carried to Jamestown, and treated well. '*Powhatans* daughter I caused to be carefully instructed in the Christian Religion,' wrote the governor, 'who, after shee had made some goode progress therein, renounced publickly her countrey Idolatry.' She took the name of Rebecca. An English colonist, John Rolfe, whose first wife had died, fell in love with her. He acknowledged the dangers of being 'in love with one whose education hath bin rude, her manners barbarous, her generation accursed, and so discrepant in all nurtriture from myselfe'. But her beauty triumphed, and they married. The value of their union for Anglo-Indian relations was not overlooked: it was suggested that Rolfe married her for the good of the plantation.

With her husband, she came to London in 1616, was received 'with festivall, pompe and state', met the King and Queen, attended a masque (one of Ben Jonson's) and 'did not only accustome herselfe to civilitie but still carried herselfe as the Daughter of a King'. She met her old friend Captain Smith. In 1628, when she had long been dead, Smith published the *Generall Historie of Virginia*. Pocahontas, who in his *True Relation* had been no more than a lovely Indian girl, now appears as the guiding spirit of the settlers, and the heroine who saved Smith's life just when her father Powhatan was about to have his skull smashed in – an account rather to be suspected.

Early in 1617 Pocahontas prepared (it seems against her will) to return to Virginia. At Gravesend she fell sick, and died. 'She made not more sorrow for her unexpected death, than joy in the beholders to heare and see her make so religious and godly an end,' wrote Smith. Rolfe married again, and died in 1623. Even the most unromantic of narratives of Pocahontas's life is full of the exile's sadness, the essential tragedy of the displaced person. In the register of burials at Gravesend she is described as 'a Virginia lady borne'.

ILLUSTRATION: Page 311.

'Atrabilious dipsomaniac'

POE, Edgar Allen, (1809–1849), American poet and short-story writer and the first 'pure artist' to be produced by America. He had to struggle always with the neurotic elements of his own nature and with the cultural atmosphere around him.

This Virginian devotee of art – 'With me poetry has not been a purpose, but a passion' – lived when Americans were ruled in art by the moral optimism of New England and in life by the struggle to make money. His dream was to be a Southern Gentleman. But circumstances were against him. His parents, who were on the stage, left him an orphan, he quarrelled with the guardian who might have made the dream come true, he was withdrawn from college, ran away to enlist, was admitted to West Point and then expelled, and took to a romantic black cape and a life of journalism. He was further affected by his marriage to a child-wife, his cousin Virginia Clemm, around whose early death he wove contradictory fantasies. It is doubtful if Poe, self-dedicated to the 'Imp of the Perverse', preferred a live wife to a romantically dead one:

For the moon never beams without bringing me dreams
  Of the beautiful Annabel Lee,
And the stars never rise but I see the bright eyes
  Of the beautiful Annabel Lee;
So, all the night-tide, I lie down by the side
Of my darling – my darling – my life and my bride
  In her sepulchre there by the sea,
  In her tomb by the side of the sea.

He was involved always in a compensatory dream world.

'An artist', he wrote, 'is an artist only by dint of his exquisite sense of Beauty ... at the same time implying an equally exquisite sense of Deformity – of disproportion.' It was this 'exquisite sense of Deformity' that informed Poe's most durable writing – the macabre tales such as *The Fall of the House of Usher* or *The Pit and the Pendulum*.

Poe has always been a problem to critics. The President of Yale refused this 'atrabilious dipsomaniac' entry into the Hall of Fame because he 'wrote like a drunkard and a man who is not accustomed to pay his debts' – *i.e.* he was not a good citizen. But it is also possible to say that he was not a good writer – at least not a good poet, thinning language down to sugar-water and, as one critic has complained, writing in characteristic rhythms (cf. the lines quoted above) which resemble waves of hair all too glossily smarmed and scented with cheap brilliantine. Poe borrowed from Coleridge, without Coleridge's safeguarding intellect, and so from English romanticism which belatedly came across the ocean. English and Americans can tell his weakness. Lacking a native sensitivity to good English or to sugar English, the French have rated him too highly. On the verge of marrying a second time, Poe died at Baltimore in 1849 after a burst of drunkenness.

The Pompadour

POMPADOUR, Jeanne-Antoinette Poisson Le Normant d'Étioles, marquise de, (1721–1764), the famous mistress of Louis XV of France. She was the first bourgeois mistress a French king had ever had: and her position at Versailles was not easy.

After the glories of the reign of the Sun king (Louis XIV) and the degeneracy of Philippe d'Orléans' Regency, the reign of Louis XV was a rippling, clear brook of mannered sensuality. Louis was a cruel, false king, the destroyer of many women: yet Pompadour – spurred on by a fortune-teller who said that she would be the most important woman in France – set her cap at him. And Louis, struck by her beauty, took her as his mistress. The Marquise de Seran – after the Pompadour's death – asked the King if he had ever been in love.

'Yes,' he said, 'with Mme de Châteauroux' (another of his mistresses).

'And with Madame de Pompadour?'

'No, I never loved her.'

'But you kept her for as long as she wanted?'

'Yes,' said Louis, 'because it would have killed her to send her away.'

For eleven years the Pompadour ruled Versailles: she had a suite of six rooms in an attic, filled with the flowers that were her delight: Christmas roses, lilies of the valley, and freakish tulips. Scents of *pot-pourri* and musk filled the air. As time went on, Louis grew more and more dependent on her soothing charm; she amused him. As he came back tired from a day's hunting, she would appear in a milkmaid's dress, bringing a glass of warm milk for him. She built a small theatre at Bellevue: in one gallery Verbreck had carved light garlands of flowers along the whole length of the walls: these were coloured by other artists, and then used to frame a series of panels by her great friend, the painter Boucher.

Her struggle against the Court was continuous: they could not ignore her, but it was possible to be very rude. The Pompadour took all the chairs out of her bedroom so that the aristocrats would have to stand. But there was an occasional humiliation. For a long time she had tried to get the services of the fashionable, and rather supercilious, hairdresser Dagé. At last he came, and the Pompadour asked why he was all the rage. 'Because I was the other one's hairdresser', he replied, meaning the Duchesse de Châteauroux.

By 1750 she was spending a million francs a year; as her beauty disappeared, she sought more and more to be remembered as a patron of the arts. Voltaire, Diderot, D'Alembert – the leading Encyclopaedists – enjoyed her support. She meddled in foreign affairs, favouring Austria because Maria Theresa had written a friendly letter to her: while Frederick the Great was snubbed because of some scurrilous doggerel he wrote about the Pompadour. Her meddling led to the disastrous Seven Years War.

'In every place where there are human beings,' she wrote to her brother, 'you will find deceit and every vice of which mortals are capable. To live by oneself, however, would be very monotonous, so one must endure them along with their faults and pretend not to notice them.' A prim judgement: but the real Pompadour. She had the abilities of a Theodora, but the inclination of a *Hausfrau*.

Her last days were sad. Louis's taste was for adolescent girls; but his affection for her remained, his only comment, as he watched her funeral procession in the rain, was 'the marquise has chosen bad weather for her journey'.

ILLUSTRATION: Plate 11.

The little wasp of Twickenham

POPE, Alexander, (1688–1744), English poet, the greatest master of satire in English, and the consummate representative of his age. His *Essay on Man* is a pithy and delightful reference book to the cross-currents of ideas by which men lived in the early eighteenth century, and though the general mass of people may not read him now, more popular phrases can be traced back to him than to any other poet in the language, with the exception of Shakespeare – *e.g.*'Fools rush in where angels fear to tread' or 'A little learning is a dangerous thing', both of which come from Pope's *Essay on Criticism.*

He was the son of the late middle age of a wholesale linen-draper and a lady of a Yorkshire county family. They were Catholics, which meant that Pope shared the social and political disabilities suffered then by those of his faith. Moreover, he was pitiable in physique, inhabitating 'a tender crazy little carcase', and in later years he referred to 'that long disease, my life'. He was about four foot six high, miserably thin, afflicted with curvature of the spine as a result of Pott's disease – a tubercular infection. He made up for his frailty by an enormous moral and physical courage. As Swinburne said of him, 'the spirit which was in Pope ... was almost as good as bodiless. And what a spirit it was! How fiery bright and dauntless!' It needed to be, for very early in his career he was viciously attacked by Grub Street, and he retorted in scathing satire which has made immortal many men who would otherwise be forgotten, not only in *The Dunciad* but in some of the *Imitations from Horace*:

> Envy must own, I live among the Great,
> No Pimp of Pleasure, and no Spy of State,
> With Eyes that pry not, Tongue that ne'er repeats,
> Fond to spread Friendships, but to cover Heats,
> To help who want, to forward who excel;
> This, all who know me, know; who love me, tell;
> And who unknown defame me, let them be
> Scriblers or Peers, alike are *Mob* to me ...

Yet if to many he may seem merely a satirist – a calling ranked too low by the sentimental queasiness of our time – there is often a vein of sadness running through his work, as, for instance, at the end of that delicious social satire, that charming game, *The Rape of the Lock*. His romantic epistle *From Heloise to Abelard* was regarded by Byron as the most passionate poem in the language; *Windsor Forest* is at once a great country poem and a great patriotic one, and his translation of Homer was for more than a century the accepted version.

He made his name very early, and if he infuriated jealous pygmies, he was the close friend of such towering figures as Swift, of such sensitive, able people as Congreve, Prior and Gay. He achieved the position of being 'caressed', as they said in those days, by the great cultured Whig lords, though in politics he was a Tory. If sometimes a touch of personal animus inspires his lines, he attacked always the mean, the ignoble, the pretentious; and what he felt he was most fighting against was the decay of standards he considered to be corroding his time, in literature, in manners, in morals, in politics, in integrity generally. Of course he was not perfect; he was too much of a human being for that. Much on the defensive, he was occasionally guilty of lies and evasions; and when fools snapped at him, he hit back hard –

> I nod in Company, I wake at Night
> Fools rush into my Head, and so I write.

He referred to himself in his youth as 'The gayest valetudinaire. Most thinking rake alive', but he was deeply meditative, and a profoundly religious Deist. Though he is most often thought of as battling furiously and intemperately with the writers of his day, as 'the little wasp of Twickenham', the truer picture of him is that of a devoted son preferring to pass most of his time in his garden and grotto, giving his time to his poetry and his friends – and his dogs – but chiefly to his poetry, which he wore himself out in perfecting.

'*I have neglected nothing*'

POUSSIN, Nicholas, (1594–1665), one of the gravest and most rewarding of the world's painters. Poussin's portrait of himself at fifty-six, in the Louvre, in Paris, expresses his own honest self-knowledge. He is the master of order, yet a man: behind him are the severe rectangles of an abstract painter; there is Poussin, heavy-featured and blue-eyed – and ill-tempered, it might seem to someone who did not value the earnestness, the concentration, and the humility also in the face and the pose.

He was the son of peasants in the Andelys district of France, who left secretly for Paris when he was eighteen, determined to become a painter. Rome and antiquity beckoned him; and adapting Titian's colouring in his own electric way, he learned to use it in canvases where men, gods, ruins, temples, trees and landscape dance in the most solemn formality. He wished to stir in us wonder at the monumental, the ordered and the noble. Rhythms are slow and solemn, the combination of colours, particularly in the range of blues and of yellow-browns like the outpourings of tea, are thrillingly peculiar.

Throughout his life in Rome, Poussin felt the vision of antiquity. A story was told of him meeting among the ruins a tourist who wished to take home some rarity to remind him of Rome. 'I can give you', said Poussin, 'the finest rarity you could desire': he picked up a handful of earth mixed with fragments of porphyry and marble: 'Here, Signore, take this to your museum, and say this is ancient Rome.'

Poussin's pictures reach an extreme of austerity, and they need learning – perhaps by way of the cool intensity of the landscapes – *The Seasons*, for example, in the Louvre, which he painted in his old age for Cardinal Richelieu; or the landscape with the recovery of the ashes of Phocion (Lord Derby, Knowsley Hall), placid, clear and complex, at once plain and as mysterious and monumental as higher mathematics, full of details (such as the figure of the woman walking under the trees, or the bathers undressing and bathing), each of which would have served later artists for a whole canvas.

Living through his eyes, drawing from nature and the antique, studying perspective, practising anatomy under a famous surgeon, and reading the classics, Poussin was able to say 'I have neglected nothing', which was no more than a simple statement of the truth.

ILLUSTRATION: Page 367.

Sense and soda-water

PRIESTLEY, Joseph, (1733–1804), English Unitarian minister and radical, who engaged in laboratory experiments 'as a relaxation from his other studies'. He invented soda-water and discovered oxygen.

Son of a cloth-finisher in Wakefield, Priestley carried to the height of genius the characteristics of a Yorkshire craftsman. He had exceptional energy, a strong sense of individual liberty and a Yorkshire accent, and was opposed to style on principle, aiming to be not 'a fine writer but ... a useful one'. Human society, he wrote in his *Essay on Government* (1768), exists for 'the good and happiness of the members'. It was from this sentence that Bentham (q.v.) derived his definition of the ideal society as that which gave the 'greatest happiness to the greatest number'. With regard to revolutions, Priestley asked: 'In the name of God ... what principles are those which ought to restrain an injured and insulted people from asserting their natural rights?'

He had strong human feelings. 'Being fond of domestic life, I got a habit of writing on any subject by the parlour fire, with my wife and children about me, without experiencing any inconvenience from such interruptions ... these are useful habits, which studious persons in general might acquire, if they would, and many persons greatly distress themselves, and others, by the idea that they can do nothing except in perfect solitude and silence.'

In 1766 he was introduced to Benjamin Franklin, and to Price, the founder of the modern theory of insurance. Franklin encouraged him to write the *History of Electricity*. Within the year, the book was written and printed, and Priestley was elected a Fellow of the Royal Society. In 1767 he became minister at Leeds, and it was while living next door to a brewery that he made experiments with the carbon dioxide from the fermentation vats, thus inventing soda-water. Priestley was recommended by Price to the statesman Lord Shelburne as librarian, and he spent seven years in his service. He accompanied the future prime minister on a grand visit to France in 1774, and told Lavoisier at dinner of his discovery of oxygen.

Meanwhile, Priestley's theological and social writings became more and more radical, which made his patron less and less comfortable; so Priestley accepted a ministry in Birmingham, where he was the associate of Boulton, James Watt and Erasmus Darwin in the famous Lunar Society. After the French Revolution, Priestley was invited to be a member of the National Convention, and was elected an Honorary Citizen of France. The Birmingham mob was incited to sack and burn his house, and those of other dissenters, on the anniversary of the fall of the Bastille. Priestley moved to London, but he was cold-shouldered for his radical views, and emigrated, in consequence, to America in 1794, where he lived out his life. He was the epitome of the radical nonconformist, and one of the most instructive figures of his time.

In the cork-lined room

PROUST, Marcel, (1871–1922), French novelist. A biography of this great writer is bound to be of secondary interest. We cannot help thinking of Proust as the 'I' (critics call him Marcel), who tells his sixteen-volume story *Remembrance of Things Past* (*À la recherche du temps perdu*) – and his personality, whom we know from the inside, must be one of the vividest egos in all literature.

But though his imaginative life so much surpassed his real life in interest, it was a superstructure upon it. He was born in Paris, the eldest son of a doctor from Illiers who had married into a cultivated Jewish family of the name of Weil. He was a sickly child and an ailing and unhealthy man, neurotic, insomniac, asthmatic and homosexual. Fortunately he inherited considerable wealth, which enabled him to gratify his taste for the society of the Faubourg Saint Germain and served as a protective shell for his hypersensitive character. His ways grew more and more peculiar with middle age. He would drive out into the country to see a landscape through the windows of a hermetically closed carriage, he would question hotel managers for hours about the habits of their guests and his huge tips to servants were a byword. For long viewed as an elegant dilettante, in his last years he secluded himself from society in a cork-lined room and devoted himself body and soul to his work. He laboured in a squalid dressing-gown or in bed. He died in 1922, when only a few volumes of his great work had been published—*Du côté de chez Swann* (*Swann's Way*) in 1913, *À l'ombre des jeunes filles en fleurs* (*Within a Budding Grove*) in 1918, and the first part of *Sodome et Gomorrhe* (*The Cities of the Plain*), which appeared in the year of his death. The remaining volumes were published posthumously, the last, *Le Temps retrouvé* (*Time Regained*) appearing only in 1927.

Readers nearly always feel tempted to look for 'keys' to Proust's work, which is flattering to the author; we know the characters and scenes so well – the dining-room at the hotel at Balbec like a great aquarium, the leafy walks round Combray, the iron table in the garden at which Swann sat talking with young Marcel's parents, Saint Loup for ever chasing his monocle, the icy stare of the Baron de Charlus – that it is hard to believe Proust's world is not real. But his characters are composite like his geography; Balbec is based partly on Concarneau in Brittany where

Proust spent holidays as a boy, partly on Cabourg in Normandy and so on, and no one has ever identified Madame Verdurin, Charlus or Morel exactly.

Proust presents us with the most sensitive of all pictures of the qualitative civilization which began disappearing for ever with the first World War; the France of the Impressionist painters, of Anatole France and of the Dreyfus case. But this is only a minimal part of his achievement. He introduced an entirely new concept of time into his novel – Henri Bergson, who was a distant relative by marriage, was elaborating his philosophy of time and creative evolution at the same period. Proust's immense sentences, with their pauses and divagations and minutiae of analysis, are necessary for his new interpretation of life in terms of time; and all goes to reinforce the tragedy of disillusion when we are shown the same people, noblemen, *nouveaux riches*, servants, first through the idyllic eyes of boyhood in the earlier volumes, then after the revelations of corruption as in *The Cities of the Plain* and the Albertine books, and the achievement of 'the act of physical possession in which, paradoxically, the possessor possesses nothing', and last of all when they are mere mummies, dressed-up dolls.

There are contradictions and mistakes in the posthumously published volumes, and had he lived there is no doubt that Proust would have added much to them – he had the habit of inserting whole pages of description and analysis into his proofs. But this does not mean that *Remembrance of Things Past* is incomplete as it stands. The volumes obey a minutely elaborate plan, and details that at first seem irrelevant, such as a description of how a woman wore her hat, or why a servant's dialect altered, are a means for reinforcing Proust's presentation of a cosmos which is a flux of change and regarding which the essential data are unknown to man.

Incense and architecture

PUGIN, Augustus Welby Northmore, (1812–1852), English architect who in part was responsible for the Houses of Parliament. Ruskin called him 'not a great architect, but one of the smallest possible or conceivable architects'; Pugin said of himself, 'I have done the work of a hundred years in forty and it has worn me out.' The work, according to Pugin, was to bring

England back to Catholicism by restoring Gothic glories. In fact, architecture of our day, which looks most removed from Pugin's revivalism, is different because Pugin lived. In modernism the functional element is Germanic, the romantic element is English springing from the seeds which Pugin sowed.

Pugin's father was a French *émigré*, his mother a fanatical protestant sectarian. As a young man he distressed his parents by dressing as a seaman, designing stage scenery and marrying a beautiful girl of seventeen, only two years younger than himself. She died a year later, whereupon he began his 'tireless search for ancient beauty, and found the Road to Rome'. He wanted to restore what he called 'the real thing' – vestments, pyxes, sedilia, rood screens, Ruskin (q.v.) pouring contempt on him as 'one who was stitched into a new creed by the gold thread on priests' petticoats, jangled into a change of conscience by the chimes of a belfry'. In 1836 he published his *Contrasts; or a Parallel between the Architecture of the 15th and 19th Centuries*, which was an architectural counterpart to Carlyle's *Past and Present* – the well-ordered medieval world was laid devastatingly alongside the squalor of the new age, the alms-house by the workhouse, etc.

Into twenty-five working years, Pugin crowded three marriages, four polemical books, two cathedrals, thirty churches, mansions, schools, a monastery – and the Houses of Parliament, the last an old subject of controversy. Barry was the architect of the Houses of Parliament. Pugin gave him full credit for the plan, and Barry attempted to conceal Pugin's share. In fact, wherever Pugin touched the work – there are eight portfolios of his drawings – the architecture blazes into life. The thrones and the Peers' Library remain as masterpieces of the Victorian Age.

For his own fame or proper recognition, Pugin was born a little too soon. He was a medievalist before Ruskin, a craftsman before William Morris wrote passionately of craftsmanship, a convert to Rome before conversion was respectable, an earnest Victorian grappling with pre-Victorian society. His fanaticism makes him seem at times a little comic. After visiting the theologian W. G. Ward at Balliol College in Oxford, he wrote, 'What an extraordinary thing that so glorious a man should be living in a room without mullions.' Apart from the Houses of Parliament, too much of his work looks thin and starved; he was accused of 'starving his roof-tree to gild his altar'.

ILLUSTRATION: Page 274.

Henry Purcell

PURCELL, Henry, (1658–1695), the greatest of English composers, 'in whose person', remarked Dryden the poet (q.v.), 'we have at length found an Englishman equal with the best abroad'.

'There is nothing in Nature that is great and beautiful,' wrote a critic of Purcell's generation, 'without Rule and Order; and the more Rule and Order, and Harmony, we find in the Objects that strike our Senses, the more Worthy and Noble we esteem them. I humbly conceive that it is the same in Art ...' Purcell's time of rule, order and harmony coincided among his elders with Dryden and Rochester in poetry, and Sir Isaac Newton in science and speculation, among those more nearly of his age with Defoe, Swift, and Congreve the dramatist. Charles II was his 'brisk and airy prince', who liked a tune, enjoyed tapping his feet in church, and sent his musician Pelham Humphrey to Lulli, the Italianate French composer, to learn how to write good church music. One might expect, then, that Purcell would vary between light and grave, within the dictates of order, between the Restoration ethos and the more solemn line and grain of Dryden, whose work he set to music.

In 1679, when he was twenty-two, Purcell became organist at Westminster Abbey, 'the famous Mr Purcell', 'the great Mr Purcell' of panegyrists, who forgot to say more about him. In that situation, Purcell stood between the poles of the gay and the grand. He was by no means impervious to Restoration comedy, and there are delectable improprieties in his catches – and broadness as well, as in a drunken piece which allows the singer rests for belching. Some of his finest music was written for ephemeral stage productions. If a play was in danger of failing, the author was instructed to scribble in 'Come, sirs, a song', and Mr Purcell was asked to write something to improve the occasion. Unhappily, when the plays descended into limbo, they dragged much of the music with them. In his instrumental sonatas Purcell confessedly imitated Italian models, with the intention of bringing 'the Seriousness and gravity of that sort of Music into vogue and reputation among our Country-men, whose humour, 'tis time now, should begin to loath the levity and balladry of our neighbours' (the French). But this 'imitative' music of Purcell's ended by being wholly Purcellian, and never more so than in the vocal music, where the melodic lines are miraculously wedded to the inflections of English speech.

To the characterization in his operas he brought a psychological insight new to English music. Not the least charming of his qualities is his immediate response to the sense of the words he is setting. Sometimes he carries this to excess, and the coupling of two words such as 'high' and 'low' will incite him to the most violent changes of pitch. The drooping of the Cupids' wings in the final chorus of *Dido and Aeneas* (1689) is an instance of a musical image of profound force. There is indeed no finer evidence of Purcell's genius than the vividness of expression and the elegiac grandeur of the *Dido and Aeneas*. When he died in 1695 – a youngish man of thirty-seven – he was appropriately buried underneath the organ of Westminster Abbey. Handel was then ten years old.

'Dead mirth of my delirious days'

PUSHKIN, Aleksandr Sergeyevich, (1799–1837). The greatest of Russian poets, and a follower of Byron, whom he far surpasses.

> As leaden as the aftermath of wine
> Is the dead mirth of my delirious days;
> And as wine waxes strong with age, so weighs
> More heavily the past on my decline.
> My path is dim. The future's troubled sea
> Foretokens only toil and grief to me.
> But oh! my friends, I do not ask to die!
> I crave more life, more dreams, more agony!
> Midmost the care, the panic, the distress,
> I know that I shall taste of happiness.

– wrote Pushkin in his poem *Elegy* (1830), shortly before his marriage to N. N. Goncharova, as though in anticipation of the grief and final tragedy it would lead to eventually.

Pushkin belonged to an old Russian family with an odd admixture of negro blood inherited from his maternal great-grandfather, General Ibrahim Hannibal, Peter the Great's 'negro' and reputedly an Abyssinian prince. It was enough to give him a negro look, clear in paintings of him and in his own self-portrait sketches. Rightly Pushkin is regarded as the founder of modern Russian literature, yet on Pushkin himself the most important influence had nothing to do with the usual aristocratic convention which he was given, and everything to do with his old nurse, Arina Rodionovna; it was she who told him the traditional Russian folk-tales, made him feel the beauties of the Russian language, and so taught him to despise the florid, artificial style affected by the Russian poets of the eighteenth century.

Everything he wrote about, Pushkin brought to life, partly because he can evoke such powerful emotion just by the sound and music of his verse (which makes his poems practically untranslatable). His poetry also is astonishingly compact without ever becoming obscure; and he has into the bargain an exquisite sense of humour which runs all through *Eugene Onegin* (1833), his greatest narrative poem, or as he calls it, his 'novel in verse', into which, according to Belinsky, 'he put in all his life, all his soul, all his love, feelings, views and ideals'.

As a result of a Court intrigue, Pushkin was killed in a duel with his wife's brother-in-law, Baron d'Anthès, a French *émigré* and the adopted son of the Dutch ambassador, whom he suspected to be his wife's lover. Turgenev, then a boy, met him at a concert a few days before his death and described him as a broad-chested man of medium height: 'I remember', he wrote 'his dark face, his African lips, the flash of his white teeth, his pendent side-whiskers, his dark jaundiced eyes with almost no eyebrows, and his curly hair. He threw a glance at me; the unceremonious way with which I stared at him must have annoyed him, for he looked vexed, shrugged – he did not seem to be in a good mood that day – and walked away. A few days later I saw him lying in his coffin ...'

ILLUSTRATION: Page 275.

Q

The average man

QUÉTELET, Adolphe, (1796–1874), Belgian statistician, inventor of the concept of the Average Man, and founder of Vital Statistics.

While an undergraduate he wrote libretti for three successful operas. His interest in science was aroused by the mathematician Garnier. He transferred his attention from literature to science by way of a study of Pascal, and his first mathematical discoveries were similar to the discoveries Pascal made in geometry. Quételet swiftly became a most admired lecturer. In Paris in 1823 he met Laplace, the French astronomer and mathematician who interested him in the theory of probability. He began to apply it to meteorology, and to wider and wider fields, and finally to the whole nature of man and human society.

He derived his concept of the Average Man (hardly a virtuous concept, though that is not Quételet's fault, when it supplies a target for journalism or advertising agents) in the first instance from his investigation of human measurements, especially of the chest measurements of Scottish soldiers, and heights of French conscripts. 'The man that I consider here is analogous to the centre of gravity in bodies; he is the mean about which oscillate the social elements; he is, so to speak, a fictitious being for whom all things proceed conformably to the average results obtained for society. If we wish to establish the basis of a social mechanics, it is he whom we should consider, without stopping to examine particular or anomalous cases.'

Quételet believed that the properties of the Average Man would guide the doctor to the best medical treatment, the writer to the most representative form of literature, and the politician to the sentiments and beliefs which formed public opinion. He foresaw the technique of the public opinion poll, market research, and advertising analysis. The biologist could discover racial characteristics, and the social scientist would be able to ascertain the laws of birth, growth, and decay of nations. He was deeply impressed by the remarkable invariability of the statistics of crime. The development of man was 'the result of his organization ... Society prepares the crime and the guilty is only the instrument by which it is accomplished.' The criminal was 'an expiatory victim for society'.

R

Gargantua and Pantagruel

RABELAIS, François, (c. 1490–1553), one of the great fertilizers of life and literature in the sixteenth century, with every Gallic quality but discipline – a vast vocabulary, an inexhaustible vitality, a (pre-cliché) Gargantuan appetite for the intellectual banquet of his age. With his head in the Republic of Letters, his feet in folklore and his broad bottom on his well-loved *pays de vache* of Touraine and Poitou, Rabelais contrived several volumes of reckless humour and noble thought, which passed through ninety-eight editions before the end of the century.

This great man added medicine to his studies in Latin, Greek, Theology, Law and Natural History. He made, in fact, a real reputation as a doctor, and his Pantagruelism – 'a certain jollity of mind, pickled in the scorn of fortune' – is a clinical attitude as well as a stoic philosophy. It was for his patients' relaxation and his own, he hinted, that he put out *Pantagruel* in time for the Lyons fair of 1533, and then slaked a thirst for overflowing life with *Gargantua* and those sequels which at last reach Cathay and that Oracle of the Bottle which announces 'Drink', as the answer to all things.

Of his personages, Gargantua, Pantagruel, Panurge, Friar John, who enter English literature through the magnificent translation of Sir Thomas Urquhart, the nearest to a character is Panurge, who is also a universal type – *l'homme moyen sensuel*, deflated by danger: 'O Destinies,' he says, 'why did you not spin me for a Cabbage-Planter? O how few are they to whom Jupiter has been so favourable as to predestinate them to plant Cabbage! They have always one Foot on the Ground and the other not far from it.'

The 'Rabelaisian' coarseness is the reverse of furtive. The prodigious drinking and eating and voiding, fighting and swiving, talking and voyaging, curiously contain the lesson of moderation in all things. Truth is Nature (Physis) who 'at her first burthen begat Beauty and Harmony'. The enemies are the offspring of Antiphysis, Calvinists and 'Popemongers' alike, 'dunces of the cowl', the ignorant and the fanatical. The Abbey of Thélème with its famous legend 'Do What Thou Wilt' implies, not libertinism, but a developed culture, since 'Men that are free, well-born, well-bred and conversant in honest companies, have naturally an instinct and spurre that prompteth them unto vertuous actions and withdraws them from vice, which is called honour.'

Rabelais paid two exciting visits to Italy, corresponded with Erasmus, and died as 'the good curé of Meudon' near Paris. The greatest French writers, and some English ones, acknowledged his influence. On the charge of atheism, which has been levelled against him, Anatole France said that Rabelais 'believed in God five days out of seven, which is a great deal'.

Saint of Islam

RABI'A of BASRA, (c. 717–801), greatest of the women saints of Islam. Every night, when she went on to her roof to pray, she began: 'O my Lord, the stars are shining and the eyes of men are closed, and kings have shut their doors and every lover is alone with his beloved, and here I am alone with Thee ...'

She was born, and lived all her long life, in Basra. She came from the poorest of homes; tradition tells that on the night of her birth there was no oil in the house, no lamp, and no clothes in which to wrap the new-born child. Her father, who already had three daughters and no son, was distressed at the birth of this fourth one (Rabi'a means 'fourth'), but Mohammed consoled him in a vision.

Her parents died in a famine while she was still a girl; the family was scattered and Rabi'a herself sold into slavery. By day she worked for her master; by night she prayed to her Lord. Her master, looking down at her through a window, overheard her: 'O my Lord, Thou knowest that the desire of my heart is to obey Thee, and that the light of my eye is in the service of thy court. If it rested with me, I should not cease for one hour from thy service, but Thou hast made me subject to a creature.' The next day her master sent for her and set her free. For a time she earned her living as a flute-player; for a time she lived as an anchoress. She never married. She made the Pilgrimage to Mecca, but found no satisfaction in the shrine: 'O my Lord, my heart is perplexed, whither shall I go? I am but a clod of earth, and that House (the Kaaba) is only a stone to me. Show Thyself in this very place.' God replied in her heart: 'O Rabi'a ... when Moses desired to see my face, I cast a few particles of my Glory upon the mountain, and it was rent in forty pieces. Be content with my Name.'

The religion of her time was founded on rewards and punishments; holiness was a dread of God, of death, of sin, of Hell-fire; its reward the pleasures of Paradise – and both Hell and Paradise are vividly described in the Koran. Rabi'a felt lost among all this. 'O my Lord, my plaint to Thee is that I am but a stranger in thy country, and lonely among thy worshippers.' The sign of sanctity was the power to work miracles; but Rabi'a said to her niece Zulfa: 'I am told they say that I find money in my place of prayer, and that I cook food in the pot without a fire. O daughter of my brother, if I had found such things in my house I would not have touched them; I tell you

that I buy my things and am blessed in them.' Then, of course, one must abjure the Devil; but when Rabi'a was asked: 'Do you hold Satan as an enemy?' she answered: 'My love for God leaves no room for hating Satan.' 'Have you no desire for Paradise?' they asked her. 'The Neighbour first, and then the House,' she said. 'Is it not enough for me that I am given leave to worship Him?'

The first biography of Rabi'a dates from four hundred years after her time, and is full of legends, some opposed to her doctrine. But there is one account of her, in old age, which sounds authentic: 'I went to Rabi'a, and she was a very old woman of eighty years, as if she were a worn-out skin almost falling down; and I saw in her house a reed-mat, and a clothes stand of Persian reed ... and perhaps there was a mat and an earthen jug and a bed of felt, which was also her prayer-carpet.' There she prayed that loveliest of all prayers: 'O my Lord, if I worship Thee from fear of Hell, burn me in Hell; and if I worship Thee from hope of Paradise, exclude me from Paradise; but if I worship Thee for Thine own sake, withhold not Thine Everlasting Beauty from me.'

Elizabeth's most sparkling courtier

RALEGH, Sir Walter (1552–1618). One of the most sparkling and extraordinary men of Elizabethan England, poet, prose writer, statesman, courtier, soldier, explorer, who ended his life under the executioner's axe.

Ralegh aspired to be the best of everything. From an obscure manor house in Devonshire and an Oxford college, soldiering in France and Ireland brought him as a proud and handsome young man to the court of Queen Elizabeth. He aspired to be the leading courtier, the Queen's favourite, he aspired to be the richest and the best dressed and the most powerful Englishman, he aspired to know the ablest and loftiest spirits of his time. He was the man of thought and letters as well as the man of action and fine steel. His love for one of the Queen's maids of honour, whom he married, brought him into disfavour, and opened up the long path to Ralegh's execution, but it also deepened experiences out of which the noblest of his poems were written.

Here was the man whose small V-shaped beard

was said to curl automatically with pride, who was the best hated man in England, and who could spend the night arguing on the immortality of the soul with a captured Roman Catholic priest, who was to be executed the next day. Here was the courtier, the favourite, and the ex-favourite, who could instruct his soul to

> Say to the Court it glows
> And shines like rotten wood,
> Say to the Church it shows
> What's good, and doth no good.
> If Church and Court reply,
> Then give them both the lie.

His career under the Queen was up and down. He conceived and financed the expedition which discovered Virginia (1585), and was responsible for the first English colony, though he never visited the North American continent himself. He went exploring to Guiana ten years later in search of gold, but his discoveries did not win back the Queen's favour. He did brilliant service in expeditions against Cadiz and to the Azores (1596 and 1597).

Elizabeth died in 1603. Before the year was out King James sent Ralegh to the Tower on a trumped-up charge of treason, for which he was farcically and scornfully tried and condemned. While he waited for execution, he wrote a superb farewell to his wife, sending her his love, to keep when he was dead, begging her not to mourn – 'Your mourning cannot avail me that am but dust', assuring her that her son was the child of a true man, who 'in his own respect, despiseth Death, and all his misshapen and ugly forms'. He was pardoned at the last moment, but after this rehearsal of death he was kept in the Tower of London, where he wrote his *History of the World*.

Ralegh always had visions of that golden country of Guiana which he had visited and never been allowed to test. The King was persuaded to release him from the Tower in 1616 – Ralegh was now an old man – to lead an expedition to the mines of Guiana. There was to be no fighting with the Spaniards. The expedition did not succeed, there was fighting with the Spaniards, and Ralegh came back in 1618 without gold. He was sent to the Tower and executed, on the old false conviction of being a traitor.

One poem by Ralegh magnificently ends

> Know that love is a careless child
> And forgets promise past,
> He is blind, he is deaf when he list
> And in faith never fast.

> His desire is a dureless content
> And a trustless joy,
> He is won with a world of despair
> And is lost with a toy.

> Of women kind such indeed is the love,
> Or the word love abused,
> Under which many childish desires
> And conceits are excused.

> But true love is a durable fire
> In the mind ever burning;
> Never sick, never old, never dead,
> From itself never turning.

Ralegh and his peerless and intelligent wife knew such a true love in the extremes of happiness, triumph, anxiety, dejection and danger. After he was beheaded, Elizabeth Ralegh is said to have kept her husband's embalmed head constantly by her, in a bag of red leather.

What happened in history

RANKE, Leopold von, (1795–1886). 'My heart leaps with happiness when I foresee the joy that executing an important work will give me,' one of this German historian's letters proclaimed, 'I swear daily to execute it without departing by a hair's breadth from the truth which I see.'

The truth which this Berlin professor saw was, he hoped, the truth, the whole truth and nothing but the truth, scientifically ascertained. He wished to present the past, in his own phrase 'as it really was'; and to this end von Ranke was the first to play the old mole in a large way among archives – particularly diplomatic archives in which he detected the chief 'facts' of history. For three years he lived in Italy, maintained by the Prussian state, buying every book, every document he could corner for the Berlin library, and in his published work he ranged through the past 'as it really was' of Prussia, France, England and the Papacy. Believing that facts could be ordered and mastered objectively, he made no allowance for the observer conditioning the observation. He was hardly aware, moreover, of social and economic history and their implications. But though history obstinately remains a myth, von Ranke was a Colossus among those German historians of the nineteenth century who revolutionized its methods. *Si monumentum requiris, circumspice*: annually, and particularly after 1918 and 1945, the archives of nations are ransacked, published and studied microscopically for those researchers searching for the past as it really was.

Discoverer of argon

RAYLEIGH, John William Strutt, third Baron, (1842–1919), English physicist and discoverer, with Ramsay, of argon and the inert gases in the atmosphere, explainer of why the sky is blue, of why we hear a musical note when we walk on stone flags beside a railing, and of a host of the properties of matter.

In his own day Rayleigh was much less famous than Lord Kelvin, yet many of the most modern ideas in aerodynamics, engineering design, and the properties of surfaces and lubrication go back to principles he was the first to elucidate. Rayleigh preferred seclusion to limelight. He was a landed aristocrat, who approached physics aristocratically and like a great landlord, maintaining a private laboratory on his estates near Chelmsford, where he chose to tackle problems which were fundamentally difficult, but not spectacular. A scientist of tremendous intellectual power, he was persuaded for a while to act as Cavendish professor at Cambridge after the premature death of Clerk-Maxwell, but he was back in his own laboratory at the first opportunity. His son, the fourth Baron Rayleigh, was also a considerable physicist, but diffident. His manner was not improved by the way in which his distinguished father would sit in the middle of the front row at his lectures at Royal Institution, and suggest corrections as they came to him.

'It is not honour I seek, but freedom'

REMBRANDT HARMENSZOON VAN RIJN, (1606–1669), a Dutchman, one of the world's major artists – painter, etcher and portraitist. 'The ugly and plebeian face by which he was favoured was accompanied by dusty and untidy clothes since it was his custom when working to wipe his brushes on himself ... When he worked, he would not have granted an audience to the first monarch in the world' (Baldinucci). Rembrandt looked deep into personality, comprehending the net of our relationships and the complex tissue of feeling and experience in which the simplest of us are involved.

Compare Pieter Bruegel (q.v.), who died in 1569, thirty-seven years before Rembrandt was born in Leyden to a prosperous miller. Bruegel painted mankind in the mass, Rembrandt painted man (and woman) in particular: he lives in a new world, which is to culminate in the novel – a world in which man is regarded as the feeling, brooding, suffering individual. In older painting a Bathsheba or a Danaë was a figure of myth: in Rembrandt's Bathsheba (1654) and Danaë (1636, Leningrad), each is a particular, individual woman, the one desired by King David and pondering her situation, the other awaiting, in every line and volume and in all the light and dark of her attitude, the onslaught of Jupiter in the shower of gold.

Rembrandt's vision quickly ripened and deepened. He moved to Amsterdam when he was twenty-five, where his portraits made him into the most wealthy and famous artist of Holland. Before he was thirty he had married the well-to-do Saskia van Uylenburgh, established himself in a good house, and was amassing the collection of art and antiques which included work by Caravaggio (q.v.), Tintoretto, Mantegna, Michelangelo and Ribera. The Dresden self-portrait of 1634 (no artist before Rembrandt painted so long and so revealing a gallery of self-portraits) shows him in the year of his marriage, extravagant, pleasure-loving, seated at table with Saskia on his knee; he wears a dashing plumed hat, and an embroidered coat with lace at the neck and wrists. On the table, a roast peacock waits to be eaten. Rembrandt laughs, and lifts a tall glass as if to toast his own success.

Rembrandt, however, was well on the way by this time to the understanding, the drama, the poetry and the superb composition of his pictures. In 1632 he had painted the *Anatomy Lesson of Dr Tulp* (Mauritshuis, The Hague), in which the spectators are dramatically related to each other and – life to death – to the corpse, a red tendon of which is raised up by the demonstrator. Blows and misfortunes came not to fuddle Rembrandt and shrivel him, but to deepen his compassionate and passionate understanding, for which he found more and more complete means of expression. In 1642 Saskia died. In the same year the huge group portrait *The Night Watch* (Rijksmuseum, Amsterdam) was badly received by those who had commissioned it, and who had expected a uniform celebration of themselves, not a selective drama of light and shade. Rembrandt turned away from the fashionable world, and the world from Rembrandt. He lost touch with his clients, and in 1657 he was declared bankrupt, only the help of his son Titus, and his housekeeper and mistress, Henrickje Stoffles, saving him from ruin. Wonderful dramas belong to this time of his life; not only the portraits, but *The Polish Rider*, that mysterious glory of the Frick Collection in New York, and the *Anatomy Lesson of Dr Deyman* (Rijksmuseum), the central portion of a painting which suffered from fire. The cleaned *Night Watch* and this *Anatomy Lesson* hang near each other in the Museum. *The Night Watch* has a wall to itself, curtains, and a special seat for spectators, a major *tour-de-force* of greater fame than it deserves. The small *Anatomy Lesson* hangs in mixed company on the wall, yet is one of the most compassionate, strong and noble images of life and death in the world's art. Rembrandt contrived an exact and electric tension here of life and death – death in the slack cadaver, life in the curled cuff of the indifferent attendant who holds the top of the skull like a chalice, and in the glittering bridge which the demonstrator makes with his knife between hand and hand, above the pink brain and the sagging scalp and hair, and dark cave gaping under the ribs.

In his portraits of beggars, old women, Jews, etc., Rembrandt painted outcasts with the sympathy and insight of an outcast. Using a limited range of browns and blacks, he heightened the psychological drama by concentrating the light on a part only of the face, rendering this light in thick rough paint, and allowing the rest of the form to disappear in shadow. 'In the autumn of his life', wrote one of his biographers, 'he kept company mostly with common people and such as practiced art... and he gave this reason for it: "If I want to give my mind diversion, then it is not honour I seek but freedom".'

Both Hendrickje and Titus died before him. He was alone and forgotten in his last years, yet he still painted with an unbroken will. A self-portrait (Cologne) shows him in a ragged smock and old cap, peering into the mirror, and smiling at what he sees – the reflection of a lined and toothless face.

ILLUSTRATION: Page 319.

Innocent sensuality

RENOIR, Pierre Auguste, (1841–1919), French artist, the always young painter of the joyfulness of art, life and nature, who wrote, 'I love pictures which make me want to stroll about in them, if they are landscapes, or to caress them, if they are women.'

Like most of the Impressionist painters who were his friends, he knew hardship and poverty during the earlier part of his life; during his later years he suffered extreme pain from gout and arthritis, which eventually crippled him; yet he remained a happy, contented man, expressing his own personal happiness in paintings which were frank, sensuous, always charming and often ravishingly beautiful, for to Renoir beauty was synonymous with happiness. In the Musée de Luxembourg is the large *Moulin de la Galette*, which he painted in 1876: in the gardens of a popular café, young men and girls are seated around the tables talking and drinking. Behind them couples are dancing under the trees. The dappled sunlight shining through the leaves and branches is represented with the brilliant colours of impressionism – pink and yellow patches of light, green, blue or purple shadows; and the whole scene has the gaiety and charm which we are apt to call the properties of a vanished period. 'The world knew how to laugh in those days!' wrote Renoir in his old age. 'Machinery had not absorbed all of life, you had leisure for enjoyment and no one was the worse for it.' Half-way through his career, after he had won fame, Renoir courageously, though logically, abandoned Impressionism for a more carefully drawn and finished style: 'About 1883 I had wrung Impressionism dry and I finally came to the conclusion that I knew neither how to paint nor how to draw. In a word, Impressionism was a blind alley as far as I was concerned.' His paintings of naked women in a pink, rounded, healthy nakedness, of cooks, housemaids, shop-girls, became a series of images of delightful fecundity and of a sensual innocence entirely uncontaminated. The learned skill behind these canvases came to a head in his large intricate painting of *The Bathers*, which gives an impression of spontaneity, though every item is exactly and faultlessly calculated.

During his last years, Renoir returned to the style of impressionism, using a 'rainbow' palette to paint the sunlit landscapes and female forms in which colour has become flesh and flesh part of nature; nothing else matters – least of all whether these glowing torsos have soul or even sense. During this time he was so crippled that he could not hold his brushes, but had to work with them strapped to his wrist, often in great pain. It was thus that Matisse found him when he visited him one day. 'Why do any more, master? Why torture yourself?' he asked. Renoir's reply was that 'the pain passes but the beauty remains'. The day before he died Renoir said, 'I am still making progress.'

Empire builder

RHODES, Cecil John, (1853–1902), the archetypal Empire builder, a sincere jingoist who confounded his critics by an altruism unsuspected until his death.

Rhodes had that singleness of purpose which is necessary for great success; he believed in himself, and never doubted the justice of his own actions. At the age of eighteen this fifth son of a country parson was earning his keep in South Africa; at thirty-six he was the head of the richest, most powerful company in the world, De Beers Consolidated Mines; at forty-nine he was dead. His patriotism was religious in its fervour: all Africa, North and South America, much of Asia, he wished to see under the British flag. He was supremely a man of the middle classes and the nineteenth century, whose dual motive was financial gain and public service. His health failed very early, and he was sent to Natal, where his brother grew cotton. Oxford, where he should have gone, became his Mecca: in 1873, recovered partly, he returned to England, and entered Oriel College. For eight years he studied, intermittently through bad health, yet all the while building up his South African interests. At last he took his degree. It was a devoted achievement, proof of a love of Oxford (rather than of learning), which was most handsomely remembered in his will.

There was in Rhodes something of the mystic, something of the stoic; he shares, with T. E. Lawrence and General Gordon, the strangeness of the successful expatriate. In his life appear key-fragments: a solitary, eight-month journey on foot and by ox-wagon through undeveloped territory; a remark after having nipped a Matabele rebellion in the bud by force of personality – 'these are the things that make life worth while'. He never had real friends, for individual friendships detracted from ability. His ideas were few, and they absorbed him entirely. There was nothing of the cultivated man about him.

Of his personality, the word demonic has been used: certainly, in the ruthless drive, in the ruthlessly held concept of a new nation which would rise powerfully under the British flag in the divided sub-continent, there was an inhuman quality. In 1890, when Rhodes was made prime minister of the Cape, his power was colossal: the prospect of an early death made him careless of policy, fond of the strong short cut. In his delicate dealings with the Dutch, he sanctioned Jameson's disastrous raid; his political stock fell, and the too simple myth of Rhodes as the scheming, selfish capitalist began. The last years of his life were spent in developing the vast territories to the north of the Zambesi that were given the name of Rhodesia as a tribute to his pioneering work.

The entire poet

RILKE, Rainer Maria, (1875–1926), German poet, born in Prague, whose influence is now European or world-wide, just as Rilke himself was at home in every part of the European Continent, from Russia to Spain, from Scandinavia to Italy.

Rilke's life was his poetry. He practised no other profession. Even his personal relationships, including an early marriage, were not allowed to interfere with his art. This led to a dilemma painfully apparent in several collections of his love-letters published since his death. Never well-to-do, often in poverty, he was able, all the same, to spend his mature years in leisured retirement – submerged in one of the great cities of Europe, or a guest in the houses of his distinguished patrons and friends. One of his patrons lent him the Château de Muzot at Sierre in Switzerland, where he wrote his last great works and died of a rare disease precipitated by the thorn of a rose that had poisoned his left hand. The rose was picked for a girl who was visiting him at the castle. Roses were the flowers of which he wrote again and again; late in his life he devoted a whole cycle of poems to their praise. His gravestone bears an inscription by himself:

> Rose, pure contradiction and delight
> Of being no one's sleep beneath so many
> Eyelids.

Yet Rilke was far from being a mere aesthete; his concern was the whole of life – and a great deal more than most of us are content to regard as the whole of life. Much of his work explores unexplored experience, groping sensitively into the world of things, plants and animals; and he was always occupied with death, which, he insisted, is 'the other half of life', a reality with which every one of us should come to terms. Death, considered as a part of existence, is as crucial in his early *Book of Hours* (1899–1903) as in his last major cycles, *Sonnets to Orpheus* (1922) and *Duino Elegies* (1912–1922).

Every country he visited, every kind of person he knew, every landscape or object that impressed him, added something to the ideas and images Rilke translated into poetry. An early visit to Russia confirmed for him the importance of pure feeling, that 'inwardness' which transforms the external world into something other than himself. His meeting with the French sculptor Rodin was also decisive; it was Rodin who taught him the importance of work for work's sake, thus opposing Rilke's tendency to be a passive receptacle for impressions that would flow out again into his poetry. *New Poems* (1907–1908) and the novel *Malte Laurids Brigge* (1903–1910) owe much to the effect of Rodin – and Paris; to Rilke's new discipline of observation, that ability to concentrate on a specific person or thing, much as a painter concentrates on his model. Here is a poem of this period, a study of a *Blue Hydrangea*:

The leaves are dry and dull, resembling
the green left over in a pot of paint,
behind the clustered blooms that have no blue
but merely mirror it from far away.

Their mirroring of it seems blurred with tears
and vague, as though they were to lose it soon;
and, as in old blue writing-paper,
there is some yellow in them, mauve and grey.

A washed-out colour as in children's pinafores,
a thing no longer worn, with nothing any more
to happen: how one feels a small life's brevity.

But suddenly the blueness seems renewed
within one of the clusters, and one sees
a touching blue rejoice before the green.

(Translated by Ruth Speirs.)

The originality of Rilke's last works is largely due to a happy combination of such minute observation with his peculiar capacity for 'inwardness'. He could never be dryly descriptive, since he was both a musical and a thoughtful poet; but now his original lyricism broadened out until it could contain the prosaic elements so evident in the free verse of the *Duino Elegies*:

Squares, o square in Paris, infinite show-place,
where the modiste Madame Lamort
winds and binds the restless ways of the world ...

Rilke never aspired to be the centre of a pseudo-religious cult. Too idolatrous admirers ought to ponder his own definition of fame as 'the aggregate of all the misunderstandings that collect around a new name'.

Stealer of fire

RIMBAUD, Arthur, (1854–1891), French poet of exalted and extreme romanticism. 'I say that one must be a *visionary* – that one must make oneself a VISIONARY,' he wrote to his schoolmaster friend, when at seventeen he was drafting a theory which owed much to occult writings. 'The poet makes himself a *visionary* through a long, immense and reasoned *derangement of all the senses*, all forms of love, of suffering, of madness; he seeks himself, he exhausts all poisons in himself to keep only their quintessences ... The poet is a true Stealer of Fire.'

Rimbaud's life was a series of flights from his strong-willed mother and his bourgeois home in the North of France – to Paris at the time of the Commune, to the poet Verlaine, with Verlaine to England, and at last out of Europe altogether, to Aden and Ethiopia. He was a boy of striking beauty, though with a peasant's body, lice in his hair, oaths in his mouth and a taste for drink and homosexual debauch. He tyrannized the bald-headed and submissive Verlaine, seduced him from his wife and baby, sent him to prison for two years in Belgium, made him blaspheme when he had been newly converted and then knocked him down. Their friendship, which produced Verlaine's *Romances sans paroles* and his own poems in verse and prose, *Les Illuminations*, was commented upon in Rimbaud's masterpiece, *Une Saison en Enfer* (A Season in Hell), the 'pagan, nigger book', in which he sardonically criticizes his life with Verlaine, and his former theories, re-affirms his alliance with the brutal under-dogs of civilization and takes his farewell of writing. 'Do I know Nature? do

I know myself? – *No more words*. I bury the dead in my belly. Shouts, drums, dance, dance, dance!'

So this boy, who developed his ideas by nineteen, had within three years or so abandoned authorship altogether. He had no more use for books, devoted himself to languages, practical affairs, atrocious hardships as a trader and traveller. He would have liked a son to bring up as 'a famous engineer, powerful and rich through science'. Rimbaud's life and writings are relevant to problems of art against science, individual mysticism against religious orthodoxy, primitivism against culture, or bohemianism in opposition to bourgeois society.

ILLUSTRATION: Page 278.

Jacobin leader

ROBESPIERRE, Maximilian, (1758–1794), French revolutionary, was the greatest of Jacobin leaders and became the symbol of the Terror. Carlyle called him 'the sea-green incorruptible'.

Robespierre came from Arras and was educated at the seminary of Louis-le-Grand, where he once presented a loyal address to Louis XVI. He set up as a provincial lawyer and specialized in philosophic enlightenment: he defended a client who had erected a lightning-conductor and resigned an official appointment rather than pass the death penalty. In 1789 he was elected to the States-General and acquired there a considerable reputation as a spokesman of democratic principles drawn from Rousseau. Wider fame came to him with the founding of the Jacobin club. He spoke there constantly; and his cold pedantic discourses corresponded exactly to the spirit of the members. In the critical year 1792 he opposed the romantic Girondists, who clamoured for foreign war; and even shrank from advocating a republic. Unlike Danton, he did not play a leading part in the overthrow of the monarchy on 10 August.

Great power came to him with the Convention, which met in September 1792. When the Jacobins seized power in May 1793 Robespierre was elected to the Committee of Public Safety and was henceforth its leading figure. While other members organized the armies, Robespierre looked after the Terror and the suppression of counter-revolution. His scruples against the death penalty now disappeared, though he always claimed that the Terror was a temporary measure. He regarded himself as the voice of the people; and therefore held that popular liberty was secured by the silencing of every voice except his own. Early in 1794 he sent Hebèrt and his followers to the guillotine for being too extreme; and then had Danton and his followers guillotined for being too moderate. He opposed the atheist trend of the revolution and established the worship of the Supreme Being, with himself as high priest. When he threatened new measures against the war-profiteers, he was overthrown and himself guillotined. With his death the Terror came to an unexpected end.

Richest man in the world

ROCKEFELLER, John Davison, (1839–1937), American industrialist, and benefactor, founder of Standard Oil, once the biggest industrial organization in the world.

Rockefeller's early life follows a traditional pattern of success: humble rural home, an atmosphere of thrift, moderate schooling. At the age of sixteen, he went to work for a commission merchant in Cleveland, Ohio. Business fascinated him; as it did every young American in that era, as though it were the exploration and conquest of a new continent, each man his own emperor. From the beginning Rockefeller worked hard, was conscientious and watched the money. One day his employer showed him a 4,000-dollar bill: 'As soon as he was gone I unlocked the safe,' he said, 'and taking out that note, stared at it with open eyes and mouth, and then replaced it, and double-locked the safe. It seemed like an awfully large sum to me, an unheard-of amount, and many times during the day did I open that safe to gaze longingly at the note.' Besides respect for money, Rockefeller acquired another habit in those early days: benefaction. Even as a poorly paid clerk, he would give away as much as five or six per cent of his salary to charity.

In that age only failure was immoral. The practices of combination and destruction that Rockefeller developed were perfectly proper in the eighteen-seventies; and early on Rockefeller had seen that oil was his way to prosperity; and by a ruthless devotion to self-interest he built up the Standard Oil Trust; all competitors squashed, all profits high.

How did he do it? 'Don't be a good fellow,' he once told a Bible class. 'Don't let good fellowship get the least hold on you ... It is my firm conviction that every downfall is traceable directly or indirectly to the victim's good fellowship, his good cheer among his friends, who come as quickly as they go. We have to apologize every day for this class of men who fill our hospitals, our asylums, our poor-houses, and the very gutters of our streets. Look on them and don't be a good fellow.'

To say that Rockefeller got nothing out of his money is to miss the point completely: all his inner needs were in business success. His life was simple, and he read little. He enjoyed talking; and one night he listened to a friend explaining the new Soviet system. The next morning Rockefeller admitted that it had given him a sleepless night. He lived to be ninety-eight, and saw himself turned in the eyes of the American public from a monster to a kindly old man. His gifts, to universities, medical centres, schools, totalled some 500,000,000 dollars.

Rockefeller was always a religious man. And he once said, and he certainly believed, that all the money he made was God's, and that he was the trustee.

ILLUSTRATION: Page 276.

Roland against the Saracens

ROLAND, (d. 778), the legendary paladin of Charlemagne's army, the hero of Roncevaux, exists historically only as a grain of truth, tucked in an old chronicle. The myth-makers, the minnesingers and troubadours of the romance-loving Middle Ages, seized this grain and turned it into a whole field of waving anecdotes.

Roland died in a rearguard action at Roncevaux in 778. It is very probable that the action did take place. Charlemagne invaded Spain in 778 to deliver the country from the Saracens. While balked before Saragossa, a Saxon revolt called him back to the Rhine. On the retreat to the Pyrenees, the rear part of his army was cut off by Basque guerillas, and destroyed. Among the slain, the chronicler records 'Hruodland, praefect of the Breton marches'. That is all we have: yet from the twelfth to the sixteenth centuries, the story of Roland grew in splendour: the small military action became a national defeat, the few Basques a vast Saracen army. The twelve peers, Roland's friendship with Oliver, Canelon's treachery, Roland's horse Vaillantif, Roland's horn Olifant, which he sounded with such final poignancy, when only himself and Oliver and two others remained alive, and Roland's sword Durandal – all these are the work of romancers.

The story's spread is a good example of the ballad tradition: the passing on of a story through successive generations orally, until at last it is written down. The French *Chanson de Roland* is the most famous account of the hero, a Roland with all the romantic qualities of the medieval epic; who, even more than the Cid (q.v.), is bygone chivalry embodied in fiction. Taillefer, who struck the first blow against the English at the battle of Hastings, chanted the fame of Roland in front of the Norman soldiers of William the Conqueror.

Whether Hruodland the praefect of the Breton marches was at all like Roland the hero does not really matter. Roland's importance is that he was the prime exemplar of chivalry.

'Je suis Ronsard'

RONSARD, Pierre de, (1525–c. 1585), French poet of unabashed pride in his own fame and performance, poet royal and chief of the group known as *La Pléiade*, the Pleiades, after the constellation and a group of Greek poets. Others were Joachim du Bellay and Remy Belleau.

What is the worst fate for a great poet? To be of historical importance; and to be known by six outstanding anthology pieces; which is the fate of Ronsard. Joachim du Bellay in the manifesto of the group *La Deffence et illustration de la langue francoyse* (1549) set out the programme: 'Leave all that old French poetry – the rondeaux, ballades, virelais, chants royaux, chansons, and all the other frippery – to verse competitions and festivals; instead sing me the odes still unknown to the Muse of France, tuning your lute to the lyre of Greece and Rome' – which applies well to Ronsard, though he only used the name of the group casually and after its work had been done. *La Pléiade* was taken up as a label by his enemies – since he made no bones about his pride, and claimed the first place; which Europe accorded him. Pope Pius V wrote him letters, Mary Stuart sent him plate and her portrait for his library; Elizabeth sent him a rich diamond; Charles IX wrote to his Christian brother, the King of Portugal, for the Order of Christ for him; Philip II of Spain was good enough to signify his approbation of Ronsard's *Discourses*. The poets, from Jan Kochanowski of Poland to Sir Philip Sidney in England and Lope de Vega in Spain, concurred. And for the rest, Ronsard told them firmly *Vous estes tous yssus de la grandeur de moy* – 'you are all the offspring of my greatness'.

Like Yeats (who loved him and resembled him in many ways), he constantly tinkered with the text of his poems; like Ben Jonson (who also resembled him), he watched the printing of every comma; and on his title page he signed himself: PIERRE DE RONSARD, GENTILHOMME VANDO-MOIS – gentleman of Vendôme. That tells us much, for a country gentleman he was, and his countryside remembers him still. Though he was bred as a court page, and lived to be a court poet; though he could flatter with the best, and tout for a benefice (he took minor orders, was a court Chaplain, and hoped for a Bishopric), yet he could say, and mean it, *Je hay la Court comme la mort* – 'I hate the Court like death.'

> When I go twenty months or more
> And do not see Vendôme
> Full then of vagabonding dreams
> And of regret and care
> To crags I make my moan,
> And caves and woods and streams.

The open air was his delight: horsemanship, hunting, steeplechasing, the tourney, fencing, tennis – and into middle age, when arthritis had already attacked him, he still practised at the vaulting-horse. To these, he added the other delights of the country gentleman of his time – music, poetry, and love, and food and drink; reading, and classical learning, and architecture. And, special to himself, Fame. He wrote at the end of his will: 'No one of my time has been so filled with fame as I; I have lived in it and loved and triumphed in it through my time past, and now I leave it to my country to garner and possess after I shall be dead.'

He was very tall, grey, and bald at thirty, and deaf, so that old age, the evanescence of things, the ravages of time, the symbolism of the falling rose which is everywhere in his verse, were more than commonplaces to him:

> My sweet young days are past,
> My early strength has cracked,

> My teeth have lost their white,
> My locks their youthful black.

About his loves, it is hard to be sure where poetry stops and autobiography begins (which is true of most Renaissance poets from Wyatt to Donne). The first of them, Cassandre Salviati, he certainly never possessed but worshipped from far off, like a true disciple of Petrarch. She was half French and half Italian, the daughter of a Florentine banker; and he saw her first at Blois, singing a Burgundian air to the lute. His last love, Hélène de Surgères, was half Spanish, and lady-in-waiting to Catherine de' Medici. According to his friends, she was not very good looking, but she was very smart and intellectual and opinionated. He fell in love with her when he was fifty; and though she was impressed, she was cold to him – and perhaps to all men. To her he wrote the most wonderful of his poems, the *Sonnets pour Hélène*, in which he no longer bothers about being an artist; but being one, can make an absurd affair both beautiful and sad. As for love's pleasures, he probably got most from his little country girl, Marie, and the Parisienne Genèvre; neither of whom was a lady, but both of whom seem to have deserved the attentions of the first poet of Europe. Genèvre he found sitting at her door in the Faubourg St Marcel in 1561. He wrote that at last she timidly enquired his name, and whether or no he had loved other women. *Je suis, dis-je, Ronsard* –

> I am, I said, Ronsard. Let that suffice:
> Whom France with song and honour prizes at such price,
> The Muses' darling, whose delightful verse
> Tokens his glory through this mighty universe.

X-Rays

RÖNTGEN, Wilhelm Conrad, (1845–1923), German physicist and discoverer of X-rays, was a careful and thorough scientist, who, like many others in the last quarter of the nineteenth century, was investigating what happens when electric sparks are sent through tubes containing gases at low pressure.

Early in 1895 Röntgen noticed that when these tubes were being operated, substances such as barium platinocyanide were apt to fluoresce, or glitter, when near to the tube, even when the whole tube was completely enclosed in black cardboard. He saw at once that he had discovered a new kind of radiation which could penetrate ordinarily opaque substances. In intense excitement, he worked almost without sleeping for two or three months, elucidating all the main features of the rays. He did not mention his discovery to a soul, not even to his wife, until he had established the main points. Then at a meeting of the Würzburg Physical and Medical Society in December 1895 he read a paper which gave a virtually complete account of the essence of the new phenomenon. In this highly condensed paper of four thousand words he had given, or hinted at, the fundamental properties of X-rays. It is difficult to think of any other discovery in the history of science which was so sudden and so complete in principle. The shock to the scientific world was tremendous. It opened the new era of experimental physics, as Rutherford was never tired of saying, and within twelve months had inspired the discovery of radioactivity.

The greatest effect of his discovery was to close the book of classical physics, and open the volume of the twentieth century.

President of the New Deal

ROOSEVELT, Franklin Delano, (1882–1945), four times President of the United States, was the towering figure of recent American history and the most celebrated President since Lincoln.

Born of a rich New York family, Roosevelt joined the Democratic party and served under President Wilson. Though crippled by infantile paralysis in the prime of life, he never slackened his public activities. He served as Governor of New York, and was elected President in 1932 by an overwhelming Democratic majority. America had touched the lowest point of the great economic crisis. Roosevelt, who never had defined economic theories, now acted resolutely on the impulse of the moment. In 1933 he inaugurated 'the New Deal', giving to America the social security and controlled economy which private enterprise had hitherto resisted. American economic life was revolutionized within a few years. The industrial workers were brought within the democratic system for the first time, and economy was revived by a liberal credit policy. The New Deal brought prosperity to the bankrupt farmers, and great schemes, such as the Tennessee Valley Authority, restored derelict areas. Roosevelt saved American capitalism, though he was not loved by the capitalists.

In foreign affairs he was originally an isolationist, repudiating all responsibility for events overseas. He accepted the proposals for American neutrality and favoured appeasement of the dictators. Gradually, however, he began to mobilize public opinion against them, though never giving a constructive lead. In 1940 he gave indirect support to Great Britain, but he kept the United States out of war until driven into it by the Japanese attack at Pearl Harbour. He then developed as a great war-leader, directing operations on the western side. He had always contrived to have his way in home politics by personal charm, and he supposed that the same methods would work with Stalin. The meetings of the Big Three at Teheran and Yalta demonstrated the limitations of this method. At the end of his life his cajoling of Stalin had ceased to work, and when he died suddenly in 1945 a break with the Soviet Union was already in sight. Roosevelt was a great phrase-maker and the first President to exploit the potentialities of radio. He had neither principles nor ideas; and his successes and failures demonstrated what improvisation can do – and what it cannot.

The trumpeter's son

ROSSINI, Gioacchino Antonio, (1792–1868), Italian composer of comic operas.

His gift was inherited. Rossini's father was municipal trumpeter – master of the gayest instrument – at Pesaro on the Adriatic. His amiable manner and his high spirits won him the nickname of Vivazza, 'the lively one', and recommended him to the Muses as the right father for the Master of Italian *opera buffa*. Gioacchino began life in the right way: he was adventurous and troublesome, he neglected his lessons, but sang like the angel he so obviously was not. His official musical training was so unsuitable that in private he was driven to studying the works of Haydn and Mozart; and he emerged upon a delighted world as a precocious but very likeable young man. His first opera, *La Cambiale de Matrimonio*, was produced when he was eighteen, and his remaining operas – no fewer than thirty-eight altogether – appeared during the next nineteen years. The success of the early works culminated in *Tancredi* (1813) and *L'Italiana in Algeri* (1813). Venice was enraptured. There was nothing Rossini would not attempt. He wrote an opera on Elizabeth of England; he married his impresario's mistress and remained on excellent terms with his impresario; in 1816 he even challenged the fame of Paisiello's vastly popular setting of Beaumarchais' comedy *The Barber of Seville* by making a version of his own. This last venture was rewarded with whistles, shouts, and laughter at the first performance, success at the second, and world-wide renown ever since. Once, when Rossini had been asked which of his operas he liked the best, this student of Mozart quickly replied, '*Don Giovanni*'. But beneath his genuine humility he must have concealed a justified pride in *The Barber*; Beethoven, the gruff and morose Beethoven, praised it to his face in the warmest terms.

Rossini was by now an international celebrity, which changed him not at all, except that he could more easily indulge his epicurean tastes. In London he sang duets with George IV, and in Paris he settled down as 'Composer to His Majesty and Inspector General of Singing' at 20,000 francs a year. This post was created specially for Rossini who, with solemn face, used to listen out of his window to the singers in the street, and explain to his friends that he was carrying out his official duties. In 1829, with the grand opera *William Tell*, Rossini abruptly closed his operatic career. He was then at the height of his fame.

During the years of silence which followed there were times in which music was almost forgotten by Rossini, who was ill both in mind and body. In 1856 the once vigorous composer, now corpulent and decrepit, was ordered to 'take the baths' in Germany. He did so, and returned to Paris a cured man. His last eleven years were enlivened by a quieter and more intimate contact with music. At his own home he held his famous *soirées musicales*, and in his leisure time wrote 186 musical trifles which he entitled *Sins of My Old Age*. In some respects these remarkable pieces look forward to the music of Chabrier and Satie (qq.v.); in their fantastic humour and apparent insouciance they seem to hide the anxiety of a sincere, sensitive artist who looked back upon his years of achievement, and realized that he had never quite reached the top.

ILLUSTRATION: Page 318.

Banker of Europe

ROTHSCHILD, Nathan Mayer, (1777–1836), German-born banker who controlled the Finance of Europe from his London office.

He was a Jew from the Frankfurt ghetto: but his father determined that his sons should get on – and they did. 'History will quote the firm of the Rothschilds', wrote the *Augsburger Allgemeine Zeitung*, 'as a remarkable example of the attainment of enormous wealth and far-reaching political influence by a shrewd spirit of speculation, perseverance, and fraternal unity, aided by fortune and wit.' Nathan came to London; and worked for a while in Manchester. When the Prince of Hesse sent him large sums to invest, he managed them so well that his fortune and reputation were made. The event that made him famous was his payment of the English army during the Peninsular War. He bought £800,000 of gold that the Government needed. 'The government sent for me and said that they must have it. When they had got it, they did not know how to get it to Portugal. I undertook all that' – an army of Rothschild agents crossed the hostile frontiers each with a small sum – 'it was the best business that I have ever done.'

Rothschild was soon a magic name. He cared little for comforts; he made no attempt to wander off into other diversions. Through his brothers in the European capitals, and a highly efficient information service (and carrier pigeons by the basketful), he was able to keep profitably ahead of his rivals.

The story of how he saved the London Stock Exchange (and possibly Europe) is coloured with fancy; but its essence is true. By 1815, Rothschild was the biggest financial power in Europe: he had paid out nearly £18,000,000 in loans on the Continent in a year. Napoleon's escape from Elba alarmed the British Government and Herries, the Clerk of the Exchequer, asked Rothschild to provide gold. As the day of the battle with Napoleon drew near, Rothschild, so the story goes, could stand the suspense no longer. He hurried to the Continent, and followed the allied armies. As he saw, on the smoking field of Waterloo, that Napoleon had been defeated, he galloped to Ostend, and took a ship to England. The next morning he entered the Stock Exchange and leant against a column in his usual way. A look at his tired face – he had been seasick all night – was enough for the anxious brokers and jobbers: Napoleon must have won. Everyone sold frantically; and Rothschilds' secret agent bought and bought. He made £1,000,000 and saved the Exchange.

There was little wit to the man: 'Sometimes, to amuse myself, I give a beggar a guinea,' he said. 'He thinks I have made a mistake, and, for fear that I should find it out, off he runs as hard as he can. I advise you to give a beggar a guinea sometimes; it is very amusing.'

Where politics and money go arm in arm, it is hard to decide who is honest or what honesty implies: Rothschild was probably as honest as any – and he was much cleverer than most. He was all powerful, and determined: when the Bank of England refused to pay a bill he had sent to them – saying that they only paid on their own notes – Rothschild went to the Bank himself, handed over one of their five-pound notes, and asked for the equivalent gold. When he had it, he produced another one, and then another: by the end of the day he had reduced the Bank's gold reserve by £210,000; and he was prepared to keep this up for two months. The Bank capitulated.

The growing complexity of international affairs meant vast powers and vast profits for such monarchs of finance as Rothschild. He died suddenly at Frankfurt. One of the carrier pigeons was despatched with a short regal message attached to its leg, *Il est mort*.

A man without a skin

ROUSSEAU, Jean Jacques, (1712–1778), was the French philosophical writer who best exemplified in the pre-revolutionary period the romantic cult of the self, and all that went with it in the way of spontaneous natural affections, sensibility, sentimentality, intense moral fervour combined with the paranoiac egoism of a Shelley or a Byron. Yet foolish as he undoubtedly was from time to time, and pathetic as some of his revelations of emotional and sexual peculiarities may seem to be, Rousseau helped immensely the emancipation of the modern spirit.

The picture of Rousseau in his heyday is not without both charm and nobility. In the rural simplicity of some, alas! only temporary shelter, the Hermitage where he composed *La Nouvelle Héloise* on gilt-edged paper dusted with azure sand, or the grotto or *donjon* of Mount Louis where he worked on his *Émile*, the reader comes upon him in extravagant Armenian dress (to facilitate dealing with his bladder complaint), engaged upon his incessant copying of music (for he must be independent) or contentedly busy with his lace-making (the results of which he will present to young mothers who promise to nurse their children themselves); and eager for another solitary walk, another hour or two of botanizing. 'With what eagerness I ran each morning at sunrise to breathe the fragrant air! ...', he remembered in his *Confessions*. 'What good *café au lait* I took tête-à-tête with my Thérèse! ... I was in the terrestrial paradise. I lived there with as much innocence, and I tasted there the same happiness.' Later, on a different refuge in the Lac de Bienne, he loved to be alone with his Linnaeus. 'As for me, who took for garden the entire isle, as soon as I needed to make or to verify any observation, I ran into the wood or meadows, the book under my arm. There, I lay on the ground beside the plant in question, to examine it on the spot at my ease.' It was this *vie égale et simple*, wholesome as a Swiss cheese and, ultimately, as over-ecstatic as a Swiss picture-postcard, which prompted the State of Nature in Rousseau's *Contrat Social* (1762): 'O nature! O my mother! here I am under your sole guard; here there is no clever and cunning man to interpose between you and me.'

Yet up to his thirty-third year Rousseau led an odd vagabonding life; the son of a dissolute watchmaker in Switzerland, he was apprenticed first to a notary, then to an engraver; he ran away to become a footman; he was rescued as a kind of servant-lover by Mme de Warens; he was secretary to a diplomatist in Venice, he invented a scheme of musical notation, he taught, quarrelled, and loved. Diderot (q.v.) finally gave him his friendship and an entrance to the Encyclopaedia. In 1749 his essay, *Discours sur les art et sciences*, won him a prize from the academy at Dijon. But, although he was a convinced republican, his romantic unstable temperament, and his sentimental deism in particular, did not really fit him to be a member of the *philosophes* and, although he found friends among many people of power and influence, his beloved independence and his solitary nature, when combined with suspicion, made a difficult life still more uneasy. Fréron, Voltaire, Helvetius, Diderot, and Montesquieu were also persecuted at times, but they had wealth or wit to protect them – Rousseau was, as his Scottish friend Hume said, 'a man without a skin'. Thus, despite his continuous literary success from 1750 to the quarrel with Diderot and beyond, he was always aware of uncertainty in his relations with the free-thinking aristocrats and the law. Threatened with arrest in Paris, he flew to Neuchâtel; despite the protection of Frederick of Prussia, he was driven from Neuchâtel (which belonged to Prussia) by a handful of Protestant clergymen to the Canton of Berne; once more expelled, he took refuge in England only to be driven away again by a cruel trick of Horace Walpole's. A period of comparative quiet in Paris followed before his death.

Rousseau's wide talents, as political thinker, musician, botanist, were always secondary to an art which never found an orthodox form. His was the eloquence of a naked sensibility, moralizing in its own interest. Rousseau's views on education (it should take place in the family circle – he abominated colleges), domestic psychology (love affairs between people of different classes were possible, but needed the sublimation of philosophy), and the foundations of democratic government (men voluntarily gave up their individual freedom to obtain the benefits of an organized State), never very logical, have given comfort to widely conflicting minds in our own age. The Nazis, the Communists, the devotees of primitive art, the autobiographical exhibitionists, the sexual revolutionaries – such sectarians who show facets of an anxious and usually godless individualism, can be traced back to this Alpine idyllist, at once too good to be true and too true to be good.

'The Homer of painting'

RUBENS, Peter Paul, (1577–1640), Flemish artist, one of the world's supremely energetic painters, exuberant, prolific, self-confident. Having in mind the decoration of the ceiling of Inigo Jones's Banqueting Hall in London, he declared, and justly, 'My courage has always been equal to any enterprise, however vast in size or diversified in subject.'

Delacroix called Rubens the Homer of Painting, he was 'the father of warmth and enthusiasm', but it is none too easy now to accept his ranges of flesh and his explosion of a vast cracker which sends bodies and draperies swirling into the air. Few painters have been more successful. Not frozen, not academic, his paintings fitted the splendour of courts in the seventeenth century; and he knew his market, well educated, a court page before he became a painter, a

courtier, a diplomat and a man of affairs. In London in 1629, in the double character of artist and diplomat, he gave Charles I (who conferred a knighthood upon him) a large painting by his own hand of *Peace and War*. In the back Minerva, Goddess of Wisdom, drives away Mars, God of War. In front symbols of fruitfulness proliferate – buxom Wealth, her arms full of gold and jewels, Happiness singing and clashing cymbals, matronly Peace offering her breast to a child, Pan stooping over a pile of fruit by which a panther is playing; and a group of children fly from the terrors of war. Movement, swirling colour, rich and satisfying contrasts of silk, satin, metal, fur, flesh, are the essence of the composition. Subject, as so often, seems the excuse for an immense pageant of sheer painting.

One does not have to be super-refined to react now and then from the fleshly mountains. Of the *Drunken Silenus* at Munich, the German critic Waagen wrote more than a century ago that here was 'Old Silenus naked and in a state of complete drunkenness led by two females, presenting every characteristic of the grossest animal nature; in the foreground perhaps a fat female faun, unconscious from beastly drunkenness, while two little fauns are hanging at her bosom and intoxicating themselves with her milk'.

It is Rubens's own fault, though one must say that another Victorian critic made amends by writing of this picture that 'there is no odour of bad whisky about it; it has a Burgundian bouquet'.

Ruskin called Rubens 'a healthy, worthy, kindhearted, courtly-phrased animal, except when he paints his children'. Easier for us to appreciate him in smaller and quieter pieces, sketches, fresh and delightful portraits such as the picture of himself and his first wife Isabella Brant and his intricate, firmly-contrived, widely inclusive landscapes, such as the view (in the National Gallery, London) from the Château de Steen, the home Rubens purchased in 1635, after the best part of a life of huge commissions and unlimited self-expenditure.

Rubens managed his orders by controlling a 'picture factory' in Antwerp, where artists worked from his small sketches, carrying out in large (unusually large) the allegories, the pagan subjects, religious subjects, etc., which the master himself completed with a few quick strokes. So strong was his personality that it stamped every product of the factory. His mastery of exuberant rhythm, his glowing dimpled flesh, his delight in the living translucency of bodies, his constant good temper in paint make him much more than one of the most painterly painters of the world – a fashionable painter. But the modern admirer must first of all, perhaps, take a course in Rubens.

As for his character, anyone who has observed how artists betray themselves under the favours of knights, businessmen, gallery directors and society hostesses, will marvel at the way in which this friend of kings and royal collectors retained his sincerity and freshness; though it may be that he had nothing in him of the greatest depth to betray.

ILLUSTRATION: Plate 12.

Merging into God

RŪMĪ, (1207–1273), mystical poet and one of the chief of Persian writers, who founded the order of Dancing Dervishes.

Jalāl'l-Dīn Rūmī is among the world's major poets; passionate and direct, his poems, above all, were meant to teach – 'does a painter paint a beautiful picture for the picture's sake?' Rūmī asks rhetorically – and the teaching converged upon one thing, the ultimate union of the soul with God, who is above the world, yet fills the world:

Mineral I died, and turned to plant,
A plant I died, then climbed to animal,
Animal I died, and now was Man.
Shall I fear death then, since
Death's made me always more?
As man again I'll die and climb
To holy angel, yet from angel still
Go on – 'All perishes but God':
My angel's soul I shall forego
And shall be then what none has known:
O may I be no more, since not-being
With deep music says that we
Return at last to Him alone.

That is man's right progress through a world in which God is everywhere, in Rūmī's pantheism;

What strange worlds roll inside the Mind's
Huge ocean which embraces all,
On which our figures float like bowls
Which fill, then sink and send
No trail of bubbles to the ocean roof.
The Spirit is so close it can't be seen.
It is a presence: drink of it! Or be
A brimming pitcher with its cold lip dry,
A rider through the miles he rides
Blind to the horse beneath his thigh.

By ourselves we are nothing, and God plays on us:

We are the flute, the music's you,
The mountain we, which echoes you,
The chessmen set in line by you,
To win or lose now moved by you.
We are the flags embroidered with the lion,
The unseen wind which ripples us is you.

These are extracts from the Mathnawī, Rūmī's immense poem of 50,000 lines composed in his old age.

Though he was born in northern Persia, Rūmī's family took refuge from the Mongols in Rum (Asia Minor), after which he was surnamed Rūmī. Eventually he made his home at Konia, the ancient Iconium visited by St Paul, which in Rūmī's day was the cultured, rich and splendid capital of the Seljuk Turks. Teacher and ecstatic, Rūmī lived in a mystical identity of love with particular disciples. The Dancing or Whirling Dervishes are members of the Mevlevi Order which he founded. They dance a mystical, symbolical dance to the music of reed-flutes. Rūmī's tomb is in one of the mosques of Konia.

A pope of art

RUSKIN, John, (1819–1900), English art critic, prose writer, social reformer, lawgiver, seer and prophet of Victorian England. 'I don't think myself a genius,' he wrote to his father, in 1857, 'but there is a strong instinct in me to draw and describe the things I love ... and neither for reputation nor for the good of others. I should like to draw St Mark's stone by stone, touch by touch.'

His father was a rich sherry merchant, his mother a strict evangelical who taught him the Bible by heart. His suburban home was happy, middle class, cultured and snobbish – an egoisme à trois. As a child he would find himself praying that the frost should not spoil the almond blossom. As an undergraduate at Oxford he 'preferred the fritillaries in Christchurch Meadow to Latin or Greek'; and in 1843 he published what one of his biographers has called among 'the most presumptuous, most poetic, most brilliant, yet most wrong-headed volumes ever published by a very young man' – the first volume of Modern Painters, intended as a passionate defence of Turner (q.v.), but in fact a vast essay on everything from hoar frost to high cloud, ivy stalks to Alpine peaks. As Ruskin's voluminous writings were unrolled, it became clear that he was a supreme artist in words (one who was to influence Proust), whose range was from intuition and eloquence to silliness. At one moment he could write of Landseer the animal painter: 'It was not by the study of Raphael that Landseer attained his eminent success, but by a healthy love of Scotch terriers'; at another he would be brilliantly defining the artist as 'a seeing and feeling creature', or declaring that 'the beginning and end and aim of all noble art' was 'that spirit and power which man may witness, but not weigh; conceive, but not comprehend; love, but not imit; and imagine, but not define;' or he would paint a stirring word picture of the Campagna of Rome:

A dull purple poisonous haze stretches level along the desert, veiling its spectral wrecks of massy ruins, on whose rents the red light rests, like a dying fire on defiled altars. The blue ridge of the Alban Mount lifts itself against a solemn space of green, clear, quiet sky. Watch-towers of dark clouds stand steadfastly along the promontories of the Apennines. From the plain to the mountains, the shattered aqueducts, pier beyond pier, melt into the darkness, like shadowy and countless troops of funeral mourners, passing from a nation's grave.'

By the eighteen-fifties Ruskin had the power to make reputations. 'The little despot', one young artist wrote, 'imagines himself the Pope of Art and would wear three crowns as a right, only they would make him look funny in London.' His position was scarcely challenged or his bluff called until 1878 when Whistler (q.v.) took proceedings against him for libel, after Ruskin had written of his art that he 'never expected to hear a coxcomb ask two hundred guineas for flinging a pot of paint in the public's face'. The pot so flung was one of Whistler's 'nocturnes'.

The farthing damages which Whistler received ended an era; but Ruskin the prose-poet of eloquence, force and intuition, the master of purple passage, remained; and the Ruskin whose medievalism (compare and see *William Morris*) brought him to strong views on the working man and to the socialist doctrines of *Unto This Last* (1860). In old age he developed a pathological propensity for charming young girls. His rejection by Rose La Touche – thirty years younger than himself – broke his heart and at last helped to undermine his reason. He confused her with Carpaccio's St Ursula. In the sane periods, Ruskin wrote his very fine autobiography *Praeterita*.

ILLUSTRATION: Plate 13.

Disintegrating the atom

RUTHERFORD, Ernest, first Baron, (1871–1937), son of a New Zealand wheelwright and farmer, of Scottish descent, pioneer of nuclear-physics, the first man to disintegrate the atom, and one of those men of science whose work may change the life of mankind.

Rutherford's childhood was spent among water-wheels in an agricultural community. He was well taught by a succession of good teachers, including Bickerton, the eccentric professor of physics at Canterbury College, who lectured on anything from tuberculosis to the collision of stars. After graduating, Rutherford began research at Canterbury, inventing the magnetic detector for radio waves. A scholarship now enabled him to go to England. His mother called out the news of his success to him while he was digging potatoes in the garden, at which he flung his spade aside, and said: 'These are the last potatoes that I shall dig.'

At Cambridge, Rutherford had an unparalleled success, in the midst of which he suddenly gave up radio research, and collaborated with J.J. Thomson (q.v.). He gave Thomson important help in the discovery of the electron, and tackled the new field of radioactivity. Within four years he and Soddy demonstrated that radioactivity is due to the spontaneous disintegration of atoms. They said, in 1902, that 'it seems not unreasonable to hope ... that radioactivity ... affords the means of obtaining information of the processes occurring within ... the atom'. Within seven years he had proved that the atom has a small nucleus. His method was simply to fire particles at the atom and observe their behaviour. Since they seldom recoiled, the atom was evidently hollow. Occasionally, however, the particles bounced back with great violence, thus showing that the atom contained a small nucleus which was relatively heavy and highly charged.

In 1912 Niels Bohr came to work with him, a young Dane who had ideas on the application of the quantum theory to Rutherford's conception of the nuclear atom. Their collaboration was one of the most fruitful in the history of science. The Rutherford–Bohr atom has been the foundation for the subsequent development of atomic physics. In 1917 Rutherford was on the track of the artificial disintegration of atoms. He noticed particles which seemed to be splinters knocked out of atoms; and during the darkest days of the First World War, Rutherford,

Continued on p. 375

UTAMARO (1753–1806) painting a phoenix on the walls of a Yoshiwara house. Self-portrait (detail) from a woodcut book.

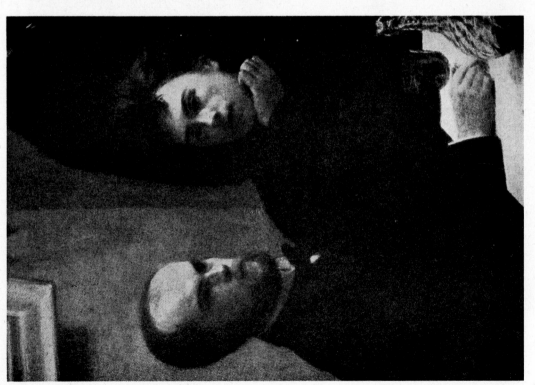

VERLAINE (1844–1896) and RIMBAUD (1854–1891). Detail from *Un Coin de Table*, by Henri Fantin-Latour.

359

VESALIUS (1514–1564) from his book *De Humani Corporis Fabrica*, published in 1543.

SIMONETTA VESPUCCI (1453–1476) by Piero di Cosimo.

GEORGE WASHINGTON (1732–1799) from *General Washington at Trenton* by John Trumbull.

CHARLES WATERTON (1782–1865) by Charles Willson Peale.

ANTOINE WIERTZ (1806–1865) self-portrait.

JOHN WESLEY (1703–1791) painted by N. Hone in 1766.

365

VAN GOGH (1853–1890). Self-portrait after severing his ear.

STRINDBERG (1849–1912).

RICHARD WAGNER (1813–1883) taken c. 1849.

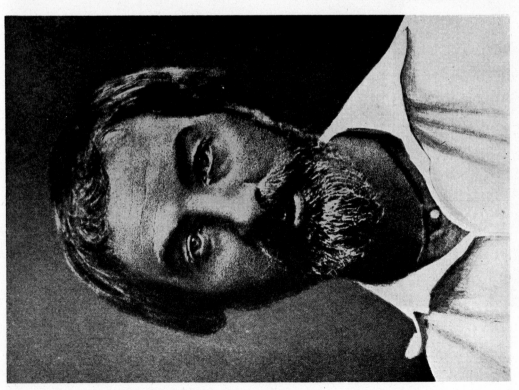

WALT WHITMAN (1819–1892).

OSCAR WILDE (1854–1900) at the age of thirty-seven.

EDWARD WHYMPER (1840–1911) aged twenty-five.

WILLIAM WORDSWORTH (1770–1850) by Benjamin Robert Haydon, 1832.

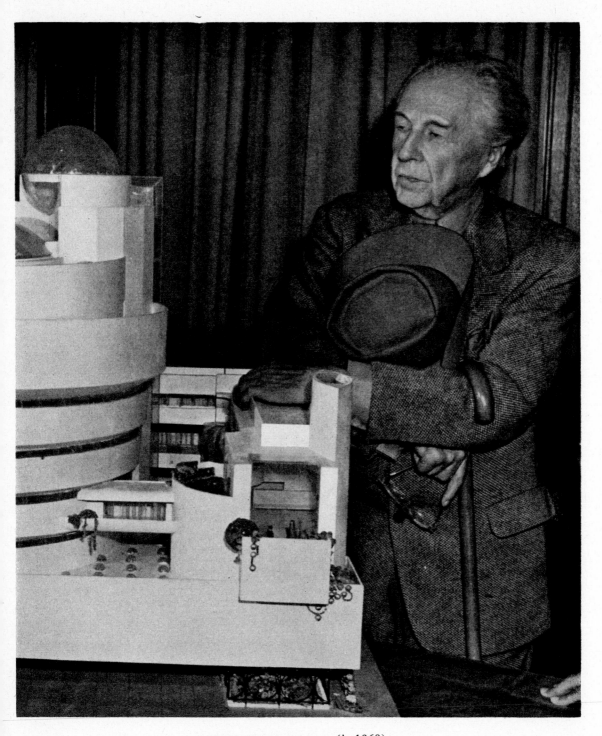

FRANK LLOYD WRIGHT (b. 1869).

WILBUR WRIGHT (1867–1912).

W. B. YEATS (1865–1939).

BRIGHAM YOUNG (1801–1877).

RICHARD TREVITHICK (1771–1833) by John Linnell.

with his one assistant, Kay, spent hour upon hour in a cellar at Manchester University, watching the little specks of light made by the atomic splinters. He even cut his military scientific committee meetings, saying: 'I have been engaged in experiments which suggest that the atom can be artificially disintegrated. If it is true, it is of far greater importance than a war.'

He published his tremendous discovery in 1919. He had accomplished the dream of the alchemists by transmuting one element into another. In the same year he succeeded J.J.Thomson as Cavendish professor at Cambridge, and created a school of nuclear research of undying fame. In his laboratory in 1932 Chadwick discovered the neutron, and Cockcroft and Walton accomplished the first disintegration of an atom by machinery. In 1937, while still in great vigour, he died after a slight operation. In 1938 his former pupil, Otto Hahn (with Fritz Strassman), discovered uranium fission.

Rutherford possessed a wonderful concern for the activities of his friends and pupils, and assessed people entirely by what they did. His greatness and his kindliness enabled him to say things which would have been unthinkable from another man. A pupil once complained to him that he lacked facilities. 'Why,' said Rutherford, '*I* could do research at the North Pole.' Rutherford hated the commercial exploitation of science. Proposals of that kind raised in him a blazing anger, and he died a relatively poor man. He never accepted a single American dollar for research, though millions were ready. 'If the British want research, they can pay for it,' he said.

There was nothing strange or mysterious about him, except his marvellous series of discoveries and his enormous influence on others. Niels Bohr once said: 'Rutherford is not a clever man, he is a great man.'

S

The chivalrous Saracen

SALADIN – in Arabic Salah-ed-din, (1138–1193), Moslem conqueror, Sultan, and opponent of the Crusaders, whose reputation for chivalry marched hand in hand with his hatred of Christians: 'Let us purge the air they breathe,' he said.

R

From the Moslem point of view, Saladin was the right man at the right time: there was a deeply felt demand for Arab unity in defence of the faith. He was not a great captain, but he was a prudent, careful man, and a good administrator. His uncle, Shirkuh, was vizier of Egypt, and on his death in 1169, Saladin succeeded him. When Nur-ed-din, the powerful sultan, died in 1174, Saladin, with very unchivalrous cunning, made himself his successor. His rapid rise alarmed the Christians of Syria and the Latin kingdom. They appealed to the West for a Crusade.

In 1187 Saladin began what was to be his final period of conquest. Egypt was his, and Syria. There now remained the destruction of the Latin kingdom. While besieging Kerak, he learned that Isabel, the sister of the adventurer Reginald de Châtillon, was celebrating her marriage inside the castle. Wine from the wedding banquet was sent to Saladin, who ordered his troops to spare the tower where Isabel and her husband would spend the night. He overran Palestine, and took Jerusalem. The fall of the Holy City shocked Europe, and three kings were soon on their way to the Holy Land: Richard Coeur de Lion of England, Philip Augustus of France and the red-bearded Frederick of Germany.

The conflict between Richard, the beau-ideal of Christian knighthood, and Saladin, his Mussulman equivalent, is legendary. A story is told that in one battle Saladin, seeing Richard unhorsed, sent him two chargers, saying that he could not see such a brave opponent without a mount. The Bishop of Salisbury told the Saracen that 'if anyone could give your noble qualities to King Richard, and his to you ... then the whole world would not furnish two such princes'. But chivalry did not deflect Saladin from his aims. Looking out over the Mediterranean, he said to his secretary: 'When, by God's help, not a Frank is left on this coast, I mean to divide my territories, and to charge my successors with my last commands. Then ... I will sail on this sea to the islands in pursuit of them, until there shall not remain on the face of this earth one unbeliever in God.'

He never lived to fulfil this promise. But he saw the Moslems united by the Peace of Ramleh (1192), which ended the Crusades and made Saladin master of the Middle East. Shortly after, Saladin died. In his last hours he ordered his standard bearer to ride through the streets of Damascus with a shroud, crying, 'Look upon all that is left of the mighty Saladin, the Conqueror of the East.'

Monsieur le pauvre

SATIE, Erik Alfred Leslie, (1866–1925), French composer. 'Erik Satie', he said himself, '... is considered to be the strangest musician of our time ... Everyone will tell you that I am not a musician. That is true. From the beginning of my career I classed myself among the phonometrographers'; and this *blagueur* of musical genius, this composer of delightful ironies, did certainly measure an ordinary F sharp, and find that it weighed ninety-three kilograms, although it came out of a very flat tenor.

Satie was the child of a French father and a Scottish mother who died when he was very young. He played the piano in a café Gaud, and wrote songs in the sentimental tradition, which he called *rudes saloperies*, though they do not deserve the insult. The café and the songs kept him alive, while he composed the *Sarabandes* (1887) and the *Gymnopédies* (1888), early works which turned their back on the world and the opulent music of the eighteen-eighties. Money did not interest him. 'Those who practise an art', he maintained, 'must live in a state of complete renunciation and humility.' So *Monsieur le Pauvre* remained poor. In the days of his fame, a publisher asked him to write a number of piano pieces. Satie was enraged because they offered him too high a price. The fee had to be reduced to a level of fitting modesty, after which he composed the twenty little pieces which he called *Divertissements* (1914), and which have been compared for their precision and lack of fuzziness and colour to Japanese prints.

This friend of Debussy in one generation and of Cocteau and of Picasso in another called himself *un vieux bolcheviste*, partly to shock his hearers, partly because he did in fact take some part in radical politics. Ironically and yet seriously he also drew a caricature of himself, and wrote under it:

'Study for a bust,
of M. Erik SATIE
painted by himself
WITH AN APOPHTHEGM:
I have come into
a very young world
in a very old time.'

and indeed Satie combined the innocent eye with a critical, ironic intelligence. No one could believe that he was wholly real. Jean Cocteau said that his nocturnal walk across Paris from Montparnasse to his home in Arcueil was not possible unless he was carried by those angels who guided, cherished and tormented him. Satie's master-work was the cantata *Socrate* (1918), an act of humility and reverence to its subject. Jacques Maritain wrote that 'Satie's lesson was the lesson of a Socrates who maliciously awakened virtue, troubled bad consciences and pricked good ones; he cleansed music of all pretension and pedantry, he thoroughly purified it'.

The group of musicians known as *Les Six*, including Honegger, Poulenc and Darius Milhaud, gathered around Satie in his old age.

Schliemann of Troy

SCHLIEMANN, Heinrich, (1822–1890), the prime hero of pre-scientific archaeology.

Son of a humble cleric, grocer's assistant, cabin boy, book-keeper, successful merchant, master of many languages, including ancient and modern Greek, this pertinacious German was obsessed from childhood by one thing – the story of the siege of Troy as told by Homer. He had once bribed a drunkard to recite Homer to him, and had wept because he could not understand the glorious words. Troy must be rediscovered: when he had made a fortune as a contractor in the Crimean War, Schliemann had the leisure, the money, and the power to back his enthusiasm.

In 1864 he brought himself and his considerable fortune to Greece. Troy he concluded to be the mound of Hissarlik in Asia Minor. In 1871, to prove his theory, he began to excavate the mound, or rather to hack his way into it. He found, not one Troy, but several; and, convinced that Troy of the legendary siege must be on the bottom level, he dug his ruthless way through the stratified remains, cutting through the city he was after – the Sixth, or Mycenaean city, of the great poem of the *Iliad*. No matter. Schliemann had pushed back the bounds of history; and, in Greece again, he now began to search for the burial-place of the Greek hero Agamemnon, to complete the tale. In the citadel of Mycenae he uncovered five out of six kingly tombs, a treasure of gold, silver, ivory and bronze, and more of what history had chosen to forget.

A telegram to the King of Greece proclaiming that he had found Agamemnon's tomb set the learned by the ears; but this romantic of the pick and shovel had fulfilled his dream. He had proved (by methods which would dement the modern, gingerly archaeologist, disciplined by scientific method), that the Heroic Age was not a myth – that Greek civilization did not just 'happen' without antecedents. A superbly obsessed amateur, Schliemann proved his hunches and stimulated the recovery of vast reaches of the past of our civilization, from Troy and Mycenae to Knossos, Knossos to Ur, and Ur to the utterly forgotten cities of Harappa and Mohenjo-Daro.

Arnold Schönberg

SCHÖNBERG, Arnold, (1874–1951), Austrian composer of the world's most unpopular music, born in Vienna, the city of the world's most popular music and most popular musicians.

Vienna was closely bound up with the decline of the Romantic movement, at the very end of which stands Schönberg, involved in a decadence and also the chief architect of a renaissance. His early music is still romantically Wagnerian upon the surface, though behind the heroic gestures of the *Gurrelieder* (1901), there are hints of disillusionment, more clear in the sudden, sinister intrusion of a banal nursery tune upon the highly cultivated proceedings of his first string-quartet (1905). The disillusionment breaks out in the frightening vision of disintegration which illuminates the last two movements of his second quartet (1908). There were outcries from people who saw their musical security being demolished. During a performance of the second quartet in Vienna, the conductor Weingartner rose from the audience and protested vigorously. But despite these and other deterrents, Schönberg continued to take tradition to pieces, not because he enjoyed destruction – all his life he considered himself an unwilling instrument of a cruel destiny – but because the parts were rusty and worn. By 1911 or thereabouts everything was dismantled and laid out on the floor according to a pattern whose meaning was clear to the composer, and, at that time, only to him. His imagination was free to wander into the unknown, where he discovered his most famous work, *Pierrot Lunaire* (1911). An artist cannot always remain free, and after writing *Pierrot*, Schönberg began slowly and painfully to put things

together again. From what he had discovered in his years of freedom he evolved a new method of organizing the materials which every composer has at his disposal. In 1924 Schönberg presented to the world the first fruits of his labour, the *Suite for Piano, opus 25*, and the *Wind Quintet, opus 26*. One may compare the development of cubism and abstract painting from about 1910, or in poetry T.S.Eliot's *The Waste Land*, published in 1922, and in fiction James Joyce's *Ulysses*, written between 1914 and 1921. Schönberg had accomplished single-handed what might have taken generations to achieve. Public rejoicing at the overthrow of the familiar tonality could hardly be expected. Indeed, it was from this time that Schönberg had to stand against a continual stream of vilification from the academies and the press. For the Nazis he was a 'degenerate' artist, and in 1933 he was deprived of his position on the faculty of the Prussian Academy of Arts. Two months later Schönberg returned to the Jewish faith which he had abandoned in 1921; three months later still, he arrived in America, where he spent the rest of his life teaching and composing. 'No art', he wrote in his introduction to his *Harmonielehre*, 'has been so hindered in its development by teachers as music, since nobody watches more closely over his property than the man who knows that, strictly speaking, it does not belong to him.'

Franz Schubert

SCHUBERT, Franz Peter, (1797–1828). Austrian composer of romantic lyrical music.

After Schubert's death, his few belongings were listed and valued. 'A quantity of old music' – his unpublished manuscripts – were valued at eight and sixpence. He lived and died in poverty, and largely in obscurity, though there were friends enough to recognize his genius. No artist comes more completely out of the text-book of romanticism. This child of poor Austrian parents was ill at ease in society (cf. Handel), preferred students and bohemians, had no fixed home, moving from lodging to lodging, was simple in character and childlike, and needed devotion and help – which were given him in good measure by his brother Ferdinand. Music welled out of him, his first Mass when he was seventeen, his symphonies – of which *The Unfinished* must be one of the best-known symphonies in the world – his operas, chamber music and, above all, his songs. He wrote for any words which came to hand. Schumann said of him that he 'would set a placard to music!' In the prodigious collection of songs, there are seventy poems by Goethe, and forty-five by Schiller. One famous song we owe to a chance meeting with a friend who sat reading Shakespeare in a beer garden. Schubert took up the volume and opened it by chance at *Hark, hark the lark*. He read it through once, looked up and remarked, 'Such a lovely melody has come into my head. If only I had some paper ...', and he at once wrote down his setting on the back of the menu.

His idol was Beethoven (q.v.), who then dominated musical Vienna. 'Who', he asked, 'can do anything after Beethoven?' In his last days, Beethoven was given some of Schubert's work and declared, 'He has a divine soul.' When he was dying he declared, 'Schubert has my soul.' Schubert carried a torch at Beethoven's funeral in 1827, and on his own death-bed (he died of typhus), he asked to be buried beside him.

One statement of Schubert is typical. Delightful music, painting, poetry is the product of delight, but not always of happiness. 'My musical works', he said, 'are the product of my genius and my misery, and what the public most relishes is that which has given me the most distress.' The poet, John Clare (q.v.), who was Schubert's contemporary and had the gift of lyricism and also appeared gay and optimistic, said much the same – that he wrote because it pleased him in sorrow – 'and when happy it made me happier and so I go on'.

ILLUSTRATION: Page 326.

Lutheran composer

SCHÜTZ, Heinrich, (1585–1672), German choral composer, who lived in an age of transition, and was great enough to make use of new discoveries evolved by others outside the ancient tradition to which he belonged by training.

Schütz came from fine, hard-working Lutheran stock, and benefited from a first-class education which included music as well as logic, rhetoric, dialectic and the usual disciplines. He was able to go to Italy to study for three years under Giovanni Gabrieli, and when he returned he brought with him some of the Italian joy in musical sumptuousness.

He added colour to the music at the court of the local Landgrave, and was noticed by the Elector of Saxony, who made him Kapellmeister at Dresden. He remained at the Elector's court, on and off, for the rest of his life, and worked with characteristic devotion at a wide range of duties, musical and administrative. In 1628 he felt a strong desire to return to Italy. He disclaimed all frivolous intentions – an unnecessary precaution for Schütz – and told the Elector that a further chance of learning the latest musical developments would be invaluable to his own composition. He added that it might be unwise to refuse to let him go, since it would upset him and make him incapable of fulfilling his court functions. This high-principled craftiness won over the Elector, and Schütz travelled to an Italy whose music was by now established in new dramatic and expressive methods, thanks to the resplendent example of Monteverdi (q.v.). Schütz paid his homage to the new style in his *Symphoniae Sacrae* (1629–1650). But by the late sixteen-forties, long after his return to Saxony, his music had changed in a way that may reflect his distaste for the growing insincerity of Italian composers, particularly the ones who were finding favour and employment in Germany. Conditions at the Elector's court had been bad for some time, as a result of the German wars, and Schütz was even reduced to paying some of the musicians out of his own pocket, in order to keep them together. He considered himself to have been poorly used, and repeatedly asked for his release. Eventually there was a reconciliation, and Schütz spent the last eleven years of his long life in quiet and happy industry. The return to the austerity of his youth, which he had made some years before, had not endeared his music to the crowd, and the austere and deeply moving dignity of *Four Passions* which Schütz wrote during his last years meant little to a public that could amuse itself with such things as an Italian Mass including trumpets and drums. Schütz's music is one of the loftiest achievements of German art. Severe, grand, the *Four Passions* and the *Seven Last Words of Christ* are so contrived that the sacred words emerge clear and audible upon the support of the music, imparting their lessons like the wall-paintings or stained glass of Protestantism. Indeed, his music is an unsurpassed revelation of the Lutheran spirit, possessive, moving and ennobling. It seems right that Schütz should have been at work on a setting of the psalmist's words 'Thy statutes have been my songs in the house of my pilgrimage' at the moment of his death.

History and romance

SCOTT, Sir Walter, (1771–1832), Scottish novelist in prose and verse.

A lawyer by profession, Scott came into writing accidentally, and continued to write because it paid and promised to enable him to live, as he wanted to, like a country gentleman. Dour, humdrum, conventionally jocose, his greatest passion the striking of a political opponent at an election meeting, he spent most of his life in his native Scotland, for the last twenty years in Abbotsford, the home he built for £76,000.

His fame began with the verse-novels, of which the first was *The Lay of the Last Minstrel* (1805). Here was a new blend of antiquity, sentiment and story-telling, coming when the reading public was ripe for knights, abbeys, owls, ivy, ruins and moonlight; and Scott now settled to a phenomenal output. Rising at five, he would begin writing at six and finish by noon, to spend the rest of the day on his legal work, roaming his estate and mingling with local society. From childhood he had been immersed in Scottish lore; and in 1814 he published *Waverley*, his first novel in prose. The success of this book with no name on the title-page was triumphant. Eight more historical, romantic novels followed in five years. Scott became the European novelist of his day, feeding mankind's dream of journeying backwards out of life into other lives and times. He was a public idol, eagerly read, honoured and fêted. If much of what he wrote is no longer readable, at least *The Antiquary* and *Old Mortality* deserve to live on.

In 1825, at the climax of his sparkling career, Scott found himself responsible for £130,000, through the fall of his publisher. With staggering industry, he wrote away a third of this debt of honour in two years; but his health was crippled and he died soon after. Slowly Scott has been overtaken by the posthumous fate of the best-seller. Time has found him out; but undoubtedly he gave the world a new kind of fiction, which in later hands is not extinct even now.

ILLUSTRATION: Page 326.

Island castaway

SELKIRK, Alexander, (1676–1721). Mariner, castaway, and the Robinson Crusoe of fact.

On the desert island of Juan Fernandez, in the Pacific, Alexander Selkirk lived by himself for four years and four months, with no company but cats and goats. As a young sailing master in a privateering galley he had quarrelled with his captain, and was put on Juan Fernandez at his own request. He changed his mind, but the captain refused to take him on board again, and sailed.

That was in 1704. In January 1709, sailors who touched at Juan Fernandez for fresh food and water found, as their captain wrote, 'a man cloath'd in goat skins who look'd wilder than the first owners of them'. Selkirk had first endured eight months of melancholy and terror, eating only when he had to eat and sleeping only when he could no longer stay awake. Ships' cats and rats had bred in large numbers, and the rats were a nuisance, nibbling at his clothes and his feet when he slept: he tamed the cats by feeding them with goat flesh; the cats dealt with the rats and 'would lie about him in hundreds'. He tamed kids and would divert himself by dancing with the kids and the cats and singing to them.

'A nature humanized'

SHAKESPEARE, William, (1564–1616), English playwright, and by universal consent the supreme dramatic poet, or dramatist and poet, of the world, active during the last years of Elizabeth I and the first half of James I's reign. Coleridge with sharp insight called him 'a nature humanized, a genial understanding directing self-consciously a power and implicit wisdom deeper than consciousness'.

Playwright is the first fact about Shakespeare; and it implies a skilled maker of plays (as *cartwright, millwright*), a task defined by Ben Jonson, who wrote that 'A good play is like a skeene of silk, which if you take by the right end you may wind off, at pleasure, on the bottome or card of your discourse, in a tale or so; how you will: but if you light in the wrong end, you will pull all into a knot, or elfe-locke; which nothing but the sheers, or a candle, will undoe or separate.' Those who believe 'Shakespeare' a borrowed name for Edward de Vere, Earl of Oxford; William Herbert, Earl of Pembroke; or Sir Francis Bacon, must prove first where their Shakespeare learnt to take the dramatic skein of silk by the right end. The personality of William Shakespeare, the player, is enigmatic, but his theatrical credentials are not in dispute.

He was baptized on 26 April, 1564, the son of John Shakespeare, glover, of Stratford-on-Avon, who rose to be Bailiff, Alderman, Justice of Peace, and who in 1576 (when William was twelve) applied for a grant of arms. Suddenly the Alderman abandoned the application and all municipal office, and became involved in lawsuits. In 1582 William, then eighteen, married Anne Hathaway, eight years his senior and four months gone with child; neither place nor exact date are known. (On 27 November a licence was taken out at Worcester for William Shakespeare to marry Anna Whateley of Temple Grafton, followed the next day by a bond of surety against impediment for him to marry Anne Hathwey of Stratford.) She bore him Susanna (baptized 26 May 1583) and the twins Hamnet and Judith (1585), of whom the boy only lived until 1596.

After a blank of more than seven years, William Shakespeare reappears as a rising playwright in London. In 1593 and 1594 he dedicated two poems (*Venus and Adonis* and *The Rape of Lucrece*) to the Earl of Southampton, adherent of the rising Court favourite, the Earl of Essex. At the end of 1594 he purchased a 'fellowship in a cry of players', the newly reorganized Lord Chamberlain's Company, headed by the Burbage family; he acted with them at the Globe Theatre and in many Court entertainments; and was always named among the first of them in play-lists and Court records. In 1596 he renewed his father's application for arms, and though it was questioned, carried it through; the next year he bought New Place, the best house in Stratford – the first of several purchases of property in his native place. In London he was only a lodger; we hear of him in 1604 in the refugee household of a Huguenot wig-maker, Christopher Mountjoy, where he helped to make an unfortunate marriage between his landlord's daughter and apprentice. After this time he acted little, though he kept up his connection with the King's Men; he was named first among them in the distribution of livery for James I's royal progress through the City. Then he retired to Stratford, where in 1607 his elder daughter Susanna married Dr John Hall, and in 1616 Judith (then thirty-one) married Thomas Quiney. Soon after, on 25 March, he made a hurried will, perplexing in several respects, and then died on 23 April.

Although each fact here has its crust of conjecture (What happened to his father, and how did William react? Was he forced into marriage, and is it by in-

tention that he lies alone in his tomb in Stratford Church? Where did he go when he left Stratford, and where did he get the money to buy his shares in the Globe company? Was he bored, or cagey, or ill, when he gave his unsatisfactory evidence in the Mountjoy suit?) one thing is clear, and it is the important thing: his status in his profession: 'The father of us Cuthbert and Richard Burbage was the first builder of Playhowses ... we built the Globe with summes of money taken up at interest, which lay heavy on us many years, and to ourselves we joyned those deserving men, Shakespeare, Hemengs, Condall, Philips, and other partners in the profittes of that they call the House ...' (*Evidence of Cuthbert Burbage before the Lord Chamberlain, 1635*).

That the plays are documents of the Globe playhouse is equally indisputable, and not only from their editing by those deserving men, Heminge and Condall, but from their pages ... Richard Burbage grows older; the boy heroines' voices break; Kemp and Cowley intrude into the text of *Much Ado about Nothing* where Dogberry and Verges should be; John Sinkler, the tall, thin man with the lantern jaw, pops in and out ('Goodman Death, Goodman Bones, thou Anatomy, thou'); Kemp goes to Rome, Armin arrives ...

These, then, are plays of occasion; and whoever made them made them in and for the Globe Theatre company and its audience: As *You* Like It, What *You* Will: 'Gentles, doe not reprehend. If you pardon, we will mend', 'Peece out our imperfections with your thoughts', 'Let your Indulgence set me free ... the Queen oblig'd him to write a play of Sir John Falstaff in Love, which I am very well assured he perform'd in a fortnight'.

Shakespeare's fundamental attitude is one of acceptance, and in that his anonymity resides. What was written by Keats applies well to Shakespeare: 'As to the poetical Character itself – It has no character – it enjoys light and shade; it lives in gusto, be it foul or fair, high or low, rich or poor, mean or elevated – It has as much delight in conceiving an Iago as an Imogen. The poet has no identity – he is certainly the most unpoetical of all God's creatures.' Shakespeare finds expression through the shape of an existing company, in a theatre whose public loved clowns, young love, sword fights, bawdry, high moral sentiments, moonlight, revenge, disguises. He never invents, but uses traditional stories, and treats them with the same respect, whether they are as august as Plutarch, or as fantastic as a *novella* of Bandello. He shapes them in an inherited convention compounded of medieval miracle and morality plays and classical scholarship with a hint of Italian *commedia dell'arte*. The rich, newly-augmented language he uses is organized through the mechanism of Renaissance rhetoric and the resources of allegory. He can still use as living things the age-old commonplaces – Fortune's Wheel, the cuckold's horns, the Seven Ages of Man (as you may see them, for instance, on the floor of Siena Cathedral, in a mosaic of 1476, from *Infans* with his hobby-horse to *Decrepitas* bowed on his two sticks and looking into his tomb).

There is present behind these things a powerful personality, but it is dispersed. One might compare Shakespeare to the slaughtered Osiris, whose body, cut small, is scattered over his fields to make them fertile. Sometimes we may feel that we get near enough to smell blood:

'I would there were no age between sixteen and three and twenty, or that youth would sleep out the rest, for there is nothing (in the betweene) but getting wenches with childe, wronging the Auncientry, stealing, fighting ...'

> 'The weariest, and most loathed worldly life
> That Age, Ache, penury, and imprisonment
> Can lay on nature, is a Paradise
> To what we feare of death ...'

'Dost thou thinke because thou art vertuous, there shall be no more Cakes and Ale?'

But because his universality consists in minute particulars we can never be sure: his porter is Macbeth's porter; his milkmaid, Cleopatra doing the chares. The voice that we think reflects his opinion or circumstance may be only the unseen power that uses him. 'A Man's life of any worth', wrote Keats again, 'is a continual allegory – and very few eyes can see the Mystery of his life, a life like the Scriptures, figurative. Shakespeare led a life of Allegory: his works are the comments on it.'

Dragon slayer

SHAW, George Bernard, (1856–1950), Irish playwright, critic, social irritant, and quizzing magnifico of modern letters. In his *Man and Superman* Don Juan says, 'I tell you that as long as I can conceive something better than myself, I cannot be easy until I am striving to bring it into existence or clearing the way for it.' Here was one principle which propelled Shaw through the best part of a hundred years of activity.

Four keys to the man are that he was born in Dublin, that he worked in an estate agents' office, that his father was a drunkard, and that his mother was dedicated to music. He carried an Irish gift of eloquent paradox to an extreme; collecting Dublin rents taught him the vile poverty of slums; he was often preoccupied in his writing, dramatic and critical, with the relation of the sexes in marriage; and he soaked himself in music during his early years, and made his first reputation as a music critic in London. Upon music Shaw superimposed a reading of Marx's *Das Kapital*. After this, social regeneration, though not Marx's revolutionary analysis, obsessed him throughout a career which swept from poverty to plenty, obscurity to world success, and the Nobel Prize for literature.

The public mask he devised was hardly the real Shaw. He was not all the time G.B.S., an outrageous Mephistophelean in knickerbockers, with a jaunty walk around the streets of London, spiky reddish eyebrows, a caricaturist's gift of a beard, and a readiness for super-pertness and paradox: Should he not be awarded the Order of Merit? He had conferred it upon himself, Shaw replied, years ago. What book would Mr Shaw like to have with him if wrecked upon a desert island? Answer: a Manual of Boatbuilding. But Shaw knew how to force his ideas upon public indifference by forcing his *persona* upon it as well. He had compelled himself to be effective as writer and speaker, though his early books failed and he was at first tremulous and shy on a platform. Socialist and one of the founders of the Fabian Society, which substituted political permeation and gradualism for the necessity of revolution, he never left his existence or his position in doubt.

Quite clearly Shaw is always for something or against something. He was against most of the nineteenth century, and in play after play he attacked its unintentional or unrealized shams. When he started, there was only one subject for the theatre – 'clandestine adultery', as he put it; a theatre slum which he cleared with the help of Ibsen, if slum can be applied to the boudoir. In a preface to his massive *Back to Methuselah*, Shaw noted a few of the dragons he had boldly faced – 'slum landlordism, doctrinaire Free Love (psuedo-Ibsenism), prostitution, militarism, marriage, history, current politics, natural Christianity, national and individual character, paradoxes of conventional society, husband hunting, questions of conscience, professional delusions and impostures ...' Dead dragons to left and to right of him, Shaw was practically and socially involved in the transformations of this century. He had nothing if not a good conceit of himself, with some foundation. He fought, that is certain – with voice, plays, prefaces and pamphlets; and with no theoretical rivals upon the Right, he had much influence in spreading the beliefs of Socialism.

Icelandic chronicler

SNORRI STURLUSON, (1179–1241), Icelandic historian and one of the greatest writers of medieval Europe.

A journey through the Borgafjord country to Reykjaholt, in South-west Iceland, where Snorri lived, and where one can still see the Snorralang, Snorri's stone bath fed from a hot spring, makes one marvel at Icelandic literature and learning in the Middle Ages. Agriculturally here is one of the richer, or less poor, districts of Iceland, but the loose tracks, the wide valleys, the low sullen mountains on each side, the grey bogs and the grey or black lava, the snipe drumming around the green home meadows of each isolated homestead, the swans flying away down some endless lake or river, give an impression of an altogether cruel, dismal and enormous land in which all one's trouble would have been to keep alive. Snorri came at the end of the great medieval period of Icelandic literature, the age of the sagas, the family histories in prose. He was wealthy by the standards of Iceland, an expert in law, a poet, as well as an historian; but also an ambitious man without scruples, in a time when Icelandic society was in upheaval, ready to cheat, sacrifice, kill, and betray. He lived partly in Iceland, partly in Norway with King Hakon, and it was by Hakon's order that he was murdered after returning to Reykjaholt.

The two books for which Snorri is known are the *Prose Edda*, in part an account of the old gods of the North (he tells, for instance, the tale of the slaying of Baldur the Beautiful with the shaft of mistletoe), in part a handbook for poets, and the *Heimskringla* (so called from the first word, meaning the 'world's circle') or Chronicle of the Kings of Norway. Snorri's preface begins, 'In this book I have had old stories written down, as I have heard them told by intelligent people, concerning chiefs who have held dominion in the northern countries.' In the prose tradition of the sagas, in language curt and lively, Snorri tells, for instance, the histories of St Olaf and Olaf Tryggvason. One of his merits is not to take sides but to state the facts as he knew them – 'a man to our knowledge', it was written of him after his death, 'most wise and fair-minded'. Again and again he makes his narrative actual and dramatic by the report of detail or incident, for instance:

'Halfdan the Black was driving from a feast in Hadeland, and it so happened that his road lay over the lake called Rand. It was in spring, and there was a great thaw. They drove across the bight called Rykinsvik, where in winter there had been a pond broken in ice for the cattle to drink at; and where the dung had fallen upon the ice, the thaw had eaten it into holes. Now as the king drove over it the ice broke, and King Halfdan and many with him perished. He was then forty years old.'

Or his description of how Einar slew Halfdan Haleg in Orkney. Halfdan had fled into the night after an encounter: 'Einar and his men lay all night without tents, and when it was light in the morning they searched the whole island and killed every man they could lay hold of. Then Einar said "What is that I see upon the isle of Ronaldsay? Is it a man or a bird? Sometimes it raises itself up, and sometimes lies down again." They went to it, and found it was Halfdan Haleg, and took him prisoner ... Thereafter Earl Einar went up to Halfdan, and cut a spreadeagle upon his back, by striking his sword through his back into his belly, dividing his ribs from the backbone down to his loins, and tearing out his lungs; and so Halfdan was killed.'

Snorri's death was in keeping for violence with many of the deaths he had described. His son-in-law, as King Hakon's agent, attacked him at Reykjaholt, when Snorri was asleep, and killed him.

All is God

SPINOZA, Benedict, (1632–1677), Dutch philosopher whose metaphysical system, as expounded in his posthumously published *Ethics*, is the most ambitious and comprehensive of modern times.

Spinoza the man is largely hidden behind his work. This accurately represents his own intentions. But what little we do know of his life reveals him as in every way admirable and lovable. His family were Portuguese Jews who had come to Amsterdam (where Spinoza was born) to escape the Inquisition, and in the tolerant Dutch community he was given an orthodox Jewish education. But though willing to conform to some extent, he could not conceal his religious doubts. They centred round the interpretation of the Bible, which seemed to be inconsistent with the discoveries of the new sciences. Neither threats nor bribes could induce him to renounce his views, and in 1656 he was excommunicated by the Jews. He continued to live quietly in Amsterdam and later at the Hague, earning his living at the highly skilled trade of polishing lenses, corresponding with other philosophers, and discussing Descartes (q.v.) in a small circle of enlightened friends. Unusually indifferent to money, Spinoza was urbane without being worldly, frugal yet not ascetic, pious but not a sectarian or a bigot, reflective by temperament yet observant of public affairs. Though he deeply impressed those who met him, he was in general reviled or ignored by Jew and Christian alike. At the early age of forty-three he died of phthisis.

The *Ethics* has been described as the most widely misunderstood work of modern philosophy, and its difficulties are certainly formidable. Its intellectual climate is fundamentally different from that of our own times. With the development of the specialized sciences, and with the insight into the distinction – based on the work of Hume and Kant – between metaphysics and experimental science, philosophy has largely withdrawn her claim, which we find unabated in Spinoza, to render the universe as a whole intelligible to a thinker who proposes to use no instrument other than his own powers of reasoning and logic. The design of the *Ethics* is geometrical, beginning with definitions, axioms, and propositions and proceeding deductively; indeed, it is part of Spinoza's claim on behalf of philosophy that he thought everything *could* be demonstrated. Most philosophers today would not accept the view that the connections between the various parts of the universe are *logical* ones; but Spinoza will always be of interest in as far as he raises, in the most uncompromising form, the question of the legitimacy and scope of metaphysical speculation.

ILLUSTRATION: Page 315.

From horse-plough to atomic pile

STALIN, (1879–1953), dictator and industrializer of Russia, who began life as Joseph Vissarionovich Djugashvili.

Lenin (q.v.), Stalin's predecessor, had not intended to found a monolithic police state whose leader's word was holy writ, but he set in motion forces which made such a state and such a leader inevitable. He had believed, (1) that the Russian revolution could only endure with the aid of a successful revolution in one of the industrially advanced countries, (2) that such a proletarian revolution in the West would not be delayed for any great while. When he died in 1924, it seemed that Trotsky, his right-hand man, would succeed. History, as Marx's colleague Engels observed, always keeps a card up her sleeve. Trotsky continued to fulminate about revolution outside Russia, while Stalin, the secretary of the Communist Party, quietly established his hold on key post after post in the Russian Government.

Abroad, Stalin was so little considered at this time that the London *Daily Worker*, the Communist paper, knew no better than to print his name as 'Stallin'. At home, to the Communist leaders, he was an able organizer, with a spaniel's fidelity to Lenin; as a Marxian theorist, they treated him with a smile. But the next few years were to wipe that smile from their faces. Since the so-called revolutionary masses of Western Europe were so unwilling to revolt, Stalin had to switch to the doctrine of socialism in a single country; and so before long Marxism (since there are always learned doctors ready to justify political necessity on theoretical grounds) had to be re-written in his support.

With great skill Stalin exploited the differences between the other leaders. One by one he removed them from authority. One by one he destroyed them, until at last all Lenin's principal comrades had been exposed as the counter-revolutionary agents of foreign imperialism. That this was improbable did not go unnoticed, and the process involved a struggle. But it became more and more dangerous to protest. Under Stalin's lethal frown, the last show of free discussion in any organ of state or party faded away. When the name of Stalin was uttered at a meeting, it became the custom for all to rise piously to their feet. From above, a system of 'criticism and self-criticism' was imposed, from which the wavering party line was exempt. This provided extra work in plenty for the informer and the secret police.

Stalin remained all the while the modest general secretary of the party, pushed forward, as policy and occasion demanded, in carefully organized public appearances. In theory, his single vote on the central committee was worth no more than the vote of any other member. But Russian history was being rewritten, no less than the theory of Marxism. The purpose was to show how tremendously Stalin had helped in the revolution by Lenin's side; and, at last, no speech could be made, no book could be published, without tribute to the all-knowing and always infallible leader.

The infallible leader, needless to say, made tragic mistakes; but he was protected from the consequences by his infallible system of terror, discipline and propaganda.

This is not to deny Stalin's ability, his force of character and his toughness: if Lenin had made Russia's political and social revolution, then Stalin was the ruthless contriver of Russia's industrial revolution. A country barely emerged from serfdom (from which England had emerged in the fourteenth century) was made literate by his efforts within a generation, and was transformed into one of the major industrial nations of the world. Stalin, it has been said, found Russia ploughing with horses, and left it with the atomic pile. His triumph did enable the Soviet Union – with British and American help – to survive Hitler's invasion of Russia. Yet after the Second World War, Stalin's imperialist expansion, and his intransigent policy in dealing with his former allies, polarized the world into two hostile groups, with the chance of catastrophe for both of them.

his amateurs, and before long he became known as a brilliant producer, but one who did not hesitate to use the stage for his purposes no matter what the dramatist's aim in his own play. In 1898 he and Nemirovich-Danchenko founded the Moscow Art Theatre; and he now produced and popularized plays by Chekhov, clashing with the playwright over his intentions when they differed from his own interpretations.

Soon, however, Stanislavsky's indefatigably questing spirit made him realize that this was not the producer's role and that it was not his business to be a stage autocrat whose word was law to the actors. Slowly he began to evolve his famous system of acting based on the idea of the subordination of the producer to the dramatist and of permitting the actor greater freedom in developing his own concept of the character he has to perform. Here in his own words is the essence of his teaching: 'The theatre must not give us a bare reflection of life, but must reflect everything in life in its inner heroic tension, in the seemingly simple forms of an ordinary day, but in reality in precise and luminous images in which all feelings are alive and in which all passions have been ennobled.' Stanislavsky embodied his ideas on acting in *An Actor's Work on Himself*, published after his death. His evolution as an actor and producer he described fully in his other famous book, *My Life in Art* (1923), which he wrote after touring the United States with his company of the Moscow Art Theatre.

Maxim Gorky called him, with some justice, 'the greatest reformer of dramatic art'. He refreshed the theatre, and his influence has gone through the world.

'The greatest reformer of dramatic art'

STANISLAVSKY, Konstantin, (1863–1938), pseudonym of Constantin Sergeyevich Alexeyev, Russian theatrical producer and founder of the Moscow Art Theatre, who reinvigorated acting and producing.

He was born in Moscow, the son of a wealthy industrialist, and was enthusiastic for acting and the theatre from early childhood, growing with his profession. He began with amateur theatricals. Family performances widened to public performances in Moscow and the provinces given by Stanislavsky and

A modern Marco Polo

STEIN, Sir Marc Aurel, (1862–1943), the greatest Asian traveller since Marco Polo.

As a schoolboy in Dresden, Aurel Stein was fascinated by the eastern campaigns of Alexander the Great, and from early on he determined to explore the ancient Bactria. He came of a cultured Hungarian Jewish family, and having an aptitude for languages, as well as a scholarly and meticulous mind, he concentrated on Oriental studies, and in 1886, after research work in the British Museum in London, he was made Principal of the Oriental College at Lahore, in

India. Though a quiet and unassuming man, he became expert in lobbying officialdom in pursuit of his plans, and his tenacity, patience, and unrivalled flair for topography served him well. After some archaeological work in Kashmir, an area he loved above all others, he started, in 1900, on the first of those Central Asian journeys which were to make him the most famous explorer of his day.

Stein made four great journeys into Sinkiang, Khotan, across the Gobi Desert, through the Pamirs, and by the jade and silk routes into ancient Transoxiana. Travelling extremely light, he covered many thousands of miles of barren and forbidding country, some of it unseen by a European since Marco Polo's day. This small, stocky man was possessed of unlimited energy, and after a day's march of thirty-six miles across burning desert, he thought nothing of writing a six-page letter to a friend, as well as keeping up a detailed and accurate log of his day's work.

From the dryness and the deserts he recovered load after load of parchments and documents, silk scrolls and banners, bronzes, beads and paintings, which are still occupying scholars as far afield as India, America, France and England. Their illumination of the prolonged intercourse between the Indian, Persian Hellenistic and Chinese civilizations has profoundly influenced the study of ancient history, and documents he found in the Cave of a Thousand Buddhas, walled up since the eleventh century, are still being collated and transcribed.

Stein's last work was devoted to his first love, Alexander, but the arduous mountain scrambles and hard marches on foot were beginning to tell on a man in his eightieth year. Receiving permission at last, after many rebuffs, to explore in Afghanistan, he reached Kabul on 19 October 1943. He caught a chill while visiting the museum, and died within a few days. One of his last utterances was: 'I have had a wonderful life, and it could not be concluded more happily than in Afghanistan, which I have wanted to visit for sixty years.' He is buried in Kabul. Books in which he wrote of his work range from *Innermost Asia* (1928) to *Old Routes of Western Iran* (1940).

'Being read in 1935'

STENDHAL, pseudonym of Henri Beyle, (1783–1842), French novelist. 'I have a ticket in a lottery,' he wrote characteristically, 'and the main prize amounts to this: being read in 1935.' Forecasting that he would be understood in a hundred years was only one example of Stendhal's eccentricity to his age. And he was uncannily right.

He was born in Grenoble – he described its provincial atmosphere in his great novel *Le Rouge et le noir* (1830). His youth was of a desultory and disorganized kind; he liked extravagances that appealed to women, and he was often short of money. For a while he was a soldier in Italy and fell in love with life in Milan; he took part in Napoleon's Russian campaign, but though he admired Napoleon, he certainly did not put war aims first. At the end of the Napoleonic wars he was able to return to Milan. Unfortunately he was expelled from Italy as a liberal in 1830, but after nine further years in Paris he managed to get appointed French consul at Civita Vecchia in the Papal States. He was no better as a consul than a soldier. He was talkative, lazy, and extremely fat, and he spent much of his time in the salons of Rome. In his latter years he suffered badly from gout, and he died in Paris in 1842.

Most French critics of the nineteenth century treated Stendhal as a minor writer; Sainte-Beuve, for nstance, maintained that his characters were 'not living beings, but ingeniously-constructed automata'. Such under-estimation is scarcely surprising, for Stendhal's life coincided with the full flow of the romantic movement, and though in his novels he made lavish use of the romantic paraphernalia then fashionable, Stendhal really belonged to the central French tradition stretching from Montaigne to the eighteenth-century novelists and *lumières* – from which the Romantics had broken. The first to perceive this was Balzac (q.v.), who described him as 'one of the most eminent masters of the literature of ideas' as contrasted with the prevalent 'literature of imagery'. But even Balzac complained of Stendhal's style, which seemed to him rough and unfinished like that of some of the seventeenth-century writers or Diderot. The observation was just, if the criticism was unfounded. Stendhal's ideal was clarity and logic, and he claimed the *Code Napoléon* as a model of French prose. He wrote *La Chartreuse de Parme* (1839) in seven weeks – much of it being dictated; and if there are unfinished sentences in it and odd constructions, no other French novelist conveys such intense vitality or hits the reader with such immediacy.

Liveliness, accuracy, and frankness combine in Stendhal with a quality of *spagnolismo* which he derived from his beloved Italy – from the complicated intrigues of Ariosto, for instance, and from the passions of the fascinating life he saw around him. He completed only two full-length novels, *Le Rouge et Le Noir* and *La Charteuse de Parme*; his other works of fiction – *L'Abbesse de Castro*, *Lucien Leuwen*, *Lamiel* and *Armance* – are short or incomplete. Apart from his autobiographical *Vie de Henri Brulard* he wrote a number of essays (the best known is *De l'amour*, the treatise or extended notebook on the birth, crystallization, and progress of love, which has given new expressions to the French language) and superb travel diaries about Italy. His private diaries are extremely outspoken and emphasize his unromantic eighteenth-century attitude to sex. Stendhal, as he himself has foreseen, was rediscovered long after his death. One of the most penetrating of his new admirers was Friedrich Nietzsche, who called him 'that remarkable anticipatory and forerunning man who with Napoleonic tempo traversed his Europe, in fact several centuries of the European soul, as a ... discoverer thereof', and as 'the most successful expression of genuine French curiosity and inventive talent ...' A distinguished devotee in the twentieth century was Marcel Proust (q.v.). Stendhal's influence on French writers of the first rank has been growing continuously in the last thirty years, and he now has an established position among the greatest talents in French literature.

ILLUSTRATION: Page 313.

Blue Danube

STRAUSS, Johann, (1825–1899), Austrian composer. An old official of the Viennese Court used to say, 'The Emperor Franz Joseph reigned till the death of Johann Strauss.'

His life began when his own father, the elder Johann Strauss, was born. His own birth was a continuation, a renewal. Strauss the elder, with enthusiasm and little training, had raised an orchestra, taught himself to write waltzes, and then conquered Europe – and even Berlin. Having presented his wife Anna with six children, he became bored with convention, and set up house with Emilie Trampusch, to whom he gave four other children. Viewing this other family with distaste, and being a determined woman, Anna Strauss resolved to challenge her prolific husband by establishing her son Johann as Pretender to the title of Waltz-King. His temperament was exactly right. He had been expelled from school for bursting into song during a class, and he much distressed the teacher his mother sent him to by playing waltzes on the church organ, explaining that they had been intended as fugues, but had somehow been diverted from sobriety.

At nineteen Johann obtained a licence to perform in public with his orchestra. His first concert began amid protests from his father's supporters, who were a trifle mollified when they heard Strauss's fine music, and were won over when he charmingly concluded his programme with one of his father's compositions. Nonetheless, the rivalry continued until the death of the elder Strauss in 1849, when the orchestras of the two men were combined.

Any critic could solemnly – and pointlessly – remark that the many waltzes by Strauss, always played, never forgotten, (the *Blue Danube* (1866), the *Tales from the Vienna Woods* (1868), the operettas, especially *Der Fledermaus* (1873) and *Der Zigeunerbaron* (1885)), were the musical froth that arose out of a hectic, frivolous and decadent Viennese society. Strauss was a genius of light music, with an imagination that did not for a moment content itself with the conventional and the cliché. If he worshipped happiness, and stands for an era that was desperately anxious to worship with him, before the death of the Austrian Empire, and the climax of Hitler and then the Russians on the Ringstrasse, both happiness and escape are part of the human situation as much as tragedy and involvement; and they no less demand their music. No one gave better supply than Strauss – even if the Danube is mud-coloured and not blue.

ILLUSTRATION: Page 312.

'I am in the present'

STRAVINSKY, Igor Feodorovich, (b. 1882), Russian composer, the modernist who with admirable good sense has declared, in his *Poetics of Music*, 'I am no more academic than I am modern, no more modern than I am conservative.'

Stravinsky tells a story of himself in the first World War. A control officer on the French border asked him his profession, to which he replied he was 'an inventor of music'. Soberly checking this against the passport, the control officer found 'composer', and Stravinsky had to explain that 'inventor of music' seemed to him a more exact definition. A year or two before, Stravinsky had undergone the Ordeal by Bayreuth: he had been persuaded by his friend Diaghilev, the impresario of the Russian ballet, to go to the Bayreuth festival to hear Wagner's *Parsifal*. Deeply religious himself, he was revolted by *Parsifal* as a religious play. The theatre-shrine seemed like a crematorium, he was disgusted by 'the murky inanities of the Art-Religion, with its heroic hardware, its arsenal of warrior mysticism and its vocabulary seasoned with an adulterated religiosity', as he says in his autobiography.

If this was the goal of composing, then Stravinsky would retire and become an 'inventor of music'.

When the war began in 1914, Stravinsky had just returned from Russia to Switzerland, beginning a separation from his own country which led him to become, first of all, a French citizen in 1934, and afterwards an American citizen in 1945 – a transformation which has left an elegant Russian underneath the change of clothes. The soil his music grows out of is still Russian, although a western sun may have melted off the picturesque snows and dried and hardened the surface. He had soon abandoned the fairy-tale atmosphere of the early ballets, *The Firebird* (1910) and *Petrushka* (1911), and by the nineteen-twenties had begun to direct his 'ferocious intellect' to problems which were entirely musical: he became the revolutionary traditionalist trying to express in contemporary idiom musical truths which had not been new in Mozart's day. He made a new version of an old classicism, the beauty of which, according to André Gide (q.v.), 'lies in its subjugated romanticism'.

A serene disquiet runs through Stravinsky's finest classical works, such as *Perséphone* (1934), the *Symphony in C* (1940) and the *Orpheus* (1947). He makes the lament of Orpheus a lament for a world that no longer has time to sing. Yet in the *Symphony of Psalms* (1930) and the recent *Mass*, the 'inventor of music' had faith enough to build a monumental religious structure. All of Stravinsky's best music has this massive, graven quality, like the quality of monuments which might be buried but which still remain monuments. Stravinsky has written of himself 'I am in the present. I cannot know what tomorrow will bring forth. I can know only what the truth is for me today. That is what I am called upon to serve, and I serve it in all lucidity'. Writers he has worked with are

André Gide (*Perséphone*), Cocteau (*Oedipus Rex*, 1927) and W.H.Auden, who wrote the libretto for the *Rake's Progress* (1947) – for all of whom there are entries in this volume.

The universal exile

STRINDBERG, Johan August, (1849–1912), Swedish playwright, poet and novelist. 'We shall soon be fifty and have danced away our milk teeth, and should be thinking of our end. But I can't help it; I must laugh when I look at Life and her tricks, damned nasty tricks at times. As you see, my life is still as stormy as ever. There have been fair intervals, enchanting idylls, but at times it's hellish torture. I am often weary of it. I have had all I wanted of life and much besides ...' (Strindberg to Leo Littmansson, 1894.)

Strindberg belongs to the period of the exiles: Ibsen, Rimbaud, Henry James, James Joyce. For all of them exile was not merely physical but spiritual, not merely inevitable but intolerable, not merely personal but universal. Of Strindberg's three wives, Siri von Essen was Finnish, Frida Uhl was Austrian, and Harriet Bosse a Norwegian; and his sixteen most important years from 1883 to 1899 were spent outside Sweden. In 1896 he wrote from Paris to Torsten Hedlund: 'Don't you realize that Sweden is the place of the exiles, of the damned who must sit and watch how the world is run without their advice being heard? The land of the non-adult, the disenfranchised, the muts.'

Yet he was a Swede, and never more at home (like all the exiles) than when he was away. 'At first the orange trees duped me, but later! ... the Mediterranean ... *humbug, Sir!*' Catholicism tremendously appealed to him, as all his later plays show; but when it came to the question of Catholic baptism for Frida Uhl's child: 'We Protestants are tolerant and pretty easy-going in matters of creed, but we do not sell our faith, still less our children.'

No Victorian melodrama is richer in coincidences than the life of this Victorian playwright. At eighteen, he found himself back in the Klara School in Stockholm where he had been so bitterly unhappy as a child, and was now equally unhappy as a teacher (an incident reflected in *A Dream Play*). At twenty-six, going to call for the first time on Siri von Essen after he had met her shopping, he found her in the very house where he had lived before his mother died in 1862. At forty-four, when he was actually on his way to marry Frida Uhl, he met Siri's old husband, Carl Wrangel, in a Berlin street. At fifty-eight, a young actor-producer came to him with a plan for a Strindberg theatre – and this man had not only the same Christian name, but the surname which Strindberg had used for himself in his novel *The Red Room* (1879): August Falck. If in his plays and his philosophy everything turns in circles, it was because in life Strindberg had found it so.

But another dramatic device is richly present in his life; the reversal of fortune – *peripeteia*, as the Greeks called it, the swift turn round. If at one moment he is living in a garret and depending for warmth on the flue that comes up from the kitchen below, the next moment he has found a royal patron, Karl XV. He sinks again to a telegraph clerk; within a couple of years (1874) he is assistant Librarian of the Royal Library, classifying the Chinese manuscripts. In 1894 his plays are the rage of Paris, and his supporters prepare a banquet for him; but Strindberg is interested only in alchemy (later, however, the banquet finds its place in *To Damascus*). The enemy of religion and morals, he stands trial for blasphemy, and then writes *Easter*, the loveliest morality play since the Middle Ages. Renowned for his cruelty to women, mad, impossible to live with, he can always find a new sweetheart, a new friend, a new reputation.

What a pity that Strindberg is so much known as just the author of *Lady Julia* (1888) and *The Father* (1887), when *The Dream Play* (1902), *The Dance of Death* (1901) and *To Damascus* (1898–1904) are not only masterpieces in their own right (and especially the first, his own favourite), but the sources of Expressionism and much that came after. They are the last cry of Romantic Man and of the dark night of the North.

ILLUSTRATION: Page 366.

Gothic pioneer

SUGER, Abbot of St Denis, (1081–1151), administrator, mystic, patron and builder, to whom Gothic architecture was immensely indebted. 'Rarely – in fact never', wrote Panofsky in his *Abbot Suger* (1944), 'has a great patron of the arts been stirred to write a retrospective account of his intentions and accomplishments'. This Suger did in his two little books, *De Administratione* and *De Consecratione*.

Of very humble birth, Suger was dedicated at an early age to the service of St Denis. His origins, small stature and Christian humility, combined with a tremendous natural vanity, caused him to sublimate all his energies in the glorification of his abbey. He was Abbot from 1122 until his death. St Denis was the 'royal' abbey – burial-place of Pepin, Charles the Bald and Hugh Capet – as well as the repository of several relics; this enabled Suger to give it a significance, territorial and political, far greater than that of most bishoprics. His account of the rebuilding of the old and decayed Carolingian church of St Denis is in the nature of an apologia. The pious were against interference with a building said to have been touched by Christ; the austere monastic orders were against Suger's enthusiasm, his flamboyant taste and his love of gold and precious stones. Suger, in replying to these unnamed critics, emphasizes that the precious things of this world could not be used too much to the Glory of God. This, in effect, was a turning point in the story of medieval art. He wrote –

Marvel not at the gold and the expense but at the craftsmanship of the work.
Bright is the noble work; but, being nobly bright, the work
Should brighten the minds so that they may travel, through the true lights,
To the True Light, where Christ is the true door.

In replanning the Abbey of St Denis, he completely destroyed the old Basilican west front and replaced it with two fine towers and three carved portals. He then rebuilt the eastern limb of the church, and in doing so developed that miracle of medieval architecture – the full French chevet of chapels radiating from an ambulatory aisle. He was more than a mere patron, concerning himself with day-to-day building work. Suger also describes several 'miracles', such as a quarry that had previously yielded only mill-stones, suddenly giving forth marble columns, and a forest that suddenly gave beams of the right length.

Suger's taste may have been fulsome. The Christian ideal until his time, at least in the West, had been one of austerity – bare stone, fustian vestments, a wooden crucifix. By the time Suger had finished with St Denis it was compared with Santa Sophia. The later styles of Gothic – English 'Decorated' and French 'Flamboyant' – flow from Suger's influence. Some of the St Denis treasures are now in the Louvre, but the high altar – as extant in the fifteenth century – may be seen in the picture of the *Mass of St Giles* by the Master of St Giles, in the National Gallery, London.

Revolution in China

SUN YAT-SEN, (1867–1925), Chinese revolutionary, Provisional President of the Chinese Republic and founder of the Kuomintang party.

Sun Yat-sen was born in 1867 in the province of Kwangtung (Canton), the son of a Chinese Christian convert. Kwangtung at that time was more affected by Western influence than any other province of China because of the proximity of Hong Kong and the large numbers of Cantonese emigrants to Malaya, Indonesia, and California. Sun entered the College of Medicine in Hong Kong in 1887 and qualified as a doctor; he started practice in Macao, but soon became involved in a revolutionary agitation which combined the old Cantonese tradition of resistance to the Manchu conquerors of China with modern Western ideas of popular sovereignty. After the failure of an attempted insurrection in 1895, Sun fled abroad and spent the next seventeen years of his life in America and England, working for a republican revolution in China. He attacked the views of those Chinese reformers who favoured a constitutional monarchy and maintained that progress could only be brought about in China through an overthrow of the reigning dynasty. His influence alarmed the authorities in Peking, who tried to strike at him even in his exile. In 1896 he was kidnapped in London and held a prisoner in the Chinese Legation; he would have been shipped back to China and executed, but he managed to smuggle a message out of the Legation, and the British Government obtained his release.

In 1911 a revolt broke out in China, beginning as an assertion of provincial rights against the central government in a matter of railway contracts, but soon developing into a movement against the Manchu dynasty. Sun returned to China and was elected Provisional President by a revolutionary assembly in Nanking. But the only effective military force in China was under the command of Yuan Shih-kai, who was prepared to arrange the abdication of the dynasty on condition that he himself was made first President of the Republic. Sun retired in Yuan's favour and the Republic was established. But it soon became clear that Yuan wished to be a dictator; the Kuomintang party, which Sun had founded, dominated the new parliament, but was powerless to control the executive which rested on the support of the army. A new civil war broke out in 1913 and Sun again had to flee abroad, this time to Japan. Later, after Yuan's death in 1916, central authority in China broke up completely, and Sun was able to return to Canton, where he set up a local government based on the Kuomintang. He maintained his power in his home province through various ups and downs of fortune until his death in 1925, but it was only afterwards that the Kuomintang advanced northwards from Canton and overran central and northern China.

After 1917 Sun's political thinking was increasingly affected by Marxism and by the example of the Russian Revolution. The chaos which had followed the attempt to set up a democratic republic in China had disillusioned him about his former liberal ideals, and he now inclined to the single-party dictatorship for rebuilding China on the model of the Bolshevik dictatorship in Russia, even though without any immediate socialist objective. At the same time the insistence of the Western Powers on payment of the foreign-administered Maritime Customs revenue to the nominal central government in Peking caused Sun to adopt a strongly pro-Soviet policy. A close working alliance was concluded in 1924 between the Kuomintang and the Chinese Communist Party, which had been founded in 1921, and Soviet political and military advisers were sent to Canton to reorganize the Kuomintang and its army. In the last year of his life, however, Sun receded somewhat from his enthusiasm for Marxism and came under the influence of Maurice William, an American anti-Marxist writer of Russian-Jewish origin. Sun's principal exposition of political theory, his *San Min Chu I* or 'Three Principles of the People' reflects both tendencies of thought, but as long as he lived Sun avoided any break with the Communists. Sun Yat-sen married one of the three famous Soong sisters, another of whom married Chiang Kai-shek (q.v.). After her husband's death Madame Sun quarrelled with her sisters and eventually threw in her lot with the Communists.

Sun Yat-sen always commanded respect, even among his political adversaries, for his personal integrity and incorruptibility. But he was never a success as a practical politician or administrator, and at the time of his death there was little to indicate that either his Kuomintang or his Communist allies were destined to obtain power over China as a whole. (*See also Tzu Hsi and Mao Tse-tung*.)

'Hero, buffoon, half demon and half dirt'

SUVOROV, Aleksandr Vasilyevich, (1729–1800), Russian Field-Marshal, Count of Rimnik, Prince of Italy, Count of the Holy Roman Empire, called 'the ever-victorious general', a character of contradictions.

Byron described him in *Childe Harold* as

'Hero, buffoon, half demon and half dirt,
Praying, instructing, desolating, plundering'!

Suvorov, the son of a Russian general, joined the army as a private at the age of twelve and was on active service at fifteen, which gives substance to his later boast: 'I am a soldier and know neither kith nor kin.' He served in numerous wars, had become a major-general by forty-nine and made himself internationally notorious for his conduct in the Russo-Turkish war of 1789–1791. After a victory at Rimnik, for which he was made a count, he had sacked Ismail, in Bessarabia, with appalling ferocity. 26,000 Turks were massacred. Transferred to Poland, Suvorov was responsible for the mass slaughter of 15,000 Poles when he captured the Praga suburb of Warsaw. For these services he was promoted Field-Marshal.

After some years of retirement, during which he fell into disgrace with the Tsar, he was recalled to take command against the French Revolutionary forces in North Italy. He drove them out in a series of quick victories, for which he was awarded the title of Prince of Italy, but Massena's defence of the Swiss Alps prevented him from advancing to the Lower Rhine, and he had to retire, losing much baggage and stores. This was Suvorov's only defeat as an army commander. He returned to Russia and died in disgrace the following year; but he was soon recognized

as a national hero; and a Russian hero he has remained ever since.

Suvorov was extremely ugly; he was small, he stooped and he was delicate from boyhood. He made great demands on his soldiers, who idolized him as 'Father Suvorov', and he lived like a private on his campaigns, preferring to sleep on a truss of hay, covered with a cloak. He never carried money or wore a watch or an overcoat, and disliked using pocket handkerchiefs. It must be said that Suvorov was one of the best-educated generals in any army of his time; he was well-read, he was fluent in eight languages, he even wrote poetry – rather badly – and often compiled his official despatches in verse. As for the buffoon in Suvorov, he played practical jokes, and sneered and gibed at his equals and inferiors, but grovelled – 'half demon and half dirt' – to his superiors. A plunderer – but he never took booty for himself; and though responsible for bloody massacres, this slight grotesque creature frequently protested that he hated bloodshed. In war his tactic was to 'march on the enemy and attack him', and from Suvorov later Russian commanders derived their doctrine of 'invincibility by weight of numbers' and the mass attack.

God's instrument

SWEDENBORG, Emanuel, (1688–1772), Swedish visionary, and natural philosopher. 'All religion has relation to life', he wrote, 'and the life of religion is to do good'.

Educated at the university of Uppsala, Swedenborg began life as a scientist, studying medicine, mathematics and astronomy, pursuing knowledge in Amsterdam and London. To Greenwich Observatory he submitted a method for calculating longitude by the moon. In Sweden he devoted himself to practical schemes of mining, metallurgy and engineering. Practical experiments in anatomy led him to speculate on the relation of soul to body, and to conclude that 'Life is one thing, nature is another'. He localized the psychological functions of the brain in the cortex, and observed the symbolic nature of dreams, which seemed to him directed to some definite end, guiding the soul.

The soul was Swedenborg's atmosphere. At fifty-five, he began to experience visions, to develop powers of clairvoyance and the power of 'communicating' with 'discarnate spirits'. *The Word Explained*, symbolic re-interpretation of the Bible, was dictated to him, so he claimed, in automatic writing. Yet Swedenborg showed no traces of insanity, he continued his practical activities, he entertained his many distinguished friends in his beautiful house and garden on the island of Södermalm, and he continued to write visionary works – of which the best known are *Heaven and Hell* (1758), *The Divine Providence* and *The Divine Love and Wisdom* (1763–4), *The Apocalypse Revealed* (1766) and *Conjugial Love* (1768) – until the end of his life.

Swedenborg's insights may not appeal to severely additive and logical minds. 'It was to Swedenborg', F.W.H. Myers wrote, 'that the unseen world appeared before all things as a realm of law.' According to his theory of 'correspondences', appearances in the spiritual world correspond to mental states; and the same is true of the natural world, in which, however, the forms so created are fixed in matter. 'The Lord's Kingdom', he held, 'is like a man; and without such a kingdom, which is like a true man (for the Lord is the only Man, and his Kingdom resembles him) no man could possibly live, since all things in heaven conspire to the conservation of the minutest things in the body.'

Swedenborg's morality was much in advance of his day: all acts were to be judged by their intention: 'with some the angels counted these as evils of sin, and with others accounted them not as evils'. This test he applied even to marriage, which he regarded as an inner, not a legal bond: 'It is the life of our love which we live, and that life is of such quality as the love is.'

Poets were indebted to this student of God and explorer of the spirit as they were indebted to the thought of Jakob Böhme (q.v.). Blake and Coleridge were influenced by him, as well as Carlyle, Balzac in France, and William James in America.

I hate that animal called Man

SWIFT, Jonathan, (1667–1745), Irish satirist and poet, and author of *Gulliver's Travels*. 'An immense genius;' Thackeray said of him, 'an awful downfall

and ruin. So great a man he seems, that thinking of him is like an empire falling.'

In his last days of loneliness and madness, a Diogenes in an Irish cabin, friends heard him muttering, 'I am what I am.' But what was Swift? For two centuries that has been the ground for a battle of books. Macaulay, the Whig historian indicting the man who went over to the Tories, called him 'the ribald priest, the perjured lover, the apostate politician, a heart burning with hatred against the whole human race, a mind richly stored with images from the dunghill and lazar house'. But then Macaulay was also the Victorian who needed rose-coloured glasses for the facts of life: Swift dissected such facts under the microscope. Swift, at least, knew what he was. He put it in his own epitaph, and Yeats has translated its mordant Latin:

> Swift has sailed into his rest;
> *Savage indignation there*
> *Cannot lacerate his breast.*
> Imitate him if you dare,
> World-besotted traveller; he
> Served human liberty.

'Principally I hate and detest that animal called man,' Swift wrote, 'although I heartily love John, Peter, Thomas and so forth.' Macaulay saw the general hate, missed the individual compassion. *Gulliver* castigates Man. The epigrams castigate the Sexes. 'A Nice Man is a Man of nasty Ideas.' 'A very little Wit is valued in a Woman, as we are pleas'd with a very few Words spoken plain by a Parrot.' But the Dublin poor, honouring Swift's charity, conducted him to his burial. He lies in the Cathedral of St Patrick, of which he was dean, beside 'Stella', the Esther Johnson of his famous and enigmatic *Journal to Stella*. In the baby-talk of his letters to her is the tenderness squeezed out of his satire. That tenderness fills his passion at young Lady Ashburnham's death: 'To see so many thousand wretches burdening the earth, while such as her die, makes me think God did never intend life for a blessing.'

Swift is all paradox. That *Gulliver's Travels* is a classic children's book is paradox pursuing him after death. The marvellous story of the floating island, the scientists seeking sunshine in cucumbers, the manikins and the horses, deceives them by a style that runs like a needle through water, and by a precision which compels the mind to turn each event, each incident, into a picture. Emerson said he described his characters as if for the police; and certainly he saw all the warts upon humanity's face. Dryden told Swift that he would never be a poet. But he was wrong, and as well as his prose, Swift's poems, in their wide range of savagery, satire, irony, raciness and fun, should not be underestimated.

ILLUSTRATION: Page 314.

T

Light pictures

TALBOT, William Henry Fox, (1800–1877), English inventor of photography, the first man to perfect a negative from which any number of prints could be made.

He was a scholarly country gentleman, living at Lacock Abbey, a nunnery turned into a country house, in Wiltshire. At Cambridge he had done well in his scientific studies. All his life he kept up researches in mathematics and physics, but it was the study of light (much to the fore since the discoveries of Newton and the work of Sir David Brewster) and later photography, that chiefly occupied him. At Como, in 1833, he was trying to paint pictures by the aid of a *camera lucida* – an advanced form of the *camera obscura*, which with the aid of a lens cast an image of the landscape on paper – and he wondered if by some means or other the image could not be fixed and made permanent.

As early as 1802 Thomas Wedgwood, the potter's son, had fixed an image on sensitized paper. Talbot worked along these lines, with no idea that in France, Louis Jacques Mandé Daguerre was doing almost the same thing. Daguerre was following Niepce, who made what he called 'heliotypes' – on glass plates covered with bitumen. When, in January 1839, it was announced to the *Académie des Sciences* in Paris that Daguerre had registered photographic images on silver-coated plates, Talbot (a little piqued) asked Faraday to announce his invention of 'Photogenic Drawing': a process that reproduced an image on chemically sensitized paper. The brightness, detail, and novelty of the daguerrotype made it at first the more popular form of photograph: but Talbot, using

paper sensitized by iodide of silver, had been able to develop and fix a negative on the paper, which could be used to print on to another paper, thus producing any number of positive prints. These pictures, called Calotypes (later, Talbotypes), ultimately led to all modern plate and film photography. To begin with, Fox Talbot was rather harsh about patents, but he then presented his ideas to the nation after an appeal had been made to him by the Presidents of the Royal Society and the Royal Academy (since photography was the child both of art and science).

Talbot's book, *The Pencil of Nature* (1844), contains the first photographs ever used for book-illustration: a 'Notice to the Reader' says, 'The plates of the present work are impressed by the agency of light alone, without any aid whatsoever from the artist's pencil.' The fading postures and blurred detail of the Calotypes appear very crude compared with the sharply defined, glossy prints of today: but Talbot's views on the boon of photography are completely up to date.

ILLUSTRATION: Page 323.

The 'Cursed Cripple'

TALLEYRAND-PÉRIGORD, Charles Maurice de, (1754–1838), French statesman, one of the most eminent diplomats of his time, civilized, witty, cynical, a trimmer of consummate success. He survived the Monarchy, the Directory, the Consulship, the Empire, and the Restoration: he withstood calumny from all directions, grew very rich, and on his death-bed signed a renunciation of all his misdeeds, thus reconciling himself with the Church.

He was unprincipled, not alone in this in his century certainly, but more so than almost any other man of similar position. It seems clear now that his claims that his actions were all for the good of France were not mere hypocrisy: in an age of reason, he abhorred enthusiasm ('*pas trop de zèle*', he said once) and preferred the skill of negotiation to the lesser arts of leadership.

From an early age Talleyrand was lame, a deformity that did not prevent him leading a life of cultivated licentiousness: by custom rather than vocation he entered the Church, and became Bishop of Autun in 1788. Autun sent him to the National Assembly in 1789: his verbal skill created a favourable impression.

While in England on a mission to Pitt, the Monarchy fell, and he was forced to flee to America. After 1794 he was able to return; his good friend Mme de Stael aided his political perferment and he became Foreign Minister in 1797. Like all good diplomats, he had an eye for straws in the wind, or stars on the ascent. He saw that the star of Buonaparte was rising, and he rose with it.

His fortunes rose as well: his avarice was unparalleled. A series of shady financial transactions with foreign powers marked his career, his supreme usefulness saving him from disgrace. In the plot that overthrew the Directory he had his two plans ready: Napoleon became First Consul, and Talleyrand stayed. He worked hard to restrict Napoleon's territorial ambition, although he had no objection to the Consul's assumption of the title of Emperor: Talleyrand found himself Grand Chamberlain, with an appropriate salary.

After Leipzig, he saw that the end was not far off. He began to consider the future. News of some alleged chicanery reached Napoleon, who began to upbraid Talleyrand with coarse accusations of perfidy. Talleyrand's only comment was: 'What a pity that such a great man should have been brought up so badly.' It was the last time that he saw Napoleon. In 1814 he was persuading the Tsar that only the return of the Bourbons could solve the problem of France. 'The republic is an impossibility,' he said, 'the regency and Bernadotte are an intrigue, the Bourbons alone are a principle.' At the Congress of Vienna, Talleyrand concluded a profitable secret alliance with England and Holland.

Under Louis XVIII he was President of the Council; at the revolution of 1830 he supported the Duke of Orleans, and was rewarded with the Embassy at London. He died in harness, and was widely mourned. The 'cursed cripple' had survived when thousands had fallen victim of their allegiances. He had been far too shrewd ever to give himself wholeheartedly.

Timur the lame

TAMERLANE, (1336–1405), was born, like his ancestor Jenghiz Khan, so it was said, with hands clenched and full of blood. When he died he had the reputation of the greatest destroyer of towns and most pitiless exterminator of people in the memory of man.

It is easy to see his appeal to the Elizabethans: the sheer enormity of his actions, the massacres, the burnings, the sweep of his kingdom, the beauty of his capital, Samarkand. Everything was here for Christopher Marlowe, whose *Tamburlaine the Great* was a dramatized chronicle of his barbarities and triumphs.

Robust by nature, fond of warlike pastimes and reading the Koran, he rose to power as governor of Transoxiana: strength, self-reliance and complete lack of loyalty were obviously qualities he possessed in good measure, for by 1369 he had survived a host of internecine struggles, and was proclaimed king of Djagatai by the Tartars. This was the beginning of the Tamerlane, *i.e.* 'Timur the lame', of history, a tall, long-bearded, white-skinned man, whose sole aim was to conquer all the nations that Jenghiz Khan had formerly held. By 1380 he was ready – with Persia as his first objective. He seems to have been lenient with those who did not oppose him: an unfortunate town that did (Sebsewar) provided the first example of his favourite punishment—2,000 of the inhabitants were encased alive in a pile of brick and mortar. He conquered Telvis, Kars, Tiflis, Var without let; at Ispahan 70,000 were slaughtered. By 1391 he was back in Samarkand, warring with his longtime enemy, Toktamish. Bagdad he occupied unresisted, and then continued the struggle with Toktamish, pursuing him nearly to the gates of Moscow. Returning to Persia, he ravaged Azov.

India was the next glittering prize; with loud assertion that his sole aim was the propagation of Islam, he marched as far as Delhi, where Mahmoud waited to oppose him. Before the battle, which he won, he cut the throats of 100,000 prisoners. With even Kashmir acknowledging him, he left India in 1399. His final campaign was against Bayezid, ruler of the Ottoman empire. 'Turkoman ant', wrote Tamerlane, 'do you dare to attack an elephant?' and defeated him. There were still new worlds for Tamerlane: impatient to conquer China, he would not wait for the spring, and led out an army of 200,000 in the winter of 1404. Taken ill, he died proclaiming his faith in God. His embalmed body was returned, as he had always returned, to Samarkand.

He was a quiet, reserved man, we are told, who disliked both lies and jokes, and who never spoke of violence, murder and pillage – a common, if ludicrous, reticence which he shares with many of the world's famous murderers.

Poetry and wine

T'AO CH'IEN, (365–427), one of the older masters of Chinese poetry, in the Chin dynasty, a poet of resignation, wisdom and tenderness.

It is hard to dwell long in prosperity;
Rise and decline cannot be reckoned on.
What were formerly lotus buds in May,
Now in the autumn are but withered seed-pods.
A heavy frost stiffens the prairie grasses –
They wilt despondently and do not quickly die.
The sun and moon come ever circling back.
Once *we* depart we do not shine again.
I ponder deeply on times long past and gone
Though to remember tears my very entrails.

That brief poem gives the individual tone, the character and directness of his work. T'ao came of a good though not rich family, preferred living on his own small estate to posts in the civil service, wrote and drank heavily – compare Li Tai-po (q.v.) and meditated, and wrote again. Indeed, being drunk loosened his tongue and his thoughts; it made him a superb conversationalist, and often inspired him to poetry. When drunk (as he claimed), he wrote this poem:

Fortune and misfortune
have no fixed abode;
This one and the other
are given us in turn.
Shao P'ing working
in his field of melons
Was much as he had been
when Lord of Tung-ling.
Cold and hot seasons
follow one another,
And the way of man
will always be like this.
The intelligent man
sees that it must be so.
Having gone so far,
he will not doubt again,
But from that moment
every day and evening
He will be happy
holding a cup of wine.

T'ao Ch'ien's marks were independence, honesty, aloofness and – not untypical of poets – a certain separation in spirit from others (though he had his friends) and from his own family. He was also known as T'ao Yin-chii, 'T'ao who lived in hiding'. He said about himself that he wrote to please himself, and so revealed his own thought. Possibly one of the stories told of him can be interpreted in that sense. Though he was not a musician, he owned a lute without strings which he would hold in his two hands; observing that he cared only for the music inside the lute – 'So why should I bother about the notes and the strings?' One poem of his especially stays in the mind:

Long I have loved to stroll among the hills and marshes,
And take my pleasure roaming the woods and fields.
Now I hold hands with a train of nieces and nephews,
Parting the hazel growth we tread the untilled wastes,
Wandering to and fro amidst the hills and mounds
Everywhere around us are dwellings of ancient men.
Here are vestiges of their wells and hearth stone,
There the rotted stumps of bamboos and mulberry groves.
I stop and ask a faggot-gatherer:
'These men – what has become of them?'
The faggot-gatherer turns to me and says:
'Once they were dead that was the end of them'.
In the same world men lead different lives;
Some at the court, some in the market place.
Indeed I know these are no empty words:
The life of man is like a shadow-play
Which must in the end return to nothingness

(Translations by William Acker.)

Terra australis incognita

TASMAN, Abel Janszoon, (c. 1603–1659), the most resourceful of the Dutch explorers, who took over from the Portuguese and the Spaniards the quest for the *terra australis incognita*. This was the great 'unknown southern land' or continent, which must stretch, so the older geographers believed, right across the Southern Pacific as a necessary balance or counterweight to the European–Asiatic land mass on the opposite side of the globe. They believed, also, that it must correspond with Marco Polo's 'golden province of Beach, which few have visited because of the cruelty of the people'.

Tasman's magnificent feat was the circumnavigation of Australia and New Guinea, in the course of which he also discovered Tasmania and New Zealand. Clearly Australia (which the Dutch called New Holland) could not be that 'golden' southern continent which had inspired so much cupidity and curiosity. Tasman did not land in New Zealand, and its possible extension towards Chile was untested. The continent, men now thought, must be somewhat smaller and less inviting than cosmographers had assumed; and this question of the *terra australis incognita* was left to be settled by the Englishman Captain Cook (q.v.). The Dutch East India Company who promoted Tasman's voyage, were not unnaturally disappointed with its commercial results.

'If any calm, a calm despair'

TENNYSON, Alfred, (1809–1892), English elegiac poet – of

> ... the chill
> November dawns and dewy-glooming downs,
> The gentle shower, the smell of dying leaves,
> And the low moan of leaden-colour'd seas.

It is rather too easy to picture Tennyson as the *grand seigneur* of Victorian poetry, with the noble features, the dark beard, the 'old master' pose given him by photographer or draughtsman, and the peerage – the only one ever conferred on an English poet for poetry – given him by Queen Victoria. The physical reality is different, a swarthy man, with loose dark hair, a slouch, badly creased clothing, and the look Rossetti has given him in his drawing. The spiritual reality is of a man 'unhappy from his uncertainty regarding the condition and destiny of man', having white lilac for his favourite flower, and maintaining an exquisite refuge in the melancholy, autumnal beauty of phrases, lines, and whole lyrics. Tennyson's vocal taste was ultra-fine – *The mellow ouzel fluted in the elm; Landscape lover; lord of language; Love's white star Beam'd thro' the Thicken'd cedar in the dusk; If any calm, a calm despair.*

Above all, he was the poet who wanted the occasion, the stimulus, but did not always wait for it. Ask Tennyson to write a poem for the nineteenth centenary of the death of Virgil, to whom he felt akin, and the result is splendid:

> ... I salute thee, Mantovano,
> I that loved thee since my day began,
> Wielder of the stateliest measure
> ever moulded by the lips of man.

Bring him within hearing of the bugle sounded at Killarney ('The bugle echoes', said Tennyson, 'were wonderful – nine times – at last like a chant of angels in the sky'), and how elegiacally fine a lyric his exacting ear and speech organs contrive –

> The splendour falls on castle walls
> And snowy summits old in story:
> The long light shakes across the lakes,
> And the world cataract leaps in glory.
> Blow, bugle, blow, set the wild echoes flying,
> Blow, bugle; answer, echoes, dying, dying, dying.
>
> O hark, O hear! how thin and clear,
> And thinner, clearer, farther going!
> O sweet and far from cliff and scar
> The horns of Elfland faintly blowing!
> Blow, let us hear the purple glens replying:
> Blow, bugle; answer, echoes, dying, dying, dying.
>
> O love, they die in yon rich sky,
> They faint on hill or field or river:
> Our echoes roll from soul to soul
> And grow for ever and for ever.
> Blow, bugle, blow, set the wild echoes flying,
> And answer, echoes, answer, dying, dying, dying.

Tennyson made the mistake of writing too much between the occasions and of attempting to justify himself in verse preachments suitable for the time – notably in the *Idylls of the King,* which stretched from 1857 to 1872. *In Memoriam* (1850) without question was his masterpiece – again a series of elegies: autumn, regret, dying falls, sonorous resignation – of which the stimuli were the death of his friend A. H. Hallam and his own fears and uncertainties. Millais the painter, when he was twenty-two, wrote in his diary 'Oct. 23, 1851. Went to bed rather late, and read *In Memoriam,* which produced a refining melancholy.' Unlike Baudelaire (q.v.) Tennyson averted his eyes and sense from all that was not 'refining': although it is said that he kept a collection of Victorian *curiosa* behind the Waverley Novels in his study. When other men's eyes grew more inclusive and honest, the old Tennyson had to exclaim at authors:

> Feed the budding rose of boyhood with the drainage of your sewer:
> Send the drain into the fountain, lest the stream should issue pure.

Outside the occasion the great man could be exceedingly little:

Fairy:	Tit, my queen, must it be so?
	Wherefore, wherefore should we go?
Titania:	I, Titania, bid you flit,
	And you dare to call me Tit! ...
	Pertest of our flickering mob
	Wouldst thou call my Oberon Ob?

When he died in the fullness of his honours, laurel from Virgil's tomb was put into his coffin, and he was taken through the Sussex starlight and put in a train en route for burial in Westminster Abbey.

ILLUSTRATION: Page 325.

Soul in pursuit of liberty

TERESA DE ÁVILA, (1515–1582), saint, visionary, poet and reformer of the Carmelites, whose writings (*e.g. The Way of Perfection*, and *The Castle of the Soul*) are models of Spanish prose. Her autobiography is held to be the finest written by any saint except Augustine, whose works she much admired.

Teresa's childhood was spent in her father's house in Ávila. There was a good library of Spanish books which he encouraged his nine sons and three daughters to read. When she was a small girl, Teresa, inspired by some Lives of the Saints, persuaded one of her brothers to run away with her from home to convert the Moors or die a martyr's death. At fourteen she was a normal child, devouring romances, loving finery and perfume and wishing 'to appear handsome'. According to herself, she formed an undesirable friendship with an older cousin, and was thereupon sent to school in a convent. At school she began to veer towards the religious life, against the opposition of her widowed father; and at nineteen she made her own decision, entering a Carmelite house where a friend was already a nun. Within a year or two she became so ill that she was fetched home to die. But she slowly recovered, though she remained a near-cripple for a long time and was delicate for the rest of her life. In these years she had begun to practise mental prayer, though she tells us she became lax in this respect, not leading the life of prayer in earnest until early middle life. She made it a rule never to speak ill of anyone – 'Hence it was understood, wherever I was, that all absent persons were secure.'

Life in a convent at that time was not exacting. Nuns often resided for long whiles away from their convent, especially if the convent was poor. St Teresa gives it as her opinion that it is better for girls to marry even 'very meanly' than to go into religious houses that have the advantages neither of this world nor of the spiritual life. Her reform of the Carmelite Order began in 1562, when against opposition she founded the Convent of St Joseph, in Ávila, the first of a number of houses, both for nuns and for monks, that she established throughout Spain during her last twenty years. The reformed nuns – the Discalzed (or Barefoot) Carmelites, they were called – were strictly enclosed, practised great austerities and severe penance, and observed the ancient rule of poverty. St Teresa held that religious communities should number not more than about twelve persons. Passionately orthodox, she wished to remove many of the abuses which had caused the Reformation, and she was herself one of the strong forces of the counter-reformation.

In the early years of her visionary life St Teresa was persecuted by a group who maintained that her visions were of evil origin. At one time she even feared that she might have to appear before the Inquisition. Despite her confessor's urging, she could not banish the vision of Jesus from her mind. He was the Heavenly Bridegroom, and she his Bride. 'Either suffer or die,' she once said; and as an angel plunged the burning tip of his lance into her side again and again she suffered and was happy at the same time. Her powerful friends and her strict conformity to the rules of Church and Order saved her. St Peter of Alcántara, mystic and ascetic, was Teresa's friend and helped to confirm her in her path. Later, she was to influence St John of the Cross (q.v.) in the same formative way.

St Teresa's account of her visions stands high in mystical writing. She describes the four states of meditation, contemplation, ecstasy and union; she developed, in ecstatic states, apparent foreknowledge of events, conversing with the absent or the dead and healing by prayer. Her visions ranged from the heights of heaven to the depths of hell; and the physical world seemed to her a place of bondage, and death a passage into life – 'I die because I may not die' is a frequent theme, as well as the refrain of her best known poem. 'O what it is', she wrote, 'for a soul, which finds herself in such a condition as this [ecstasy] to be brought to return again, to converse in the world, and to behold the comedy, or puppet show of this miserable life ... and now she cries out aloud ... and begs of his Divine Majesty to set her at liberty. –

And this is often done with so very great an impulse of mind, that the soul would get presently out of the body, in pursuit of this liberty: and in the mean time, seeing she is not freed, she walks up and down the world, like one sold for a slave, to serve and drudge in a strange country: and that which afflicts her yet more, is that she cannot meet with many, who will lament with her, and desire that which she desires.'

All Teresa's accounts of her spiritual life were written under obedience, for her confessor; and they show her warm humanity, her capacity for friendship, her courage, her administrative ability, her energy and her spiritual greatness.

Back to the Stone Age

THOMSEN, Christian Jurgensen, (1788–1865), Danish archaeologist, who navigated and charted history before history and helped to make sense of the most ancient story of man.

Before Thomsen's day the certain tale of man petered out with the earliest records of literature. Beyond, backwards, were seas of time not unlike the unexplored Atlantic before Columbus and Cabot. These seas were not regarded as very wide: push across them, and you would come to the act of creation in 4004 B.C. Thomsen was in charge of the young National Museum at Copenhagen, where he was faced with the usual mix-middle of objects, which were clearly ancient in a cloudy indeterminate way. Taking a hint from a Danish historian, he conceived a plan for dividing his exhibits chronologically. Man must have moved technologically from stage to stage, and Thomsen postulated three stages: (1) when men used stone of various kinds (especially flint) for weapons and tools, (2) when they learnt to use bronze, (3) when, as we still do, they used iron. So the Museum was arranged and divided into Stone Age, Bronze Age and Iron Age, the one following the other.

Thomsen published his classification in 1836. Thus three small boats were provided for navigating the unknown seas or the misty dimension which archaeologists were adding to our story. Excavation proved Thomsen's brilliant hypothesis to be accurate, more or less; and man had now the first crude chart of his own antiquity. Since then the old chart has been divided and sub-divided, and it is now out-moded. Thomsen so liked his Three-Age system (and with some reason) that his coat of arms was heraldically coloured grey for the Stone Age, bronze for the Bronze Age and black for the Iron Age.

Into the Atomic Age

THOMSON, Sir Joseph John, (1856–1940), English physicist and discoverer of the electron.

Thomson's father died early, so the family were unable to pay the premium for him to become an engineer, and he was sent to the newly-opened Owens College in Manchester, because it was cheaper, at the age of fourteen. He graduated in engineering, and then went with a scholarship to Cambridge, where he did excellently in mathematics. In 1881 he published his first important paper, showing that an electrically-charged body increases in mass with increases in speed. He even calculated that the mass of the earth is increased by 650 tons, because it is a charged body moving through space.

The premature death of Clerk Maxwell in 1879 left the Cavendish professorship of experimental physics vacant, and J. J. Thomson, who had taken his Cambridge degree in mathematics and had very little experience as an experimenter, was elected in 1884, at the age of twenty-eight. During the next decade Thomson devoted more and more effort to experiment and to organizing laboratory research. His reward came in 1897, with his conclusive proof of the existence of the electron, one of the great discoveries of all time, which led to the whole modern science of electronics. The fact that electrons could be derived from any atom showed that atoms had a structure. Thus Thomson also founded the science of atomic structure, and showed how Mendeleev's Periodic Table of the Chemical Elements naturally arose from it.

In spite of his tremendous experimental achievements, Thomson was very clumsy with his hands. He saw experiments in his imagination, and then made his nimble-fingered assistants handle the apparatus, the assistants praying that he would keep out of the way. Thomson indeed was like a general, one of those who created the modern idea of organized scientific research; he could tell his many gifted officers what to do and co-ordinate their doings in a grand scheme. Utterly different in temperament was Thomson's great pupil and successor Rutherford (q.v.), no general, but a hero of research, who rushed forward at the head of his troops and then returned victoriously with trophies from the unknown. Shrewd and humorous, Thomson could hold together the highly gifted and often highly strung research students who came to him at Cambridge. So he, and they, set the theme of research in experimental physics for the twentieth century – the discovery of the secrets of the atom.

ILLUSTRATION: Page 320.

'Heal yourselves, doctors: by God, I live'

THOREAU, Henry David, (1817–1862), American naturalist, poet and prose-writer: 'The greater part of what my neighbours call good I believe in my soul to be bad', wrote Thoreau in *Walden, or Life in the Woods* (1854), the most famous of his books.

Nearly all his life he passed in Concord, Massachusetts, where his father and the family made pencils in a shed attached to their house. According to his great friend Emerson (q.v.), he knew the country round Concord like a fox or a bird, threading it by his own paths. In 1845 he built a hut on the edge of the green, deep and still waters of Walden Pond. There he meditated for two years, confirming for himself the values of self-reliance, simplicity of need, communion with bird, beast and plant, and delight in man's natural environment. This hermit's life deepened his criticism of human society – the society of neighbours nearby in Concord and of the world at large.

Living what he preached, no American was more tender, yet more resolute and more passionate for the dignity of the individual. At Harvard it was the rule to wear black coats in chapel. The young Thoreau rejected this interference: he wore a green coat. In Concord in 1845 he refused to pay the poll tax, and was arrested. 'I was put into jail as I was going to the shoemaker's to get a shoe which was mended. When I was let out the next morning' – against his wish the tax had been paid for him – 'I proceeded to finish my errand, and, having put on my mended shoe, joined a huckleberry party.' In half an hour, he was high up in a huckleberry field where 'the State was nowhere to

be seen'. So he wrote about himself in *Civil Disobedience*, the classic and characteristic essay which moved Mahatma Gandhi (q.v.) in his campaign of non-resistance against English rule in India. In Great Britain, Thoreau's teaching on human dignity and freedom also helped to shape the ideas of the Labour Party which in the end gave their freedom to India and Pakistan.

As well as *Walden*, notable writings by Thoreau are *A Week on the Concord and Merrimack Rivers* (1849), *Cape Cod* (1865), the portions of his Journal in the collected *Writings of Henry David Thoreau* and the *Familiar Letters of Henry David Thoreau*.

'Heal yourselves, doctors; by God, I live' – these words by Thoreau fit a life and a message admirably American.

Passionate for fame

TINTORETTO, properly called Jacopo Robusti, (1518–1594), Venetian painter. 'He had a passionate desire for fame and his one thought was to achieve immortality through his work,' wrote Carlo Ridolfi, the 17th century historian of Venetian art; and though there may be other reasons for continuing to be an artist, Tintoretto's life was dedicated to the expansion of the language of painting; he was always making experiments in aid of a more total expression, and he spent his entire life in Venice, devoting himself in proud isolation and austere glory to the most tremendous labours any artist had yet attempted.

As a young man Tintoretto nailed to his studio door the sign 'Titian's colour; Michelangelo's drawing', and in an attempt to achieve the maximum of drama, force and impetuosity of movement in his pictures, he tried new effects of light, shade and colour; he let the light flicker across his canvases; he contrasted the emotional highlights of his scenes with rich warm shadows and cool half-lights. He worked far into the night, experimenting with wax or clay figures hung on threads, allowing them to move in flickering candlelight until he had the effect he wanted. As he grew older, he worked, not like other artists, from carefully prepared drawings, but directly on to the canvas, painting spontaneously and impetuously, gaining still more vitality and violence of movement.

In 1563 the Scuola di San Rocco, a religious

brotherhood of Venice, decided to have their refectory ceiling decorated and asked several painters, including Tintoretto, to submit designs. While the other artists were preparing drawings, he painted a full-size picture; when the committee assembled to judge the designs and award the commission, they found that Tintoretto had already had his picture put into place, saying that this was his way of preparing a design and if they did not wish to recompense him he would make them a gift of the painting. For the next twenty-three years he worked for this fraternity, painting on the walls of the Scuola, where they may still be seen, a prodigious series of episodes from the Old and New Testaments, of which the *Crucifixion* is the masterpiece.

At the same time he worked for other churches in Venice, for private patrons and for the Venetian Republic. However, the new sea routes to the East, and the struggle against the Turks, were sapping the wealth of Venice; though she was to remain a luxury city for another two hundred years. The restraints were felt by Tintoretto, who expressed them in an even greater emotionalism and by even more theatrical contrasts of flickering light and dark shadows.

In 1588, at the age of seventy, he began his most grandiose painting, the *Paradise* for the hall of the Grand Council in the Doge's Palace. Thirty feet high and seventy-four feet long, this painting contains more than five hundred figures arranged in concentric circles. Tintoretto was working up to the last day of his life. 'Beautiful colours', he once remarked, 'are for sale in the shops of the Rialto, but good drawing can be had only from the casket of the painter's talent by patient study and sleepless nights.'

Painter of splendour and luxury

TITIAN, (1477–1576), the painter in whom Venetian colour, splendour, luxury and worldliness were fulfilled.

A few very great writers, artists, composers, etc., work on and on into an old age still fresh and unrepetitive. Titian – Tiziano Vecellio – was one of them, living and painting till he was close upon a hundred; when he died, not of old age, but the plague.

Through that long while he stands more for the wealth, the power, the silks and the velvets – and the courtesans – of Venice, richest of Italian cities, than for a startling change in the nature of art. With Titian painting becomes an entertainment, which cannot be said of his young contemporary Giorgione or his predecessor Giovanni Bellini (q.v.).

Able to make an oil-painting into a splendid object and ornament, Titian was always employed and always famous. He was always 'a most healthy and fortunate man,' Vasari wrote, 'beyond any of his fellows, receiving only favours from heaven.' His house at Venice was frequented 'by all the princes, learned men and gallants of his time, for to genius he added also the most courtly manners'; and Vasari thought his work would endure 'as long as the memory of famous men', which is true and not true. Artist after artist has been moved by Titian and by his living vibrancy of colour, yet one may doubt if many of his enormous number of pictures much appeal to the modern popular consciousness. He lives somewhat by the momentum of his fame.

Before Titian, the picture was an interpretation by means of art. Titian made it into a display of art. His portraits may be grand – this master was sought for by kings and emperors and was the official artist of the Doges of Venice – but in penetration he is at times limited. If he paints a religious subject, or an altarpiece, it is a splendid exercise, which, in the end, hardly satisfies our religious need. Or if he paints a subject from myth or history, Titian no longer seems possessed by the classical world as a revelation of innocence and perfection. In fact, he was not the innocent painter, but the courtier's painter. Like his friend Aretino the poet, Titian is most himself among the courtesans of Venice. He responded passionately to the light and colours and contours of the bodies of women. What posterity has called his paintings of Venus – for instance, the Venus with a lap dog and an organist – are perfect renderings of the young, ripe, experienced and naked bodies of Venetian prostitutes. Danaë awaiting Jupiter in a shower of gold belongs, not to myth, but to this same earthly and mortal order of Venetian girls.

Titian, in brief, is the superb amorist. If he is also the dignified master of effects and the entertainer who revolutionized art, his amazing talent was not matched by his mental power. Michelangelo, after calling on Titian, declared that he had 'ability and a charming, vivacious style' – he was helped by nature, but to be supreme he needed the help of 'art and design'. A fair criticism of his greatness.

ILLUSTRATION: Page 317.

Author of 'War and Peace'

TOLSTOY, Leo Nikolayevich, (1828–1910). 'To be good', wrote this supreme Russian novelist in his diary in 1851, 'all literary work must come singing out of the writer's soul'; and in his old age he added, 'Write only when you leave a piece of flesh in the ink-well every time you dip your pen.'

Most of his time Tolstoy spent on his estate of Yasnaya Polyana, near Tula, where as a child he and his three elder brothers had searched for the magic 'green stick' which would reveal the secret of happiness to mankind. His whole life was, in a way, a continuation of that quest. His ideal as a boy, he wrote in his first published work, the autobiographical trilogy *Childhood, Boyhood* and *Youth* (1852–1856) was 'to reform all mankind', though he realized that at first he would have 'to improve himself, become the master of all the virtues and be happy'. As a student at Kazan university, he took Jean Jacques Rousseau (q.v.) for his spiritual guide and wore his portrait in a medallion round his neck. Ten years later, after falling again and again a victim to the temptations of the flesh, he was struck by 'a great and tremendous idea' of founding a new religion, which would offer felicity to men 'on earth, and not in a future life'. By that time his position as a writer was firmly established. After his visits abroad in 1857 and 1860 he gave up literature and opened a school in Yasnaya Polyana based on his own system of 'free education'. His marriage in 1862 to Sofia Bers, the daughter of a well-known Moscow physician, brought him a period of spiritual calm and happiness during which he wrote his two world-famous novels, *War and Peace* (1864–1869) and *Anna Karenina* (1873–1877).

'Tolstoy', wrote Maxim Gorky (q.v.) in appreciation of his great novels, 'has done a truly tremendous thing: he has provided us with an epitome of an age, and he has done it with astonishing truthfulness, force and beauty ... From him we can learn what I consider one of the chief merits of creative writing, I mean the art of representing people in the round. When you read him – and I am not exaggerating – you get the impression of the physical presence of his heroes, so cleverly are his characters moulded: they seem to stand before you and you cannot help feeling you could touch them with your hand.'

The years after the publication of *Anna Karenina* were years of spiritual struggle which ended when he actually did found a new religion, based chiefly on Christ's injunction, 'Resist not him that is evil'. At first his teachings were extraordinarily successful both in Russia and abroad, where his influence (and the influence of Thoreau (q.v.)) can be seen in Gandhi's acceptance of his doctrine of non-resistance. The new beliefs did not end Tolstoy's perpetual wrestling with his soul. According to Gorky, Tolstoy 'was on very indeterminate terms with God, and at times they remind me of the expression: "two bears in one lair".' They did, though, make him into one of the most powerful men in Russia. 'We have two Tsars: Nicholas II and Leo Tolstoy,' Alexy Suvorin, one of the most influential newspaper owners in Russia noted in his diary. 'Which of the two is more powerful? Nicholas II cannot do anything with Tolstoy, he cannot share his throne, whereas Tolstoy is undoubtedly shaking the throne of Nicholas and his dynasty.'

The innate contradiction between his religious beliefs and 'the wild life of plenty amidst want' which was forced on him by his family drove him at last into flight from Yasnaya Polyana on the night of 28 October 1910. He caught pneumonia in the train and died on 7 November in the house of the station-master of Astapovo (now renamed Leo Tolstoy). He was buried in the grounds of Yasnaya Polyana, near the spot where he and his brothers had been looking for 'the green stick'.

ILLUSTRATION: Page 316.

Scourge of heresy

TORQUEMADA, Tomás de, (1420–1498), the famous Inquisitor-General of Spain, whose reign of terror in the name of faith set a pattern too familiar in our own time. There was little difference between the Holy Offices of the Inquisition and the torture chambers of the Third Reich. In each case the protagonists believed in the right of their own cause, in either case the most sadistic impulses were at work behind a wealth of polemic.

It has been said that Torquemada was the perfect agent: of King Ferdinand, of Rome, of the Inquisition. Ferdinand was jealous of the wealthy Moors and Jews of Castile: he alleged that they had embraced Christianity for its privileges, not through faith. From Sixtus IV he obtained a bull authorizing an Inquisition: it was the first organized witch-hunt. In 1482 Torquemada, a devout Dominican, was made inquisitor-general for Castile, later for Aragon and Barcelona. He reorganized the tribunals that were already in existence, and standardized the procedure. The tribunals met regularly, and they judged without appeal; allegations were investigated, with the customary help of torture; there was no defence, as the accusers were never revealed.

Torquemada was noted for the excessive piety, and modesty, of the religious fanatic. His severity towards those suspected of heresy was several times objected to; but he was a faithful son of Rome, and all attempts to remove him failed. Each pope in succession praised his zeal: Innocent VIII extended his jurisdiction to the whole of Spain. Torquemada's enthusiasm grew with his success. By 1488 there were not enough prisons for all the accused, and Spain smoked with fires in which heretics were being destroyed.

The *auto-da-fé* (the act of faith) was a masterpiece of showmanship. All the condemned were led to the place of execution. There were the impenitents, who were to be burnt, the relapsed repentants, who had the privilege of being strangled before being burnt, and those who were declared to be forgiven by the Church, and sentenced to incarceration for life. The scene was deliberately planned to resemble the popular idea of the last judgement. Sentence was read, and the fires were lit.

The effect on Spain was disastrous: for centuries the spirit of the Inquisition survived, inculcating an atmosphere in which the slightest question was regarded as revolt, and all doubt was heresy. It is not too far-fetched to say that Spain is still affected by Torquemada's policy. However, his faith did not sustain him wholly: he travelled with a bodyguard of 250 armed men, and was in constant dread of being poisoned.

Disobedient, slow, obstinate and spoiled . . . very inattentive

TREVITHICK, Richard, (1771–1833), English inventor and engineer. He devised the high-pressure steam engine, which made possible the first locomotives and the railways.

Trevithick was a Cornishman and a product of the Industrial Revolution in Cornwall, in the heyday of Cornish tin and copper mining. His father was a mine-manager; and though he never got beyond the three R's at school and his teacher reported him 'a disobedient, slow, obstinate, spoiled boy, frequently absent and very inattentive', he grew up among engines. His father was among the first to install the engines built by James Watt to pump out the mines, and Trevithick himself, 'an uncommon quick-spirited man and the strongest ever known', 'full of fun and good humour, and a good story-teller', became technical adviser to the mine-managers who wanted to avoid paying royalties on their Watt engines. Watt's engine had a separate condenser and used steam at only a few pounds' boiler pressure. The boiler was little more than a hot-water tank, and though Watt avoided the problem of making strong boilers and cylinders which would withstand high pressures by making efficient use of the pressure of the atmosphere, his engine had disadvantages. Not only was steam limited to such low pressure, the condenser was bulky and heavy, and needed cooling water. So the Watt engine was condemned to be stationary. The steam-engine could only be put on wheels by making it light and compact, with high-pressure steam to give great energy in a little space. This Trevithick achieved.

He invented his new engine in 1800. Thirty-five years younger than Watt, he had come just at the right time for the next advance, though he had his obstacles and setbacks. Thus in 1803 he installed one of his high-pressure engines at Greenwich, and the cast-iron boiler blew up. Trevithick described the accident in his illiterate way, 'one pice of the boiler, its abt one Inch thick and abt 500 lb' was thrown nearly 125 yards; 'it killed 3 on the spot and one other is sence dead of his wounds ... I believe that Mr B. and Watt is abt to do mee every engurey in their power for they have don their outemost to repoart the exploseion both in the newspapers and private letters very different to what it really is ...'

Trevithick was not dismayed. Years later, he wrote that 'the late Mr James Watt ... said ... that I deserved hanging for bringing into use the high pressure engine'. Trevithick built engines and boilers working at pressures of 150 lb. This led him to great improvements in boiler design. He invented the Cornish boiler, in which the flames are taken from the outside, and put through a flue inside the boiler. He wrote that the idea was 'like maney other wild fanceys that flyes through the brain'; and from this he advanced to tubular boilers and superheaters. He solved the new problems by a natural talent for engineering design, devising remarkably simple and clean constructions. Sanguine and choleric in temperament, he was exactly the reverse of the melancholy, reflective, infinitely critical Watt.

In 1804, he built a tramway locomotive which hauled, according to his description, 'ten tons of Iron, five waggons, and 70 Men ... 9 miles which we perform'd in 4 hours and 5 Mints, but we had to cut down som trees and remove Large rocks out of road'. This was at Penydaren in Wales, and Trevithick thereby won a bet of £500. A year later, he built a locomotive at Newcastle, which was the ancestor of the railway locomotive built by Stephenson.

In 1811, Uvillé, a speculator in Peru, whose silver mines 14,000 feet high in the Andes, were flooded, applied to Boulton and Watt for a pumping engine. They pointed out that their engines could not work efficiently at the low atmospheric pressure of such a great altitude. While wandering through Fitzroy Square, Uvillé saw a model of Trevithick's high-pressure engine, which was free from this limitation. He returned to Peru, and persuaded his partners to secure Trevithick engines, and sailed once more to England to purchase them. Four engines were shipped to Peru and carried in parts on mule back through the Andes. Trevithick himself followed in 1815, and it is to these Andean mines, or mountains rather, that he points in the portrait of him by Blake's friend John Linnell.

Trevithick became involved in the Peruvian Civil War, and was conscripted by Bolivar (q.v.), for whose cavalry, according to Francis Trevithick, 'he invented and made a carbine with a short barrel of large bore'.

In the midst of mining adventures he made £2500 by salving a wreck. He was urged to send £2000 to his wife. 'Instead of this', wrote Liddell, 'he embarked the money in some Utopian scheme for pearl fishing at Panama, and lost all.' He returned to England in 1827, after further adventures in Central America. He was penniless. He died in 1833, and was buried in Dartford, in a place reserved for the poor, unmarked by any stone.

ILLUSTRATION: Page 374.

The Shakespeare of China

TU FU, (712–770), gravest and greatest of the poets of China.

There are poets whose greatness is conceded automatically, though their poems no longer touch us.

Tu Fu, like Shakespeare, rises above time because he was deeply tender for human life, and fixed his tenderness in the tough precision of his art. Moreover, Tu Fu lived in a time like our own: the peace of the T'ang empire was broken, and he knew rebellion, war, abandoned gardens and farms, misery, poverty, and the loneliness and despair of refugees –

While the evening here is approaching the mountain paths,
I come to this high-up chamber, very close to the Water Gate.
Thin clouds rest on the edges of cliffs;
A lonely moon turns among the waves.

A line of cranes in flight is silent;
A pack of wolves baying over their prey breaks the quiet.
I cannot sleep because I am concerned about wars,
Because I am powerless to amend the world.

Though born of a family of scholars, Tu Fu was not very successful under the Brilliant Emperor, Hsuan-tsung (685–762), and his successors. He held different appointments, but would have given more service than he was allowed to give, since, unlike his friend, the great Li Po (q.v.), he was not the poet of wildness and impulse. Sane, balanced, deep, Tu Fu wanted peace, friendship, happiness and good government. Instead he had to see the empire disrupted by An Lu-shan's rebellion and by Tibetan invaders. Separated from his family in 756, he wrote of his wife watching the same moon, with the dew on her scented hair and the night chilly to her delicate arms, and he asked

When can we both lean by the wind-blown curtains
And see the tears dry on each other's face?

A few years later, in a long autobiographical poem, he presented himself as an old, sick stranger in a distant region, out of favour:

The autumn wind is blowing in this mournful ravine;
The unhappy green orchid can offer only faint fragrance.

This poet, who confessed his love of wine and bamboos bending in the wind, had too much of the bitterness of the northern snow –

Wind-driven leaves are flying with the snow.
Mixed with rain, the flakes seldom show the pattern of a flower

– whereas he preferred the snow sprinkling the red-lacquered roofs of the court.

If he had more troubles than the white hairs on his head, if he lived with wasps in the dust and scorpions in the sand, or compared himself to a gull 'blown about between heaven and earth', he maintained always a self-knowledge and a Confucian serenity. He was the shabby parrot of his own poem:

The parrot seems to be sad;
Perhaps it is wise enough to remember
    its separation from its kin.
The green feathers are now a bit shabby;
Still the red beak betrays too much knowledge.
While you vainly wait for the day
    when the cage will be opened,
The branch on which you used to perch
    has rotted away.
Men pet you, and also harm you.
What is the use of being a rare bird?

Tu Fu complained that much of his poetry was only written to console himself, but his consolation consoles us. In one of his last poems, composed with the moonlight on his knees, this poet who stated but never whined, and who always maintained an inner serenity, asked if understanding the 'ultimate unity of coming and going' was not 'the secret of immortality': here and beyond, there was just one stillness.

Not long before he died at fifty-eight, when he was sick on one of his journeys with the double fever of malaria and of life, he asked:

What good will the villagers accomplish
    by smiting drums to invoke
The spirits that can do nothing, or by
    shooting the birds
That merely resemble the owls of ill luck?

Ivan Turgenev

TURGENEV, Ivan Sergeyevich, (1818–1883). 'During the whole of my literary life I strove to represent conscientiously and impartially what Shakespeare calls *the body and pressure of time* and the fast changing physiognomy of the Russians of the educated classes, who mostly served as the object of my observations,' wrote Turgenev in the introduction to the 1880 edition of his complete works.

For the greater part of his childhood this Russian novelist and short-story writer lived on his mother's estate of Spasskoye, not far from Oryol. It was at Spasskoye that he obtained his first-hand knowledge of the countryside, his passion for shooting and his familiarity with the lives of the peasants – whose maltreatment at the hands of his self-willed and despotic mother made him swear 'a Hannibal oath' not to rest till he had brought about the abolition of serfdom. This he helped to do with his *Diary of a Sportsman* (1852), a book that aroused the conscience of the Russian ruling class against the iniquities of serfdom. But he had turned to prose only after trying his hand at poetry, which he began writing as a student in Moscow and Petersburg. Most of the stories of the *Diary of a Sportsman* and most of his plays were written during his first visit to France between 1847 and 1850, which he spent mostly at Courtavenel, the country house of the opera singer Pauline Viardot, with whom Turgenev was in love. Two years after his return to Russia he was arrested for publishing an obituary of Gogol (q.v.) in a Moscow paper, and spent a month in a police cell, where he wrote his famous story *Mumu* (1852).

Then followed eighteen months under house arrest at Spasskoye, of which the outcome was Turgenev's first novel, *Rudin* (1856), the first of his profound studies of character and social environment. His second novel, *A Gentleman's Nest* (1858), he began in Rome and finished at Spasskoye; it was his greatest success. His third novel, *On the Eve* (1859), did less well, and his fourth, *Fathers and Sons* (1861), certainly his greatest novel, raised a storm. Turgenev, a constitutionalist who believed in gradual reform, was accused of lampooning the revolutionaries in the person of his hero Bazarov. He replied that he shared all Bazarov's views, except those on art. This made no impression, and the agitation against him became so hysterical that he preferred to spend the next ten years in Baden-Baden, next door to Pauline Viardot and her family. There he wrote his fifth novel, *Smoke* (1867). Exposing the pretensions of both the Russian reactionaries and revolutionaries, it released another flood of abuse against him.

During the Franco-Prussian War he lived for a short time in England and then settled in France, spending his winters in Paris and his summers in Bougival, where he wrote his last and longest novel, *Virgin Soil* (1877), in which he gave a brilliant appraisal of the revolutionary movement in Russia, his last short stories, and *Poems in Prose* (1878–1882), his autobiographical and philosophical musings on the meaning of life and man's destiny.

ILLUSTRATION: Page 322.

Painter and worshipper of light

TURNER, Joseph Mallord William, (1775–1851), worshipper of light, nature, energy; and the greatest of English painters.

Small, ugly, vital, with keen blue eyes, Turner was the son of a London barber and of a butcher's daughter of ungovernable temper, which brought her to the mad-house. As a boy Turner was 'singular', 'silent', 'exclusively devoted to his drawing', intolerant of society, indifferent to theatres or music, and with no 'faculty for friendship'. As a man he took care that little should be known of his private life: he was secretive, lonely (he never married), sharp-tongued in self-defence, stingy and always immensely active, energetic and productive.

He grew up in a revolutionary period of self-expression (Napoleon was six, Beethoven five when he was born). For John Constable (q.v.) the Lord was in the still small voice. For Turner the Lord – Himself – was in the wind, the earthquake and the fire. Brilliant from the first, the Royal Academy in London made him a full academician when he was twenty-seven, although older eyes marked him as a dangerous innovator, whose pictures were blotchings of disordered and too brilliant colour.

Turner's paintings of storm and mountain were nevertheless popular; and he amassed wealth, partly by book illustrations, until he could paint as he pleased. From the age of about thirty-two until his death, he more and more worshipped light, eventually dissolving his subjects into a swirl of colour, as if each canvas contained a revolving catherine-wheel. He could afford to be a joke, ridiculed and insulted by the critics, who talked of the 'dotage of his art' or the 'wonderful fruits of a diseased eye and a reckless hand'. Lost in his swirling triangles of pink, blue, yellow and green, Turner, still young, original and powerful in his seventies, did not care a button. The new inventions of his old age he also accepted as wonders of nature and subjects for dissolution in light – whether they were rockets, steam-tugs, paddle-boats, the railway train or the iron furnace.

Turner's art, like Constable's, is the expression of feelings; these feelings include not only exultation, in storm or in the swirl of colour, but pastoral feelings of delight in the quiet stillness and gentleness of scenery, as in oil sketches painted on the Thames in 1807.

Turner made the mistake of leaving his unsold pictures, drawings, etc., to his country. The bequest included nearly all his late 'abstract' paintings. The concentration of these in the national collections in London has prevented that understanding of his genius which would have followed had they only been scattered round the galleries of the world.

A story of Turner in his old age suggests that the work he realized appeared to him only a shadow, or a flash, of all he had felt. A young American admirer met him at a London picture-dealer's, and stammered out praise for his pictures. 'I wish they were all put in a blunderbuss', was Turner's reply, 'and fired off.'

ILLUSTRATION: Page 321.

Mississippi pilot

TWAIN, Mark, (1835–1910), American novelist and humorist. Of his *Tom Sawyer* he said 'it is simply a hymn, put into prose form to give it a worldly air' – which applies equally to his greatest book *Huckleberry Finn*. Ernest Hemingway has remarked of *Huckleberry Finn* that it is the source of all modern American literature. W. H. Auden has called it a book essential for understanding the United States. In both volumes Mark Twain wrote a hymn to childhood, and to the pre-industrial childhood of America, to lost youth and to the river Mississippi. He never recaptured the quality of these two masterpieces. Indeed, when he did attempt books about an adult Tom Sawyer, he uttered the disastrous truth in his remark that Tom could not be carried into maturity – because 'he would just lie like all the other one-horse men of literature and the reader would conceive a hearty contempt for him'.

Samuel Langhorne Clemens lived as a child at Hannibal, Mo., taking the nom-de-plume of Mark Twain when he became a journalist. But that was after he had worked as a printer, apprenticed himself to the 'stupendous task of learning the twelve hundred miles of the Mississippi River' in its powerful, sullen, muddy windings between St Louis and New Orleans, become one of the best pilots on the river, and then lost his vocation when river traffic was stopped by the Civil War. 'Mark Twain' was the two fathom call made by those who heaved the lead on the river-boats. As for fighting, 'I was a *soldier* for two weeks once in the beginning of the war,' he wrote, 'and was hunted like a rat the whole time.' He was happier when he lit out for the West and worked as a miner. Turning back to journalism, he took a voyage which led to his travel book, *The Innocents Abroad* – this made him as a humorist – and to his marriage. A fellow passenger showed him a miniature of his sister: Twain determined to marry the girl; he did, and the effects of that marriage are still debated. This much is clear, that Mark Twain rebelled violently against the strait-laced atmosphere of his youth, and that his wife fought the rebellion. 'Change *breech-clout*,' she would note on his MSS. 'It's a word that you love and I abominate. I would take that and *offal* out of the language.'

Because Twain loved his wife, it was only in his imagination now that he could 'light out for the Territory'. He was her captive; he was also, like Scott, the captive of circumstance, for he was ruined in a publishing venture and had to write pot-boilers to pay off the liabilities he was determined to meet. He was captive also of his temperament, always ready to surrender to the saccharine, the sentimental, and the brash. Consequently, most of his books are by-passed by contemporary taste, but not *Huckleberry Finn*, which emerges decisively as a monumental book, the *David Copperfield* of nineteenth-century America.

Twain put into the book every detail of the known and familiar landscape of his early years; he paints the whole hard, coarse truth of life on the Mississippi. Nothing is missed, the squalor, the immorality, the blood-feuds, the race-hate of white and black, the impassiveness and mercilessness of the great waterway, at which a European will stare in helplessness and amazement. Yet the realism is penetrated with romance, and lifted into poetry both by Twain's vision and the language in which he expresses it. The language catches the poetry and accuracy of speech in a primitive community. It does not imitate, it *is* colloquial American of the period. Twain's vision can only be illustrated in quotation – in such a passage as – 'When I got there it was all still and Sunday-like, and hot and sunshiny – the hands was gone to the fields: and there was them kind of faint dronings of bugs and flies in the air that makes it seem so lonesome and like everybody's dead ...'

man. Tylor introduced the comparative study of human institutions, for which he worked out a method he himself applied, by way of illustration, to the laws of marriage and descent. By showing that 'the development of institutions may be investigated on a basis of tabulation and classification', Tylor removed man's proper study of man from fantasy at last to facts.

He was the son of a London brass founder and Quaker, and entered his father's business. A breakdown in health sent him on a convalescent voyage, during which he visited Mexico with the ethnologist Henry Christy. Tylor made notes on Mexico and Mexicans and published a book on them, *Anahuac*, in 1861 – a step towards his great work *Researches into the Early History of Mankind and the Development of Civilization* (1865). This revealed immense reading, as well as the skilful comparison of data which were assembled in altogether new perspectives. Ten years went by, and Tylor published his famous *Primitive Culture*, in which he elaborated his animistic theory of religion: the idea of a god, he supposed, evolved from a prior notion of a soul, spirit or *anima*, which could exist independently of the body, and after death – 'The idea of souls, demons, deities and any other classes of spiritual beings', he wrote, 'are conceptions of a similar nature throughout, the conception of souls being the original one in the series.' Tylor believed that primitive man evolved his notion of the soul from his sense of the biological principles which distinguish living bodies from dead ones, and from his acquaintance with 'those human shapes which appear in dreams and visions'; and by combining the biological attributes of a living being with the shapes observed in visions, Tylor went beyond Herbert Spencer's earlier theory that the original god was the dead chieftain.

This convinced evolutionist had a power of generalization comparable with that of Charles Darwin (q.v.). He was both scientist and artist: the combination required for the full understanding of mankind.

Man's proper study

TYLOR, Sir Edward Burnett, (1832–1917), founder of modern evolutionary anthropology, the science of

'Motherly and auspicious'

TZU HSI, (1835–1908), Empress Dowager and effective ruler of China for nearly half a century.

Best known to history by the title of Tzu Hsi, meaning 'Motherly and Auspicious', bestowed on her in 1861, her original name was Yehonala; born of a noble Manchu family, she entered the imperial harem as a concubine in 1852 at the age of seventeen. Four years later she bore to the emperor Hsien Feng his only son and was elevated to the rank of *kweifei* or concubine of the first class; her grade was still secondary to that of the Empress-consort Sakota, but she was a much stronger personality, and acquired predominant influence over the Emperor. When the Emperor became seriously ill in the summer of 1861, a group of princes planned to seize power on his death through a regency council; they accused Yehonala of an intrigue with Jung Lu, a young officer of the imperial guards, and had her excluded from the Emperor's presence. She managed, however, to take possession of the imperial seal, without which the dying Emperor's decree appointing the regents could not be lawfully promulgated. The conspirators did not dare to take the seal from her by force, and with the aid of troops gathered by Jung Lu, she had them arrested and executed or banished. Sakota and Yehonala were then proclaimed joint regents for the five-year-old successor to the throne, receiving the titles of Tzu An and Tzu Hsi; in practice all power was in the hands of Tzu Hsi. She governed the empire without a rival until her son, the Emperor T'ung Chih, came of age and assumed full governing authority in 1873. But T'ung Chih died of small-pox two years later; Tzu Hsi obtained the succession for her sister's son, then aged four, and resumed the regency. The new Emperor, Kuang Hsu, did not assume sole power until 1889, and even then the Empress Dowager retained great influence in affairs of state. In 1898, after defeat in war by Japan and the humiliation of China by the ensuing exactions of the Western Powers, there was a great outburst of patriotic feeling among the educated classes and a demand for administrative reforms of the kind which had already turned Japan into a strong modern state. Kuang Hsu was sympathetic to reform, and on the advice of the leader of the reform party, Kang Yu-wei, issued a series of decrees introducing radical changes into the whole system of government. Tzu Hsi and Jung Lu disapproved of some of these measures, and the reformers planned to arrest them both, execute Jung Lu and subject the Empress Dowager to virtual imprisonment. But with her unfailing skill in the art of *coups d'état* she forestalled her enemies, arresting all the leaders of the reform party who were

unable to escape abroad, and making the Emperor her prisoner. Once more until her death in 1908 she held supreme governing power, keeping Kuang Hsu in strict captivity, and when at last the time came for her to die, she saw to it that he died first. Her last political act was to proclaim a new Emperor – the three-year old Pu Yi, who was to be the last monarch of the Manchu dynasty – and a new regent.

In 1900 Tzu Hsi was involved in the attempt of the 'Boxers' to drive all foreigners out of China. The I Ho Ch'uan or Fists of Righteous Harmony – whence the nickname of 'Boxers' given them by the British residents in China – were a secret society which gained strong popular support by agitation against foreigners and won over a number of high officials with influence at Court. Tzu Hsi was persuaded by this faction to authorize an ultimatum requiring the envoys of foreign Powers and their armed guards to leave Peking. Jung Lu, however, together with the most powerful of the provincial governors, opposed this policy as certain to bring disaster on China, and he was able to prevent the Chinese army's heavy guns from being used against the Legations on the pretext that the noise of artillery gave the Empress Dowager a headache. An international expeditionary force marched to Peking to relieve the Legations, and Tzu Hsi, with the captive Emperor, disguised as peasants, escaped from the palace in a cart; they went to Sian, far in the interior, and only returned to Peking after a peace settlement.

Living always in the seclusion which old Chinese custom imposed on the women of the imperial palace, lacking any modern education and profoundly ignorant of the world outside China, Tzu Hsi could not help being reactionary in her sympathies and unable to comprehend the basic problems which faced China during her lifetime. She had, though, a remarkable flair for government; she was an acute judge of men and she showed appreciation of ability in the selection of her ministers. That the *ancien régime* in China survived as long as it did without utter collapse was largely due to the capacity of statesmen such as Prince Kung, Li Hung-chang and Yuan Shih-hai, whom Tzu Hsi favoured and promoted to high office.

Apart from politics, her outstanding characteristic was her passion for private theatricals; and to her own dramatic impersonations of Buddhist divinities she owed the nickname of 'the Old Buddha' by which she was colloquially known in China. (*See also Sun Yat-sen.*)

U

'Oh, what a delight is perspective!'

UCCELLO, Paolo, (1397–1475), early master of painting in the new age of science, who was born and lived most of his life in Florence. In Uccello's day Florence was the creative capital of Europe, indeed of mankind; and down to Michelangelo (born in the year Uccello died) the great artists of the city were more than painters: they enquired into the world with scientific curiosity and passion. Uccello delighted to discuss geometry with the mathematician Giovanni Manetti; and in paintings he was passionate to represent things as we see them in their relative positions and sizes (perspective). So objects in his pictures were surrounded with space. The process was novel, a step in the revelation of the palpable world.

It has often been said that Uccello damaged his paintings by making them exercises in perspective. His passion for this 'true' perspective art was so strong that it would keep him at work all night standing at his writing-table. When his wife begged him to go to bed, Uccello would reply like a man in a trance, 'Oh, what a delight is perspective!' In fact perspective does help to endow the few great pictures by him which have survived with a sharply, solidly, emotionally powerful strangeness, as though everything was newly revealed in vision or hallucination. This is wonderfully true of three incidents Uccello painted of the Rout of San Romano (a battle in which the Sienese were defeated by the Florentines): the horses from hoof to nostril and tail-bells to rolling eyeball, the broken lances, the vizored figures, the curving crossbows – every item and the action as a whole are frozen into the strangest perspective poetry. These three pictures, now in the National Gallery in London, the Louvre in Paris and the Uffizi in Florence, were painted for the bedroom of Lorenzo de' Medici, the Lord of Florence.

Uccello died in poverty, so often the fate of artists. He wrote at the foot of a tax return in 1469, 'I am old and I have no means of livelihood, my wife is ill and I cannot work any more.'

T

Kitagawa Utamaro

UTAMARO, Kitagawa, (1753–1806), Japanese artist. In Japan he is considered the greatest designer of coloured wood-cut prints in the tradition of the *Ukiyoya*, the Pictures of the Passing World (*see Hiroshige and Hokusai*).

First of all, he made illustrated theatre books and prints of actors, which caused no stir; and he was destitute when the publisher Tsutaya Jusaburo invited him to live in his house and illustrate books for him. There he stayed from about 1781 probably until Tsutaya's death in 1797, meeting other artists and writers, including Bakin, the Japanese novelist. By the late eighties and early nineties he had found his style. His *Shell Book* (1790) and *Book of Birds and Flowers* (1791) for colour, drawing and design are two of the most beautiful of the world's illustrated books. In the seventeen-nineties he designed his *Types of Love* and *Women's Physiognomies*, printed in delicate colours often on bold yellow grounds, or grounds of pink or white mica. These prints of beautiful women, courtesans of the Yoshiwara, the licensed pleasure quarter of old Tokyo, made him famous. Utamaro excelled in compositions running over several sheets, of which the *Awabi Fishers* in three sheets, the *Silkworm Culture*, and the Susuhaki (or house cleaning at the end of the year) are among the best known; he also invented a new 'brocade style' of richly patterned colour.

Utamaro was a proud, independent man. In 1805 he was imprisoned (or confined to his house) for depicting Hideyoshi, the celebrated ancestor of the ruling Shogun, relaxing in idle luxury; and he criticized poor work by his fellow artists for the discredit it brought upon the *Ukiyoye*. Publishers, he said, should come to him and pay his fee, 'which was as high as his nose'. The West began to notice Utamaro in the eighties when he was 'discovered' by French painters. The varied landscapes and genre scenes of Hokusai and Hiroshige are more appealing at first sight, but Arthur Morrison, the historian of Japanese painting, could reasonably claim that as a 'painter of the human figure in an exquisitely synthetic convention Utamaro has few rivals East or West'. More than one of Utamaro's self-portraits show him painting on the walls of a Yoshiwara house, with the beauties he has immortalized.

ILLUSTRATION: Page 359.

Pessimist without despair

VALÉRY, Paul, (1871–1945). Of this French poet T.S. Eliot once wrote: 'It is he who will remain to posterity the representative poet, the symbol of the poet, of the first half of the twentieth century – not Yeats, not Rilke, nor anyone else', which may or may not be true.

Valéry was born in 1871, the same year as Marcel Proust (q.v.), at Sète on the Mediterranean. Some critics have thought him too peculiarly French ever to be understood outside his country; but for all his 'Frenchness' his forebears were exclusively Italian and Corsican and his family name was originally Valéri. His youth was passed in the South. He studied at Montpellier and at a very early age wrote a number of poems that Mallarmé, the greatest living poet, found extremely promising. He also developed an important friendship with Pierre Louys, the author of *Sappho* and other evocations of Greek life and customs. Then and always Valéry looked towards Greek and classical ideals.

But despite this excellent beginning, at the age of twenty-one he suddenly decided to give up writing poetry – a resolve in which he persevered for twenty-five years. Instead he devoted himself to science and mathematics – they remained his passion all his life – and practical work. He spent a short period in London, where he found a job in the press service of Cecil Rhodes's Chartered Company, but soon had to leave because the climate made him ill. Back in Paris he worked at the War Ministry, which was then busy developing the afterwards-famous cannon known as 'Seventy-fives'. Valéry was a methodical and competent official, interested in detail; and, as well, he wrote a much-discussed essay on the expansion of Germany.

Valéry's abandonment of poetry by no means meant the abandonment of a concern for literature. He frequented the society of Mallarmé, Heredia and Henri de Regnier, as well as that of mathematicians and scientists, and he won the reputation of an 'exquisite' cerebral writer with his *Introduction à la vie de Léonard de Vinci* and *La Soirée avec Monsieur Teste*. Monsieur Teste has always been taken to represent a side of Valéry's own character; he is a man who is supreme in the purely intellectual world of ideas but who is incapable of facing life.

M. Teste has been held to reflect Valéry's renunciation of poetry – but in retrospect this long silence seems to have been a necessary preparation. For when he did turn once again to poetry, in 1917 and with *La Jeune Parque*, it was to astonish his contemporaries with a masterpiece of discipline and classical order which was alike in the tradition of Racine and yet emphatically the declaration of a singular new talent. Surely the most elegant poem in modern times, *La Jeune Parque* is sometimes described as the most difficult in French – the difficulty coming at least in part from the kind of cerebral 'Narcissism' present in other masterpieces too, such as *Le Serpent. Le Cimetière Marin*, whose scene is the graveyard in Sète where Valéry is now buried, had a wider popular appeal. It is equally representative (and, alas, untranslatable):

> Ce toit tranquille, ou marchent des colombes
> Entre les pins palpite, entre les tombes.
> Midi le juste y compose de feux
> La mer, la mer toujours recommencée!
> O récompense après une pensée
> Qu'un long regard sur le calme des dieux!
>
> This peaceful roof on which the pigeons strut
> Trembles among the pines, among the tombs,
> There exact midday puts in order with its flames
> The sea, the sea for ever re-begun!
> O the reward after a time of thought
> Of a long glance on the calm of the gods!

– a literal translation which conveys only a fraction of the original.

The twenties and thirties were for Valéry years of apotheosis. His total of verse was not large, but his prose-writings were vast; of these *Eupalinos,* and *L'Ame de la danse,* stand out. In 1927 he was elected to the Académie Française. He began to be appreciated abroad, was decorated by various governments, made honorary doctor at Oxford, and appointed professor at the Collège de France. He wrote many *discours* and introductions to books and his reflections (extremely impersonal – the very opposite of Gide's) went to swell out his volumes of *Variétés*. His last important work was on the theme of Faust, which he interpreted in the new 'Valérian' or cerebral way.

Valéry was in many things typically Mediter-ranean. He was an excellent conversationalist and talked quickly in a deaf voice like M. Teste. He had no Nordic inhibitions but was moderate in all his habits. In mind he was rationalistic, scientific and sceptical. He loved his family and in politics he was something of an anarchist. The critic, Albert Béguin, once called him 'an optimist without hope', but it would be equally accurate to call him 'a pessimist without despair'.

'Belief even unto martyrdom'

VAN GOGH, Vincent, (1853–1890). This passion-ate and excessive painter, who made pigment into tropical flames, was born in the flat misty north at Groot-Zundert in Holland, where his father was a clergyman.

Much of his life was spent in a tragically slow strug-gle to discover himself as an artist. His brief flowering came at Arles, in the South of France, where he painted brilliant canvases: a tormented ravine, a canary-yellow drawbridge against a hot blue sky, a yellow chair with a straw seat on which rests a pipe, a café at night in which the furniture seems to shrivel under pulsating enormously magnified lamps. 'Oh, the beautiful sun of midsummer!' he wrote in one of his letters to his devoted brother, Theo. 'It beats upon my head, and I do not doubt that it makes one a little queer.' It was this sun which dominated his last works, in which foliage writhes like flame; reds, blues and yellows consume the canvas; and the vigorous brush-strokes themselves curve and whirl and explode with the dynamics of heat. Queer these works certainly were – Cézanne, to whom he showed them, replied, 'To be honest, they are the paintings of a madman.' Analogous, perhaps are some of the poems of Ger-ard Manley Hopkins (q.v.), his contemporary

> The glassy peartree leaves and blooms, they brush
> The descending blue; that blue is all in a rush
> With richness ...

or some of the ecstasies of Walt Whitman (q.v.).

Van Gogh passed his youth in frustrated oscilla-tions between the two family interests of religion and art-dealing. He worked in the art-business at the Hague, Paris and London; he was a schoolmaster in England, and a bookseller at Dordrecht, and for a long time he preferred sickly religiosity of content to any tough passion or form. He tried hard to be a pastor, even after he had failed his examinations, and spent a period doing pastoral work amongst the typhus-stricken peasants and miners of the Borinage. Only very gradually did the vivacity of Amsterdam and Paris awaken in him a desire for colour.

At Arles, where he settled in 1888, he formed the idea of a 'House of Friends' under the belief that a painting should be made as a group effort. But the visit of Gauguin, who was to collaborate in the pro-ject, was not a success. An attack of insanity drove him to the local hospital, later to the asylum at St Remy and finally to Auvers and the companionship of his friend Dr Grachet, whom he drew and who described his vocation in phrases suitable for an epi-taph: 'The words "love of art" are scarcely applicable to him. One ought to say: belief even unto martyr-dom.' Van Gogh continued to paint vigorously and to write his fascinating letters up to the day when he went out, stood against a tree, and shot himself.

ILLUSTRATION: Page 366.

Under the microscope

VAN LEEUWENHOEK, Antony, (1632–1723), draper at Delft in Holland and founder of micro-scopy.

The Dutch had already developed the manufac-ture of spectacles, and this humble and ingenious man spent his spare time in making improved lenses, and directing them upon a world of unsuspected beings. A fellow citizen brought his work to the no-tice of the new Royal Society of London, and in 1673 he was invited to send his observations. He replied, 'I have oft-times been besought, by divers gentlemen, to set down on paper what I have beheld through my newly invented *Microscopia*: but I have generally de-clined; first, because I have no style, or pen, where-with to express my thoughts properly; secondly, be-cause I have not been brought up to the languages of arts, but only to business; and in the third place, be-cause I do not gladly suffer contradiction or censure from others ... my observations and thoughts are the outcome of my own unaided impulse and curiosity alone ... so pray take not amiss my poor pen' – whereupon Van Leeuwenhoek despatched to the Royal Society a marvellous stream of three hundred papers, over a period of fifty years.

His lenses consisted of single tiny particles of glass. He had a special skill in making them, and had natural eyesight of extraordinary acuity. Van Leeuwenhoek's discoveries were innumerable. He was the first man to give accurate descriptions of yeast globules and of the red corpuscles of the blood, the first to observe bacteria and spermatozoa. 'I well know', he wrote, 'there are whole universities that will not believe there are living creatures in the male seed, but such things do not worry me. I know I am in the right.' The wonderful Dutchman worked on, 'ignorant of all other men's thoughts', until he was ninety-one. His fame drew visitors and not always welcome interruption from all over the world. Peter the Great called at Delft in 1698, and invited Van Leeuwenhoek to demonstrate 'his incomparable magnifying-glasses'. Van Leeuwenhoek had the honour of showing him 'the marvellous circulation [of the blood] in the tail of an eel'.

ILLUSTRATION: Page 224.

Revenge by forgery

VAN MEEGEREN, Henricus Anthonius, (1889–1947), forger and the special hobgoblin of Dutch (and other) art historians, since so many of them were deluded by his incompetent fabrications of Vermeer.

In 1937 a *Christ at Emmaus* by Johannes Vermeer, unknown and with a vague pedigree, was brought to the celebrated Dutch art historian, Dr A. Bredius. His excitement was considerable. Here was a religious painting by this rare master akin to an early unique work of his in the National Gallery at Edinburgh; here was a document of his first style, a find which Dr Bredius quickly certified as genuine, and which he announced with the proper solemnity in the leading journal of English connoisseurs and art historians. The painting was for sale; and since a relic so precious and of such religious penetration must at all costs be retained by Vermeer's countrymen, the Rembrandt Society and the Dutch Government acquired it. Sanctified by a price of more than £50,000, the new Vermeer was hung in the great Boymans Museum at Rotterdam.

Other Vermeers came to light, though behind the screen of war and the German occupation of the Netherlands. In 1945, when the Germans had been expelled, Dutch Field Security searched busily for collaborators and discovered that the German air chief, Hermann Goering, had been sold Vermeer's *Woman taken in Adultery*. It had cost him other works of art to the value of £165,000. Who had sold this Dutch masterpiece to the enemy? There had been intermediaries, but the thread ran back to Han Van Meegeren, as he was known, who was arrested, and then reversed the position by declaring that he, and not Vermeer, had painted the picture by which Goering had been duped. Moreover Van Meegeren tactlessly confessed to having painted five other expensive Vermeers, including that master work so confidently certified by Dr Bredius, so eagerly discussed by art historians, so patriotically and so expensively purchased by the Rembrandt Society – and public funds. Under surveillance, this feeble artist, of 'small stature, old before his time, but intelligent and with an extremely clear brain and great cunning', painted a Vermeer of *Jesus among the Doctors* in order to prove his confession.

For a Dutch legal enquiry the Rotterdam picture was X-rayed and probed scientifically; and the enquiry pronounced it a modern work. Little Van Meegeren was arrested, tried as a forger, and sentenced to a year's imprisonment. Exchanges in court between the President and Dr Hannema, war-time director of the Boymans Museum, should please the ironist for all time. It was bought, was it not, for its merit? 'Certainly. Vermeers are uncommon, after all.' Had its origin been discussed? 'Yes, but it was all very vague', and Dr Hannema now stated that 'None of us liked it, but we were afraid it would be sold to Germany.'

While art historians cringed (though less than they should have done, since the *Christ at Emmaus* is a masterpiece of impudence, lax draughtsmanship and cheap religiosity), Han Van Meegeren's story was uncovered – his days at the Institute of Technology in Delft (Vermeer's own town), his early habit of making drawings in imitation of Dutch seventeenth century art, his brief successes and more decisive failures as a painter of excruciating banality, and the stimulus to forgery and revenge (Van Meegeren spoke of his 'plan for vengeance') in his damaged self-esteem. His fabrications had now been sold for some £600,000, he had enjoyed wealth and what was, in fact, a somewhat mean-spirited self-gratification – not a loud rumbling laugh at academic pretension blended with self-interest. Still, the lessons are plain enough – that the conferring of a thousand degrees upon a thousand art historians (or upon the academic purveyors of any other art) does not automatically confer on them the rare gifts of open-eyed sensibility and judgement; and that most of us are readier to venerate works of art as if they were the miracle-working toenails of the elect, than to be honest towards them as works which enhance our living.

Dr Bredius died before he could know of the dunce's cap he had placed upon his own ears, and the forger did not live to undergo his prison sentence. He died soon after the trial.

Sea route to India

VASCO DA GAMA, (1460–1524), discoverer of the sea route to India and Portuguese national hero celebrated in the *Lusiads* by the poet Camoens, who sailed in his wake fifty years later. Da Gama, wrote Camoens

> ... saw all heaven resolved
> To make of Lisbon a new Rome;

but the reality, though impressive enough, was more prosaic. Da Gama's voyage opened up the commerce of the east to the western world, yet it was only the logical consummation of the work of Henry the Navigator (q.v.) and his efforts to find a sea route to the east, more particularly of the rounding of the Cape of Good Hope by Bartholomew Diaz (an achievement ranked by some as higher than that of Columbus). Diaz designed some of Da Gama's ships, and men who had sailed with Diaz strengthened his crew.

The most notable thing about Da Gama's voyage down the African coast was that he decided to strike boldly across the open sea after passing Cape Verde, which caused him to be ninety-six days out of sight of land; but he avoided the equatorial doldrums by which Diaz had been held up. This was the route followed by all sailing-ships until sail became obsolete. Once Da Gama had rounded the southern extremity of Africa and started the journey northwards through the Indian Ocean, he was within short sailing distance of seas regularly traversed by Muslim traders, and thereafter his difficulties were chiefly diplomatic. Muslim traders did not welcome Christian competi-

tion. A Hindu pilot whom Da Gama took for a Christian (possibly confusing 'Krishna' with 'Christ') conducted him from Malindi across the Indian Ocean to Calicut on the Malabar coast, where he disappointed the local ruler by the paltriness of his gifts. The Hindus were willing to trade, but Da Gama had more trouble with the Muslims.

Da Gama returned to Lisbon after some two-thirds of his crew had died of scurvy. A fleet was then despatched under Cabral to establish a Portuguese trading station at Calicut. Cabral's Atlantic course was too far westward, with the result that he accidentally discovered Brazil. The men Cabral left at Calicut were murdered at the instigation of Muslim traders, and Da Gama led a punitive expedition which bombarded Calicut, treated the inhabitants with appalling savagery, and established 'favourable trading relations' with them. This led to the foundation of the Portuguese Indian empire, of which a fragment remains in Goa.

First of 'modern' artists

VELASQUEZ, Diego Rodríguez de Silva y, (1599–1660). Manet, the so-called Father of Impressionism, called this Spanish master 'the painter of painters', revering him for his detached and more or less impersonal style, his way of recording visual impressions. In a sense he was the first of 'modern' artists.

Early in his painting life Velasquez was summoned to Madrid by the chief minister of Philip IV, whom he painted from boyhood to age. King, child, dwarf, dress, skin, fish or eggs were to Velasquez occasions of light and tone. *Philip IV when Young*, in the National Gallery in London, is less an individual or a king than a man in clothes created by a technique of combining prodigious skill and somewhat limited sensibility. Velasquez observes the exact degree and effect of light. Forms nearest the eye are in full light; subtle, carefully calculated brush-strokes of varying tone convey the receding forms, and between the two Velasquez creates an impression of the reality of space. The ground of the dress is a simple rubbing of this brown paint, on which he touches in the heavy silver brocade with crisp separate strokes of grey and white of extraordinary liveliness and freedom.

Fifteen years later he painted another picture of

Philip (also in the National Gallery), a head-and-shoulders portrait showing the culmination of his cool impersonality; with a gradation of tones and soft silvery paint he records the face of this tired king in his black dress embroidered with gold. It was such pictures as these which caused modern artists to engage themselves in a selection of optical appearances rather than in the expression of profound ideas. Velasquez and Constable and those whom they influenced in the nineteenth century have introduced us to the beauties of a calmly observed visual world, which has led paradoxically to the disappearance of 'nature' in painting and the development of abstract art. Not, of course, that Velasquez put what was 'real' upon canvas. Picasso has said of him, 'Through art we express our conception of what nature is not. Velasquez left us his idea of the people of his epoch. Undoubtedly they differed from his painting of them; yet the only Philip IV we can conceive is the one by Velasquez', and long ago the French painter Delacroix remarked how 'strange a thing it would be and how wonderful' to join the visual style of Velasquez to the (meaningful) style of Michelangelo.

ILLUSTRATION: Page 324.

Giovanni Verga

VERGA, Giovanni, (1840–1922), commonly imagined to be the librettist of Mascagni's opera *Cavalleria Rusticana,* did not write a libretto in all of his long life, but was certainly one of the greatest of Italian novelists.

His short story *Cavalleria Rusticana,* on which the opera was based, is not one of his best; and his other work became known in the English-speaking world only through the translations of D. H. Lawrence. These translations are more Laurentian than Vergan; so that it has been Verga's misfortune to be thought of as an appendage of two men – Lawrence and Mascagni – who were lesser than himself. He was not more fortunate in his own country. In the first twenty years after its publication the sales of *I Malavoglia* (1881), the first of his two great novels (the title of the English translation is *The House by the Medlar Tree*), reached five thousand copies, a pitiful figure for a writer of Verga's magnitude. The amount of critical attention paid him by his countrymen is minute in comparison with that lavished upon their great novel-

ists by the critics of other countries, and no Italian has yet thought it worth while to write his biography. *I Malavoglia, Mastro-Don Gesualdo* (1889) and a few volumes of short stories are Verga's finest work. Six years after *I Malavoglia* he wrote to a friend that it was 'a failure, a total and complete failure ... Many have spoken ill of it, and those who have not avoid me as if I had committed a crime ... The worst of it is that I am not convinced of the failure, and if I had to write the book again I should write it in exactly the same way.' Lack of appreciation dried up his genius.

In the sixties and seventies Verga had written romantic stories about ladies and gentlemen in the fashion of his time, but 'one day, I don't know how, there fell into my hands a kind of ship's log, a pretty illiterate and ungrammatical handwritten document in which a skipper succinctly described certain adventures that had happened to him in his sailing ship. It was shipshape stuff, without a superfluous phrase, brief. It struck me, and I re-read it; it was what I had long been looking for without realizing it.' After this he wrote about the peasants and fishermen of the neighbourhood of Catania in Sicily, where he was born and where he died. *I Malavoglia* and *Mastro-Don Gesualdo* were intended to be the first two parts of a trilogy to be called *I Vinti* ('The Defeated') – Verga was always more fascinated by failure than by success. Each part of the trilogy was to be set higher in the social scale; and it was not only disappointment at the reception of the first two parts that made him abandon the third after writing only one chapter; it was lack of artistic sympathy with the refined susceptibilities of the educated. To Verga the artist, the sufferings and strivings of his semi-literate peasants and fishermen, talking an unintelligible provincial dialect, alone were 'real'. In some sense, indeed, Verga is an Italian Thomas Hardy.

Il pleut dans mon cœur

VERLAINE, Paul, (1844–1896), the most popular of the French *poètes maudits*; he lacked the depth and force of his young companion, Rimbaud (q.v.), but wrote many haunting verses that have a permanent place in French literature.

Nothing about Verlaine is more striking than the

contrast between the purity of his short musical poems and the almost unredeemed squalour of his personal life. Born in 1844 at Metz, he rapidly reached prominence among the 'young Parnassiens' for his early volumes of verse, *Poèmes saturniens* (1867), *Fêtes galantes* (1869) and *La bonne chanson* (1870). As a civil servant in Paris he was dismissed for alleged sympathy with the Commune. He had become addicted to drink and dissipation in his youth, reforming for a while when he married Mathilde Mauté de Fleurville, who provided a little money; but the change was not to last. His bald dome-like head above moustaches and a sprout of beard is somehow eloquent of his self-pitying and dissipated character.

His marriage was broken up in 1871 by the arrival of Arthur Rimbaud in Paris, Rimbaud being then seventeen. The man and the boy fell under one another's spell and together they plunged into a life of drunkenness and debauchery. Verlaine called Rimbaud 'my great radiant sin', and said he was damning himself. When he returned home drunk he tried to set fire to his wife's hair, threatened to cut her throat with a razor and on one occasion threw his little baby son against the wall, nearly killing him. Mathilde made several efforts to separate him from Rimbaud, once following him to Brussels where there was a reconciliation. But next day he escaped, leaving an insulting note behind for his 'miserable ginger-haired fairy', his 'mouse princess', saying that he had gone back to Rimbaud.

In September 1872 the poets arrived in London and stayed in Soho off the Tottenham Court Road. Much of their time they spent pub-crawling and getting drunk. Verlaine found pubs very inferior to cafés. 'O lamentable infériorité des Anglo-Saxons,' he wrote; and 'A flat black bug, that is London.' At Christmas Rimbaud went home to Charleville, and alone in the foreign metropolis, watching the rain, Verlaine wrote typically limpid verses:

> Il pleut dans mon cœur
> Comme il pleut sur la ville
> Quelle est cette langueur
> Qui pénètre mon cœur ...

After further scandalous outbursts and vicissitudes we find Verlaine and Rimbaud living in Camden Town on Verlaine's mother's money. But this only meant more drunken quarrels between the two poets. When Verlaine left for Brussels Rimbaud followed him and the brawling continued there. In Brussels Verlaine shot Rimbaud in the wrist, was arrested and sentenced to three years' imprisonment.

When he emerged he was fervently religious. He saw Rimbaud once more, but the relationship was over. Verlaine's poetry – *Sagesse* (1881), much of it written in gaol, *Jadis et Naguère* (1884), *Parallèlement* (1889) and *Chansons pour elle* (1891) – was now dominated by religious feeling. Yet he was unable to give up drinking, and he became a familiar and pathetic figure in Paris, hiccupping home to his squalid lodgings. But if he lived like a pig he wrote on occasion like an angel.

ILLUSTRATION: Page 359.

Under the knife

VESALIUS, Andreas, (1514–1564), born at Brussels, was the founder of modern biology. As a boy he had dissected animals, and as a student at Paris he realized that the teaching of biology was archaic. So he went south to Padua. There the students (who at that time chose their own professors) elected to be taught by this young Belgian of twenty-three, who impressed them by his tremendous ability to work and his enthusiasm as an expositor.

The tradition of teaching anatomy demanded that the professor should read his students the descriptions left by the Greek physician Galen, while an illiterate demonstrator handled the dissected parts. Vesalius substituted experience for authority: he based his course on his own investigations of animal structure, thus bringing out the contradictions in Galen's anatomy, which had been taught virtually without question for more than a thousand years. In 1543, when he was still only twenty-eight, Vesalius published his superb *De humani corporis fabrica*, a human anatomy new and modern in outlook, and magnificently illustrated with engravings which combine the full artistry and science of the age.

This masterpiece by Vesalius and the *Revolutions of the Celestial Spheres* by Copernicus (q.v.) appeared in the same year, and it is a striking fact that these two manifestoes of modern science, produced simultaneously, should have been written by men from the North and West, who had both studied in Italy. Both of them, in fact, examined the knowledge and spirit of the Renaissance in a detached way, both were unconsciously adopting this knowledge and spirit on behalf of those northern societies which were to dominate the world. The independence and directness of

Vesalius fit in well with the rise of the Netherlands politically, industrially and artistically.

ILLUSTRATION: Page 360.

Amerigo: America

VESPUCCI, Amerigo, (1454–1512), Italian merchant and adventurer and one of the most controversial figures in the whole history of exploration. His name, because of a letter he sent to his former employer in Florence in 1503, came to be given to the American continent.

'And it is lawful to call it a new world', Vespucci wrote of America, 'because none of these countries were known to our ancestors, and to all who hear about them, they will be entirely new.' That statement in his letter was unobjectionable, though it does show how outmoded the views of Vespucci's friend, Columbus, had become within a few years, for Columbus (q.v.) still obstinately maintained that the land he had discovered was part of eastern Asia. However, three sentences further on, Vespucci unwittingly prepared his own immortality. 'I have found a continent', he wrote about his last voyage, in a phrase which has caused trouble and confusion without end.

In Spain and Portugal, from which the explorers of the new world had sailed, there was no lack of reliable information about the discoveries across the Atlantic. There it would not have occurred to anyone to name the new continent after Vespucci; and there Vespucci's famous letter to Lorenzo di Medici was not printed in his lifetime. In Italy, Germany and France, the letter was immediately printed, and gave the first generally available information about the new world, going through edition after edition. So Amerigo's name was bestowed on America by men of learning and cosmographers who were remote from Spain and Portugal and knew nothing of navigation. Columbus's friends in Spain were naturally indignant: it seemed an attempt to deprive Columbus of his glory, and the Columbus–Vespucci controversy has not altogether died away even now. In Vespucci's defence, it should be said that 'I have found a continent' does not necessarily imply a claim to have found it before everyone else. With Columbus, however, he remained always on the best of terms.

Vespucci did not go to sea until he was nearly fifty, at which age a successful business man does not usually become a professional pilot. With two of the four expeditions he described, he never sailed; with the other two, he must have sailed not as pilot, but perhaps as cosmographer. Much of the information he gives was false or defective. Yet Vespucci secured the post of Chief Pilot from the Spanish king – but a king who dismissed Columbus and was known for his bad appointments.

La bella Simonetta

VESPUCCI, Simonetta, (1453–1476), a Genoese girl whose symbolic beauty was immortalized in the years of the Florentine Renaissance.

The Bella Simonetta came to Florence when she was sixteen, the young wife of Marco Vespucci. She attracted Giuliano de' Medici, the brother of Lorenzo the Magnificent, ruler of Florence, and the two were well matched in beauty and character. Lorenzo said that Simonetta had sweetness and beauty without parallel: all young men, her manner was so gentle and so winning, felt that she loved them. All young women forbore jealousy and praised her beauty and gentleness. She figured especially in Giuliano's tournament in 1475, which was held in the Piazza San Croce. Poliziano describes her beauty in his poem The Joust. He pictures a young huntsman – Giuliano – riding through the woods after a phantom stag put in his way by Cupid. He reaches a clearing and there he sees a marvellous apparition – either girl or goddess, though his bewildered senses give him no certain answer:

> Candid the Lady was and yet as candid
> Her gown that leaves and roses did adorn;
> The winding ringlets of her golden head
> Descend those brows where pity conquers scorn;
> Softly about her smiled the green-monthed glade
> As it would grow less horrid and forlorn,
> Each gesture royal, yet a most gentle maid
> Whose single glance the brawling winds allayed.
>
> Forth flash those eyes in soft inazured light
> For Cupid hides his torches in those eyes;
> The air about her muted by delight
> Wherever those Love-bearing orbs she plies;
> Hued red as roses, as the privet white,
> Upon her face some holy gladness lies.
> The wind is stilled by her divine tongue's sound,
> Birds in their wild speech her praise resound.

There as she sat upon a grassy mound,
With every flower that ever nature made
She wove a garland that she might be crowned,
And with those flowers her tunic was arrayed,
When first she saw the youth she turned her round,
Seeing that youth her eyes grew half afraid;
Then, raising the border of her gown, she rose,
Her lap, a garden filled with every flower that grows.

A year after the tournament La Bella Simonetta was dead – of consumption; she died in April, and was carried to her grave on an open bier so that all could see her beauty. Lorenzo in his commentary on his own poems writes of seeing a very bright star in the west, as he walked with a friend talking of the loss of Simonetta. It was 'of such a splendour that it far outshone the other stars'. At first astonished, he turned and said that 'the soul of that most gentle lady has either been transformed into a new star or united with it'. Two more years, and the handsome, steadfast Giuliano was killed at Mass in the Duomo, stabbed nineteen times with a hysterical violence.

The story that Simonetta was painted by Botticelli in the *Primavera* and again in the Birth of Venus, was invented in the nineteenth century, and is certainly untrue. Nonetheless she was a symbol to the Florentines of beauty and its evanescence; and if Botticelli (q.v.) never made her after her death into the central figure of his great mythologies, she was pictured – as Cleopatra, with the asp – in Piero di Cosimo's famous portrait.

ILLUSTRATION: Page 361.

Sixty years a queen

VICTORIA, (1819–1901), Queen of England and Empress of India, reigned longest of British monarchs and gave her name to the Victorian age. 'We are not amused', if applied to an improper story, was appropriate enough; but she would, no doubt, prefer to be remembered by her firm political judgement: 'She will *never* be the Queen of a democratic monarchy.'

Victoria was the only daughter of Edward, Duke of Kent, himself the fourth son of George III. Her father died soon after her birth; and she was brought up in melancholy seclusion by her mother. On seeing a genealogical table, which made it clear to her that she would succeed to the throne, she exclaimed: 'I will be good'; and on her accession in 1837 she immediately insisted on a separate bedroom from her mother.

To begin with, Victoria regarded herself as a Whig Queen and refused to dismiss her court-ladies in 1839 at the request of Sir Robert Peel, prospective Conservative Prime Minister. Her cousin, Albert of Saxe-Coburg-Gotha, whom she married in 1840, taught her a more detached constitutional duty: the Queen should accept the vagaries of party and should stand critical and experienced, above the battle. This doctrine she applied with considerable success; and Albert, acting in her name, became a moderating influence in politics. In 1861 Albert died of typhoid fever. Victoria shut herself up at Balmoral or Osborne, and for many years she refused to take any part in public life. The flattery of Disraeli persuaded her to emerge and to open parliament in 1876 – the year when she became Empress of India. She fell foul of Gladstone, especially over his proposals for Irish Home Rule; and she did her best to prevent the return of the Liberals to office. But her complaints and her expostulations were a nuisance which had no serious effect; and she might just as well have acted the impartial role with which she was credited by public opinion. She celebrated her Jubilee in 1887 and her Diamond Jubilee in 1897 – the latter a festival of Empire; and in extreme old age, the Queen's dumpy figure – propelled back and forwards, as it seemed, by a concealed spring – became a symbol of respectability and imperial grandeur.

In reality she knew nothing of her Empire, which she never visited; she tolerated dissolute living in her ministers (and even her Prime Minister) so long as it was concealed from the middle-class public; and, like many women of a passionate nature, she disliked her children, whom she regarded as the inevitable, but heavy, price of her married bliss. She was more German than English in character and appearance – but then, so was Victorian England.

The great detective

VIDOCQ, Eugène François, (1775–1857), French criminal and detective, who founded the Paris *Service de Sûreté*, and whose romantic life on both sides of the law made him the prototype of the master-mind detective of crime-fiction.

The chief witness of Vidocq's exploits is Vidocq in

his *Mémoires* (1828), brashly written by a ghost probably, and not by Vidocq himself. He was a baker's son, a soldier, a deserter, a jail-bird, who was condemned to the galleys, a master of escapes and disguises, and last of all an informer, a police spy, founding a detective department with himself at the head. His methods were new. He represents the change from the old catch-them-in-the-act policing to planned investigation of crime and criminals. His life as an investigator was not without difficulties. 'Without women and duels I should have the Cross of the Legion of Honour, and I should have mounted to the top of the ladder.' When arresting Sablin, a robber, he had to act as midwife to Mme Sablin. 'The lady having fallen into a chair, groaned very bitterly ... a midwife was needed, but who was going to search for her? ... I recalled to mind the Grand Monarque (Louis XIV) performing the office of accoucheur to La Vallière. Why, said I, should I be more delicate than he? I immediately took off my coat, and in less than twenty-five minutes Mme Sablin was delivered.'

As a scourge and an inverted papa of all criminals, Vidocq always watched the fettering of chain-gang prisoners who were off to the galleys. He served for twenty years until 1827, retired, started a paper-mill in which the labour was provided by ex-convicts, and soon tried to return to the Sûreté, fabricating a criminal case, so it is said, and then 'solving' it to show how indispensable he was. One story goes that he died in poverty, another that when he left the Sûreté he owned half a million francs. The truth about him is not easily come by. Just as the criminals were surprised when one of their accomplices turned out to be Vidocq, so it may well be that Vidocq fooled the police equally – when it suited him. He writes of one Beaumont who had robbed the police.

'In effect, to have robbed the police was the height of address. Is not a robbery of this nature the *chef d'œuvre* of its kind, and can it do otherwise than make its perpetrator a hero in the eyes of his admirers? Who should dare to compare with him? Beaumont had robbed the police!!! Hang yourself, Brave Crillon! hang yourself, Coignard! hang yourself, Pertruisard! hang yourself, Callet! – to him, you are but of Saint-Jean. What is it to have robbed golden services? To have carried off the treasure of the army of the Rhine? To have carried off the military chest? – Beaumont had robbed the police! Hang yourselves! – or go to England, they will hang you there!' There is an admiring nostalgia in this that does not reveal Vidocq's own opinion: but it is silly

to look too far. If we get too close, he will put on another disguise. And suddenly he will not be there at all. Vidocq collected Dutch paintings, models of tropical fruit and instruments of torture. Balzac knew him and he makes his first bow in literature as the redoubtable Vautrin, once in the galleys, whose character in the wonderful novel *Le Père Goriot* (1835) is all force and iron and sinister determination. Emile Gaboriau (1835–1873) made out of him the M. Lecoq of his pioneering detective stories.

Poet of love and poverty

VILLON, François, (b. 1431), the first great French poet.

We do not know many facts about Villon's life, and most that we do know come from his poems. He appears to have been born in 1431, and his real name was probably des Loges or Montcorbier. He studied at the University of Paris but plainly lacked the qualities needed for a man of learning. In 1455 he killed a man in a quarrel, and thereafter lived a Bohemian life with thieves, vagabonds, and prostitutes for company. He was once saved from the gallows and we hear of him emerging from prison at Meung-sur-Loire in 1461. We do not know when he died.

Villon expresses his thoughts and problems, those of an outcast, with simplicity and directness. His life was strangely like that of a nineteenth-century *poète damné*, but only in externals. Villon rose above all his troubles with a cheerfulness or at least a resignation which sometimes seems almost superhuman to the modern reader. One of his favourite themes is the transitoriness of human life – *mais où sont les neiges d'antan* – where are the snows of yester-year? His examples are often lurid, even macabre, as befitting one who lived under the gallows, but he treats his characters with deep sympathy. The prostitute laments her old age spent crouching in a row with other 'poor silly old women' – reflecting such is the outcome of human beauty as she counts her ruined charms:

Les bras cours et les mains contraites,
Les espaulles toutes bossues,
Mamelles, quoy! toutes retraites ...

Shoulders all a hump,
Short arms, contracted hands, and
Breasts! – well, breasts all shrunk ...

Or, after a hair-raising description of death from which there is no escape, he ends up with a tenderness of humour:

> Corps feminin qui tant est tendre
> Poly, souef, si precieux,
> Te fauldra il ces maulx attendre?
> Oy, ou tout vif aller es cieulx

> A woman's body which is so tender,
> Polished, lissom, of such price,
> Must it look forward to these ills?
> It must, or go alive to Paradise!

Villon's religion is truly medieval. He prays to Our Lady: 'You, noble virgin and princess, bore Jesus who reigns', and he nails to the mast the faith in which he intends to live and die; but he also appeals against Death's severity for robbing him of his mistress. We are lost in wonder at the poem he wrote about himself and his companions when they lay under sentence of death; death he accepts calmly, but he appeals for brotherly feeling and understanding. We see their corpses swaying from the gallows, as Villon meant us to:

> La pluye nous a buez et lavez
> Et le soleil desechez et noircis:
> Pies, corbeaulx, nous ont les yeux cavez
> Et arraché la barbe et les sourcilz ...

> The rain's washed over us, we're dried
> And blackened by the sun, and crows and pies
> Have plucked our eyebrows and our beards
> And hollowed out the sockets of our eyes.

But he also says:

> Se freres vous clamons, pas n'en devez
> Avoir desdaing, quoique fusmes occis
> Par justice ...

> If we name you brothers, you should
> Have no disdain of us who by the law
> Are slain

And typical of the Middle Ages at their best is Villon's love of the poor and his sense of pity. There is a Franciscan quality about his attitudes and his adjectives. In Villon's eyes poverty staked a claim to heaven. This 'poor little scholar who was named François Villon', as he wrote of himself in famous lines, was not only a great French poet, but one of the most attractively human and natural of all poets.

The gadfly of Europe

VOLTAIRE, François Marie Arouet de, (1694–1778), French writer and individualist, who sparkled and flashed with erratic brilliance among the outmoded ideas of Europe, and helped to sow liberty in the human mind.

A few weeks before his death, Voltaire returned – after many years' exile – to Paris. The entire Academy – but not the bishops – welcomed him. The crowd cried, 'Hail to the Universal Man!' It was the voice of the eighteenth century acclaiming in just terms its most typical and controversial figure, its champion of clarity and reason. He had fought all his life against the mighty windmills of Church and State – as he imagined them. He had lived to see his name supreme above all European intellectuals; his fame was renowned throughout the civilized world. And now his own country had recognized the prophet: it was a triumph indeed.

He began as the darling of the nobility. In his twenties he was a fashionable playwright at the French court, and the holder of a royal pension. But that ended when, after a quarrel, the Chevalier de Rohan-Chabot set his roughs on Voltaire to beat him up. Voltaire appealed to the great Sully for revenge; but Sully smiled – he was related to Rohan. From then, Voltaire was the implacable enemy of caste: he used all his intellect and wit to undermine the foundations of the *ancien régime*.

He wrote incessantly: plays, poetry, essays, countless letters. 'Much to be pitied are they who need the help of religion to be honest men,' he said. And it was Voltaire who published with glee a remark he found in the will of Jean Messelier, who died in 1733: 'I should like to see – and this will be the final and the most ardent of my wishes – the last king strangled with the guts of the last priest.'

When his famous visit to Frederick the Great (the triumphant mind meeting the triumphant materialist) ended in a quarrel, Voltaire's pamphlet on the subject was burned in the streets of Berlin. The two men had respected but not admired each other. When Voltaire spoke to Frederick of his 'friendship' with Emilie de Breteuil, marquise du Châtelet (his mistress for sixteen years), Frederick genially enquired: 'Would you have me believe that during all that time you talked of nothing but philosophy to the most charming woman in France?' Emilie died when Voltaire was fifty-five: there was to be a long twilight. Each time that he felt like dying he would remind himself that three or four princes would profit by his death – they paid him annuities – 'then I take courage from pure malice and I conspire against them with rhubarb and sobriety'. Boswell visited him and found an old man in 'a slate-blue, fine frieze greatcoat night-gown, and three-knotted wig ... at last we came upon religion. Then did he rage.'

Of his enormous literary output, little more than *Candide* lives universally today. And, with reservations, it represents Voltaire's ethos. He believed with Dr Pangloss (for whom the philosopher Leibniz was the model), that everything is for the best in the best of all possible worlds. It is said that his last words were '*Déjà les flammes*' – The flames, so soon! But he had little to fear, since his rage was against the earthly representatives of Divine Rule.

Today, the complete man is a recurring ideal: and Voltaire is often put forward as an example. But though he read widely and was in touch with all sides of contemporary knowledge, he was rarely more than a brilliant *littérateur*, a gadfly who plagued Europe, or a searchlight turned this way and that. His greatest achievement was that he opened the dusty windows of men's minds with his scepticism, and showed them the power of private thought over public law.

ILLUSTRATION: Plate 14.

'*Melodramatic rhetorician of the senses*'

WAGNER, Wilhelm Richard, (1813–1883), German composer, whose life was in some ways a perversion of Beethoven's ideal of the artist-aristocrat. He rebelled against the lifeless rules by which lifeless teachers tried to bind him: 'For me', he wrote in *Mein Leben*, his autobiography, 'music was a spirit, a noble and mystic monster, and any attempt to regulate it seemed to lower it in my eyes.'

Nietzsche described him as 'a melodramatic rhetorician of the senses', and from childhood Wagner's spirit expanded into darkness and storm. 'The excitements of horror', he wrote in his autobiography, 'and of fear of ghosts formed quite a special factor in the development of my spiritual life';

and in the years of his success and fame he delighted to live in a lurid *mis en scène* – silk-hung walls, thick soft carpets, himself clad in suits of coloured satin. To some degree Wagner always inhabited a moral vacuum. As a young man, when with his wife he was on the way to try his luck in Paris, Wagner stopped for a month or so in Boulogne, where he was introduced to Meyerbeer, the German-Jewish operatic composer, whose kindness to them was returned years later when Wagner wrote a pamphlet entitled *Judaism in Music* (1869). In this he called Meyerbeer 'a wretched Jew banker to whom it occurred to write operas'. In Paris from 1839 to 1842 and afterwards in Dresden he developed a grudge against the world which denied him wealth, luxury and success, and in the revolutionary year of 1848 paraded the Dresden streets with a musket, having to escape to Weimar and then to Zürich. Success came to him with the performance of *Lohengrin* at Weimar in 1850. Working intermittently on the gigantic tetralogy of *The Ring*, completing *Tristan and Isolde* (1857–1859), *The Meistersingers* (1862–1867), finding in 1864 a patron in the King of Bavaria, Wagner slowly turned himself into a romantic, sensational, pseudo-mystical institution, altogether above good and evil. At the Dresden Court he collected a strange entourage consisting of himself, the musician von Bülow and von Bülow's wife Cosima, who was his mistress. Baudelaire (q.v.) had written to him in 1860 to say that he owed Wagner 'the greatest musical pleasure' he had ever experienced, that he found in his works 'the solemnity of the grand sounds of Nature', the 'supreme utterance of a soul at its highest paroxysm'.

At Bayreuth he was able to build a theatre, a shrine for Wagner, opened in 1876 with a complete performance of *The Ring*, which dives deep into the murkier regions of the German soul.

Wagner's masterpiece was *Tristan and Isolde*, revolutionary by reducing the singers to equality with the orchestra, and for beginning the disintegration of the key system, the reorganization of tonality, over which Schönberg was to preside nearly a century later.

ILLUSTRATION: Page 367.

A poet of Emperors

WALTHER VON DER VOGELWEIDE, (c. 1170–1230), the most original and versatile of the minnesingers (or love minstrels) who wrote in Middle High German.

Unlike some of the minnesingers who flourished in Western Germany, Walther, an Austrian, did not try to emulate the subtleties and artificialities of the French poets, but tended to the directness of popular verse. Generally speaking, his love poetry does not comply with the conventions of 'higher' or courtly love, which demanded that the poem should be addressed to a married lady of distinction. His most characteristic love lyrics glorify 'lower' or natural love, like this song of a young girl:

> Under the lime-tree
> By the heath,
> Where with my well-beloved I lay,
> You can go and see –
> Pleasant both –
> Flowers and grass we broke that day.
> Where the forest meets the dale:
> Tandaradee!
>   Sweetly sang the nightingale.
>
> Here we were meeting;
> But already
> My well-beloved was waiting there.
> Such was his greeting,
> Gracious Lady,
> That ever since I've walked on air.
> Did he kiss me? Yes, and well:
> Tandaradee!
>   Look how red my lips are still.
>
> With the wild flowers
> There my love
> Made a lavish bed for me;
> This bed of ours,
> Should you pass above,
> Will make you laugh most heartily.
> By the roses you can trace –
> Tandaradee! –
>   Where my head lay in that place.
>
> Had anyone seen us
> Lying there,
> (God grant none did!) I'd be ashamed.
> What passed between us
> Is our affair,
> Never to be known or named
> But by us and a small bird –
> Tandaradee! –
>   Which may never breathe a word.

Besides the love poetry proper, Walther wrote much religious, political and didactic verse, as well as a commentary on the principal events of his time. Walther's treatment of his powerful patrons – mostly emperors, kings and prelates – was candid to the point of bluntness.

It was his last and most generous patron, the Emperor Frederick II, who granted him a small fief, for which Walther returned the most sincere, joyful thanks; but when Frederick was excommunicated for preferring Sicily to the Holy Land, Walther could not approve, but composed his impassioned lament for the declining age of chivalry:

> Alas, how ill and meanly
>   do the young behave
> Whose bearing once was courtly,
>   generous and brave ...
> The wild birds on the branches
>   are troubled by our wailing;
> No wonder that my courage,
>   my very faith is failing.
> Woe, what am I saying
>   in my foolish scorn?
> Who seeks this life's enjoyment
>   the other has forsworn
> For ever more, alas!

As in other poems of his last years, he goes on to renounce the world:

> Without, the world is lovely,
>   white, red and green,
> But black it is in colour,
>   dark as death within.
> Whomsoever it has misguided,
>   behold his consolation:
> Though great his sin, no matter:
>   small penance wins salvation ...
> If only on that voyage,
>   the dear one, I could go,
> Then 'hail' I should be singing,
>   never 'alas' or 'woe',
> Never again 'alas'.

(The translations are by Michael Hamburger.)

America's last Englishman and first American

WASHINGTON, George, (1732–1799), Commander-in-Chief of the Army of Independence and first President of the United States.

Washington was a typical Virginian planter, of British antecedents and aristocratic connections, who seemed little fitted by circumstance for the noble, energetic role played in the foundation of American liberty. Throughout his life he was interested in estate management and speculation in western lands; he first became surveyor through the encouragement of the Fairfax family, whose vast territory lay near Mount Vernon; he was a slave-owner, though of a somewhat moderate kind; to this serene if prosaic life was added, however, much frontier experience as a result of his mission to warn the French away from the Ohio in the winter of 1753 and his soldiering during the French and Indian War, when he showed both courage and organizing ability during the retreat of General Braddock. At the early age of twenty-three he was given command of the Virginian forces, having to protect a frontier of three hundred and fifty miles with a mere seven hundred men. He also attended the House of Burgesses where he showed himself a realistic judge of the difficulties with Britain: 'Shall we after this whine and cry for relief?' was his comment when the import negotiations broke down.

In 1774 Virginia sent him as one of its seven delegates to the first Continental Congress. Here again his opinion was forthright: 'More blood will be spilled on this occasion, if the ministry are determined to push matters to extremes, than history has ever yet found instances of in the annals of North America,' he declared, and it has been remarked that he was the only delegate to appear constantly in uniform when the Congress convened for the second time. After the battle of Bunker Hill in 1775 he offered his services for the Boston campaign in a famous single sentence and it seemed to surprise nobody, although there was later to be much backbiting and intrigue, that he was given the leadership of the whole army.

Washington brought great qualities to his task: under his cold exterior he hid much dash and fire, as he had shown with General Braddock; he had faith in the Union and the greatest determination to secure its victory; but, more important than this, he was almost universally respected for his moral qualities, his disinterestedness and his probity. If there still seems some mystery as to why the mantle should have fallen so inevitably and conclusively on his shoulder, if his strategy seems at times too European and orthodox, and his celebrated aloofness too chilly to make him a good judge of character, his moral qualities proved invaluable during the retreat through New Jersey, the delaying actions at Trenton and Princeton, the defence of the approaches to Philadelphia, and during the bitter winter at Valley Forge. He had much to contend with on his own side, amongst the senior ranks of the army; the Conway cabal and the rivalry of Gates, the appalling shock administered by Benedict Arnold and rather inhumanly responded to by the execution of Major André, not to speak of the widespread corruption which affected commanders as brave and valuable as Greene. Again and again Washington grew bitter in reproach. Referring to 'those murderers of our cause, the monopolizers, the forestallers, the engrossers', he went on, 'I would to God that one of the most atrocious in each state was hung in gibbets on a gallows five times as high as the one prepared by Haman.' On another occasion he wrote, 'And shall we at last become the victims of our own abominable lust for gain? Forbid it Heaven! Forbid it all and every state in the Union! by enacting and enforcing efficacious laws for checking the growth of these monstrous evils ...' Perhaps Washington's chief contribution was to keep for so long, and in such hard-pressed circumstances, the scattered elements of rebellion together, to invest them with dignity of purpose, and to convince the British – as he certainly did – that they were opposed by forces far more formidable than was in fact the case.

Although Washington had been determined to take New York, it was in his own state of Virginia that victory came, a victory surprising in itself and only gained with the aid of the French and of Washington's mercurial French friend, Lafayette. It has been said that the only men surprised by Cornwallis's surrender at Yorktown were the two chief protagonists, Washington and George III. Washington was still worried; 'the temper of the army is much soured, and has become more irritable than at any period since the beginning of the war', he wrote out of his awareness of the possibility of military rebellion and dictatorship, with himself probably cast for the lead. Facing the murmuring officers of his army at Newburgh in March 1783, he made a gesture characteristic of him: 'Gentlemen, you will permit me to put on my spectacles, for I have not only grown grey, but almost blind, in the service of my country.' The warrior 'panted for retirement', and wished to 'become a private citizen on the banks of the Potomac'.

Nevertheless a reluctant Washington was to be twice president of the country he had helped to form. He had to face much criticism in this office, as well as the ambitions and intellectual attainments of Jefferson and Madison; but he held his course firm and never more so than when he resisted attempts to entangle the United States with the French revolutionary war, thus forecasting the Monroe doctrine of no colonization and no European finger in America. Political faction he little understood, 'Why, then, when some of the best citizens of the United States, men of Discernment, uniform and tried patriots, who have no sinister views to promote, but are chaste in their ways of thinking and acting, are to be found some on one side and some on the other of the questions which have caused this agitation, should either of you [Jefferson and Hamilton] be so tenacious of your opinions as to make no allowance for those of the others?' Finally released from office, he spent the last two and a half years of his life back at Mount Vernon. Still concerned with foreign policy, for 'Peace with all the world is my sincere wish' but also able to draft, within three days of his death, a document of nearly ten thousand words planning the rotation of crops on his farms up till the year 1803, he died within seventeen days of the nineteenth century – at once the last Englishman and the first American of his country.

ILLUSTRATION: Page 362.

An English Eccentric

WATERTON, Charles, (1782–1865), English eccentric and naturalist. A house on an island in a lake surrounded by a park was the right setting for this peculiar squire of Walton Hall, near Wakefield in Yorkshire. The many acres of the park were girdled with a wall eight feet high. Inside, Charles Waterton protected his trees and his birds – even his weasels (though the larger foxes and badgers were expelled), the weasels occupying a corner under rocks, near a rock-hewn grotto in which twice a year he gave dinner to a hundred lunatics from the local asylum.

Waterton was set apart to some degree by belonging to a Roman Catholic family at a time when Catholics still suffered from legal and educational disabilities. His family owned sugar estates in British Guiana, which he visited as a young man, so beginning those travels described in his once famous *Wanderings in South America* (1825); but this book is rather tediously written in a way ill according with Waterton's real character and liveliness. As a naturalist his passion above all was for birds, which he collected in the New World and to which he gave protection at home, turning his park into a bird sanctuary before bird sanctuaries were thought of, arranging nesting-boxes, building an owl-tower, and even an artificial quarry in which there were nesting-holes for sand-martins. Waterton had a tenderness for living creatures – which extended even to a bug he found crawling on his neck as he travelled by steamer on the St Lawrence. Addressing the bug, he asked it if it was journeying from the United States to Canada or from Canada to the United States. He spared the bug, and threw it among the baggage nearby, recommending it 'to get ashore at the first opportunity'. He was tender to his trees, delighting to climb them, perch himself among the branches, and there take out his Virgil; but his natural history had its unnatural side, its grotesque humour. He delighted in odd trees – a lime with seven trunks known as the Seven Deadly Sins, a filbert which grew from the hole in a millstone, the two together being known as 'John Bull and the National Debt' – and also in taxidermic satire and fantasy – the Nondescript, for example, a howler monkey fashioned into a hairy bust, a parody of the neo-classic head and shoulders of gentleman or statesman; or the stuffed figures called 'England's Reformation Zoologically Illustrated', which included John Knox as a black frog. At the foot of his grand staircase he set the monstrous head of a sheep with horns growing from the ears, he dissected a rotting gorilla in his drawing-room, he grafted mistletoe on his trees, he slept always with his head on a hollowed-out block of beechwood.

Waterton never grew up. The young man who climbed to the lightning conductor above the dome of St Peter's in Rome, where he left his gloves, climbed oak trees in his park at eighty-three or scratched the back of his head with his big toe at seventy-seven. One of his intimates describing 'the playful levity' of his 'octogenarian friend', wrote that Waterton once received him by imitating a savage dog and barking at him from under the table. On his death, he was buried near his own lake, after a funeral voyage in the coal boat he always had called 'Charon's Ferry'. Waterton was most admirably painted by his American friend, Charles Willson Peale of Philadelphia. From Rembrandt Peale he bought a portrait of Washington, whose health he always drank on July 4th – in water.

ILLUSTRATION: Page 363.

Radiolocation

WATSON-WATT, Sir Robert Alexander, (b. 1892), was the chief British creator of radar, the device for detecting the approach of aircraft by means of the reflection of radio waves, which was a necessary instrument in the defeat of the German air force in the second world war. Radar is short for ra(dio) d(etection) a(nd) r(anging).

After the war of 1914–1918, Watson-Watt became superintendent of the Radio Department at the National Physical Laboratory, where he investigated the origin and nature of the 'atmospherics' which disturb radio reception. He developed ways of finding their origin on the earth's surface and recording on cathode-ray tubes the shape of the electro-magnetic waves which carry them. In 1934, after the rise of Hitler, the threat of air bombardment became serious and new counter-measures were searched for. The public demanded 'death rays' which would destroy aircraft. Watson-Watt was asked if such rays were conceivable: scarcely, he reported with great speed; though in theory aircraft could be detected by the reflection of radio waves. Experiments to see whether the radio-waves sent out by the powerful transmitter at Rugby might be reflected from a passing aircraft were at once successful, and orders were given for the development under Watson-Watt of a 'detective' system. When war broke out, Britain was decently girdled and protected by radar stations.

Watson-Watt had ably presented radar to statesmen and soldiers, a brilliant advocate in that marginal zone between science and affairs. He knew the technique necessary in our world for securing the proper use of science.

Dreamer of love

WATTEAU, Jean Antoine, (1684–1721), French painter of the beauty, transience and poignancy of life.

In Paris, poor, obscure, living from hand to mouth, Watteau first copied religious pictures in a workshop on the Pont Notre Dame; he designed stage sets, and worked for the decorative painter Audran, who was also keeper of the Luxembourg Gardens. Here this son of a tiler and carpenter at Valennciennes found the vistas of trees and statues and the setting for his poignant dreams of the *fête gallante*.

All the elements of Watteau's art may be seen in his most famous picture, *L'Embarquement pour Cythère* (in the Louvre, in Paris), which he painted as his diploma work for the Academy. Across a gently sloping, grassy hillock, overshadowed by dark trees, the lovers rise to walk slowly down to the edge of the sea, where a boat waits to take them to the Island of Love. Here and there a girl is coquettish and unwilling, her partner tenderly persuades her, while Cupids flutter overhead and a statue of Venus regards them. A soft golden light gleams on grey, blue, yellow and pink silks and satins. 'With what elegance', remarked Gautier, 'the lady about to enter the boat holds up the train of her skirt behind her with a little movement of her hand! Only Watteau can seize in their flight these feminine movements.' Always indeed the marvel in Watteau's work is the truth, tenderness and elegance of the drawing. He is a knowledgeable and supreme draughtsman, redeeming the artificiality of his situations with underlying honesty.

At the time when he painted the *Embarkation*, Watteau was already seriously ill with consumption. He visited London, consulted Queen Anne's physician, and returned to Paris to die, when he was only thirty-seven, in the arms of his friend Gersaint, the picture-dealer. According to Gersaint, he 'was of average height and weak constitution; his disposition was anxious and changeable; he was self-willed; he had a wanton truant wit but his conduct was virtuous. He was impatient and timid; cold and embarrassed in his manner of receiving; discreet and reserved with strangers, but a good though difficult friend; misanthropic, even malicious and caustic in his criticism, always dissatisfied with himself and others and forgiving with difficulty'. Gersaint said he had often witnessed 'the impatience and disgust with which his own productions inspired him. I have sometimes seen him totally efface completed pictures ... on one occasion, much against his will, I even wrenched one from his destructive grasp, an action which greatly upset him.'

Sometimes this melancholy, precise and poetic painter turned his wit against himself: 'The last resort is the hospital, isn't it? That is where no one is refused admission.' For enjoying Watteau's dream world of fairy parks, where nothing is important except the ritual of love and the fingering of a lute, it is best to visit the Louvre in Paris and the Wallace Collection in London.

The Iron Duke

WELLINGTON, Arthur Wellesley, first Duke of, (1769–1852), the victor of Waterloo – 'Waterloo and recovered Christendom!' –, most stable and self-possessed of soldiers, and the outstanding example of military common sense.

In the war against France up to the year 1814 Wellington never commanded in the main theatre. Napoleon was overborne by the mass uprising of Europe against him. Yet the contribution made to his defeat by Wellington's campaigns in the Iberian Peninsula was very great. No force comparable in size to the one he led had managed to achieve so much. French armies several times the strength of his own were contained, defeated, and worn out with the aid of the Spanish guerillas. The Peninsular War was one of the most successful 'side shows' known to history. It was largely defensive because Wellington was always faced by superior numbers in the theatre of war and more often than not on the field of battle as well; but it ended in a completely successful offensive. Wellington in the Hundred Days, the Waterloo campaign, said: 'By God! I don't think it would have been done if I had not been there!' It was true. No other soldier in Europe could have won the battle. Judge him again by results, and Wellington's importance was immense. The results he owed to the application of an overwhelming common sense, fortified by experience and contemplation. He had no lofty mind – witness the way in which he had fixed officers' Lisbon leave at two days, 'forty-eight hours, which is as long as any reasonable man can wish to stay in bed with some woman'. Yet the extremely practical and at the same time frequently mordant advice which he gave over scores of years on every conceivable topic ends by giving delight as well as forcing one's admiration.

Translated into fighting, it was the same thing. Here was a sensible strategist, not a great one. But he was great in tactics. He was never afraid; and he led troops who were not easily unsettled. Changing from soldier into politician four years after Waterloo and becoming Prime Minister in 1828, he showed the same qualities, where they were less advantageous. He lacked imagination, as Goya (q.v.) discovered when Wellington sat to him and caused the despatch of a plaster cast towards his head. Yet in politics as in war he could rise to the occasion in great style, as he did over the Bill for the emancipation of the Catholics which was passed during his premiership. Wellington never climbed the heights. Nelson (q.v.) we could love, but hardly Wellington. But he is an historical character who lives by achievement and by horse-sense.

ILLUSTRATION: Plate 15.

Free citizen of the New World

WELLS, Herbert George, (1866–1946), English novelist and propagandist for a World State. A decade before his death he composed his own obituary, and wrote in it: 'The most interesting thing about Wells was his refusal to accept the social inferiority to which he seemed to have been born and the tenacity with which he insisted upon his role as a free citizen of the new world.'

Wells had the large aim of grappling with the universe. Until the last days when, an old man under the bombs of the London blitz, he wrote *Mind at the End of its Tether*, he faced the world blithely with all the answers. In his journey from a London suburb, and a draper's counter, to becoming the self-appointed Public Relations Officer of the World State, he contrived, by releasing his own personality through his writing, to give simultaneous release to millions. He used the novel as a safety-valve for his passions and his propaganda. 'I was disposed to regard a novel', he said, 'as about as much an art form as a market place or a boulevard. It had not even necessarily to get anywhere. You went by it on your various occasions.' Henry James (q.v.) and Wells had a famous exchange over the notion that the novel is merely a waste-paper basket for ideas. Wells parodied James mercilessly in *Boon*. Yet Wells's novels diminish, James's increase in stature. However, his claim is certainly true: 'I have become a symbol against the authoritative, the dull, the presumptuously established, against all that is hateful and hostile to youth and tomorrow.' He released a whole generation from the Victorian straitjacket. It is curious now to recall that St Loe Strachey, editor of the London *Spectator*, led a deputation to the Home Secretary asking him to ban Wells's novel, *Ann Veronica*, as subversive of family life. Wells became a world-figure. He shot from an interview with Roosevelt to an interview with Stalin. But he was an innovator as well as a liberator. He virtually created Science Fiction. He was always a jump ahead.

Though he said, 'I am a journalist all the time and what I write *goes now* – and will presently die', his stories and some of his novels have a long lease of life. Readers can hardly become indifferent to such brilliantly told narratives as *The First Men in the Moon*, *The Invisible Man* or *The Food of the Gods*.

Modern poet of China

WEN YI-TUO, (1896–1946), one of the chief poets of modern China, whose poems issue in part from a blend of the ancient Chinese and the modern European traditions, and stand for a new energy and a new consciousness in China.

Wen Yi-tuo was trained as an artist in the vast Chicago Art Institute, but he gave up painting for writing poems and teaching in the Chinese universities. Like T.S.Eliot (q.v.), he was modernist and traditionalist in one, a reformer of poetry, a revolutionary scholar and intellectual. Both are poets of a small output, but whereas Eliot has been inclined to praise form and then to dispense with strictness of form in his own writing, Wen Yi-tuo more strictly combined practice and precept. His ruthless gravity also suggests a certain kinship with Eliot; he would have sympathized with the Eliotesque imagery of rat's feet and gasworks, but as a Chinese poet, he felt and thought more richly through the world of objects, as in his famous *Dead Water*:

Here is a ditch of dead and hopeless water:
No breeze can raise a ripple on it.
Best to throw in it scraps of rusty iron and copper,
And pour out in it the refuse of meat and soup.

Perhaps the copper will burn green as emeralds,
Perhaps the rusty iron will assume the shape of peach
    blossoms.
Let grease weave a layer of silky gauze
And bacteria puff patches of cloud and haze.

So let the dead water ferment into green wine
Littered with floating pearls of white foam.
Small pearls cackle aloud and become big pearls,
Only to be burst like gnats to rob the vintage.

And so this ditch of dead and hopeless water
May boast a touch of brightness:
If the toads cannot endure the deadly silence,
The water may burst out singing.

Here is a ditch of dead and hopeless water,
A region where beauty can never stay.
Better abandon it to evil –
Then, perhaps, some beauty will come out of it.
                           (*Translated by Ho Yung.*)

Wen Yi-tuo was killed by Chiang Kai-shek's soldiers in 1946.

'All the world my parish'

WESLEY, John, (1703–1791), English evangelist, founder of the Methodist Church, tireless instigator of one of the greatest of religious revivals.

Wesley himself would probably have rejected that description. To the end of his long life he refused to admit a separation of Methodists from the Church of England. By instinct and inspiration he was a High Churchman and (in politics) a Tory. His inspiration began with Thomas à Kempis, and continued even more powerfully with Jeremy Taylor, master of English devotion and of devotional prose. As a young don at Oxford he was inclined to believe that the clergy should not marry, was dubious about some of the Thirty-nine Articles as Calvinistic, and was much occupied with details of ritual. The name Methodist arises from Oxford meetings of the Holy Club, to which Wesley and his brother belonged. The members were variously nicknamed Methodists, Bible Moths, Enthusiasts and Supererogation Men, and the Club became notorious because they took Communion once a week, instead of three times a year, like other decent Protestants.

The basis of Wesley's work was simple enough. 'God, in Scripture, commands me, according to my power, to instruct the ignorant, reform the wicked, confirm the virtuous. Man forbids me to do this in another's parish; that is, in effect, to do it at all, seeing that I have now no parish of my own, nor probably ever shall ... I look' – how fine a statement this is – 'upon the world as my parish.'

By not admitting separation, Wesley made difficulties for himself. He could appoint no ministers, for example, still less any bishops, without declaring himself cut off from the Church, and he was driven to such expedients as having people ordained by an Eastern Orthodox Bishop. After the American War of Independence, when at the end of his life he wanted to ensure the continuity of Methodism in America, he 'set aside' an Anglican clergyman, Dr Thomas Coke (who had been driven out of his parish as a Methodist sympathizer), and appointed him 'superintendent' of the Methodist Societies in America. On arrival, however, Dr Coke called himself a Bishop, and appointed a second Bishop, Asbury; and the Methodist Episcopal Church of America has Bishops to this day; while the Methodist Church in England has so far failed to 'take Episcopacy into its system'.

Wesley was created by Methodism as much as Methodism was formed by him; this is true in spite of his dominating personality, untameable courage and energy. He went where the need was (after a series of false starts that would have crushed a lesser man), and once he had broken through the crust of indifference and apathy to the unsatisfied passions below, their volcanic rush carried all before it. That he was able to keep any control at all was due to what he had learnt from the Moravian Brethren, to whom he had been linked for a while.

Like many great religious teachers, Wesley was extremely attractive to women, but his relations with them seem like some curious anti-masque or satyr-play to the high seriousness of his calling. From Varanese (Sarah Kirkham?) and Sophy Hopkey to Grace Murray and the extraordinary marriage with Mrs Vazeille ('My brother', wrote Charles Wesley, 'has married a ferret') – the episodes of Wesley's love affairs are like grotesques scribbled by Rowlandson, or a spiritual *Tom Jones* with the bed left out. ('I am free from the foolish passion that the world calls love.') These things only make Wesley a human being as well as a great man. When he died (2 March 1791) the Church of England burial service was, of course, used. When the words were heard: 'Forasmuch as it hath pleased Almighty God to take unto himself the soul of our dear ... Father' (substituted, with the most tender emphasis, for *Brother*) the crowd broke into uncontrollable weeping.

ILLUSTRATION: Page 365.

'A combative artist named Whistler'

WHISTLER, James Abbott McNeill, (1834–1903), American-born painter, wit and controversialist in defence of art, author of *The Gentle Art of Making Enemies* (1890), one of the wittiest of all statements of the artist against the crowd.

> There's a combative artist named Whistler
> Who is, like his own hog's-hairs, a bristler;
> A tube of white lead and a punch on the head
> Offer varied attractions to Whistler.
> (*D. G. Rossetti.*)

When a friend remarked that the Thames one evening looked like one of his pictures, Whistler replied, 'Nature is looking up!' By pen and brush he fought the dogma that art is superficial imitation: rather, in his view, 'art for art's sake'. Nature contains the elements, he wrote, the artist's job is to pick and choose and combine: 'To say to the painter, that nature is to be taken as she is, is to say to the player, that he may sit on the piano'; and he charged nature with producing as often as not 'a very foolish sunset', which is given foolish and unlimited admiration. 'Listen!' he said in the famous *Ten O'Clock Lecture*. 'There never was an artistic period. There never was an art-loving nation.' He infuriated the Victorian public by giving his pictures titles which suggested only their sentiment or their arrangements of colour and shape – *Harmony in Grey and Green, Nocturne*, etc. – rather than titles which told a story. Also, prepared either to slap the public's face or flick the public with insults, he told them that 'the vast majority of English folk cannot and will not consider a picture as a picture, apart from any story it may be supposed to tell'; he went on, 'My picture of *A Harmony in Grey and Gold* is an illustration of my meaning – a snow scene with a single black figure and a lighted tavern. I care nothing for the past, present or future of the black figure, placed there because the black was wanted at that spot. All that I know is that my combination of grey and gold is the basis of the picture. Art should be independent of all clap-trap – should stand alone and appeal to the artistic sense of eye or ear, without confounding this with emotions entirely foreign to it, as devotion, pity, love, patriotism, and the like. All these have no kind of concern with it; and that is why I insist on calling my works "arrangements" and "harmonies".' No painter ever expresses the whole of art; but the case Whistler argued so wittily and with such insolence was a truth for Whistler's time, necessary as a recall to first principles.

In 1878 came the famous case of Whistler versus Ruskin. Whistler exhibited his picture of *Old Battersea Bridge*. Inspired by the simple pattern of Japanese prints, he painted his scene with a wash of liquid colour, the shape of the bridge silhouetted against sky and water, and a few flecks of the brush here and there to suggest lights, or dark figures. Ruskin (q.v.) thereupon wrote of the 'ill-educated conceit of the artist', which 'nearly approached the aspect of wilful imposture'. He had seen and heard 'much of cockney impudence before now; but never expected to hear a coxcomb ask two hundred guineas for flinging a pot of paint in the public's face'. Whistler sued for libel. In the trial the Attorney-General asked him how long it had taken him to paint the picture. Whistler replied, a few days. 'Then you ask two hundred guineas for the work of a few days?' 'No, I ask it for the knowledge of a life-time.' Whistler's damages of one farthing seemed a moral victory for Ruskin, but the trial exploded some of the pretentiousness of the time. The panjandrums of accepted art, from the over-cultivated Burne-Jones to the under-cultivated Frith, the painter of *Derby Day* who had stated in his autobiography that it was a toss-up whether he became a painter or an auctioneer, were ranged against Whistler in the witness-box; and their mixed ideals emerged shaky and battered.

Whistler's wit, vivacity, rudeness, sharpness, his unconventional appearance and behaviour, drew notice to him; but they now give a false *fin-de-siècle* notion of his painting. Decorativeness and a twilit dreaminess are not half of his achievement; influenced by Velasquez and Degas (qq.v.), he was toughly and wirily able to present things as they appear, in paint and etching as well. Whistler is better understood by those who have studied him in the Freer Gallery at Washington, D.C., where paintings in sharp clean colour are honestly delicious in themselves and contain seeds of much that was to come in modern painting.

ILLUSTRATION: Plate 16.

Bats, worms, wild geese

WHITE, Gilbert, (1720–1793), English naturalist and writer.

The Natural History and Antiquities of Selborne, in the County of Southampton, Gilbert White's one great book, appeared in 1789, has gone ever since into edition after edition, and has made the village and the parish of Selborne a living place for thousands who have never been there. Few men of genius are nourished enough by their environment: White, a cleric and Fellow of Oriel College, Oxford, and a contemporary of Linnaeus (q.v.) thrived at Selborne like the hobo of the Big Rock Candy Mountains paddling on his lake of stew. He had a disposition lazy enough to make him the greatest of all amateur naturalists.

In his late forties he began to exchange letters with Thomas Pennant, the zoologist, and the lawyer, amateur naturalist and antiquary, Daines Barrington; and began to keep a journal of his observations of natural history in a series of entry books designed by Barrington. The correspondence soon became the outward expression of White's monomania, White's endless curiosity about the birds, the mammals, the reptiles, insects and plants of Selborne. In 1771, or thereabouts, when he was fifty, the idea of publication occurred to him, but he was a modest procrastinating man. When he was sixty-eight, *The Natural History of Selborne* at last appeared.

White was the great learner; a natural scientist eternally dissatisfied with the evidence of his senses, an inveterate questioner, a devoted chronicler, an accurate reporter, a tolerant and humorous commentator. He made mistakes, but fewer than seems possible; he made the discoveries (without fieldglasses) that cut nearly the last folded pages of the list of birds and mammals native to Great Britain. White made the true distinction between the three British leaf-warblers and he was the first to identify in Britain the noctule bat and the harvest-mouse. He was the first critical writer to state the principle of protective coloration among animals. He knew that many birds hold territories; and that earthworms are 'the greatest promoters of vegetation'. He knew about those wonders of avian adaptation, the nightjars and swifts, and swallows and martins, and wrote of them in a benign mixture of scientific respect and ordinary affection. 'My remarks', he once went so far as to say, 'are the result of many years' observation; and are, I trust, true on the whole.' But he went on, 'though I do not pretend to say that they are perfectly void of mistake, or that a more nice observer might not make many additions, since subjects of this kind are inexhaustible'.

The *Natural History* shows White most emphatically, perhaps, as an ornithologist, though his interest in mammals was profound, and his observations on the habits of the field-cricket do not appear to have been extended, or even confirmed, until 1945. The book moves in an apparently desultory but compelling way from (for instance) the quail, the corncrake and black game to migration – and often back to migration, the problem that perhaps puzzled White most – from his beloved leaf-warblers to weasels, from the drumming of snipe to the mating of frogs.

Many books have been written of such creatures. No one has written of them with such style and spirit. White's honest accuracy, and his clarity and felicity of expression, combined in a work of art of which there have been a hundred and fifty editions since 1789. White's *Selborne* became the inspiration of a movement – to take nature to pieces, to learn nature's nature, to put the pieces together again – which swept England and now sweeps the world. It has had that effect because White with his clear eighteenth-century mind had no wish to be mysterious. His only bias was towards investigation of the nature of the external world. His language is terse and simple:

'When brown owls hoot their throats swell as big as an hen's egg.'

'A good monography of worms would afford much entertainment and information at the same time, and would open a large and new field in natural history. Worms work most in the spring; but by no means lie torpid in the dead months; are out every mild night in the winter, as any person may be convinced that will take the pains to examine his grass-plot with a candle; are hermaphrodites, and much addicted to venery, and consequently very prolific.'

'Aquatic and gregarious birds, especially the nocturnal that shift their quarters in the dark, are very noisy and loquacious; as cranes, wild-geese, wild-ducks, and the like; their perpetual clamour prevents them from dispersing and losing their companions.'

With such records of observations White did not want to *charm* anybody (as people now say that he does); he did not even want especially to influence anybody, or do more than put the natural history of his lovely and beloved parish into a book. Books such as *Walden* by Thoreau (q.v.) descend from *The Natural History of Selborne*.

'Night, sleep, death and the stars'

WHITMAN, Walt, (1819–1892), the major poet of America's age of expansion in the nineteenth century, 'non-literary and non-decorous', as he described himself, tackling life, love and death with the energy, the assurance and the character of an archaic seer making revelations to the modern world.

Born on Long Island, where his family had lived since the seventeenth century, Whitman was the son of a carpenter and farmer. West Hills was soon exchanged for Brooklyn, so Whitman grew up to feel and enjoy the pulse of a developing democratic urbanism, backed by all the vast extension of America. He knew the individual and the crowd, the work, the muscle, the sweat, the ferries and the great star-sparkling hood of the sky overhead. His own observation was never dulled and his strength was never cramped by a long conventional schooling, though it was by teaching he lived for a while and then by work (but first as a compositor) for newspapers and magazines. In his reading Whitman cosmologically swallowed Aeschylus, for example, Homer, Dante, Shakespeare, the Bible; also the romantic prose poems of Ossian (written in fact by James Macpherson, 1736–1796), which had once thrilled Europe, but were then outmoded. Indeed, Whitman mixed the grandeur of a psalmist in himself with some quantity of Ossianic vapouring.

In 1855 appeared the first product of the huge ferment within this man, the first slender edition of *Leaves of Grass*, in which the world was given a new poetry in some ways akin to Courbet's painting, Rodin's sculpture or Wagner's music. Included was the famous – in contemporary opinion the infamous – *Song of Myself*, outraging propriety in such lines as

I believe in the flesh and the appetites,
Seeing, hearing, feeling, are miracles, and each part and tag of me is a miracle.
Divine am I inside and out, and I make holy whatever I touch or am touch'd from,
The scent of these arm-pits aroma finer than prayer,
This head more than churches, bibles and all the creeds ...

When poetic language, English or American, had a false nobility, Whitman's at its best was genuinely noble. The poems have a compulsive rhythm, even if they lack a close, expected shape. It was this absence of shape, or this apparent freedom, which has always caused a distrust of Whitman in the name of art; but only among those who cabin poetry too much and subscribe to a rule that poetry must not vary with the poet. The poems rise often to a splendour, to memorable wholes (read *Passage to India*) and memorable lines which never stale – *Out of the cradle endlessly* rocking, or *A march in the ranks hard-prest and the road unknown*, or the hushed lines which so greatly open the poem to Abraham Lincoln:

> When lilacs last in the dooryard bloom'd
> And the great star early droop'd in the western sky in the night,
> I mourn'd, and yet shall mourn with ever-returning spring.

His prose also rises nobly and tenderly in *Specimen Days*, for example, in terrifying scenes out of the American Civil War.

As Courbet (q.v.) was found outrageous in painting, so Whitman repelled and attracted the English and Americans of his day. His inclusiveness, his celebration of the common healthy worker, his indifference to sexual conventions, his celebration of the flesh – all seemed as debatable as the 'formless' form and the manner of his poems. Yet translation into many languages speaks for Whitman's universality, as he pondered 'night, sleep, death and the stars'. So, too, does admiration of him by poets as various as the Jesuit poet Hopkins in England (a guarded admiration and sympathy since Hopkins felt Whitman to be a rogue), Laforgue in France, or García Lorca in Spain.

ILLUSTRATION: Page 367.

One man, one mountain

WHYMPER, Edward, (1840–1911), most famous of all English mountaineers, whose ascent of the Matterhorn, the last great unclimbed summit of the Alps, ended the Golden Age of mountaineering in 1865. 'He was resolved to do the Matterhorn, and equally resolved, when that was done, to give up mountaineering because there were no more *new* great mountains to be conquered', said a fellow climber.

Whymper saw mountains as an affront to man's conquest of nature. Competition with nature rather than the Alpine idealism of his contemporaries drove him upwards, and his contacts with other mountaineers were seldom prolonged or cordial. He was by training a wood-engraver. A commission to draw a number of sketches brought him first to the Alps, when he was twenty. He climbed with determination for the next five years and then abandoned serious

mountaineering – by which time he was a legend. Many new peaks fell to Whymper, but it was the lean white pinnacle of the Matterhorn which fascinated him. Only after six unsuccessful attempts did he stand at last on its apex with three friends and three guides, in 1865, proving that Man, in the shape of Edward Whymper, had conquered. On the descent, four of the party fell 4,000 feet to their death. Echoes of the disaster girdled the world, and delayed the development of mountaineering for a decade. For Whymper there was 'never glad confident morning again'; and his initial reluctance to explain the details of the accident caused much concern. There was argument over the composition of the party and its rivalry with a party of Italians who failed to reach the top. 'Is it life? Is it duty? Is it common sense?' the London *Times* asked, in a leading article, of all mountaineering.

Whymper was not the most experienced amateur of his day, but his drama of one man against one mountain swamped the facts. To thousands, Whymper *was* mountaineering from 1865 to the end of his life. His famous *Scrambles amongst the Alps* and *Travels Amongst the Great Andes of the Equator* underlined the illusion. The books, dramatically illustrated by himself, ran through edition after edition, and in their pages one hears, even now, the thunder of the falling rocks. To the end Whymper was tough. 'When I come, I shall come in the old style', he wrote before his last visit to Switzerland at the age of seventy. He would take his chance of finding a room: 'If none can be had, I shall camp out.' Argumentative and lonely, his abnormalities – which included a delight in walking naked in crowded hotels – made him always an unclubbable man.

ILLUSTRATION: Page 369.

'Shocking specimen of stupidity and rascality'

WIERTZ, Antoine, (1806–1865), Belgian painter, and a type specimen of the false artists who exist in every age, deluding their world as well as themselves. 'Pride,' Wiertz inscribed over his painting-room, 'the virtue which inspires masterpieces and wounds other men's self-esteem. Modesty, the mask which flatters the self-esteem of other men in order to attract praise.' But Wiertz mistook pride for talent.

His father fought in the ranks for Napoleon, and filled Wiertz with notions of glory; and he determined to out-master the masters of art. In the Museum at Antwerp one day the young Wiertz pretended not to see the Prince of Orange. His teacher reproving him, Wiertz replied, 'Why should I take my hat off to that fellow, when' – he pointed to pictures by Rubens – 'I've never taken it off to this one?' Above all others it was Rubens (q.v.) he wished to surpass. In 1842 he finished a *Revolt of Hell against Heaven*, an enormous painting, thirty-four feet high, and then offered it to Antwerp Cathedral, on one condition – that it should hang next to the triptych of the *Descent from the Cross* by Rubens. The Cathedral declined. Wiertz at this period had declared his ambition in the saying, 'Portraits for soup, pictures for glory.' His pictures were so large it was hard to find a big enough studio. The *Revolt of Hell* had been painted in an empty church. In Brussels he hired an empty factory to paint a *Triumph of Christ*, which was accepted by the Brussels Salon and was then too big for the gallery.

These pictures for glory, he announced – come failure, come destitution – were not for sale; though the Russian government offered 100,000 francs, and the Prince of Prussia 300,000 francs, for the *Triumph of Christ*. However, Wiertz had the idea that his country – a young country which had been free of the Dutch only for a few years – might require an art hero and might finance him; and he persuaded the Belgian government to build him a vast studio, with living quarters. In return the State was to have his pictures when he died. The canvases still crowd the studio (now the Musée Wiertz, in a leafy side-street of Brussels), a mixture of the pseudo-heroic, the pseudo-moral, the sententious, the sentimental, the horrific, morbid and lascivious – *The Beacon of Golgotha, The Last Cannon* – peace scrapping the last cannon over the dead of all the battles of history – *The Premature Burial, The Thoughts and Visions of a Severed Head, Suicide, Hunger, Madness, Crime* – in which the mad mother stews her child's leg over a fire made of the furniture.

Baudelaire (q.v.), fine art critic as well as poet, found Wiertz the right painter for *les Belges* of that day, whom he loathed for blowing themselves up with beer, barking at the moon, vomiting like Englishmen, jeering at Heaven and believing in progress. 'Wiertz,' he jotted down, 'the great painter around here. Painting in the manner of the Encyclopaedists, philosophic and humanitarian pretensions. Shocking specimen of stupidity and rascality.' A self-portrait of 1860 shows Wiertz, cloaked and bearded, gazing at a ladder which climbs to the upper reaches of a canvas.

ILLUSTRATION: Page 364.

'I am dying beyond my means'

WILDE, Oscar Fingall O'Flahertie Wills, (1854–1900), Irish dramatist, wit and poet.

'Nothing is so dangerous as being too modern; one is apt to grow old-fashioned quite suddenly', Wilde wrote in *An Ideal Husband*, his comedy which disproved its own epigram by becoming a successful film more than half a century after it was written. He also declared in *The Picture of Dorian Gray* the principle which he lived by, and which destroyed him: 'There is only one thing in the world worse than being talked about, and that is not being talked about.'

Wilde was born in Dublin, the son of a bluestocking poetess and of a distinguished ear-surgeon, whose life was overshadowed, like his son's, by a trial for a sexual offence. As a young man he conquered London by a combination of arrogance and wit, and with a glitter which was often pure gold. There, too, he cut his name down to Oscar Wilde: 'A name which is destined to be in everybody's mouth must not be too long. It comes so expensively in the advertisements.'

At first he contrived to be talked about by carrying aestheticism to an 'O Altitudo!'. He dressed in fantastically affected clothes and stepped into fame when Gilbert satirized him as Bunthorne in his comic opera *Patience*. However, his aestheticism, and the notion of Wilde-Bunthorne simpering with a lily through Piccadilly were partially belied by the way in which he outdrank Rocky Mountain miners and cowboys during a tour in the United States. The cowboys had to admit that Wilde could drink any of them under the table and then carry them home two at a time.

He continued to be talked about as a highly succesful dramatist. The London stage of the nineties saw, one after the other, *Lady Windermere's Fan, A Woman of No Importance, An Ideal Husband* and *The Importance of Being Earnest*, in which he combined style and stylishness as they had never been combined since the seventeenth century. His plays brought him sudden wealth, and he indulged what he called 'that inordinate passion for pleasure, which is the secret of remaining young'.

Not all his epigrams had a core of truth; but when, in *A Woman of No Importance*, Lord Illingworth said, 'The Book of Life began with a woman and a man in a garden', and Mrs Allomby replied, 'It ends with Revelations', Wilde, *mutatis mutandis*, was being prophetic, since his own Paradise was to end in revelations of the blackest kind. An equivocal and extravagant friendship with Lord Alfred Douglas led to an action in 1895 with his father, the Marquess of Queensberry; in this Wilde was compelled by the merciless cross-questioning of Sir Edward Carson, whose hard facts he thought he could dissolve with bright epigrams, to admit to quite unequivocal relations with a number of shabby young men. This famous trial was a turning-point in English cultural history; it was the end of the Nineties, and of the cult, which had been invaluable to a certain degree, of Art for Art's sake. Wilde disappeared to prison, and his plays went out of production. In *The Ballad of Reading Gaol*, a great poem, and *De Profundis*, he expressed both his contrition and his anger with Lord Alfred Douglas; when released, he retired to France, where his last days made it clear that both his contrition and his anger had been nominal.

'I am dying', he said at the end, 'beyond my means.' In his life and his writings he had already taken paradox and hyperbole to the unforgettable limit, and his modernity seems likely to become, not old-fashioned, but immortal.

ILLUSTRATION: Page 368.

'So very stern was he and hot'

WILLIAM THE CONQUEROR, (1027–1087), King of England, 'So very stern was he and hot', wrote a near contemporary chronicler, 'that no man durst do anything against his will.' William was the bastard son of Robert 'the Devil', Duke of Normandy, and of a tanner's daughter, named Arlette. In later life, when he was besieging Alençon and the citizens hung out raw hides on their walls to taunt his base birth, he was so infuriated that as soon as the town fell, he had its leading officials flayed alive.

He succeeded to his father's duchy when he was still a boy, and he was confronted with all the baronial turbulence that followed in medieval times when the ruler was under age. By his mid-twenties, he had tamed his Norman barons, and had conquered the province of Maine. Now came England's turn. William was cousin to the childless Edward the Confessor, who had promised to make him his heir. Already Norman clerics and knights were infiltrating into England; and from King Edward's most powerful nobleman, Harold Godwinson, who fell into his hands by shipwreck, William had exacted an oath of allegiance. When King Edward died, and Harold was elected King by the Witangemot, William, with the blessing of the Pope, invaded England to claim his inheritance. The tragedy of Hastings followed in September 1066; and William was crowned King. A few thousand Norman knights and men-at-arms had conquered a country containing about a million and a half inhabitants.

Lands were now shared out among the Conqueror's companions, and the Norman methods of government introduced, though at first with some circumspection. 'I will', declared William to the citizens of London, 'that ye be worthy of all the laws that ye were worthy of in King Edward's day.' But the Anglo-Saxon resistance here and there in the shires, and a serious rising in the North, sharpened William's purpose. Within twenty years of his landing, a large part of the refractory England north of the Trent had been laid waste, and throughout the kingdom there remained only two major land-holders of Anglo-Saxon stock, and one English bishop. All over the rest of the country, the feudal rule of Norman knights, squires and clerics had been ruthlessly imposed upon the surviving English institutions. To this feudal structure there were three chief aspects: it was a system of land-holding, a method of securing service to the King in peace and in war, and it also provided the basis for taxation – and William was 'a merciless taxer'. William's great Domesday Book of 1085 represented a codification of the system, with these three requirements in mind. It was a formidable statistical achievement: 'So narrowly did he cause his survey to be made that there was not one single hide nor rood of land nor – it is shameful to tell, but he thought it no shame to do – was there an ox, cow or swine that was not set down in it.'

In person, according to William of Malmesbury, William 'was of moderate height, immense corpulence, going rather bald in front; of such great strength of arm that no one could bend the bow that he drew when his horse was at full gallop'. Chief among his diversions was stag-hunting – 'he loved the tall stags like a father', wrote one chronicler; and when he received protests against the extensive encroachments of his hunting forests, 'he was so sturdy that he recked nought of them'. His overbearing power of will, his furious temper and his remarkable capacity for government he passed in large measure to his two sons who in turn succeeded him, William Rufus and Henry I. The results have been immense. On the Norman state the father and sons established, all of English and much of world history have been built: and this Norman settlement decided the future of the English language and of that English culture which is so un-German among a people so much of German stock.

'Poetry is emotion recollected in tranquillity'

WORDSWORTH, William, (1770–1850). English poet who looked for the essence of human values in communion with nature.

A bronze-coloured face, thick ugly ears, an enormous nose, sensual lips, a 'convulsive inclination to laughter' about his mouth, strange eyes that could assume 'an appearance the most solemn and spiritual that it is possible for the human eye to wear', full of a light 'radiating from some far spiritual world' – such was the look of this poet of the English Lake District, who wrote of communion with nature as the way to love, and the way to

> the great thought
> By which we live, Infinity and God.

Wordsworth lived among the mountains and the lakes as a schoolboy, and then returned to them as a mature poet, eventually dying at Grasmere in a melancholic state near to madness – so justifying his own statement that

> We poets in our youth begin in gladness
> But thereof comes in the end despondency and madness.

His friend Coleridge saw greatness in Wordsworth as a man because for so long he fought this inclination to melancholy, stiffness and moodiness, and made himself a happy man against his own nature.

Wordsworth was a poet of opposites and contra-

dictions. Reserved, severe, lofty, gaunt, yet smiling; slow, solemn, majestic in his conversation. Nevertheless passion broke his reserve when he was a young man, in his love affair with the French girl, Annette Vallon, by whom he had a child. He attempted a reform of English poetic language by basing his poems upon common speech, or employing, as he wrote, 'a selection of language really used by men'. All good poetry he described (and it certainly applies to his own) as 'the spontaneous overflow of powerful feelings', taking its origin 'from emotion recollected in tranquillity'. A poet is always 'a man speaking to men' – excellently true of Wordsworth, in such a poem as the sonnet composed on Westminster Bridge, in London, on 3 September 1802:

> Earth has not anything to show more fair:
> Dull would he be of soul who could pass by
> A sight so touching in its majesty:
> This City now doth like a garment wear
> The beauty of the morning; silent, bare,
> Ships, towers, domes, theatres, and temples lie
> Open unto the fields, and to the sky;
> All bright and glittering in the smokeless air.
> Never did sun more beautifully steep
> In his first splendour, valley, rock, or hill;
> Ne'er saw I, never felt, a calm so deep!
> The river glideth at his own sweet will:
> Dear God! the very houses seem asleep;
> And all that mighty heart is lying still.

Gerard Manley Hopkins considered Wordsworth one of those very few men who give a shock to human nature and set it trembling. The shock, he thought, was received from Wordsworth's Ode, *Intimations of Immortality from Recollections of Early Childhood*. Much of Wordsworth's most splendid and durable verse will be found in the long autobiographical poem, *The Prelude, or Growth of a Poet's Mind* (1799–1805).

ILLUSTRATION: Page 370.

'Organic architecture'

WRIGHT, Frank Lloyd, (b. 1869), Welsh-born American architect who has built in every state in the Union. If Le Corbusier (q.v.) is the *enfant terrible* of the Modern Movement, Lloyd Wright is its prophet. He is the pioneer of 'organic architecture', whose mottoes are: 'Truth against the World', and 'The Hypocrite hates the Radical'.

The Modern Movement has two facets: the revolt against the machine – William Morris's 'Art will die out if the system lasts' – and the exploitation of the machine, summed up in Lloyd Wright's comment upon Chicago seen at night, 'If this power must be uprooted that civilization may live, then civilization is doomed.' Wright is an eccentric, but not a crank. A crank dabbles in small departures from the norm; Lloyd Wright has dabbled in big ones. He recognized, a quarter of a century before the foundation of the English MARS Group, which has the same view, that the artist must enter into partnership with science and industry. Nevertheless, loathing the eighteenth century, he is in the great line of Romantics, and he looks to Carlyle's *Past and Present* for its emphasis upon the well-ordered life; to Walt Whitman and Ruskin for adoration of Nature; to Shelley, Samuel Butler and Kropotkin for their revolt in the cause of freedom; to Morris and Lethaby for aesthetic solutions and honest craftsmanship. His dominant passion is love of nature; his autobiography is full of the poetry and colour of desert and forest.

The result of Lloyd Wright's philosophy has been (*a*) the 'Usonian' (American) house, organic with nature, *i.e.* moulded to the site and exploiting beauty of materials, and (*b*) his 'modern' buildings such as the Oak Park Unity Temple, near Chicago, for which the drawings were made in 1906 and which was the first reinforced concrete monolith, and the Larkin Soap Factory at Buffalo (1903), which was the first sealed and air-conditioned building.

Real fame came with the Imperial Hotel, Tokyo (1916) – a lavish reinforced concrete group with Aztec-like decorations – and the congratulatory telegram from the Emperor upon the fact that these buildings survived the great earthquake in 1923. The culmination of his 'organic architecture' was the house named Falling Waters (1936), at Bear Run, Pennsylvania, a sublime adaptation of concrete terraces and openly planned rooms at several levels to a rock and forest site. The culmination of his scientific techniques was the Johnson Wax Factory at Racine, Wisconsin, with its mushroom-like concrete columns and its walls of glass tube.

Lloyd Wright's own days are now divided, according to season, between his home at Spring Green, Wisconsin – a wide-spreading stone and timber house in a landscape like that of the Cotswolds in England – and the famous house near Phoenix in the Arizona desert, built of red teak and rock, with canvas roofs to give translucent light. In both homes he runs the Taliesin training scheme for his apprentices. The life is poetic, well-ordered and highly patriarchal.

Honours came to him late, after a life of achievement, quarrels, domestic drama and even melodrama, including two disastrous fires, one of them arson, which destroyed two homes. In 1941 he received the medal of the Royal Institute of British Architects, in 1948 the gold medal of the American Institute of Architects. Colleagues, there is no doubt, had been jealous and disliked his arrogance – even more than the fact that he had good reason and a good basis for arrogance. In 1951 an exhibition of Lloyd Wright's work filled a whole floor of the Strozzi Palace in Florence, and the whole of the École des Beaux Arts in Paris. Failure to raise funds prevented its display in England.

ILLUSTRATION: Page 371.

Powered, sustained and controlled flight

WRIGHT, Wilbur, (1867–1912), and Orville, (1871–1948), American aviation pioneers; the first men to achieve powered, sustained and controlled flight in an aeroplane, and so bring about the present age of practical flying.

Sons of a bishop in Dayton, Ohio, they first showed their enterprise by producing a small but successful newspaper; then turned to selling, repairing and finally manufacturing bicycles – the occupation which alone gave them a living and enabled them to spend their spare time on flying experiments. They were inspired by the German gliding pioneer Otto Lilienthal (killed in 1896) and they studied – from 1900 onwards – every available work on aeronautics. In 1900 they had built and flown their first glider. They adopted the biplane glider type of another American pioneer, Octave Chanute, but during the years 1900, 1901 and 1902 completely transformed it, both aerodynamically and from the standpoint of control.

After intensive research and experiment, including more than a thousand glides on the three gliders they built, they designed and constructed their first powered aeroplane (as well as the engine) in 1903; which they named the *Flyer*. At Kitty Hawk, on the coast of North Carolina, the first successful flight was made on 17 December 1903, with Orville as pilot.

The essential elements were lift, propulsion and, above all, the system of control by the combined 'warping' (twisting) of the wing-tips and turning of the rudder to produce banked turns, with a forward elevator for climbing and diving. *Powered, sustained* and *controlled* – these are the three words to keep in mind in estimating the Wrights' achievement: singly, or paired, they are words which had spelt achievement before; but the Wrights first combined all three to produce practical powered flying.

Through a combination of misunderstanding, stupidity and secretiveness (only secretiveness applying to the Wrights), the world did not know of their triumph until late in 1906; they did not fly in public until the summer of 1908. By 1908, although they had not been in the air once in 1906 and 1907, they had made great strides in secret and had evolved an eminently practical two-seater aeroplane from the primitive biplane of 1903. Flight endurance had advanced from twelve seconds in 1903 to thirty-eight minutes in 1905. Orville's public flights at Fort Myer, U.S.A., in 1908, and Wilbur's near Le Mans in France during the same year, revolutionized aviation, which had lately been making an independent but wavering start chiefly in France, based on second-hand acquaintance with the Wright gliders and the application of Hargrave's box-kite. If the Wright machines had been flown publicly in 1905, the evolution of the aeroplane would have quickened. As it happened, the pooling of the basic ideas, American and European, did not become general until 1909, when the Wrights were almost as much influenced by their rivals as their rivals had been by them.

Wilbur Wright died in 1912, and Orville soon ceased to be active in flying. The brothers formed a modest and devoted team – both were ingenious, pertinacious and methodical – and they attacked the problem of practical flight with a quiet confidence in their ultimate success.

ILLUSTRATION: Page 372.

Apostle of the Indies

XAVIER, St Francis, (1506–1552), Francisco de Yasu y Xavier, Spanish Jesuit, founder of the Christian mission to the Japanese, is held to have been the greatest missionary since the Apostles; he was also one of the greatest of early travellers, voyaging to India, China and Japan.

Of a noble Navarre family in decline, he went to the university of Paris: and there, while full of hopes of fame and honour to be had from learning, he fell in with Ignatius Loyola. Loyola's ideal, an apostolic life in poverty and chastity, at last won Xavier over. It was no easy task to find his vocation – 'the hardest clay I have ever moulded', said Loyola – but once assured, Xavier humbled his pride, and threw himself into his new world.

Each religious order has its distinguishing characteristics; the Jesuits, more than any other, represent evangelism at its most powerful, industrious and planned. It is no distance from the zealot to the fanatic: but Xavier never took the step to bigotry. All his short life he remained the true holy man, faithful and tolerant. He worked in the Portuguese colonial empire of the East: there, first in Southern India, then in the Islands of the East Indies, he led the lapsed back to the Church, and converted unbelievers to the faith.

The sight of a man who can give up everything for a belief is both elevating and saddening: Xavier, passing close by his mother's house on the way to take ship for the East, knowing that he was not likely to see her or his friends again, would not turn aside from his work to see them. He would visit them in Heaven, he said.

In the East, Xavier lived only on rice and water, slept only three hours a night. He was the first systematic missionary, and set the pattern for all that followed: he would learn the languages of the countries he visited, use native helpers and translate devotional works into native tongues.

Tales of the new-found Japanese suggested that among them, cultured, populous, he might lay the foundation of the Church in the East. He voyaged there, and was well received; but the good work he did was all in vain, as it turned out. In 1552 he started for China, then barred to the world. Alone, he managed to reach Sancian, an island near the Chinese mainland: but no one would take him over. A fever laid him low, and shortly after he died. His body was eventually carried to Goa, the capital of the Portuguese empire in the East, and displayed in miracle-working splendour. St Francis Xavier's last words were, 'In thee, O Lord, I have hoped: I shall not be confounded for ever.'

A Chinese Pompadour

YANG KUEI-FEI, (719–756), was consort or Imperial Concubine of the T'ang emperor Hsüan-tsung. Ever since, she has been celebrated in legend and literature and on the stage as one of the four loveliest women of China.

Kuei-fei's birth was heralded by a meteor which slowly lit up her parents' bed and then hit the ground with a noise like thunder, clearly foretelling for the child a notable career. Perfection of figure, skin, and features, and teeth like jasmine buds (though, as H.A.Giles oddly put it in his *Chinese Biographical Dictionary*, she was 'specially noted as being the only fat lady among China's historical beauties') – to all such corporeal delights this Chinese Pompadour added intelligence, inexpressible charm and gaiety.

First she was the favourite of the Emperor's eighteenth son. Then she was brought to the Emperor's notice and shared his life for more than twenty years until the peace of the T'ang empire was broken by the revolt of An Lu-shan, who had been her lover behind the Emperor's back. The Emperor's rapturous fulfilment in this most artful as well as most exquisite of women distracted him from the business of state, and the extravagance for which she was responsible was to blame partly for the civil war which ravaged China. After the Emperor was forced to abandon the capital, his troops mutinied and killed Kuei-fei's sisters who had been maintained in a scarcely virtuous splendour, and her brother Yang Kuo-chung, the Prime Minister. They also demanded the life of Kuei-fei, to which the Emperor had to agree. Accounts say that his Chief Eunuch strangled her, also that she hanged herself from an old pear tree with a silken cord, climbing first on a round oak stool. Kuei-fei's beauty was celebrated in her own time by the great Li Po (q.v.), herself holding the stone ink-slab while he composed. In his famous poem *The Everlasting Wrong*, the third of the great T'ang poets, Po Chu-i, long afterwards described her life with the Emperor:

> In a warm bed netted with hibiscus
> she passed the spring nights –

– her death:

> Knitting her moth eye-brows, death caught her among the horses,
> Her hairpins scattered over the earth, no one picking them up –
> Kingfisher feathers, gold birds, combs of jade.
> The Emperor hid his face, unable to save her ...
> Who will share with him the kingfisher quilts of old?

– and finally her ghostly reappearance.

Custom and ceremony

YEATS, William Butler, (1865–1939), Anglo-Irish poet:

> We were the last romantics – chose for theme
> Traditional sanctity and loveliness;
> Whatever's written in what poets name
> The books of the people; whatever most can bless
> The mind of man or elevate a rhyme;
> But all is changed, that high horse riderless,
> Though mounted in that saddle Homer rode
> Where the swan drifts upon a darkening flood.

Many converging lines met in this 'last romantic', son of a portrait-painter who was a Protestant and a liberal humanitarian. When he was eight or nine, his family moved from Ireland to London, where 'I told myself that whatever I most cared for had been taken away'. Ireland moulded Yeats partly by exile from Ireland, though he spent holidays in Sligo, and came back to live in Dublin when he was sixteen. As an art student he first met theosophy and its practitioners in Dublin, and back in London he knew Madame Blavatsky, joined an occult group, the Society of the Golden Dawn, and learnt of symbols and their evocative power. Poets he knew included Henley, William Morris, Lionel Johnson and Oscar Wilde; he delighted in William Blake, interpreting the symbolism of his *Prophetic Books*. Images of romantic infinity and suggestiveness haunted him in other men's poetry. Favourite lines from Blake were

> ... Etinthus, queen of waters, how thou shinest in the sky!
> My daughter, how do I rejoice! for thy children flock around
> Like the gay fishes on the wave, when the cold moon drinks the dew.

- and from Burns

> The wan moon is setting ayont the white wave
> And time is setting with me, oh!

Another source of symbolic thought in Yeats was Irish folk-lore, the tales which had seeped through time into Ireland, and were transmitted orally, and the elaborate fairy faith. Characteristically, Yeats wished to test the reality of the fairy faith, and went in search of the Queen of the Fairies on 'a far western sandy shore. We talked of the Dinny Math or faery people, and came in the midst of our talk to a notable haunt of theirs, a shallow cave amid black rocks, with its reflection under it in wet sea sand.' He then asked his companion to call out to the Queen, and he saw in a trance-like state a tall, beautiful woman with four trains of attendants. Doubly characteristic was the question Yeats asked of her – 'whether she and her people were not dramatizations of our moods?', a question that the Queen of the Dinny Math did not understand. It was one Yeats returned to later on in his prose book *A Vision* (1926), when he drew from the spirits who dictated to him a confession that they came to give him images for poetry. Just as Yeats saw the reflection of the cave on the wet sand when he went in search of the Fairy Queen, so his early poetry is not so vapid and dreamy as one may think. Dreams are not dreamy, and these poems could be as sharp as the strange *Cap and Bells* (actually 'given' to him in a dream), which begins:

> The jester walked in the garden:
> The garden had fallen still;
> He bade his soul rise upward
> And stand on her window-sill.
>
> It rose in a straight blue garment,
> When owls began to call:
> It had grown wise-tongued by thinking
> Of a quiet and light foot fall;
>
> But the young queen would not listen;
> She rose in her pale night-gown;
> She drew in the heavy casement
> And pushed the latches down.
>
> He bade his heart go out to her,
> When the owls called out no more;
> In a red and quivering garment
> It sang to her through the door ...

Ireland, and the beauty of Maud Gonne, who would never marry him and to whom he wrote love poems for many years, absorbed him and he began to link his poet's vocation to the destiny of Young Ireland. He reflected that races had had 'their first unity from a mythology, that marries them to rock and hill'. Might not Irish mythological stories be made once more to work upon the Irish, and might their political passion not be deepened so that 'all, artist and poet, craftsman and day-labourer, would accept a common design?' He believed in 'a nation-wide multiform reverie, every mind passing through a stream of suggestion, and all streams acting and reacting upon one another', and hoped for an Irish unity of culture, a 'literature which, though made by many minds, would seem the work of a single mind, and turn our places of beauty and legendary association into holy symbols'. Later on he abandoned such hopes, and realized that a modern nation cannot return to this unity. A patriot, but not a democrat, Yeats found little satisfaction in the tendencies of our world. He wrote in *The Second Coming*:

> Things fall apart; the centre cannot hold;
> Mere anarchy is loosed upon the world,
> The blood-dimmed tide is loosed, and everywhere
> The ceremony of innocence is drowned;
> The best lack all conviction, while the worst
> Are full of passionate intensity –

he ended the poem by asking what new birth our age was producing

> And what rough beast, its turn come round at last,
> Slouches towards Bethlehem to be born?

With *Responsibilities* (1914) and *The Wild Swans at Coole* (1917) Yeats began to alter, clarify and crystallize his way of writing, becoming unmistakably the major poet. He replaced the symbolic personae of Irish myth, Diarmuid and Grania, etc., and the grey cromlech, with more concrete figures from the world of the actual – yet for abstract ends.

> 'Time to put off the world and go somewhere
> And find my health again in the sea air'
> *Beggar to beggar cried, being frenzy-struck,*
> 'And make my soul before my pate is bare.'

Love, politics, religion, philosophy – he expressed abstraction of thought in the realism of image, losing nothing of his lyricism as the thought became more abstract, nothing of his mastery of refrain, and his ability to be splendid in the barest of words. Yeats was above all creed, religious or political. He saw human history against the grand scale of the eternal, which gave life to his words.

ILLUSTRATION: Page 373.

Leader of the Mormons

YOUNG, Brigham, (1801–1877), second President of the Church of Jesus Christ of Latter Day Saints (called Mormons); and Founder of the State of Utah. 'What was your object in coming here?' asked the Mormon leader John Taylor, when Utah was threatened in 1857 with invasion by United States troops, 'Was it to rebel against the general government?' Brigham Young replied that it was 'To get away from Christians', – from Christian charity.

Brigham Young was not the founder of the Mormon church, but its St Paul, or, to use an even closer comparison, its Stalin. He was four years older than Joseph Smith, who in 1830 published *The Book of Mormon* from which the movement had its nickname. Joseph Smith claimed to have translated this work from hieroglyphics on golden plates which he had dug up, and which give in hermetic form the ancient history of North America, from the time when Lehi, Sarrah, and their four sons left Jerusalem in 600 B.C. and wandered into the wilderness of Arabia. Smith and Young both came from the same state, Vermont, both had the same background of the restless frontier-drifters, and both experienced the religious revivals which swept around like forest-fires. Young was baptized into the new faith in 1832.

The Mormon church grew rapidly, and soon Brigham Young was their most successful missionary. By 1839 he was the first of Smith's twelve apostles, and when *Joseph the Seer* grew ill in 1841, he hurried home from England to take charge of administration.

At home, the Mormons were now receiving a fiery baptism of persecution. They had gathered first out of the Eastern states into Ohio; and from there had branched out in the early thirties to Jackson County in Missouri, which had been divinely set apart, they maintained, as their inheritance. Other settlers saw with dismay the irruption of twelve hundred Mormons, who set about clearing land, building townships, declaring God's promises, and voting as a unit in elections. Mormon leaders were caught, tarred and feathered, or whipped; homesteads were burnt and families driven into the woods. A little Mormon boy, begging for his life at Haun's Mill in 1838 when he saw 18 killed around him, was told 'Nits make lice' as they blew out his brains. Driven out of Missouri the Mormons made a new settlement in a mosquito-infested bog on the banks of the Mississippi in Illinois. Within five years they had made the wilderness blossom, and then trouble started all over again. A fresh cause of offence was now given to the *Gentiles*, since the need of polygamy had been revealed to Joseph Smith. This was in 1844. Joseph Smith and his brother Hyrum were taken to jail at Carthage. The mob broke open the jail and lynched them. The Mormon community was delirious with grief and panic, and threatened to disintegrate. Brigham Young now showed his greatness; he assumed command, and with courage, skill, forethought, and persistence, resolved to lead the Latter Day Saints once more into the wilderness. But where? If our enemies will give us just ten years unmolested, we will ask 'no more of them; we will never be driven again.'

Young decided, from all the enquiries that he could make, that the district round the great Salt Lake, Utah, was the promised land. It was not an inviting one, but that was an advantage; it would not be coveted by the Gentiles. Young first led a pilot expedition to plot the road to the new land, and survey the difficulties; and to establish a reception centre. His capital city was planned from the start. As the Mormons arrived in their mule- and ox-waggons, they were despatched in parties, each party with its quota of mechanics and necessary specialists, to occupy the strategic valleys which were well watered. Irrigation schemes were started, and industries to make the province self-sufficient. Young proved, as the Quakers had proved long before, that it was possible to be friends with the Indians if you treated them properly, so much so that the Indians were soon distinguishing between Mormons and the 'Mericats' on whom they still preyed.

The United States government was unable to tolerate the state within a state which Utah looked like becoming. (It had still been Mexican territory when the Mormons first went there.) In 1857, a full-scale expeditionary force was despatched against the territory; but war was avoided, although there were some tragic incidents. Young was made first governor of the Territory, but refused to give way at the end of his term of office; and remained the real master of Utah until his death in 1877, when he was survived by 17 widows; a benevolent despot, a legend in his lifetime, and proof once more of the integrating power of a faith. It was poverty, persecution, their millennial visions, and the quality of their leaders that had given the Mormons their unity and drive.

ILLUSTRATION: Page 374.

'Phenomenon Young'

YOUNG, Thomas, (1773–1829), English scientist, interpreter of Egyptian hieroglyphs, founder of physiological optics and the modern wave theory of light, and introducer of the term 'energy' in its modern scientific meaning.

This child of Somersetshire Quakers perfectly exemplified the infant prodigy. He could read fluently at two; at six he began Latin, at eight Greek, mathematics, mechanics and general science. At thirteen he turned to Hebrew, Chaldaic, Syriac and Persian. At fourteen he was tutor in classics to one of the Gurney family. Arabic, French, Italian and Spanish he added to his languages. At nineteen he began to qualify in medicine. At twenty he published his discovery that the accommodation of the eye in vision is due to the curvature of the crystalline lens. At twenty-one he was elected a Fellow of the Royal Society. He proceeded to Edinburgh to study chemistry, then to Göttingen, where he mastered music and horsemanship, and at last to Cambridge in 1797, when he had already been an F.R.S. for three years. At Cambridge they called him 'Phenomenon Young'.

Young propounded the theory that colour sensations are due to structures in the retina which are sensitive to red, green, and violet; and he founded not only the modern wave-theory of light, but the modern theory of elasticity, which has its memorial in the coefficient of elasticity known as 'Young's Modulus'.

Possibly Young was the most learned Englishman that ever lived, but he spread himself too widely, and his fame suffered in consequence.

Young's fantastic combination of literary and scientific powers enabled him to decipher the famous stone discovered at Rosetta at the mouth of the Nile in 1799. On the stone are three parallel inscriptions in hieroglyphic characters, demotic characters (the cursive writing which succeeded hieroglyphics) and Greek. Young took a careful copy of these with him to Worthing during his summer visit of 1814, and in a few weeks had deciphered about one half of the hieroglyphics. He described his work at the time as 'the first step towards any authentic information respecting the ancient history and letters of Egypt'.

Z

Monk and skull

ZURBARÁN, Francisco de, (1598–1662), Spanish painter of the sombre ecstasies of the monastic life.

Monks of Zurbarán, white Carthusians, who in the shadow
Glide noiselessly over the flagstones of the dead,
Murmuring Our Fathers and Aves numberless,
What are you expiating by such great remorse,
O tonsured phantoms ... ?

– asked the French poet Gautier. Yet the monks are anything but phantoms: in white or brown robes, sometimes torn and patched, with a skull in their hands, they are solid and firm, and Zurbarán gains his effect of mystery precisely by contrast between the painted reality of his monks and the invisible words of ecstasy which come from their lips or the invisible thoughts which so visibly possess them. Zurbarán was a peasant's son born in a village in the Estramadura, who studied with obscure painters in Seville, and accepted commissions early in his career from the Convent of Our Lady of Ransom, a sisterhood concerned with the ransoming of captives. He had his later successes as official painter of Seville and in painting a number of pictures for Philip IV, but he remained unique and solitary, achieving his often dream-like effects by this tension between inner vision and outer naturalism. He created no more impressive image than the *Franciscan* (1639) in the National Gallery in London. Velasquez (q.v.) delights in what he sees, Zurbarán in all that he knows and feels or imagines. Where El Greco (q.v.) had paraded the subjects of religious ecstasy, Zurbarán simplified everything to the strongest, most spare, and most convincing image. He is among the most haunting of all painters. He worked on for monasteries and convents of Madrid and Seville, but towards the end his painting loses its force, and the strange personality breaks up. He seems to have drained his vision dry.

THE END

ACKNOWLEDGEMENTS

Acknowledgements and thanks for the right to reproduce illustrations are due to the persons and institutions listed below. The following abbreviations have been used:–B.M. *British Museum, London;* N.P.G. *National Portrait Gallery, London;* V & A. *Victoria & Albert Museum, London;* P.P. *Picture Post Library, London;* M.C. *Mansell Collection, London;* S.C.R. *Society for Cultural Relations with Soviet Russia, London;* U.S.I.S. *United States Information Service, London.*

COLOR PLATES. *Plates* 1 *and* 2 V & A. 3 Prado, Madrid and Thames & Hudson, London. 4 Louvre, Paris and Fine Art Engravers, London. 5 N.P.G. 6 Metropolitan Museum, New York and Fine Art Engravers, London. 7 Royal Society and R.B.Fleming, London. 8 Fama Press, London and Prof. Emil Korner, Scotland. 9 Louvre, Paris and Fine Art Engravers, London. 10 N.P.G. 11 Wallace Collection, London. 12 Alte Pinakothek, Munich and Fama Press, London. 14 A.M.H.de Lessert, Geneva. 15 By gracious permission of Her Majesty the Queen. *Endpapers* Musée de Versailles and L.Laniepce, Paris.

BLACK AND WHITE PLATES. *Page* 23 Vizzavona, Paris and Syndics of the Fitzwilliam Museum, Cambridge. 24 P.P. 25 M.C. 26 Prof. Johannes Widmann, Leipzig. 27 P.P. 28 Vizzavona, Paris. 29 M.C. 30 Royal Society and R.B. Fleming, London, and P.P. 31 N.P.G. and P.P. 32 P.P. 33 H.Gernsheim, London. 34 M.C. 35 N.P.G. 36 and 37 P.P. 38 Albertina, Vienna and P.P. 71 Northampton Public Library and City Art Gallery, Manchester. 72 P.P. 74 P.P. 75 Svenska Portrattarkivet, National Museum, Stockholm. 76 Kingston-upon-Hull Corporation and H.Abba. 77 Sir Bruce Ingram and City Museum and Art Gallery, Birmingham. 78 M.Schwarzkopf, Zurich and Michel Molinare, London. 79 United Artists Corporation, London. 80 and 81 N.P.G. 82 B.M. 83 U.S.I.S. 84 P.P. 85 N.P.G. 86 P.P. and H.Gernsheim, London. 119 Royal Society and R.B.Fleming, London and P.P. 120 Vizzavona, Paris. 121 Dean and Chapter, St Paul's Cathedral and R.B.Fleming. 122 P.P. 123 P.P. 124 M.C. 125 Phaidon Press, London. 126 H. Gernsheim, London, and P.P. 127 H.Gernsheim, London and U.S.I.S. 128 P.P. 129 M.C. 130 P.P. 131 Quintin Gurney, Norfolk and Friends House, London. 132 and 133 P.P. 134 U.S.I.S. and Miss Anna Freud. 167 P.P. and Marquis of Cholmondeley and A.C.Cooper, London. 168 Roland Leten, Ghent. 169 Rafael Nadal, London. 170 S.C.R. 171 H.Gernsheim, London. 172 M.C. 173 N.P.G. 174 P.P. and Württembergische Landesbibliothek, Stuttgart. 175 N.P.G. and B.M. and R.B.Fleming. 176 and 177 M.C. 178 N.P.G. 179 Scottish National Portrait Gallery, Edinburgh. 180 B.M. and R.B.Fleming, London. 181 P.P. 182 S.C.R. 215 U.S.I.S. and P.P. 216 M.C. 217 Felix Mann. 218 Yale University Art Gallery, U.S.A. 219 N.P.G. 220 P.P. 221 N.P.G. 222 P.P. 223 National Maritime Museum, Greenwich and Drummond Young, Edinburgh. 224 Rijksmuseum, Amsterdam. 225 Royal Society and R.B.Fleming, London. 226 Museum and Art Gallery, Leipzig. 227 and 228 P.P. 229 M.C. 230 Arts Council, London and M.C. 263 Soiceta Colombaria, Florence and Phaidon Press, London. 264 By gracious permission of Her Majesty the Queen. 265 M.C. 266 Ferdinandeum, Innsbruck. 267 Mozart Museum, Salzburg. 268 Steichen Camera Company, New York and Victor Gollancz, London. 269 P.P. 270 P.P. 271 S.C.R. and N.P.G. 272 Historical Society of Pennyslvania, U.S.A. and Friends House, London. 273 N.P.G. 274 N.P.G. 275 P.P. 276 Bettmann Archives, New York. 277 P.P. 278 Anthony Richmond, England. 311 P.P. 312 and 313 P.P. 314 Bodleian Library, Oxford. 315 Herzog August Bibliothek, Wolfenbüttel. 316 and 317 M.C. 318 M.C. and P.P. 319 Uffize Gallery, Florence and Fine Art Engravers, London and Vizzavona, Paris. 320 N.P.G. 321 Sheffield Corporation. 322 S.C.R. 323 P.P. 324 M.C. 325 City Museum and Art Gallery, Birmingham. 326 P.P. and M.C. 359 B.M. and R.B.Fleming, London and Vizzavona, Paris. 360 Wellcome Historical Museum, London. 361 M.C. 362 Yale University Art Gallery, U.S.A. 363 N.P.G. 364 P.P. 365 N.P.G. 366 Home House Trustees, Courtauld Institute, London and Swedish Institute, London. 367 Bettman Archives, New York and P.P. 368 H.Gernsheim, London. 370 N.P.G. 371 U.S.I.S. 372 Science Museum, London. 373 British Broadcasting Corporation, London. 374 Science Museum, London and P.P.

For permission to include copyright material we are indebted to the following: P. 10 *Collected Shorter Poems and New Year Letter* by W.H.Auden (Faber & Faber Ltd). P. 104 *An Introduction to Welsh Poetry* by Gwyn Williams (Faber & Faber Ltd). P. 139 *Collected Poems of T.S.Eliot* (Faber & Faber Ltd). Pp. 210–11 *Conversations with Kafka* by Gustav Janouch, trans. Goronwy Rees (Derek Verschoyle Ltd). *Letters to Milena* by Franz Kafka, ed. Willi Haas, trans. Willa & Edwin Muir (Secker & Warburg Ltd). *The Journals of S.Kierkegaard* ed. & trans. Alexander Dru (O.U.P.). P. 256 *The White Pony* ed. Robert Payne (George Allen & Unwin Ltd). P. 349 *Springtime* by Rainer Maria Rilke, trans. Ruth Speirs (Peter Owen Ltd). P. 394 *T'ao the Hermit* trans. William Acker (Thames & Hudson Ltd). P. 406 *Tu Fu* by William Hung (Harvard University Press). P. 424 *Contemporary Chinese Poetry* ed. Robert Payne (Routledge & Kegan Paul Ltd). Pp. 434–5 *Collected Poems of W.B.Yeats* (Macmillan & Co Ltd). *Spy cartoons from* Vanity Fair *reproduced by kind permission of The National Magazine Co. Ltd.*

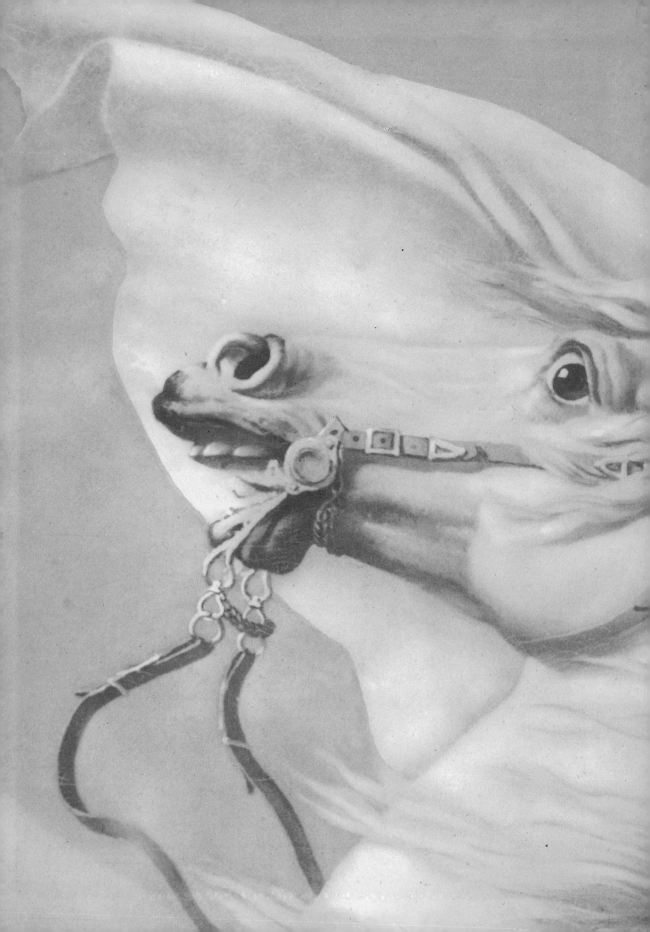